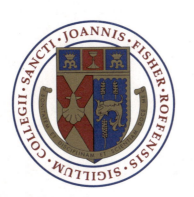

LAVOISIER

LAVOISIER

Chemist, Biologist, Economist

—

Jean-Pierre Poirier

translated from the French
by Rebecca Balinski

PENN

UNIVERSITY OF PENNSYLVANIA PRESS

Philadelphia

Originally published 1993 as *Antoine Laurent de Lavoisier, 1743–1794* by Editions
Pygmalion/Gérard Watelet, Paris
Copyright © 1993 Editions Pygmalion/Gérard Watelet, Paris

English translation revised and expanded by the author
Copyright © 1996 Jean-Pierre Poirier

Printed in the United States of America on acid-free paper

10 9 8 7 6 5 4 3 2 1

Published by
University of Pennsylvania Press
Philadelphia, Pennsylvania 19104-6097

Library of Congress Cataloging-in-Publication Data
Poirier, Jean Pierre.
[Antoine Laurent de Lavoisier, 1743–1794. English]
Lavoisier, chemist, biologist, economist / Jean-Pierre Poirier ;
translated by Rebecca Balinski.
    p.   cm. — (Chemical sciences in society series)
Includes bibliographical references (p.   –   ) and index.
ISBN 0-8122-3365-4 (cloth : alk. paper)
    1. Lavoisier, Antoine Laurent, 1743–1794. 2. Chemists—France—
Biography. I. Title. II. Series.
QD22.L4P6513   1996
540'.92—dc20
[B]   96-35738
                                                                    CIP

Contents

French Terms

Agiotage — Stock exchange manipulation

Aides — Tobacco and alcohol taxes

Arrêt — Official decision having the force of law

Arts et métiers — Arts and Trades

Assemblée Constituante — Constituent Assembly

Assemblée des notables — Assembly of Notables

Assemblée Legislative — Legislative Assembly

Assemblée provinciale de l'Orléanais — Provincial Assembly of Orléans

Assignat — Paper currency issued in 1790 on the security of nationalized clerical and royal property, printed and distributed by the special bank for the repayment of the short-term debt. Made legal tender on April 17, 1790, the assignat ceased to bear interest and became a simple banknote. By 1795, inflation had rendered the assignat nearly worthless

Assignation — Payment order drawn on a particular revenue and assigned to it

Bailliage — Local electoral unit

Billet d'escompte — Bill of exchange

Billet de banque — Banknote

Bureau de consultation des Arts et Métiers — Advisory Board of Arts and Trades

Bureau des impositions — Taxation Office

Bureau des subsistances de Paris — Paris Food Commission

Cahier de doléances — Register of Grievances

Caisse — A fund independently managed by an accountant

Caisse d'Escompte — Discount Bank

Caisse de l'Extraordinaire — Special Bank

Caissier — Cashier or Clerical manager of a *caisse*

Capitation — Combination of a poll and income taxes

Chambre des Comptes — Chamber of Accounts

Comité d'Administration de l'Agriculture — Committee on Agriculture

Comité d'Instruction publique — Committee on Public Education

Comité de Comptabilité — Accounting Committee

Comité de Salubrité — Committee on Public Health

Comité de Salut public — Committee of Public Safety

Comité de Sûreté générale — Committee of General Security

Comité de Trésorerie — Treasury Committee

Comité des Finances—Finance Committee

Comité des Impositions—Taxation Committee

Comité des Monnaies—Currency Committee

Comité ecclésiastique—Ecclesiastical Committee

Comité des Contributions publiques—Taxation Committee

Commissaire de la Trésorerie—Treasury Commissioner

Commission d'Agriculture et des Arts—Commission on Agriculture and Arts

Commission des Monnaies—Commission on Currency

Commission des Poids et Mesures—Commission on Weights and Measures

Compte—Current account

Contribution mobilière—Tax on personal income

Contribution patriotique—Patriotic tax

Contributions foncière—Tax on income from land

Contributions publique—Public taxation

Contrôle général des Finances—General Control of Finance

Contrôleur général des Finances—Controller General of Finance

Corporations, maîtrises, jurandes—Professional guilds

Corvée—Tax paid by peasants through labor on roadways

Croupe—Crupper, or the rump of a horse. The allusion is to a person who rides along behind the saddle, a free-loader, so to say. Share in the profits of the General Farm taken from a Farmer General and assigned by the King to a person outside the administration

Dette exigible—Short-term debt made up of advances to the government by financiers and bankers, and requiring urgent repayment

*Dette constitué*e—Long-term debt, consolidated, payable to individual investors in life annuities

Dîme—Tithe collected by the Church

Élection—District

Entrées—Duties on goods entering Paris

État au vrai—Accountant's report on receipts and expenditures

États généraux—States General

Fermage—Land tenure system

Ferme générale—General Farm

Fermier général—Farmer General

Financier—A person known to have interests in the farms, state-owned companies, enterprises or affairs concerning the *finances*, that is the Royal Treasury

Fonds d'avance—Capital investment

Gabelles—Salt taxes

Lit de justice—A decision imposed by the king over parliament's opposition

Maison du Roi et de la Reine—Royal Household

Nitrière—Nitrate works

Octroi—Tollgate

Patente—Tax on commercial income

Ponts et Chaussées—Roads and Bridges Service

Postes et Messageries—Mail and Stagecoach Services

Receveur—Tax collector

Receveur général des Finances—Head of tax collection for the Ministry of Finance

Régie—Government administrative body responsible to the Royal Council

Régie des Poudres et Salpêtres—Gunpowder and Saltpeter Administration

Régisseur—Director of a *Régie* (Tobacco, Gunpowder and Saltpeter, and so forth)

Registre de prospectus or registre des prévisions budgétaires—Register of Budgetary Forecasts

Rescription—Payment order drawn by an accountant on a cashier

Revenu national—Gross national product or net national product

Salpêtrier—Saltpeter manufacturer, saltpeter man

Setier—Unit of capacity for grains—156 liters (or 12 bushels of 13 liters)

Société d'Agriculture—Society of Agriculture

Subsistances—Food supplies including grain purchases

Taille—Old feudal tax of two types: the *taille réelle* levied in the *pays d'Etats* by the provincial assemblies, assessed against the value of real property; the *taille personnelle*, levied in the *pays d'élection* by the central government, a direct assessment of the individual income

Trésorier général des Finances—General Treasurer of Finance

Traites—Customs duties

Vingtièmes—Twentieth or 5% tax on income

Foreword

THE SPIRIT OF ACCOUNTANCY raised to genius, there is the hallmark of the Lavoisier whom Jean-Pierre Poirier portrays in the first biography that does equal justice to all facets of an extraordinary career. To be sure, chemistry remains the centerpiece. Lavoisier himself considered that it was in founding the new chemistry that he gave his measure, and history has largely ratified his self-estimate, according him the leading role that Isaac Newton played in physics, Charles Darwin in evolutionary biology, Albert Einstein in relativity, and Niels Bohr in quantum mechanics. All were prime movers in transformations of a scope that, as if anticipating political events, Lavoisier called a revolution in his science.

Poirier refines our understanding of Lavoisier's reformation of chemistry, its replacement of phlogiston by oxygen in the theory of combustion, its adoption of the systematic nomenclature in use ever since, its dependence on the principle of conservation of matter, its rigorously quantitative mode of analysis. He gives due weight to the importance of Lavoisier's study of respiration both for physiology and for the early history of organic chemistry, and goes beyond recent scholarship in attributing to Lavoisier comprehension of the metabolic role of the liver. In all this Poirier brings out, as Lavoisier on the whole did not, the parts of others, of predecessors, associates, and opponents. Science is always a collective enterprise, and here we have the whole cast, French, British, and European, and not merely the protagonist, the ultimately tragic protagonist. For Jean-Pierre Poirier, putting matters in perspective does not entail any belittling of Lavoisier's stature nor any subordination of the content of his science to the social and political context, which is equally well delineated.

Still, the overall story of the chemical revolution is familiar, and it is mainly in his account of Lavoisier's further concerns that Poirier breaks new ground. Beyond the mere facts of his having been a partner in the Tax Farm, an administrator of the Gunpowder Service, and a model farmer, little has been known of how Lavoisier actually spent his days. As a rule, chemistry occupied only the hours before breakfast and in the evenings.

For the rest, his life was that of a financier, economist, and liberal administrator, a "grand commis d'état." No mere investor in the Tax Farm, Lavoisier had direct responsibility for specific operations and for setting broad policy. Its practices, if not formally corrupt, do appear invidious enough to make the odium it incurred inevitable. Lavoisier's participation was both effective in general and self-serving in particular. Money was greatly important to him, as it is to many wealthy people, and finance a realm in which he made himself as expert as he did in science.

This biography is, and has to be, economic history no less than history of science. In 1788 Lavoisier became chairman of the board of the Discount Bank, founded by Turgot in 1776, and forerunner of the Banque de France. His responsibilities there, together with agricultural experimentation on his own farm and a program of general agrarian reform developed in company with Pierre-Samuel Dupont de Nemours, led him into broad study of the measure of national wealth and productivity. Indeed, his involvement in the Revolution itself was as much that of financier and economist as of scientist. He served as a consultant on finance to the National Assembly in 1790–91 and a commissioner of the Treasury from April 1791 until February 1792. Lavoisier's success in administering the service, and his failure to persuade the Assembly to adopt sound fiscal policy, offer an instructive instance of the interplay of expertise with politics in revolutionary circumstance. He was very bad at politics: "This piece of writing will be as cool as reason (froid comme la raison)," he wrote in the preamble to his estimate of the state of national finances in January 1792, a season of intense political heat.

In everything he did, his method was that of the balance sheet, carried over from quantitative chemical analysis wherein nothing is lost and the weight of the products of a reaction must equal the weight of the reagents. Even so, in the refining of crude saltpetre for the munitions industry, in the balancing of the cost of seed, manure, land, and labor against the value of agricultural produce, in the collection of taxes and transmission of the proceeds to the Crown, in overseeing the proportion of reserves to notes issued by the Discount Bank, in the double entry bookkeeping required of Treasury clerks, in his estimates of national wealth—in all these enterprises, meticulous attention to fact and rigorous control over quantity were the conditions of success. In prison awaiting trial and execution, he labored over his own accounts and over the final accounting of the Tax Farm.

Poirier brings everyone around Lavoisier to life—Dupont de Nemours, Fourcroy, Guyton-Morveau, Hassenfratz, Turgot, Guettard, and most notably his wife. Madame Lavoisier becomes a person in her own right, as a child bride, as an intelligent young matron in the Paris of salons, as a widow and pathetic embarrassment outliving her time. Lavoisier himself we do not come to know. It is not the author's fault. No one ever did. It does not appear that Lavoisier was capable of intimacy. He wished to be right, not to be known, let alone to be liked. Poirier is not the sort of biographer who would seek to penetrate that reserve in search of feelings to which the sources offer no clue. He has fully combed those sources, is as faithful to them as Lavoisier to his balances, and tells us all we can expect to know in the liveliest possible manner.

CHARLES C. GILLISPIE
Princeton University

Acknowledgments

Most historians of science agree that when the Revolutionary Tribunal in Paris sentenced Antoine Laurent Lavoisier to death on May 8, 1794, France lost the father of modern chemistry and biology. But this collector of indirect taxes who became a director of the tobacco and gunpowder industries, an important landowner, a powerful banker, an early advocate of the French Revolution, and, finally, a civil servant at the National Treasury, was also a precursor of modern economic thought. He developed a highly original approach to economics—both scientific and practical—that was similar to his quantitative approach to chemistry.

Writing the biography of this remarkable man has occupied me for so many years that it sometimes seems that I have devoted all my working life to it. However, I previously spent ten years practicing medicine and twenty-five as director of research and development in the pharmaceutical industry. Since therapeutics is primarily the art of finding new chemical treatments for biological disorders, I became familiar in those years with the history of biology, chemistry, and economics. And so I was bound to encounter Antoine Laurent Lavoisier sooner or later. The fateful meeting occurred when I bought a manuscript entitled *De la Situation du Trésor Public au 1er Juin 1791* from a knowledgeable Parisian bookseller, Bernard Clavreuil. The fact that Lavoisier, along with Condorcet, was one of the authors of the report stimulated my curiosity. How had the father of the chemical revolution come to be a civil servant at such a crucial time? Could this unexpected and certainly unpopular position explain his perplexing end? The acquisition of this manuscript marked the beginning of an incessant quest for more information and led me to libraries and rare bookshops not just in Paris but in London, Edinburgh, Amsterdam, Philadelphia, Princeton, Ithaca, Wilmington, and New York as well. Anatole France wrote in *Le jardin d'Epicure*:

Is there any activity more honorable than collecting books? Actually, those who engage in it are rather like children who build sandcastles at the seashore; they labor in vain because all that they construct will shortly disappear. The same is true for collections of books and paintings; it is the vicissitudes of existence and the brevity of life that are responsible. The sea washes away the piles of sand, the auctioneer breaks up the collections. And yet, there is absolutely nothing more satisfying than building sandcastles when one is ten and collections when one is sixty. (Paris: Calmann-Levy, 1921, 96–97).

Rare manuscripts and books can do much more than simply make up a collection. They contain vivid testimonies from the past and important insights that help us focus on the present through the perspective of the past. But they cannot always be easily found, even in the best public libraries. For access to many of the texts consulted in my research, I am greatly indebted to a number of rare book-dealers who provided me with invaluable advice, as well as documents.

It was extremely heartening that my early research on Lavoisier as an economist was considered to be a valid contribution by such specialists as Paule Ameller and Jean-Claude Toutain, Research Directors at CNRS, and Gérard Duru, professor of economics at the Université Claude Bernard of Lyon. Christian Labrousse, professor of economics at the Université Panthéon-Assas of Paris, encouraged me to investigate further Lavoisier's role in public affairs by writing a doctoral thesis in economics. The thesis, presented in 1992, explored Lavoisier's many contributions—the metric system and decimal division, the Bank of France, the National Treasury, national statistics and accounting, budgetary forecasts, the balancing of the receipts and expenditures of the State—as well as his concern for social questions and public health.

In 1993 a vast amount of unpublished information was made available when le comte Guy de Chabrol donated more than 1000 documents to the Archives of the Paris Academy of Science, and 350 of Lavoisier's manuscripts, which had been lost for 25 years, were returned. These latter papers had been in Clermont-Ferrand, where a bibliophile had discovered them in 1970, spilling forth from a wall cupboard plastered over for years in the house of René Fric, the editor of the three first fascicles of Lavoisier's correspondence. It was then that I decided to write a complete biography of Lavoisier, with the goals of establishing the links between the multidisciplinary activities of his brilliant mind and grasping the logic of his life and death.

The Lavoisier Collection of the Archives de l'Académie des Sciences de Paris was the main source of information for this work. Special thanks are due to Christiane Demeulenaere-Douyère, Curator, and her colleague Claudine Pourret, for having greatly facilitated my access to these documents.

The joint work at the Lavoisier Committee of the Academy of Science, responsible for publishing Lavoisier's *Correspondance*, in which I participate, has been a considerable source of enrichment. I would like especially to thank my colleagues in this small group, which carries on the work begun by René Fric and continued by Michelle Goupil. The frequent meetings with René Taton, Michel Valentin, Patrice Bret, Emmanuel Grison, Bruno Belhoste, Philippe Savoie, and Yves Noël are always occasions for vivid evocations and more precise definitions of Lavoisier's contribution. They have enabled me to clarify obscure periods in Lavoisier's career, in particular his political activity on the eve of the French Revolution and his role in overseeing the finances of the state during that crucial time dating from July 1789 to February 1792.

I wish to thank all those who provided assistance for my research in Paris, at the Archives Nationales and the Departmental and Municipal Archives. At the Bibliothèque Nationale, special thanks are due to Bruno Blasselle, director of the Département des Livres Imprimés, and at the National Assembly Library, to Michel Ameller and Ghislain Wouters. I would also like to thank staff members of the Bibliothèque Mazarine, the Bibliothèque Sainte Geneviève, the Bibliothèque Cujas, the Bibliothèque de la Ville de Paris as well as the libraries at the Sorbonne, the Institut de France, the Cité des Sciences, the Museum of Natural History, the Academy of Medicine, the Faculty of Medicine, the Faculty of Pharmacy, the Arsenal, the National Conservatory of Arts and Trades and the French Society of Agriculture. Finally, I obtained important information from departmental archives and municipal libraries located in Clermont-Ferrand, Orléans, Blois, Limoges and Angoulême.

In London, the British Library and the Royal Society Library and Archives made available sources concerning contributions by Joseph Black, Joseph Priestley, Richard Kirwan, David MacBride, John Pringle, Stephen Hales, Charles Blagden, and many others. The National Library of Scotland in Edinburgh provided valuable testimony on James Hall's sojourn in Paris during the Revolution and the frequent contacts he had with Lavoisier. My thanks are due to these libraries for access to the collections and for permission to quote a number of documents.

In the United States, a prime source of information was the Lavoisier Collection at Cornell University. L. Pearce Williams introduced me to staff members, in particular David Corson, who kindly helped me to explore it. I was able to consult most of its 324 manuscripts, including Jean Etienne Guettard's records of the geological investigations with Lavoisier, unpublished lecture notes of Guillaume François Rouelle and Joseph Black, Lavoisier's laboratory worksheets recording the experiments on the large-scale decomposition and synthesis of water carried out with Jean Baptiste Meusnier in 1785, letters and reports on Mesmerism, and such diverse topics as street lighting, the effects of heat, meteorology, the decimal system, and the new weights and measures. Furthermore, Lavoisier's participation in public affairs—the

General Farm, the Gunpowder and Saltpeter Administration, the Discount
Bank, the Committee on Agriculture, the Orléans Provincial Assembly—is
distinctly reflected in the wealth of correspondence, notes, invoices, receipts
and leases I saw there. The printed material of the collection consists of 1288
titles contained in 2012 volumes, and makes up more than 90 percent of the
705 entries in the standard *Bibliography of the Works of Antoine Laurent Lavoisier* by Duveen and Klickstein (London, 1954) and its *Supplement* (London,
1965). Using this same material, Marco Beretta recently published *Bibliotheca
Lavoisieriana: The Catalogue of the Library of Antoine Laurent Lavoisier*, which
sheds new light on the nature and impact of Lavoisier's sources.

Two other American sources of documents regarding Lavoisier and his
epoch are the Hagley Museum and Library in Wilmington, Delaware, and
the Houghton Library at Harvard University. In the former, with special assistance from Marjorie McNinch, I consulted manuscripts written by Quesnay, Turgot, and Du Pont de Nemours. In the latter, Leslie A. Morris helped
me to reconstitute the correspondence between Du Pont de Nemours and
Madame Lavoisier.

Fruitful visits were made to other libraries in the United States. I would
like to express my thanks to Roy E. Goodman at the American Philosophical
Society Library in Philadelphia and to staff members at the Princeton University Library, the New York Public Library, and the Rockefeller University
Library.

Patricia Smith and Alison A. Anderson, from the University of Pennsylvania Press, gave invaluable help in preparing the manuscript for the publisher. They saved me from many subtle inconsistencies and errors by their
advice and meticulous copyediting.

I wish to thank Rebecca Balinski for the translation of a difficult text
covering a variety of disciplines and often using antiquated terminology. We
hope that her thorough knowledge of the French language and our permanent and friendly exchanges during almost two years in Paris were able to
render something of the clarity and elegance of Lavoisier's beautifully flowing style.

I am greatly indebted to those British and American scholars who have
created a vast literature describing Antoine Laurent Lavoisier's achievements,
especially William R. Albury, Keith M. Baker, I. Bernard Cohen, Maurice
Crosland, Robert Darnton, Arthur Donovan, Jerry B. Gough, Henry Guerlac, Douglas McKie, Seymour H. Mauskopf, Robert Multhauf, Carleton E.
Perrin, Rhoda Rappaport, William A. Smeaton, Robert Siegfried, and Norton Wise.

I give special thanks to the two referees who, while recommending my
work for publication, suggested that I clarify and reinforce certain points that

had not been developed in the French version. Since professors Hahn and Holmes kindly gave the University of Pennsylvania Press their permission to reveal their identities, I would like to emphasize how much I am indebted to them.

Roger Hahn, professor of history of science at the University of California, Berkeley, through his major book, *The Anatomy of a Scientific Institution: The Paris Academy of Science, 1666–1803*, helped me understand what Lavoisier, this elitist manager, learned from the jarring events of the French Revolution and from his contacts with some of the "lesser" artisans.

Frederic L. Holmes, professor of history of medicine at Yale University, author of *Eighteenth Century Chemistry as an Investigative Entreprise* and *Lavoisier and the Chemistry of Life*, through his thorough and comprehensive analysis, helped me greatly to perceive how Lavoisier established the foundations for the fields of organic chemistry and biochemistry. His study of Lavoisier's views on the physiology of respiration and Charles A. Culotta's *History of Respiratory Theory: Lavoisier to Paul Bert, 1777–1880* provided me with stimulating insights.

The studies on *French Finances at the End of Eighteenth Century* by John F. Bosher, on *The Taxation Committee in the Constituent Assembly* by Kenneth Margerison, on *French Finances and the American War* by Robert D. Harris, on *French Administrators and French Scientists* by Harold T. Parker, and on *The French Tobacco Monopoly* by Jacob Price, were very helpful concerning Lavoisier's achievements as an economist.

An International Symposium and several other celebrations, held in Paris in May 1994 on the 200th anniversary of Lavoisier's death, highlighted his role as the founder of modern scientific experimental methodology, well before Claude Bernard, who, incidentally, paid him tribute. These commemorations were occasions to meet distinguished scholars who gave me a more complete picture of the relevant and pervasive influence of German, Swedish and Italian chemists on Lavoisier's thinking.

Maurice Crosland suggested that I be more explicit on the quantitative nature of Lavoisier's science; he emphasized that the oxygen theory is not just a theory of combustion but also includes theories of composition and acidity.

Bernadette Bensaude-Vincent's *Lavoisier: Mémoires d'une révolution*, Ferdinando Abbri's *Le terre, l'acqua e le arie*, and Marco Beretta's *From Galileo to Lavoisier: The Enlightenment of Matter* were incentives to reexamine the concept of chemical revolution. Was chemistry before Lavoisier a structured discipline, a rational, coherent system that could be called a science? More recently, Bernadette Bensaude-Vincent and Ferdinando Abbri, have published the proceedings of a workshop focused on the diffusion of the new nomenclature, *Lavoisier in European Context: Negotiating a New Language for Chemistry*.

Keiko Kawashima's work on Madame Lavoisier's scientific contribution led me to give more attention to an inadequately explored aspect of her personality and deepened my appreciation of this energetic and intelligent lady.

I am especially obliged to Professor Joshua Lederberg, a recipient of the Nobel prize for his work in genetics and former President of the Rockefeller University, for his authoritative comments on the history of science, and for pointing out Madame Lavoisier's role in her husband's career as a chemist and a politician. And I would also like to express my gratitude to his wife, Marguerite, a psychiatrist at the Memorial Sloan-Kettering Cancer Center, like me a native of Charente, that tranquil region of France famous for its cognac and native sons, Jean Monnet and François Mitterrand. The Lederbergs' gracious hospitality, expert advice, and introductions to leading American scholars were of inestimable aid.

At their home, I met Arnold Thackray, Executive Director of the Chemical Heritage Foundation, who instigated this revised presentation of Antoine Laurent Lavoisier's biography. I am greatly indebted to him, and to Theodor Benfey, Editor of *Chemical Heritage*, the News Magazine of the Chemical Heritage Foundation, for their help and advice.

My major debt is to Charles C. Gillispie, whose works inspired my approach to history of science. Following his example, I tried to write a history of the interactions between "science and polity" and to relate them to the movement for governmental reform and economic modernization in France. I received much help and encouragement from discussions with him, in both Paris and Princeton, and from a close, uninterrupted correspondence. His counsel, advice, and criticism have greatly improved this biography. I would like to express my gratitude for his support, and for the great honor he has done me in writing the preface to this book.

And, finally, I would like to dedicate this book to Dr. Marie Poirier-Comar, my wife, whose persevering and inventive collaboration brought methodicalness, rigor and intuitive sensitivity to its writing.

Prologue

Certain authors, speaking of their works, say, "My book,"
"My commentary," "My history," etc. They resemble middle-
class people who have a house of their own, and always have
"My house" on their lips. They would do better to say, "Our
book," "Our commentary," "Our history," etc., because there
is in them usually more of other people's than their own.

—Blaise Pascal, *Pensées*, translated by W. F. Trotter
(New York: Random House, 1941), Pensée 43, p. 15.

Paris, February 1789. The chemical revolution is well under way and
Antoine Laurent Lavoisier, a respected scientist and influential Academician of Science, has just published its crowning achievement, the *Traité élémentaire de chimie*. The book has had a rapid success throughout Europe and
even in America. With it the foundations of modern chemistry have been laid.

Marie Anne Lavoisier is both muse and secretary to her husband. Wanting to celebrate this success, in which she has had a part, by a work of art, she
has asked Jean Henri Hassenfratz, the director of the Arsenal Laboratory, for
ideas. Imbued with the current taste for allegory, he has suggested one of two
subjects: the combat of oxygen against phlogiston, three-quarters won, or
else the genius of the new chemistry bringing down the phlogiston hypothesis.[1] But a much simpler and better idea has been chosen, a double portrait
showing husband and wife at the summit of their social success, well earned
by effort and talent.

The fashionable painter Jacques Louis David has agreed to execute the
work for the considerable sum of 7,000 livres ($280,000 in 1996).[2] The result is
an immense classical canvas of intriguing composition. Curiously, it is Marie
Anne Lavoisier, small and rather plump, who occupies the foreground. Her
unsmiling eyes gaze directly ahead. Her nose is long and straight, her lips
tightly closed. A small wrinkle at the right-hand corner of her mouth suggests

Figure 1. Portrait of M. and Mme Lavoisier by Jacques Louis David. Metropolitan Museum of Art, New York.

a strong character, assertive and unconcerned about trying to please. Her intelligent face is crowned by a mass of blond curls ending in long tresses at her waist. Against the grey background of a bourgeois salon, the young woman, wearing a filmy white dress trimmed in fine lace and blue silk, is standing beside her husband. Somewhat protective and maternal, she is leaning forward and rests her left hand on his shoulder. The other hand only lightly touches the table. She seems distracted, as though she is there just for an instant. Her mind is elsewhere.

Lavoisier is dressed in richly textured black, highlighted by a white lace jabot and cuffs, and is seated at a table covered with crimson velvet falling to the floor. Atop his broad forehead sits a short wig, curled and powdered. His large eyes and protruding nose contrast with the thin, tight mouth and small chin. His face expresses gentleness, indeed timidity, as does the way he is sitting on the edge of the chair. But the right leg is stretched forward, as if to show off the engraved silver buckle on the elegant black shoe. He is correcting proofs of a book, but has turned away for an instant to look at his wife. The goose quill in his hand remains immobile. He looks expectant. His work has been interrupted and he is impatient to get back to it.

The instruments around him evoke his career and his two major scientific contributions. On the table, beside the inkwell, the mercury gasometer calls to mind the liberation of oxygen from oxide of mercury and the determination of the composition of air. On the floor, the large glass balloon evokes the determination of the composition of water. At Lavoisier's feet, the light plays on the copper of the cylindrical hydrometer for the study of the density of the mineral waters.

On the left-hand side of the painting, a large portfolio, standing on an armchair, contains the first examples of the thirteen plates illustrating Lavoisier's work, drawn and engraved by Madame Lavoisier, under David's supervision.

But there is something bizarre about the portrait. It is as if Madame Lavoisier were the leading figure. Her husband's docile attitude is surprising in someone who has been showered with the highest honors. Did David perceive a weakness in him? Is it diffidence, doubt, or dissatisfaction that causes Lavoisier to seek approval in his wife's eyes? Could a secret dissension explain the visibly cold attitude between this ostensibly close couple? Or has the anti-establishment David, who finds it hard to adapt to his role as official painter of bourgeois success, simply been gratuitously roguish?

Whatever the case, as David composes the portrait, Antoine Laurent Lavoisier's success is total. At forty-five, he is an eminent bourgeois—ennobled, wealthy, powerful—equally at home in scientific, aristocratic, financial, and governmental circles. A man who has succeeded in everything, he undoubtedly still has an exceptional future ahead. Since his birth in Paris on August 26, 1743, fortune has always smiled on him.

I

Youth

A Family of Lawyers

THE LAVOISIER FAMILY ORIGINATED in Villers-Cotterêts near Soissons, and had begun its climb up the social ladder a century before Antoine Laurent was born. The ancestor, Antoine, was a postillion in the King's Stables. By 1620, he had been succeeded by a postmaster who became the owner of the Hôtellerie de l'Ange on the marketplace. His grandson, Nicolas, was a sheriff's officer and owned several town houses. His successor, an attorney for the bailiwick of Villers-Cotterêts, married in 1705 a wealthy heiress, Jeanne Waroquier, daughter of a lawyer in Pierrefonds. Their first child, Jean Antoine, was sent to study in Paris. Ambitious and hardworking, he also became a lawyer. At the beginning of his career, he was encouraged by his maternal uncle, Jacques Waroquier, attorney at the Parlement de Paris, the highest court of justice under the old Régime. Unmarried, Waroquier left his law practice to his nephew when he retired.[1] Provided with an excellent position, Jean Antoine married, on June 4, 1742, the beautiful but fragile Emilie, daughter of Clément Punctis, another lawyer, and Marie Thérèse Frère. The couple lived on the Cul-de-Sac Pecquet in the parish of Saint Merri in Paris.[2] They led the comfortable and dignified existence typical of a milieu of lawyers concerned with respectability.

Antoine Laurent, their first child, was baptized at the church of Saint Merri. The godmother was the maternal grandmother; the godfather was a great-uncle and cleric, Laurent Waroquier, principal of the Beauvais grammar school. The child's first years were spent in the family residence, surrounded by the gardens of the imposing mansions of the La Trémoille and Mesme families and the La Merci monastery. He was two when his sister, Marie Marguerite Emilie, was born. And only a year later, on March 24, 1746, his mother died.

In 1748 Jean Antoine went with his two children to live with his mother-in-law, who had been widowed shortly before. Madame Punctis lived with her second daughter, Constance, in a handsome mansion on the rue du four Saint-Eustache.³ Constance was kindhearted and had a keen sense of family duty. Although she was only twenty, she renounced the idea of marriage so as to devote herself to the education of her nephew and niece. The days were filled with lessons, but they were cheerful. There were frequent outings to the Tuileries. Vacations were spent at Villers-Cotterêts on the family domain, and it was there that Antoine Laurent began to learn about rural life. But the child remained permanently marked by the two years without a maternal presence. Overly solemn for a small boy, he preferred study to games. Moreover, when he was 11, his father, wanting him to have the best education possible, enrolled him in the Collège Mazarin to study classics.

The Collège Mazarin

Formerly called the School of the Four Nations, the Collège Mazarin was built, according to Mazarin's wish, on the site of the Nesle mansion.⁴ In the beginning, it had been a free military school for sixty impoverished young noblemen who came from the Protestant provinces captured by Louis XIV and united with France by the treaties of Munster and the Pyrenees. They were taught fencing, riding, the martial arts, and mathematics. Each pupil had a private room and his own silver cutlery in the refectory. Later financial difficulties arose. The number of boarders was reduced to thirty and numerous day students were admitted. Spiteful gossip said that the Collège Mazarin was "the most beautiful and prestigious as well as the wealthiest of the Paris secondary schools, but that it was also the poorest in qualified teachers and educated schoolboys."⁵ The judgment was too harsh: the teaching was quite good. In particular, the college was the only one in Paris where sciences and mathematics were taught along with history and literature. This originality would determine Antoine Laurent's destiny. In 1754 he joined 1,000 other young men when he entered the school as a day pupil. He was already a privileged person. Only 11, he had just inherited 45,600 livres, his part of the legacy left by his maternal great-grandfather, Christophe Frère, a meat merchant and burgess of Paris.⁶ Such an important fortune ($1.8 million in 1996) coming so early in his life was bound to instill a taste for sums and exact accounts in this future theoretician of balanced budgets.

A serious student, he was interested in all subjects: theater, poetry, essays, satire, and rhetoric. Attracted by Jean Jacques Rousseau's work, he tried to write a play based on *La nouvelle Héloïse*, but abandoned it after six pages. He competed for prizes from the provincial Academies. For Besançon, he examined "whether desire to perpetuate one's name and actions in men's memories conforms to nature and reason"; for Amiens, "whether the rectitude of heart is as necessary in the quest for truth as is soundness of mind."

Lavoisier did not retain a favorable memory of the first notions of chemistry as presented by Louis C. de La Planche:

I was surprised to see how much obscurity surrounded the approaches to the science. In the first steps, one began by assuming rather than proving. I was presented with words that could not be defined for me, or at least could be defined only by borrowing from subject matter that was completely unknown to me, and that I could acquire only by studying all of chemistry. Therefore, in beginning to teach me science, he supposed that I already knew it.[7]

La Planche estimated that it took three years to learn chemistry. In the first, one got to know the terms, learned its "dictionary." At the end of the second year, ideas should begin to sort themselves out. The third year should be the one of true learning. Lavoisier, however, judged the end result to be decidedly insufficient:

When the chemistry course ended, I wanted to take stock of what I had learned. I felt fairly confident about everything concerning the composition of mineral salts, the preparation of mineral acids—the only things about which there then existed exact and positive knowledge. But it seemed that I had retained only the vaguest ideas about all the rest of the science.[8]

In 1760 Lavoisier received the second prize in the general competition for French composition in rhetoric class. That same year, he suffered another heartbreak when his sister died at the age of 15. All the affection of the family was then focused on the young man whose earnestness, enthusiasm for study, and intelligence attracted all who met him. In addition to rhetoric, the curriculum at the Collège Mazarin reserved a year for mathematics and the exact sciences. A renowned professor, the Abbé Nicolas Louis de La Caille, would play a decisive role in turning the young student's interest toward the sciences. Assistant astronomer at the Royal Academy of Science, La Caille, along with César François Cassini de Thury, had been a member of the commission responsible for the verification of the meridian line. In 1754 he had just returned from a three-year expedition to the Cape of Good Hope. Equipped with a quarter-circle with a radius of three feet and a 32-inch telescope, he had located the positions of 9,766 stars and described them in his famous *Caelum Australe Stelliferum*.

La Caille had published his *Leçons élémentaires de Mathématiques ou Elé-*

ments d'algèbre et de géométrie, "first because of the difficulty students had in writing down precisely things that were new and that they did not understand; secondly, because having to dictate courses is a loss of valuable time."[9] Breaking with the past, La Caille had written the book in French and not in Latin; "because of its clarity, French is much more suitable than Latin for explaining the principles of a science that is particularly dependent on evidence."[10]

From La Caille, Lavoisier received a taste for exact calculation and logical reasoning, freed from all pedantry, that would mark him forever. "I was accustomed to the rigorous reasoning of mathematicians. They never take up a proposition until the one preceding it has been determined. Everything is connected, from the definition of the point and the line up to the most sublime truths of transcendent geometry."[11]

Lavoisier left the college in June 1761, forgoing the two years of philosophy that would have led to the baccalauréat.[12] He had not yet chosen his career. His father was pushing him toward law, a profession in which the elder Lavoisier could serve as guide and assure his son a good position. And, in the end, he entered the School of Law. At the same time, following La Caille's advice, he began studying meteorology, hoping to discover the laws governing the "movements of the atmosphere." He started a series of barometric observations that he pursued throughout his life.

La Caille died in March 1762, and afterward Lavoisier discovered other subjects. He learned botany at the Jardin du Roi, known today as the Jardin des Plantes, with Bernard de Jussieu, who took him along on his "philosophic walks." He acquired the rudiments of anatomy at the School of Medicine, and witnessed the Abbé Jean Antoine Nollet's experiments with electricity.

Decidedly Lavoisier preferred work to pleasure. Every moment was devoted to study. He became a bit of a recluse, even neglecting to do certain favors asked of him by Monsieur de Troncq, a friend of his father. To escape the obligations of social life, he would claim to be ill and, at one point, he stopped all nourishment except milk. His family was worried. Monsieur de Troncq sent him fine wheat flour, butter, and some good advice: "Your health, my dear mathematician, is like that of almost all educated people whose minds are stronger than their bodies. So, spend less time on your studies and remember that one more year on earth is better than a hundred in men's memories."[13]

A year later, in 1763, the young man was still withdrawn. His diligence in scientific studies benefited from this state, but his social disposition suffered.

Guettard, the Misanthrope

During this period Lavoisier discovered his father's friend Jean Etienne Guettard, who, although he was a pious and good man, declared himself to be a misanthrope. Guettard had entered the Royal Academy of Science in 1743 as a botanist, and in 1748 the duc d'Orléans had asked him to be the curator of his natural history collection.

Guettard was a "fighting animal," a quarreler whose frankness shocked his contemporaries. To a new colleague at the Academy of Science who thanked him for his support, he replied, "You owe me nothing. If I had not considered the vote justified, I would not have cast it, because I do not like you." [14]

Like so many men of this period, Guettard had an encyclopedic mind that investigated mineralogy, geology, and chemistry, all new sciences just beginning to penetrate France under German and Scandinavian influence. Baron Paul Henry d'Holbach had just translated Johann Gottschalk Wallerius's *Mineralogy* and Georg Ernst Stahl's *Treatise on Sulphur*, which contained the complete explanation of the phlogiston theory. During the summer of 1763, Guettard traveled up and down the Valois region with Lavoisier, initiating him to mineralogical and geological observation.[15] It was the younger man who wrote the accounts of the trip.[16] He also started to catalogue his collection of mineralogical samples and noted that certain sedimentary layers rich in fossils "are horizontal, which proves that they were not brought about by a sudden change, but had the opportunity to assume their natural position." [17]

On September 6, 1763, Lavoisier passed the first two examinations for the Bachelor of Law degree. On October 24, after observing an aurora borealis at Villers-Cotterêts, he wrote his first scientific report, sounding more like a poet than an astronomer when he described the luminous rays resembling "quite closely the folds, the chiaroscuro and shadows of a white drapery." [18]

Rouelle's Chemistry Course

Guettard advised Lavoisier to attend the chemistry course taught by Guillaume François Rouelle, since the precise identification of geological veins and their character required chemical analysis. For example, by pouring a mineral acid on kaolin samples, it was possible to demonstrate the presence of limestone residues, since they provoked an effervescence.[19]

The idea that natural phenomena were to be observed and analyzed rather than philosophized about was beginning to be accepted. But mineralogy and mineral chemistry had to be studied together. Chemistry had progressed in France thanks to men like Nicolas Lémery and Pierre Joseph Macquer, professor of chemistry at the Jardin du Roi and member of the Royal Academy. Rouelle, however, was the first chemist to teach geology. He was also an enthusiast for the experimental method. "Chemistry is not looking for fruitless reasoning, it seeks only facts."[20] His public lectures at the Jardin du Roi, on plants, animals and minerals, were very popular. Denis Diderot had attended them in 1754, taking notes that he carefully corrected and reproduced. Lavoisier owned and annotated one of these "polycopies."[21]

All the prominent chemists of the time—Pierre Joseph Macquer, Jean Baptiste Bucquet, Pierre Bayen, Jean d'Arcet, Gabriel François Venel, and Antoine Alexis Cadet—had attended Rouelle's course. However, Lavoisier would later say that "joined with the celebrated professor's methodical way of presenting his ideas was a great deal of vagueness in expressing them."[22]

Tall and lanky, Rouelle paid no heed to either his appearance or his language. When someone once pointed this out to him, he retorted: "Where are we? At the Academy of Proper Speech?" He came to the lecture hall in full dress: a velvet morning coat, a well-powdered wig, and a small hat clasped under his arm. Calm enough as he began to speak, he gradually warmed up, laid down his hat, removed his wig—revealing a thick mop of red hair—and loosened his tie. Then, continuing to lecture, he unbuttoned his coat and vest, took them off, one after the other, and went on in his shirt sleeves. Carried away by what he was saying, he once declared to his listeners: "You can see very well, Gentlemen, the cauldron over the flames. Well, if I were to stop stirring it for one moment, there would be an explosion that would blow us to the rooftops."[23] While speaking these words, he forgot the cauldron and the explosion occurred, blowing out window panes and sending the students, terrified, to the garden. Along with his public lectures, Rouelle started, in 1762, a private chemistry course in his pharmacy, at the corner of the rue Jacob and the rue des Deux Anges. Lavoisier came to do lab work and, with a select group, to listen to Rouelle tackle difficult subjects, such as that of the "philosophers' stone."[24]

F. L. Holmes and a recent historiographic school consider that chemistry, before Lavoisier, was not any more an empirical craft; centered around the chemistry of acids, bases, and neutral salts, it was already a coherent and structured discipline. Repeated failures in attempts to transmute metals had led to the understanding that each metal had its own identity and could not be transformed into another. Nevertheless the old concepts developed by Aristotle were still being accepted. Rouelle was still trying to reconcile the alchemists' daydreams with the theory of the four elements: fire, earth, water,

and air. The latter was based on centuries of philosophical musing and un-
demonstrated scientific hypotheses:

We call principles or else elements, simple, homogeneous, indivisible, unchanging and
insensible bodies, more or less mobile depending on their different shapes, stature and
mass, which vary among themselves by their volume and particular aspect. It is impossible to perceive them in isolation and separated from each other, unless they come
together in great numbers. Therefore, their particular aspect is impossible to determine and it would be ridiculous to claim otherwise as several physicists have done.
What can be ascertained is that their numbers are limited, but nevertheless their various combinations suffice to form all the bodies found in Nature. We recognize four
principles or elements: phlogiston or fire, earth, water and air. A fifth, Becher's mercurial principle, might even be added.[25]

But how was the conception of unchanging elements compatible with
their changing states, Lavoisier was asking? How, for example, could one explain that water could exist in solid, liquid or vaporous states? Anne Robert
Jacques Turgot had written in the *Encyclopédie* that these changes were linked
to variations in temperature; and these variations depended upon the amount
of the matter of fire combined with them. "Air is not a separate element,"
Lavoisier wrote in 1766. "It is a compound. It is water turned into vapor, or,
to be more precise, it results from the combination of water and the matter
of fire."[26] Behind this question, another was emerging: might this matter of
fire be the same as Stahl's phlogiston, popularized in Paris through Rouelle's
lectures?

Stahl's Mysterious Phlogiston

A German physician and chemist, Georg Ernst Stahl, claimed that elements
were material beings, endowed with weight and well-defined qualities.[27] He
had demonstrated the basic fact that the combustion of sulfur, carbon, and
phosphorus brought about the same chemical process as the transformation
of metals into calces or oxides. He was above all the author of an original
theory making it possible to explain combustion: all bodies contain phlogiston, the "principle of combustibility." It is imperceptible, but becomes visible
when it escapes them to become fire. During their combustion, the phlogiston contained in the bodies changes from a combined state to a free state.
The richest combustible substances (charcoal, oils, fats, sulfur, phosphorus)
are also the richest in phlogiston.

Stahl believed that metals were compound bodies; each metal was made
of calx (oxide) and phlogiston. According to his theory, when a metal was

subjected to intense heat, the phlogiston escaped and calx remained. For this reason, the operation was called calcination. Conversely, he believed that if a metallic calx was heated in the presence of charcoal, then the lost phlogiston would be restored, and the calx would regain the characteristics of metal: ductility, elasticity, and malleability. All chemists had seen metallurgists extract from the soil metallic calces that did not have the properties of metals. These properties could be restored by heating the calces, shielded from air, in the presence of charcoal. This kind of observation gave Stahl's theory a certain plausibility. A burning substance certainly gives the impression that something is escaping from it. And yet, as we know today, it is just the contrary: the substance is absorbing the oxygen of atmospheric air. Similarly, when a metallic calx is heated in the presence of charcoal, it seems that something is being added to it. Here again, it is just the opposite: one obtains a metal and carbonic gas (the oxygen of the calx having combined with the charcoal). Calx is thus a compound body; metal is a simple one.

Lavoisier clearly saw that Stahl's theory was contradictory: the calcination of the metal ought to reduce its weight, since according to him, there was a loss of phlogiston. But this was not the case. The weight of the metallic calx produced was greater than that of the original metal. Then of what value was the theory? To tell the truth, scientists throughout Europe, and Stahl himself, recognized and accepted the contradiction. "We know very well that the weight of metals increases during their calcination. But this fact, far from invalidating the phlogiston theory simply confirms it. Because phlogiston, being lighter than air, tends to lift up the substance with which it is compounded and causes it to lose a part of its weight. Therefore, the substance weighs more after having lost its phlogiston."[28] Phlogiston, then, was said to be endowed with a negative weight, a daring theoretical advance that shocked nobody at the time.

Bold Early Ventures

As for Lavoisier, he was becoming impatient. He realized that he had "spent four years studying a science founded on only a small number of facts, that it had been formed from absolutely incoherent ideas and unproven suppositions, that the method of teaching chemistry was inexistent, and that no one had the slightest idea of its logic." "I then recognized," he said, "the necessity of starting my chemical education afresh, of getting rid of everything I had learned except facts, and of arranging them methodically in my mind so as to conform to the inherent course of nature."[29]

This young man of twenty-one, so self-confident and passionately fond of logic, qualified as Licentiate of Law on July 26, 1764. He was soon admitted to the Parlement de Paris. From his identity papers, we see that he was relatively tall (5 feet, 4 inches or 1.71 meters).[30] He had fair coloring with chestnut brown hair and brown eyes. His forehead was prominent, his nose long and hooked. But his mouth was small, his lips thin, and his chin somewhat receding. The look in his eyes was gentle and attentive, but the set of his face was reserved and a little severe. His rather strict attire and slightly stiff grace reflected a natural aloofness. In fact, he was rather timid and felt more at ease in the lecture hall or his study, surrounded by books, than in society. Intelligence was his strong point. It was sharp, penetrating, analytical, and very critical. His powers of concentration were great and he had an intense intellectual curiosity. He was interested in everything. But his very sound, intransigent, and rather caustic mind was not rapid. Lavoisier liked to build on solid bases, to advance by successive deductions. He allowed himself a synthetic conclusion only after having exhausted and verified all the particulars of a problem.[31]

In 1764, at the request of Antoine Gabriel de Sartine, Deputy Commissioner of Police, the Royal Academy of Science sponsored a competition with a prize of 2,000 livres, to determine "the best means of lighting city streets, by combining brightness, simplicity of maintenance, and economy."[32] Lavoisier entered the competition. To conduct his tests and sensitize his view, he covered the wall of his study with black cloth and shut himself up in darkness for six weeks. He compared all possible types of street lamps, and even suggested having them publicly tested on the rue Croix des Petits-Champs, or near Saint-Eustache. His seventy page report which, according to the rules, had to remain anonymous, was recognizable by the proud motto placed at the top of the first page: "*Signabit viam flammis.*"[33] Brought up with high principles, Lavoisier lyrically expressed his desire to dedicate his enthusiasm, intelligence and knowledge to serving the State.

It was his first approach to the phenomena of combustion: whether simple lanterns (with candles or oil), or reflecting ones (that is, with mirrors), they both required a combustible. He concluded that olive oil was the best one. As for the fuel, oxygen, he would identify it only ten years later.

Unable to decide on one winner, the Academy of Science shared the prize among three competitors and presented Lavoisier with a medal on August 9, 1766. For the first time his name was cited, albeit misspelled, in the *Avant-Coureur*: "There was a paper full of curious research and the best physics, done by M. Ravoisier (sic) whom the Academy of Science praised. The king awarded him a gold medal, which was publicly presented by the president of the Academy."[34]

In fact, for some time Lavoisier had nursed the ambition of entering the Academy of Science, that is, of taking up "an honorable profession and, in a way, a public function."[35] Created along with the Académie Française in 1666 by Jean Baptiste Colbert, Louis XIV's chief minister, the Royal Academy of Science was "made up of mathematicians and physicists," who met in the king's library. In 1669, Louis XIV made it a royal academy having the right to meet regularly in the Louvre.

A hundred years later, the Academy of Science had become an assembly of experts responsible for realizing scientific studies requested by royal power. It was a high civil administration whose modes of recruitment and remuneration were strictly codified. There were fifty-four members, of whom twelve were honorary, eighteen were pensionnaires (the only ones to receive an annual salary, 2,000 livres; $80,000 in 1996), twelve were associates, and twelve were assistants. The members were divided into six groups. The mathematical sciences had three (geometry, astronomy, and mechanics), as did the physical sciences (chemistry, anatomy, and botany).[36]

To protect any possible discoveries made in their research, members of the Academy had the secretary initial the pages of their reports as they wrote them. Or else, before witnesses, they left their finished works with him, in sealed, dated, and numbered envelopes that were kept in the archives. Before publication, all reports were submitted to a commission for approval.

The Academy of Science in Paris inspired national research in collaboration with thirty-two provincial Academies, totaling about 2,500 Academicians. Its only European rivals were the Royal Society in London, the Royal Swedish Academy of Science in Stockholm, and the Institute in Bologna.

First Paper, "The Analysis of Gypsum"

On February 27, 1765 Lavoisier presented his first official paper at the Academy of Science. He spoke as a "visiting scientist" since he was not yet a member. The subject chosen, "The Analysis of Gypsum," situated at the junction of geology, mineralogy, and chemistry, had been suggested by Guettard. Thus Lavoisier's first scientific text was devoted to an analytical study. Here we can already see his analytical mind at work. Throughout his life, he would be the outspoken champion of analysis.

He had undertaken "a very considerable study" of all mineral substances. His predecessors, he said, had lacked imagination in limiting themselves to the study of metallic substances, when an infinity of mineral substances were to be found in nature. "Most soils, stones and crystallizations are absolutely new substances for the chemist. Their examination can provide an inexhaustable source of experiments and discoveries."[37] But, Lavoisier continued, it is not enough to discover new mineral substances, one must have an accurate analytical method to study them. He believed that in this domain Johann Heinrich Pott, the author of *Lithéognosie* (Mineralogy), had hardly contributed to the body of knowledge. "The path I have followed in analyzing mineral substances is entirely different. I have attempted to copy nature. Since water, the almost universal solvent that nothing resists, is the principal agent it employs, it is also the one I have used."[38] When he calcined gypsum, he noted that it gave off a light vapor. Collected in a container, this vapor resembled distilled water and weighed a quarter of the initial weight of gypsum. It was the water of crystallization. When he returned it to the gypsum crystals, they rapidly absorbed it and formed a mass. Plasterers called this operation "tempering the plaster."

Lavoisier had just perfected the double demonstration method that he would use throughout his scientific career. First, decompose a supposedly simple substance into its elements, then recompose it from those same elements.

The first quarrels relating to the precedence of publication were already starting. Lavoisier learned that Antoine Baumé had just published a study on plaster in the *Gazette d'Epidaure* and felt obliged to explain:

Persons who have my interests at heart, having pointed out to me that precise experiments conducted on the same subject by two different persons could only serve to confirm each other, and that, moreover, M. Baumé's announcement contained nothing but generalities, and that the work he referred to had not yet been published, I acknowledged their observations and decided to present this paper as it was then, without changing anything.[39]

The referees named by the Academy of Science, Henri Louis Duhamel du Monceau and Bernard de Jussieu, judiciously chosen because they were friends of Lavoisier's father, accepted the text for the *Savants étrangers* collection.[40] They remarked that most of the evidence set forth by Lavoisier was not entirely new, "but no one has treated this subject matter so methodically and broadly as he, and one is especially indebted to him for his ingenious explanation reducing the phenomenon of plaster of Paris to the simple laws of crystallization, and for determining the amount of water needed for the dissolution of gypsum."[41]

However, Lavoisier had made an original test not mentioned by the referees. Having learned from metallurgists that calcination transforms metal into calx and causes it to lose its metallic qualities, he had calcined gypsum instead of heating it, and its properties had changed. It no longer formed a mass in water, but a crumbly, powdery heap. Were the two situations analogous? "I could make a few conjectures," he wrote, "I might even succeed in making them probable, but they would be out of place in a chemistry paper, in which one must proceed only with experiment in hand. Perhaps the continuation of my work will give me some insight into this phenomenon."[42]

On March 19, 1766, in a second paper on gypsum, he showed that it was formed from chalk and sulfuric acid, and that its solubility depended on the acid content. He explained that, at the base of mountains, gypsums are rich in acid; they are false alabasters. In other places, where the sea remained for centuries, depositing enormous masses of shells, acid is rare but limestone abounds: it is *lapis specularis*. He had begun to see that geological laws govern the nature of soils and the arrangement of sedimentary strata. He wanted to "convey just how important the analysis of these mineral substances is for shedding light on the past of nature. It will inevitably lead to a theory explaining the changes that have occurred on the surface of the earth."[43]

Lavoisier felt that the time was right for pursuing his candidacy for membership in the Academy of Science. In April he suggested to the president and permanent secretary that an additional class in experimental physics be created. He would hope to join it, as would Baumé and the younger Rouelle, Hilaire Marin. Lavoisier argued cleverly, referring to the past successes of the physics group from 1666 to 1699, when Christian Huygens, the Abbé Edme Mariotte, and Claude Perrault were members, and deploring the fact that the lack of qualified candidates had made it impossible to maintain the group. "This is why progress in experimental physics came to a halt in France, and why foreigners profited from our spoils. Because, it must be admitted, membership in the Academy serves more than anything else to form minds and to kindle in young souls the competitive fire that impels them to great discoveries."[44]

The reopening of this section, he argued, would be justified by the large number of qualified candidates. "A crowd of them exists, several have already shown great promise. Why should we discourage young talent?"[45] It would be, he continued, a way of lessening the dependence on foreigners, of assuring the distinction of France and that of Daniel Trudaine, director of the Bureau of Commerce. Finally, with a minimum expenditure of a thousand écus per year, the State could acquire seven scientists.[46]

But the proposition was judged to be too daring. The day after its rejection, Lavoisier, along with Baumé and the younger Rouelle, proposed himself as a candidate for a place as assistant in the chemistry group. But he would have to wait two years before being accepted.

From Mineralogy to Geology

Lavoisier was undaunted by vast projects and, while waiting, confidently decided to construct a theory of the formation of earth. "This immense work," he announced with his habitual juvenile magniloquence, "will provide exact information on the previous boundaries of the sea, on the bed it covered and the former arrangements of the continents. In a word, it will be a systematic description of global changes, based on reliable experiments and observations." [47]

Starting from the works of his teachers—the comte de Buffon, Guettard and Rouelle—he constructed his own theory. [48] The crust of the earth, he said, is formed from an old soil, made from mountainous granite masses with a low fossil content, and a new soil, fossiliferous and sedimentary. The rocks of the old soil are "arranged in perpendicular layers or inclined toward the horizon. They are of quartz, granite, shale, slate and talcose stone. [49] The sediments, he continued, are of four types: "lime soils and stones, gypsum soils and stones, pebbles or flint and clayey soil." [50]

Like Rouelle, Lavoisier at first conceived of only one period of sedimentation. He considered that the waters, in receding, had isolated the continents and given a complex distribution to the maritime basins and continents. There were two kinds of beds: pelagic beds, formed in deep seas and made up of almost pure calx, mixed with shell fragments accumulated over the centuries, and littoral beds along the coasts, complex in nature with, from top to bottom pebbles, coarse sand, fine sand, clay, and siliceous soil.

The theory did not explain the existence of littoral beds within pelagic beds; and when Lavoisier observed a sandbed enclosed with a layer of calx, he considered it "accidental." [51] But in the autumn of 1766, a trip to Brie showed him that the alternation of calx with sandy layers was much more common than he had thought. The cyclical ebb and flow of the ocean had undoubtedly deposited a succession of sedimentary beds. To measure their thickness, altitude and extent, he drew contour lines using a barometer. Beginning in the vicinity of Paris, he then proceeded to Etampes and Orléans. He planned to continue on to Blois and Tours and determine the height of all the mountains of the region.

This study of sedimentary phenomena and the stratigraphy of soils had more than merely theoretical objectives. It was also a means of making an inventory of the mineralogical resources of France. The questionnaries Lavoisier sent to his provincial correspondents are revealing. He wanted to know about the places where chalk, building stone, limestone, and sand were extracted. Were there marble, slate, sandstone, iron ore, coal, or "any other interesting raw materials for the arts and commerce?"[52]

Here the word "arts" designated the emerging industrial activities in which the duc d'Orléans, Guettard's patron, was interested. Lavoisier's curiosity about geology was spurred by Guettard's important project, the *Atlas minéralogique de la France*, which was to be an inventory of "the quarries, excavating mines, mineral springs, and all raw materials contained in the earth."[53] Jean Baptiste Bertin, the Minister who was supporting the project, had chosen Guettard to head the official expedition to explore Lorraine and Alsace.

Research in the Vosges Mountains

Guettard asked Lavoisier to accompany him on his expedition to the Vosges Mountains. It was made on horseback because the roads were in poor condition. Lavoisier took along all the instruments needed for his observations: a box of chemical reagents, three thermometers, and a barometer. He also had a silver hydrometer for measuring the density of mineral waters and a tiny silver mortar. A small oblong box, covered with dogfish skin, or green galuchat, contained a single piece of vermeil tableware: at one end it had three prongs, on the other a curved knife blade.[54]

The two men left on June 14, 1767, accompanied by a servant, Joseph. Already that evening Lavoisier mailed his first letter from Brie-Comte-Robert. "Animals and people are delighted and in good health. The horses seem especially gay and have good appetites. So there is every reason to hope that all will go well."[55] After Provins and Troyes, they reached the Château de Lancques, near Chaumont, where their hosts were the Briaucourts. To show his appreciation for their hospitality, Lavoisier asked his father, who was to join them at Bourbonne-les-Bains, to put several bottles of ratafia in his carriage. Then he added, "If you could also bring a few Roman candles and pinwheels, they would greatly amuse the family at Lancques. Also, Madame de Briaucourt would like to have goldfish to put in her moats. There are many of them at the Palais Royal. Could you get half a dozen small ones for her? You can transport them in a wide-necked bottle or a tin bowl."[56] In spite of his desire to please, Lavoisier's father confessed to being a bit put out:

We shall get the goldfish, but the problem will be transporting them. They cannot be cut off from the air, which means that we shall have to hold the container in our lap. And even so, it is not at all certain that any will survive. They will fight in a bottle or jar and may kill each other. You have given me a nasty and extremely awkward errand, but I shall overlook the trouble and effort when I think that I shall be meeting you very soon.[57]

The two scientists had less frivolous activities and they had to do everything themselves. It was not enough to collect rock fragments and carry them back to the inn. They then had to sort, label, wrap, and catalogue them. Boxes had to be constructed, then packed and sent to the Ministry, along with a notification of their dispatch. Finally, a copy of the catalogue had to be posted. The weather was not always clement. The travelers endured heavy rains and storms and their wardrobes suffered; "I think it will be necessary to have a suit made for the autumn," Lavoisier wrote his aunt. "The one I have is ruined, more yellow than green. I believe, unless you think otherwise, that it should be made of wool, green, or some other color if you prefer, so long as it is a color appropriate for the country. It should be trimmed with a narrow gold braid."[58] Painstaking as usual, Lavoisier returned to the subject several days later. "In my next-to-last letter, I mentioned having a suit made. Instead of green, perhaps iron grey would be better. I believe it would be more practical."[59]

Aunt Constance immediately took care of everything. "I bought the cloth for your suit on Tuesday and have given it to the tailor. I hesitated quite a while, since you had seemed uncertain about the color. Following M. Viqui's advice, and that of M. Desvue, I chose green, since iron grey is not in fashion, whereas green is very much so. They did not hesitate in urging me to choose green. Besides, M. Desvue had no grey cloth. The fabric is magnificent, and I think you will be pleased with it as well as the border. I suggested to the tailor that he put buttons on the fab and the small pockets to hold your pistols more securely."[60]

The route lay through Bourbonne-les-Bains, Vesoul, Villersexel, Lure, Ronchamp, Luxeuil. The travelers stayed for a few days in Giromagny and climbed the Ballon d'Alsace. Their itinerary took them to Bussang, Belfort, Montbéliard, Altkirch, and finally Basel. They took readings from the barometer and thermometer several times a day. They studied the soils, topography, and vegetation of the various regions and analyzed the mineral and drinking waters. They visited mines, factories, a steelmill, a workshop for bleaching cloth, freestone quarries, and works for producing rubble stone, calx, and plaster.

They were in Basel, Switzerland, on July 25, met the mathematician

Daniel Bernouilli and a number of scientists, and began to dream of political freedom. "Basel is a most agreeable town. It exudes comfort and liberty. The government is aristocratic. All citizens are equal and can equally aspire to high offices in the Republic."[61] Thus, twenty years before the French Revolution, Lavoisier was already expressing the secret aspirations that were going to trigger it.

After Basel they visited Mulhouse, Thann, and Gerardmer, where they climbed to the Grand Ballon, the highest point of the Vosges Mountains. They were accompanied by an artist who made a series of drawings of the panorama. Lavoisier recorded the readings of the thermometer and barometer, the temperature and density of mineral waters. He was also a curious observer of peasant life: "The life led in these mountains is quite remarkable. The dairy farmers, who are ordinarily very well off, eat neither bread nor meat. Nor does one find any wine among them. They live from a fresh low-fat cheese, quite dry, that they shape into large loaves. They drink only water or milk."[62] In Colmar, on August 14, Guettard wrote:

One would hardly put a dog outside in this weather. But we have to keep going. Such are the pleasures of mineralogy. For this profession, you have to be made of iron. One day you are utterly soaked with rain, the next with perspiration, and on still another, by both—the rain from above, the perspiration from within. Then a plague of burning rays grills you like a smoked herring. We are quite well roasted by now. In addition to all that, we have to laden ourselves with stones, make packages, and scribble down our observations. We eat in a hurry and whatever we can find. Is this a life for a Christian?"[63]

Finally, on September 3, they reached Strasbourg, a stopping place much looked forward to by Lavoisier. Lavoisier met there a number of scientists, including the chemist Friedrich Ludwig Ehrmann. In the big bookstore called König, he bought twelve in quarto volumes of the *Acta Physico-Medica*, published by the "Society of the Curious about Nature"; the *Commentaries on Medical Science* from the Leipzig Academy of Science; Agricola's *De re metallica*; chemical works by Johann Joachim Becher, Frederick Cartheuser, Howard Gruber, Frederick Hoffmann, Martin Lister, Jan Baptist Van Helmont, John Mayow, Petrus Van Musschenbroek, Georg Ernst Stahl, Emanuel Swedenborg, Johann Gottschalk Wallerius, and Samuel Widmer; numerous books on hydrology and geology and several on medicine. Finally, he bought the six volumes missing from his collection of the *Memoirs of the Academy of Science of Berlin* and other works unavailable in France.

The bill amounted to 533 livres and 5 sous ($20,000). But König was a sensible shopkeeper. "I flatter myself that you will be satisfied," he said, "when

I let you have all the books for the round sum of 500 livres, especially since I am not charging you for packing and transportation."[64] The large, well-packed crate addressed to "M. Lavoisier, libri, Paris" weighed 288 pounds. The 118 works it contained already attested to the keen appetite for knowledge that led Lavoisier to build a very fine library. At every possible occasion, he acquired scientific works, especially German and Swedish ones that, since they were written in Latin, were more accessible to him than English publications. His vocation as a collector had begun to flourish when he had purchased in May 1766 some items from Jean Hellot's Library: "The catalogue listed 2,128 titles, both printed and manuscript, more than half of which dealt with natural sciences. Many of the works of chemistry were rare or by authors not very well known in France. Hellot also owned a unique collection of 63 treatises devoted to the chemical analysis of mineral water."[65] Several of these books on mineral waters had a direct link with the program of work in the Vosges; others reflected Lavoisier's approach to scientific questions; furthermore, he had a genuine taste for bibliophily. In addition to books and mineral samples, his passion for collecting would take on diverse forms throughout his life, and include public functions and responsibilities, money, stocks, real estate, land.

The mineralogists' return trip took them through Saverne, Sarrebourg, Baccarat, and Remiremont. The stopover at Cormont was quite uncomfortable:

We are housed in a drafty barn-like structure where the odor of a heap of onions left to dry has gone to our heads. We sleep on miserable feather beds only two inches thick. We scoured the village in search of two blankets, because the custom here is to use the feather beds for cover, even in summer. However, we had been told that we could be comfortably accommodated here. This is not the first time, alas, that we have experienced the same fate, but nowhere else was it quite as bad.[66]

They returned to Paris on October 19, 1767, after passing through Plombières, Epinal, Luxeuil, Mirecourt, Nancy, and Bourbonne-les-Bains, and immediately began sorting their notes. These four months over hill and dale had hardly advanced the theory of the earth, because of the great geological disorder of the regions explored. But the analysis of mineral waters had convinced Lavoisier that there existed a close relationship between them and the soils from which they gushed forth:

For the mineralogist there is no surer guide than the examination of waters. Because water is the favorite agent of nature. It is water that covers the insides of mine veins and all sorts of crystals that we admire and choose to adorn the shelves of our display cabinets. It is water that, filtering through the hardest stones, forms the crystal and the diamond. And it is also water that, combining metallic dissolvents with the saps of quartz and crystalline, forms precious stones.[67]

The young chemist did not yet realize that his interest in water would eventually lead him to question the nature of this element, to see it as a compound body, and to determine its exact composition.

2

Farmer General and Academician

AT TWENTY-FOUR, Lavoisier had reached the age for choosing a profession. The bar definitely did not appeal to him, and the annual salary of 2,000 livres that he might expect from the Royal Academy of Science would not allow him to live according to his tastes and ambitions. In March 1768 Antoine Chaumont de La Galaizière, Intendant from Lorraine, suggested that he enter the *Ferme générale* or General Farm, a private company with sixty stockholders, in charge of collecting indirect taxes for the king; *gabelle* (salt tax), *aides* (tobacco and alcohol taxes), *traites* (customs duties), and *entrées* (taxes on goods entering Paris). One of the Farmers General, François Baudon, seventy-four years old, wanted to sell his holdings. The assets of the General Farm totaled 93.6 million livres; each member's part amounted to 1,560,000 livres. On May 2, 1768 Lavoisier purchased a third of Baudon's share for 520,000 livres ($21 million in 1996), of which 68,000 were a down payment.[1] Malicious gossip claimed that Cromot de Bourg, Baudon's son-in-law, received half the sum for having slightly forced Baudon's hand. Although Lavoisier had made a good investment, he had chosen a highly unpopular profession.[2]

The Farm contracted six-year leases with the Controller-General of Finance and paid in advance to the royal Treasury a stipulated sum in each year of the lease. The amount to be paid annually, representing the taxes to collect, was fixed after negotiation, and handed over to the Treasury. At the beginning of the eighteenth century it totaled 75 million livres. It soon reached 130, and was at 152 million by 1774. Signed by a straw man, generally the manservant of the Controller-General, the lease bore his name: thus the one for the period 1768–1774 was known as the "Alaterre lease."

The profit of the General Farm came from the difference between the sum paid to the Treasury and the sum of the taxes collected, once the expenses and salaries of 30,000 employees had been deducted. The profit could not be calculated when the lease expired because there were always debts to be paid, stocks to be inventoried, and legal proceedings to be settled. This complex operation might stretch over several years, and during the duration of the lease the stockholders received sums corresponding to the profit from the on-going lease plus belated settlements from the preceding one. The finances of the State being in comparable disorder, it was very difficult to determine the exact amount of inflows and outflows for each fiscal year.

The annual income of a Farmer General included a fixed remuneration of 24,000 livres, 4,200 livres for office expenses and a travel allowance of 1,500 livres per month during inspection tours. There was also a 10 percent interest on the first million livres invested, and 6 percent for the remaining 560,000 livres. Finally, as an advance, each member was given a part of the profit that would be calculated at the end of the lease. Therefore his gross income came to 145,000 livres per year, but once the interest on loans, bribes, *croupes* or crup-pers, and living allowances were deducted, real income amounted to between 60,000 and 120,000 livres per year (between $2.4 and 4.8 million in 1996).

The king often threatened to reduce the profits of the Farm and even to put taxes under direct state control. But the Farm provided 40 to 50 percent of his resources, lent him money, and made up a powerful pressure group capable of blocking any reform. Placing money in the Farm remained a guar-antee of high return with no risk.

The French found indirect taxes hard to endure and tried to escape them. Fraud and contraband were widespread and very harshly punished. "The ac-count of the import duty and salt tax would suffice to explain the unpopu-larity of the General Farm. To have earned it, the Farmers General had no need to be overly zealous. It was enough to carry out their duty, simply and routinely."[3] In one year, for the smuggling of salt alone, there were almost 4,000 domiciliary seizures, and on the roads, 2,500 men, 2,000 women, and 6,000 children were arrested, while almost 1,200 horses and 56 carts were con-fiscated. "The condemnations to the galleys exceeded 200 and, in short, of the 6,000 convicts in penal servitude, a third had been sent there for smuggling."[4]

The Tobacco Commission

The General Farm had no director, and the jobs were divided up among the members. Each one held one or several positions, whether on *committees* that made decisions, on *commissions* that carried them out, or as *inspectors* who veri-fied the efficiency of the operations on the spot.

In the beginning, Lavoisier was a *tourneur*, that is a regional inspector, for the Tobacco Commission. His territory included the Marne, Champagne, and Ardennes regions. His supervisor was Jacques Paulze de Chasteignolles, who was not only a Farmer General but a lawyer at the Parlement de Paris, a Royal Prosecutor, and a director of the East India Company. Paulze advised Lavoisier, as he had already done for his own son, Balthazar Jacques, to be honest and considerate to all, and wary of confiding in anybody. He should have irreproachably moral behavior and never let himself be tempted by gambling. He ought to know the population, industries, trade, communications, workforce, and salaries in each town he inspected. "The amount of duties collected by the General Farm," Paulze said, "is proportional to alcohol consumption, which is always proportional to the number and the wealth of the consumers. A Farmer General has to be aware of all these elements."[5]

The Farm held a monopoly on the production, importation, and sale of tobacco; and it levied taxes on the sales. The stakes were high, since duties brought in nearly 30 million livres every year. Unknown before the sixteenth century, tobacco had conquered Europe in two hundred years and had rapidly become an important source of the income of the State.[6] But since 1759 income had fallen by more than 20 percent, from 34 to 26 million livres. Uneasy, the General Farm appointed a committee of specialists to investigate the matter—made up of MM. Geoffroy Chalut de Vérin, Charles de Mazières, Jean François Verdun de Montchiroux, Claude François Rougeot, Clément de Laâge de Bellefaye, Alexandre Philibert Pierre Parceval de Gonneville, Gilbert Georges de Montcloux, François Puissant de La Villeguérie, and Jacques Paulze de Chasteignolles. The simple enumeration of the commissioners' names amusingly underlines the desire of all these bourgeois, who had only recently become wealthy, to acquire noble particles and titles. Lavoisier would not escape this shortcoming.

After four years of persistent effort, a young Farmer General, Jacques Delahante, discovered how the fraud worked. Tobacco was delivered by the Farm to dealers in three different forms: in plugs for chewing, shredded and blended for pipes, and in *bouts* or ends that were grated into powder for snufftakers. The dealers had devised a way of selling several of these ends tied together with strings. They looked like sausages, but were called "carrots" because they were grated in the same way. Dealers mixed smuggled ends with those coming from the Farm. Thus the Farm decided to discourage fraud by making its own carrots.

Taking snuff soon became the fashion and customers no longer wanted carrots but ground tobacco. The dealers rushed to satisfy them by grinding the contraband tobacco with the legal product and returned to the good old days of the smuggled ends. They sold not only contraband tobacco, which was ten times cheaper than the tobacco of the Farm, at high prices, but also a variety of pulverizable substances that cost them nothing at all. Certain Farmers General then proposed that the Farm take over the grinding and direct sale of tobacco. Some attempts were made in secure territories, in particular in Lorraine, Lavoisier's preserve. Others thought it preferable to leave this privilige to the dealers. It was the beginning of the quarrel between the "pro-graters" and the "anti-graters," and it continued for forty years.

Lavoisier's main responsibility was to fight contraband and fraud among retailers. Tobacco was being smuggled into France by land or sea, circulated in clandestine networks, and then hidden before surfacing in the shops. The dealers had found a new way to improve their profit. They mixed this tobacco with tobacco from the Farm and then added ash and water. Lavoisier used his skills as an analyst to check the quality of the tobacco being sold by the dealers. He wrote to his director:

You know that ash is the most commonly used substance in the mixtures. Fortunately, chemistry provides sure, unequivocal means of recognizing ash in almost all of the substances with which it is mixed. When a spirit of vitriol, *aqua fortis* or some other acid solution is poured on ash, there is an immediate very intense effervescent reaction, accompanied by an easily detected noise. Ash mixed with tobacco retains this property; therefore, it is a sure means of recognizing if the tobacco has been adulterated by the addition of ash. Moreover, by the greater or lesser intensity of the effervescent reaction, one can judge approximately the proportion of ash to tobacco.[7]

Mixtures were rare at Charleville, where recent dismissals had intimidated dealers. At Sainte-Menehould, on the contrary, cheating was widespread. In Vitry, the tobacco not only was mixed with ash, but was extremely humid. It fermented, heated up, and acquired a disagreeable odor most likely to repel tobacco lovers.

Lavoisier asked, however, whether the Farm should not profit from certain recipes used by dealers, in particular Patin's. "His tobacco enjoys a very good reputation in the province. [. . .] The very small portion of ash that is added gives it a particularly pungent flavor that consumers look for. Perhaps the farm could gain some advantage by adding a bit of this liquid mixture when the tobacco is fabricated."[8]

Gradually, on the important question of *mouillade* or moistening, which would become the source of so many passionate disputes and serious accusations, Lavoisier defined the doctrine of the Farm: there was a legitimate moistening, practiced in factories, and necessary to production. "Tobacco, when ready for consumption, is a vegetable that has undergone a first stage of fermentation. But we know that fermentation cannot take place without the help of water."[9] However, a sense of moderation had to be kept: "Tobacco when moistened easily ferments, and its temperature rises. It begins to smell sour. [. . .] I believe that in general we must be extremely cautious about adding water to tobacco. It would be better to make slight sacrifices than to run the risk of displeasing the public."[10] The acceptable amount of water was 6 pounds, 5 ounces per hundredweight of grated tobacco, or 6.3 percent. This quantity of added water was reimbursed to the dealers by the seventeenth ounce of tobacco the Farm delivered without cost for each order of sixteen ounces.

But the moistening practiced by the dealers to increase their profits was unacceptable: they risked "putrefying" the tobacco, and that would harm the reputation and legitimate interests of the Farm. Lavoisier inspected them in every town and knew how to exercise his authority. He decided who was to be kept or replaced, and did not hesitate to dismiss the guilty. In Vitry, Suzanne Regnault, suspected of mixing, made a good impression.

I found in this young woman a sincerity and frankness that I've seen nowhere else. Besides, everybody in Vitry takes an interest in her, and it is a great advantage for a dealer to have the confidence of the public. She insists that if her tobacco was mixed, she never knew about it, and she suspects that only the grater could have done it. Monsieur Rougeot is keenly interested in this dealer. From the way she spoke to me, I would be tempted to believe that the mixtures were indeed made without her knowledge.[11]

In Chalons Lavoisier suspected a *receveur* of having removed samples of questionable tobacco from a parcel sent to Paulze. And he urged the dismissal of Sieur Marlin, half of whose tobacco was made up of foreign substances. He was more tolerant concerning the Widow Ducloir:

Although the corrupt practices of the dealer have been well proven, I think I should bring to your attention a few motives that will convince you to suspend her dismissal. First, she is the widow of a former military officer, and the tobacco dealership was given to her as a kind of reparation. Second, she is responsible for a very large family and has no other means of supporting them. Third, Monsieur d'Auteroche, in particular, has a special interest in her. Fourth, she sells a great deal of tobacco.[12]

Independent of the humanitarian feelings that prompted him, it is highly likely that Lavoisier was not insensitive to the fact that the widow Ducloir's patron was Monsieur d'Auteroche and that Madame Regnault's patron was Monsieur Rougeot, both his colleagues in the Farm.

Every day he inspected and spoke with the customs squads, going over the customs boundaries, and adjusting them if necessary to make surveillance easier. He slept at the home of Sieur Lannoy, a customs officer in the small village of Heitz l'Evêque, and noted, "One can learn a great deal from subordinates when one can put them at ease."[13] But the conversations, as it turned out, were not entirely favorable to his host. When it was proposed that Lannoy be promoted to the rank of captain, Lavoisier commented:

Of all the horsemen I know, this employee is the one who seems to have the best education, the broadest outlook, the greatest shrewdness and energy. But I must tell you also that he is not popular with the other employees. They claim that he has a quick and hotheaded temper, that he is excessively proud and unsociable, that he is very difficult in general, and even that there is something deceitful in his character.[14]

Lavoisier's functions as an inspector were an extraordinary occasion to discover administrative organization in the field, to see the practical problems it posed, to learn how to judge men, and to familiarize himself with commerical and industrial methods. He sent Paulze a series of brief reports on the principal officials of the region. His superior could feel very pleased with such a competent and efficient collaborator. Lavoisier was well-organized, knew how to adapt means to ends and was adept at matching tasks with his employees' abilities.

Concurrently, he continued his inventory of the mineral resources of the kingdom for the future *Atlas minéralogique de la France*, which was to include 230 mineralogical maps corresponding exactly to geographical ones. The required budget was 300,000 livres ($12 million). But both funds and time were lacking. Lavoisier suggested reducing the project to 28 maps and the budget to 45,000 livres ($1.8 million). He had found some financiers who would lend the money, he said, if the Minister would contribute 18,000 livres, payable in four years. But Jean Baptiste Bertin had no money, and particular interests stood in the way.

At the public session of the Academy of Science in the spring of 1770, Guettard paid tribute to his young collaborator. "The detailed observations on certain districts were made by Monsieur Lavoisier alone. Obliged to travel in the interests of a company to which he is attached, he kept a record of his observations. From this effort, more than sixteen individual maps have resulted. Altogether the maps cover quite a large area of this kingdom."[15]

The financial, political, and human events were going to persist for the next ten years. The *Atlas*, which finally appeared in 1778, had only twenty-six maps, of which sixteen were attributed to Lavoisier. The economic purpose of the work appeared clearly in the foreword written by Guettard:

It is not for miners alone that this mineralogical map of France is essential. It will be helpful to all landowners wishing to profit from the natural resources their property contains: calcareous stones and pebbles, quarries for building stone, marble, lime, clay, marl and coalmines. [. . .] Manufacturers will find the information necessary for establishing factories producing tiles, bricks, pottery, earthenware and porcelain. By consulting it, producers of woolen cloth will often be able to find close at hand the fuller's earth that they are sometimes obliged to transport from afar.[16]

Admission to the Royal Academy of Science

Théodore Baron d'Enouville, known for his research on borax and potassium chloride, died on March 10, 1768, freeing a place for an assistant chemist at the Academy of Science. For two years, Lavoisier had been a candidate, along with Antoine Baumé (a pharmacist), Jacques François Demachy (a chemist), Jacques Christophe Valmont de Bomare (a demonstrator in natural history), Antoine Monnet and Balthazar Sage (mineralogists), and Gabriel Jars (a metallurgist). Jars, who was his most serious competitor, had directed the development of silver-bearing lead mines in Brittany and coal mines in Anjou. From his numerous foreign missions, he had brought back processes for manufacturing red lead.

Jars was backed by Buffon, the treasurer, and the minister, the comte de Saint-Florentin. Lavoisier could count on the votes of his father's friends, the astronomer Giacomo Maraldi and Henri Louis Duhamel du Monceau, as well as those of Bernard de Jussieu and Pierre Joseph Macquer. "I helped to elect Lavoisier," said Joseph Jerôme Lalande, the astronomer, "although he was younger and less well known, because I felt that a young man—educated, intelligent and energetic—whom fortune had exempted from taking up another profession, would naturally be very useful to science."[17] The fact that Lavoisier was a Farmer General did not bother his future colleagues. One of them even remarked: "That's just fine! The dinners he will serve us will be all the better!"

The election was held on May 18, 1768. Lavoisier had the highest number of votes, Jars the second highest. The definitive choice was left to the minister Saint-Florentin and the king. In consideration for his outstanding service to France, Jars was chosen. However, an additional temporary place of assistant chemist was created for Lavoisier, it being understood that he would be named officially, without an election, when the next vacancy occurred.

On Wednesday, June 1, 1768, a month after he had joined the General Farm, Lavoisier sat for the first time at the Royal Academy of Science. He was already familiar with the scene. In 1678 Louis XIV had left the Louvre and permanently settled with the court in his new palace at Versailles. The Academy, located until that time in the King's Library, on ground level, had moved in 1699 to the King's apartment on the first floor. The academicians

took possession of four rooms designated by "D" on Jacques François Blondel's plan of the Louvre dated 1752. They held session in the salle Henri II,
the king's old antechamber. They entered from the Cour Carrée, by the staircase to the left under the Tour de l'Horloge, mounted to the first story, and
passed through the Salle des Etats. Meetings were held weekly, on Wednesdays and Saturdays from three to five in the hall, hung with tapestries from the
king's collection and decorated by a large conventional painting by Antoine
Coypel, "Minerva Looking at the Portrait of Louis XIV." Public galleries had
been built, and there were also a library, a physics laboratory, and a natural history exhibition room with a number of animal skeletons. Lavoisier sat
with the other assistant chemists on a bench at the back of the hall, behind
the armchairs of the associate members, facing the president and director. The
salaried members, the secretary, and the treasurer were seated along the sides.

Today the rooms corresponding to the Academy of Science in the Louvre
are part of department 7, first floor, Sully wing; they are Salle Henri II or Salle
33 des Antiquités grecques, étrusques et romaines, Salle Clarac or Salle 35 des
Antiquités grecques, étrusques et romaines, and Salle des Sept-Cheminées or
Salle 74 des Peintures françaises. Salle 33, under a ceiling decorated since 1953
by *Les oiseaux*, a large painting by Braque, exhibits Roman jewels and silver-
ware. Salle 35 is mostly devoted to Etruscan terra cottas and ceramics. Salle
74 presents large French paintings from the XIXth century.[18]

As Lavoisier began his official career as a chemist, he was musing over an
article in the *Encyclopédie* where Gabriel François Venel prophecied, "It is obvious that the revolution that would place chemistry in the rank it deserves—
which would at least place it beside experimental physics—can be carried out
only by a clever, enthusiastic, and bold chemist who, finding himself in a
favorable position and skillfully profiting from a few fortunate circumstances,
can attract the attention of scientists, first by a noisy ostentation and a determined, assertive tone. And then by reason, if his first arms have stirred up
prejudice."[19]

Lavoisier, determined to realize this program, filled at least the first of
Venel's conditions: he found himself "in a favorable position."

The Waters of the Yvette

One of the first technical studies Lavoisier did for the Academy was the
evaluation of a project proposed by the engineer Antoine de Parcieux, known
for his demographic research. To supply Paris with drinking water, Parcieux

proposed bringing it by aqueduct from a small river, the Yvette, which had its source near Longjumeau. Voltaire wrote the engineer: "You have a plan to give Paris the water it lacks and save us at last from the disgrace and ridicule of constantly hearing the shout, 'A l'eau,' and seeing women enclosed in oblong hoops, carrying two buckets of water weighing 30 pounds up five floors for use in a privy. Be so kind as to tell me how many beasts of burden with two hands and two feet there are in France."[20]

The aqueduct would cost 8 million livres but fill an urgent need. The only drinking water in the city was supplied by watercarriers who took it from the Seine. But the river also served as a sewer and the quality of the water was dubious. The problem was to find financial backing for the project. Voltaire was skeptical:

The Hôtel de Ville in Paris is not the Capitol. It will not begrudge money for a Comic Opera, but will complain about building aqueducts worthy of Augustus. I passionately hope I am wrong. I would so much like to see the Yvette waters form a large pool around Louis XV's statue. I would so much like to know that all houses in Paris, like those in London, are being supplied with water.[21]

The government hesitated because of the high cost of the project. Finally the plan was indeed ruled out because the Opera, which had just burned, had to be rebuilt. Voltaire, undeceived, wrote ironically, "The maids of the Opera have prevailed over the nymphs of the Yvette."[22]

Antoine de Parcieux died at the end of 1768. His aqueduct was immediately the object of a vehement attack by Father Félicien de Saint-Norbert. Lavoisier, who had been studying the proposal, contested the validity of the criticism and declared at the Academy that Parcieux's project was the most advantageous of all those being considered. "It is the least expensive, considering the mass of water it will provide, and the one most suitable for the capital."[23] But still the financial state of the city made it impossible to go ahead with the project.

The Yvette Aqueduct opened a debate on methods of chemical analysis. To choose the best water, the Academy asked for a comparative analysis of water from different rivers near Paris, and imposed two methods to be used: measuring either the density of the water or the residue of mineral salts left after evaporation.

Lavoisier advocated the former method, hydrometry. The reliability of the latter was contested by Jean Baptiste Le Roy, a professor of medicine at Montpellier. He claimed that distillation could not provide pure water, since all water contained a rather significant amount of earth, so closely united with the water that almost all of it passed through the distillation process.

But a small amount of earth did separate from the water and remain in the still. This, he pointed out, had led numerous scientists to believe errone-ously that water was transformed into earth during the distillation process. Lavoisier came close to sharing Le Roy's opinion. "It can be considered as a sufficiently established truth that water, reduced to vapor, carries with it a small portion of salts that it retains in dissolution."[24] He did not think that it was a change in nature—water is not transformed into salts or earth—but rather a change of state. When subjected to heat, the mineral salts dissolved in the water passed from a liquid to a gaseous state. If the analysis by evaporation was unreliable, the measure of density, on the contrary, allowed exact calcu-lations. Robert Boyle's hydrometer (now called a densimeter) could measure the specific weight of a water sample according to its salt content, and its den-sities could be determined by comparison with distilled water. Lavoisier had already used this technique at the Farm to calculate the strength of alcoholic drinks and, hence, the duties to be paid to the city agencies. He had several models of the hydrometer made in copper and silver. They were topped by small cups on which weights could be placed and—a most important innova-tion—graduated in decimal units.[25] Thus he could read directly the density of the different water samples containing known amounts of three salts: Glau-ber salt (sodium sulfate), sea salt (sodium chloride), and selenite or gypsum salts (calcium sulfate). To determine the amount of any one of these salts in a water sample, it sufficed to compare its density value to those on the table. But the method had its drawbacks. The temperature had to be constant, and the water could contain only one salt. Unfortunately, most mineral waters contain several.

On March 23, 1768, even before being admitted to the Royal Academy, Lavoisier had presented his research on hydrometers and one hundred sixty densimetric measures. For the first time he referred to current social ideas. Medicinal waters, he said, had their uses, but it was much more important to study drinking waters. "It is on them that the strength and health of citi-zens depend, and even if the former have sometimes revived persons precious to the State, the latter, in continuously re-establishing the order and equilib-rium of the animal system, save the lives of a much greater number of persons every day. The examination of mineral waters strictly speaking interests only a small, dwindling portion of society. That of common waters interests all of society and principally that active part whose arms are both the strength and the wealth of the State."[26] Logical with himself, he thereafter devoted his time to studying the problem of providing drinking water for Parisians.

The Transmutation of Water into Earth

Le Roy's thesis disagreed with earlier observations as well as with recent research. Many scientists accepted the possibility of a transmutation of water into earth, which would explain the mysterious phenomenon that plants and trees do not need additional supplies of earth to grow, but only water. Jan Baptist Van Helmont had been the first to formulate the idea more than a century earlier. This Brussels physician had planted a five-pound willow in a container filled with 200 pounds of earth. He had covered it with a perforated lid and had watered the earth for five years with rainwater. At the end of the experiment, the willow weighed 169 pounds and 3 ounces. Since the weight of the soil had remained constant, and only rainwater had been used, Van Helmont believed that the additional weight could only have come from the transformation of the water. The same experiment using squash, cucumbers, pumpkins, hyacinth bulbs, mint, hempseed grains, and oats always gave the same results.

Moreover, Robert Boyle, Hermann Boerhaave, Etienne François Geoffroy Saint-Hilaire, and Andreas Sigismund Margraff had observed that the same quantity of water, subjected to repeated distillations, always left a solid residue in the still. Lavoisier came to ask himself whether his analyses of mineral water, made according to a standard sample of distilled water, were always valid. Distilling the same sample of water repeatedly, he compared the results with rainwater. One of two things had to be true: either the earth, originating outside the water, would be progressively eliminated by successive distillations, or else there would be continuous transmutation of water into earth, and each distillation would produce the same weight of earth. As distillation went forward, the density and the residue diminished. Therefore there was no transmutation and the residue came necessarily from the retort itself, because the soda or potash used to make glass were eminently soluble.

To show that the glass of the retort had dissolved, Lavoisier boiled three pounds of rainwater (1.468 grams) in a "pelican," a glass still whose narrow upper part had two curved hollow handles that opened into the wider base, thus resembling the form of the bird. The vapor condensed in the cooler upper part of the vessel and flowed down through the handles toward the base. After boiling the water for a hundred days, Lavoisier found that the pelican contained an earthy residue whose weight equaled the weight loss of the vessel. From that he concluded that water does not change into earth, but that prolonged boiling attacks glass and dissolves part of it.

However, he did not reach this result quite as simply as he claimed. Certainly he carefully weighed all the elements of the experiment and kept a record of inflows and outflows. The total weight of the vessel and its contents did not change, but the weight loss of the vessel was 12.5 grains more than the weight of the residue. What happened to the missing 12.5 grains? Lavoisier thought that they had remained in the residual water of the pelican in the form of salts in solution. In fact, the density of this water had increased and the hydrometer showed that it contained 15.5 grains of salts. At evaporation, it had exactly the same weight as the residue.

But there was a new problem. Where did the 3 extra grains come from? An ordinary mind would have thought that a part of the water had changed into earth. "Lavoisier, on the contrary, let it pass. For him, this increase of three grains proved nothing. It was a minor event in the experiment."[27]

In spite of the imperfection of the experimental protocol and the daring of the interpretations, Lavoisier had for the first time used a scientific method and defined a chemical composition from the criteria of weight. He relied completely on the principle of the conservation of matter: nothing is destroyed, nothing is created; matter only changes form. If he was not the author of the principle, he was the first to apply it systematically. His belief in its absolute and universal value would help him succeed in finding the true significance of his experiments, even when their results were disappointing or misleading.

On November 14, 1770, at the public reopening of the Royal Academy, Lavoisier read a paper describing his tests on the nature of water. He had proved that water could not be transmuted into earth. The residue observed after prolonged distillation came from the glass of the container. And rainwater contained scarcely one-twentieth of a grain of sea salt per pound, thus it was pure. "Water from a fountain or the Seine is as pure as rainwater after having been distilled once or twice, at moderate heat, in a metal still."[28]

The Academy published papers only after two or three years. But Lavoisier was in a hurry. He got on well with the cleric Rozier, who was launching a new journal, *Les observations sur la physique, sur l'histoire naturelle et sur les arts*. The first issue of July 1771 contained an essay by Bengt Ferner, a Swedish scientist who believed in the transmutation of water into earth. A footnote drew attention to Lavoisier's recent paper. The second issue published a summary of the famous paper, emphasizing that "M. Lavoisier's clear and precise style, the natural way in which he presents his ideas, his great descriptive powers, all contribute to fixing the principal facts firmly in memory."[29] The journal might have added that "Lavoisier had produced the first example of the methods, both experimental and intellectual, that lay at the heart of his revolution; he had argued from gravimetric grounds that the 'earth' that appeared in water distillled over a long time could not be composed of water."[30]

Henceforth he was going to base all his demonstrations on the use of the scale and the verification of the weights of inflows and outflows.

Work at the Royal Academy of Science

Lavoisier very soon became known at the Royal Academy of Science. Since he was among the youngest members, was full of enthusiasm and wrote easily, he was given all sorts of subjects to examine. With unfailing regularity, he produced reports on antimephitic pumps, the gas in cesspools, peat bogs, and many other topics of uneven interest.

Lazzaro Spallanzani claimed that if the heads of snails were cut off, they grew new ones. Voltaire agreed. "They move, they cling to a wall, they stretch the neck. But there is no semblance of a head, except one. Here we have two well-recognized marvels: animals who live without heads and those who re-produce them." [31]

Lavoisier tried the experiment. Three out of seven of his subjects died. Two refused to emerge from their shells. Finally, a single one seemingly re-sumed normal movements. The *Avant Coureur* rather exaggerated the results: "Monsieur Lavoisier showed the Royal Academy of Science, of which he is a member, a snail whose head he had himself cut off. He had kept and observed the snail very carefully. The snail did indeed grow a new head entirely similar to the first one, except that, unlike the first head, it was no longer the same color as the rest of the body." [32]

Somewhat embarrassed by this obtrusive publicity, Lavoisier wrote to the paper to say that the experiment was not finished; then, after three months, he announced that the head had partially grown back. But the de-bate continued. Valmont de Bomare contended that the heads did not grow back. Finally, Spallanzani put an end to the controversy by saying that differ-ent techniques and races of snails explained the divergent results.

Another subject for study arose when the inhabitants of Lucé, a small town in the Maine region, saw and heard on September 13, 1768, at 4:30 p.m., a stone fall from the sky after a very loud thunderclap. Terrified, they had fled at first. But their curiosity got the better of them and they soon returned to the site. The stone, half buried in the earth, was so hot and burning that it was impossible to touch. It was triangular, black in color and weighed seven and a half pounds. The parish priest, Father Bachelay, removed a piece of the stone and sent it to the Academy of Science. The analysis revealed that the stone was made up of 8.5 percent sulfur, 36 percent iron, and 55.5 percent vit-rifiable earth. The Academy concluded, "The stone could not have originated with the thunder, or have fallen from the sky. Neither was it formed by mineral substances fused by the fire of the thunder. The stone is nothing but a kind of pyritic sandstone. There is nothing unusual about it."[33] It was only at the end of the century that the existence of meteorites was acknowledged. The peasants had been right, the Academicians wrong.

During the summer of 1769, returning from a long inspection tour for the Tobacco Commission in the Chalons region, Lavoisier learned of Jars's sudden death. He was to replace him at the Academy, but his tasks would remain as disjointed as ever. He was asked to report on the divining rod, a forked hazel stick that certain scientists believed could detect springs and metallic veins. They attributed this power to the action of corpuscles in water and metals. The Church condemned the practice as diabolical and the Academy was skeptical. A water diviner recommended by the duc d'Ayen was invited to Macquer's country house near Le Bourget. After supper, when it was dark, Lavoisier and Macquer led the diviner to a forest bordered on one side by a pond, on the other by a stream. But no water was found. Lavoisier concluded:

The talents of a diviner are far from being as wonderful as commonly believed. There is water everywhere, and it is rare that one digs a well without finding it. The reported detections, to which some people attach great importance, are only natural. Since the stick sometimes turns as a result of the involuntary movements of the one holding it, it is possible that several honest persons have been misled, and have attributed to an exterior cause an effect that depended only on themselves.[34]

Another amazing phenomenon delighted the newspapers. It was said that a child in Montélimar could detect water with his eyes, seeing through earth and rock. He was called the child hydroscope. Lavoisier refused to have the child come to Paris. Such a step would have given the affair an appearance of credibility that would have dishonored the Academy. He was indignant:

Philosophy can only bemoan the fact that in an enlightened century, persons whose professions, knowledge, and reputations raise them above the commonplace, publicly revive old errors whose absurdity has long been recognized and against which true scientists have never ceased to protest.[35]

All the government turned to the Academy for advice. The Deputy Commissioner of Police, Antoine Raymond Gabriel de Sartine, asked about the possible dangers of fireworks that replaced powder with hydrogen, a new gas just discovered by the English scientist Henry Cavendish (he had named it "inflammable air"). Lavoisier was an expert on the subject of fireworks. In 1768 he had left at the Academy—in sealed envelopes—his personal formulas for rockets colored blue and yellow. The blue had been obtained by mixing zinc, sulfur, saltpeter, and charcoal; the yellow by mixing sodium and salt-peter. "On the whole," Lavoisier answered, "it is obvious that the new tech-nique that Sieur Ruggieri wants to use would expose his workers to some danger, especially in the beginning. But assuming they take the precautions he has indicated, the dangers of using inflammable air would be fewer than those to which using powder exposes them."[36]

The Secretary of the Navy consulted Lavoisier on the quality of various colonial products; he was told that Cayenne indigo was a better dye than the one coming from Santo Domingo, but inferior to the one from Guatemala. As for the cloves from Cayenne, they were attractive to the eye and entirely suitable for cooking: "From this point of view, they can compete with the Dutch cloves, since some spice merchants having an expertise in such matters, prefer them."[37] The expertise in this case came from his friend, Jean Baptiste Pluvinet, the pharmacist on the rue des Lombards, where Lavoisier bought the reagents for his experiments.

The list of subjects submitted to the Academicians was endless: tech-niques for wallpapering and laundering, a theory of colors, fireplace construc-tion, a machine for hoisting boats from the water, cheese-making, engraving of coats-of-arms, tobacco grating, paper-making, fabrication of rouge for the cheeks.

Lavoisier was always available. "The Academy of Science," he said, "would be tempted to believe that nothing related to the domestic arts or what interests society is alien to it. Thus it sometimes deals with subjects that might seem, at first glance, futile and insignificant."[38] In fact, the Academy fulfilled its mission. It gave technical advice to the State on questions of gen-eral interest such as town planning, equipment, and weaponry. In its public service, it helped scientists and artisans to have their inventions recognized and protected.

Regarding technical analyses, it was sometimes led to take part in signifi-cant debates between competing industrial projects. The debate about sup-plying Paris with water from the Yvette was renewed in 1771. Claude François Joseph d'Auxiron, a retired artillery captain, proposed bringing the water, not by aqueduct but by a pumping system driven by four steam engines. Lavoisier made a systematic study of the three steam-driven engines existing in France: one at Bois-Bossu, in Hainaut, described in the *Encyclopédie*; another one at Montrelais near Ingrande, on the Loire; and the engine at Anzin near Valen-ciennes. He calculated their power, their coal consumption, and the resulting pollution. He concluded that to supply Paris with the waters of the Yvette, one would need seven steam engines (each one costing 120,000 livres), a 110-

foot-high tower for distributing the water, and thirty-three employees to feed the furnaces with coal day and night. The annual operating costs could vary from 200,000 to 600,000 livres, depending on the height to which the water was pumped and the amount of water to be furnished. But the expenditure would have to be renewed each year, whereas with Parcieux's project it would be made only once. Moreover, it was not certain that one could transport the needed coal by river if water levels were low, or rivers frozen or flooded. Finally—and here it was the hygienist who spoke—the thick smoke that the combustion of such an enormous mass of coal would continuously spread over Paris would surely bother the inhabitants.

According to the lowest estimates, coal consumption would be set at sixteen tons every twenty-four hours. But even so, the considerable amount of sulfur, ammonia and empyreumatic oil that would continuously rise in the air and mix with the atmosphere of the city would not be harmful, but there is no doubt that it would have a very disagreeable odor.[39]

However, Lavoisier himself refrained from pronouncing and merely compared Auxiron's proposal to Parcieux's. But it is easy to see where his sympathies lay. In the end, the Yvette canal was never constructed. It was only during the First Empire that the Ourcq Canal was built instead.

The Academicians and civil servants eager to help inventors and entrepreneurs played an important role in the industrialization of France. It was thanks to their technical approval that projects had access to a channel of financing or realization—the Bureau of Commerce or the royal manufactures of Gobelins, Saint-Gobain, and Sèvres. Lavoisier was especially familiar with this aspect of the Academy's proliferating activities. He did not yet participate in the important debates of specialized commissions on fundamental research. He was both too young and too often away from Paris, obliged to travel regularly to Picardy and Champagne for the General Farm.

Marriage

During his sojourns in Paris Lavoisier met in his director's house many prominent men: the Abbé Guillaume Thomas Raynal whom Paulze had helped to write the *Histoire philosophique et politique des établissements et du commerce des Européens dans les deux Indes*; other famous economists: Robert Anne Jacques Turgot, Pierre Samuel Dupont, Trudaine de Montigny, Véron de Forbonnais; many civil servants: Jean-Baptiste Bertin, Gabriel de Sartine, Lamoignon de Malesherbes; several academicians: d'Alembert, Condorcet, Bernard de Jussieu, Cassini de Thury, Jean Étienne Guettard, Duhamel du Monceau; and naturally, many Farmers General.

The Farmers General held a special place in society. Coming from families with banking, mercantile, or legal backgrounds, they frequented the important men of the kingdom, and owned fine residences both in town and in the country. Their taste and elegant life style distanced them from the people, but they were not integrated into the aristocracy. Nor did the political world like them very much. "Soon there will remain only the Farmers General and their financial rivals whose loans can support a government burdened with debt and lacking credit as well as resources. When that happens, they will control the government."[40]

Lavoisier gradually discovered this milieu during his work sessions at the headquarters of the Farm on the rue de Grenelle-Saint-Honoré, at the Hôtel de Longueville on the Place du Carrousel, where the Tobacco Commission was housed, or at the Hôtel de Bretonvilliers on the Ile Saint-Louis.

Jacques Paulze had just lost his wife, Claudine Thoynet, niece of the Abbé Terray who, as Controller General of Finance, supervised the General Farm. The baron Auget de Montyon formulates a severe judgment on Abbé Joseph Marie Terray:

Terray was a most extraordinary being, and happily a rare breed. His exterior was hard, sinister, even frightening. He was very tall but stooped, and had a gloomy face with wild eyes that stared downwards, a sign of duplicity and treachery. His manners were inelegant,his tone of voice crude, and his conversations curt. He had no openness of spirit or trust. He judged all humanity unfavorably, because he judged it according to the way he was. He very seldom laughed and his humour was caustic. In affairs of State, he never argued, never disposed of an objection, and even admitted that it was sound, but he never changed his mind.[41]

The judgment was too harsh. Indeed, the Abbé Terray's imposition of radical economic measures and the partial bankruptcy of the finances of the State had made him very unpopular. But by reducing expenditures, spreading out the repayment of the debt and increasing revenues, he had reestablished the overall equilibrium of the royal Treasury. His success would be illustrated by the reduction of yields on government stocks, which would fall from 12 percent in 1770 to 6 percent at the time of his departure.

Madame Paulze's close ties to power had resulted in a certain vanity. Returning one day from a family property near Geneva, and passing through Ferney, she had notified Voltaire that she would like to meet him. The irascible old man had rejected her request. "Tell Madame Paulze that I have only one grudge left, and that I hold it against her uncle."[42]

The Paulzes' only daughter, Marie Anne Pierrette, born in 1758, had been educated in a convent at Montbrison. After her mother's death, she was brought back to Paris by her father to be his hostess. Only thirteen, she had very blue eyes and brown hair, a fresh complexion, and small mouth. Already very feminine, she filled her role with charm and authority.

Lavoisier, whose studies and trips had given him little time to mix with fashionable women, felt more at ease in the young girl's company. He talked with her about geology, chemistry, or astronomy, and told her about his travels. She listened with interest and admiration and reciprocated by playing several tunes on the harp or harpsichord. He remembered having studied harmony and spoke learnedly of the qualities of the music and those of the musician. The evenings passed happily in the intimacy of this lively and warm family setting.

The social games of the period gave an opportunity for friendly banter. The "Game of Good Fortune" was played with a square box on whose bottom was written a series of inscriptions in a circle: "Love, Teeth, Sabot, Heart, Shoelace, Bed, Rooster, Card." In the center, a tiny cardboard angel, concealing a magnet, turned on a pivot and pointed to one of the words. Turn by turn, the players illustrated the word chosen by chance with whimsical commentaries. The rules were the same for the games called "Wonderful Oracles" and "Love Compass." When one knew the laws of magnetism, it was easy to have the needle point to a chosen word by turning the box in the desired direction. It was a discreet way of encouraging destiny and addressing gallant or amusing messages to one's partner.[43]

Before Lavoisier had been able to question himself on the nature of the feeling that was developing between him and Marie Anne Pierrette, an incident caused by the Abbé Terray, the great-uncle, speeded up matters. Terray had fallen under the spell of the baronne de La Garde, who wanted at all costs to arrange the marriage of her brother, the comte d'Amerval, to Marie Anne. Terray put pressure on Paulze, who, at the risk of jeopardizing his position, replied:

My dear Uncle, when you spoke to me about my daughter's marriage, I considered this project as being far in the future, and I had to think about how a prospective husband might be matched in age, character, fortune and other affinities with my daughter. I find that M. d'Amerval offers no advantages in any of these categories. He is fifty, my daughter is only thirteen. He does not even have 1,500 francs in annual income, and my daughter, without being rich, can at this time bring double that amount to her husband. You do not know his character, but he cannot suit my daughter, you, or me. I already have certain information on the subject. My daughter has a definite aversion to him, and I shall certainly not force her.[44]

Irritated, Terray threatened to remove Paulze from his post as director
of the Tobacco Commission. However, Michel Bouret, one of three brothers
who had entered the Farm thanks to Madame de Pompadour's patronage,
interceded. Bouret, made wealthy by speculation on wheat, had spent 42 million livres on mere follies, but was not lacking in tact. On Paulze's behalf he
wrote to Terray, "I am angry that he has displeased you, but his conduct at the
Farm will continue to please you and his talents will permit you to negotiate
a good lease. He is the only man who can re-establish order in the different
parts of the Farm."[45]

Paulze kept his job, but fearing a new offensive from his uncle, he decided to forestall him. Lavoisier, his young and brilliant colleague, would be
an ideal son-in-law, he thought. Twenty-eight years old, of impressive stature, he was well-off and quite good looking. Obviously he did not displease
Marie-Anne. Sounded out, Lavoisier saw all the advantages of this flattering
offer and accepted without hesitation.

Terray was a good sport, and was present when the marriage contract
was signed on December 4, 1771. Marie Anne brought a dowry of 80,000
livres—20,000 to be paid immediately and the balance in six years. Lavoisier
brought 170,000 livres from his private fortune, 250,000 livres as advances
from his father, and 50,000 promised by his aunt, Constance Punctis, as an
inheritance. He was therefore much wealthier than his bride. But he owed a
million livres because he now held half of a share in the Farm, which had cost
him 780,000 livres. After paying the interest on the loans, his annual income
was about 20,000 livres ($800,000), a sum allowing the young couple to live
very comfortably.

Attending the reception after the signing were the Minister Bertin; the
Deputy Commissioner of Police, Sartine; Jean Charles Philibert Trudaine de
Montigny, intendant of Finance; several Farmers General: Michel Bouret,
Jean Claude Douet, Antoine Gaspard Grimod de La Reynière, Louis Bal-
thazar Danger-Bagneux, Pierre Faventines, François Baudon, Jean Robert
Tronchin, François Puissant, Etienne Gigault de Crisenoy, Jacques Delahante
and Jean François Didelot; several Academicians: d'Alembert, Cassini and Jus-
sieu; la duchesse de Mortemart, la marquise d'Asfeld, la comtesse d'Amerval,
Madame de Chavigny, and Madame de Rozière.

The religious marriage took place on December 16 in the chapel of the
Hôtel des Finances, on the rue Neuve des Petits Champs. The very simple
ceremony was celebrated by the parish priest at Saint-Roch, in the presence of
family and witnesses. For the bride, the witnesses were Terray and his brother,
Terray de Rozière; for the groom, Charles Martin Husson, honorary coun-
sellor at the Parlement de Paris, and Jacques Delahante. The young couple

moved into a house, bought for them by Lavoisier's father, on the rue Neuve des Bons Enfants, near the gardens of the Palais Royal.

The Education of an Economist

When Lavoisier entered the milieu of financiers and senior civil servants, he readily adopted its political and economic ideas. For these partisans of the mercantilist system, the formation of riches was based on money and the welfare of the State. The prosperity of the nation was the result of a balance of payments surplus. Therefore, imports had to be limited by imposing high duties on foreign products and exportation of national products had to be stimulated through financial aid and creation of State industries. This is the way Colbert had proceeded a century earlier.

These protectionist views were defended by François Véron-Duverger de Forbonnais, Terray's colleague and Paulze's friend. Lavoisier's library included Forbonnais's two basic works, the *Eléments du commerce* (1754) and *Recherches et considérations sur les finances* (1758).

Regarding taxes, Forbonnais favored a sharing of public expenditures based on each person's fortune. He opposed the *taille*, the direct tax imposed on non-nobles, which discouraged the well-off bourgeois from developing their lands. He preferred indirect to direct taxation, but wanted to reduce the cost of collecting it.

From Forbonnais's arguments, Lavoisier retained the principles of economic calculation: consumption is the exact reflection of production; production makes it possible to calculate the value of the invested capital; on a balance sheet of inflows-outflows, one can liken the total production agriculture to that of a unique producer.

Paulze's advice had probably been Lavoisier's first notion of the links between socio-economic and demographic factors. At this point, he was very far from the arguments of the Physiocrats. He had not yet met Pierre Samuel Dupont and Anne Robert Jacques Turgot, who would play a decisive role in his education as an economist. He defended the simple ideas that made the rounds of the financial circles, and was favorable to import duties, price controls and regulation of money supply. He acquired a taste for studying economic phenomena, and in October 1772 he read the *Essays on Commerce* by David Hume, the Scottish philosopher, historian, and economist much appreciated in Paris. This big man with a very sharp mind had studied economics not as a merchant but as a philosopher, and, prior to the Physiocrats, had published important texts on trade, money, and interest rates. Lavoisier read them attentively, with pen in hand, and filled more than seventy "reading cards." Contact with Hume familiarized him with a thought that was both mercantilist and liberal, while maintaining the legitimacy of a certain protectionism.

Hume felt that the power of the sovereign and the fortune of the State required the prosperity of trade and manufacture. He considered that "the real riches and force of the State consisted in piles of grain, stores of textiles, and supplies of arms and munitions."[46] A kingdom that develops its foreign trade encourages its industries and produces more luxury goods than one living in autarky. It is wealthier, more powerful, and happier. It is the luxurious techniques that support the progress of industry and commerce, creating a bourgeoisie capable of promoting reforms.

Hume did not believe in a strict balance of payments policy. The profit of one country did not necessarily produce the misfortune of another. It was more advantageous, he felt, for a country to be surrounded by rich nations than by poor ones, just as one can do business more successfully with a rich man than a poor one. He preferred indirect taxes, because taxpayers do not notice them as long as a certain threshold is not passed: "a time comes when raising taxes diminishes rather than increases the amount collected."[47]

One of the reading notes taken by Lavoisier, under the heading of "Population," expressed his understanding of the links between the creation of wealth and socio-economic conditions.

When I look through the census figures of the population of France, I see only sums added together. They tell me nothing. I wish they would specify that in a certain province the square league of land contains such and such a number of inhabitants, that, in another, it contains fewer because the type of cultivation is different. It should indicate that in one place it is the fertility of the soil that determines population, in another it is smuggling that ravages the countryside, and in still another it is excessive taxes that drive the cultivator from his fields and plough.[48]

In 1772 the Académie Française announced the theme "Colbert's Eulogy" for its essay competition, thus reflecting the support of the government for an interventionist policy, a regulation of economic life, and assistance to industrial development. Ten years earlier, it had asked for essays in praise of Sully, the model for the Physiocrats and partisans of liberalism.

Lavoisier decided to enter the competition. He started his essay by depicting the economic situation of France in Colbert's time. But it was merely a literary device, because his description reflected conditions existing in 1771: the constant rise in taxes, the stringency applied to their collection, and the harsh punishments of imprisonment and executions for their nonpayment; the incessant creation of new taxes; the delay in payment of pensions; the accumulation of debts; the increasing expenses of the king's household; the four to five year backlogs in the bookkeeping of the Treasury; the ruinous loans. "Finally, there is incredibly widespread misappropriation in financial and business circles."[49] He expressed the indignation of the senior civil servants who saw the worsening economic situation in France and feared its social consequences. He put into Colbert's mouth the principles of good administration that were his own: the equilibrium of the prosperity of a nation is fragile; to preserve it, the statesman must have two objectives: an increase in population and a healthy trade to absorb the surplus money that threatens to stifle industry.

In practice Lavoisier proposed Forbonnais's formulas: stopping the grain export to bring down the price and increase domestic consumption; adding to the reserves of the Royal Treasury to reduce the monetary surplus; halting inflation by provoking a fall in prices and cutting manpower costs. The wealth of the State, he argued, did not depend on its monetary reserves. It was useless to try to attract foreign money. Money is a fluid whose movements necessarily end up in a state of equilibrium.

If by some device one manages to delay its movement, to accumulate it beyond its natural level in some part or other of Europe, the state having that excess is punished by the increasing costs within its borders of all types of manpower. The necessary rise in production costs, of its commodities, stops exportation. Its industry and trade flag, up to the point that, through imperceptible channels, the overflow leaks out.[50]

Lavoisier the natural scientist and Lavoisier the economist were practitioners of one and the same approach. There was one important link, his commitment to measurement. His concern to balance inflows and outflows in economics as in chemistry was inspired by physics:

Money attracts commodities and commodities attract money; that means, for example, that if we consider two neighboring states, isolated like two persons, with one having all the money and the other all the commodities, a necessary equilibrium will soon be established between them. Each one will have about half the money and half the commodities. This level, which cannot be disturbed because of the physical order of things, pretty well exists in all European States. [. . .] If we succeeded in accumulating a greater part of the money available in Europe, our manpower costs would necessarily increase and our manufactures would decline, until the overflow leaked out and we would then regain our limits.[51]

At the same time, in a more practical approach Lavoisier felt that a rationalization of taxation would improve the situation of the finances of the State:

Colbert saw the issue of taxation in a new way. He saw that most of the king's revenue consists of a partial interest in the public wealth, that the king, through taxation, has a greater or lesser interest in every kind of commerce without being directly responsible for it, from which he concluded that everything that tends to increase commerce at the same time contributes to the royal finances. [. . .] He was not concerned whether this or that tax pertained to the king's domains or whether it was old or new; what mattered was whether it was a burden to the people, whether it hindered the collection of taxes on other forms of revenue that were more abundant or more easily taxed.[52]

Lavoisier never finished the manuscript, and instead, withdrew from the competition. One may wonder whether he had become aware of the simplistic character of his economic conceptions, or whether he was asked by the General Farm to leave the field open to another competitor, Jacques Necker, an influential banker and financier.

A Banker Tempted by Politics

Necker had arrived in Paris from Geneva in 1747. At first a simple bookkeeper for the Isaac Vernet Bank, he was soon a partner in the Thélusson and Necker Bank, which became one of the most important in Paris in less than ten years. Necker's methods were efficacious, and sometimes on the limit of accepted practices.

In 1762 he financed a speculation on English annuities, devalued in France during the Seven Years' War. The prices were expected to rise when peace came. Alerted by Sainte-Foy that it was imminent, Necker made a successful transaction. When his informant demanded his share, Necker pretended that he had not acted after all, and pocketed the profit: 1,800,000 livres.

The State bonds issued by French agents in Canada had lost 80 percent of their value. With the help of the duc de Choiseul and the Abbé Terray, Necker bought a large number cheaply, sent them to London and had himself reimbursed for their face value as English property, according to the Treaty of 1763.[53]

In 1764 the Thélusson and Necker Bank made important profits in trading wheat and corn. The bank also owned shares in the East India Company, the situation oif which was disastrous. Its possessions wiped out, its trading posts and ships destroyed, it was 60 million livres in debt. When it was about to be liquidated, its directors—notably Terray, Paulze, Raynal, and Claude Antoine Nicolas Valdec de Lessart—called on Necker to manage the process. Thanks to him, the company obtained the king's authorization to conduct its affairs independently. In four years, the debts were settled, the trading posts and ships rebuilt, and trade was thriving as it had in its best days.[54] Necker had made a great deal of money because his bank had served as an intermediary with the Bourdieu and Chollet Bank in London. In June 1768 Louis XV wanted to re-establish government supervision of the East India Company, but Necker argued that it should remain independent. "This company set up all the Indian settlements. It changed two uncultivated and deserted islands (France and Bourbon) into two commercial and cultivated ones. It built the town of Pondichéry and all the flourishing settlements that aroused the envy of other nations before the last war. It might be said that this company created the town of Lorient."[55]

In 1772, when he was named ambassador of the Genevan Republic in Paris on the condition that he cut all visible ties with his bank, Necker ceded his place to his brother, Louis de Germany, but remained a silent partner. At that time his fortune was estimated at from 5 to 8 million livres. ($200 to 320 million).[56]

Terray methodically exploited the system of periodic bankruptcies, each time relieving the budget of the State of 40 million livres. He regularly borrowed important sums from Necker, writing to him in July 1772: "We implore you to rescue us before the end of the day. Please lend us the sum that is vitally needed. Time is running out. You are our only recourse."[57] Necker replied by sending a million livres and cleverly left it up to Terray to set the interest rate.[58] In the year 1772 alone, Necker lent no less than 4 million livres to the Treasury. Such favors are not forgotten.

Necker began to nourish political ambitions and even contemplated succeeding Terray one day. The General Farm was favorable, but to obtain the post Necker had to show that he was a writer and a philosopher, and that his political views were sound. In particular, he had to convince the General Farm and the financial world that he was not envisaging challenging established situations by imprudent reforms, as those "desperados" who called themselves Economistes or Physiocrats were threatening to do.

Already in 1769 he had taken a stand against them in his brochure on the East India Company. A new occasion to demonstrate his talents arose with the competition for the best "Colbert's Eulogy." Lavoisier, as we know, stepped aside for his rival.

In Necker's one hundred page memoir, praise for Colbert was disposed of rather casually, but it was followed by thirty-four pages of short notes in small print. They made up both a treatise on economic policy and a concrete program for government.[59] Criticizing the Physiocrats and their dogmatism, Necker wrote:

In looking at Colbert's operations, one sees that he did not blindly embrace any one system. One never tires of admiring his wisdom and moderation. He always seemed to be ahead of the game played by the men of our century who exaggerate all the fundamental maxims of conduct so as to hide from themselves their incapacity to define their limits, and, by exaggerating, give an appearance of strength to their thoughts.[60]

Far from limiting his mission to tax collection and control of expenditures, the good administrator should, according to him, concern himself with the fate of the people and the economy of the nation. He should increase the power of the State without harming particular interests. He should define the fair relationship between wealth and taxation, between agriculture, industry and commerce. Rather than a unique land tax, he should prefer a tax on production and consumption.

Necker was against the free export of grains, favorable to a State monopoly on trade with India and China and to borrowing when public credit allowed it. It was precisely the program desired by the General Farm. The coincidence was not fortuitous. In total, Necker rejected wild liberalism and praised the centralizing State whose intervention was necessary as much for economic development as for social aid. Institutional reform, however, should be carried out gradually, progressively, "without upheavals, without upsetting habits and common sense; and without excessive zeal, which would only produce new resistance."[61]

3

Fixed Air and Pneumatic Chemistry

LAVOISIER'S EARLY SCIENTIFIC APPROACH to chemistry was, in keeping with the spirit of the times, dominated by the Aristotelian theory of the four elements: earth, water, air and fire. The earth and its minerals were the first to interest him. Next came water—its analysis, density, effects on nature and urban uses; its transmutation into earth had not held him for very long. In 1772 a third element, air, became his major subject of inspiration and study. It would absorb him for several years. He would discover a new discipline, coming from England: pneumatic chemistry, the chemistry of gases. Until then considered as inert matter, playing a purely mechanical role in combustion and calcination, gases were about to be credited with an active function in chemical reactions. But to draw Lavoisier's attention to this new chemistry, the diamonds of a wealthy Parisian jeweler, the indiscretions of a Portuguese monk in London, and the burning glasses of the Saint-Gobain factory would be needed.

Do Diamonds Burn?

On April 25, 1772 the duc de Croÿ stopped in to visit Antoine Alexis Cadet, the apothecary. He later wrote:

I found the furnaces lit and everyone very busy. Monsieur Lavoisier, Farmer General and Academy member, and somebody else were trying to distill a diamond. It has been proven many times and, in particular, by Monsieur Rouelle's famous experiment six months ago, that a diamond can be volatilized. When I returned at seven in the evening, the diamonds had not changed, because they had been enclosed in retorts; they burn and disappear only if exposed to air. These experiments are putting lots of diamonds in the fire! [1]

It is true that for some time everybody had been making a frantic effort to burn diamonds. As early as 1694 at the court of Cosimo III, Grand Duke of

Tuscany, two Florentine scientists, Giuseppe Averani and Cipriano Targioni, used burning glasses, large lenses of bi-convex glass, to focus sun rays on diamonds so that they calcined. François I, Austrian Emperor, had described the same experiment to Guettard in May 1760. Diamonds and rubies worth 6,000 florins had been enclosed in cone-shaped crucibles and subjected to intense fire for twenty-four hours. When the crucibles were opened, "the rubies had not changed, but the diamonds had completely disappeared, to the point that not the slightest trace was found."[2] This imperial extravagance dumbfounded Guettard.

But soon other scientists were imitating the emperor.[3] Robert Boyle, one of the great English chemists of the seventeenth century, looking for medicinal virtues, had unsuccessfully tried to collect the emanations of diamonds. In the spring of 1768, Jean d'Arcet, medical doctor and chemist at the Sèvres factory, used the large kilns for his research on the effects of fire on diamonds. He thus discovered that two of them—one placed in a closed and sealed porcelain crucible, the other in a crucible fitted with a perforated cover—after being exposed to the heat of the kiln, had completely disappeared, "just as a drop of the purest water would have done."[4]

The Royal Academy of Science had greeted these results with polite interest, but had refused to express an opinion, judging the evidence to be insufficient. Jean d'Arcet then carried on with a series of tests and confirmed that "all diamonds are volatile in themselves to a rather inferior degree of fire, and do not need air."[5]

Still skeptical, Macquer tried his own experiment on July 24, 1771, "in the presence of seventeen very well educated persons," including d'Arcet and Rouelle. After twenty minutes, he half-opened the furnace, pulled out the cupel and showed it to the group. Without knowing it, they were participating in a scientific discovery. The red color of the diamond was more glowing and luminous than that of the cupel, and the gem was "completely enveloped in a faint, phosphoric-like flame."[6] Thirty minutes later, the diamond had completely disappeared.

D'Arcet started his tests again in August, in the company of the younger Rouelle and the pharmacist Pierre François Mitouard. There followed experiments by Augustin Roux, Mademoiselle de Lespinasse's physician, Balthazar Georges Sage, the mineralogist, and many others. Macquer concluded: "The destructibility of diamond by fire has been proven and even demonstrated by numerous and completely authentic experiments. But how it happens remains to be seen."[7]

Was it the effect of a simple volatilization, comparable to what happens to air when it is heated? Was it a combustion, similar to that of wine spirits?

Or was it a decrepitation, the diamond being reduced to "particles so fine that they can no longer be perceived by our senses?"[8]

To find out, Lavoisier, Macquer and Cadet set to work in Cadet's laboratory, and were soon joined by Nicolas Le Blanc, a jeweler, who was worried about the effects on his clientele of the discovery that diamonds burn. Moreover, all the jewelers, lapidaries, and diamond merchants were incredulous. They had the habit of subjecting diamonds with certain blemishes "to rather intense heat for more or less long periods, and now feared that this heat could diminish or destroy them. Those who carried out this procedure were very careful, without knowing why, to surround their diamonds with a kind of cement, containing charcoal dust, and to enclose everything in crucibles as tightly sealed as possible."[9]

Le Blanc brought along a diamond, inserted it in a paste made of chalk and charcoal dust, and put it in a closed and hermetically sealed crucible. After heating it intensely for three hours, he removed the crucible and let it cool. When he opened it, he saw that the stone had completely disappeared, without a trace, except its form in the cement that had enclosed it."[10]

Diamonds could definitely be destroyed by fire. But Maillard, another jeweler, was convinced that they could not be destroyed by heat alone, that the contact with air was necessary. To demonstrate his theory he placed his diamonds in the bowl of a tobacco pipe filled with charcoal dust. The pipe was closed with a small strip of sheet metal and covered by sand moistened with salt water. It was then placed in a crucible coated with dry chalk, itself contained in two other crucibles joined together. All the joints were hermetically sealed.[11] "It is surely easy to conceive of and produce more exact devices than that of the jewelers to guarantee the access of air to the diamonds," Macquer wrote condescendingly, "but since the diamonds they use are their own, and the objective is to convince them, it is better to let them do it their way."[12]

Heated for two hours, the diamonds emerged intact. But somebody suggested that it was perhaps because of the inadequate draught of the furnace. Another furnace with a large pipe and grill was brought in. The fire was so intense that after two hours everything had softened, lost its shape, and was ready to run. They stopped feeding the fire and let the furnace cool. Maillard, who had never seen diamonds put to such a severe test, cautiously searched for them in the ashes. Macquer wrote ironically, "Seeing M. Maillard so delicately collecting the ashes from the furnace, I said to him jokingly that if he wanted absolutely to retrieve his diamonds, it would be better to have the chimney swept and to look for them in the soot rather than in the ash."[13]

But Macquer's triumph was short-lived. Once the vitrified coating surrounding them had been broken, the three diamonds were found to be just as sound as before the test. They had kept their form, the sharp edges of their facets, and their brilliance, and their weight was unchanged. They had simply acquired a superficial blackish film that disappeared after cleaning with a buff wheel. The conclusion was that diamonds were certainly combustible, but only on contact with air.

Lavoisier himself was persuaded that diamonds burned easily when exposed to air, and that, when shielded from it, could withstand intense fire without being volatilized. But it was necessary to understand better the role played by the materials surrounding them.[14] He placed three diamonds in three clay pipe stems. The first one was empty; the second was filled with chalk and the third with charcoal dust. Each receptacle was placed in a container made up of two crucibles with sealed edges forming a hermetic sphere. The temperature of the furnaces was raised to the maximum degree for two and a half hours. At the end of the experiment, Lavoisier observed:

The diamond that had been placed in the powdered charcoal had lost neither weight nor brilliance. The one that had been enclosed in chalk had lost a bit more than a fifth of its weight, was completely tarnished, and its angles were blunted; it was also covered with a greyish crust like an uncut diamond. The diamond exposed to fire without protection had also lost almost a fifth of its weight, its color and brilliance had been considerably altered, and what was very remarkable, it was jet black.[15]

On April 29, 1772, at the public session of the Academy, Lavoisier reported the results of tests done on thirty-one diamonds. In the absence of air, protected by charcoal dust, the diamonds remained "absolutely unchanged." In the presence of air, they were destroyed, but he still did not know how this happened. Macquer, Maillard, and Mitouard thought that they burned, Cadet that they decrepitated, and d'Arcet and the Rouelle brothers that they were volatilized. Lavoisier, who did not really agree with any of them, was somewhat embarrassed. He leaned rather more toward volatilization or decrepitation. An argument started between the scientists. Always cautious, the Royal Academy of Science rendered a verdict that contradicted no one, and yet was irrefutable scientifically speaking. (1) The conflicting results could be explained by the different experimental conditions. (2) The temperatures were different and, in any case, inadequate. It would be necessary to go back to the Florentines' technique and use a burning glass. Cadet and Mathurin Jacques Brisson immediately requested authorization to use the large lens made at the beginning of the century by comte Ehrenfried Walter von Tschirnhausen and then a part of the collection of "curiosities" at the Academy.

Magellan, Intelligence Agent

At the same time in London, a certain João Jacinto de Magalhaens or Magellan, a Portuguese monk who was a descendant of the famous navigator, was practicing scientific espionage with talent and discretion. He worked for France and continuously informed Daniel Trudaine of all the scientific and technical inventions made in England.[16]

In 1769, when Daniel Trudaine died, his son Jean Charles Philibert Trudaine de Montigny replaced him as director of the Bureau of Commerce. He was much more interested than his father in the activities of the Royal Academy of Science of which he was a member. In 1771 he had Magellan named a corresponding member of the Academy and appointed Macquer as his interlocutor.

Magellan was well-informed about everything, and knew the instrument manufacturers John Bird and Jesse Ramsden and the scientists William Watson and James Watt. He was also a friend of Benjamin Franklin and the economist Richard Price, both of whom were members of the Royal Society.

The Royal Society had been created officially in 1663, three years before its rival in Paris. It had forty resident members, and welcomed foreign scientists, such as Benjamin Franklin, a self-taught specialist in electricity, who had come to London to negotiate tariffs on American trade. Franklin and Richard Price had helped to elect a professional theologian and amateur man of science, Joseph Priestley, who would soon make a name for himself.

Magellan was one of the first to understand just how valuable the rapid and general communication of discoveries could be to the sciences, and to practice this correspondence in the center most favorable to its success, London itself.[17] On May 4, 1771 he sent Macquer some elastic gum, or rubber, and the English translation of Macquer's *Dictionary of Chemistry* done by James Keir, a Birmingham chemist. The translator had enriched the English version with several comments, "the author not having been acquainted with some very late discoveries, specially those important ones concerning fixable air, made by Dr. Black, professor of chemistry in the University of Edinburgh, by Dr. MacBride of Dublin and by the Honorable Mr. Cavendish."[18] These omissions were corrected by added notes.

Rather offended, Macquer had asked for more information about this "fixable air" or "fixed air" (carbonic gas, or carbon dioxide, CO_2), a gas still unknown in Paris. On October 25 Magellan drew his attention to a series of recent publications on the subject by the German chemists Johann Friedrich Meyer, Joseph Franz Jacquin and Heinrich Johann Nepomuk Crantz.

Meanwhile, on March 19, 1772, an important event occurred in London when Priestley presented his *Experiments and Observations on Different Kinds of Air* to the Royal Society. For a year he had lived in Leeds, next to a brewery, and for his experiments he had used the thick layer of fixed air that is always found at the surface of fermenting beer. He showed his friends that lighted candles, live charcoals, and burning twigs were extinguished immediately by this gas. Animals could not breathe it without dying. Only plants could live and develop in it; they even had the power to make the gas breathable again and to regenerate atmospheric air. "Experiments made in the year 1772 abundantly confirmed my conclusion concerning the restoration of air in which candles had burned out by plants growing in it. [...] Besides, the plant which I have found to be the most effectual of any that I have tried for this purpose is spinach, which is of quick growth, but will seldom thrive long in water."[19]

When Priestley informed Franklin of this phenomenon, the American was hardly surprised, and he responded:

That the vegetable creation should restore the air which is spoiled by the animal part of it, looks like a rational system, and seems to be of a piece with the rest. [...] I hope this will give some check to the rage of destroying trees that grow near houses, which has accompanied our late improvements in gardening, from an opinion of their being unwholesome. I am certain, from long observation, that there is nothing unhealthy in the air of woods; for we Americans have every where our country habitations in the midst of woods, and no people on earth enjoy better health, or are more prolific.[20]

Two physicians, John Pringle and David MacBride, observed that fermentation and the production of fixed air accompanying it were capable of halting the putrefaction of animal substances. Why not, they asked, use fixed air to treat scurvy, putrid fevers, throat and lung inflammations, and cancers? With this goal in view, Priestley devised a preparation of fixed air in the form of artificially gaseous water. "The readiest method of preparing this water for use is to agitate it strongly with a large surface exposed to the fixed air. By this means more than an equal bulk of air may be communicated to a large quantity of water in the space of a few minutes."[21]

As of March 20, Magellan had informed Macquer of Priestley's formula. "Yesterday, one continued to read Mr. Priestley's paper on fixed air at the Royal Society. There was also a paper by a physician or surgeon who cured putrid fever by administering fixed air through the patient's anus."[22] Ten days later, on April 1, Macquer spoke about all this at the Academy of Science. Lavoisier was present but paid little attention to the information; his handwritten notes made no mention of it.[23]

The Abbé Rozier, however, took it up again in his journal:

Mr. Priestley has explained how nature compensates for this enormous quantity of air consumed or destroyed by fire and flame. And he has proved by experiments that plant vegetation contributes toward its replacement and the restoration of its qualities. He has shown that air, vitiated and infected by vapors given off by matter tending toward corruption and already corrupted, can be replenished and restored by the fixed air that escapes from a fermenting body.[24]

Lavoisier still did not react. To attract his attention, the information had to pass by official channels. On July 5 Magellan sent Trudaine de Montigny a copy of Priestley's latest work, *Directions for Impregnating Water with Fixed Air*, which had appeared in London in June. On July 7 Magellan returned to the attack because the affair was assuming the importance of a military secret. Priestley had proposed to the Lords of the Admiralty to treat scurvy by water impregnated with fixed air. In that period of naval wars, the crews of the ships were constantly exposed to this terrible ailment, and their effectiveness in battle suffered as a result. Hence it was essential that the new therapy should be known and evaluated in France.

When he received the message, Trudaine de Montigny was just setting up a chemistry laboratory in his château at Montigny-Lencoup near the Fontainebleau forest. On July 14 he sent the pamphlet to Lavoisier, asking him to translate it and circulate it among the medical corps.

May I ask you to repeat these experiments and add your own observations. Since the value of these new discoveries depends on the rapidity with which they can be applied, I hope that you will not be long in getting out this little work. Desiring to satisfy M. Magalhaens, I could think of no one better to perform this service than you. I know your precision regarding details of physics and chemistry, and I know that I am obliging you by giving you the possibility to do something useful.[25]

In spite of the polite phrases, the letter seemed more like an order. Trudaine de Montigny was a very important person whom Lavoisier appreciated and respected. In 1772, he was a senior member of the Council of State, a high official in the Finance Ministry, and vice-president of the Academy of Science.

The letter determined Lavoisier's new specialization in the study of fixed air and he acknowledged it in 1774 in his dedication to Montigny of the *Opuscules physiques et chymiques*. "It is to you I am indebted for the initial idea. It was you who urged me to undertake its preparation and publication, who more than once directed me in the choice of experiments, and who often explained their consequences to me. And finally, it was you who desired that most of them be done or repeated in front of you."[26]

For the historians of science who often try to retrace the progression of the great scientific discoveries, it is interesting to note that Lavoisier's orientation toward the chemistry of gases, which was decisive for his career, resulted not from a sudden flash of inspiration but from an official request made by a high government official belonging to the Academy of Science. Trudaine de Montigny's role in Lavoisier's scientific development must not be overlooked.

The Burning Glasses

But for the moment, along with Cadet and Brisson, Lavoisier was still pursuing his research on diamonds. After having been relegated for sixty years to the collection of instruments in the "Curiosities Room" of the Academy, the large burning glass, four feet in diameter, was removed from it with great ceremony. It had been used between 1702 and 1709 by Etienne François Geoffroy and Guillaume Homberg for their studies of fusion and volatilization of metals at high temperatures. A second glass, of the same diameter, but with a shorter focal length, was lent by the comte Théophile Malo Corret de La Tour d'Auvergne. Thus the Academicians had two of the most powerful lenses ever made at their disposal.

During their trials, Geoffroy and Homberg had demonstrated that the calcination of antimony, lead, tin and mercury produced ashes heavier than the original metal. Nicolas Lémery's *Cours de chymie* specified that in calcining four ounces of alloy of antimony with moderate heat, they had observed emanating vapors for an hour and a half. At the end of the experiment, the antimony was transformed into a grey powder, exceeding by two and a half drachmas its original weight: "This increase was all the more surprising since the smoke that had escaped from the substance should have diminished its weight. Therefore, a greater amount of fire particles must have replaced what escaped."[27] They had not collected the abundant vapors given off by the metals during the tests. However, Lavoisier noted, "All metals give off vapors or smoke when the burning glass is used. It would be very interesting to invent an instrument for collecting and condensing them. Rock crystal vessels might do, but it must be seen if they can resist the heat of burning glass."[28] He began to anticipate that air could well be a part of mineral substances. Two facts reinforced his conviction. On the one hand, metallic reductions were always accompanied by a considerable effervescence at the point when the metallic calx changed to the metal state. According to Macquer's first edition of the *Dictionnaire de chymie*, "the effervescences are accompanied by bubbles, small jets of vapor and a slight noise or quivering. All these phenomena are due to the air that is discharged or develops in almost all dissolving processes."[29] And in the *Encyclopédie* Venel wrote that an effervescence was nothing more than a sudden release of air.

On the other hand, Balthazar Georges Sage had shown in his *Eléments de minéralogie docimastique* that metals no longer produced effervescence after prolonged exposure to the intense heat of the burning glass. They ceased to be malleable and soluble in acids.

Lavoisier, too, considered effervescence of metallic calxes to be "a sudden discharge of the air that was somehow dissolved in them. [. . .] Most metals do not produce effervescence after a prolonged exposure to the flame of the burning glass . Undoubtedly the intense heat to which they are subjected removes the air that had been a part of their composition. What is most particular is that metals in this state are no longer malleable, and that they are virtually indissoluble."[30]

Finally, the experiments with burning glasses were an excellent opportunity for an in-depth study of the airs released by mineral substances during combustion.

Pneumatic Chemistry

Lavoisier was aware that the French were behind in the study of airs, but since Trudaine de Montigny was interested, he was quite willing to explore this new field. "Master's and doctoral theses and all sorts of papers on the subject appear in England, Germany, and Holland," he wrote. "French chemists alone seem to take no part in this interesting question."[31]

Before defining his research program, Lavoisier read or reread everything that had been published on fixed air, and, more generally, "on the elastic emanations that escape from matter during combustion, fermentation, and effervescences."[32] Calling "silvan spirit" this elastic fluid that is released during the fermentation of organic matter, the explosion of gunpowder, and the combustion of coal, the Swiss Paracelsus had been the first to describe it. Jan Baptist Van Helmont, his disciple, had invented the word "gas" to designate these elastic fluids, which he differentiated from vapors.[33] He did not succeed in collecting them, but established that silvan spirit, our carbonic gas, results from the combustion of coal, from the effect of vinegar on carbonate of lime, from the fermentation of grape juice, and that it can be found in caves. He distinguished nonflammable gases from inflammable ones.

Later Robert Boyle understood that these gases represented, along with solids and liquids, a third important class of substances. He managed to collect them with a pneumatic trough and discovered hydrogen, without identifying it, by having sulfuric acid act on nails. His student, John Mayow, using a burning glass, heated saltpeter (potassium nitrate) in an airless bell jar and observed that something was escaping from it, a gas he sometimes called "vital spirit," sometimes "nitro-aerial spirit." He had unknowingly detected oxygen as early as 1674. He noted that the combustion of a candle or the breath of a mouse took away "its elastic force."

In 1735 Stephen Hales, Vicar at Teddington in Middlesex, observed while cultivating his garden that plants absorb a large amount of air through their roots and leaves. "Finding by many experiments that the air is plentifully inspired by vegetables, not only at their roots, but also through several parts of their trunks and branches, this put me upon making a more particular inquiry into the nature of the air, and to discover, if possible, wherein its great importance to the life and support of vegetables might consist."[34] Subjecting all sorts of substances to combustion, Hales collected released gas with the help of two kinds of pneumatic vessels. One was a glass bell jar filled with water, turned upside down on a container also filled with water and having in its center a vertical rod ending in a small pedestal. On the pedestal he placed an animal, a candle, or a substance to be calcined. The variations in water levels within the bell jar gave the measure of the gas produced or consumed. From his experiments, Hales concluded that all matter contained a great amount of atmospheric air, which was fixed in it: "Thus upon the whole, we see that air abounds in animal, vegetable, and mineral substances; in all which it bears a considerable part; if all the parts of matter were only endued with a strongly attracting power, whole nature would then immediately become one unactive cohering lump; wherefore it was absolutely necessary, in order to the actuating and enlivening this vast mass of attracting matter, that there should be every where, intermixed with it, a due proportion of strongly rebelling elastick particles, which might enliven the whole mass, by the incessant action between them and the attracting particles."[35]

Lavoisier agreed with Hales's conclusions: "In Nature, air exists in two forms. Sometimes it is seen as a very rare, very dilatable, very elastic fluid; this is the air we breathe. Sometimes it is fixed in matter; it is intimately combined with it; in that situation air loses all the properties that it had previously; air is no longer fluid, it becomes a solid."[36]

From his wide reading, Lavoisier retained several essential ideas: the metallic calces could contain not only phlogiston, but also gases. But there were two conceptions of the presence of air in matter: for some, it was atmospheric air, the one we breathe, that was fixed; for others, fixed air was a distinct air, a different gas. Finally, it could be said that fixed air was "a real

Proteus that—sometimes fixed, sometimes volatile—must be counted among chemical principles and occupy a rank previously denied to it." [37]

In 1772 Lavoisier did not yet know about Joseph Black's work. A chemistry professor in Edinburgh, the Scotsman had demonstrated in 1756 the existence of fixed air in magnesia alba, which had been long used and valued as a mild and tasteless purgative. "We may therefore safely conclude that the volatile matter lost in the calcination of magnesia is mostly air; and hence the calcined magnesia does not emit air or make effervescence when mixed with acids." [38]

But the *Experiments upon Magnesia Alba* had not been not well received in France at their publication in 1758. Rouelle and Demachy had questioned the experiments. Macquer had not mentioned them in the 1766 edition of his *Dictionnaire de chymie.*

In 1764 David MacBride had declared that fixed air was an elastic fluid different from atmospheric air and that it had "the deleterious quality of suffocating animals." [39] At the same time, Henry Cavendish, a wealthy aristocrat and talented chemist, had announced at the Royal Society that carbon combustion notably diminished the volume of air in which it burned and produced fixed air.

It was finally thanks to Priestley that Lavoisier discovered fixed air. Priestley had judged that fixed air was not harmful and could be breathed. He even thought that it improved air tainted by animal respiration and putrefaction. It could, he thought, contribute to urban hygiene. "If fixed air tends to correct air which has been injured by animal respiration or putrefaction, lime kilns, which discharge great quantities of fixed air, may be wholesome in the neighbourhood of populous cities, the atmosphere of which must abound with putrid effluvia." [40]

Thus, while the doctrine of fixed air had been accepted in England, studies in pneumatic chemistry had aroused little interest in France, up to the time of Magellan's letter. "They were known in France," Antoine François de Fourcroy, Lavoisier's student, would later write, "and received the attention they deserved only more than twelve years after their publication, and after scientific discussions on fixed air and the alkalis had been the subject of several very distinguished works growing out of a large number of experiments and discoveries in Germany, England, and Holland." [41]

In the Jardin de l'Infante

On August 8, 1772 Lavoisier wrote up the program of experiments to be done with the burning glasses, in collaboration with Cadet and Brisson. Thanks to the extreme heat that could be obtained, they hoped to end the debate on diamonds' properties, repeat the tests done by Homberg and Geoffroy on metals, and perhaps gain an understanding of the nature of Stahl's phlogiston.

Lavoisier's past experience as a geologist inspired him with the idea of adding to the tests on metals "a series of experiments on soils, stones, mines, and an infinity of mineral substances."[42] But the instructions written by Trudaine de Montigny on July 14 had given him an additional idea. Since gases seemed to be a part of minerals and metals, one ought to be able to collect the ones released during calcination, measure their volume, and analyze them by adapting a pneumatic trough to the burning glass. He still thought that fixed air was simply fixed atmospheric air and indicated this from the sub-title of his program: "On Fixed Air, or Rather on the Air Contained in Matter." "It seems to be constant that air is a part—a very large part—of most minerals, even of metals. No chemist, however, has yet included air in the definition of either metals or mineral matter."[43]

Actually, Lavoisier was not the first to envisage the presence of air in metals and minerals, since Black had preceded him. But he did not know this. Nor did he know that air was not a component of metals, but of calxes or metallic oxides; that it was not atmospheric air in its totality that they contained, but one of its components, oxygen; and that fixed air was not atmospheric air fixed in matter, but carbon dioxide. These were precisely the points he was going to elucidate in the following years.

In any case, the experiments with the burning lenses were the first opportunity for Lavoisier to study the role of air as chemical agent in combustions. In this respect, he was breaking new ground, because up to that time in France, air had been considered only as a physical agent. Aware of the originality of his program, Lavoisier had the paper initialed by Jean-Paul Grandjean de Fouchy, secretary of the Academy.

From the first tests, the scientists were disappointed by the performances of the Tschirnhausen lenses. "The narrow focus means that one can test the effect of the sun only on very small amounts of material."[44] They needed a wider lens, but it was impossible to cast in one piece a glass that would be sufficiently large, thick, and flawless. They had the idea of using two large convex glasses with a radius of eight feet, joined by their edges. The space separating them would be filled by 140 pints of alcohol. Thanks to an excep-

Figure 2. The diamond experiments with the burning glass. Private collection.

tional subsidy given by Trudaine de Montigny, Lavoisier and his colleagues were able to arrange for the use of a large "liquor lens" (Figure 2). The glasses were donated by Saint-Gobain.[45] The optical machine, operated by cranks, was placed on a wooden platform with six wheels, capable of holding eight to ten persons. The rays of the sun, caught by the large lens, were recaptured by a second, smaller one that concentrated them on the focus of the experiment, producing an intense heat. A complicated apparatus made up of cranks and cogwheels made it possible to regulate the angle and orientation of the lenses, depending on the position of the sun.

A group of assistants were in charge of adjusting and moving the machine while the four scientists, wearing wigs and dark glasses, proceeded with the tests, installed as if they were on the poop deck of a ship. They worked outside the Louvre in the Jardin de l'Infante, on the vast terrace facing south that stretched between the palace and the banks of the Seine. Elegant women and the curious came to stroll there and observed the scene with amazement. One hundred ninety experiments were performed from August 14, 1772 to October 13, 1772. Cadet and Brisson repeated many times what most interested them, the tests on metals and minerals. Mitouard brought samples of minerals, diaphoretic antimony, and even a ruby. The gem "was exposed to the focus on a hard sandstone. It did not smoke, or melt or lose it color. It was only slightly attached to its support."[46]

In 1773, from March 14 to August 14, Lavoisier carried out a new series of nineteen experiments on diamonds. He placed them under a glass pneumatic trough so as to collect the escaping gases. But the glass jar broke as a result of the high temperatures, and the gases could not be collected. In the end, the question of the mechanism responsible for the destruction of diamonds remained unanswered. But already a new question was intriguing Lavoisier: if metals can fix air, could the presence of this air explain their increase in weight when they are transformed into calces (oxides) by calcination?

4

The Calcination of Metals

ANOTHER IMPORTANT QUESTION still remained unanswered: why did the weight of metals increase when they were transformed into calces (oxides) by calcination? The fact that calcined metals increased in weight had been long established, since 1630 when Dr. Jean Rey had published his *Essays sur la recherche de la cause pour laquelle l'étain et le plomb augmentent de poids quand on les calcine.*

Lavoisier had read the collection of the *Mémoires de l'Académie des Sciences* since the creation of the academy. In 1667 the secretary wrote in his report:

It would be quite natural to believe that a body cannot become heavier unless it is combined with another appreciable material. But M. Du Clos demonstrated to the Academy that a pound of régule of antimony, finely ground into an impalpable dust and then reduced to ashes after an exposure during one hour to a burning glass, increased its weight by 1/10, although while burning it produced a thick white smoke. [. . .] He also found that sulfurous minerals, such as pewter and lead, increase in weight when calcined. [. . .] M. Du Clos conjectured that the air that flowed constantly toward the flames, deposited on these burning materials, filled with sulfurs from the soil, more volatile sulfurated particles that permanently combined with them and formed those observed filaments, which apparently are responsible for the increase in weight.[1]

Following Georg Ernst Stahl's theory calcined metals released phlogiston. In Lavoisier's opinion, the theory had a fundamental contradiction. Since phlogiston was a ponderous body, the metals ought to lose weight; on the contrary, their weight increased. The principle of conservation of mass and the equation between inflows and outflows made the theory unacceptable. What then was he to think? Do calcined metals capture a gas or do they release phlogiston? Lavoisier was not the only person in France to be stymied by this dilemma.

The Theories of Guyton de Morveau

Louis Bernard Guyton de Morveau was one of the first to attempt to resolve the dilemma. This Dijon jurist had created a laboratory and a chemistry
course with the aid of works by two famous Parisian chemists, Pierre Joseph
Macquer and Antoine Baumé, and had rapidly acquired an excellent reputation. His first scientific work was precisely a *Mémoire sur les phénomènes de
l'air dans la combustion*, published in 1768. He was trying to shed some light
on the debate over phlogiston that opposed his colleague in Dijon, Dr. Jean-
Pierre Chardenon to Father Laurent Béraut, a Jesuit who was a mathematics
professor at the Collège de Lyon.

From 1747 Béraut had maintained that the increase in the weight of
metals during calcination was due to the fixation of "aerial corpuscles."[2]
Chardenon argued that it resulted from the loss of phlogiston, which, due to
its negative weight, "gave wings to earthly molecules" and allowed them to
escape gravity. Béraut ridiculed this theory pointing out that it was refuted
by all astronomers and upholders of the universal laws of gravitation.

In 1770 Guyton presented his *Dissertation sur le phlogistique considéré
comme corps grave* in Dijon. He tried without much success to support his
colleague in Dijon, arguing that the addition of phlogiston made the metal
lighter because phlogiston was specifically lighter than air.

Fortunately, his experimental work was better than this theories. He
demonstrated incontestably that all metals increase in weight when calcination transforms them into calces. He proved it by calcining copper shavings,
iron and steel filings, tin, antimony, bismuth, and zinc. He also showed that
calcination requires the presence of air and that it cannot occur in closed re-
ceptacles containing little air.

Guyton's text was published in 1772 in *Digressions académiques*.[3] The importance of his work was immediately recognized in Paris, but each scientist
interpreted it in his own way. Baumé approved "the broad views proposed by
this clever physicist."[4] According to Macquer, it brought out "the fundamental fact of the increase in absolute weight of bodies once their inflammable
principle is removed."[5] Lavoisier, although sparing in his compliments, admitted that *Digressions académiques* was "marked with the genius of observation, and contained the results of the most complete, interesting and exact
experiments that existed on the calcination of metals."[6] It was surely the least
he could say, since he was going to borrow Guyton's two demonstrations
showing that metals grew heavier in becoming metallic calces, and that this
increase in weight was due to the fixation of air.

Jean Antoine Nicolas Caritat, marquis de Condorcet, a young and brilliant mathematician and protégé of Jean le Rond d'Alembert, had entered the Academy in 1769. He commented: "After extensive research, M. de Morveau has established that this increase in weight is real and general for all metals, in spite of the denials of certain chemists."[7] In a recently discovered letter to Guyton de Morveau, Condorcet showed himself to be a convinced phlogistician, in total disagreement with Lavoisier:

At the opening session of the Academy, M. Lavoisier read a paper in which he attributes another cause to the weight increase in calcined metals. According to him, the increase results from the air that combines with the metals during calcination. But during the reduction, the air separates from them and the metals are no longer in the form of calces. Using a burning glass, M. Lavoisier has calcined and reduced the metals placed under a bell jar and they absorbed air during calcination just as they released it during reduction. According to you, the increase in weight is due to the difference between the weight of air and that of phlogiston; but since the difference is less than if phlogiston were weightless, and the increase in weight is on the contrary greater than if one had added to the metal a volume of air equal to its total weight, it necessarily follows that the air replacing the phlogiston has a greater density than atmospheric air, and this can be expected from that "principle of bodies air" or fixed air. M. Lavoisier seems to think that this air explains the difference in weight existing between metallic calces and metals and that the presence of phlogiston is not necessary for the metallic state. It seems to me that this assertion needs to be proved by precise experiments, because if ever there was anything established in chemistry, it is surely the theory of phlogiston.[8]

Turgot's Ideas

Still another person from the provinces had ideas about why metals gain weight during calcination. Anne Robert Jacques Turgot, intendant of Limoges, was a philosopher and economist as well as an amateur chemist. At Denis Diderot's request, he had written the article on "expansibility" for the grand *Encyclopédie*.[9]

Condorcet helped Turgot to forget that Limoges was very far from Paris by keeping up a regular correspondence with him. It was he who pointed out that, according to Guyton de Morveau, "unlike other bodies, phlogiston is not attracted by each molecule of earthly matter, but on the contrary is impelled by forces that give it a direction contrary to that of gravity."[10]

Although a professed advocate of the phlogiston theory, Turgot answered that Guyton was not a good scientist and that he reasoned as poorly as Hermann Boerhaave, "that ignorant charlatan, so much copied by our bad physicists and praised by his medical colleagues."[11] Turgot did not believe in the existence of fixed air as a particular gas distinct from common air. For him, this fixedness was only an accidental and passing state, not a constituent property of the gas. The gas described by the Scottish chemists "is not fixed air, but rather air that was fixed for a certain time and no longer is. It is the air released from the combination in which it had been fixed. The appellation 'fixed air' is therefore inappropriate and must be banned."[12]

According to him, the weight gain of metals was due to the fixation of atmospheric air, which took the place of the lighter phlogiston. Like Guyton de Morveau, he tried to find a compromise between the weight increase and Stahl's theory, but his explanation was hardly any better:

The increase in weight occurring in metal is due to the air which, in the combustion process, combines with the metallic earth and replaces the phlogiston, which is burned and which, without being of an absolute lightness, is incomparably less heavy than air, apparently because it contains less matter.[13]

Condorcet suggested to Turgot that he and Balthazar Georges Sage carry out an experiment that would advance the debate on fixed air. It entailed reducing lead calx with charcoal in a closed retort connected to a container filled with limewater. If the water precipitated, it would prove that the reduction of the lead calx produced fixed air. Turgot considered this experiment useless, and the opportunity was missed. But one can imagine that when he came to Paris and met Lavoisier at Paulze's parties he spoke to him about it.

The Fixation of Air by Phosphorus

In 1772 the French scientists were getting acquainted with phosphorus, a body not found in its pure state in nature and very difficult to prepare. This curious substance, phosphorescent in the dark, burned spontaneously when it came into contact with air, producing phosphoric acid, and the weight of the acid produced was greater than that of the original phosphorus. At the beginning of the year, Sage had specified that the weight of the acid formed was three times that of the phosphorus, and this increase supposedly was due to the addition of humidity from the atmospheric air.

In May the Abbé François Rozier published an article by Giovanni Francesco Cigna, a professor of anatomy in Turin, showing that two grains of phosphorus, burned under a glass bell jar, consumed twenty-three inches of air. But Cigna did not establish a link either with the fixation of air by phosphorus or with its increase in weight. Guyton in turn burned twenty-two grains of phosphorus and collected thirty-seven grains of phosphoric acid. The additional fifteen grains, he said, could not be explained solely by the absorption of the humidity of air. Mitouard, candidate for the post of adjunct chemist at the Academy, was trying to improve the method of producing phosphorus.[14] He too had noted this increase in the weight of the acid. But did it come from the humidity of air or from air itself?

Lavoisier commented that "what is most remarkable is that, regardless of the degree of concentration to which one brings the acid, its weight is always greater than that of the phosphoric powder used."[15] He suspected that the increase in weight came from the air absorbed by the burning phosphorus, and on September 10 he purchased from Mitouard, for about 45 livres ($1,800), one ounce of excellent phosphorus imported from Germany. "I wanted to prove that the phosphorus absorbed air during its combustion: using a wire, I tightly attached a pneumatic flask to the neck of a bottle in which I had previously put fifteen grains of phosphorus."[16]

The note breaks off in mid-sentence. Perhaps he was interrupted, or was the experiment a failure? But it is certain that he returned to it. He was convinced that phosphorus absorbs air when it burns and is transformed into phosphoric acid. On October 20 he placed eight grains of phosphorus in a small capsule of agate and covered it with a glass bell jar. He directed the focus of a burning glass on the phosphorus, which burst into a brilliant flame. A fluffy white cloud arose and settled on the inside surface of the bell jar; then within a few minutes, the vapors condensed into clear drops of phosphoric acid. "The quantity of acid derived from the phosphorus is considerably greater than the quantity of phosphorus that produced it," he noted. "This increase in weight, the proportion of which is difficult to observe accurately, comes from the air that is fixed in this process."[17]

To eliminate the role of the humidity contained in the atmospheric air, he diluted the acid formed in a large volume of distilled water, collected this solution in a bottle, marked the level and weighed the bottle. Then he emptied the bottle, filled it with distilled water up to the same level and weighed it again. The difference between the two weights represented the weight of the phosphoric acid formed, which was much greater than that of the initial weight of the phosphorus. The increase could not be attributed to the absorption of air since the role of humidity had been ruled out.

He repeated the experiment with sulfur that he calcined under a glass bell jar. The results being less good, he did not give figures.[18] But he noted that the quantity of sulfuric acid obtained was much greater than the quantity of sulfur used.[19]

On the basis of these two experiments he proposed in principle that every combustion or calcination of a metal or "a great number of solid and liquid bodies is accompanied by weight increase and absorption of air."[20] Indeed tin, heated in an hermetically closed container filled with air, was transformed into a calx (oxide) which was heavier; at the same time the air inside the container diminished. The increase in the weight of the calx was equal to the decrease in the weight of the air.

But what Lavoisier had performed in this case was a synthesis: metal + air. Faithful to his method, he had to verify this by analysis: calx − air. Thus he reversed the operation and reduced the lead calx or litharge (lead monoxide), to lead.[21] In a closed receptacle containing charcoal, the heated litharge was transformed into metallic lead, lost weight and released a very important volume of gas. The validity of his scientific approach had been confirmed, he thought. But, in fact, he had been misled: the gas he had collected after the reduction was not that contained by the oxide, oxygen. In contact with the charcoal, it had been transformed into carbon dioxide (CO_2).

He was, however, in no less a hurry to protect his discovery. "Since it is difficult when conversing with friends not to let drop something that could put them on the right path," he took unusual precautions.[22] On November 1, 1772 he deposited a sealed envelope with the secretary of the Academy. It contained his assertion that the increase in weight observed in the combustion of sulfur and phosphorus was the result of the fixation of an immense quantity of air, and that the same was true for the weight increase of metals during calcination. "Since this discovery seemed to me to be one of the most interesting that had been made since Stahl's, I felt that I ought to ensure that it remained my property."[23] Lavoisier was well aware of the innovative character of his approach to combustion and of the threat it posed to Stahl's phlogiston. And, in fact, this note has been considered by many historians to be the birth certificate of modern chemistry. But he was not the only one to have plunged into the study of gases. There was a regular correspondence between French and English scientists. New experiments incited keen rivalries and their authors fought ferociously over the paternity of discoveries. The competition was going to be very tough, not only from the English side—from Priestley in particular—but also from the French. In addition to Mitouard, three young scientists had recently entered the lists: Jean Baptiste Bucquet, Hilaire Marin Rouelle, and Pierre Bayen.

Bucquet, a physician and chemistry professor in Paris, had done a series of experiments in the laboratory of the duc de La Rochefoucauld d'Enville. In April 1773 he had presented the first original French publication on fixed air at the Royal Academy of Science.[24] He had also worked for almost a year in Lavoisier's laboratory, where he was responsible for carrying out a part of the program set up by Trudaine de Montigny. He had demonstrated that fixed air obtained by the action of acids on chalk and weak alkalis is always the same, regardless of the acid used, and that it is identical with the air released by fermentations, but different from atmospheric air and from inflammable gas produced by the action of acids on metals (hydrogen). "Although these experiments were closely linked to those published before M. Bucquet's, especially those done by M. Priestley, they are no less valuable for physics," Lavoisier amiably commented on June 12, 1773. "It would be impossible to overdo experiments on such a thorny subject, parts of which are still obscure."[25]

In May 1773 Hilaire Marin Rouelle, known as Rouelle the younger, established in the *Journal de Médecine* a clear distinction between fixed air, which dissolves in water and cannot be ignited, and inflammable gas (hydrogen), insoluble in water and which can be easily ignated.[26] He disagreed with Priestley as to the beneficial character of fixed air. "I have a strong suspicion that wherever it is gathered in quantity and has no contact with atmospheric air, it can become dangerous and perhaps fatal."[27] Rouelle knew what he was talking about: the day he had almost perished from asphyxiation after breathing fixed air from a bottle had left a very bad memory. Johann Friedrich Meyer had had the same misadventure.

Pierre Bayen, a military pharmacist who was a friend of Rouelle and Venel, produced fixed air by applying intense heat to samples of siderite (ferrous carbonate). The gas was absorbed by potassium carbonate, which produced a crystalline salt, bicarbonate of potassium. From this Bayen concluded that the mineral siderite was composed of one part of fixed air and three parts of metallic iron. These were his beginnings in pneumatic chemistry. His path would soon cross Lavoisier's.

Only Baumé resisted the general trend. He was absolutely convinced that "fixed air would never bring about a total revolution in chemistry and change the order of acquired knowledge."[28] According to him, there was only one kind of air, although it could enter into an infinite number of combinations. Fixed air was only ordinary air, and "the new properties that will be found in it will always be due to extraneous substances and not to the air itself."[29] He expressed exactly the opinion of Turgot who, as might be expected, considered him to be "a man of merit."[30]

At this point, Lavoisier was no longer seeking to demonstrate that air could enter into the composition of bodies—that had already been proven—nor to establish the existence of fixed air. He had stepped over a new threshold in trying to specify its nature: sometimes this gas was soluble in water, capable of precipitating limewater, extinguishing candlelight and killing animals; at other times, it was insoluble and caused candles to burn brightly.

Lavoisier did not know that there was a very simple reason for this variability in results: in the former case he was dealing with carbon dioxide and in the latter with oxygen. In any case, he was convinced that the chemistry of gases warranted a detailed study and was bound to produce important discoveries in the end.

The Research Program

Therefore on February 20, 1773 Lavoisier wrote out at the beginning of his first laboratory register, the famous plan of action cited by all historians of science.[31]

Before undertaking the long series of experiments I intend to carry out on the elastic fluid released from bodies—whether by fermentation, distillation, or various combinations—and on the air absorbed during the combustion of a great number of substances, I believe that I should write down a few reflections, so as to formulate the plan I must follow. However numerous the experiments done by MM. Hales, Black, MacBride, Jacquin, Crantz, Priestley and Smeth on this subject, they nevertheless fall short of forming a complete body of theory. [. . .] The importance of the subject has committed me to reviewing all this work, which seems likely to bring about a revolution in physics and chemistry. I feel that I should regard everything done before as mere information. I have decided to repeat everything, taking new precautions, so that what we learn about air that becomes fixed or is released from bodies can be linked with already established knowledge and a new theory can be formulated.[32]

The great question was still whether fixed air was atmospheric air, only a part of it, or a different gas. To find the answer, it was necessary to study all the circumstances in which air became fixed or was released. Consequently, Lavoisier was going to examine successively "vegetation, animal respiration, combustion, calcination in certain circumstances, and certain chemical combinations."[33] He followed this plan to the letter for twenty years, exploring all of mineral, vegetable, and animal chemistry. His entire scientific work was contained in the few lines of this program.

In February he tackled the calcination of lead and the reduction of minium (red lead), which he believed to be a combination of lead and atmospheric air. He wrote in his first laboratory notebook:

Air combined with lead in minium is not this fixed air, which has such an aptitude for combining with alkalis. It is undoubtedly atmospheric air. It can also be that this air released from lead is not sufficiently charged with phlogiston to combine with the alkalis, because, according to some researchers, fixed air is an air combined with phlogiston; but I confess that all this presents a great deal of uncertainty.[34]

In March he took up the tests on the combustion of phosphorus and the calcination of metals. He produced fixed air by having chalk react with acid, and tried, like Priestley, to make it salubrious by having it bubble in water. He thought that, by removing its fixed or phlogisticated part in this way, he could produce common air, suitable for respiration and combustion. Elsewhere he took an opposite approach and wondered whether fixed air could be converted into atmospheric air by adding phlogiston.[35]

Somewhat uncertain, but always in a rush, he wanted to have something original to announce to the Easter session of the Academy. As luck would have it, the laboratory was not ready, and "the different machines were not yet finished, because the workers have been slow."[36] On March 29 he discovered that the calcination of lead in a closed retort stopped after a certain time and he wrote in his laboratory notebook:

I was surprised to see that the lead was no longer calcining. I then began to suspect that contact with a circulating air is necessary for the formation of metallic calx; even perhaps that not all the air we breathe enters into the metals being calcined, but only a portion, which is not found abundantly in a given mass of air.[37]

By detecting the compound nature of air, he was on the right track. On August 2, 1773 Trudaine de Montigny, always attentive to Lavoisier's research, posed three questions. Could metal be calcined in the vacuum of a pneumatic machine? If so, any idea of the fixation of air was excluded. Could metal be calcined in a minimum quantity of air, so that the air would be completely absorbed? If so, that would mean that atmospheric air became fixed in its totality and that it was made up of a single component. Finally, could one collect the residual gas after the calcination of a metal and see whether it supported animal respiration and the flame of a candle? If it did, then atmospheric air was made up of only a single gas. If not, then calcination would have removed from atmospheric air a component indispensable for combustion and respiration. "I believe," Trudaine de Montigny wrote, "that these experiments would shed considerable light on the fixed air theory."[38] They would also have opened up many other paths for research, but at that time Lavoisier was concentrating on publishing his results on fixed air before the English and the French.

The *Opuscules physiques et chymiques*

Lavoisier could not wait for the appearance of the *Mémoires* of the Royal Academy of Science, whose usual delay was two years, and published the *Opuscules physiques et chymiques* on his own. "The keen interest that scientists seem to be showing in this subject and the increasing research being done everywhere would undoubtedly have been a sufficient reason for my decision, and I had no need to look for another."[39]

Written in three months, from September to November 1773, the *Opuscules physiques et chymiques* were approved on December 7 by the committee of the Academy composed of Trudaine de Montigny, Pierre Joseph Macquer, Jean Baptiste Le Roy, and Antoine Alexis Cadet. In fact—perhaps to save time, perhaps at his colleagues' request—it was Lavoisier who wrote the referees' report. One thousand two hundred and fifty copies of the work were printed by three Parisian publishers. Thirty of them were delivered to Trudaine de Montigny and twelve to the Court. Lavoisier presented the text to the Academy on January 8, 1774.

The first part, a *Précis historique sur les émanations élastiques qui se dégagent des corps pendant la combustion, pendant la fermentation et pendant les effervescences*, summarized in 184 pages everything that had been written on fixed air. The various authors received unequal treatment. Lavoisier quoted Priestley amply, but did not entirely do justice to Black. He mentioned that he had extracted fixed air from "magnesia, chalky earth, and in general all kinds of earth, that are reduced to quick lime when calcined."[40] Lavoisier then, analyzed Black's work in five rather dry pages and attributed to Nicolas Joseph Jacquin the merit of having completed the work. He devoted twenty pages to Johann Friedrich Meyer and Heinrich Johann Nepomuk Crantz, who were hostile to Black. The account on Cavendish's work is defective.

The second part described in 167 pages Lavoisier's own experiments. They confirmed his working hypothesis formulated at the start:

I began to suspect that atmospheric air, or some sort of elastic fluid contained in air, was in a great many circumstances likely to become fixed, to combine itself with metals; that the addition of this substance resulted in the phenomena of calcination, the increase in weight of metals converted into calces and perhaps many other phenomena for which physicists had not yet given any satisfying explanation.[41]

Another essential idea appeared. He no longer considered atmospheric air as a simple element, but as a compound one, a mixture:

Not all the air that we breathe is likely to fix itself and enter into the combination of metallic calces, but the atmosphere contains a particular elastic fluid that is mixed with air, and it is at the moment when the quantity of this fluid within the bell jar is exhausted that calcination can no longer occur.[42]

The assertion was not followed by demonstration, but it was correct. Lavoisier was not yet in a position "to decide if the part of the elastic fluid produced by the effervescences and reductions that can be combined is a substance essentially different from air, or if it is air itself to which it has been added or from which it has removed something."[43]

The *Opuscules physiques et chymiques* were in advance over anything which had gone before and established Lavoisier's reputation as a chemist. He presented his discoveries modestly and paid tribute to his precursors. He sent copies to French and foreign scientists and to the best-known academic societies, such as those in London, Edinburgh, and Stockholm. He announced that a second volume, dedicated to elastic fluid, would be forthcoming, but it never appeared. The announced chapters would appear fifteen years later in the *Traité élémentaire de chimie*.

5

The Oxygen Dispute

AT THE BEGINNING OF 1774 *mercurius calcinatus per se* (red calx of mercury or mercury oxide) was arousing the curiosity of the scientific community. A substance inherited from alchemists, until then it had been known especially by apothecaries who used it for treating venereal diseases. By calcining liquid mercury for several weeks at a high temperature, one obtained this red oxide which, heated to a still higher temperature, would be retransformed into liquid mercury.

This reduction without charcoal—without the addition of phlogiston, in Stahl's system—did not seem logical. The fact had been pointed out by Rouelle in his course and by Macquer in the 1766 edition of his *Dictionnaire de chymie*, but no interpretation had been given.

Lavoisier was bound to be interested in *mercurius calcinatus*. Reductions without charcoal could deliver him from his conceptual impasse. Since the end of the summer of 1772, he had known that at the time of calcination a gas contained in air combined with metals and transformed them into calces. He suspected that the reduction of these calces with charcoal discharged a different gas, which had the properties of fixed air.

At the time of his experiments using the burning glasses on diamonds, he had succeeded in reducing iron oxide without charcoal, but had been unable to identify the gas produced. On September 16, for the 19th experiment, he had placed *mercurius calcinatus* in a stoneware cup, and under the effect of the heat produced by the burning glass, had seen gray droplets of metallic mercury gush forth from the cup. He had just witnessed a partial reduction of the mercury oxide without charcoal, but had not understood the significance of what he had observed. He limited himself to noting in the report: "we have attributed this revivification to the contact with iron, which we shall verify."[1] Two years later he still had not confirmed by synthesis what he had accidentally revealed by analysis. If he was a long time in perceiving the interest of the *mercurius calcinatus*, others were more perspicacious.

Bayen's Publications

Mercury oxide could be obtained by a method simpler than calcination. The mercury was dissolved in nitric acid, and the resulting solution was treated by evaporation or precipitated through a base, soda or caustic potash.[2] It gave a salt which, moderately heated, was transformed into a red powder similar to *mercurius calcinatus*, but contained impurities. A chemist who wanted to work with genuine mercury calx had to get it from a trusted pharmacist, or else make it himself.

Pierre Bayen, a pharmacist in the French army, was, according to his assistant, Antoine Augustin Parmentier, "the most distinguished pharmacist existing not only in France but in all of Europe." He knew perfectly well how to make mercury solutions in nitric acid for analyzing the mineral waters from Bagnères and Luchon.[3] By precipitating these solutions through potassium carbonate, ammonium carbonate or caustic potash, he could obtain many different mercury oxides: nitrates, carbonates, and hydroxides. Bayen observed that, heated moderately in retorts, these oxides discharged a gas while losing weight. On heating them with charcoal, he obtained fixed air that he could identify by its odor, its slightly acrid taste, and its action on iron filings. But more important was his discovery that the oxides could be reduced without the addition of charcoal. In that case he obtained a gas he did not identify: it would have sufficed to introduce a lighted candle under the water trough to understand that it was a different gas and to discover oxygen.

In any case, he noted the essential fact that Lavoisier had not yet demonstrated: "They all reduce themselves independently and without addition, and in so doing they lose one eighth of their weight."[4] A good observer, he lacked boldness as a theoretician. His interpretations reflect this shyness: "an unknown cause had the effect of making a metallic calx heavier than the metal was before the combustion."[5]

In April he specified that the weight increase of oxides was due to the fixation of the elastic fluid described by Lavoisier in his *Opuscules physiques et chymiques*, pointing out that this fact challenged the very existence of phlogiston. But could the phlogiston come from a source other than the charcoal? From the rays of the sun passing through the burning glasses or electric fluid, for example?

On May 20, 1774 Nicolas Christian de Thy, Count de Milly, a colonel in the dragoons and an amateur chemist, known for his studies on Dresden china, presented to the Royal Academy of Science a memoir on the reduction of metallic calces by electric fluid. He claimed to demonstrate that this fluid was phlogiston. Lavoisier, Brisson, Baumé, and Cadet verified his results on July 28 in Brisson's laboratory. They used a *mercurius calcinatus* made by Cadet, who sold it for 18 livres (or $720) an ounce. However, Baumé contested the quality of Cadet's product and at the next meeting brought along his own sample, supposedly impossible to reduce without charcoal and which he sold for 48 livres (or $1,920) an ounce. Cadet asserted that this *mercurius calcinatus* could very well be reduced, just like all the others, without phlogiston. Baumé was indignant, the quarrel grew more acrimonious, and a new committee was named.

Lavoisier, Brisson, and Sage resumed the tests on September 3 and continued until November 19. Baumé refused to participate. All the samples of *mercurius calcinatus* were easily reduced by using heat without charcoal, and the quantity of liquid mercury collected was diminished by about one-twelfth. The plan had been to collect the gases discharged during the operation by adapting pneumatic troughs to the retorts, but the samples were small, and the slight volume of gas obtained was too diluted in the air of the retort to be analyzed. For a second time, Lavoisier had witnessed the reduction of mercury calx without charcoal, and the simultaneous production of oxygen. He did not perceive the importance of the event and merely made a simple observation: "The comparative experiments that we have just reported demonstrate the similarity existing between the samples of *mercurius calcinatus per se* of MM. Baumé and Cadet respectively, and show that both are reducible without addition."[6]

Priestley's Dephlogisticated Air

Fourcroy would later write: "That discovery and the difference of this air from atmospheric air was reserved for Priestley. He made it precisely while Bayen was publicizing his research and while Lavoisier was laying the first foundation of his doctrine on the calcination of metals and combustion."[7]

Priestley had just acquired a burning glass of small dimensions, more practical than the mirror he had previously used. He thus calcined different substances and collected the discharged gases in a mercury trough. It was on August 1, 1774 that he first observed that the gas from *mercurius calcinatus per se* had very particular characteristics: "But what surprised me more than I can well express, was that a candle burned in this air with a remarkably vigorous flame, very much like that enlarged flame with which a candle burns in nitrous air, exposed to iron or liver of sulfur. [. . .] I was utterly at a loss how to account for it."[8]

The flame resembled the one obtained when he plunged a candle in nitrous air (nitrous oxide), a gas he had discovered in 1772 and that he used for the test of nitrous air, which was supposed to measure the "goodness of air."[9] Since nitric acid was not used in the preparation of the genuine *mercurius calcinatus*, this new gas could not be nitrous air. Moreover, its flame was larger, more brilliant, and hotter. But perhaps his *mercurius calcinatus* had mixed with ordinary red precipitate, prepared by dissolving mercury in nitric acid; that could give rise to error. He started over again with ordinary red precipitate and then used calcined mercury of good quality, and both times he collected a considerable quantity of the unknown gas. "This experiment would have satisfied a moderate skeptic," he noted, but he wanted to be certain. For that, he needed an excellent calcined mercury like the one found in Paris. In October 1774 an opportunity arose for him to accompany his patron, Lord Shelbourne, to Paris. "Knowing that there were several very eminent chymists in that place, I did not omit the opportunity, by means of my friend Mr. Magellan, to get an ounce of *mercurius calcinatus* prepared by Mr. Cadet, of the genuineness of which, there could not possibly be any suspicion."[10]

His presence could not pass unnoticed and he told the French about his recent discovery: "I frequently mentioned my surprize at the kind of air which I had got from this preparation to Mr. Lavoisier, Mr. Le Roy and several other philosophers, who honoured me with their notice in that city, and who, I daresay, cannot fail to recollect the circumstance."[11] In 1800 Priestley still remembered perfectly the dinner at Lavoisier's house:

Having made the discovery some time before I was in Paris, in the year 1774, I mentioned it at the table of Mr. Lavoisier, when most of the philosophical people of the city were present, saying that it was a kind of air in which a candle burned much better than in common air, but that I had not then given it a name. At this, all the company, and Mr. and Mrs. Lavoisier as much as any, expressed great surprise. I told them that I had gotten it from *precipitate per se* and also from red lead. Speaking French very imperfectly and being little acquainted with the terms of chemistry, I said *plomb rouge*, which was not understood till Mr. Macquer said I must mean *minium*.[12]

Priestley acknowledged having been mistaken about the nature of the new gas. He did not even suspect that it was salubrious and suitable for respiration. During his stay in Paris, however, he had given two capital pieces of information to the French: not only did the calcined mercury contain a gas that could be discharged by the simple application of heat, but this gas also sustained combustion much better than did atmospheric air.

Returning to England in November, Priestley went back to work. Subjecting the calcined mercury purchased from Cadet to moderate heat, he again obtained the unknown gas. In it a candle burned more brilliantly than in atmospheric air and it was breathable. "In this ignorance of the real nature of this kind of air, I continued from this time [November] to the 1st of March following. [. . .] But, in the course of this month, I not only ascertained the nature of this kind of air, though very gradually, but was led by it to the complete discovery of the constitution of the air we breathe."[13]

It was only in March 1775 that he subjected the new gas to the test of nitrous air. At first contact, the gas diminished by a fifth, just as it did with atmospheric air, and the mixture had the same red color. On March 8 he placed a mouse in a glass receptacle containing two measures of the new gas. Instead of surviving fifteen minutes as it would have in atmospheric air, it was still alive after half an hour; when it was removed, it was simply cold and rapidly regained its strength. "This experiment with the mouse, when I had reflected upon it some time, gave me so much suspicion that the air in which I had put it was better than common air, that I was induced, the day after, to apply the test of nitrous air to a small part of that very quantity of air which the mouse had breathed so long."[14]

The test was positive; the gas diminished in volume. Priestley repeated the process: the gas diminished still more. He once again placed the mouse in it and it survived for half an hour. This gas was decidedly much better than common air. Priestley named it dephlogisticated air because, according to him, it contained less phlogiston than did atmospheric air; it was five to six times "better" than atmospheric air. It could be kept in tanks or bellows and used to bring the heat of an oven to very high temperatures. When mixed with hydrogen in certain proportions, it formed an explosive mixture. One could even envisage medical applications, in particular the treatment of pulmonary consumption. Finally, he tested the air on himself, by breathing it through a siphon: "I fancied that my breast felt peculiarly light and easy for some time afterwards. Who can tell but that, in time, this pure air may become a fashionable article in luxury. Hitherto, only two mice and myself have had the privilege of breathing it."[15]

Scheele's Fire Air

The list of competitors for the discovery of oxygen was not yet closed however. A modest Swedish researcher, Carl Wilhelm Scheele, had discovered it three or perhaps four years earlier. He worked in Uppsala in a shop behind the pharmacy that supplied the famous professor Torbern Olof Bergman with his chemical reagents. A correspondent of Macquer at the Academy of Science since 1768, Bergman had admitted that "Swedish discoveries, little known up to now because of distance and our language, cannot be accepted in one day."[16]

Scheele was an excellent bench scientist. "His cleverness made up for everything, and with limited equipment, he knew how to carry out the most delicate experiments, isolate the most hidden bodies, produce the most unforeseen compounds and attain the most important discoveries. Nature seemed to want to console him for the misfortunes inflicted on him by men, and to delight in sharing with him its most beautiful secrets. He never touched a body without making a discovery."[17]

On November 16, 1772—and undoubtedly even as early as 1771—he had discovered that manganese oxide, when heated to incandescence, discharged a gas that he called "fire air." Before both Priestley and Lavoisier, he had obtained oxygen by heating manganese oxide, mercury oxide, silver carbonate, magnesium nitrate and potassium nitrate. Each time, the charcoal powder became incandescent on contact with the discharged oxygen and burned up rapidly. "I have often taken great pleasure in observing the extraordinarily brilliant sparks produced by heat alone, when reducing in a retort metallic calces with which only a small amount of charcoal dust has been mixed."[18] Finally Scheele realized his masterly experiment:

I had wanted for a long time to have a little calcined mercury to see if it would also produce fire air while being reduced. [. . .] I placed over the flame a portion of this calcined mercury in a small glass retort to whose neck I had attached an empty air bag. Once the retort began to turn red, the air bag began to expand and the reduced mercury immediately rose in the neck of the retort. It did not rise from red precipitate, as happens with mercury calx prepared with nitrous acid. The air obtained was pure fire air.[19]

Scheele had definitely discovered oxygen and described its properties, but he attributed them to phlogiston. He disapproved of Priestley's having named it dephlogisticated air. No one today contests the priority of Scheele's discovery of oxygen. It is Lavoisier's attitude that remains to be explained. On April 12, 1774 Lavoisier sent two copies of his *Opuscules physiques et chymiques* to Wargentin, Secretary of the Academy of Science in Stockholm. He included a friendly letter for Bergman and added a postscript: "I take the liberty of sending a copy for Mr. Scheele."[20]

On September 30, 1774 Scheele thanked Lavoisier for the book and suggested a protocol for producing a large quantity of fire air using burning glasses. It required dissolving silver in nitric acid, precipitating it by using potassium carbonate, washing and drying the precipitate of the silver carbonate and then subjecting it to the fire of the burning glass, taking the precaution of placing a little quick lime under the bell jar to absorb the fixed air discharged during the operation.[21]

Having obtained only an incomplete decomposition of the silver carbonate and a light discharge of fire air in his furnace, Scheele was expecting more convincing results from the Lavoisier's burning glass: "It is by this means that I hope you will see how much air is produced during the reduction, and whether a lighted candle will maintain its flame and animals survive in it. I should be much obliged if you could let me know the result of this experiment."[22]

Lavoisier received Scheele's letter on October 15, 1774, but he did not answer it.[23] He was undoubtedly very busy, but it seems to be a weak excuse for a man who was usually so punctual in his correspondence. The Swedish historians of science have still not forgiven him for what was much more than simple rudeness. It is difficult to disagree with them.

The Turin School, Beccaria, and Cigna

At the public session of the Academy of Science on November 12, 1774 Lavoisier announced officially:

Atmospheric air is not a simple body, but is composed of very different substances, and the work that I have undertaken on the calcination and revivification of mercury calx has only confirmed my opinion. Without going into the consequences of this work, I believe that I can announce here that the totality of atmospheric air is not in a breathable state; that it is the salubrious portion that combines with metals during their calcination and that what remains after calcination is a kind of *mofette* (nitrogen), incapable of sustaining animal respiration or the burning of bodies.[24]

A few days later, in December 1774, he announced his discovery to the readers of *Observations sur la physique*.

I believe I am in a position to confirm that air, however pure one can suppose it to be, divested of all humidity and every substance extraneous to its existence and composition, far from being a simple being, an element, as has been commonly thought, must on the contrary be placed at least in the mixed class, and perhaps even in the compound one.[25]

But he received a letter written on November 1774 from Gianbatista Cesare Beccaria, a priest in Turin, who, by calcining tin and lead in closed retorts, had demonstrated that calcination of metals could not be pursued after some time. His nephew, Giovanni Francesco Cigna, had confirmed the results in 1759:

Father Beccaria has shown that by placing lead or pewter filings in hermetically sealed glass vessels and exposing them to fire so as to calcine them, he could reduce only a portion to calces, and that the greater the capacity of the vessels, the greater the portion of calces formed.[26]

In 1772 Cigna had published in Abbé Rozier's journal his own results on the diminution in the volume of air caused by burning phosphorus in a sealed retort; he had written: "Two grains of phosphorus, lighted and enclosed in a container, absorb 28 inches of air."[27] But he had failed to understand that the absorbed air combined with the phosphorus by a chemical reaction to produce an oxide. Instead, he accepted the interpretation given by Hales in *Vegetable Staticks* and wrote: "The flames diminished the movement of air, not by absorbing it, but by exhaling vapors that reduced the repulsive force of the parts of the fluid with which they had mixed."[28]

Apparently Lavoisier had been unaware of Cigna's paper and did not mention it in his historical review of all earlier work on fixed air, from Hales to Priestley, contained in the *Opuscules physiques et chimiques*. But in 1774, after the publication of the work, the comte de Saluces asked him to acknowledge Beccaria's and Cigna's contributions. And in December 1774 Lavoisier answered in Abbé Rozier's journal:

It is important to me that the public be convinced as soon as possible that I have no intention of taking over somebody else's work, and I am convinced that scrupulousness in literature and physics is no less essential than in morals. Although Father Beccaria's experiment removes some of the novelty from my own, I nevertheless admit that his letter pleased me greatly and that I was delighted to see adopted and confirmed by a celebrated physicist the theory of the weight gain of metallic calces, which I believe I was the first to develop and which now seems to be as solidly established as a fact can be in physics and chemistry.[29]

The Air of *Mercurius Calcinatus per se*

In March 1775 Lavoisier resumed his tests on calcined mercury. He heated an ounce of it in a retort with forty-eight grains of charcoal powder and collected in a water trough sixty-four cubic inches of a gas that dissolved in water, precipitated limewater, combined with alkalis by removing their causticity, extinguished candles and killed animals in a few seconds.[30] It was definitely fixed air. He again heated an ounce of calcined mercury, but this time without charcoal, and he obtained seven gros eighteen grains of liquid mercury and seventy-eight cubic inches of a radically different gas that did not mix with water, precipitate limewater, combine with fixed alkalis, or diminish their causticity; it permitted the calcination of metals; in it, candles and charcoal burned brilliantly and animals breathed normally. It was oxygen, but he did not yet know it. "The experiment with the candle has been repeated twice, and in large earthenware jars. The effect is delightful; the flame is much larger, clearer and more beautiful than in common air, but without color other than the ordinary flame."[31]

Thanks to these tests both with and without charcoal, he had understood the mechanism of the formation of fixed air (CO_2) with charcoal. His written account of the tests was placed in a sealed envelope and left at the Academy on March 24, 1775. The metallic calces "give fixed air only because the common air they contain is converted into fixed air by the combustion of the charcoal, as it happens with mercury."[32] On the other hand, he had not succeeded in dissociating oxygen from atmospheric air. At the Easter reopening of the Academy on April 26, he declared, "The principle that combines with metals during their calcination, and increases their weight and transforms them into the state of calx, is neither a component part of air nor a particular acid existing in the atmosphere, it is *air itself, in its entirety, unaltered and not decomposed.*"[33]

At the same time, and rather contradictorily, he asserted that this gas was "*pure air, more breathable, if it can be said, than atmospheric air* and more likely to sustain flames and the combustion of bodies."[34] Oxygen did not yet have a true identity, and the composition of air remained to be established.

Priestley's Accusations

In Birmingham Priestley was annoyed. He was convinced that it was he who had given Lavoisier the idea of using *mercurius calcinatus*, during the dinner they had had together in October 1774. He denounced Lavoisier's borrowing and the gaps in his reasoning:

After I left Paris, where I procured the mercurius calcinatus above mentioned, and had spoken of the experiments that I had made, and that I intended to make with it, he (Lavoisier) began his experiments upon the same substance, and presently found what I have called dephlogisticated air, but without investigating the nature of it, and indeed, without being fully apprised of the degree of its purity. And though he says *it seems to be* more fit for respiration than common air, he does not say that he has made any trial to determine how long an animal could live in it. He therefore inferred, as I have said that I myself had once done, that this substance had, during the process of calcination imbibed atmospherical air, not in part, but in whole. But then he extends his conclusion, and, as it appears to me, without any evidence, to all the metallic calces; saying that, very probably, they would all of them yield only common air, if, like *mercurius calcinatus*, they could be reduced without addition."[35]

Lavoisier insisted that he had begun his research in April 1774. He admitted, however, that "for the tests done on *mercurius calcinatus* he had first used the burning glass during the month of November 1774."[36] The coincidence is disturbing. It cannot be denied that Lavoisier was kept informed very precisely of the evolution of Priestley's ideas. Between 1772 and 1777, Magellan sent thirteen letters describing English scientific work, in particular that of Priestley.[37] Lavoisier could answer that Priestley had no monopoly on *mercurius calcinatus*, and that the conversation over dinner had at most simply spurred him on to use this interesting reagent. Besides, neither one of them knew that he was about to discover oxygen. But there were embarrassing witnesses such as Edmond C. Genet, who would relate in 1783:

I also had the advantage during my stay at Birmingham of becoming acquainted with Dr. Priestley who had the kindness to repeat for my gratification his most interesting experiments on air and gases of which I sent an account to the Academy of Paris. At that time, Lavoisier was pursuing the same subject, and I was surprised on my return to hear him read a memorial at one of the sittings of the Academy which was simply a repetition in different words of Priestley's experiments which I had reported. He laughed, and said to me, "My friend, you know that those who start the hare do not always catch it".[38]

An Unknown Precursor, Jean Rey

Priestley was not the only one to be annoyed. In February 1775 Bayen had again tried to identify the elastic fluid discharged by the *mercurius calcinatus*. Heating the substance in a glass retort, he had collected the gas produced in a water trough. With charcoal, he had obtained fixed air. Without it, he had obtained oxygen, but he did not see the difference. Fourcroy severely commented in the *Dictionnaire de chimie*:

In reading over all of Bayen's experiments, one is surprised that he came so near to the real goal without ever reaching it. Several times he succeeded in enclosing this elastic fluid in an apparatus he had built, and of which he was very proud. He measured and weighed it. He determined that its weight was greater than that of the atmosphere, but he never made the single step that was as simple as necessary for reaching the exposition of this discovery.[39]

Even so, Bayen would have liked very much to be mentioned by Lavoisier.[40] To get his revenge, in January 1775 he republished a book by Jean Rey that had appeared a century and a half earlier. An apothecary from Bergerac had asked this Perigourdian doctor why he had recuperated 2 lbs 13 ounces of tin after calcining only 2 lbs. 6 ounces. Jean Rey had answered that the weight gain of metals during calcination was due to the fixation of air.[41] Completely aware of the novelty of his thesis, he considered the fact as "something that until now has not been understood."[42]

Bayen asked the Abbé Rozier to publish this information; then chemists everywhere would know that Jean Rey had guessed, before Lavoisier, the cause of the gain weight of metals when they are converted into calces. And Bayen concluded: "The cause is precisely the same as that whose truth has just been demonstrated by the experiments described by M. Lavoisier during the most recent public session of the Academy of Science."[43]

Lavoisier was furious and later gave his own appreciation in *Réflexions sur le phlogistique*:

However demonstrative the experiments on which I based myself, I began, according to common practice, by questioning the facts. Furthermore, those who seek to persuade the public that everything new is not true or that everything true is not new, have succeeded in finding the first germ of this discovery in an earlier author. Without examining the authenticity of the work that has just been so hastily brought out in a new edition, I have noted with some pleasure that the impartial public has judged that a vague assertion, thrown out by chance and backed up by no experiments and heretofore unknown to scientists, has not prevented me from being regarded as the discoverer of the cause for the weight gain of metallic calces.[44]

Certainly Lavoisier was unaware of Jean Rey's work before undertaking his own tests, but he was unjust as to the quality of the work. One very reasonable clarification of this affair, written or at least approved by Lavoisier, appeared in the *Histoire de l'Académie des Sciences*:

There was something in this idea, as in many others just as ingenious and true that are found in writers living in unenlightened centuries (because genius existed in all of them), but because proof was lacking, because of the numerous errors with which these ideas were combined, because of their clash with philosophical principles then in use, they have been forgotten. Such ideas are attributed to their original authors only after having presented themselves anew to other scholars and been further developed, since only then do they become easy to notice.[45]

A beautiful, serene reflection on the slow maturation of scientific ideas. A note written in pencil on the flyleaf of the copy at the British Museum of the new edition of Jean Rey's work could raise a doubt: "Lavoisier and his friends bought all the copies of the Gobet edition of Jean Rey they could find and this work has become very rare."[46]

Lavoisier would have lost nothing, however, by acknowledging Jean Rey's merits. In fact, he eventually did when he wrote in 1792:

Jean Rey, in a work published in 1630 describing his research on the reasons for which lead and pewter increase in weight when they are oxidized, developed views that are so profound and analogous to what experience has since confirmed, so much in conformity with the doctrine of saturation and affinities, that for a long time I could not help thinking that Jean Rey's *Essays* had been composed at a much later date than is indicated on the frontispiece of the work.[47]

In any case, the debate did not establish the validity of Bayen's claims. According to Marcelin Berthelot: "When things were clarified, Bayen resumed his experiments and claimed both the discovery of oxygen and all its theory. But his contemporaries did not accept his protests and neither can posterity."[48]

Regarding the discovery of oxygen, the events can thus be summarized as follows: Priestley was the first to announce that he had discovered the new gas in August 1774, but he thought that it was "dephlogisticated" atmospheric air. In November Lavoisier rediscovered it, but, he too, confused it with atmospheric air. In March 1775 Priestley specified that the new gas was different from atmospheric air, in that it was purer. Finally, in 1777 Lavoisier established the exact quantitative composition of atmospheric air.

Far away in the Northern mists, Scheele, the self-effacing Swede, had preceded both of them. He had made the discovery in 1771, but announced it only in 1777 in his *Treatise on Fire and Air*, without daring to claim his discovery for fear that he would be accused of plagiarism. Therefore, he remained outside the great debate of the new chemistry that was about to be born. This outstanding researcher nevertheless deserved to occupy his place as the discoverer of numerous bodies on which the rapid expansion of chemistry was based: chlorine, manganese, baryta, silicon fluoride, mineral acids (hydrofluoric, arsenic, molybdic, tungstic), organic acids (tartaric, mucic, lactic, uric, prussic, oxalic, citric, malic, gallic), and glycerol, murexide, aldehyde, casein.[49]

Lavoisier's original contribution was to understand that not only metals, but all combustible bodies, absorb uniquely the breathable portion of air while burning, and that the quantity of this air equals the weight gain of the calces or acids produced. "It is this point in Lavoisier's discovery that was specifically his: thus determined, it was suspected only in 1774, and clearly announced in 1775," Cuvier wrote.[50]

A long road remained to be traveled. Lavoisier still needed several years before completely freeing oxygen from the ambiguities and confusions surrounding it and before giving it its true personality, distinct from carbonic gas, nitrogen, atmospheric air, and phlogiston.

6

The Turgot Years

LOUIS XV LEFT HIS GRANDSON the difficult task of deciding who would replace the Abbé Terray as Controller-General of Finance, thereby upsetting all the plans elaborated by the General Farm. In order to replenish the treasury and stimulate the whole economy of the nation, it was crucial to form a new government as soon as possible. This government would implement a vast program of administrative and fiscal reforms directed toward liberalizing the economy. Aware that he was too young to reign, Louis XVI chose as his mentor Jean Frédéric Phélypeaux, comte de Maurepas, a clever and opportunistic politician who was seventy-four years old. It happened that Madame de Maurepas was a friend of the Abbé de Véri, a great admirer of Turgot. Both the abbé and the duchesse de La Rouchefoucauld d'Enville urged that Turgot be named Controller General. But the king hesitated because the candidate, close to the Encyclopedists, did not go to Mass. To which Maurepas replied, "Do you think, Sire, that the Abbé Terray goes to Mass every day!"

In the end, on July 14, 1774, Turgot was appointed to the Ministry of the Navy. Condorcet was among the first to rejoice: "Nothing better could happen for France and human reason. Never before has a monarchical advisor combined to such a degree virtue, courage, impartiality, dedication to public welfare, wisdom and the zeal to spread it."[1]

On the following August 24, after having "passed the test," Turgot was moved up to Finance and suggested to the king his famous motto: "No bankruptcy, no tax increase, no borrowing." Turgot addressed himself to improving agricultural production and reducing the expenditures of the Court, to attacking abuses, cutting back on privileges, freeing commerce and industry from stifling regulations and monopolies, and to modernizing the administration.

As Controller General, his power was considerable. He was responsible for budgetary and fiscal questions, public credit, and the financial and administrative oversight of various groups. He also controlled trade and manufacturing and public works and buildings. He dismissed Terray's collaborators and replaced them by his Physiocrat friends, Pierre Samuel Dupont, Condorcet, the Abbé Morellet, and Jean de Vaines, his former colleague, administrator of State property in Limoges.[2]

In his eyes, the most urgent matter was to restore the freedom of the grain trade, which his predecessor had abolished:

The freer, livelier, and broader trade is, the more promptly, efficiently, and abundantly people are supplied, and the more uniform the prices, because they are much closer to the average and habitual price on which salaries are necessarily based. The efforts of the government to supply grain cannot be as successful. Its attention, divided among too many objectives, cannot be as active as that of merchants, concerned with their trade alone. The government learns only in retrospect, and hence knows less precisely both needs and resources. Its agents, having no interest in the economy, buy at higher prices, transport at greater cost, and store with fewer precautions.[3]

This liberal profession of faith announced a series of reforms of the various farms, those financial companies to which royal power had delegated administrative jobs. Several of them had become quite inefficient and costly, and their poor functioning posed serious problems.

Turgot began by modifying the Rousselle, the company dealing with mortgages, public record taxes, and taxes on the sales of buildings, and then created a new company for state-owned properties. He ceased giving leases for mail and stagecoach services and created a company of royal Messageries. The carriages, less expensive, safer, and faster, were christened *Turgotines*. Two others reforms, that of the General Farm and the replacement of the Gunpowder Farm by a State controlled company, directly concerned Lavoisier.

The Reform of the General Farm

In September 1774 Turgot had asked the General Farm for a report on its organization, income, and operating costs. The Farmers General were to sign a new lease for the usual duration of six years, and time was running out. Lavoisier, whose talents as a writer and accountant were well known at the General Farm, received the task of preparing a very complete account.[4]

The annual income of the General Farm, for the previous leases, had been on average about 175 million livres ($7 billion): 55 for the *gabelles* or salt tax, 19 for customs duties, 40 for taxes on alcohol and products entering Paris, 35 for tobacco, 23 for State properties, and 3 for products coming from America (primarily tobacco from Virginia). The income expected for each year of the next lease would reach 200 million livres ($8 billion) and the expenses about 47 million livres; thus the king would receive only 152 million. But he was forced to accept this deduction of 25 percent; to free himself of it, he would have to reimburse the sixty Farmers General for their invested capital of 93.6 million livres ($3.75 billion). "And how could he have raised that sum, when by exhausting every means of borrowing, he barely managed to cover the deficit of everyday operation of the kingdom?"[5] If the lease was in deficit or made no profit, the Farmers General turned to the king, who decided what indemnity they would be paid.[6]

The conditions for the new lease, Lavoisier pointed out, were less advantageous for the Farmers General than they seemed.[7] The annual remuneration for each of them was fixed at 161,800 livres ($6.5 million), a sum that corresponded to a fixed salary of 24,000 livres ($900,000), office expenses of 4,200 livres ($168,000), and an interest of 133,600 livres ($5.3 million) on the invested capital of 1,560,000 livres ($62 million).

After the deduction of a 10 percent provision for depreciation, there remained 145,620 livres ($5.8 million), from which 93,600 livres ($3.7 million) for interest on loans and notary fees had to be subtracted. "Thus, insisted Lavoisier, "there remained for each Farmer General only 52,000 livres per year [$2.1 million]. One will no doubt agree that what the Farmer General has left to support his household and bring up his family will provide only very modest resources for economizing and investing with the end of seeking far from certain profit as a means of providing for his children's future."[8]

With Lavoisier, the lawyer's talent prevailed over the calculator's rigor. Terray had estimated the annual income of a Farmer General to be 100,000 livres ($4 million). Nicolas François Mollien, who spent six years at the Farm from 1776 to 1782, gave a much higher figure:

For each of the sixty Farmers General, the profits were to be more than 200,000 livres (over $8 million) for each of the six years. In addition, they realized a $5\frac{2}{3}$ percent interest on their capital outlay, which amounted to 1,560,000 francs for each Farmer General. Thus, for each year of the 1774 lease, a Farmer General received a dividend of almost 300,000 francs [$12 million] which meant that he was realizing 20 percent per year on his capital outlay.[9]

Mollien calculated that the sixty Farmers General thus withdrew 18 million livres ($720 million) for their personal remuneration, without counting the salaries and operating costs of their assistants. It is true that they also had to face heavy expenses: a collective gift of 300,000 livres had to be made to the Controller General when the new lease was signed; and there were the annual charity donation of 18,000 livres ($720,000), the bribe of 150,000 livres

($6 million) paid by each member at his nomination, and finally the croupes and pensions.[10]

The croupes were shares in the company given by the king to persons outside the administration of the Farm. Without participating in any work, they received a portion of the profits. The sums given them represented 1,250,000 livres ($50 million).

The pensions, totaling 400,000 livres ($16 million) were attributed by the king to members of his entourage: the Dauphin and his sisters and aunts received an eighth of the sum; the duc de Bourgogne's nurse was paid 10,000 livres; Madame du Barry's doctor received 10,000 livres, the Abbé Voisenon 3,000, and a certain opera singer 2,000, and so forth.[11]

Finally, the Farmers had to give Christmas gifts and bonuses to the intendants, ministers, and court dignitaries. Until 1774 the names of the beneficiaries remained a secret, but when the lease was to be renewed, Terray sent a confidential circular letter to the Farmers General asking them to draw up a list. When an administrative assistant leaked this list to the newspapers, Jean Baptiste Coquereau reports that "an immense uproar was created in Parisian circles. Indiscriminately mixed together, the recipients—from the monarch to the lowliest of his subjects, all sheltered from the tax collectors—were dividing up the spoils of France."[12]

In his report, Lavoisier did not envisage reducing the share of the Farmers General to the benefit of the Royal Treasury. However, he suggested that one could economize on operating costs: 400,000 livres on the salt tax, 100,000 on tobacco and at least 300,000 on the offices of the Farm. Moreover, the elimination of privileges in certain provinces and a uniform collection throughout the kingdom would reduce expenses by more than 4 million livres ($160 million).

Dreading Turgot's reforms, the Farmers General had rushed to sign with Terray the lease being negotiated in 1774, and Turgot had to be satisfied with only partial changes. He did manage to get Terray to return the bribe of 300,000 livres that he had pocketed after the signing of the lease, and gave the money to hospitals. Louis XVI refused to do away with the croupes and pensions, but promised that in the future he would no longer grant "its particular favors to persons outside the General Farm."[13]

Turgot next took on the *gabelles*, the taxes on salt. "It has been shown that they cost the Nation at least 80 million livres, for the 50 million or so they bring to the King; and furthermore, that they are exceedingly harmful to agriculture, trade, human liberty, fertility of earth, and maintenance of livestock."[14]

He wanted to abolish this unpopular and uneconomical tax and replace it by another more modern one that would save the nation 30 million livres, but time was lacking and most Farmers General, frightened by his real or supposed plans, were hostile to him. Certain ones, however, did him justice: "Among them must be mentioned MM. de Verdun, Augeard, and de Lavoisier."[15]

On the other hand, the places at the General Farm were henceforth to be reserved for experienced men: "The sons of Farmers General will be called to occupy their fathers' places only after they have reached at least the age of twenty-five and after they have been tested in different jobs in which they have proven their capacity."[16]

The fears of the Farmers General in 1774 were completely unjustified. Thanks to Turgot's liberal measures, trade and consumption grew and so did the profits of the General Farm. Dupont saw this as proof of the advantages of liberalism. But he added: "It is true that several good wine harvests contributed to this extraordinary profit."[17]

Lavoisier's influence at the General Farm was constantly growing. He took an active part in its administration and attended the daily working meetings of the Committees responsible for taxes collected on salt, tobacco, alcoholic drinks, playing cards, oils, soap, and goods entering Paris. At the same time, he was in charge of the saltworks in Franche-Comté, Lorraine, and Trois-Evêchés, the management of aides, and the accounting and personnel of the General Farm. He controlled the salaries of 30,000 employees, and verified the data provided to him by the administration. During his numerous travels in the provinces, he also gathered data on the economic and social life in France which would later be invaluable for his economic and financial studies.

The one reform Turgot did not succeed in realizing was that of the gauging of vessels. This process concerned the calculation of the contents of wine casks at tollgates. This failure implicated Lavoisier and the General Farm. Of all the duties collected by the Farm at the entries into Paris, those affecting wine and alcohol were the most unpopular. Tax-evaders would stop at nothing to avoid payment. Louis Sébastien Mercier described in his *Tableau de Paris* a world of fake wet nurses with alcohol-filled tin breasts, supposed sufferers from gout dragging cylindrical legs, and smugglers using hollowed tree trunks and stones to transport their wares. He also told about the discovery of two hundred feet of tin pipe passing under the tollgate to end up in an innkeeper's casks.

Even honest citizens complained of the way these duties were calculated. Since the end of the seventeenth century, the employees of the Farm had determined the contents of casks by using a graduated ruler called a *velte*. Introduced into the cask obliquely, it measured the distance from the stopper to the bottom and gave the capacity of the cask in setiers and pints. But these estimations were often greater than the actual content and hence the duties imposed were excessive. The Farm, which was the beneficiary of this method, did not want to change it and accused the City gaugers of doing their work badly. In 1772 it had managed to have them replaced by its own employees, whom it considered more reliable, but who escaped all outside control.

Alerted to the problem, Turgot created on December 22, 1775 a "Royal Commission of Gauging" whose task was to define a rigorous method of measurement. Dez, a mathematics professor at the Ecole Militaire, developed a theory based on complicated mathematical calculations; its complexity precisely suited the General Farm because it ensured its monopoly on control of the city tollgates.[18] But the employees objected to the inconvenience of the system. Dez forthwith invented thirteen others.[19] Finally, Dez's original method and gauge were adopted and made obligatory. Condorcet who was constantly and outspokenly denouncing the schemes of the General Farm, complained to Turgot:

My colleague Lavoisier has conducted himself in this affair as eminently suited to be the Abbé Terray's nephew and M. de La Paulze's son-in-law. He began by wanting to use his *petite géometrie* against the plan itself. Happily, M. de Laplace had already approved the memoir and M. Lavoisier did not dare risk an academic quarrel with him. [. . .] Finally, to save time, M. Lavoisier wants the city of Paris to be consulted. Instead of using what he knows about these matters to make his colleagues more reasonable, he is only trying to furnish them with arguments. Farewell. I have spoken too much about this matter, but all these chiselers put me in such bad humor and my only remedy is to confide in the one person who can repair the damage done, unless it is absolutely irreparable.[20]

Condorcet accused Lavoisier of concealing more than fifty petitions from wine merchants who claimed to be victims of the gaugers and he suggested creating a corps of inspectors responsible for overseeing the assistants of the Farm and submitting contentious cases to the superintendent of the police. But Turgot had many more important reforms to undertake.

The Gunpowder and Saltpeter Administration

In collaboration with Lavoisier, Turgot had already undertaken the reform of the Gunpowder Farm, a private company supplying gunpowder to the Nation. The situation required emergency measures. It was said that the disastrous defeat of France in the Seven Years' War had been due to the lack of gunpowder.

The Gunpowder Farm was, like the General Farm, a private company of financiers who signed a six-year lease with the king in exchange for the exclusive right to manufacture and sell gunpowder and its principal ingredient, saltpeter. It had no organic link with the General Farm, but Lavoisier, responsible for the salt tax, was on the lookout for fraud regarding salt, one of the byproducts of the manufacture of saltpeter that the workers sometimes sold on the unofficial market. This was the point of departure for the reform he proposed to Turgot. He saw in it an opportunity to satisfy both his personal ambitions and the general interest.

Under the current lease, the Gunpowder Farm was obligated to furnish the royal arsenals with one million pounds of gunpowder per year at a price of 6 sous per pound; since one livre equaled 20 sous, the farm had a total market of 300,000 livres ($12 million). The actual cost of the gunpowder being 12 sous per pound, the theoretical value of the supply was 600,000 livres ($24 million) and the king thought that he was saving money. But he was deluding himself because he had to pay the saltpeter manufacturers a supplement of 60,000 livres ($2.4 million) each year. In wartime, he gave them subsidies that could reach the same amount. In addition, he gave the Gunpowder Farm an annual insurance of 27,000 livres covering risk of fire and explosions.

For an invested capital of 4 million livres the profits of the Gunpowder Farm were considerable: "It began by dividing 15 percent of this capital among its members every year. Then at the end of its lease, it divided up a mass of profits that had several times risen to 15 percent more annually. And it found that everything was going very well indeed."[21] The lease "filled its shareholders' coffers with gold, but failed to fill the King's arsenals with gunpowder."[22] The Farm even made an extra profit by selling gunpowder to the public at 29 sous per pound, but the King himself earned nothing from it.

Finally, "for more than sixty years, not a sou has entered the Royal Treasury from the production of the Gunpowder Farm. On the contrary, the Treasury has annually disbursed a great deal of money to pay for gunpowder and the charges remaining on the King's account on that part of public state income."[23]

No clause in the lease obliged the Farm to ensure the defense of the kingdom. If, at the end of the year, the royal orders did not attain the million pounds foreseen by the contract, the king lost the balance. And if he needed more than a million pounds, he was forced to seek it elsewhere. "The result of this clause was that in wartime the defense of the Nation was not ensured, because it often used up to three and four million pounds of gunpowder."[24]

The gunpowder was composed of three ingredients according to the old rule of the "six, ace, ace": 75 percent saltpeter, 12.5 percent charcoal, and 12.5 percent sulfur. What France lacked most was saltpeter, or *nitre* (potassium nitrate), efflorescences which develop on demolition sites and damp old walls. Its production was the highest in Europe: it had gone as high as 1,600,000 pounds per year. But the nation needed double that amount.[25] The twenty Parisian saltpeter manufacturers and the eight hundred or so in the rest of France were far from guaranteeing a sufficient production.

Furthermore, the Gunpowder Farmers preferred to import a cheaper saltpeter from India. "The domestic yield was neglected. The Farmers purchased abroad and left the kingdom without product, and the citizen without work, so as to enrich our neighbors while impoverishing France."[26]

At the end of the Seven Years' War, the route to India was closed to French vessels. The loss of the Indian colonies, the main source of saltpeter, made matters worse. Hence once again saltpeter was sought in demolition rubble, cellars, storerooms, attics, stables, and cowsheds. In accordance with the right of the State to search for saltpeter, it was even legal for the saltpeter men to go into private houses and collect saltpeter from walls. They profited from this law to obtain cheap room and board and firewood, and to drink the peasants' wine. "Their work, even when they had collected only 800 tons of saltpeter, cost the provinces at least 600,000 livres ($24 million) per year, not counting what people gave them to avoid having their property searched. The result was that individuals paid quite considerable sums to these workers without the State acquiring the saltpeter it needed."[27]

The saltpeter men collected earth and rubble that they crushed into powder with heavy blocks. This powder was then leached in barrels filled with water. Potash or wood ash was added to obtain a raw saltpeter. Next this mixture was cooked in large copper cauldrons. After evaporation, there remained yellowish crystals of saltpeter and salt. This saltpeter from the first cooking was sold to the Gunpowder Farm, which had the monopoly on the refining and the two recrystallizations necessary for obtaining the final white powder. As for the salt, it had to be turned over to the General Farm, which held the monopoly on it.

But the saltpeter men cheated on the amounts produced and sold part of it on the unofficial market. For that reason, the General Farm had a right to inspect salt production at the Gunpowder Farm. When making his inspections, Lavoisier discovered the mediocrity and archaic character of the organization producing saltpeter and gunpowder. In his opinion, a State controlled company operating on a profit-sharing basis would provide excellent administrators for moderate salaries since they would be at the same time stockholders.

The lease still had four and a half years to go, but Turgot decided to rescind it and turn over to Lavoisier, d'Ormesson, and Dupont the responsibility for creating a less biassed and more controllable body, a Gunpowder and Saltpeter Administration. "As long as France was subjected to arbitrary power," Lavoisier would explain in 1792, "the ministers and courtiers viewed financial affairs simply as means of enriching their participants and protegés. Thus all capital was placed in companies or farms. The entrepreneurs were most often only figureheads for the most powerful persons, and this kind of corruption extended all the way up to the ministers' offices, to the administrators themselves."[28]

Turgot was less rigorous in 1775. On March 30 he named four commissioners. Three of them came from the old Gunpowder Farm: Louis Claude Marthe Barbault de Glatigny, Jean Baptiste Paul Antoine Clouet, and Jean Pierre Le Faucheux. The fourth was "M. de Lavoisier, as well known for his chemical expertise, essential for this kind of administration, as for the energy, ability and honesty that he brings to that part of the management of various farms for which he is responsible as Farmer General."[29]This excellent calculator had no doubt also noted that the return on the capital invested in the Gunpowder Farm was still higher than the substantial 20 percent of the General Farm.

As a first step, the former owners had to be reimbursed. Turgot decided that the commissioners would pay them four million livres ($160 million) after four years. In the meantime, they would earn an interest of 11 percent on this sum. But even so, the arrangement did not prevent them from protesting loudly that nothing was sacred any more and that their property was being undermined.

Responsible for the production, control, and refining of saltpeter and the manufacture of gunpowder, the commissioners received a fixed salary of 2,400 livres ($96,000) per year and a bonus on sales: 1 sou for every pound of gunpowder sold beyond 800 million, 2 sous after sales of 900 million, and 6 deniers for each pound of saltpeter. In the end the annual remuneration rose to 16,000 livres ($640,000).

If Lavoisier had a clear view of the profits, he was perfectly aware too of the geopolitical dimension of the task:

A State such as France, vast and surrounded by neighbors jealous of its strength, rivals for its trade, and ever ready to upset its prosperity and peace, is forced by its very situation and scattered possessions to concern itself with everything that happens in Europe, America and Asia. Regardless of what is happening there, it must be able to obtain within its own borders all the saltpeter and gunpowder necessary for arming its fleets, supplying its armies, defending its borders, and storing and protecting its harvests; and also for stimulating its manufacturing activity, the exploitation of its mines, its public works and trade.[30]

Owing to the danger involved in the manufacture of gunpowder, no factory existed in Paris. The closest one was in Essonne, 33 kilometers from Paris, where, on the banks of the Seine, small isolated mills produced powder. In each one, a hydraulic wheel turned two shafts equipped with twelve cams that alternately lifted the same number of pestles. These pestles, arranged in two rows, pounded the contents of the mortars, made from hollowing out wooden blocks, at a rate of fifty-four times per minute. Each mortar contained twenty pounds of saltpeter, charcoal, and sulfur, to which a little water had been added. The crushed powder was transferred to other mortars at regular intervals. Otherwise, the impact of the pestles caused the powder to settle and heat up. This indispensable operation was repeated seven or eight times. At the end of the pounding, which lasted twenty-one hours, the mixture was removed from the mortars and left to dry for several days. Then it went to the "granary" where it was sifted onto an animal skin pierced with numerous holes. The gunpowder was then dried a second time and resifted before being put in bags of one hundred to two hundred pounds that were stored in enclosed barrels.

Everything would have been simple if the saltpeter supply had been adequate. This was far from the case. Both quantity and quality left much to be desired. At every delivery, disputes arose over whether the saltpeter had come from the first cooking, because there was no reliable method for determining its purity. Du Pont commented later:

The art of the saltpeter manufacturer, perfected in Sweden, Prussia, and India, was at its most rudimentary stages in France. We only knew about demolishing and leaching old buildings and we were unaware that artificial sources of nitrate could be constructed. Nitrate works could have collected the immense quantity of this substance which, dissolved in the air or ready to be formed by its means, asks only to settle on a soil prepared to attract and receive it.[31]

At Lavoisier's request, Turgot asked the Academy to create a prize of 4,000 livres ($160,000) to study means of increasing the production of saltpeter and eliminating the search in private houses.[32] Five judges, Lavoisier, Macquer, Sage, Cadet, and Mathieu Tillet, were appointed. They would have the use of a laboratory that was sufficiently large for verifying the results announced by the competitors. The fact that Lavoisier was a member of both the Gunpowder and Saltpeter Administration and the prize committee made certain Academicians hesitate: would there not be a conflict of interest? Lavoisier replied that the production of gunpowder and saltpeter was no longer a private undertaking, but the responsibility of a State-owned company; hence its officials could have only the interest of the State at heart. The Academy accepted the argument and, given the urgency, proceeded with unusual speed. Turgot's order left Versailles on August 17, 1775. The program for awarding the prize was ready on September 2.

In the meantime, Lavoisier took a certain number of practical steps. He forbade saltpeter men to enter cellars, wine storerooms, and private quarters of residences. Henceforth the search was to be limited to stables, sheepfolds, dovecotes, empty barns, and other farmyard sites surrounding houses. He encouraged the collection and crushing of demolition rubble and recommended using mills turned by horses. But the saltpeter men, hostile to any progress threatening their employment, refused to use them. They continued to crush the rubble with their own force.[33]

At the Gunpowder Administration, Lavoisier created a training program for the workers, including courses in chemistry and mathematics and lectures on the composition of saltpeter and gunpowder and the construction of mills and refineries. He reinforced controls of the leaching processes and the quality of the wood ash, refusing that used by washerwomen because a part of its potash had already been lost. He sent technicians to India to study the reasons for the abundance of saltpeter in that country and published a book containing all the information that had appeared on the subject. He built new factories, refineries, and warehouses. France would soon have seventeen gunpowder factories and thirteen saltpeter refineries.

The Arsenal Residence

In April 1776, a year after being appointed to the Gunpowder and Saltpeter Administration, Lavoisier moved into the Arsenal near the Bastille.[34] Gunpowder had not been manufactured there for a long time. The Grand Arsenal, surrounded by five courtyards, overlooked the Seine. It was inhabited by the marquis de Paulmy d'Argenson, a senior minister and the governor of the Arsenal, who had one of the finest libraries in Paris, with more than one hundred thousand volumes and ten thousand manuscripts.

The Petit Arsenal, surrounded by two courtyards, served as a gunpowder warehouse for the Bastille and communicated with it. It was there that Lavoisier had a private apartment, a large library, and an immense laboratory in the attic (Figure 3).. The adjoining sheds would soon harbor thousands of retorts, flasks, and other glass vessels; gradually, valuable measuring instruments—scales, gasometers, barometers, hydrometers, and calorimeters—would be added.

Figure 3. Lavoisier's laboratory. Musée des Arts et Métiers, Paris.

Lavoisier's schedule was very strict. He got up at five and did scientific work from six to nine in the morning. From then to seven in the evening, he went first to the General Farm, and then spent the afternoons at the Gunpowder Administration and the Academy of Science. After supper, he returned to his laboratory for three hours, from 7 to 10. Thus every day he spent six hours on scientific work. Saturdays were completely reserved for experiments to be done with his students. "For him," his wife would later write, "it was a blissful day. A few enlightened friends, a few young people, considering it an honor to be able to participate in his experiments, gathered in the laboratory in the morning. It was there that they ate lunch, discussed, and created the theory that immortalized its author. It was there that one had to see and hear that man whose mind was so sound, talent so pure and genius so lofty. It was from his conversation there that the nobility of his moral principles could be judged."[35]

Madame Lavoisier shared in his research. She had taken lessons in chemistry, first from her husband and then from Bucquet. She had learned English so as to be able to read and translate chemical works, and studied drawing with Jacques Louis David and Latin with a Monsieur Thiriot. In the laboratory she always sat at a small table placed somewhat to the side. While Lavoisier and his collaborators bustled about, she noted down the protocols of the experiments and the figures of the results they called out in loud voices. She copied into the laboratory registers the notes her husband had scribbled on the backs of letters, envelopes, or playing cards that an "in" book had recommended as saving space and time in filing. Not satisfied with making very precise drawings of complex groupings of retorts and measuring devices, she sketched the most spectacular scenes from life. The thirteen plates she drew and engraved for the *Traité élémentaire de chimie* reveal, however, more application than genius.

To tell the truth, it there had been only chemistry and laboratory work, she would have become a bit bored. Such activity was quite austere for a young woman of twenty who enjoyed social life. Happily, her role was not limited to that of an assistant secretary. Since her adolescence, she had known how to entertain and be a good hostess. She was her husband's best public relations agent and everyone who met her praised her vivacity, her talents as a conversationalist, and her intelligence. Like Lavoisier, she was interested in everything, not only in the sciences, but in the arts. They often went to the Opera and never missed a painting exhibition. But she was also interested in political life and held progressive ideas. She wanted to see France, like England, endowed with a constitutional monarchy, which would give more power and freedom to the enlightened bourgeoisie.

The Lavoisier laboratory and salon at the Arsenal quickly became the setting for much frequented social occasions, mixing mathematicians, chemists, astronomers, philosophers, economists, Farmers General, and aristocrats. The couple entertained at dinner every Monday. Friends could simply show up without letting her know. They were also hosts to numerous foreign scientists. Some of them were English, such as Blagden, Watt, Priestley, Arthur Young, and Sir James Hall. Others were Americans, such as Benjamin Franklin and Gouverneur Morris, Dutchmen like Martinus Van Marum, Swiss like Horace Benedict de Saussure. Italian scientists too, such as Giuseppe Angelo de Saluces and Marsilio Landriani and still many more, could be seen there. The Swedish astronomer Anders-Johan Lexell visited the salon several times and commented: "M. Lavoisier is a pleasing looking young man, a very clever and painstaking chemist. He has a beautiful wife who is fond of literature and presides over the Academicians when they go to his house for a cup of tea after the Academy meetings."[36]

It was a very happy period. Under Turgot a freer, lighter atmosphere reigned in Paris. On October 1, 1775 Lavoisier commented:

We are no longer in those dark and ignorant times when the administration seemed to fear being enlightened about those things that it was most important for it to learn or go into more deeply. Today the minister is not afraid to ask publicly for the information he needs. He calls on scientists from all sides to aid the arts and, by associating in a way the literary body with the administration, he brings them closer to the true goal of their institution."[37]

Turgot's economic policy was beginning to bear fruit: the State budget had been stabilized, there were signs of growth in purchasing power and an increase in productivity. The creation of new financial resources was going to allow for the profound reform of institutions: the Caisse d'Escompte or Discount Bank, created in March 1776, should be bringing a credit of 10 million livres ($400 million) at 4 percent; the loan from Holland ought to produce 45 million livres ($1.8 billion) of ready cash. The financiers were showing interest in industry and beginning to hope that investing in it would be just as profitable as investing in agriculture. Numerous Academicians, following Lavoisier's example, simultaneously carried out scientific functions and industrial responsibilities, in particular in the chemical sector, which was the most active. The manufactures of Saint-Gobain glass and Sèvres porcelain offered the most attractive posts, but the textile, dyeing, paper, mining, and metallurgical industries were also developing rapidly, and all needed technical directors and scientific advisors.[38]

The theories of the modern Physiocrats encouraged the scientists to move in this new direction.

The Modern Physiocrats

Lavoisier had learned much from his contacts with Turgot and Dupont. The latter had led him to discover François Quesnay and his doctrine, founded on the natural order. Following Dupont, who had invented the term "physiocratie," or natural government, the doctrine could be summed up in one sentence: "Obtaining the greatest possible increase in enjoyment by the greatest possible decrease in expenditures is the perfection of economic conduct."[39]

Quesnay, a master surgeon by the age of twenty-four, had become a doctor of medicine in 1774 and had risen to the position of consulting physician to Madame de Pompadour and Louis XV. He was given lodgings in Versailles, where he held regular meetings with his disciples. Collectively known as Economists in their own time and later referred to as Physiocrats, they included the marquis de Mirabeau, Pierre Samuel Dupont de Nemours, the

Abbé Nicolas Baudeau, Paul Pierre Le Mercier de la Rivière, and Guillaume François Le Trosne. They discarded the mercantilist belief that wealth and its increase were due to trade. Wealth, they said, circulated on its own from one class of society to another, coming and going by always identical channels. This continuous circulation sustained the life of the social body, just as the circulation of blood sustained animal life. Since they thought that private interest always paralleled the common interest, then in a free regime, the world took care of itself. It simply had to be left alone.

Quesnay distinguished three social classes: (1) the productive class, composed exclusively of farmers, because the earth is the source of all goods and it alone generates a *produit net* (the surplus of wealth that is produced by agriculture and can be accumulated); (2) the propertied class and all those who exercise a form of sovereignty, sovereignty being linked to ownership; and, finally, (3) the sterile class, which creates no wealth and includes representatives of industry, commerce, and the liberal professions.

The natural order supposed the freedom of domestic as well as foreign trade and the freedom of labor. The State was to provide the guarantee for this natural order, but its interventions were to be limited to protecting property, spreading public instruction, and executing public works.

The views on taxes were an essential aspect of the doctrine. Quesnay had proposed a unique tax on property owners; its rate was to be fixed at one third of the net product. A national income of 2 billion livres ($80 billion) would bring the State 600 million livres ($24 billion); indirect taxes, taxes on consumption that were deemed unjust, would be abolished.

Lavoisier had gradually freed himself from the mercantilist yoke of an obsession with the balance of payments. He no longer believed that the accumulation of precious metals and prohibitive regulations were the secret of the strength of a nation. He had let himself be attracted by a liberal system that left a greater sphere of activity to individual initiative. But he did not feel entirely comfortable, because the doctrine of "laisser faire, laisser passer" had its detractors. Among these, were the Farmers General, who considered these ideas frankly subversive. Instead of free competition, they preferred a strong central power, with which it was easier to negotiate advantageous agreements.

The freedom of trade and the exportation of wheat were at the heart of the debate. Colbert had abolished it, Quesnay had re-established it in 1763, and then the Abbé Terray had abolished it anew. Turgot had restored it once again. The Abbé Galiani and Necker would use this as a weapon against him.

Lavoisier was curious to learn about these laws that the Physiocrats saw at the origin of economic phenomena, especially since Dupont was so categorical:

Until Quesnay economic science has been only a conjectural science in which one could reason at most only by induction; since the ingenious invention of the system of the *Tableau économique*, it has become an exact science, all of whose points can be subjected to demonstrations that are as rigorous and unquestionable as those of geometry and algebra.[40]

In 1775 Dupont tackled the political domain. The difficulties of France, he wrote in his *Mémoire sur les municipalités*, corrected by Turgot, stem from the fact that it has no Constitution. Dupont recommended the abolition of all orders and their replacement by a pyramid of elected assemblies. At the base would be the town councils, or village assemblies, elected by the inhabitants and responsible for apportioning taxes, maintaining roads, providing a police force, and aiding the poor. They would be followed by district and provincial councils and, at the summit, the highest council or the general assembly of the kingdom.

All indirect taxes and city tolls would be abolished and replaced by a direct tax paid by all landowners, regardless of class. Finally, to form minds to be virtuous, impartial, honorable, and zealous, a general plan for public education was foreseen. It was to be crowned by a Council of National Education.

Lavoisier would adopt many of these political ideas. He thought, like Turgot, that agriculture was not the only source of wealth, and that trade and industry should be encouraged. Trade should be unrestricted because, when it is completely and permanently free, wealth spreads, agriculture flourishes, the arts are cultivated, each citizen makes his living in a work he chooses, and everything is turned to good account. On the contrary, attacks on free trade have disastrous results: wars, tolls, customs duties, controls, exclusive privileges, indirect taxes, unstable currency, government borrowing, restrictions on the grain market, excessive luxury, speculation, private financial companies. All these factors lead to disorder and destitution.

Labor should be free and the abusive privileges of corporations opposed. Did the worker's salary not represent his share as co-owner in the creation of the product? Free competition should be practiced everywhere. Monetary loans and interest rates should also be free. Interest was as legitimate as charges on money exchange, because it represented transportation charges in time just as the exchange rate represented transportation charges in space.

The creation of the Discount Bank illustrated this idea. Jean-François Panchaud, a Genevan banker installed in Paris, Pierre Auguste Caron de Beaumarchais, the creator of Figaro, and Thomas Sutton, comte de Clonard, administrator of the East India Company, suggested to Turgot that they could help him with his policy of low interest rates. They proposed a bank that would discount bills of exchange at an interest rate never surpassing 4 percent per year, whereas the usual rate was 6 percent. Turgot attracted by the perspective of a deposit of guarantee of 10 million livres ($400 million) in the royal treasury, decided to "work toward this very favorable revolution," and authorized the creation of the Discount Bank. The former East India Company and the General Farm played a role in its founding and kept men from their ranks on its board of directors: Lavoisier was to become, twelve years later, on the eve of the French Revolution, president of this board. Regardless of the fact that he belonged to the General Farm, he was favorable to the ideas of the new economists and appreciated their political arithmetics. He was convinced that economics could become a true science if it was based on reason. The Abbé Condillac remarked: "This is a time when every good citizen should be seeking truth. That would suffice for finding it. One no longer needs courage to dare to tell the truth, and its discovery would not be lost under the present reign."[41] It was a prediction that turned out to be more than a little imprudent.

Turgot's Dismissal

In January 1776 Turgot presented the king with six new decrees, of liberal inspiration but which upset many interests and ways of doing things. He wanted to abolish the corvée (forced labor), corporations, and maitrises (guilds) throughout the kingdom. He also proposed eliminating the grain inspectors and government agencies at Paris quays, markets, and ports as well as the Caisse de Poissy, an organism for transactions between stockbreeders and butchers. Finally, he wanted to readjust taxes on tallows.

His hand being forced by Turgot, Louis XVI, the supposedly all-powerful king, had the edicts passed in bed of justice. But he was exasperated by these incessant reforms, applied so suddenly, and by the violent protests of "all the notables, the Parlements, the financiers, the women at the Court and the devout." It was just a bit too much. On May, 12, 1776 Turgot was dismissed by the king. He had been in charge of the ministry of Finance for 20 months.

The perspicacious Trudaine de Montigny had warned him: "Be careful that every counselor at the Parliament considers the edicts as the end of your ministry. Should that misfortune occur, I believe that the king's authority would be irretrievably lost."[42]

There was still another reason for Turgot's dismissal. Anxious to spare the finances of France, he had meddled in foreign affairs and was opposed to all aid to the American insurgents. His friend, Abbé Joseph Alphonse de Véri commented:

M. Turgot may not be as good at negotiation as other ministers, but he has a deeper commitment to the real interests of France than they have. An assured knowledge of what is good for the nation, coupled with a strong character, is the essential basis for political science. Today's Ministers, whose talents are very much inferior to M. Turgot's, consider themselves superior because of their experience in the political arena. They say that, totally wrapped up in his profound ideas for domestic perfection, he does not understand the foreign aspect; after all, a Controller General is expected principally to find money and do nothing more.[43]

Then who could fill this job of Controller General of Finance better than a banker? Jacques Necker's hour had come.

The New Chemistry

I N APRIL 1775 and again in April 1778, Lavoisier presented at the public sessions of the Academy of Science a memoir entitled "On the Nature
of the Principle That Unites with Metals During Combustion and Increases
Their Weight." On the two occasions the title was the same, but the theoretical content of the memoir had evolved a great deal. In that interval of
three years Lavoisier had succeeded in synthesizing his conceptions of the
true nature of oxygen and the various phenomena connected with it: oxidations and reductions, combustions, formation of acids, animal respiration,
and composition of atmospheric air. In his mind, the different subjects were
constantly mixed, associated, and combined. Each one was enriched by the
progress of the others and the whole formed the basis for the new chemistry
that was in gestation. F. L. Holmes comments:

It is not accidental that he presented his first theory of respiration in the same memoir in which he described the analysis and synthesis of atmosphere by the calcination
and reduction of mercury or that he included the next stage in the development of his
theory of respiration in his memoir on a general theory of combustion. Theses problems formed a network of investigations, not one of which can be fully understood
unless we follow them together.[1]

Animal Respiration

In August 1773, when, at Trudaine de Montigny's request, Lavoisier was trying to confirm whether the residual gas after calcination of metals would allow
animals to breathe, animals had served him only as laboratory reagents for
distinguishing two sorts of gases: those that sustain candle flames and animal
respiration and those that, like fixed air, extinguish candles and kill animals.
He was acting not as a physiologist, but as a chemist.

However, since Harvey had described the circulation of blood in 1628, scientists had understood that respiration was a vital function. In 1637 Descartes had asserted:

The true purpose of respiration is to carry enough fresh air to the lungs so that the blood, which comes to them from the right-hand concavity of the heart, where it has been rarefied and transformed into vapors, thickens and is reconverted into blood, before flowing back into the left-hand concavity, without which it would be unable to nourish the fire existing there.[2]

The Oxford chemists—Boyle, Hales, Mayow—had confirmed that air was indispensable for respiration and that it "changed black or venous blood into red or arterial blood."[3] But it was Boerhaave who had posed the fundamental question of the relationship between gaseous exchanges and energy production:

Who can say whether there exists in air a hidden virtue for sustaining the life that animals and vegetables derive from it, whether that virtue can be exhausted, and whether it is not due to this exhaustion that animals who no longer find it die? Several chemists have announced the existence of a vital element in the air, but they have not said either what it was or how it worked. Happy the man who will discover it.[4]

In 1757 Black had demonstrated that respiration transformed atmospheric air into fixed air, fatal for animals, and in 1774 Lavoisier summarized in the *Opuscules physiques et chymiques* what he had retained of the research made by his predecessor:

We know at least that this function is so essential to the existence of animals that they soon perish if their lungs are not inflated at almost every moment by the elastic fluid that makes up our atmosphere. But it is easy to see that the elastic fluid of the effervescences, or that of the metallic reductions, is not at all capable of filling this function of the animal system; that it, unlike the air we breathe, cannot inflate the lungs of animals.[5]

On March 26, 1775 Lavoisier announced at the Academy that he had identified the part of atmospheric air that was more specific to respiration: it was "a purer, more breathable air than atmospheric air."[6] He decided to call it "eminently breathable air." It was oxygen. By April 1776 he had understood that atmospheric air was a real compound body of which one-sixth was his eminently breathable air. It was this air then that was absorbed in calcination and the formation of acids. The remainder was a *mofette*, or a gas unfit for breathing and combustion (nitrogen).

On Sunday October 13 Trudaine de Montigny invited him to study at his laboratory at Montigny-Lencoup the effects on animals of different kinds of air. In four days, Lavoisier carried out sixteen experiments on the respiration of sparrows. Placed under a pneumatic trough, a sparrow seemed unaffected for a few seconds; it was only dozing slightly. But after a quarter of an hour it began to thrash about, its breathing became difficult and rapid, and convulsive movements appeared. It died in fifty-five minutes. The residual air under the bell jar was different from atmospheric air. It precipitated limewater, extinguished candles, and did not sustain the life of a second bird. It resembled the residual air remaining after the calcination of mercury. A closer examination, however, revealed two differences: "First, the decrease in volume had been much less in the latter case than in the former; second, the breathed air precipitated limewater, whereas the air from the calcination did not alter it."[7]

Lavoisier had differentiated fixed air from oxygen: during respiration, oxygen was progressively replaced by fixed air. He concluded: "It would appear that respiration absorbs atmospheric air and expels a contaminated part of it."[8] But he still had to distinguish the gas remaining under the bell jar after the calcination of mercury—nitrogen—from the one existing after the respiration of the bird, which contained fixed air as well. This was a question for a biologist.

Another question was left to him, whether the lung was the place where oxygen coming from atmospheric air was exchanged for fixed air resulting from internal combustions. He leaned toward this opinion and even applied the analogy between combustion and respiration to the change in the color of blood: in passing through the lungs to become arterial, the venous blood, like mercury, acquired a red color after contact with the oxygen of atmospheric air.

The Composition of Air

Lavoisier's memoir of April 1777, "Experiments on the Respiration of Animals, the Nature of Air and its Changes During Breathing," described the analysis and synthesis of atmospheric air.[9]

Obtaining the two components of atmospheric air was easy: eminently breathable air (oxygen) was discharged by the reduction of *mercurius calcinatus per se* by simple heating; the mofette was remaining after animal respiration (nitrogen) as long as the fixed air (CO_2) it contained had been removed by quick lime. And, finally, atmospheric air could be reconstituted by mixing eminently breathable air and mofette. Analysis and synthesis were associated and complementary; inflows equaled outflows. Lavoisier concluded with satisfaction: "Here is the most complete kind of proof that can be attained in chemistry, the decomposition of air followed by its recomposition."[10]

On May 10 Joseph II, Marie Antoinette's brother, attended the meeting at the Academy of Science. To interest the august visitor, Lavoisier repeated the series of experiments on gases that he had just performed. Fixed air, heavier than ordinary air, could be decanted from one receptacle to another; if it was poured into an open jar containing a bird, the animal reacted with convulsive movements and died in less than a minute. Atmospheric air, eminently breathable air, and mofette had different effects on the flame of a candle.

The presence of important people from the Court provided a good opportunity to explain the link between this new knowledge and hygiene in public places:

After men or animals have breathed for a long time in an enclosed space, the air, which originally contained only one kind of harmful elastic fluid, namely the mephitic, noxious part which makes up three-quarters of atmospheric air, then contains two, since fixed air has been formed. But what is very remarkable is that these different airs do not combine as long as they are not agitated. On the contrary, they are distributed in space according to their specific gravity.[11]

Lavoisier explained that the mofette (nitrogen), the lightest of the three, rises toward the ceiling; ordinary air occupies the middle level; and fixed air, the heaviest, occupies the lowest. Architects should take this into account when planning the construction and ventilation of theaters, prisons, and hospitals:

A very remarkable observation for which we are indebted to M. Duhamel, is that the Saint Louis Hospital, which was built in Paris more than two centuries ago, appears to have been constructed in large part on these principles, and almost all the precautions that I have just mentioned were taken when arranging its rooms.[12]

Lavoisier also took the occasion to express the displeasure of the Academicians at not having been consulted about the reconstruction of the Hôtel Dieu hospital that had been partially destroyed by fire:

It would no doubt be very humiliating for the nation if, after the theory on air based on exact and reliable experiments, one committed in the eighteenth century the construction errors that were foreseen and avoided in the sixteenth.[13]

The Formation of Acids

Lavoisier had already established in 1772 that, in burning, phosphorus was transformed into phosphoric acid. He had mentioned the fact in 1774, in the *Opuscules physiques et chymiques*. Returning to the subject in 1777, he showed that phosphorus, burned under a glass bell jar in the presence of air, produced two and a half times its weight in phosphoric acid. The weight gain corresponded exactly to the quantity of air absorbed, or one-fifth of the total air. The rest was mofette.

In the combustion of charcoal, eminently breathable air or vital air generated carbonic gas, which, with water vapor, produced carbonic acid: the weight of the gas formed was equal to that of the vital air added to that of the charcoal. It was also true in the combustion of sulfur: the combining of the substance with vital air produced vitriolic acid. Again, the weight of the acid formed was equal to the total weight of the elements entering the reaction.

From these observations Lavoisier derived a general law: all acids are formed from air "or from an elastic substance contained in air," and from an element particular to each acid, combined with caloric, or matter of fire.[14] Since vital air transforms everything it touches into acid, it seemed appropriate to name this element *principe oxygine* (from the Greek, "that which generates acids"). This principe oxygine, when combined with charcoal, generated chalky acid or fixed air; with sulfur, vitriolic acid; with nitrous air, nitric acid; with phosphorus, phosphoric acid. With metallic substances, it formed metallic calces.

The theory was also applicable to organic chemistry: when sugar was added, the principe oxygine formed oxalic acid, and Lavoisier was hoping to show soon "that by similar processes one can unite this same principle to animal horn, silk, animal lymph, wax, essential oils, pressed oil, manna, starch, arsenic, iron, and probably a great many other substances of the three kingdoms, and thus convert them into real acids."[15]

We now know that the theory of acidity was too rigid. It could not take into account hydrochloric acid, sulfurated hydrogen, and hydrocyanic acid. But the role of oxygen in the formation of the oxy-acids was nonetheless clearly shown. The comparison of the oxidation of metals and the formation of acids led to another consequence: carbon, sulfur, and phosphorus, until then considered as simple sources of phlogiston, became separate elements, capable of entering into the formation of compound bodies. Thus was instituted a new group of simple bodies, the ones that in a later period would be named metalloids.

Finally, the oxygen theory was not only a theory of combustion. As Maurice Crosland writes, it included a theory of acidity and a theory of composition:

Attention to the oxygen theory, whether of combustion, caloric, acidity or the more general concept of oxidation, has diverted attention from another equally important achievement of Lavoisier, that of reinterpreting chemical composition. [. . .] It was a necessary corollary of the oxygen theory that a calx formed in the calcination of a metal could no longer be considered a simple substance but a compound. Metals were now simple substances, as were sulfur, phosphorus and carbon. Lavoisier was later to make a list of these simple substances, or elements, and this list has been called "one of the milestones of modern chemistry."[16]

Combustion in General

Lavoisier's concept of combustion was not entirely clear. Combustion, he felt, was a combination between bodies that burn and air; the bodies found in air a caloric or matter of fire, "a very subtle, elastic fluid that surrounds the planet we inhabit, penetrates with more or less ease the bodies composing it and tends, when it is free, to reach an equilibrium in all of them."[17] This fluid was the dissolvant of a great number of bodies, and combined with them just as water does with salts or acids with metals. In gases the caloric dissolved the principle of each gas and transmitted its elasticity to it. During combustion the burning body took possession of the eminently breathable part of air, which increased its weight, and the caloric, which had no weight, was discharged. The flame, heat, and light were produced at this moment. The phenomenon was instantaneous in the combustion of sulfur, phosphorus or charcoal. It was slower in the calcination of metals.

Nevertheless Lavoisier's efforts to explain the different states of matter and the nature of gases by a single theory were not completely satisfactory, and he would have to spend a few more years on the subject. He continued to be bothered by the still unclear distinction between his conception of oxygen and that of Priestley. Priestley's dephlogisticated air was atmospheric air without phlogiston. Lavoisier's eminently breathable air was the principe oxygine combined with matter of fire. He was aware that his matter of fire was strangely comparable to phlogiston, and he wrote to Thomas Henry: "I shall be forced to disagree with M. Priestley from time to time, but I can be mistaken, and in spite of the pride natural to every individual, I confess that I often have more confidence in M. Priestley's ideas than in my own."[18]

Lavoisier's contemporaries argued that he was simply replacing the phlogiston by the caloric and transferring it from the combustible substance to the air. To them, his theory was just the inverse of Stahl's and they christened it the antiphlogistic theory. Henry Guerlac comments: "There is something to this view. Like phlogiston, the matter of fire was a weightless fluid (or at least too tenuous to be weighted); nevertheless, unlike phlogiston, which defied measurement, both the intensity (temperature) and the extensive measure of the fire (the heat produced in a given period of time), could be precisely measured."[19]

An initial rather prudent attack on phlogiston appeared on November 12, 1777 in Lavoisier's famous "Memoir on Combustion in General":

If one asks the partisans of Stahl's doctrine to prove the existence of matter of fire in combustible bodies, they necessarily fall into a vicious circle, and are obliged to answer that combustible bodies contain matter of fire because they burn, and that they burn because they contain matter of fire. But it is plain to see that in the final analysis, they are explaining combustion by combustion.

The existence of matter of fire, of phlogiston, in metals, in sulfur, and so forth, is really nothing but an hypothesis, a supposition, which, once granted, explains, I must admit, some of the phenomena of calcination and combustion; but, if I can establish that these same phenomena can be explained in a much more natural way by the opposite hypothesis, that is to say without supposing the existence of matter of fire or phlogiston in combustible bodies, then Stahl's system will be shaken to its foundations.[20]

As early as 1750, in St. Petersburg, the Russian scientist Michael Vassilievitch Lomonosov, a former student of Johann Friedrich Henckel, to whom Meissen china owed its reputation, had studied the nature of heat and the constitution of matter. He had noted the weight gain of metals changed into calces, and asserted that the heat was propagated as a result of the movement of molecules. Lavoisier had probably read Lomonosov's theories in the *Novi Commentarii Academiae Scientiarum Imperialis Petropolitanae*, published in 1750, and Russian biographers of Lavoisier criticize him for failing to acknowledge his source.[21] In fact, writes H. M. Leicester, "Lomonosov still considered air to be a purely physical medium which could not enter into chemical reactions. Therefore his suggestion was that the increase in weight could come from something flying around in the air, a view not very different from the idea of nitroaerial particles in the theories of Hooke, Mayow and others."[22] Finally nothing indicates that Lavoisier had profited from Lomonosov's theories.

The Arsenal School

In January 1777 Lavoisier began to work with Jean Baptiste Bucquet, a young professor of chemistry and natural history at the Medical School, who also gave private courses in his laboratory on the rue Jacob. The two men were the same age and had studied chemistry with the same professors, La Planche and Rouelle. They became interested in pneumatic chemistry at the same time and had a keen liking for each other. Among Lavoisier's thirteen laboratory notebooks, large in-folio registers bound in pale gold calfskin, volume V contains a part written by Bucquet. It is entitled *Année 1777. Produit du cours de M. Bucquet*. It was the chemistry course given at the Arsenal laboratory to Madame Lavoisier and a few other select students. In rendering this service to his overworked patron, Bucquet profited to repeat—in good conditions and with a critical eye—the classic experiments of mineral chemistry. The two scientists discussed the results "to clarify various points of theory and complete different sections of chemistry that still remained imperfect."[23]

One feature of this original form of scientific collaboration was to study the phenomena of asphyxia among various animal species. Bucquet contributed his broad knowledge of techniques for animal experimentation, and Lavoisier his new theories on the chemistry of gases. Their common efforts resulted in the simultaneous presentation of twenty-six chemical memoirs at the Academy in January 1778. Thanks to this imposing amount of work, Bucquet was elected as an assistant chemist on January 17, but he was soon afterward stricken with cancer. He had to give up his courses in 1779 and died at the beginning of 1780.

For some time one of his students, Antoine François de Fourcroy, had been coming to work at the Arsenal laboratory. Fourcroy, who had no financial means, had studied medicine under difficult conditions. He had been helped, however, by Félix Vicq d'Azyr, a brilliant professor of anatomy and a friend of his father's. In August 1778, Vicq d'Azyr became permanent secretary of the Société Royale de Médecine.

The hostility of the Faculty of Medicine toward its rival prevented Fourcroy from obtaining a grant, and he would have a very hard time getting his medical degree in 1780. A collection had to be taken up among his friends to enable him to pay for his diploma. But a diploma was not enough; to become a teacher he needed the title of "regent doctor," and the Faculty refused to award it to him. He lived by his wits, copying manuscripts and translating. He also gave lessons and came to assist Bucquet in Lavoisier's laboratory. When Bucquet could no longer teach his courses, Fourcroy replaced, then succeeded him, and enjoyed a great success. He bought from his widow Bucquet's laboratory on the rue Jacob—the one that had earlier belonged to Rouelle—and gave private lessons there.

At the Arsenal Lavoisier worked, surrounded by his students. An entire day of each week was devoted to experiments.

In the morning, several enlightened friends whose cooperation he had requested, would gather in his laboratory. He even accepted very young people whose shrewdness he had recognized and certain workers who were especially skillful in producing accurate instruments. He always announced his plans to the assistants with great clarity. Each one made suggestions about their execution; and everything that was considered plausible was soon put to the test.[24]

This is how the new chemical theory was gradually born.

Dr. Marat's Thesis

Constantly sought after by young talents avid for fame, Lavoisier also had sometimes to discourage excessive claims. Those made by one particularly ambitious person, Dr. Jean Paul Marat, who bombarded him with memoirs and cutting recriminations, made his life very difficult.

Born in the canton of Neuchâtel on May 24, 1743, to a Sardinian father and Swiss mother, Marat had left home when he was sixteen. After six years in France and eleven in England and Scotland, he had obtained a medical degree in Edinburgh. Marat had returned to Paris in 1777. Seeking to integrate himself into high society, the author of *Chains of Slavery* had successfully treated the Marquise de Laubespine for a lung infection, thanks to a medication, *eau factice anti-pulmonique*, he had created. Moving in with his patient, who lived at the corner of the rue de Bourgogne and the rue de Grenelle, in the heart of the aristocratic neighborhood, he had been appointed physician to the comte d'Artois's bodyguards and soon attracted a wealthy clientele, able to pay him the considerable fee of one louis per consultation.[25] In 1778 he initiated a series of experiments on fire, electricity, and light and began to lay siege to the Academy of Science, which alone could give him the official recognition he longed for.

Comte Yves Marie Desmarets de Maillebois, an honorary academician known for his kindness, had asked Trudaine de Montigny, Le Roy, and Sage to observe Marat's experiments. Benjamin Franklin had been in Paris since December 23, 1776 as the representative of the new United States government. Solicited by Marat on several occasions he had finally agreed to join the academicians and even to participate in an experiment. Franklin and the academicians took place in a darkened room traversed by a single ray of light focused on the optical lens of a microscope. The divergent ray that it produced was projected on a sheet of paper. By inserting the flame of a candle between the microscope and the paper, Marat obtained an enlarged image of the flame, surmounted by moving shadows created by the hot air. With an array of burning bodies or an incandescent cannonball, he produced other images of varying dimensions and intensity, depending on the temperature of the bodies. For him, these exhalations of heated bodies were made up of "igneous fluid."

Diverging from the official doctrine defined by Macquer in his *Dictionnaire de chymie*, he did not consider fire an element and explained: "The present theory concerning fire is like the one about colors before Newton; fire is considered a form of matter whereas it is only a modification of a particular fluid."[26] According to him, fire resulted from the activation of particles of the igneous fluid contained in the bodies, and his method made the phenomenon visible.

One of the academicians, Sage, has given a vivid account of the experiment: "M. Marat sets out to show us the igneous fluid in a tangible manner. He exposes to the solar microscope a metal ball that he then heats and around which one perceives an undulating sphere of vapors. M. Franklin, having exposed his bald head to the focus of the microscope, we see it surrounded by undulating vapors that all end in spiral. They look like those flames through which painters symbolize Genius."[27]

But the experts remained prudent and went no further than declaring on April 17, 1779 that the experiments had been carried out by an ingenious method that opened up to physicists a vast field of research on the emanations from heated bodies and the evaporation of fluids. They took no stand on the theoretical aspects of the debate.

On June 16 Marat had asked Maillebois to choose a new group of experts to assess his discoveries on light and his theory of colors. Le Roy and Cousin went to witness 202 experiments which, according to Marat, demonstrated three errors made by Newton: the refraction indexes in the seven colors of the prism were inexact; there were not seven basic colors, but only three—red, blue, and yellow; and they were a result not of refraction but of diffraction.

At that point, the Academy decided to send additional referees and designated Lavoisier. However, Marat declared that "he did not want Lavoisier to see his experiments."[28] He pointed out that they could be carried out only when the sun was shining. But the sky was covered and the sun never appeared. The visitors finally left. There was talk of setting another date, but the months passed. Marat, appalled that he had been forgotten, lost patience, and on April 27 1779 he asked Condorcet, Secretary of the Academy, to "be so kind as to let him know about the decision of the Academy concerning the report on his experiments."[29] Condorcet answered that the commissioners had promised the report for Saturday, but on Saturday nothing came. The date was postponed several times, but finally on May 10, the Academy expressed an opinion: the experiments did not prove what the author thought; they did not conform to the accepted optical laws. "It would be useless to go into details to make them known, since the commissioners do not regard them as being worthy of the approval or backing of the Academy."[30]

It would take much more to discourage Marat, who announced in the newspapers a series of public courses on the nature of fire. The beauty and novelty of the spectacle offered by his experiments, he declared, would alone suffice to stimulate curiosity, but they had, of course, a more important objective: that of broadening the knowledge of human mind. In his *Recherches physiques sur le feu* he presented picturesque theories. According to him, the flame of a candle confined to a limited space goes out because "the air, violently expanded by the flame and unable to escape, drastically compresses and smothers it."[31]

There was hardly anything in this to attract the specialist in combustion phenomena and the father of the principe oxygine. On June 10, 1780 Lavoisier called the attention of the Academy to an article in the *Journal de Paris* presenting "the observations by which M. Marat had made the element of fire visible as if they had been approved by the Academy. There is nothing of the sort in the report on his work. The Academy has asked M. Le Roy to reply to this assertion."[32]

Indeed, a brief, curt response appeared in the press, triggering a polemic between the Abbé Joseph Jacques Fillassier, spokesman for Marat, and Le Roy. Lavoisier paid little attention to it. Moreover, Marat's course was unsuccessful. But Marat knew who had denounced him. Lavoisier had just made a permanent enemy. He was indifferent to the opinion of those whom he did not recognize as peers. Besides, his own theories were far from being unanimously accepted, and he preferred to do battle on that terrain.

Threats to Phlogiston

Macquer, author of the famous *Dictionnaire de chymie*, had reached the summit of his career and did not like to question well-established ideas. He found Lavoisier's challenge to phlogiston hard to accept and wrote to Guyton de Morveau on January 4, 1778:

> For some time now, M. Lavoisier has been frightening me by a great discovery that he was reserving in petto and which was quite simply going to destroy completely the theory of phlogiston or compound fire. His confident air was making me deathly afraid. What would have happened to our old chemistry if an entirely different structure had had to be built? As for myself, I confess, I would have given up the fight. M. Lavoisier has just described his discovery; I confess that I now feel much less weight on my stomach.[33]

Nevertheless, Lavoiser was a man to be treated with tact. The same year, in the 1778 edition of his *Dictionnaire de chymie*, Macquer wrote prudently:

M. Lavoisier, in publishing his excellent experiments to which we have just referred, seems to have had a rather strong temptation to conclude that they proved that metals take on the form of calx only to the extent that they are combined with a considerable quantity of gaseous matter, and that, once deprived of this matter, they regain all their metallic properties. If this were proven, it would destroy the entire phlogiston doctrine, that is the theory of fire. However, this good physicist has resisted the temptation, at least until now, and has refrained from making a clear-cut decision on this delicate point. His prudence is all the more commendable because it is the distinctive characteristic of all those who truly possess the spirit of chemistry.[34]

Lavoisier was thus publicly absolved from the major sin "of imagining that one can lead chemistry along at such a rapid pace, and [. . .] thus overturn in an instant the beautiful unity of one of the greatest theories to which the genius of chemistry has risen."[35] Ironically, it was Bayen who received Macquer's reprimand. He did not belong to the Academy, and yet he had had the audacity to consider Lavoisier's conjectures as demonstrated truths: "In spite of the very sincere esteem I have for M. Bayen's talents and his fine experiments, I am bound to say that for a subject of such importance, I believe his decision to have been rash."[36]

Macquer had misjudged the importance of the new theories, but on one point he was unmistaken: the resistance of some, the force of habit of others, were going to slow down the progress of the new chemistry. Certain chemists—Antoine Grimoald Monnet, Balthazar Georges Sage, Antoine Baumé, Jean d'Arcet, George Green, Richard Kirwan, Jean Sénebier, Marsilio Landriani, Jean Claude de Lamétherie, and Joseph Priestley—attacked them openly. Jean Raymond, who would be Fourcroy's demonstrator at the future Ecole Polytechnique, painted a heroic tableau of the battle:

A renowned chemist, M. Baumé, joined forces with M. Sage and the good hearted M. d'Arcet, who had been struggling alone, to stop the wheels of the triumphal chariot of the new doctrine. These three chemists composed the triumvirate of Stahl's school. Fourcroy represented Lavoisier's. He was then the only athlete to defend and propagate the principles of the new chemistry. But this formidable champion, shielded by Lavoisier's experiments and armed with his eloquence as an orator and his sometimes cutting sarcasms, fought valiantly without stopping, demolishing his adversaries and rallying all the scholars under the banner of pneumatic chemistry of which he was the most zealous and persuasive advocate.[37]

At this point in his career, Lavoisier had made the major discoveries of the chemical revolution: he had defined oxygen as an element and combustion and calcination as chemical reactions. Unquestionably, he had borrowed experimental facts in particular from Hooke, Mayow, and Priestley but he was the author of the system he was proposing, which stated that there existed in atmospheric air a particular gas endowed with previously unknown properties. This gas—eminently breathable air or vital air—fixed itself to metals during their calcination and the result was the formation of oxides. It also fixed itself in the same way to another class of elements not yet identified, that of metalloids, to form acids. This gas was one of the constituent elements of atmospheric air. Its presence was indispensable to all combustion. Exploring the unknown domain of physiology, Lavoisier had even formulated new ideas: animal respiration was comparable to a combustion and this combustion was responsible for animal heat.

Of course the concepts of pneumatic chemistry that he had introduced in France came from England. But, much better than the English, he had known how to sketch out a global theory. Lavoisier, it is true, had a tendency to present his findings as discoveries and leave some doubt as to their exact nature. Was it the experimental fact that was new, or the interpretation he gave to it? The latter often prevailed. But was this any less to his credit? It has often been said that a collection of experimental facts, unconnected and uninterpreted as a whole, no more makes up a scientific theory than a pile of bricks makes a house. As Charles C. Gillispie humorously puts it:

The French, it often seems, formulate things and the English do them. In the chemical revolution, at any rate, pneumatic chemistry was the achievement of the English experimental school, while theoretical chemistry expressed the French instinct for formal elegance.[38]

8

The First Necker Ministry

THE MODERATE, TOLERANT MAN with an unruffled and flexible mind who would replace Turgot as Controller General of Finance was none other than Jacques Necker. Lavoisier, as a good servant of the State, adapted to the change. On August 30 he wrote to his father-in-law in his typical low-keyed style: "All our ministers are holding up well and M. Necker is gaining supporters."[1]

The magician of credit immediately launched his important borrowing policy—soon to reach 530 million livres—to finance the current expenses and the American Revolution. But to economize he did away with the posts of six intendants from Finance and four from Commerce and dismissed 36 of the 48 Receivers General of Finance responsible for collecting direct taxes—the *taille, capitation*, and *vingtième*—and 19 Treasurers of the Royal household.

Necker also intended to reform the General Farm, but would have to wait until the Laurent David lease was up in October 1780. For the time being, he had to be content with changing some details in the Royal lottery and the Mail and Stagecoach companies.

Pro-Graters Versus Anti-Graters

In the Tobacco Committee of the General Farm, the quarrel between the pro-graters and anti-graters had become more heated. Should the Farm grate the tobacco itself or leave it to the retailers? Delahante, president of the Committee, was in favor of having the Farm control the grating. This arrangement would bring numerous advantages for both the State and the public, who would be ensured of better tobacco. But the plan was opposed by the retailers and gave the provincial parliaments another reason to defy the government.

At the end of 1777 Necker felt that he had to intervene and asked the advice of the General Farm about which handling was preferable.[2] A plenary meeting brought together thirty-three Farmers General on April 2, 1778.

Nineteen memoirs were presented: fourteen advocated grating by the Farm; four opposed it; the last one, read by M. de Varanchan, belonged "to the eternal school of the goat and the cabbage; after having related all the advantages and disadvantages of each system, he reached no conclusion."[3]

Meeting followed meeting until July 1778. At a final encounter, the pro-graters Etienne Marie Delahante and Charles René Parseval de Frileuse confronted their adversaries Jacques Paulze and Gilbert Georges de Montcloux before three neutral judges, Jean Baptiste Roslin d'Ivry, Alexandre Victor de Saint-Amand, et Michel Pignon. "The advocates, having announced that they had exhausted the subject and had nothing more to say, the judges declared the debate closed. They formulated their advice and gave it to the minister during October. But just what the advice was, was never known because it was kept in greatest secrecy. Thus ended the 1778 campaign. M. Delahante was temporarily silenced."[4]

Nevertheless Delahante was not defeated.

Among the colleagues openly supporting his plan, he was particularly happy to count M. Lavoisier, whose influence in the General Farm was growing daily. M. Lavoisier, however, was in a rather difficult position. As son-in-law of M. Paulze, he had tried repeatedly to disarm his opposition. Unsuccessful, and wishing to avoid domestic discord, he had not wanted to take the role in the debate that his merit would have assigned him. But in practice his support of the new arrangement was never in doubt.[5]

Delahante did not succeed in persuading his colleagues to impose the monopoly of the Farm on grating tobacco. He limited himself to encouraging local experiments in provincial factories.

On June 22, 1778 Lavoisier wrote to him that he had visited the Morlaix factory: "I have just traveled across Brittany where I saw one of your greatest producers of powdered tobacco. The more I think about it, the more I am convinced that although the grating conditions are not the best possible, they are at least infinitely superior to those we had before."[6] He had noted that the grating technique was satisfactory but that productivity could be improved by using horses rather than men to turn the mills, and he added:

I am also afraid that the moistening may be excessive. After water has been added, the tobacco is likely to ferment and overheat and then it acquires a sour odor. I recall having noted the beginnings of such changes in the tobacco sent to the Clermontois, and it seems that the tobacco I saw in Brittany and Nantes had the same characteristics. I believe that in general one must be extremely cautious when using the moistening process; it is better to make slight sacrifices than to risk dissatisfying the public.[7]

It was nevertheless the discontent of the public over the moistening of tobacco, added to financial grievances, that would lead in 1794 to the condemnation of the Farmers General by the Revolutionary Tribunal.

The Gunpowder and Saltpeter Administration

The Gunpowder and Saltpeter Administration was also evolving. Lavoisier wanted to encourage the industrial production of saltpeter by creating artificial nitrate works, those sheds inspired by the Swedish model, under which were built pyramids made up of successive layers of earth mixed with ashes, manure, and rotting matter soaked regularly with urine and liquid waste.

To encourage investors, in 1777 Lavoisier wrote his *Instruction sur l'établissement des nitrières et sur la fabrication du salpêtre*. Actually a manual, illustrated with engravings, it gave very detailed technical instructions: how to choose the site, build the sheds, and find soils containing saltpeter; how to set up the pyramids under the sheds and how to water and leach them; how to use a hydrometer to measure the saltpeter content of water; how to refine, using potash or the leaching of ashes; and how to evaporate and crystallize saltpeter.[8]

He even calculated the profit to be gained from nitrate works consisting of ten sheds. The initial investment would be 32,900 livres ($1.3 million), and the annual operating costs would be around 7,000 livres ($280,000). The turnover would be 12,000 livres ($480,000). Hence the profit—5,000 livres—would represent slightly more than 15 percent of the capital outlay. It would thus be a very worthwhile undertaking, but its success would depend on economizing on construction and equipment. Everything that was not indispensable should be excluded. "Neither would it seem advisable to set up more than fifteen or twenty sheds in the first year. Before making a large investment in a venture, one should be assured of the product; and it is wisest to make additional investments only after realizing profits."[9]

But the incentives proved to be of no avail and investors were few. Help came, however, from the duc de La Rochefoucauld d'Enville. Having observed that rich deposits of saltpeter formed spontaneously on the chalky cliffs in the vicinity of his château at La Roche-Guyon, near Pontoise, he made a very careful study that Lavoisier published in the *Mémoires de mathématique et de physique*, more commonly called the *Savants étrangers* collection since it was mainly devoted to the works of non-members of the Academy of Science. With the help of Lavoisier, Bucquet, and Clouet, La Rochefoucauld created artificial nitrate works in the farmyard of the château in March 1777.[10]

The following year, seeking saltpeter sources, Lavoisier explored from Blois to Tours the quarries on the banks of the Loire river at Saumur and Montsoreau, the banks of the Loire river at Vendôme, the Vienne valley at Chinon, Chatellerault, Poitiers, Ruffec, and the Charente basin at Angoulême, Saintes, and Saint-Savinien.[11]

Lavoisier's efforts to reorganize the Gunpowder Administration bore their fruits. The production of saltpeter went from 1.7 million pounds in 1775 to 2 million in 1777, and Lavoisier announced that it would soon reach 3.5 million. The plan was to be producing 3.8 million in 1788. The price had dropped sharply, and was only 7 sous per pound.

The Administration manufactured several qualities of gunpowder. Along with that used by the military, reserved for the arsenals, it also produced a gunpowder for hunters, called poudre à giboyer, and a poudre royale that was more potent. There were also the explosives used in quarries and, finally, the poudre de traite or "traders powder," of inferior quality, that was sold to slave traders in ports; it was used as a currency for buying slaves.[12]

The Administration soon had a reserve of 5 million pounds of gunpowder stored in its warehouses, enough to provide for two or three campaigns, and French gunpowder became the best in Europe. Its range, which had been from 70 to 80 toises during the Seven Years' War, reached 115 to 130 toises in 1778.[13] The English navy began to complain about the inferior quality of its gunpowder.

A part of the production was exported to Holland and Spain. Large quantities—1.7 million pounds—were sent to the American insurgents within two years. Lavoisier proudly wrote in 1789: "The Kingdom was able to furnish gunpowder to all the King's friends and allies in the last war; it can truthfully be said that it is to these supplies that North America owes its freedom."[14]

At the peak of its success, the Gunpowder Administration employed 1,100 workers in forty factories. There were powder factories and saltpeter refineries in Colmar, Nancy, Besançon, Dijon, Toulouse, Bordeaux, Tours, and Rouen; powder factories in Saint-Omer, Mézières, Metz, Marseille, Montpellier, Perpignan, Saint Jean d'Angely, Brest, and Essonne; and simple saltpeter refineries in Lyon, Saumur, Orléans, Châlons-sur-Marne, and at the Paris Arsenal.

In 1778 Lavoisier consulted Benjamin Franklin about reconstructing the gunpowder warehouse at the Arsenal and sent him an invitation to dinner, accompanied by rather obvious flattery:

Every moment of your existence is dedicated either to the education or welfare of your fellow men, and posterity should know that amid the political whirlwind, while the great Franklin was shaking and setting in motion all the powers of the two worlds, he could still find the time to reassure Parisian residents by designing a warehouse shielded from all incidents.[15]

But the basic research on the chemical nature of saltpeter and the detonation of gunpowder was hardly advancing. It was precisely from this research, however, that Lavoisier was expecting decisive progress. If it had been possible to determine the constituent elements of nitric acid and the mechanism of its formation, saltpeter could have been produced from synthesis. According to earlier research, four elements were necessary: an acid, rotting matter, chalky earth, and air. "It is quite possible," wrote Lavoisier, "that air itself is a constituent part of acid, or that it provides some substance, gaseous or otherwise, that without being nitrous acid, could nevertheless be one of the ingredients necessary for its formation."[16] In spite of his efforts, he would never discover the complete schema of this synthesis. There was not enough known then to allow him to analyze the complexity of the reactions involved in the formation of nitric acid.

In 1780 the Academy was to award the "saltpeter prize." Thirty-eight reports had been submitted, but they contained few new ideas and no demonstrations. The Academy admitted that the time limit had been too restricted and postponed the deadline until 1782. The amount of the prize was increased to 8,000 livres ($320,000). The first prize was eventually awarded to the Thouvenel brothers from Nancy; one was a doctor, the other a Commissioner for Gunpowder. But their study was more economic than scientific and did not contribute new chemical information.

In 1786 Lavoisier would publish the various memoirs in the *Recueil des Mémoires sur la formation et la fabrication du salpêtre*, which appeared in volume XI of the *Savants étrangers* collection. The close control that the commission of the Academy exercised over writing style only prolonged the delays. Shortly before their publication, Sage again pointed out to Lavoisier a grammatical error to which he was prone: " One must not write *'désirer de faire connaître,'* but *'désirer faire connaître'*; the verb *'désirer'* does not take the *'de.'* "[17]

The Reform of the General Farm

One year before the Laurent David lease was due to expire, Necker had still not opened discussions for the new lease that was to begin on October 1, 1780. The Farmers General were worried, for good reason, because Necker envisaged breaking up the General Farm and reducing its profits.

The stakes were considerable, because the Farm provided the Royal Treasury with a regular income of close to 200 million livres ($8 billion) per year. After difficult negotiations, a compromise was reached, dividing the indirect taxes among three companies: (1) A general State-owned Company would collect the duties for alcoholic drinks; (2) the administration of the Domaines would collect, along with income from royal property, the droits domaniaux;

(3) the General Farm would continue collecting the taxes on salt, tobacco, traites, and entries into Paris, that is, all the customs duties on merchandise coming from the provinces and foreign countries.

The new lease, called Nicolas Salzard, was more advantageous to the State. The number of Farmers General was reduced from sixty to forty and the posts for assistants were abolished. If the collected taxes surpassed by 3 million livres the amount stipulated by the lease, the profits were to be divided evenly between the Farmers General and the Treasury. In exchange, croupes and pensions were to be eliminated. The advance payment made by each Farmer on entering was reduced from 1,560,000 to 1,200,000 livres. The interest paid on these funds was lowered from 10 to 7 percent. On the other hand, the Farmers' fixed salary was raised from 24,000 livres ($960,000) to 32,000 livres ($1.3 million).

The new status corresponded more to a governmental administrative body than to a farm, since the Farmers shared their profits with the State. Nevertheless their portion remained quite important. It would reach 75,000 livres ($3 million) per year. This was Necker's usual method. He abolished as many posts as possible in Finance, but then generously compensated the former occupants so as not to arouse violent reactions.

Lavoisier belonged to the group of forty Farmers General participating in the new lease. He was responsible for the overall direction of collecting duties on merchandise entering Paris as well as for the accounts of the Saltworks in Franche-Comté, Lorraine, and Trois-Evêchés. The years spent in contact with the worlds of finance and high administration had given him a taste for economics. Dupont, Chief Inspector of Manufacturing, had just benefited from Benjamin Franklin's support. Necker had asked him to overhaul the Bureau of the Balance of Trade, a body dependent on the General Farm, and he showed real talents as a statistician. Lavoisier was increasingly attracted by these subjects. Furthermore, he now found himself the possessor of quite a handsome sum of money inherited after his father's recent death, and he was looking for an investment. It seemed to him that land was a sound one. Agriculture, principal source of wealth according to the Physiocrats, should be the major productive activity of the nation. In France, however, it was very backward. Collapsing under the weight of costs and taxes and paralyzed by the lack of capital, it remained encased in archaic conditions.

Wealthy nobles, among whom were the ducs Etienne François de Choiseul, François Alexandre Frédéric de La Rochefoucauld-Liancourt, and Armand Joseph de Charost, and the marquis de Turbilly, had set up model farms on their vast properties to introduce new agricultural techniques and encourage the peasants to clear abandoned land, drain marshes and use the best seed.

Scientists such as Antoine Augustin Parmentier, Louis Jean Marie Daubenton, Mathieu Tillet, André Thouin, the Abbé Henri Alexandre Tessier, Sarcey de Sutières, and Duhamel du Monceau contributed their knowledge to this modernizing venture.

Lavoisier, who had made his first trials on the property at Le Bourget, inherited from his father, decided to become, like them, an important landowner. He wanted to carry out a scientific agronomic experiment and to make an investment. Simultaneously he wanted to test his ideas as an economist, as he wrote in *De quelques expériences d'agriculture et réflexions sur leur relation avec l'économie politique*, a report presented at the Society of Agriculture in 1788:

It is not simply in armchairs that economics must be studied; it is only by a well planned investigation of an extensive development of land, by sustained calculations over a number of years on the distribution of recurring wealth, that one can form an accurate idea of what contributes to the prosperity of a large kingdom.[18]

Freschines

The property where he created his model farm was in Beauce, on a road leading from Vendôme to Blois, at a point just halfway between the two towns. On March 21, 1778 he bought from Field Marshal comte Jean-Baptiste Donatien de Rochambeau, who was leaving for America, 127 hectares (about 254 acres) of wheatland in Villefrancoeur, and a few days later, he purchased a property of 694 hectares (1400 acres) at Freschines, in the same region. By 1784 he would have put together by successive acquisitions a domain consisting of 1,129 hectares (2,258 acres) for a total investment of 389,000 livres ($15.5 million).[19]

The agricultural situation was disastrous. The average wheat yield was ten hectoliters per hectare, or five times the amount of seed used. Lavoisier quickly understood that lack of fertilizer was the basic problem. The soil was good, but the means of the farmer were insufficient. Most of them had no more than four or five cows and eighty sheep. They could just barely feed the animals during the winter and used the animal fertilizer, the only kind known, sparingly, four carts per hectare.

To increase the fertilizer supply, more livestock were needed, and that meant producing more forage. Creating meadows was not the greatest problem because there was plenty of land lying fallow. But one still had to know what sort of pasturage to sow. After three years of trials, Lavoisier had noted that alfalfa was regularly destroyed by a parasite, the cuscute. Sainfoin and clover, on the other hand, did well, especially during years with heavy rainfalls. He bought twenty cows and 500 sheep. From June to October, the latter were penned up in an area covering fifteen hectares (thirty acres) that they fertilized. The extra manure made it possible to spread the fields with six rather than four carts per hectare. Progressively, he arrived at twelve carts per hectare.

His scientific approach and habitual use of balance sheets suited the situation perfectly. Everything was classified according to expenses and revenues. It was counted and weighed, just as for a laboratory experiment. He had very precise maps and plans showing the acreage and use of each parcel of land. Thus he could compare yields. For ordinary production, he checked the weight of ten or twenty sheafs per cart and calculated an average. For the experimental cultivation, each sheaf was weighed, and at threshing time, the weights of the grain, chaff, and straw were all recorded. This precise measurement allowed him to estimate the production of each field and assess the effects of his improvements. The results obtained every year were recorded in registers.

He imported breeds chosen to improve the local livestock. To protect them from epizootic diseases, which he attributed to poor hygienic conditions, he insisted that the sheepfolds and cowsheds be cleaned often and kept well ventilated. As for the sheep, they could live outside, since they were bothered only by prolonged rainfall, not by dry cold. The growing herds brought more abundant harvests, thanks to more fertilizer, and they also provided the farmers with extra meat, milk, butter, and marketable products—wool for mills, skins for tanneries. Crafts, such as the spinning of cotton and wool, began to supplement agricultural work during the winter months.

Hoping to diversify these crafts, Lavoisier and his wife visited a property near the Essonne gunpowder factory, where fifty-two Indians from Pondichéry were spinning cotton. Like a true ethnologist, he noted meticulously their physical characteristics and lifestyle. As a man of taste, however, he judged the quality of their printed calico to be inferior to that of the Bengalis, and lost interest in the experiment.

In agriculture, he was discovering, progress was slow. After eight years he had created only fifteen hectares of meadows, one hectare for turnips or rutabagas, one for beets, and one for potatoes. Nevertheless he could boast with the pride of a peasant: "I have far more fodder than my barns and granaries can hold; at last, my oat harvest considerably surpasses my consumption."[20] But the success for wheat was less spectacular. Although the straw yield had doubled, that of grain had increased only slightly, because the seed was of poor quality.

He had spent almost 120,000 livres ($4.8 million), and in spite of all his careful attention and thrift, he did not even realize an income of 5 percent on the invested capital. He concluded:

It is no doubt for this reason that the well-off farmers living near Paris who manage to save some money prefer to place it in public loans and funds rather than use it for the improvement of agriculture. This is obvious proof that the State deficit keeps the interest rate on money in France too high. Here is an insurmountable obstacle to the improvement of agriculture, and probably of a great number of other industries; it is vital to public prosperity for the government to consider means of reducing it.[21]

Therefore agriculture could progress in France thanks only to wealthy landowners, ready to sacrifice a part of their capital for developing their land, or to comfortably-off farmers behaving like owners, as a result of twenty-seven-year leases.

The peculiarities of the tax system also jeopardized the success of Lavoisier's efforts. To encourage his farmers to increase their livestock and create artificial grazing lands, he granted a bonus for each cow or sheep beyond the fixed quota. But an obstacle existed, one that a Farmer General should have been able to foresee. It was the taille, the tax that rose in proportion to the affluence of the farmer, wealth being assessed by the number of livestock. Hence the wealthiest paid the highest taille. "All the effect of my incentives was destroyed by counter-incentives, and my plans were destroyed before having been formed."[22]

Lavoisier's contemporaries, "armchair agronomists," looked especially at the scientific aspect of agricultural questions. They sought to popularize the new cultivation methods, but had no idea of the economic difficulties that made them ineffective. Lavoisier stood out from them because he saw things as an economist. The goal of the studies he had undertaken was not simply to improve agricultural techniques:

They have still another objective that I regard as more important, that of providing the economists with definite data about the distribution of territorial wealth. I tried to determine the farmer's net income precisely, after deducting his expenses for all the land under his cultivation: (1) the number of sheaves for the owner of the tithe; (2) the number for the wages of the harvesters; (3) the number for the wages of the threshers; (4) the number for the next season's sowing; (5) the number for the maintenance of livestock, harness and equipment, vehicles, and so forth; (6) the number for the food of the farmer and his family; (7) the number for the rent paid to the landowner; (8) the number for the land-tax and the various taxes on commodities.[23]

Once the accounts were made, the landowner took about a third of the harvest, taxes almost as much, and "there remained about a third for the farmer for his upkeep, exploitation costs, the repayment of interest on loans and various other expenses."[24] Nevertheless, Lavoisier was hoping to contribute to the prosperity of the nation by stimulating public opinion and by inducing the great landlords, the capitalists, and the rich people to put their money in agriculture:

Such an investment does not permit the brilliant speculations that occur on the stock-market or on the fluctuation of public loans, but it is not charged with the same risks and the same reverses; the successes obtained draw tears from no one; they are, on the contrary, accompanied by the blessings of the poor. A wealthy landowner cannot cultivate and improve his farm without spreading confort and well-being around him. Rich and abundant crops, a numerous population, and a prosperous countryside are the reward of his efforts.[25]

Three times a year Lavoisier left Paris to spend fifteen days or three weeks at Freschines. "Whenever possible, I choose the periods of fall sowing, spring sowing and harvests."[26] He took the time to discuss the results with his land-owning neighbors and his farmers, and, after analyzing them, depicted them on charts. He greatly enjoyed his role; Madame Lavoisier would later relate:

He could be seen at each of his annual visits mixing with all the inhabitants, acting as a judge to restore peace between two neighbors or return a son to paternal obedience, setting an example of all the patriarchal virtues, and looking after the ill not only with his deniers but his visits, treatments, and encouragements toward patience and hope. He founded a school for the young generation, and always had commodities delivered at below market prices out of consideration for the scruples of most of the inhabitants, who, too proud to accept help openly, were all the more to be pitied.[27]

Lavoisier paid the teacher of the free school a salary of 400 livres ($15,000) per year. The local curé did not look favorably on this competition.

The Lavoisiers lived in the château, a handsome rectangular building of three stories overlooking a lawn surrounded by large old trees. The main entrance, reached by a long flight of stone steps, opened into a hall decorated with elegant stucco. The reception rooms on the ground floor offered a fine view of the countryside. In one, a set of armchairs was covered with tapestries depicting animals from Jean de La Fontaine's fables. In another, the gilded chairs were upholstered in a red flower-patterned damask with touches of white, blue, and yellow. Gracing the dining room were two mahogany sideboards and a large table whose center was adorned by a wooden fountain painted to look like marble.[28]

On the other side of the grand salon was the wood-paneled library, considerably smaller than the one in Paris. "Unfortunately no inventory of the library has survived and the only mention of the number of volumes is of the 358 restored to Madame Lavoisier sometime in 1795."[29] Among these were the *Mémoires pour servir à l'histoire de Brandebourg*, an *Histoire d'Angleterre*, Abel Boyer's *English Dictionary*, and *Le gentilhomme cultivateur* by Jean Baptiste Dupuy-Demportes—a compilation of the *Course of Study in Agriculture* by John Hill. In the library Lavoisier kept six large registers to record the results of agronomic experiments as well as a few scientific instruments.

Upstairs, each of the six bedrooms, three of which had adjoining bathrooms, was decorated with different colored hangings: red damask with blue flowers, blue damask with white flowers, red moire with green flowers, red and white striped moire. The furniture was painted. "On the third floor, the rooms were less luxurious, the furniture less handsome, and the hangings were made of printed calico, cotton woven in a flame pattern and painted fabric."[30]

At the entrance to the property, close to the stable, there was a vast building decorated by a finely sculptured large stone escutcheon bearing Lavoisier's initials. It was there that he carried out chemical experiments applicable to agriculture.

Madame Lavoisier was less enthusiastic than her husband about agriculture. A Parisian since her father had taken her from the convent, she was accustomed to society and entertained a great deal. In the country, she missed the intellectual atmosphere she liked. The neighbors who came to dine had politically conservative ideas that were far from her own. In the beginning she promoted the development of local trades and industries, such as the carding and spinning of cotton and the production of hosiery. These occupations could provide the families with an additional income, especially in winter. But she eventually lost interest and preferred to stay in Paris with their friends. Among them Pierre Samuel Dupont had become one of the closest. Since 1776 and Turgot's fall, this very amusing man—inventive, imaginative, full of enthusiasm and an adventurous spirit—had been a frequent guest and Madame Lavoisier had grown accustomed to his company. She was not at first attracted to him, but his infectious cheerfulness, witty eloquence, and generous and nonconformist views held a certain fascination for her. With him she discovered a new world, that of political ideas.

In that domain, Dupont was unbeatable. He had read everything and expounded with brilliance the economic theory of the Physiocrats. Madame Lavoisier was twenty-five, and had been married for eleven years to a man who paid less and less attention to her. He was constantly attending meetings at the Academy, the Gunpowder Administration, or the General Farm. Or else he was in his laboratory. The rest of the time, he was away from Paris buying land in the Vendômois.

Gradually Madame Lavoisier let herself be captivated and enjoyed being flirtatious; Dupont became her lover in 1781, during one of Lavoisier's numerous absences. The date of 1781 is confirmed by several of Dupont's letters to Madame Lavoisier. In one letter written on October 23, 1798, he recalls "seventeen years of intimacy."[31] In another letter from April 1815, he writes: "The inviolable and tender affection that I had vowed to you for thirty-four years."[32] The kind of affair Madame Lavoisier was having with Dupont was common in Paris where young women were often married to older men before they were sixteen. In such a society eternal fidelity was rare and reciprocal fidelity even more so. After a few years the women fell in love with somebody else and began a liaison, and the men acquired mistresses.

Madame Lavoisier and her husband were henceforth to be merely friends and partners. Their life did not seem to be disturbed by the presence of Dupont, who remained Lavoisier's loyal and sincere friend. Did Lavoisier know about the liaison? Was he affected by it? Did he find consolations? No one knows. His personal life remained a mystery. Perhaps this man who was so active in speculations of the mind had an undemanding affectivity and sensuality.

At the Lavoisiers' Dupont often encountered Franklin, another table companion and friend. Madame Lavoisier painted Franklin's portrait while the three men discussed the Anglo-American War. Franklin and Dupont explained to Lavoisier that one was heading toward a premature peace and brandished the specter of the absolute weapon: "They say that the English have made cylindrical bullets weighing 68 pounds, which they shoot from cannons of 24 mm with strong charges of powder, and that the hits are terrible. It is very necessary to imitate, as soon as we can, these fatal inventions so as not to be the only victims."[33]

Even if we ignore the outcome of this recommendation, we know for certain that Franklin was happy with his portrait. On October 23, 1788 he wrote from Philadelphia:

I have a long time been disabled from writing to my dear friend by a severe bout of gout, or I should sooner have returned my thanks for her very kind present of the portrait which she has herself done me the honor to make of me. It is allowed by those who have seen it to have great merit as a picture in every respect; but what particularly endears it to me, is the hand that drew it.[34]

Madame Lavoisier, curious about everything, also attended series of lectures at the Lycée, the elegant private college created by François Pilâtre de Rozier in 1781, where Lavoisier and other Academicians came to teach modern sciences to the socially prominent. One of Madame Lavoisier's fellow students, the baron François Auguste de Frénilly, left an ironic description of her:

She was young, but not pretty. Somewhat pedantic, she had an excessively high opinion of herself. Moreover, she was particulaly thrifty to say the least. While the courses were in fashion, she would borrow her father's carriage to come to the Lycée which was near the Palais Royal. After following two or three science lectures, she would have herself driven to the home of my uncle, M. de Saint-Wast, and then send the paternal carriage back. After supper, she would put on her walking shoes, take her lackey's arm and go by foot from the Tuileries to the Arsenal.[35]

Frénilly attributed to extreme frugality Madame Lavoisier's penchant for evening walks through the deserted streets of Paris. But perhaps it could also be explained by her desire to conceal her affair with Dupont from her social set.

Charitable Ideas

During those years, Lavoisier had become a true financial expert. His industrial experience with the Gunpowder and Tobacco Administrations and his agricultural undertakings had given him practical bases. His theoretical knowledge came from his activities at the Academy of Science and the General Farm. He had remained faithful to meetings of the Société d'Emulation at the Hôtel de Soubise, presided over by the Abbé Nicolas Baudeau, the last survivor of the reign of the Physiocrats. There he could still run into aristocrats, members of the legal profession, clerics, scientists, including Condorcet, a few merchants and bankers, and an occasional literary hack. The company was interested in the useful arts such as how to replace natural indigo and manufacture needles, locks, stills, oars, and guns. "And if, along with these popularizations of a technical order, an economic problem was taken up, the main concern was how to help the manufacturers protect themselves from English and German competition, and also how to stimulate agricultural production."[36]

But it was Necker who had the greatest influence on Lavoisier between 1776 and 1781. Lavoisier knew his first writings regarding the East India Company in 1769, his *Eloge de Colbert* in 1773, which had made them rivals for a short time, and his major text, *Sur la législation et le commerce des grains*, written in 1775. Like the Physiocrats, Necker believed in the primacy of agriculture, source of all wealth, based on ownership of land and population growth. But he also reserved a place for commerce and industry. On the other hand, he knew that the inevitable consequence of demographic growth was pressure on salaries; hence the State should intervene to protect workers. "All they have is their strength. All they can sell is their labor."[37]

The welfare of the people required economic growth, stable prices, and fiscal equity. The role of the State was to keep prices, in particular that of bread, as low as possible and protect the poor against the monopolists. This is why Necker opposed an unrestricted grain trade, which caused prices to rise. He was aware of the conflict between the respective interests of the landowners and the people. "Those who have a share in the goods of the earth will ask only for liberty and justice. Those who have nothing need your humanity and compassion. In a word, they need political laws that lighten the burden placed on them by property."[38] Luxury, he felt, was not bad in itself, especially if it contributed to the development of an elite capable of defending liberty. The enlightenment provided by wealth prevented the enslavement of thought .

Necker specified a reform program inspired by the philanthropic spirit. Its two essential themes were enlightened despotism and administrative decentralization. For Turgot's dogmatic liberalism, he substituted economic growth eased by State interventionism. Moreover, this Swiss Anglophile, European before his time, was addressing himself not to France alone, but to all monarchies concerned for the welfare of their populations. "The national strength must not be paid for by an excessive individual sacrifice, because one must always remember that this strength itself is a good only insofar as it is a guarantee of happiness."[39]

Having gained power, Necker acted prudently. He set up a more efficient and thrifty financial administration, sought a dialogue with middlemen and aided the most underprivileged. He was going to turn his attention to all charitable institutions: prisons, infirmaries, hospitals, homes for the elderly, and orphanages. From 1780 he had the Academy of Science share in his "charitable ideas."

Lavoisier readily adhered to Necker's vision of Physiocratic thought tinged with State interventionism and social concerns. He found in it his own vision of society; the State should undertake a major administrative and financial reform in France, but the objective must be to better the welfare of the people. Madame Necker, a sincerely generous person, assisted her husband. She was even, a journalist wrote, "General-Manager in this undertaking." Lavoisier was going to support her with devotion.

On January 26, 1780 Necker submitted to the Academy a plan for transforming the Cordeliers Convent into a prison for debtors.[40] This plan fell within a general reorganization of prisons of which Paris had three: the great and little Châtelets, formerly fortresses, and the Fort l'Evêque, formerly an episcopal residence. Over the years, "for lack of building sites or suitable housing, prisoners detained for debts, and who were often guilty only through improvidence, were mixed with men degraded by crime and debauchery. Soon corrupted by this harmful society, they left the prisons only to spread the vices they had acquired there."[41]

Lavoisier headed the commission which, composed of Duhamel du Monceau, Montigny, Tillet, Le Roy, and Jacques René Tenon, began by studying Jean Colombier's memoir and the plans of Jean Michel Moreau, architect for the King and the city of Paris, and then plunged into the prison world itself. There they ran into several difficulties. On March 25, 1780 Lavoisier wrote to Madame Necker:

Would you believe that although prisons are in a way open to the public, we are finding it hard to visit them? At first our mission appeared to offend several magistrates. We had to be extremely adroit and take endless precautions so that our contribution to an operation so worthy of a good administration would not meet with disapproval. Fortunately, we have succeeded in winning them over. And after having encountered several obstacles initially, we have subsequently congratulated ourselves on the attentions, even the consideration, of the magistrates and the orders they have given that nothing be hidden.[42]

Three months later, on March 17, the report was ready. These prisons, already too small when they were built, were enormously overcrowded; the administration packed eight hundred to a thousand prisoners into 1,000 square meters allowing one square meter for each prisoner. Worse still were the sanitary conditions:

The courtyards and exercise spaces are very small, and the height of the buildings makes ventilation difficult. The cells, into which too many prisoners have been placed, are extremely small and have low ceilings. Their layout is such that fresh air and light are rare and the existing air, foul and already contaminated, easily moves from one cell to another. Openings are narrow and badly placed. The prisoners' pallets are filled with straw that is often rotten, and they are so crammed together that it is almost impossible for them to lie down normally. Latrines and urine pipes cross most of the tiny rooms; the loathsome stench of sewers is inescapable. There are cells for solitary confinement where water seeps in at the vaults, where the prisoners' clothes rot away on their bodies, and in which prisoners are forced to relieve themselves on the floor. Most of the floors are covered with stagnant water because it cannot flow out. Everywhere there is mire, vermin, and decomposition. Such was the sight offered by the three prisons that one is questioning whether to demolish or reform. It is a sight that would have been inconceivable had we not witnessed it ourselves.[43]

The convent of the Cordeliers was badly suited to be a prison because of a lack of both water and structural solidity. The Commission recommended the Celestins.[44] Whatever the place chosen, four essential conditions had to be met: cleanliness, abundant water supply, good ventilation, and standards of hygiene. Windows and other openings were to be large and numerous and air should be permanently circulating, from the bottom up. The water would be provided by the Bièvre or Yvette Canal. In the meantime, prisoners could collect rainwater and use wells. Latrines and cesspools would be removed from the proximity of the cells and drained by underground sewers emptying into the Seine. To prevent the spread of contagious diseases it was essential to have proper ventilation, wash the floors regularly and thoroughly, allow the prisoners frequent baths and changes of clothing, and disinfect the premises at least once a year with chlorine, using Guyton de Morveau's method.

Covered walkways should be built for exercise when it rained. The number of benches should make it possible for everyone to sit down. Prisoners should be fed by the State and not depend on the charity of citizens. Military and civil prisoners should be separated, as should be the debtors from the criminals. An infirmary conforming to Tenon's plans was indispensable. Finally, "it is only fair that prisoners work to pay for at least a part of their food. A regular and reasonable occupation is necessary for their health as well as for maintaining peace and order and for banishing idleness, more dangerous in these sanctuaries of crime and debauchery than elsewhere."[45]

Caring for the ill was another priority of government policy. A commission headed by Dr. Colombier was set up to examine ways of improving Parisian hospitals. There was a question of breaking up the Hôtel-Dieu, which had burned in 1772, into several units, and locating them on the outskirts of the city. The situation was actually disastrous. According to Tenon's study, Paris had forty-eight hospitals. All were old and most of them had only a few dozen beds. The Hôtel-Dieu, by contrast, could accommodate three thousand patients. In the article "Hôpital" of the *Encyclopèdie* Denis Diderot wrote:

But although it was the largest and wealthiest, it was also the most frightening of all. Imagine a long string of adjoining wards where people suffering from every conceivable illness have been placed, where three or four, even five or six, people have often been crammed into the same bed, the living next to the dying and the dead. The foul air coming from the exhalations of this multitude of ailing bodies transports the stinking germs of their infirmities from one patient to the other. And everywhere one looks, there is pain and agony, offered up and accepted. This is what the Hôtel-Dieu is like. Also, among these wretched people are those who will leave the hospital with illnesses they did not come with, and who, once outside, are going to pass them on to their households and associates. Others, not entirely cured of their afflictions, will spend the rest of their lives in a convalescence as cruel as the illness itself. And the balance, except for those few with a robust nature, will perish. Reforms of the Hôtel-Dieu have been proposed at various times, but they could never be carried out. It has remained a gaping abyss where men's lives, along with the benefactors' alms, are going to vanish.[46]

Louis Sébastien Mercier vehemently confirmed this opinion: "What incredible insensitivity! What a cruel charity our hospitals offer! Their help is fatal. They are deceptive and disastrous traps. In them, death is a hundred times sadder and more horrible for a pauper than one under his own roof, left to himself and nature."[47]

But the Archbishop of Paris and the nuns of the hospital blocked the plan for decentralizing the Hôtel Dieu. On April 22, 1781 Louis XVI specified: "We are therefore restricted to arranging this hospital so that it can accommodate at least three thousand patients, one to each bed, separated on the basis of the major types of illnesses. Also men and women should be placed in separate quarters, and there should be special rooms and areas where convalescents can walk."[48]

Necker tried to obtain the permanent opening of the Saint-Louis Hospital, which functioned only during epidemics. He experienced still another setback. His only success would be the creation on land belonging to the parishes of Saint-Sulpice and Gros-Caillou, next to the Hospice de Charité, of the hospital that bears his name today. Wanting to reform the hospitals of the kingdom, Necker needed to study a model one so as to determine precisely the daily cost of good care for one patient having a bed to himself. This small hospital with 128 beds was endowed with an income of 42,000 livres ($1.7 million) paid for by the royal lottery. One doctor, two surgeons, and twelve nuns from the Order of Saint Vincent de Paul gave excellent care for a daily cost of 16 sous 6 deniers ($32), the lowest in Paris.

The Academy and Public Health

Lavoisier's ideas concerning public health reflected his personality and taste for order, propriety, and cleanliness. He could be seen every day looking elegant, neat, and immaculate, just the way David painted him. Anything dirty and malodorous disgusted him. He was obsessed by ventilation, hygiene, and running water. He could always be counted on to support efforts to improve ventilation in public premises or protect the drinking water of the Parisians. This interest for the purity of air and water could also be explained by his penchant for analysis, since the search for impurities is the objective of chemical analysis. However that may be, the Academy recognized his competence in these domains and called on him. These interventions in social issues and public health hardly displeased him. In 1778 he verified the conclusions of a study by Parmentier on the risks of pollution of the Seine by the cesspools flowing into it. This impure water was being drunk by Parisians, and, since the plans for supplying the city with water from the Yvette had not worked out, it was necessary at least to try and limit the pollution.

Somebody proposed replacing fixed cesspools by movable ones that could be emptied outside the city walls. Although the idea was deemed interesting, there was no follow up. With Auguste Denis Fougeroux de Bondaroy, Lavoisier studied a disinfecting process using vinegar, but it proved to be ineffective. During the experiment a worker died from asphyxiation, and they recommended giving preference to anti-mephitic pumps.

He also studied the preservation and falsification of cider and perry, the fermented beverage made from pears, and the ideal strength of meat bouillon destined for the ill. As for the sailors' diet during long sea voyages, he concluded that the basis should be provided by rice, pasta, fresh bread, grape jelly, pickled sorrel, and vegetables preserved in barrels.

In 1781 the Academy consulted him about a subject on which his expertise had been recognized ever since that distant time when he had competed for the prize for the best method of lighting city streets. The Paris Opera having been destroyed by fire, he was asked to study means of lighting it once it was reconstructed. This time his report was written from a social as well as a technical angle, since he was a lover of light and lyric opera:

Three objectives must be met in lighting a theater: lighting the stage and its sets, lighting the actor, and lighting the audience. But one cannot truly call theaters those elongated rectangles, those tennis courts in which stages have often been built, where one part of the audience has been condemned to see nothing and the other to hear nothing. [. . .] The method of lighting the stage and audience was equally barbaric. Quite a large number of center lights were suspended from the ceilings, some lit up the proscenium, and others the house. There are few listening to me who have not seen members of an audience disturbed so that the tallow candles of the lights could be snuffed out. Certainly no one has forgotten how much these hanging lights obstructed the view of a part of the audience, principally those in the boxes of the upper circle. Consequently, following public complaints, most of them have been eliminated.[49]

The center lights over the proscenium had been replaced by footlights, the tallow and oil by wax, and the several fixtures in the upper gallery by a unique, lighter one. But these modifications were still unsatisfactory. It was impossible to read the libretto during the performance. Lavoisier proposed a comprehensive plan. For the house, a subdued lighting; for the scenery and stage, overhead lights placed in the flies; for the actors, footlights; and finally, for the audience, elliptical lights placed inside the ceiling. The hygienist was also concerned with salubrity: "Such lights would serve as ventilators continuously renewing the air in the house. Indeed, every burning body heats the surrounding air; the heated air expands and becomes lighter; it rises and is replaced by fresh air, which heats up in its turn and rises like the first. Hence the air is constantly being replenished."[50]

Le comte Charles Claude d'Angiviller, director of the King's Buildings, converted the salon of the large paintings in the Louvre into a theater whose walls were thirty-nine feet high. Lavoisier, assisted by Meunier, Aimé Argand, and Antoine Quinquet, lanternmakers, tested different types of lighting. Together they devised quite powerful oil lamps. A very thin circular wick holder left room for a central duct where the air circulated, and a glass tube connected with the exterior accelerated the draught that passed through the flame, according to the principle used by chemists for their furnaces.[51]

At the beginning of 1781, Madame Necker once again called on Lavoisier to help with a reform of the Hôtel-Dieu, but coming events would decide differently.[52]

Monsieur Necker's Blue Tale

On Monday February 19, 1781 Necker's *Compte rendu au Roi* (Report to the King) began to be sold in Paris for 3 livres ($120) a copy. Making public what had usually been reserved for the king alone was a real innovation. Necker "called on the nation to acquaint itself with and examine public administration, thus for the first time, making State business everybody's business."[53]

The first part of the book described his efforts to re-establish public credit, improve administration, and increase the prosperity of the State and the welfare of the people. The second part was a statement of the receipts and expenses of the Royal Treasury for 1781, and showed a surplus of 10 million livres ($400 million). The report was meant to be an argument for the work already done and a promise to carry on with reforms. It was also intended to strengthen public credit and facilitate future borrowing by demonstrating, with the use of a few artful accounting devices, the sound health of the royal finances. These tricks did not pass unnoticed, and the witty, alluding to the color of the paper used in the luxurious copies and to the analogy between the French words *compte* (account) and *conte* (tale), referred to the work as "Le conte bleu de M. Necker" (M. Necker's Blue Tale).

This tedious book had the greatest success ever known in France, with the exception of the Bible. The 100,000 copies sold made Necker the most famous man in the kingdom. But his constant appeals to public opinion were perceived as attacks on the royal dignity. Le comte Charles Gravier de Vergennes, Minister of Foreign Affairs said to Louis XVI that Necker was undermining the French monarchy, basing his conduct "on the example of England which publishes its accounts, an example for which Your Majesty's predecessors have shown such considerable and justified aversion." [54]

And in the end, the popularity of Necker's *Compte rendu* put the seal on its author's downfall. On May 19, 1781 Necker was dismissed. The prison reform as well as that of the hospitals was thus postponed indefinitely.

9
―――――

The Crowning Achievement of
the Chemical Revolution

I N THE DAYS FOLLOWING NECKER'S DISMISSAL in 1781, Lavoisier was impatient to return to his laboratory. He had just read a book published by Magellan, *Essai sur la nouvelle théorie du feu élémentaire*. This essay summarized the ideas on latent and specific heat of Joseph Black, the Scottish physician and chemist, and his disciples, William Irvine and Adair Crawford.

Lavoisier was thus led toward Aristotle's fourth element, fire, so difficult to define, but at the heart of the chemical revolution. Since 1766 he had been trying to work out a theory of heat. Its essential feature was that in principle "all substances of nature, when not decomposed by heat, are capable of assuming three states of matter: solid, liquid, or aeriform fluid. The state depended upon the amount of heat, of matter of fire, with which the substance was combined."[1]

Since matter of fire could not be weighed, Lavoisier was wondering how heat could be measured. Crawford's *Experiments and Observations on Animal Heat*, published in 1779, offered a new method, the method of mixtures, for measuring specific heat of different bodies.

The Memoir on Heat

Joseph Black had proposed the concept of latent heat in 1762. According to him, the passage of a body from one state to another—for example, the transformation of ice into water or water into vapor—required the absorption of significant quantities of heat. But this heat, he said, stays hidden; it cannot be detected with a thermometer because it is a "latent heat". He had noted that to bring different bodies of equal weight to the same temperature different quantities of heat were needed. The quantity needed by each body was its "specific heat." In Black's system the specific heat of water represented the unit, those of other bodies were its decimal fractions. If two substances of equal weight but different temperatures were mixed, their respective temperatures would vary in opposite directions until they reached an equilibrium that depended on their specific heats. Crawford's method of mixtures derived from this postulate.

Another reason for Lavoisier to be interested in Crawford's work was that his theory of animal heat resembled Lavoisier's own ideas. Crawford thought that, since animal respiration transforms atmospheric air into fixed air and the specific heat of the former is greater than that of the latter, a great quantity of heat is gained in this way, maintaining animal heat. Lavoisier, on his side, thought that respiration was a form of combustion that discharged heat; the eminently breathable air was decomposed in the lungs and released matter of fire. Wanting to apply Crawford's method to his own work, Lavoisier resumed his research on heat. For this program, he enlisted the cooperation of his junior colleague Pierre Simon Laplace, who had gained a reputation at the Academy of Science for his brilliant papers in pure mathematics. As Roger Hahn points out, "Lavoisier was perfectly capable of doing the mathematical calculations himself. He was, after all, an expert accountant at the General Farm. He knew how to weigh, calculate, and reason as well as any mathematician."[2]

Laplace's expertise in designing scientific instruments would appear to be a much more determining factor in Lavoisier's choice. His young associate had been an adjunct member of the Section of Mechanics at the Academy of Science since 1773 and had already helped Lavoisier to perfect a barometer and a dilatometer for solids. Laplace would have preferred spending his time with geometry, and hesitated at first. In a letter addressed to Lavoisier on March 6, 1782 he explained: "I am almost useless to you in the experiments you are doing on the dilation of bodies; but I shall calculate them with a true pleasure. Therefore, would you leave the journal of these experiments at the Academy on Saturday or another day, and I shall give you the corresponding dilations."[3] But Laplace was obligated to Lavoisier, who had lent him a considerable sum of money to help his father pay his debts. Fearing that a refusal might offend his elder colleague, all powerful at the Academy, he accepted the proposition on March 6, 1782.

In November the two men measured the specific heats of a certain number of bodies, using the method of mixtures. They soon realized that the method was unsuitable for substances of very different densities such as water and mercury, for nonmiscible liquids, and for substances that reacted chemically with each other. Finally, it could not measure the heat discharged from combustion, chemical reactions, and respiration. And these were precisely the subjects that interested Lavoisier.

Basing themselves on the principle of the conservation of mass, the two scientists formulated a fundamental law of thermochemistry: "All variations in heat, whether real or apparent, that a system of bodies undergoes in changing of state are reproduced in reverse order when the system goes back to its former state."[4] A new method for measuring heat ensued. The amount of heat given off by a cooling body was proportional to the amount of ice that melted on contact with it, and the weight of the water produced made it possible to measure it. It was the principle of the ice calorimeter, a real innovation.[5]

They had Pierre Naudin, a tinsmith, build a container with three concentric compartments (Figure 4). An object or animal could be placed in the central chamber. It was surrounded by a chamber filled with ice at zero degrees. The outside compartment was also packed with ice that absorbed the exterior heat and insulated the two other sections. The heat produced by the body in the first one caused the ice in the middle one to melt, and the water resulting from this fusion was drained by a faucet so that it could be collected and weighed.

Using ice meant that the work had to be done in winter. As luck would have it, the winter of 1782–1783 was mild. Nevertheless, they were able to carry out their major demonstration on January 28. To show that respiration was comparable to a slow combustion similar to that of charcoal, they placed a guinea pig in the calorimeter. The animal consumed oxygen, produced fixed air, and generated heat that melted a certain amount of ice. They next determined the weight of charcoal whose combustion would melt the same amount of ice and produce the same amount of fixed air.

They supposed that this combustion took place in the lungs and that the heat produced was transmitted to the blood when it passed through them, and was then spread throughout the organism. "Thus the air we breathe serves two purposes, equally necessary for our survival: it removes from the blood the base of fixed air whose excess would be very harmful; and the heat that this combination leaves in the lungs compensates for the continuous loss of heat to the atmosphere and surrounding bodies."[6] The results would be presented to the Academy on June 28, 1783, in the famous "Memoir on Heat."[7]

The homeothermic mechanism thus conceived rested on three phenomena that contributed to the distribution of heat throughout the body and kept it constant: oxidation produced heat and fixed air; the circulating blood transmitted the heat received in the lungs to the extremities of the body: "The heat developed in this combustion is transmitted to the blood, which passes

Figure 4. The ice calorimeter of Pierre Simon de Laplace and Lavoisier. Musée des Arts et Métiers, Paris.

through the lungs and from there is spread throughout the animal system."[8] And finally, pulmonary exhalation lowered the temperature when it rose excessively high.

Lavoisier was mistaken on one point, the combustion site was not in the lungs. It would be more than a century before it was discovered that the combustion takes place in the mitochondria of the cells of tissues. But in his conclusion, he set forth the concept of the utmost importance for the progress of animal physiology, the concept of basal metabolism:

Whenever an animal is in a stable and resting state, whenever it can live for a considerable time without suffering in its environment, in general whenever the circumstances in which it is found do not appreciably alter its blood and body fluids, so that after several hours the animal's system undergoes no perceptible change, the conservation of its animal heat is due, at least in large measure, to the heat produced by the combination of pure air breathed by the animal with the base of fixed air provided by the blood.[9]

James Hall, a young Scottish scientist passing through Paris, met Lavoisier and was surprised to hear him say that he did not know about Black's work on latent heat. He asked his uncle: "Pray enquire of Black himself and let me know the date of the discovery; for they are wonderfully candid here and are ready to give every man his due."[10] Black wrote the note asked of him by Hall's uncle. Lavoisier, the duc de La Rochefoucauld, and several others "were all surprised to find that the discovery of latent heat was really his due and did him full credit as the first mover of the present system of chemistry; latent heat and fixed air are two of its foundation stones".[11]

Even if Laplace had some regret at leaving mathematics, his enthusiasm for the experiments was strong. During the winter of 1783–1784, he wrote to Lavoisier, asking that they be resumed and extended, notably by comparing the specific heats of metals and of their oxides. These determination were carried out in the winter and spring of 1784. Then they resumed their experiments on animals. There had been, in fact, a discrepancy between the results measured by direct calorimetry on the guinea pig (13 ounces of melted ice) and those calculated on the basis of the fixed air that it produced ($10\frac{1}{2}$ ounces). Actually, the animal had exhaled less carbonic gas than the amount of inhaled oxygen would have led one to expect. Lavoisier and Laplace were probably disappointed to see that the ice calorimeter did not yield the accuracy they had expected. They announced: "We intend to repeat and to vary these experiments by determining the quantities of heat renewed in different kinds of animals, and by inquiring whether, in all of them, this quantity of heat is always proportional to the quantities of fixed air produced in respiration."[12]

These projected experiments were never realized and it was the end of their collaborative efforts. Nevertheless they had demonstrated the possibility and significance of thermal measurements and "suggested in no incertain voice that an experimental and theoretical science of heat was possible and of the utmost importance for physics and chemistry. It is hard to conceive of the accomplishments of Gay-Lussac, Fourier, Carnot, and Dulong and Petit, emerging with such rapidity, without the preparatory achievement of their influential compatriots Laplace and Lavoisier."[13]

As for Lavoisier, he came to think that the evolution of oxygen during respiration was perhaps more complex than had been foreseen; he supposed that one part was transformed into carbonic gas, while the other combined with hydrogen to form water. The reason he envisaged this hypothesis, the first exposition of the existence of a pulmonary perspiration, is that on June 24 he had succeeded in synthesizing water from oxygen and hydrogen, at the same time as Cavendish in London and Monge in Mézières.

Water Is No Simple Substance

Henry Cavendish, a wealthy English scientist, had discovered hydrogen in 1766. He had obtained it by applying sulfuric or hydrochloric acid to iron, zinc or tin, and had collected it in a mercury trough. He had named this gas, which was lighter than air and burned readily, "inflammable gas."

In March 1774 Lavoisier had undertaken a series of tests on the combustion of this gas. The combustion, he felt, ought to bring about the fixation of a portion of atmospheric air and a weight gain. But the experiment was badly conceived. He had placed diluted sulfuric acid and iron in an open flask and set fire to the hydrogen thus obtained at the neck of the vessel. To his great disappointment, he had observed a weight loss of 39 grains, due, we know today, to the evaporation into the surrounding air of the small amount of water formed. One year later, in April 1775 he had returned to these tests using closed flasks (Figure 5), but he had made the new error of collecting the gases in a water pneumatic trough. Since the product of the combustion was precisely water, he could not detect its presence.

At the beginning of 1776 Macquer, who had been surprised to read in Priestley's work that fixed and inflammable air could be mixed without having the latter lose its capacity to ignite, had tried the experiment. It had obviously been negative. To be absolutely certain that the flame of hydrogen was "accompanied by no sooty smoke," he had covered it with a white porcelain saucer. The spot where the flame touched the saucer remained perfectly white. "It was covered only with quite perceptible droplets of a clear, water-

Figure 5. Balloon flask for the water synthesis experiments. Musée des Arts et Métiers, Paris.

like liquid, which in fact appeared to us to be merely pure water." [14] Macquer thought that this water came from surrounding humidity. In fact, since hydrogen had combined with the oxygen of the atmosphere, he had just achieved, without knowing it, the first experimental synthesis of water (H_2O). But how could he have conceived of anything so strange, since in his eyes water was an element, a simple, indivisible substance that could never be decomposed, transformed, or synthesized?

In September 1777, along with Bucquet, Lavoisier had attempted to bring hydrogen into the general theory of the formation of acids. Since an acid is formed when sulfur, phosphorus, or charcoal is burned, the combustion of hydrogen should also produce an acid. They expected to obtain carbonic acid. They had dissolved iron in sulfuric acid to obtain hydrogen and collected the gas in a six-pint bottle turned upside down. Once it had been set upright, they had lit the gas escaping from the neck. But the burning gas did not precipitate limewater. Thus the combustion of hydrogen did not produce carbonic gas.

After Bucquet's death, Lavoisier had undertaken a new series of tests by filling a closed bottle containing two ounces of limewater with hydrogen. The cork was pierced by a pointed copper tube that carried into the bottle oxygen coming from a pneumatic chest." [15] When he set fire to the hydrogen, "a beautiful spear of very brilliant flame" formed at the end of the copper tube. The oxygen and hydrogen burned very well together; the limewater was not precipitated; no acid was formed.

Lavoisier was disappointed, but this gave him the idea for another experiment that he reported, in April 1782, at the public session of the Academy of Science. A stream of oxygen directed into a piece of charcoal burned at such a high temperature that it melted platinum. Franklin, observer of this experiment, considered this fire "much more powerful than that of the strongest burning mirror, indeed the strongest fire we yet know." [16]

In 1781 John Warltire had observed that a mixture of air and hydrogen, ignited by an electric spark, produced humidity. Priestley too observed that after the spark the inside surface of the tank was covered with dew. Always an excellent observer but a mediocre theoretician, Priestley spoke about this to Cavendish and wrote to Lavoisier: "I have just carried out some experiments on inflammable air that Dr. Franklin no doubt showed you. They seem to prove that inflammable air is nothing other than phlogiston." [17] For many years, Priestley was to keep the same idea and never could accept Lavoisier's antiphlogistic theory.

In the spring of 1783 Cavendish confirmed that the amount of water produced by the combustion of hydrogen and oxygen was too great to be attributed to the water vapor present in these gases. And since the weights of the bodies brought together were unchanged, one could not attribute it to the fixation or discharge of phlogiston. He had revealed a capital fact, but encumbered by phlogiston had misinterpreted it. He believed that hydrogen contained water and phlogiston, and that oxygen contained water but no phlogiston. Thus, he concluded, the formation of water resulted from the combustion of the two gases, the missing phlogiston in one being compensated by the supply from the other. His observation spread throughout the scientific world. He spoke about his tests to one of his friends, the physicist Charles Blagden, who visited Paris in June 1783.[18] "M. Blagden informed us," Lavoisier wrote," that in London M. Cavendish had already tried to burn inflammable air in closed containers and that he had obtained a very perceptible amount of water." [19]

On June 24 Lavoisier and Laplace carried out in their turn the decisive experiment on the synthesis of water in the presence of Blagden, Fourcroy, Meusnier, Achille Pierre Dionis du Séjour, Alexandre Théophile Vandermonde, and Adrien Marie Legendre. They had two pneumatic gasholders, one filled with hydrogen, the other with oxygen. The pipes, whose flow was controlled by faucets, led to a mercury pneumatic trough. They determined the right proportion of the two gases by trial and error; it was the one that produced the most beautiful and brilliant flame. They then introduced the burner into the pipe leading to the pneumatic trough, and let the gases burn up completely. The surface of the bell jar was covered with vapors that formed into drops and ran in all directions. In fifteen to twenty minutes, the surface of mercury was covered with water.

The water and mercury were recovered together in a plate placed under the bell jar. The mixture was poured into a glass funnel. Heavier, the mercury ran through before the water, which was as pure as distilled water. Lavoisier noted in his laboratory register, "The amount of water can be estimated at 3 gros [11.46 grams]. We should have been able to collect 1 ounce, 1 gros and 12 grains of water [30.40 grams]. Therefore, we must suppose a loss of two-thirds of the air or else a weight loss."[20]

The precision of the results left something to be desired, but time was pressing. The following day, June 25, Lavoisier and Laplace announced to the Academy: "Water is not a simple substance, it is composed weight for weight of inflammable air and vital air."[21] But they had not measured the quantities of gas consumed, and Laplace insisted on the fact that they did not know whether this quantity of water represented the exact weight of airs consumed. He suggested that the experiment should be repeated with all possible attention.

Lavoisier did not consider that this imperfect result stood in the way of his theory. In his *Memoir Whose Object Is to Prove That Water Is No Simple Substance*, presented on June 25, he was unequivocal: "If one burns a little less than two parts of aqueous inflammable air under a bell jar with one part of vital air, assuming that both are perfectly pure, the totality of the two airs is absorbed and one finds on the surface of the mercury a quantity of water equal in weight to that of the two airs used."[22]

He was in a great hurry to publish, knowing that a young professor of mathematics at the Engineering School in Mézières, Gaspard Monge, member of the Academy since 1780, was trying to demonstrate the same thing. Indeed, a few days later, Vandermonde read to the Academy a letter from Monge relating his experiments done in June and July. Lavoisier, worried at first, was in the end satisfied to see that Monge's studies confirmed his own and by their precision even vindicated the wager he had made that the gases and water were of equivalent weights. His commentary was flattering: "He worked without loss, so that his experiment is much more conclusive than ours and leaves nothing to be desired. The result he obtained was pure water, whose weight turned out to be almost the same as that of the two airs."[23]

Therefore the fact that water was not an element but a compound body had at last been established. Meanwhile, Blagden, who was still in Paris, and Magellan, who had continued his scientific correspondence, kept him informed of Priestley's recent works.[24] The Birmingham chemist had announced at the Royal Society on June 26 that inflammable air and phlogiston were the same thing. Seeking to reduce lead oxide with hydrogen, he had paid no heed to a capital fact that Lavoisier had spotted. The gases had disappeared during the reaction; oxygen and hydrogen had combined and Priestley had formed water without suspecting it.

Finally, at the Royal Society on January 15, 1784, Cavendish was the first to present the quantitative and qualitative composition of water. Thus began a debate that has never ended. Blagden accused Lavoisier of having profited from information coming from Cavendish. Lavoisier refused Cavendish's interpretation of the results: dephlogisticated air was not water deprived of its phlogiston. And he recalled having obtained water by reducing lead calx with charcoal powder in a closed container. Concerned about establishing the priority of his discoveries, he specified, "I recorded this fact, that I could not then explain, in the volume of *Opuscules physiques et chymiques*, which I published in 1774. (See chapter V of *Opuscules*)."[25]

In spite of Blagden's indiscretions, Lavoisier was completely within his rights to claim a part of the discovery, since it was he who correctly interpreted the facts. But, although he had achieved the synthesis of water, he still had to decompose it. And for that he needed a simple method allowing him to produce the two components—hydrogen in particular—separately.

The "Montgolfières" and the "Charlières"

In the meantime, the great scientific and technical event that captured France's imagination in 1783 was the Montgolfier brothers' aerostatic machine. Etienne de Montgolfier ran a paper mill created by his father in Annonay. Joseph, his brother, lived in Avignon; he had a lively imagination, but his absent-mindedness was extraordinary. One day he left an inn forgetting to take his horse. Another time, he forgot his wife. Both brothers were interested in science. They knew that Priestley had discovered oxygen in 1774, and Cavendish hydrogen in 1776. Joseph thought that if a balloon could be inflated with a gas lighter than air, then it would rise into the skies. Dreaming one day in front of a fire burning in the hearth, he imagined that the force that drove the smoke into the flue could be used to lift balloons. In November 1782, for the first time, a small paper balloon, inflated with hot air, rose to a height of 70 feet above Avignon. A few days later, another balloon broke away from its ropes and rose to 150 toises (900 feet) before falling on the nearby hills.

On June 4, 1783 a large balloon made of canvas and lined with paper, containing 754 cubic meters of hot air produced by burning straw, soared into the sky with all Annonay as witnesses. "It is quite amazing to see," Lavoisier wrote, "a hollow globe, 35 feet in diameter, made of canvas and paper weighing 450 pounds, cover a distance of 1,200 toises [7,200 feet] while rising quite high."[26]

The Academy of Science, impressed by the demonstration, decided to take charge of the future experiments and appointed a committee, composed of Lavoisier, Nicolas Desmarest, the Abbé Charles Bossut, Le Roy, and Monge. Mathieu Tillet, Mathurin Jacques Brisson, Cadet, and Condorcet would soon join them.

Lavoisier was assisted by Jean Baptiste Meusnier de La Place, an engineering officer who was in charge of the *Recueil des machines approuvées par l'Académie*, a publication which was forty years behind the times. Meusnier, who was doing his best to bring the enterprise up to date, had worked with Lavoisier three years earlier on the plans for the gunpowder warehouses at the Arsenal and on the machine for distilling seawater. Appreciating his qualities as a physicist and technician, Lavoisier had invited him on the previous June 24 to participate in his experiment on the synthesis of water. Later he would have him join his studies on the production of hydrogen and the composition and decomposition of water.

The Academy wanted to give an equal chance to the hydrogen balloons of the physicist Jacques Charles and the Robert brothers, who were well-known makers of scientific instruments. On August 27, in the Champ de Mars, they flew a balloon inflated with hydrogen and covered with silk, waterproofed by a rubber-based varnish. Soon there erupted a quarrel accompanied by a fierce competition for State subsidies between partisans of the hot air Montgolfières and the advocates of the hydrogen filled Charlières. The dispute entertained Parisians throughout the summer.

The amateurs of Charles's *Globes célestes* call the Montgolfier balloons *Globes terrestres*. To which the hot air enthusiasts retort that Professor Charles's motto could have been *Carolus expectat* (*Charles attend* = Charlatan) and that it was simpler and more ecological to heat a balloon with straw than to resort to a foul-smelling vitriol-based chemistry that was both complicated and dangerous.[27]

The Montgolfier brothers had the famous wallpaper factory headed by Jean Baptiste Réveillon construct a balloon measuring 45,000 cubic feet. It was destroyed by wind and rain during the first trial on September 12. "This contretemps was all the more regrettable since the king, who had ordered the experiment to be carried out before him at Versailles, had fixed the day for Friday the 19th of the same month."[28] The date could not be postponed because numerous French and foreign diplomats had already gathered in Versailles for the signing of the peace treaty freeing America from English rule. In four days, Réveillon managed to make another balloon in canvas and cotton, painted in tempera on two sides with the king's colors, gold and royal blue. On Thursday the 18th, a new test was successful, but the balloon was torn. It was hastily repaired and transported to Versailles where everything was ready for its installation.

On the 19th, as foreseen, before the king and queen and all the court, "the Réveillon," pumped full of hot air and carrying several farmyard animals in a Gondola, flew off. It rose to almost 300 toises (1,800 feet) and stayed aloft for ten minutes, but the tear reopened, and the balloon came down, landing gently on some tree branches. The animals were unharmed. Lavoisier commented:

After so many experiments, it was no longer possible to doubt the effectiveness of the Montgolfiers aerostat, but it was important to understand better their method for lifting up this machine and especially to find out whether an aerostat with a sufficient capacity could also carry men, and to what extent they could control it.[29]

Réveillon built a new balloon with a diameter of forty-five feet and a height of seventy. It had a wickerwork gondola, and a portable stove made it possible to burn straw during the flight, and thus to replenish the balloon with hot air. The problem was to find aeronauts to manoeuver it. A young and handsome adventurer, Jean François Pilâtre de Rozier, whom the Benedictines had deemed "scatterbrained, dissipated, keen on pleasure and unamenable to studies," but who had the duc de La Rochefoucauld-Liancourt as his patron, presented himself to Lavoisier. He had earned something of a scientific reputation in society as a "swallower of hydrogen," which he inhaled and then breathed out as it burned. But Lavoisier had a more serious reason for being interested in him. Pilâtre had perfected a kind of diving suit connected to an air tank which, he said, could protect sanitary service workers from suffocation provoked by mephitic gas. Lavoisier asked for a demonstration: "Pilâtre put on the rubberized suit and went to the bottom of a foul cesspool. He lay down on the excrement under a layer of thirty feet of mephitic gas and stayed there for thirty-four minutes, or until he had exhausted his reserve of air. His invention was duly approved by the Academy of Science and the Royal Society of Medicine."[30]

Lavoisier sent him to Etienne de Montgolfier, who added him to his crew. He proved himself to be both courageous and clever during the preliminary tests carried out with the captive balloon. On November 21, watched by the Dauphin and the court, Pilâtre de Rozier and the marquis d'Arlandes lifted off from the garden of the Château de la Muette, crossed the Seine, flew over Paris, and, after seventeen minutes, landed on the road to Fontaine-bleau. Lavoisier commented: "They rose or fell, depending on whether they stoked or slackened the fire, and by this sole means, they avoided, if it can be said, the dreaded pitfalls of such a navigation and went on to alight smoothly just where they chose."[31] But what made the balloon fly? It was clear that the combustion of straw produced heat, and that it in turn expanded the trapped air. A part of this air escaped, while the other part, lighter than the outside air, allowed the balloon to rise. And Lavoisier concluded: "The cause of its ascent must be attributed to the rarefaction of the air inside the aerostat, brought about by the fire."[32]

On December 1, 1783, at the Tuileries, the Academy of Science was wit-ness to a new feat. This time, the physicist Charles flew off, with the younger Robert brother on board, in a red and yellow hydrogen balloon that carried them to Nesles-la-Vallée, forty kilometers north of Paris. Benjamin Franklin witnessed this second ascent of human passengers in a hydrogen balloon:

Between one and two o'clock all eyes were gratified with seeing it rise majestically from among the trees, and ascend gradually above the buildings, a most beautiful spec-tacle. When it was about two hundred feet high, the brave adventurers held out and waved a little white pennant, on both sides of their car, to salute the spectators, who returned loud claps of applause. The wind was very little, so that the object, though moving to the northward, continued long in view; and it was a great while before the admiring people began to disperse. The persons embarked were M. Charles, profes-sor of experimental philosophy and a zealous promoter of that science; and one of the Messieurs Robert, the very ingenious constructors of the machine.[33]

Thus the world's first two balloon flights, based on different technolo-gies, occurred within ten days of each other.[34] Should hot air be preferable to hydrogen? Lavoisier arbitrated like a true Solomon; the Montgolfiers' tech-nique with its simplicity and rapidity had great advantages for civil uses; but inflammable air made it possible to use smaller aerostats for an equivalent load, required no work from its passengers, and seemed to be much better adapted to scientific uses, such as meteorological observations.[35]

The general usefulness of aerostats was beginning to be explored. The Montgolfiers suggested: "They could lift weights to certain heights; they could cross over mountain peaks or reach heretofore unattainable ones; they could descend into valleys or otherwise inaccessible spots, and, at night, they could be used to raise beacons that would convey various signals whether on land or at sea."[36]

The Academy of Science also had its ideas: "The aerostat could be used in many ways for the study of physics, such as learning more about the velocities and directions of atmospheric winds, or carrying electroscopes to altitudes higher than those that can be reached by kites; finally, as we have already said, they could reach the upper cloud regions where one could observe meteors." [37]

The Academy awarded the Montgolfiers a prize of 600 livres ($24,000) and decided that the memoir reporting their experiments would be published in the *Recueil des Savants Etrangers*. But since expenses for further study and experiments surpassed its means, the king was asked to take over some of the costs. The royal power agreed but insisted on military applications, and soon conflicts of authority with the Academy cropped up. After delicate negotiations between the duc de La Rochefoucauld and the baron de Breteuil, a settlement was reached. The Montgolfier Commission of the Academy had made its points. On December 23 it was succeeded by the Aerostats Commission made up of Lavoisier, Condorcet, Brisson, La Rochefoucauld, the Abbé Bossut, Le Roy, Claude Louis Berthollet, and Charles Augustin Coulomb.

During the first meeting on the 27th, Lavoisier defined the priorities. The first was to reduce the weight and permeability of the covering of the balloons and to improve its resistance. Monge and Hollenveiger proposed parchment softened by soaking in soapy water, scratched, and greased with a mixture of spermaceti and almond oil. Charles used a silk cloth coated with elastic gum dissolved in linseed oil. Nicolas Fortin suggested lining the insides with a very thin sheet of tin. Lavoisier and Berthollet proposed a double thickness of woven silk coated with a varnish: "Birdlime used for catching birds has been successfully tested; this substance dissolves with effervescence in linseed oil, and the result is an excellent varnish, as flexible as elastic gum." [38]

A way still had to be found for controlling the rise and descent of the balloons without having to dump ballast or waste gas. In his "Memoir on the Equilibrium of Aerostatic Machines," Meusnier described a means of controlling their altitude by inflating or deflating a small balloon filled with atmospheric air and placed within the larger balloon filled with hydrogen. To steer the balloons, he recommended using elongated aerostats, propelled and directed by revolving oars. "One cannot hope to lead them in a direction opposing the wind, but it is quite probable that one could follow an oblique line that would diverge no more than 15 to 20 degrees from the direction of a moderate wind. With a given wind, one could go where one wanted within a quarter-circle of the compass." [39]

In Dijon, Guyton de Morveau placed sails, similar to those used on boats, on his balloon measuring 350 m3. It had oars, a rudder, and small sails interspersed among the suspension shrouds. On April 25, 1784 he attempted a flight with a specific course. Departing from the main square of Dijon, in front of the cathedral, at the foot of the highest tower, the balloon was driven downward by wind gusts before it could get aloft. The situation immediately became dangerous. The aeronauts could not communicate, even by signs, with their assistants on the ground, who were responsible for casting off. They decided to dump all the available ballast. The assistants, dragged along by the combined forces of the wind and the balloon, eventually released the ropes, and the balloon instantly shot up above the spires of Saint-Bénigne and flew away. After a flight of one hour, as the sun was setting, the balloon began to deflate, and it was time to land. The navigators estimated that they were near Auxonne.

We decided to use all our rigging to guide ourselves toward this point. But the bal-loon had been badly damaged by the wind blast we had experienced at the beginning. The rudder was dislocated, one of the oars had been broken at its neck and had fallen off as soon as we had tried to use it to fly away from Dijon. The other oar on the same side had become entangled in one of the four large ropes and we had had to cut it off. Consequently, we had left only two oars which, since they were on the same side, were absolutely useless during most of our smooth flight."[40]

A light wind arose, carrying them along toward the east and bringing them closer to their destination. Since the balloon was deflating, all the bal-last had to be unloaded so as to cushion the landing. Finally, the gondola alit lightly on a copse, but only a second later it bounced upward. The crew had to hang on to tree branches to hold it down and avoid being thrown onto the surrounding trees. After their calls for help, several peasants approached uneasily and knelt down before the balloon. A bolder one declared that he would gladly help the passengers if they promised to do him no harm. The experiment was over. It had been an outright success.

Incorrigible, Guyton started over again on June 12, 1784, in a balloon filled with hydrogen. With a light wind blowing from north-north-east, he managed to steer his balloon and land at Etrevaux, twenty kilometers to the east of Dijon. Lavoisier commended his feat but, like Kirwan, he thought that these kinds of experiments were no longer suitable to Guyton de Mor-veau's age or condition, and "should be left to young physicists."[41]

But the real priority was to find a practical, reliable, and economical method for producing hydrogen. As early as December 6, Lavoisier and Ber-thollet had brought the problem before the Academy. The technique used was actually rudimentary. Into a barrel filled with iron filings, one inserted a pipe carrying sulfuric acid and water; the hydrogen formed was carried into the balloon by another pipe. But the reaction produced a large amount of water vapor that also went into the balloon, where it condensed and added to the weight of the balloon. If the balloon was made of paper, the vapor softened the covering, which became porous and hence allowed gas to escape.

Bergman had pointed out shortly before in his *Dissertatio chemica de analysi ferri* that there was another method for producing hydrogen from iron filings. Through simple exposure to water, the filings would become oxidized and discharge a great amount of hydrogen. Laplace stated that when the water was heated the yield was higher, but it still remained low. Lavoisier, however, was looking for a means of mass production of hydrogen. With Meusnier, he studied another technique that consisted of decomposing the water vapor by having it pass over an incandescent iron bar. Finally, on April 21, 1784, they produced hydrogen by having water pass drop by drop through an iron gun barrel heated to incandescence. The tests, carried out in the Arsenal laboratory, were closely linked with the program of experiments on the analysis and synthesis of water. In decomposing, the water discharged two gases, hydrogen and oxygen, but in these conditions only hydrogen was recuperated.

The Analysis and Synthesis of Water

Lavoisier, assisted by Meusnier and Berthollet, then had the instrument maker Pierre Mégnie construct sophisticated equipment, a large combustion flask and two large gasometers. Arthur Young, given the privilege of visiting the laboratory, was full of admiration for the equipment as well as for the apartment:

In the apparatus for aerial experiments, nothing makes so great a figure as the machine for burning inflammable and vital air, to make or deposit water; it is a splendid machine. Three vessels are held in suspension with indexes for marking the immediate variations of their weights; two, that are as large as half hogsheads, contain the one inflammable, the other the vital air, and a tube of communication passes to the third, were the two airs unite and burn; by contrivances, too complex to describe without plates, the loss of weight of the two airs, as indicated by their respective balances, equal at every moment to the gain in the third vessel from the formation or deposition of the water, it not being yet ascertained whether the water be actually made or deposited. If accurate (of which I must confess I have little conception), it is a noble machine. M. Lavoisier, when the structure of it was commended, said, *Mais oui, Monsieur, et même par un artiste Français*! with an accent of voice that admitted their general inferiority to ours.[42]

From February 27 to March 1, 1785 Lavoisier carried out the great experiment on the analysis and synthesis of water. It was witnessed by more than thirty scientists, physicists, surveyors and naturalists and supervised by a commission named by the Academy of Science. At first Lavoisier and Meusnier extracted the two constituent gases from water. The water, contained in a funnel with a bent joint closed by a faucet, dripped drop by drop and ran through an iron gun barrel heated to incandescence and became decomposed into hydrogen and oxygen. A water pneumatic trough collected the hydrogen; the oxygen was not kept. A part of the water vapor escaped during decomposition and was condensed in a coil and ended up in a flask. The oxygen, produced separately by heating calcined mercury was collected in a gasometer. For the synthesis, the large glass flask with three pipes received the oxygen and hydrogen simultaneously. An electric spark produced the combustion of the two gases. Five and a half ounces of water were collected.

Lavoisier could then assert that "water is not an element, that it is on the contrary composed of two very distinct principles, the base of vital air and that of hydrogen gas; and that these two principles enter into an approximate relationship of 85 to 15 respectively."[43] He had attained a double goal. One, practical, perfected a method for a large scale production of hydrogen to be used for inflating aerostats. The other, theoretical, confirmed the validity of his previous analysis by synthesis. He could not resist the pleasure of giving instructions to others:

Since these are the only means that can disclose the principles of natural substances, the importance for chemists of using them in their experiments cannot be too strongly emphasized. It is true that by insisting on measuring and calculating everything, one makes the chemical operations more difficult and longer. But one is well compensated for the increased work by the immense advantage of never having to retrace one's steps.[44]

The composition of water had been definitely established by the work of Cavendish, Lavoisier, and Monge, but on April 29 James Watt claimed priority for the discovery before the Royal Society. He accused "those rich people, members of Academies," of scientific piracy, and presented personal theories devoid of experimental demonstration and entirely impregnated with phlogiston. They were in sharp contrast to the daring and innovative character of Lavoisier's conceptions. His text simply revealed the determination with which all scientists claimed the paternity of discovery. Lavoisier, who was no less touchy in this domain, felt obligated to make a clarification:

The composition of water had first been suspected after the observation made by several French and English physicists that, in burning vital air and hydrogen gas together, a considerable amount of water resulted. Cavendish, of the Royal Society of London, was, according to Blagden, secretary of the same Society, the first person to observe this. But he did not go as far as concluding that water was composed of these two substances. Besides, it is certain that Lavoisier, Laplace and Monge had not been informed of Cavendish's work when they undertook at the same time, during June 1783, the same experiment, which they carried out, without communication of the results, by different means.[45]

A century later, Berthelot will express a moderate judgment:

Although Lavoisier did not fully initiate the facts, although Cavendish preceded him
in this regard, although Monge and Priestley participated in their progressive study,
it is incontestable that Lavoisier was the first to see the theory clearly. It was a theory
that their earlier work on the role of oxygen in the formation of oxides and acids had
led all the enlightened chemists of the epoch to sense. But it was Lavoisier who first
dared to announce clearly and publicly the composition of water. It was a truth that
became one of the cornerstones of chemical science."[46]

Ecological Visions

In 1785 Meusnier conceived of a huge aerostat capable of going round the
world, with a crew of twenty-four men, a staff of six officers, and supplies
to last sixty days. The estimated cost reached 3,300,000 livres ($132 million).
Monge, Meusnier's former teacher and friend, presented the project to the
king. "Louis XVI then wanted to see the overall plan and hear its author. He
was enchanted as he had been by the first balloon flight, and he would have
backed the project had it not been for the enormous expense it would have
entailed."[47]

Then Meusnier pulled out of his portfolio a more modest plan, a balloon
for scientific observation with a crew of six men. It would cost only 370,000
livres ($14.8 million). But the king had other concerns: his financial straits,
the affair of the queen's necklace, and the project for the around-the-world
voyage of Jean François de Galaup, comte de La Pérouse.

Lavoisier himself was completely absorbed in a great number of subjects:
the polemic over the construction of a toll wall around Paris, the meetings
of the Committee on Agriculture, the project for the mineralogical atlas of
France that had re-emerged, and the battle over phlogiston that was just beginning. As for Meusnier, whose special leave had expired, he was transferred
to Cherbourg in August. He was replaced by a new disciple, Armand Seguin,
a talented but opportunistic young chemist who launched himself into a profound study of respiration.

On February 15, 1785 the Society of Medicine asked Lavoisier to speak to
its members on a subject he knew well, the salubrity of air in public places. To
interest an audience of doctors, he needed to take up practical questions. What
alterations took place in air during respiration? What was the effect on the
lungs? What were the health disorders that could result from it? What methods could be used to prevent or treat them? In his paper, entitled "Changes in
Breathed Air," Lavoisier presented the doctors with a new idea: respiration is

not only a combustion of carbon resulting in the formation of carbonic gas, but also a combustion of hydrogen resulting in the formation of water. He announced a series of memoirs on the subject and then returned to the central theme of his talk: "The salubrity of air is bound to be more or less reduced in theaters, public meeting halls, hospital wards and all places where large numbers of people congregate, especially if the air circulates slowly and with difficulty."[48] To be salubrious, air should not vary significantly from proportions that he estimated to be those of atmospheric air: 25 percent vital air, 75 percent nitrogen.[49] Hence, the importance of adequate ventilation.

His vision of the risks of contagious diseases was prophetic:

It is frightening to think that in a large gathering the air breathed by each individual has passed and repassed a great many times—either wholly or partially—through the lungs of all the audience and has been laden with more or less putrid exhalations. But what is the nature of these emanations? To what extent are they different from one subject to another, in the elderly or the young, the ill or healthy? What are the illnesses likely to be spread by this kind of communication? What precautions could be taken to neutralize or destroy the dangerous influence of these emanations? There is perhaps not one of these points whose examination cannot be subjected to experiment, and there is nothing more important for the preservation of the human species.[50]

Lavoisier's conclusion sounds very modern and could be endorsed by today's ecologists: "All arts move rapidly toward perfection; but the art of living in society, of preserving the vigor and health of large numbers of individuals sharing limited space, of making large towns more salubrious and contagious diseases less communicable is still in its infancy."[51]

10

A Senior Civil Servant

L AVOISIER NOW ENTERED A NEW PHASE of his career as a top-ranking civil servant. At the Academy of Science, of which he was made director in 1785, he was responsible for the most important questions: those with political, economic, or social dimensions, such as the Mesmer affair, the La Pérouse expedition, the transfer of the Hôtel-Dieu.

At the General Farm, he was involved in the major decisions concerning the manufacture and sale of tobacco, and the import duties on all merchandise entering Paris. He was in charge of the accounts of the salt-works in Franche-Comté, Lorraine, and the Trois-Evêchés. He took a personal initiative fraught with consequences in proposing the construction of a customs wall around Paris. But above all, he was appointed by d'Ormesson to the Committee of Administration, the most important of the committees of the Farm, which negotiated the amount of the lease with the Controller General of Finance. "This Company of forty associates has only six who work," the marquis Paulmy d'Argenson remarked, "the others understand absolutely nothing about it and are good only for collecting their profits."[1] No doubt, Lavoisier belonged to the former group.

Mesmer's Tub

The Mesmer affair opened a scientific debate that has never ended for a number of philosophers, psychoanalysts, and psychologists. Fashionable Parisians had begun to frequent the salon of a Viennese doctor named Frantz Anton Mesmer, who, since February 1778, had claimed to cure all illnesses by animal magnetism. According to him, all individuals possessed, in varying degrees, a magnetic fluid which was spread throughout the universe and was transmittable from one person to another. Since he possessed this fluid in abundance, he could pass it on to his patients with a beneficial effect for their health. He had decorated his mansion on the Place Vendôme with refined taste. There, in semi-darkness, his patients inhaled the most exquisite perfumes while listening to soothing music. Enthroned in the middle of the room, surrounded by armchairs, was the wooden tub that supposedly produced the magnetic fluid. Filled with water, crushed glass, and iron filings, it was covered by a wooden lid containing several holes. From each hole emerged an iron bar bent at a right angle. There was one for each patient, who applied it to the ailing part of his or her body. The participants held hands so as to form a chain and transmit the fluid to each other. The method was said to allow both the diagnosis and treatment of any illness and required no particular preparation, except "extreme cleanliness and abstinence from tobacco."

Individual treatments involved a more elaborate technique. The doctor and his patient were seated face to face, with the former squeezing the thighs of the latter—most often a woman—between his knees, while his hands caressed the clothing, eyes, cheeks and arms of the patient. Then he lightly applied his hands to the abdomen and left them there for a moment.[2]

The duchesse de Chaulnes, a close friend of Queen Marie Antoinette, and the princesse de Lamballe, the Grand Master of the Scottish Lodge, had found this therapy miraculous, and their friends were all rushing to follow their example.

Mesmer's success was so great that he recruited a pupil, Dr. Charles Deslon, who replaced him when he was absent and began giving public lectures on magnetism. In the meantime, the master became increasingly demanding, insisting that the king give him a château with its lands. Otherwise, he threatened, he would abandon France and its ailing citizens, "regardless of the loss to humanity."

The baron Louis Augustin Le Tonnelier de Breteuil, Secretary of State for the Royal Household, offered him 20,000 livres ($800,000) of income and an annual salary of 10,000, but Mesmer refused it and left Paris for Spain. After his friends, including La Fayette, had raised the fabulous sum of 340,000 livres ($13.6 million) on his behalf, he finally returned to Paris.

Seeking acceptance by the learned institutions of the capital, Mesmer successively tried to obtain it from the Academy of Science, the Society of Medicine, and its rival, the Faculty of Medicine. He obtained only a threefold rebuff.

Berthollet attended his course on magnetism but saw "nothing in the convulsions, spasms, indeed outbursts, that Mesmer claims are produced by the magnetic processes, that cannot be entirely attributed to the imagination.[3]

But Mesmer's success grew even greater. Imitators opened clinico-magnetic consulting rooms and dormitories where the moral climate was questionable. The government began to worry, and the official representatives of science and medicine felt obliged to protect their authority. In the name of the Academy of Science, Lavoisier insisted:

The government cannot appear unconcerned about a question interesting the health and life of citizens, and since, according to Mesmer's system, anyone can cure a patient simply by practicing magnetism, the entire science of medicine becomes useless; the schools should be closed, the system of instruction changed, the institutions considered as repositories of medical knowledge destroyed, and everything limited to the study of magnetism.[4]

Given the rivalries among the scholarly societies, on April 2, 1784 Breteuil created two committees to study mesmerism. One committee was composed of members of the Academy of Science—Lavoisier, Franklin, Bailly, and Le Roy—and of the Paris Faculty of Medicine—Jean d'Arcet, Joseph Ignace Guillotin, Jean Borie, and Sallin. The other was made up exclusively of members of the Society of Medicine: Pierre Isaac Poissonnier, Mauduyt de La Varenne, François Andry, Caille, and Antoine Laurent de Jussieu.

Franklin was housebound in Passy with gout and Lavoisier was the prime mover in this investigation. An expert in accounting and political arithmetic, he spontaneously adopted the same approach in the scientific domain and, for the benefit of his medical colleagues, drew up recommendations that prefigured the modern methodology of clinical trials:

The art of drawing conclusions after experiments and observations consists in evaluating probabilities and estimating whether they are sufficiently significant or repeated to constitute proof. This kind of calculation is more complicated and difficult than one might think. It requires great wisdom, and in general is beyond the forces of the common run of men.

It is on errors in this kind of calculation that the success of charlatans, sorcerers and alchemists is based, and that in earlier times was based the power of magicians, enchanters and all who have either deluded themselves or sought to take advantage of public gullibility.

It is in medicine that the difficulty of evaluating probabilities is greatest. Since the life principle in animals is an always active force continuously tending to overcome obstacles, since nature left to itself cures many illnesses, then when remedies are used it is infinitely difficult to determine what can be attributed to nature and what to the remedies. Also, whereas most people consider the cure as proof of the effectiveness of a remedy, a wise man regards it as the result of a lesser or greater degree of probability, and this probability can become certainty only after large numbers of related facts have been collected.[5]

The committee members took seriously the testing on themselves and volunteers of the effects of magnetism. By magnetizing patients while facing them, results were obtained that could not be reproduced by magnetizing them without their knowing it. Other subjects experienced the same effects when they were only led to believe that they were being magnetized.

Lavoisier and his colleagues were categorical: "Having demonstrated that the imagination without magnetism produces convulsions and that magnetism without imagination produces nothing, they have concluded that there is no proof of the existence of animal magnetic fluid."[6] This is what they had predicted, and for them as for the general public the affair was closed. But on August 11, 1784 a secret report written by Bailly was sent to the king. The effectiveness of the method could well have a cause affecting morality:

This cause is the influence given by nature to one sex over another to hold and arouse it. It is always men who magnetize women. The relations established then are undoubtedly only those of an ailing woman to her doctor, but this doctor is a man. Regardless of the stage of an illness, it does not strip us of our sex, or entirely shield us from the power of the opposite one. Illnesses can weaken these impressions without ever destroying them. Moreover, most of the women drawn to magnetism are not really ill. Many of them come for treatment simply because they have nothing else to do and are looking for distraction. Others, who may suffer some minor discomfort, nevertheless retain their freshness and strength: their senses are intact; their youth has kept all its sensibility. They have enough charm to act on the doctor; and enough health to react to the doctor; thus the danger is reciprocal.

The sustained proximity, the indispensable touching, the communication of personal heat, the meeting of eyes, are the known ways of Nature and the means that it has always used for inevitably bringing about the communication of sensations and affection. The man who magnetizes usually has the woman's knees clasped in his. Consequently, the knees and the lower parts of the two bodies are in contact. The hand is pressed against the hypochondrium, and sometimes still lower on the ovaries.[7] Thus the touch is applied to many parts of the body, and in particular to the area of its most sensitive parts. Often the man, having his left hand thus applied, passes the right hand behind the body of the woman. Both parties then move toward each other so as to favor this twofold touching; they become as close as possible, face almost touches face, and they inhale each other's breath. All physical impressions are instantaneously shared, and the mutual sexual attraction is bound to act with all its force. It is not surprising that the senses are aroused. The imagination, acting at the same time, spreads a certain disorder in the system. It suspends judgment, and distracts attention. The women cannot be aware of what they are experiencing, they ignore their state.

The doctors of the committee, present and attentive to the treatment, carefully observed what took place. Leading up to this kind of climax, the face gradually became redder, the eyes fiery. It is the sign by which nature announces desire. The woman lowered her head and covered her eyes with her hand. The usual sense of modesty was prevailing without her realizing it, and prompted her to hide herself. However, the crisis continued and the eye became cloudy. It was an unequivocal sign of the total disturbance of the senses. This disarray went unnoticed by the one experiencing it, but it did not escape the doctors' watchful eyes. Once this sign appeared, the eyelids became humid, breathing was rapid and broken, the chest rose and fell rapidly. Convulsions, as well as rapid and brusk movements either of limbs or the whole body set in. With vivacious and sensitive women, the final stage, the culmination of the gentlest of emotions, was often a convulsion, followed by langor, exhaustion and a kind of falling asleep of the senses, that is a necessary rest after strong agitation.

The proof that this convulsive state, however extraordinary it might appear to those observing it, was not painful, but only natural for those experiencing it, was that once it had ceased, it left no distressing trace. Recalling it was not unpleasant, the women felt better and had no reluctance to repeat the experience.[8]

For Lavoisier and his colleagues, the explanation was clear. It was sheer charlatanism. They reported officially to the Academy in 1784:

Nothing proves the existence of animal magnetic fluid; this inexistant fluid is consequently useless. The violent effects that one observes in public treatment stem from the touching, from the activated imagination and that unconscious imitation that causes us to repeat what strikes our senses in spite of ourselves.[9]

Deslon published a refutation that merited attention:

There will henceforth remain only one problem to resolve. What does cause these effects? Is it magnetism? Or else must one add to the pharmacopoeia of medicine the three new means that the committee members have come up with to explain them: *imagination, imitation* or *touching*? While waiting for scientists to agree on this major question, one hundred eleven sick persons, who are not afraid to speak out, inform all those who wish to hear that a new blessing has been brought to men, and that one obtains in magnetism rooms the healing of illnesses that have resisted the art of medicine.[10]

Mesmerism was supported by a large part of public opinion. Numerous pamphlets appeared and the Academy tried to make it look ridiculous. Lavoisier proposed to Breteuil that he send up a balloon, carrying a dummy wearing a wooden tub on its head, and have it drop anti-Mesmer leaflets.

A. L. de Jussieu was the only one of the members of the committee to express a nuanced opinion. Certainly he condemned the magic aspects of the magnetism, but considered that the physical influence of a man on another was a reality. The results observed on a subject in a coma, a blind person, or a patient whose back was turned could not be explained by imagination alone. "The medicine of touching has been practiced in all times and in all nations; but left in unsuitable hands, administered unmethodically, relegated to particular and popular means, it has always languished in obscurity."[11] His opinion, which opened the way for psychoanalysis, suggestion, and hypnosis, would make him a hero to nonconformist doctors.

The dispute took a new direction, however, when Mesmer's defenders

Jacques Pierre Brissot de Warville, Jean Jacques d'Eprémesnil, and Jean Louis Carra set off a genuine cultural revolution. Mesmer's tub, like Marat's optical theories, began to provoke a questioning of official scientists and the Academy, who were accused of tyranny. Only public opinion should decide on the merits of a scientist, declared J. P. Brissot:

The scientific empire should contain no despots, aristocrats or electors. It should offer the image of a perfect republic. In it, the most useful merit is simply to be honored by it. To accept that a despot, aristocrats or electors are supposed to certify genius by their seal of approval, is to violate the nature of things, the freedom of the human mind. It would conspire against public opinion which alone has the right to crown genius. It would be to introduce a revolting despotism, to make a tyrant of each elector and slaves of all the other scientists.[12]

Thus began a campaign of which Dr. Jean Paul Marat, the painter Jacques Louis David, and Sébastien Roch Nicolas de Chamfort would be the spokesmen. They did not support Mesmer, but they agreed with him to criticize the Academicians, who were reproached by turns for their dependence on royal authority, their elitism, their mandarin power, and their conformism. Marat lit into their inefficiency:

They get up late, spend the morning having breakfast, reading the *Journal de Paris*, and receiving or paying calls. They dine in restaurants and afterwards they go to the theater and then to an intimate supper. And if they have been able to find a few free moments, they have used them to stock their memory with the latest news as topics for their social chatter. This is virtually what their daily life is like from one year to the next?[13]

But the Academicians also had their defenders, among whom was Condorcet, Secretary of the Academy of Science:

The primary task of academies is to serve as a permanent barrier to charlatanism in all its forms, and that is why so many people complain about them; the second task is to maintain good scientific methods and see to it that no branch of science is ever completely abandoned. A very important third task is to become independent of popular opinion without disdaining it. A chemist, an anatomist, a geometer, a member of the Academy, has no need to perform tricks of charlatans to enjoy the reputation of a scientist among the ignorant. It is up to his works to earn him celebrity or glory.[14]

Director of the Academy

In 1785 Lavoisier was named Director of the Academy for one year. He insisted that he had absolutely no desire to play the tyrant and that his peers had the right to choose their administrators. He made sure that they approved of his nomination, especially since a clash of authority had already opposed him to the President of the Academy, the duc Jean Paul François d'Ayen.

The duc, an amiable and powerful nobleman, held open house every Sunday for the Academicians and foreign scientists passing through Paris. "The French noblemen who apply themselves to the sciences," the Swedish astronomer Lexell remarked, "are much less pretentious than the scientists themselves. In paying their compliments to the scientists, they do not take into account their quality; on the contrary, they consider themselves honored when the scientists come to call on them." [15]

The duc had, however, developed with his friend La Rochefoucauld-Liancourt, and without consulting Lavoisier, a project for reforming the Academy. To satisfy the repeated requests of numerous candidates for membership, they would have created an additional fourteen permanent places and eight for associates. The king was to provide 15,000 livres ($600,000) to this end, and two new classes—one for general physics and natural history, one for mineralogy—were to be added to those already existing.

But according to Lavoisier, the Academy already had too many members (more than eighty, including the associates), which explained, he felt, its tumultuous meetings. Moreover, in his opinion, increasing the number of places would inevitably result in their depreciation. There had never before been so much pretension to knowledge and so few scientists worthy of entering the Academy. "Thus it is not the Academy that is lacking in scientists, but qualified scientists who are lacking. And if, in these circumstances, you have to make a certain number of appointments, then you have no choice but to call on mediocre talents, on that half-knowledge, more dangerous than ignorance, and the charlatanism and intrigue that accompany it." [16]

On April 13 he formed a special committee composed of thirteen members. [17] He suggested an alternative plan that would create the two additional classes, but abolish the posts of assistants and keep only three permanent members and three associates for each class. Instead of six classes of seven Academicians, there would be eight classes of six. Hence the increase would amount to only six posts, and given that five were supernumeraries, it would actually amount to only one.

Finally, as a quite spectacular innovation, he called for a vote: "Was his plan advantageous or not to the sciences and the Academy?" [18] There were eleven votes for the plan, two against. Lavoisier had won. The creation of eight posts for associate Academicians living in the kingdom was unanimously rejected. However, the duc d'Ayen and the duc de La Rochefoucauld made it known that these deliberations could not be binding for the Academy, since the special committee had been only an advisory group.

On April 16, without waiting, Lavoisier transmitted his counter-proposition to the baron de Breteuil and asked him to speed up the decision so as to avoid complaints of string-pulling and preferential treatment. The same day, he received from Breteuil's assistant a letter of apology. Since he knew that Lavoisier was a touchy man, jealous of his independence, he was conciliatory. Lavoisier, in turn, could also be diplomatic with the powerful: "There is perhaps less division and more harmony in the Academy than you have been led to believe," he replied to Breteuil. "The peaceful manner in which everything was carried out, the facility and speed with which the votes were cast, are proof of this. But one point on which we all agree is that since the beginning of the scientific revival, scientific groups have never received benefits as numerous and significant as under your ministry."[19]

Lavoisier fulfilled his functions as director with very great efficiency. He was involved with choosing the papers to be presented at the public sessions and the awarding of prizes. He kept after Condorcet, who tended to neglect his duties as Permanent Secretary and did not always meet the deadline for delivering the texts for the eulogies and the *History of the Academy*. He called meetings of the committee members responsible for compiling the instructions for La Pérouse's voyage, and obtained from the General Farm useful information on the French kingdom, such as the state of navigable rivers and canals. Bombarded by to many candidacies at the Academy of Science, he had to elaborate strategies acceptable to all parties. He promoted the membership of Jean Baptiste Charles Meusnier, the Abbé René Juste Haüy, and the geographer Jean Nicolas Buache de La Neuville. On the other hand, he held back the rise of the industrialist Jacques Constantin Périer, who had established the Creusot Company and the Chaillot Foundry. Meusnier's candidacy was supported at the Academy by La Rochefoucauld et Condorcet. Périer was a protégé of the duc d'Orléans and the baron de Breteuil, who, as Secretary of State for the Royal Household, had the final decision. Caught between his feeling of justice, his friendship for Meusnier, and the strong backing given to an overly powerful candidate, Lavoisier was hesitating:

I continue to believe that if rigorous justice requires that the younger M. Meusnier, rather than M. Périer, be third associate, then these principles of justice can be balanced by a great many considerations that the duc de La Rochefoucauld and M. de Condorcet will understand better than I. And if there is favor in what M. Meusnier proposes, one can justify it by solid motives, that will not be humiliating for M. Périer. In any case, the latter will have advanced one rank. Why should he alone, who entered the Academy as a supernumerary and almost against the wishes of the Academy, advance two?"[20]

In addition to his various jobs at the General Farm, the Gunpowder Administration, the laboratory, and his social obligations, Lavoisier had to present, in accordance with a complex ceremony, the new Academicians — three in January, three in July — to the royal family and ministers. Besides all that, he had to keep abreast of the scientific work in progress and supervise the activities of the different classes and committees. Thus he was involved in two government projects in the hands of the Academy, the transfer of the Hôtel-Dieu and the Lapérouse expedition.

The Transfer of the Hôtel-Dieu

In 1785 the baron de Breteuil reopened the debate on hospitals that had been in abeyance for four years. He had Jacques René Tenon study the possibility of transferring the Hôtel-Dieu to a site away from the heart of Paris. Tenon conducted a very detailed survey of hospitals in France, England, and Italy, found out a great deal about hygiene, and wrote a memoir that is a masterpiece of clarity and modernism. He based on man's measurements those of his environment. He calculated the ideal dimensions of a hospital ward on the basis of the respiratory needs of the patients and was particularly concerned with ventilation in dormitories.

His memoir was accompanied by an architectural project by Bernard Poyet who proposed constructing a new Hôtel-Dieu on the Ile aux Cygnes, a small island in the middle of the Seine, opposite the Champ de Mars. The hospital was to have a circular form with a large central courtyard, on the model of the Coliseum in Rome. The estimated cost was 12 million livres ($480 million).

The Academy, asked to give its opinion, appointed a committee headed by Lavoisier. It included Darcet, Bailly, Laplace, Coulomb, and three doctors: Tenon, Louis Jean Marie Daubenton, and Joseph Marie François de Lassone. They set right to work, but in spite of appeals to the archbishop, the committee members were refused access to the Hôtel-Dieu by the administration. They were forced to meet the doctors on the outside of the hospital, and to base their statistics on birth, baptismal and death certificates from Paris and its suburbs. Bailly wrote:

For more than half a century, the transfer of the Hôtel-Dieu has been recommended by all enlightened persons. The present location of the hospital in the center of the city, the small space it occupies, the sight of wards where several patients are crammed into the same bed, the peculiarity that all the vices of the regime have established, add to the suffering and anguish of the poor, forced to seek refuge there. In a word, there exists a terrifying mortality rate that is out of all proportion with that of most large European hospitals. All these are ills on which it is impossible to look without heart-break and indignation.[21]

The Hôtel-Dieu cared for three to four thousand patients each day in twenty-five wards containing a total of 1,219 beds. The number of patients, however, could rise to as high as six to seven thousand during epidemics. Several patients—three or four, indeed, sometimes five or six—lay in the same bed and hence became overheated and could neither move nor sleep. The transmission of contagious and parasitic diseases was naturally facilitated by these conditions: "A sick person just admitted to the hospital is often placed in the bed and sheets of a scabies infected corpse."[22]

The operating rooms were exposed to the dust of the street and the din of traffic; furthermore, they were poorly ventilated. Lavoisier estimated that patients could hardly find the vital minimum of necessary air: "A man could not live more than twenty-four hours if he had only three cubic feet of air that was not being replaced."[23]

All the patients were mixed together, the contagious and the insane lay alongside all the others. The result was that the illnesses lasted twice as long at the Hôtel-Dieu as at the Charité hospital, and the death rate was twice as high.

And, finally, the buildings had been constructed on stocks of combustible material, which meant living with the constant fear of a fire like the one in 1772. "Our conclusion is that this structure needs to be reformed, set up and operated on better principles, on a much bigger site," the committee wrote. 'The Hôtel-Dieu, as it is, is inadequate, inconvenient, and eminently unhealthy. The necessity of its transfer to a more suitable place has been invincibly demonstrated."[24]

They recommended that it be abolished completely and replaced by four smaller hospitals: Saint-Louis in the North, Sainte-Anne in the South, la Roquette in the East, and in the West, the abbey of Sainte Périne de Chaillot or a building to be constructed on lands belonging to the Ecole Militaire. They had chosen these four places at some distance from the Seine so as to avoid the fog and humidity common to its vicinity. Moreover, it was for this reason that they had rejected the Ile aux Cygnes as a possible location. Drinkable water would be brought to the hospitals by fire engines.

Some people criticized the plan for four separate hospitals, arguing that the ill risked being carried all over Paris before finding a place. The committee answered that it was simply a matter of organization:

To be admitted to one of the hospitals, one will do exactly what one does to be admitted at the hospital of la Charité: send somebody to find out if there is a vacant bed. But also there would be a clearing house in the center of Paris. Every evening each hospital would submit a report on its situation to this office and, by consulting the register, one could find out where the patient should be sent.[25]

The proposed organizational plan insisted on the necessity of creating isolated pavilions for contagious illnesses and wards with adequate air and light, and, in general, of grouping patients according to the nature of their illnesses.

For the first time, men of science defined the mission of the hospital as one reserved to the treatment of sick people: "Hospitals are tools or, if you wish, machines for treating the ill," Tenon wrote. Louis XVI adopted these conclusions on June 22, 1787. The Academy of Architecture organized a competition for the construction of the four hospitals. Breteuil started a fund-raising campaign to finance the project but ran into resistance from the Church, and left the government. The Hospitals Committee was dissolved, and everything was left hanging.

The La Pérouse Expedition

In 1785 it was the La Pérouse expedition, intended to circumnavigate the globe, that was Louis XVI's major undertaking. The King had himself written very precise instructions, specifying the itinerary and the political and commercial objectives.

The determination of the scientific objectives had been entrusted to the Academy of Science and its associates, the Society of Medicine and the Jardin du Roi. Lavoisier had planned an encyclopedic program encompassing physics, astronomy, geography, mineralogy, the natural sciences, botany, medicine, pharmacy, and meteorology. Condorcet, Buffon, and Jussieu had decided which scientists would go along.

The best navigational instruments were given to La Pérouse: a mobile quarter-circle made by Claude Langlois, an ebony and ivory octant, a sextant made by Edward Nairne in London, a *cercle de réflexion de Borda* made by Etienne Lenoir, and marine clocks made by Ferdinand Berthoud. "If we live up to the minister's expectations," La Pérouse wrote, "this voyage will certainly be remembered by posterity and our names will linger on over the centuries long after those of Cook and Magellan."[26]

Lavoisier personally tended to a subject especially close to his heart: the method of distilling sea water with a cucurbit, a large retort so named because of its cucumber shaped form. The production of fresh water during long sea voyages by desalination still provoked debate. Lavoisier felt that objections were absurd and expressed an interesting idea for the times:

Water, from the sea or any other place where it is spread over a considerable surface, is carried up to the atmosphere in the form of vapors by the action of heat. These vapors are subsequently condensed by the coolness of the atmosphere; they collect and fall back to earth in the form of rain and dew, from which all springs, fountains and rivers are formed. The process of artificial distillation in no way differs from that of nature except for the small scale of the operation.[27]

The most developed and solid distilling apparatus, that of Dr. Pierre Isaac Poissonier, general director of hospitals in ports and colonies, had been tested in 1763 on the vessel *Les Six Corps*, while La Pérouse was on board. He had deemed the results satisfactory, and consequently Poissonnier had received a pension of 6,000 livres ($240,000). After 1764 the distilling apparatus became standard equipment aboard ships. But its functioning posed the problem of an adequate supply of firewood. The comte de Bougainville had observed during his return voyage from Tahiti that when water began to grow scarce, so did the wood.

In February 1773 Magellan sent Trudaine de Montigny the description of an apparatus designed by Dr. William Irvine and used by Captain Phipps during his trip to the North Pole. Trudaine de Montigny and Pierre Etienne Bourgeois de Boynes, Minister of the Navy, commissioned Lavoisier to make a model in tin. Improving the original, Lavoisier, for 650 livres ($26,000), produced a perfect still that corresponded to a set objective; it used only a small quantity of charcoal and gave twelve to fifteen pints of fresh water per hour; this water could be used, "like the purest water, for everything."[28] Meat and vegetables also could be cooked perfectly in it. From this model, Lavoisier made the stills destined for La Pérouse.

The tests took place on June 17, 1785 and the lieutenant general commander of the Navy declared: "The new cucurbit adapted to the kitchen of *L'Astrolabe* appears to be highly ingenious and its production is quite considerable, less often interrupted and more rapid than the one previously used. I have given orders to install the same cucurbit in the kitchen of *La Boussole*."[29] On August 1, 1785 La Pérouse sailed from Brest for his voyage around the world. He would not return, and no one would ever know just how well Lavoisier's cucurbits performed.

The Tobacco War

The grating and moistening of tobacco continued to divide the Farmers General and to stir up public opinion. Necker's efforts to transform the General Farm into a public administration led the Treasury to intervene in the quarrel that was dragging along between pro-graters and anti-graters.

In 1782 Jean François Joly de Fleury, the new Minister of Finance, enjoined the General Farm to take a position. The administrative committee of the Farm asked each of the nine correspondents of the Tobacco Commission to write a memoir and then reviewed the question on August 22. Four of the members did not take a clear stand; Gilbert Georges de Montcloux recommended that grating be forbidden in the factories; the four others— Claude François Rougeot, Nicolas Jacques Papillon d'Auteroche, Geoffroy Saint-Hilaire, and Lavoisier—were in favor of grating by the factories. M. Lavoisier has finally kicked over his father-in-law's traces, Jacques Delahante, Director of the Tobacco Committee, exclaimed triumphantly. "His memoir was not the first official tribute he had given to the grating system. He had already written, in the same spirit, a long memoir advocating a complete reorganization of tobacco sales in Paris."[30]

The committee then came to a vote. Of the eleven members, ten pronounced in favor of grating by the factories. Only one member, Paulze, was opposed. Delahante had won. He hurriedly informed the minister so as to obtain at last the authorization to organize the Farm's monopoly on grating. But by that time Fleury had left the Finance Ministry.

In 1783 Charles Alexandre de Calonne had risen to the post of Controller General of Finance, thanks to the queen's patronage. It was a nomination that caused general displeasure: "He may not have the voice of the people," it was said, "but he will have its money."[31] Calonne, by nature already little inclined to take decisions, feared the opposition of the Parlements and refused to take sides on the grating dispute. Dealing with the quarrels of the Parlements over political and religious issues gave him quite enough to do, and he left the General Farm to fight the magistracy on its own. He was facing a difficult political and financial situation. The participation of France in the American War for Independence had cost it a great deal. During the period of unofficial aid to America (1776–1778), it had supplied weapons, logistic support, technical assistance, and financial backing. The arms were shipped from Lisbon under cover of an import-export firm, the Roderigue Hortalez Company, run in fact by Pierre Augustin Caron de Beaumarchais, author of the *Barber of Seville* and the *Marriage of Figaro*. By May 2, 1776 it had already sent weapons worth a million livres. As for the financial aid, it was all the more appreciated since it was provided in coin. In a single crossing, the frigate *La Concorde* had carried a million livres in solid silver specie.

During the period of declared war (1778–1782), France had increased its aid to the rebels. The Farmers General had lent a million livres, Beaumarchais 3 million, and the king 34 million, bringing the total to 38 million.[32] In 1777 and 1778 the total French aid in currency came to about 47.5 million livres.[33] Rochambeau's expeditionary corps (8,000 men) also paid in currency for all its ammunition, food, and other supplies purchased in America, and thus brought additional economic assistance.

To establish the total amount spent by France until the peace in 1783, the costs for soldiers and officers—their salaries, weapons, and transportation—and those of constructing and maintaining the French ships involved, as well as the naval losses incurred from the war and storms, must also be added. Contemporaries estimated the total expense to be somewhere between 1 and 1.2 billion livres. Joseph Cambon, deputy at the Convention, member of the first Committee of Public Safety, and then president of the Finance Committee until 1795, went even further: "It is important to remember," he wrote, "that the war in America cost France, according to a generally accepted estimation, about 1.5 billion livres."[34] Modern authors confirm this figure, which would equal 60 billion dollars today.[35]

Bankruptcy was becoming inevitable. Certainly the American War for Independence was far from being the unique cause, but its expense and the overly clever borrowing schemes of Necker and Calonne undoubtedly accelerated the day of reckoning. Necker's ruinous borrowing (530 million livres between 1776 and 1781) and Calonne's, of an equivalent magnitude, did not suffice to compensate for these expenditures, and simply aggravated the financial crisis.

The total debt of France then reached, according to Necker, 3.4 billion livres. The best modern studies estimate the total debt to have been close to 5 billion livres, entailing an annual expense of more than 318 million livres in interest, a sum equal to the entire financial resources of the State.[36]

Unfortunately Calonne's talents were no match for the financial difficulties he had to face. Although he had a quick and open mind, an enormous capacity for work, and perfect manners and style, the concern for his own pleasures absorbed him at the expense of his concern for the State, and his methods were somewhat specious. "During the Assemblée des Notables, he used a singular ruse to dispense himself from presenting a work promised on a certain day; he simply set fire to his office at Versailles, so as to have an excuse for the delay caused by his negligence."[37]

Calonne did, however, try to re-establish financial equilibrium and reduce the deficit. The convocation of the Etats généraux, destined in principle solely to find new financial resources, had been awaited impatiently by all those who were seeking more profound reforms of society. It became inscribed in the train of events, and the French Revolution was bound to be its consequence.

Calonne obtained a considerable re-evaluation of leases from the various farms and companies. He adopted measures that reduced the severity and arbitrariness of tax collection, and proposed the elimination of aides, the salt tax, and the monopoly on the cultivation of tobacco.

The General Farm, the prime target of his reforms, wanted no part of these changes. Therefore it seized the first available pretext to revive the quarrel over grating tobacco, and thus to embarrass the minister by asking him to arbitrate. It was an inextricable question even for Lavoisier, who commented after an especially confused discussion: "It seems indispensable in the circumstances, that *M. le Contrôleur* explain himself openly—either verbally or in writing, with regard to the company."[38]

Calonne prudently dodged the issue. In a number of cities—Paris, Nancy, Metz, Dijon, Aix, Pau, Bordeaux, Montauban, Clermont-Ferrand—the General Farm went ahead and set up a new grating system without too much difficulty. But in Rouen, Montpellier, and Rennes the dealers, upset at losing a source of profit, started a vast publicity campaign, claiming that the Farmers General were trying to increase their profits at the expense of the people.

In Grenoble a parliamentary ruling forced the Farmers to accept the competition with the dealers. In Languedoc there was a succession of scandals involving cheating by tobacco dealers, followed by the complaints of the consumers and the reports and second assessments of the experts.

In Brittany, traditionally opposed to the monopoly of the Farm, and the favored region for smuggling, the quarrel was even sharper. For the Brittany magistrates, the grating issue provided a perfect occasion for defying the government. They accused the General Farm of trying to poison the citizens by selling them excessively moistened products that had fermented. "According to them, since the dealers no longer grate the tobacco, the crews of the Newfoundland fleet have been dropping like flies, and the workers in the Morlaix factory have experienced a new form of slavery."[39]

The American War for Independence, by hindering the arrival of tobacco shipments from Virginia, had prevented the General Farm from maintaining the quality of its product . According to the *Mémoires secrets* of Louis Petit de Bachaumont, the efforts of the Farm to maintain the quantity at least, by using tobacco from other sources, obtained only "grievous results and complaints throughout the country."

The quarrel dragged on. Necker got involved, and without going beyond the stage of general ideas, he recommended that the Farmers control the quality of the production in the factories, increase the number of grating workshops, and reduce the difference in the prices of grated and ungrated tobacco. But no arbitration was provided on the important questions: who was to have the monopoly of the cultivation and sale of tobacco, and how to divide up the profits among the State, the Farmers General, and the dealers.

Baumé and Cadet had been appointed to examine the tobacco of the Farm seized in Brittany. The barrels contained a pasty, elastic, humid cold mass, blackish in color, firmly adhesive to the touch. Its flavor was acrid and salty and its odor nauseating, similar to that of opium. They immediately attributed the deterioration of the tobacco to excessive humidity. "Our analyses establish that 100 pounds of tobacco in a barrel and in the bad condition in which we found it, reduced to its intrinsic quantity of perfectly dry tobacco, contain: 35 to 36 pounds of water, 7 of salt, 1 of sand and earth, and 56 to 57 of tobacco."[40]

In Rennes the Parlement had 160 tons of this tobacco burned, but the discontent reached all the way up to the king: "The Farmers General are once again making a bad deal with their tobacco." said a confidential letter. "The avid financiers cried out in protest, but it was suggested that they calm down, so that this affair, in which they seemed to be somewhat in the wrong, did not become inflamed, especially given the fiery spirits found in Brittany."[41]

Calonne, believing that he had found a solution acceptable to all, forbade the Farm to carry out the final moistening, considered to be the cause of the fermentation of tobacco, and decided that it should be entrusted to the dealers, to be done when the tobacco was sold to consumers. Contrary to his hopes, the compromise satisfied nobody: "The Farm could not admit that in Brittany its operations led to fermentations that did not occur in the other provinces, and the dealers did not find in the final moistening process, as they did in the grating, the means of selling smuggled tobacco."[42]

On April 29, 1785 Jacques Jacques Delahante, managed to get the parliamentary rulings annulled by the Supreme Court of Appeal.[43] Lavoisier, cleared of involvement in the fermented tobacco scandal by Cadet and Baumé, kept a copy of their report, but asked that it not be published so as not to harm his colleagues at the General Farm.

Perhaps to distract himself from his worries, Lavoisier spent a week at home, from July 12 to 19, overseeing an experiment on the manufacture of chocolate. He specified that two qualities of cocoa should be mixed. One, excellent but too fatty, came from the Carraque coast in Africa. The other, "much inferior to the former," grew in the American islands. He weighed all the ingredients—the cocoa, cinnamon, sugar, and vanilla—that he had bought from his friend Pluvinet, the grocer-hardware shop proprietor in the rue des Lombards, and carefully noted their cost, without overlooking the price of the charcoal, the rent for the utensils, and the salary of one worker— 40 sous a day and several bottles of wine. Sixty-two pounds of chocolate were produced, costing him 2.6 livres (about $90.00) per pound, and he recorded the results in a brief report entitled "A Good Way to Make Chocolate."

The General Farm's Wall Around Paris

Lavoisier, however, was confronted with the much more serious problem of collecting duties on goods entering Paris. He had kept a close watch on the records of the taxes collected and, according to his calculations, the merchandise officially coming into Paris represented only four-fifths of the needs of the inhabitants. Hence he concluded that one-fifth was being smuggled in.

The fraud was facilitated by the expansion of the city. Houses were built on the edges of the suburbs, and many had two exits, one within and the other beyond the tollgates, which were only simple wooden fences. Only the main thoroughfares had special barriers manned by officers of customs. Numerous small streets led directly to the countryside.

Moreover, the religious communities and the Intendants of the Bastille and the Invalides, who were exempted from paying taxes, profited by engaging in contraband and selling alcohols and wines on the unofficial market. "Everybody cursed the customs officers in their frockcoats, who earn a paltry one hundred pistoles a year, but who are ever suspicious, never budge from their position, who would even spot a mouse crossing the barrier. They stop every passing carriage, open the door with a jerk and snap, 'Are you carrying anything contrary to the King's orders?' Then they climb in, make an awkward inspection, climb down and slam the door. You would like to tell them to go to the devil, but they could not care less."[44] Nevertheless, the smugglers never lacked for ingenuity:

A smuggler rents a coach in which he drives out of Paris every evening, as if he were going to his house in the country. At the rear of the vehicle he places two very tall footmen dressed exactly alike. But one of them is made of wicker and is empty. The following day, the empty space is filled with prohibited merchandise, and the smuggler returns to Paris. Once they reach the tollgate, the real footman jumps down, and politely opens the door for the customs officer who, accustomed to seeing pass daily the occupant of the coach, does not bother to look very closely. He simply casts a quick glance. The false footman, of course, does not move from his seat, and the other

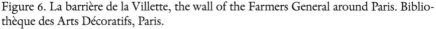

Figure 6. La barrière de la Villette, the wall of the Farmers General around Paris. Bibliothèque des Arts Décoratifs, Paris.

one, once the inspection has been made or supposedly made, climbs back up beside him. The coachman cracks his whip, the horses move away, and once again the Farm has been outwitted.[45]

In 1779 Lavoisier had proposed the construction of a wall around Paris, as a means of controlling the smuggling of alcohols and tobacco. But his memoir had been filed away. In 1787, however, Calonne accepted the plan and turned it over to Claude Nicolas Ledoux, a very gifted architect, who gave free rein to his fantasy and constructed an impenetrable wall interspersed with magnificent pavilions to serve as tollgates (Figure 6). "These tollgates differ as much by their form and size as by their interior layout. Some resemble caves, others tombs and churches. Still others are as splendid as palaces. The architect has been unsparing in his fantastic designs."[46]

Little concerned about cost, Ledoux spent 30 million livres ($1.2 billion). No doubt Lavoisier encouraged him. Architecture was an art that appealed to him since it was characterized by calculation, order and symmetry; it was serious and its creations were meant to endure. Given Lavoisier's attitude, the monumental character of these pavilions built to serve as tollgates becomes more understandable. Lavoisier had been consulted about them, as was normal since he was the author of the project. He had even had the idea of surrounding the wall with a circular boulevard for heavy hauling, forbidden within Paris. Besides, had he not already studied with Poyet the proposal for the circular hospital on the Ile aux Cygnes, and built warehouses and factories for the Gunpowder and the Tobacco administrations? He had a passion for building, the best pastime, he felt, for a man of reason and calculation, who was also an achiever. Pasteur would call him "the lawmaker of chemistry." One could also call this constructor of scientific and economic systems, conceived to serve and endure, an "architect."

This affair made Lavoisier very unpopular; in the fashionable salons, a play on words was often repeated: "Le mur murant Paris rend Paris murmurant". ("The wall walling in Paris has made Paris complain"). The wall rallied against him both those who were scandalized by the excessive expenditure and those who had profited from smuggling goods into the city, and he was exposed to public condemnation by all the lampoonists.

The wall that is going to make the capital an immense prison is in general opposed by Parisians, and does not even have the unanimous approval of the General Farm. What is strange is that this odious fiscal monument is the work of M. Lavoisier, the only one of the forty pillars of the State [the Farmers General] who is a member of the Academy of Science. He is a chemist and practical jokers say that he wanted to put Paris in a cucurbit whose receptacle would be the Farmers' cashbox.[47]

In an anonymous lampoon, *Réclamation d'un citoyen contre la nouvelle enceinte de Paris élevée par les fermiers généraux*, Jacques Antoine Dulaure condemned him in the name of hygiene:

You, vile inventor of a tyrannical project, who have no fear of sacrificing the honor and life of your fellow citizens to your insatiable greed, be assured that whatever the titles with which you adorn yourself, the riches with which you glorify yourself, only hate and disgrace await you. The Farm owes you gold, but the country owes you its curse. You are guilty of the new oppression exercised by the financiers against your fellow citizens. The calamities that will result from it, the epidemics, the deaths of numerous men caused by unhealthy air, the misfortunes, the disorders inevitable in an over populated and sprawling city will be your crimes. Your children will be ashamed to have you as a father and your name will become an insult. Everybody confirms that M. Lavoisier, of the Academy of Science, is the beneficent patriot to whom we owe the ingenious and salutary invention of imprisoning the French capital. After the death of this Academician, the colleagues responsible for his eulogy will do him a favor by removing this act from his biography. The General Farm can erect his statue on the walls he has invented, but the Academy ought to be ashamed of his membership. It is said that a Field Marshal of France, the duc de Nivernois, whose opinion on this wall was sought, replied: "I think that the author of the plan should be hanged." Luckily for M. Lavoisier, his advice has not yet been followed.[48]

Louis Sebastien Mercier gave in *Le nouveau Paris* his personal interpretation, which was more political:[49]

It is true that it was Lavoisier of the Academy of Science who was responsible for these burdensome and useless tollgates, a new oppression exercised by the financiers on their fellow citizens. But, alas, this great physicist, Lavoisier, was also a Farmer General. [. . .] One recalls the complaints of the Parisians against this offensive wall. Its secret objective was to control and contain the city, several of its tollgates being genuine fortresses.[49]

Lavoisier prepared a note for the newspapers in which he declined all responsibility for the wall, pretending that it was the decision of the government. But he gave up the idea of sending it and chose to ignore the whole affair, absorbed as he was in his administrative and scientific tasks. As usual, he cut himself off, protected himself from the vexations of life in society, and took refuge in work. Would the new wall have stopped contraband?

The General Farm would not have the time to find out; its days were numbered. The year 1789 would put an end to its activities and its wall. From July 13, the tollgates at the principal entries to Paris were burned and the walls demolished. An unrealized plan from 1793 proposed transforming the burned tollgates into a fragmented museum of the Revolution. But the nineteenth century destroyed almost all of them. Of the forty-five edifices constructed by Ledoux, only four remain today: the Denfert pavillon (Place Denfert-Rochereau), the Trône pavillon (Place de la Nation), the Parc Monceau and La Villette Rotundas.[50]

The Nicolas Salzard lease of the General Farm expired in 1786. The profit of each Farmer was 75,000 livres ($3 million) per year. As for Lavoisier, between 1768 and 1786 he had gained 1,200,000 livres ($48 million), an indication of just how wisely the initial investment had been managed. The following lease, called Jean Baptiste Mager, was signed in 1786, but would not reach its expiration date. The General Farm would be abolished by the National Assembly on March, 20, 1791.

Paris Slaughterhouses

On January 20, 1787 the Academy was asked to provide a plan for creating slaughterhouses on the outskirts of Paris. It was a difficult task touching on public health, the collection of customs duties and the monopoly exercised by the butchers. Lavoisier, Daubenton, Tillet, Bailly, Laplace, Coulomb, and Darcet were asked to make a study.

Every year in Paris three hundred butchers slaughtered 90,0000 steers, 100,000 calves, and 300,000 sheep. The slaughterhouses, which were also called *tueries* ("killing places"), were installed in the most populated neighborhoods: in Saint-Germain des Près, on the rue des Boucheries, and at the Croix Rouge; in the Faubourg Saint-Martin; on the rue Montmartre; on the Montagne Sainte-Geneviève and in the Gros Caillou.

The inhabitants complained. The animals who had to be led through the streets created great disorder. Those who escaped caused accidents. The odors from manure, the blood that ran into the streams, and the melted fat were a public nuisance. Moreover, the stoves used to liquefy the fat often caused fires.

The authors of the report assessed the health hazards. Could not the putrid emanations favor the appearance and spread of the plague and other contagious diseases? "It is difficult to answer the question precisely and rigorously and to reach a conclusion as to the salubrity or insalubrity of air in the shops of the butchers as well as in surrounding areas, because it seems that no direct experiments or sustained research have ever been done in this area. They could only be long and difficult."[51]

The proposed solution was simply to construct vast slaughterhouses with cowsheds, granaries, storehouses, drinking troughs, and so forth, outside the city. Each butcher would have his own place. Contractors came forward with offers to carry out the plan. The Academy did not wish to give an opinion as to how the project should be financed. Combining hygiene and Physiocracy, it did, however, insist on two points: the slaughterhouses should be built at some distance from the city—in Vieux-Neuilly or else on the Ile aux Cygnes—and they should not have an exclusive privilege:

The advantage and prosperity of trade depends on its freedom. It would be desirable that the meat trade be perfectly free; but since it has been left exclusively to a corporation and to privileged merchants, the least one can do is not to introduce new obstacles and allow the slaughtering right to whoever wants it. The company whose policy it is to slaughter on a large scale and hence be able to sell at a lower price, will always have the advantage over the small enterprise.[52]

But Lavoisier did not forget the interests of the General Farm:

In these plans, most of which were conceived before the wall of the Farm was constructed, the slaughterhouses were to be placed outside the tollgates. But now that the tollgates have been placed further from the center of the city, perhaps it would be better for the collection of duties to place the slaughterhouses within them, very close to the inside walls. They would still be isolated enough and yet they would be closer to the center of the city.[53]

No decision was taken by the government, and the cahiers de doléances (registers of grievances) of the city brought to the meeting of the States General in 1789 repeated almost word for the word the list of inconveniences resulting from having the slaughterhouses in the heart of Paris.

The Tools of Communication

T HE MEMOIRS OF THE NEW CHEMISTRY began in 1776 and continued until 1782, when the last one was published. The most important are those dating from 1777 when phlogiston was finally dismissed. The ideas in them have just begun to germinate and one speaks of them as if they were new discoveries, whereas they are at least ten years old." [1] These are Lavoisier's own words, written in 1785 to James Hall, the young Scottish chemist who had a talent for asking searching questions.

It is certainly true that from 1777 to 1785, in spite of all his efforts and the publication of numerous memoirs, Lavoisier remained alone in considering air as sole agent in chemical reactions; other chemists did not abandon phlogiston. Although they accepted the value of his experiments and the veracity of his results, they still endeavored to find a more or less acceptable compromise between his theories and Stahl's phlogiston. But after the analysis and synthesis of water, hesitation was no longer possible.

The *Réflexions sur le phlogistique*

Lavoisier, who had waited until 1785 because of the reservations of the scientific community, decided to go on the offensive. [2] Feeling strong enough to speak out strongly, on June 23, 1785 he presented to the Academy of Science the first part of his decisive memoir, *Les Réflexions sur le phlogistique* ("Reflections on Phlogiston"). He made a frontal attack: "The time has come for me to explain myself more precisely and categorically on an opinion that I regard as a disastrous error for chemistry. It has retarded its progress considerably, by the bad philosophical practice it has introduced." [3] After recalling the internal contradiction of Stahl's system, he went on in an ironic tone:

Chemists have made of phlogiston a vague principle that has not been rigorously defined and, hence, it can be adapted to any explanation one wants to give for it. Sometimes the principle is heavy, sometimes not; sometimes it is free fire, sometimes it is fire combined with the earthy element; sometimes it passes through the pores of the vessels, sometimes they are impermeable to it. It can explain both causticity and non-causticity, translucence and opaqueness, colors and the absence of colors. It is a veritable Proteus that changes form every second. Chemistry must be subjected to more rigorous reasoning, the facts that daily enrich this science must be stripped away from what mere arguments and prejudices add to it; what comes from fact and observation must be separated from what is systematic and hypothetical.[4]

According to him, any body having the capacity to decompose vital air into its two components, principe oxygine and matter of fire, was a combustible. At the moment of combustion, the principe oxygine abandoned the matter of fire, combined with the burning body and increased its weight. Thus the phenomena of combustion and calcination were explained more simply without phlogiston, which was an imaginary being whose existence was useless.

Actually, the matter of fire described by Lavoisier was not so different from phlogiston: the sole point distinguishing them was that the former was placed in oxygen, whereas the latter was in the combustible body. It could be reasonably argued that his theory was only the inverse of Stahl's.

Some people today also reproach him for having placed chemistry and physics in an impasse by replacing phlogiston by the matter of fire. Of the two conceptions of the nature of heat—heat-substance and heat-movement—existing at that time, he chose the wrong one, that of the imponderable material substance.

He showed himself, however, to be conciliatory: "I do no expect my ideas to be adopted all at once. The human mind adapts to a way of looking at things, and those who have held a certain concept of nature throughout their careers accept new ideas with difficulty. Therefore, only time will confirm or destroy the opinions I have presented."[5]

An Essay on Phlogiston

But his adversaries had just launched a counter-offensive. Richard Kirwan, an Irish chemist and mineralogist, a fellow of the Royal Society from 1780, corresponded with the whole of scientific Europe. In 1787, he published in London *An Essay on Phlogiston and the Constitution of Acids*, which was a direct attack on Lavoisier's theory. Kirwan credited him with two merits:

M. Lavoisier was undoubtedly the first who proved, by direct and exact experiments, that the weight which metals gain by calcination corresponds with that of the air which they absorb; he was also the first who published that the atmosphere consists of two distinct fluids, the one fit for the purposes of respiration and combustion, which he therefore calls *vital* or *pure air*; the other unfit for either purpose, and thence called *foul* or *mephitic air*; and that in the atmosphere the proportion of the first was to that of the last nearly as 1 to 4.[6]

What followed was less nice. Kirwan recalled that the discovery of dephlogisticated air belonged to Priestley, the caloric theory to Crawford, and the discovery of the composition of water to Cavendish. Lavoisier, he said, had been casting doubt on the very existence of phlogiston for a long time. But this position was untenable now that it had been proven that inflammable bodies like metals discharged inflammable gas when exposed to acids. It was surely the proof that phlogiston existed and was no different from hydrogen. Kirwan's usage of the word "inflammable" needs some interpreting. Today we say that hydrogen is inflammable, that gasoline is inflammable, but we find it difficult to say that iron and zinc are inflammable; they oxidize, or rust, but they do not burn. Kirwan, following Sthal's theory, considered that any body which contained phlogiston was inflammable. Since iron and zinc discharged inflammable gas when exposed to acids, these metals necessarily contained phlogiston; consequently they were "inflammable."

Kirwan went on to say that the experiments on the decomposition of water provided no arguments against phlogiston. Discharged hydrogen did not come from water, as Lavoisier claimed, but from iron.

For the metals that principally afford it, as iron and zinc, are by themselves, and in the total absence of water, perfectly inflammable, and therefore should be deemed to possess the same principle of inflammability as vegetable and animal substances, whose inflammability, without any controversy, is attributed to the presence of inflammable air, whereas water can be inflamed in no circumstances whatsoever.[7]

Throughout the twelve chapters of his work, Kirwan sought to demonstrate the presence of hydrogen in acids, fixed air, sulfur, phosphorus, sugar, charcoal, and metals. The phlogiston doctrine, he insisted, had been born in Germany and Sweden, the countries most advanced in mineralogy and metallurgy, and their faith in it had remained unshakable. Kirwan decided to call Lavoisier's theory on combustion *antiphlogistic hypothesis*, and commented:

This hypothesis has been advanced in an enlightened age and country; it is recommendable by its simplicity, and it owes its origin to a philosopher of great eminence, who was the first that introduced an almost mathematical precision into experimental philosophy. [. . .] The theory that must be accounted the least probable is the one which fails oftenest in explaining the phaenomena, is more arbitrary in its application, and less countenanced by the general rules of philosophic reasoning.[8]

Kirwan's work was favorably received in Europe, especially in England, Germany, and Sweden. In France the first to rally to Lavoisier's new chemistry were the mathematicians: Laplace, Cousin, Vandermonde. Lavoisier observed with satisfaction that the young, who were discovering chemistry with open minds, no longer believed in Stahl's phlogiston. But established chemists were more resistant.

However, on April 6 Berthollet announced publicly his conversion to the theory.[9] At the same time, Fourcroy introduced the theory in his course, but he attempted to have it co-exist with the old one and would not be definitively convinced of its validity until the first trimester of 1786. It was Fourcroy, however, who more than anybody else would contribute to spreading the new chemistry through his teaching.

On July 13 Lavoisier read to the Academy of Science the second half of his "Reflections on Phlogiston." One man in the audience was listening with special attention. He was Martinus Van Marum, a Dutch doctor who taught philosophy and mathematics in Haarlem and directed the Teyler Museum. With a generator of static electricity, he had succeeded by repeated discharges in reducing calcined metals. From this result, he had concluded that phlogiston was simply the matter of electricity and had come to Paris to present his findings.

The meeting was turbulent: "M. Lavoisier read, among other things a memorandum on the different sorts of air. But the violent objections which were raised against it, in consequence of which the reading was repeatedly interrupted, and the fact that the lecturer and his opponents spoke simultaneously allowed me to hear very little of it."[10] Somewhat surprised by the virulence of the discussion, Van Marum went to see Lavoisier, who invited him to lunch, but he was not free. It was Monge, who, in three working sessions, explained to Van Marum the most recent theories on gases and combustion. The latter went away half-convinced.

As for Guyton de Morveau, he was converted while he was editing the *Dictionnaire de chimie* of the *Encyclopédie méthodique*, as a result of which the work contains two contradictory "Forewords." The first one keeps its distance from Lavoisier: "We are far from adopting entirely the explanation in which this learned chemist believes that he can completely dismiss phlogiston."[11] Three years later and six hundred pages further along, the second "Foreword" renounced phlogiston: "This doctrine that has reigned for so long in chemical schools throughout Europe is only a hypothesis and can no longer be supported."[12]

Soon Monge, Meusnier, Chaptal, and Louis Lefèvre de Gineau would join the three pioneers and adhere by turns to the "antiphlogiston theory."

The group of converts spared no effort to spread its ideas. In September 1787 they all met in Dijon at the home of Guyton de Morveau. The discussions about phlogiston made good progress in his vast laboratory, which, later, was visited by Arthur Young:

The view of this great chymist's laboratory will shew that he is not idle: It consists of two large rooms, admirably furnished indeed. There are six or seven different furnaces (of which Macquer's is the most powerful), and such a variety and extent of apparatus, as I have seen nowhere else, with a furniture of specimens from the three kingdoms, as looks truly like business. There are little writing desks, with pens and papers, scattered everywhere, and in his library also, which is convenient. He has a large course of eudiometrical experiments going on at present, particularly with Fontana's and Volta's eudiometers.[13]

Young goes on to describe eudiometers, a pair of scales made in Paris, an air pump, burning lenses, a respirator, and "an abundance of new and most ingenious inventions for facilitating enquiries in the new philosophy of air."[14]

Kirwan, whose faith in phlogiston was as strong as ever, had made an attempt in 1786 to win back Guyton, whom he felt was faltering: "To tell the truth, you become even more valuable to me than ever; because, now that Scheele, the great Scheele, is dead, I no longer know where to find true chemical genius, if not in you."[15]

Guyton, embarrassed, replied later: "M. Beddoes was visiting one day last autumn when Messrs. Lavoisier, Monge and Fourcroy came to call. A few days later I had the visit of the Chevalier Marsilio Landriani. As you can see, the chemists have been out in force in Dijon. On leaving, M. Landriani wrote to M. Jean Sénebier that only a thread still connected chemistry with phlogiston."[16]

In March 1787 Lavoisier received a long letter from Van Marum who, having repeated all the experiments on the calcination of metals, had concluded that "metal calcination consists in the metal uniting with the principle of vital air [. . .] You will see moreover that I have almost entirely adopted your theory, having rejected phlogiston, which I now regard as a useless hypothesis and inadequate."[17]

The French Translation of *An Essay on Phlogiston*

In the meantime, Lavoisier and his friends had mounted the perfect counterattack against Kirwan's efforts. They decided to publish a French translation of *An Essay on Phlogiston* with a systematic refutation of Kirwan's ideas. Madame Lavoisier translated it, helped by Madame Picardet, Guyton de Morveau's assistant. The book appeared at the beginning of 1788 under the signatures of six authors. Each of them wrote critical notes disproving the existence of phlogiston in the domain that he had particularly studied. Lavoisier's five notes went back to material in previous publications. Meusnier wrote nothing, but Lavoisier cited him as co-author of the experiment on the decomposition of water. Monge wrote a single note on the properties of iron and its conversion into steel. Berthollet and Fourcroy wrote three notes each: the former's subjects were nitric acid, muriatic acid, and *eau régale*; the latter's were oxalic acid, the calcination of metals, and their dissolution. Guyton de Morveau contributed two notes: one on phosphoric acid and the other by way of a conclusion. He asserted that in the end there was no proof of the existence of phlogiston, nor any proof of its identity with hydrogen. If one confined oneself to the facts of weight analysis, the unique solid basis, all phenomena could be explained much more simply without phlogiston.

Lavoisier went further and pointed out that, even if all combustible bodies contained hydrogen, oxygen would still be necessary for their combustion: "The antiphlogistic doctrine will not be less obliged to come to the assistance of the ancient doctrine to explain the phenomena of calcination and combustion."[18]

A few months later, Arthur Young visited Guyton de Morveau. "We had," he wrote, "some conversation on the interesting topic to all philosophers, phlogiston; Mr. de Morveau contends vehemently for its nonexistence; treats Dr. Priestley's last publication as wide of the question; and declares that he considers the controversy as much decided as the question of liberty is in France."[19]

Guyton introduced him to Madame Picardet, who "is as agreeable in conversation as she is learned in the closet; a very pleasing unaffected woman; she has translated Scheele from the German, and a part of Mr. Kirwan's from the English; a treasure to Mr. de Morveau, for she is able and willing to converse with him on chemical subjects and on any others that tend either to instruct or please."[20] Guyton de Morveau invited Young to dinner.

It was a rich day to me; the great and just reputation of Mr. de Morveau, for being not only the first chemist of France, but one of the greatest that Europe has to boast, was alone sufficient to render his company interesting; but to find such a man void of affectation, free from those airs of superiority which are sometimes found in celebrated characters, and that reserve which oftener throws a veil over their talents, as well as conceals their deficiencies for which it is intended, was very pleasing.[21]

Young, who was above all an agronomist, wanted to see Guyton direct his research toward applications to agriculture. Guyton agreed that it offered an excellent field of investigations and that discoveries were bound to be made, but he had no time to get involved. Young noted:

It is clear from his conversation that his views are entirely occupied by the non-existence of phlogiston, except a little on the means of establishing and enforcing the new nomenclature. [. . .] I took the liberty of telling him that a man who can devise the experiments which shall be most conclusive in ascertaining the questions of a science, and has talents to draw all the usefull conclusions of them, should be entirely employed in experiments, and their register; and if I were king or minister of France, I would make that employment so profitable to him, that he should do nothing else. He laughed and asked me, if I were such an advocate for working, and such an enemy to writing, what I thought of my friend Dr. Priestley. And he then explained to the two other gentlemen the great philosopher's attention to metaphysics and polemic divinity.[22]

In 1789 Kirwan produced a new edition of *An Essay on Phlogiston*, with a translation of the adverse commentaries by the French scientists and additional remarks by the author. The translator was William Nicholson, man of science and inventor. In his preface, he commented on Lavoisier's taste for results "carried to five places of figures," and wrote ironically:

If it be denied that these results are pretended to be true in the last figures, I must beg leave to observe that these long rows of figures, which in some instances extend to a thousand times the nicety of experiment, serve only to exhibit a parade which true science has no need of: and, more than this, that when the real degree of accuracy in experiments is thus hidden from our contemplation, we are somewhat disposed to doubt whether the *exactitude scrupuleuse* of the experiments be indeed such as to render the proofs *de l'ordre demonstratif*.[23]

The Method of Chemical Nomenclature

In 1787 Lavoisier and Guyton de Morveau took an important new initiative on the part of the antiphlogisticians. For a long time and especially in writing the *Dictionnaire de chimie*, Guyton de Morveau had been bothered by the inadequacy of the technical vocabulary. He often found himself at a loss when trying to designate certain substances and, reluctant to use paraphrases that only misled the reader, he wanted to find invariable and unambiguous appellations. But at that point there was still a long way to go before achieving the ideal precision.

Certain metals were designated by referring to pagan gods: Venus for copper, Jupiter for tin, Mars for iron. This was why iron oxide had come to be called "astringent Mars saffron." Other substances were designated according to their properties or origins, the names of their inventors, or terms inherited from alchemy. Thus sufuric acid was "oil of vitriol"; a mixture of potassium hydroxide and potassium carbonate was known as "oil of tartar per deliquium"; zinc oxide as "philosophic wool"; calcium acetate as "shrimp eyes salt"; magnesium carbonate as Epsom salt; tin chloride as "Libavius smoking liquor"; sodium tartrate as "Seignette salt."

The number of identified bodies had suddenly exploded. There had been seven metals; now, all of a sudden, there were seventeen. Martin Henri Klaproth added uranium in 1789. There were five types of earths. Stone was subdivided into quartz, clay, marble, and spar. The chemistry of gases was constantly being enriched by new elastic fluids: nitrous air, muriatic acid air, alkaline air, diminished nitrous air, vitriolic acid air, fixed air, inflammable air, dephlogisticated air, nitrous acid vapor.

"Let us ask ourselves," Guyton concluded, "if it is possible to find our way about in this chaos. Does not the understanding of such a nomenclature require more effort than the understanding of the science itself? Let us admit the necessity for reforming the language and seek to establish the principles that must determine the choices of names in all circumstances."[24]

Moreover, chemistry had begun to have numerous practical applications, in crafts and nascent industries, that made it necessary to have a written and oral method accessible to all. Guyton was keenly aware of just how much artisans were indebted to his discipline:

It is from chemistry that the dyer acquired all the processes for extracting, toning and fixing his colors; through it, the starcher, brewer and distiller control their fermentations. It is chemistry that has allowed the cabinetmaker to vary the shades of his veneers, the varnisher to dissolve resins, the tanner to tan leathers and soften hides. It is also chemistry that taught so many manufacturers how to remove the grease from wool and to smooth out silks. It alone can add some perfection to all these arts. It alone can correct old formulas and acquire new ones for simplifying procedures or reaching the same end more economically.[25]

The French had been obliged to borrow English, German, and Swedish technical terms, and these foreign languages presented an obstacle to the spread of knowledge. To complicate matters even further, the keepers of the hardware shops used a different terminology from that of scientists. There *vitriol de Mars* became *couperose verte* ("green blotches"), and zinc vitriol was called *couperose blanche* ("white blotches").

For a long time, Guyton had been determined to snatch chemistry from obscurity and make it accessible to everybody. As early as May 1782 he had written a memoir on chemical designations, the necessity for improving the system, and rules for doing so, followed by a table of chemical nomenclature. According to him, a rational chemical language should respect five fundamental principles.

"First principle: a phrase is not a name. Chemical beings and products must have names that apply in all circumstances, without one's having to resort to circumlocutions. [. . .]

Second principle: the designations should, as much as possible, conform to the nature of the things themselves."[26] Consequently, the primitive name belongs to the simple, unmodified substance; the compound name should evoke the nature of the constituents and nothing else. Lead acetate should replace "Saturn sugar" and silver muriate the "horned moon."

Third principle: when a substance is poorly defined, "it is better to give it a name expressing nothing than one that could convey a false idea."[27]

Fourth principle: new designations should be formed from Greek or Latin roots so that they can be memorized thanks to their meaning.

Fifth principle: "The designations should be carefully matched with the genius of the language for which they are being formed."[28]

Thus the genius of the French language required that one designate substances derived from chalk, tallow, ants, and sorrel by the epithets *crétacé, sébacé, formicin,* and *oxalin,* not by *crayacé, suifacé, fourmieux,* and *oseillique.*

Bergman encouraged Guyton in this direction: "Do not honor any inappropriate designation. Those who know already will understand; those who do not yet know will understand sooner."[29] Guyton's friends at the Paris Royal Academy of Science were less convinced of the necessity for changing the vocabulary and were very cool to his suggestions. In 1786 he came to explain himself to them, and presented his ideas to Lavoisier, Berthollet, and Fourcroy at the Arsenal. Lavoisier, captivated, asked him to join his research team. In order to perfect the chemical revolution, a new language—precise, clear, and logical—would of course be a considerable asset. But in Guyton's proposition Lavoisier saw also a new idea, that of using semantic analysis as the equivalent of chemical analysis. He reasoned that, since nothing is either lost or created, it is possible to determine the nature of a compound body by analysis. Similarly, if one gives an exact designation to simple elements, one should be able to define compound bodies by combining words in the way one combines bodies.

The objective of languages is not only, as is commonly believed, to express ideas and images by signs. Languages are also genuine analytical methods, with the aid of which we proceed from the known to the unknown. [. . .] An analytical method is a language; a language is an analytical method, and these two expressions are, in a certain sense, synonyms.[30]

It was owing to these working discussions on the new nomenclature that Guyton de Morveau was converted to the antiphlogiston theory, whereas as far as Lavoisier was concerned, he saw his propaganda weapon, a well-made language, emerge from them.

Lavoisier returned to the ideas of Condillac, whose reflections on the mechanisms for acquiring knowledge had greatly influenced the educational and scientific worlds: "The arts of speaking, writing, discourse and thinking are in the end only one art. In fact, when one knows how to think, one knows how to argue, and there is nothing more to speaking and writing well than simply speaking the way one thinks and writing the way one speaks."[31]

He appreciated the rigor, clarity, and easily accessible character of Condillac's thought: one must beware of reasoning that can lead us astray, and continuously put it to the experimental test. We must keep only facts, which are truths given by nature and hence cannot deceive us. Truth must be sought only in the linking of experiments and observations.

The Academicians were at last ready to hear this message. Ten years earlier they had been much less receptive, but the irritating problem of an imprecise chemical nomenclature had hampered both their work and everyday life. In 1778, after the *Journal de Paris* had reported Lavoisier's trip in search of soils containing saltpeter, the chemist had them publish a correction:

You announced, Gentlemen, in the June 14 edition of your newspaper, that I had discovered in Touraine rocks covered with efflorescence of *Natrum* or alkali of soda. Allow me to point out that this observation was not made by me alone. I was traveling with M. Clouet, Director of the Gunpowder Administration and my colleague, and it was made by both of us, just as all the others we made regarding natural saltpeter.[32]

That might have been the end of the matter. But a young pharmacy student, the son of Professor Vidal who taught medicine at Montpellier, wanting to make himself known, pointed out in a letter to the newspaper on July 15 that the substance called *nitrum alkalisé* had been discovered by Henri de Boulainvilliers, mentioned by Jean Hellot in memoirs read at the Royal Academy of Science, and published in translation in a book by Schlueter, *De la fonte des mines*. Unfortunately, he had had the idea of ending his letter in a mocking tone: "I hope that M. Lavoisier will not hold it against me for having robbed him of the honor of this discovery. His observation regarding it is no less interesting. Besides he has acquired so much in chemistry that this trifling matter will not cast a shadow on his glory."[33]

Lavoisier, cut to the quick, wrote a letter to the newspaper on July 24 that revealed both the failings of the old nomenclature and his own—his excessive touchiness and lack of humor:

M. Vidal junior has no knowledge of the work that we did on the saltpeter that is found naturally in France in certain quarries, in particular in those containing chalk and tufa. Otherwise, he would be aware that we have not claimed anybody's discoveries, that we have made the greatest effort to render justice to all who have instructed us, and that we know at least as well as he what has been written on this matter. It seems that M. Vidal is no better informed on the purpose of the trip that we have just made for the king. It was not Lorraine we visited, as his letter states, but Touraine, a part of Anjou, Saintonge, Brittany, etc. It was not *nitrum alkalisé* that we found in efflorescence on the rocks but *natrum*, something quite different, which a pharmacy student should not confuse, since one is a vegetable alkali, the other a mineral one. In the presence of vitriolic acid, one forms vitriolized tartar, the other one Glauber salt, etc. At the same time, we inform him, and all those who could be tempted like him to attack us without knowing the purpose of our work or the means we have used to carry it out, that we have made a rule not to reply to critics in the future. Our occupations leave us no time for getting involved in literary discussions. We regard the Academy of Science as the only court before which we should naturally appear. We have already submitted the first part of our work to be judged by it, and it is unlikely that we shall refuse its jurisdiction to subject ourselves to M. Vidal's judgment.[34]

In March 1787, after six months of assiduous effort pursued in daily meetings, the four chemists were finally ready for the great reform: "M. de Morveau is presently in Paris," Lavoisier wrote to Meusnier," and we are profiting from the occasion to work with him on a chemical nomenclature. At the moment, this is perhaps the most urgent matter for the advancement of the sciences."[35]

Fourcroy was very well suited to this group of admirers of fine language. At the age of thirty, he had already entered the Academy of Science, was continuing his private course on the rue Jacob, and had succeeded Macquer as tenured professor in the chemistry chair at the Jardin du Roy, a well paid post that was very much in the public eye.

His oratorical talent was equal to his ambitions. He had a "logical method, the ability to extemporize, and such precision and elegance in his use of words that it was as if they had been chosen only after long consideration. And yet they were spoken with such liveliness, brilliance and novelty that they seemed to be spontaneous. He had a flexible, sonorous, silvery voice that lent itself to his movements and penetrated into the innermost recesses of the largest auditorium. Nature had given him everything."[36] So wrote Georges Cuvier.

He kept himself informed of the latest progress in chemistry, announced the most recent discoveries, and brought modern science within reach of all.

In a certain way, he built his success on others' ideas, those of Lavoisier and Guyton in particular, but he was also the best popularizer of the new chemistry.

Berthollet was the fourth member of the group. Born in Turin in 1748, a doctor and chemist and member of the Royal Academy since 1780, he had just succeeded Macquer as director of dyeing at the Gobelins factory. He had a laboratory there for his research and discovered the bleaching property of liquid chlorine and subsequently developed a technique for bleaching fabrics. As a result, there was born, with the help of Lavoisier and the duc d'Orléans, a company for weaving and bleaching linen located on the rue de Montparnasse.

Rallied to the new chemistry in 1785, Berthollet became a regular visitor at the Arsenal, where he was to be found gathered round Lavoisier and his wife, Guyton, Fourcroy, Hassenfratz, Adet, and, later, Seguin. Lavoisier had set up a system of working in teams: with it, diverse talents formed "by their joint efforts a collective being that possessed enlightenment, knowledge and means that would have been impossible to find in isolated individuals."[37]

Beyond the team, they benefited from the advice given by a group of geometers from the Academy headed by Laplace and Monge. Lavoisier was one of the first scientists in France to possess such a clear vision of a multidisciplinary work: "This is the way that all sciences help each other and mutually lend strength to build together the great edifice of human knowledge."[38]

On April 18, 1787 Lavoisier presented his "Memoir on the Necessity for Reforming and Improving Chemical Nomenclature" at the Academy. It was the kickoff, so to speak. In his scientific talk he distinguished three things:

The series of facts that make up science; the ideas that recall the facts; and the words that express them. The word ought to bring about the birth of the idea; the idea should depict the fact; they are three imprints from the same stamp. And since it is words that preserve and transmit ideas, the result is that it would be impossible to improve science without improving its language. However true the facts, however exact the ideas it would bring into existence, they would still transmit only false impressions if one did not have the precise expressions for rendering them. The perfection of the nomenclature of chemistry, envisaged from this perspective, consists of rendering ideas and facts in their exact truth, without omitting anything of what they present, and especially without adding anything to them: it must be nothing more than a faithful mirror.[39]

Fifteen days later, on May 2, Fourcroy presented his table of simple substances. They numbered thirty-three and were divided into five groups. The first group contained five substances: light, caloric, oxygen, hydrogen, and nitrogen.[40] The second contained the nonmetallic substances: sulfur, phosphorus, and carbon that are transformed into acids, nitrogen since it is a base for nitric acid, and three radicals still undescribed but whose theoretical existence was recognized: "the muriatic, fluoric, and boracic radicals." The third group was made up of the seventeen oxidizable and acidifiable metals: antimony, silver, arsenic, bismuth, cobalt, copper, tin, iron, manganese, mercury, molybdenum, nickel, gold, platinum, lead, tungsten, and zinc. The fourth group was composed of five types of earth: chalk, magnesium, barite, alumina, and silica.[41] The fifth group consisted of the three alkalis: potassium hydroxide, soda, and ammonia.[42]

Fourcroy then explained the new method for creating the names of compound bodies from their components. The strong reliance on Greek for creating the new designations expressed the authors' twofold determination: to avoid Swedish and German terms, which were incompatible with French, but also to exclude Latin, language of the Vatican and the Jesuits, whose teaching role the authors wanted to reduce.

After the Revolution, however, Fourcroy gave a purely esthetic justification for the choice of a new name:

To the advantage of having no connection with already known words and hence of avoiding confusion with names belonging to different substances, they added that of offering to the ear soft and pleasant sounds, easy to pronounce and sometimes even harmonious, thus the advantage of coming nearer to the genius of the French language whose softness and easy pronunciation have made it the most widespread idiom in the world.[43]

The authors hoped that their method would have a universal value and could be adapted to future discoveries: "So long as it is a method of naming rather than a nomenclature, it will adapt itself naturally to the works that will come afterwards. It will mark out in advance the place and name of the new substances that can be discovered, and require only a few local and particular adjustments."[44]

What impresses the reader about this passage is its confidence in the future. As Marco Beretta writes, "Lavoisier asserts that an entirely new nomenclature will last forever, with only occasional minor amendments. It is striking to see that, so far, he has been proven right and that the language of inorganic chemistry still uses the words of the naming method that he outlined in 1787."[45] And Ferdinando Abbri remarks that the mental shift provoked by Lavoisier's definition of simple substances implied a method of conceiving all chemical operations a priori. Chemistry was now to be regarded as the science of chemical changes rather than the investigation of the composition of matter.[46]

In postulating that all substances discovered in the future would be automatically designated according to the permanent principles of the new method of nomenclature, Lavoisier was adopting Condillac's idea that language is not only an analytical method but also one of discovery.

On May 5 Jean Henri Hassenfratz and Pierre Auguste Adet, who had both worked in Lavoisier's laboratory, presented in their turn two reports proposing that new characters be used in chemical notation. The simple bodies would be represented by a range of conventional characters: the straight line, half circle, circle, triangle and square. Their juxtaposition would give the nature and quantity of simple substances associated in a compound body. Lavoisier was not enthusiastic. Already in 1782 he had attempted a notation of this kind, inspired by Geoffroy and Bergman, but had abandoned it.

Disregarding the graphics of Hassenfratz and Adet, he gave a complete exposition of the new chemistry: the role of oxygen, the composition of air and water, the theory of acids, and the uselessness of phlogiston. He hoped that the Academy would "continue to regard favorably a new doctrine that had been formed within it, that had already absorbed nearly twenty years of work, that the force of argument and facts had obliged several celebrated chemists to adopt, and in favor of which a much greater number appeared to be deciding at this very moment."[47]

The referees named by the Academy of Science, Baumé, Darcet, and Sage, did not commit themselves on the new nomenclature. They said that it should be subjected to the test of time, the impact of experience, the sway of opinions, and public judgment. In this way, it would be known whether it was a linking of truths or an error. "In the former case, it will give still another solid base to human knowledge; in the latter, it will fall into oblivion like all the unfounded theories and systems of physics that will have preceded it."[48]

The *Journal Encyclopédique* in Liège poked fun at them. Were they incapable of giving a definitive judgment straightaway? "The nomenclature is either good or bad. In the former case, the Academy should adopt it, because it cannot remain indecisive without slowing up the progress of science. [. . .] If it is bad, why not condemn it straight-away?"[49]

To spread the new method, the authors decided to publish it themselves in 1787 under the title of *Méthode de nomenclature chimique*. At that time, only two scientific journals reached a wide audience: the *Recueil des Mémoires de l'Académie Royale des Sciences*, whose volumes were always several years behind, and the Abbé Rozier's *Observations sur la Physique*, which in 1787 had passed into the hands of a partisan of the phlogiston theory, Jean Claude de La Métherie. He would obviously do nothing for the new chemistry. On the contrary, he criticized its semantic innovations, arguing, for example, that since water contains a large quantity of hydrogen, "the word oxygen is inappropriate and it would be be more logical to call it hydrogen (from the greek Udor = water)." [50]

Other adversaries suggested calling hydrogen "oléogène," since oil contained a high proportion of it. Kirwan fulminated unstintingly against a nomenclature which "is untranslatable, revolting, systematic and unintelligible for the greater part of those who cultivate practical chemistry" (26 July 1788). [51]

Nevertheless, the method was rapidly adopted. And, at last, chemistry disposed of a clear language. One would no longer speak of powder of algaroth, salt of alembroth, pompholix, phagedenic water, turbith mineral, or colcothar.

The work would be printed in seven editions in France, two in Germany, and one in England, Spain, and Italy respectively. In all editions of his *Eléments d'histoire naturelle et de chimie*, Fourcroy went back to the texts of which he was the author. They were translated into all languages. The tables and dictionary of chemical terms were reprinted in numerous encyclopedic works used by chemistry professors.

The method would undergo enrichment and changes. The essential role attributed to oxygen in the formation of acids would be challenged. Hardly had the new nomenclature become known when Berthollet established the acid character of two compounds without oxygen: hydrogen sulfide or hydrosulfurous acid, and prussic acid or hydrocyanic acid. Soon afterward, another oxygenless acid, hydrochloric acid, would be discovered. On the other hand, the dualist conception of the composition of salts had to be abandoned.

Two centuries later, the importance of the reform appears clearly to historians of science: "There was a before and an after 1787," writes B. Bensaude-Vincent. *"La méthode de nomenclature* introduced such a rupture in the history of chemistry that the natural language of the old chemists became a foreign language for us. All of chemistry was profoundly modified. These names are the baptismal certificates of a new rational, experimental, quantitative, and rigorous science. The typical example of a revolution." [52]

The *Annales de chimie*

Lavoisier began to contemplate founding a new journal following the model of the *Annales* of the German chemist Lorenz Florent Friedrich von Crell. Adet would be in charge. But a special "permission" was required and it was refused by the State Censor. The Academy of Science could have used its own "privilege" and dispensed with the authorization, but it feared retaliatory measures.

On July 29, 1787 Lavoisier and his colleagues asked the baron de Breteuil to intervene on their behalf, but his efforts were far from satisfactory. They were authorized to publish only the faithful translation of Crell's journal, but without adding anything new or producing more than one volume each trimester. This arrangement could not suit them since their goal was precisely to bring out original memoirs in French as rapidly as possible. "If M. Adet were restricted to the mere translation of a German journal, he would present only an incomplete picture of the discoveries being made daily, and the whole point of his work would be lost, for the public and for himself."[53] They then attempted to obtain at least the authorization to sell Crell's journal on a subscription basis under the title of *Annales chimiques* and to include extracts from French, English, Italian, and German memoirs.

Repeated interventions were unsuccessful. Adet, discouraged and without financial resources, sought a post as a doctor in Santo Domingo. Lavoisier took up his case with Condorcet, and wrote to the Minister of the Navy. But in vain. Adet was in despair. He had nothing more on which to live, and his creditors were demanding to be paid 288 livres ($11,500). He borrowed half the sum from Lavoisier and the other half from Fourcroy but, on the settlement date, he was still insolvent. Lavoisier reimbursed Fourcroy and advanced an additional 600 livres to the unfortunate Adet.

By the end of 1788 the Censor, who had more to worry about than keeping watch over the scientific press, finally gave his approval. On December 23, Lavoisier asked the Academy to name referees for examining the first four volumes of the *Annales de chimie*.

The journal finally appeared one month before the opening of the Etats généraux in April 1789. Its contributors were Guyton de Morveau, Lavoisier, Monge, Berthollet, Fourcroy, the baron de Dietrich, Hassenfratz, and Adet, who was editorial secretary. Lavoisier was the treasurer and the real boss.[54] The *Annales de chimie* contained numerous publications by him on chemistry and related subjects such as mineralogy, meteorology, physics, physiology and the production of saltpeter. He also included the reports he had presented to the Academy on prisons, hospitals and slaughterhouses, a plan for the creation of a steam pump for supplying Paris with drinkable water, as well as the *Résultat de quelques expériences d'agriculture et réflexions sur leurs relations avec l'économie politique*, an article on the experiments carried out during the ten years in Freschines, and several texts on the new weights and measures.

The editors' aims were "to establish communications and active correspondence among all European men of science, to hasten the progress of a science, the dominant study of which sufficiently demonstates its importance and to bring together in a useful way published work dispersed in a large number of volumes." It should be noted, states Maurice Crosland, "that the first aim stated above was to facilitate co-operation between *savants* in different countries. Europe is specifically mentioned because America did not yet have an established scientific community."[55]

The journal had a great success, in particular in France and England. Lavoisier's new chemistry would eventually captivate the entire scientific community by its coherent vision of chemical phenomena and its logical language. In 1788 Joseph François Bonjour referred to it as "the new theory of the French chemists," which angered Lavoisier: "This theory is not, as I have heard it said, the theory of French chemists. It is my theory, and it is a property that I claim before my contemporaries and posterity."[56]

Eighteen volumes of the *Annales de chimie* would be published between April 1789 and November 1793, the date on which the journal would cease to appear for some time.

The *Traité élémentaire de chimie*

This new science, however, lacked a catechism. Lavoisier spent almost all of 1788 writing the *Traité élémentaire de chimie* (*Elements of Chemistry*) a work that was the crowning achievement of his undertaking. On January 17, 1789 he had the first copies in hand.

The initial goal of the work had been to develop the memoir of April 1787 on the necessity for a new nomenclature, but it had been imperceptibly transformed into an educational text. Originally, the book was addressed to the enlightened people who wanted to discover the essential principles of the new chemistry. In fact, as Maurice Daumas has shown, Lavoisier had long intended, perhaps for more than twelve years, to write a book for beginners in chemistry. And finally he had found himself gradually led to rethink all the teaching of chemistry:

I have imposed upon myself, as a law, never to advance but from what is known to what is unknown; never to form any conclusion which is not an immediate consequence necessarily flowing from observation and experiment; and always to arrange the facts, and the conclusions which are drawn from them, in such an order as shall render it most easy for beginners in the study of chemistry thoroughly to understand them. Hence I have been obliged to depart from the usual order of courses of lectures and of treatises upon chemistry, which always assume the first principle of the science as known, when the pupil or the reader should never be supposed to know them till they have been explained in subsequent lessons.[57]

And he added: "It is not to the history of the science, or of the human mind, that we are to attend in an elementary treatise. Our only aim ought to be ease and perspicuity, and with the utmost care to keep every thing out of view which might draw aside the student's attention; it is a road which we should be continually rendering more smooth, and from which we should endeavour to remove every obstacle which can occasion delay."[58]

The first part of the book was devoted to the essential points of the new chemistry: the composition of air and water, the role of oxygen in combustion and in the formation of acids and oxides, the theory of heat and the role of caloric, the composition of vegetable and animal substances. "The bases of the vegetable acids were shown to consist either of hydrogen and carbon or of hydrogen, carbon and phosphorus, while animal acids were more compound, their bases generally consisting of combinations of carbon, phosphorus, hydrogen and azote (nitrogen)."[59] In chapter XIII, on vinous fermentation, Lavoisier gave the first explicit statement of the law of the conservation of matter in chemical reactions: "in all the operations of art and nature, nothing is created; an equal quantity of matter exists both before and after the operation."

The second part of the book described the compounds of the acids with various bases, giving extensive tables of these compounds. They are the first modern list of the chemical elements. "Lavoisier had removed from the table given in 1787 in the new nomenclature the radicals of the organic acids, because they had been shown to be compound of hydrogen and carbon, but he retained the earths, although he suspected that they were compounds, probably oxides, and he omitted the alkalis because they were evidently compounds. The list therefore contained thirty-three elements, including light and caloric."[60]

The third part depicted the instruments and experimental methods of new chemistry (see Figure 7), and recalled the rules of a true scientific approach: "We must trust to nothing but facts: these are presented to us by nature, and cannot deceive. We ought, in every insrtance, to submit our reasoning to the test of experiment, and never to search for truth but by the natural road of experiment and observation."[61]

Lavoisier refused to speak of affinities, although it was a fashionable subject: "MM. Geoffroy, Gellert, Bergman, Scheele, de Morveau, Kirwan, and many others, have collected a number of particular facts on this subject, which only wait for a proper arrangement."[62]

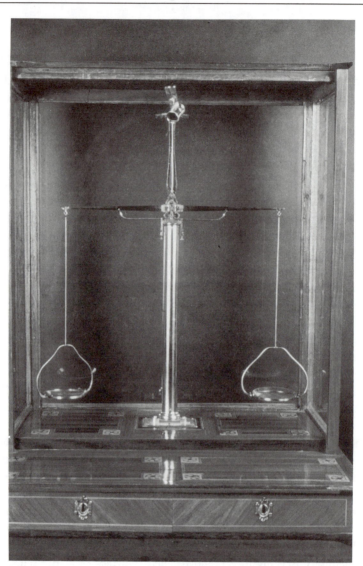

Figure 7. Precision balance by Pierre Bernard Mégnié. Musée des Arts et Métiers, Paris.

As for whether simple bodies were made up of elementary particles, it was too soon to answer: "Thus, as chemistry advances towards perfection, by dividing and subdividing, it is impossible to say where it is to end; and these things we at present suppose simple may soon be found quite otherwise. All we dare venture to affirm of any substance is that it must be considered as simple in the present state of our knowledge, and so far as chemical analysis has hitherto been able to show."[63]

It would be up to the younger chemists to complete the work, but their contributions should be of the highest quality: "Every edifice which is intended to resist the ravages of time should be built upon a sure foundation; and, in the present state of chemistry, to attempt discoveries by experiments, either not perfectly exact, or not sufficiently rigorous, will serve only to interrupt its progress, instead of contributing to its advancement."[64]

The thirteen plates illustrating the work had been engraved by Madame Lavoisier. They gave an extremely precise and accurate picture of the instruments used by her husband. The eleventh plate contains, however, one small error in the joining of the pipes that carry the gases discharged from the combustion of oils to the two balloons destined to hold the carbonic gas by bubbling in potassium hydroxide.

The treatise received the simultaneous approval of the Academy of Science, the Agricultural Society, and the Society of Medicine. Nevertheless, Lavoisier was not completely satisfied with the first edition. Joseph Marie Cuchet, the publisher, had chosen a small format, in-octavo, and the book was too thick. There were 32 pages of introduction, 12 for contents, 558 for the text, 13 for the plates, and 33 containing laudatory commentary from various societies.

In Lavoisier's eyes the book lacked elegance, and the appearance of the four copies bound in single volumes with red morocco for the king, the queen, the comte de Provence, and the comte d'Artois was not, he felt, at all refined. Had he not been in such a hurry, he would have had the work bound in two thinner volumes. But the bookbinder, overwhelmed as always, had been so slow that he had to let it pass and send the copies to Versailles as they were.[65]

There would be nine editions in France, five in England, three in America, Germany, and Italy respectively, two in Holland, and one each in Spain and Mexico. Gradually, the new chemistry was conquering France, Europe and the world. But something was still lacking as far as Lavoisier was concerned: the public rallying of Benjamin Franklin. On February 2, 1790 Lavoisier sent the American two copies with the following note:

As you will see in the preface, I sought to reach the truth by linking facts, to eliminate argument as much as possible, because it is often a false instrument that deceives us, and replace it by the torch of observation and experiment. This path that had not previously been followed in chemistry led me to arrange my work in a completely new order, and chemistry has become much closer than it was to experimental physics. [. . .] Here then is the revolution that has taken place in an important branch of human knowledge since your departure from Europe. I shall consider this revolution as well advanced and even completely achieved if you join our ranks.[66]

Others, whose approval Lavoisier did not solicit, judged the father of the chemical revolution severely. Marat, who had not forgotten "the imputations of ignorance, incompetence and charlatanism" leveled at him by the Academicians, would get his revenge in "Modern Charlatans," a pamphlet written in 1791:

At the head of them all would have to come Lavoisier, the putative father of all the discoveries that have made such a splash. Because he has no ideas of his own, he makes do with those of others. But since he almost never knows how to appreciate them, he abandons them as rashly as he took them up, and he changes systems as often as he changes his shoes. In the space of six months, I saw him adhere, one after the other, to the new theories of matter of fire, ignited fluid and latent heat. In a still shorter space of time, I saw him develop a passion for pure phlogiston and then ruthlessly proscribe it. A while ago, after Cavendish, he found the precious secret of making water with water. Next, having dreamt that this liquid was only a mixture of pure air and inflammable air, he transformed it into the king of fuels. If you ask me what he did to be so much lauded, I would answer that he managed to get himself an income of 100,000 livres, that he produced the plan to turn Paris into a vast prison and that he changed the terms acid into oxygine, phlogiston into nitrogen, marine into muriatic, and nitrous into nitric and nitrac. These are his claims to immortality. Trusting in his great deeds he is now resting on his laurels.[67]

Several recent works have analyzed the effects of the conceptual rupture desired by Lavoisier on the development of modern chemistry. Some emphasize the philosophical bases of the reform and the influence of the rationalist approach used by Descartes and Condillac. Others consider, on the contrary, that Lavoisier remained above all an experimentalist, inspired by Newton, Bacon, Boyle, and Priestley. This quarrel over the origins of modern chemistry—French, philosophical, and rationalist, or English, naturalist, and experimental—has been going on for two centuries. Lavoisier, who was nurtured on the French rationalist tradition while recognizing the value of the English scientific approach, was capable of synthesizing the two cultures. To reduce his scientific method to one or the other influence is to impoverish it. His complex personality escapes all classification. Endowed above all with a down-to-earth mind, he was not very much attracted by philosophical speculations and abstract systems. Had he not, after all, abandoned two years of philosophy included in the curriculum at the Collège des Quatre Nations so as to study science?

On the other hand, his interest in Condillac's thought was not limited to the philosophy of science but was very pragmatic and also included the economic principles developed in *Le commerce et le gouvernement considérés relativement l'un à l'autre*. Finally, he was fully aware of the universal value of his contribution and rejected nationalistic views in science. Thus he would say in 1791 regarding the project for standardization of weights and measures: "It belongs equally to all nations of the earth. It does not establish the pre-eminence of one nation over another. All can adopt it without wounding their national pride, which is hardly less potent than individual pride."[68]

And when, in 1793, the Academy of Science wanted to limit to French artisans the competition "for the best pocket watch for determining longitudes at sea," Lavoisier would be indignant at this protectionist measure: "Thus even in this century of knowledge and equality, even in the eyes of one of the most enlightened and instructed societies in Europe, there still exists a difference between men who cover the surface of the earth! There still exist national distinctions among scientists and artisans! "[69]

On the whole, the success of the conceptual rupture created by Lavoisier is based on three original characteristics. First, as I. Bernard Cohen had written, "the chemical revolution has a primary place among revolutions in science in that it is the first generally recognized major one to have been called a revolution by its chief author."[70] Second, this celebrated revolution concerned not only chemistry but biology and economics as well, as we shall see. Thus Lavoisier occupies a nodal point in the network. Describing the role of "great men," Norton Wise explains that "their power as individuals resides not so much in their creative genius, which is genuine enough, but in their having constructed themselves, their ideas, their technologies, and their realities so as to play a crucial role in stabilizing a cultural network."[71] Third, Lavoisier was the first chemist to have recourse to such a powerful and organized communications policy which included both a newly created language and a range of publications intended for a diverse readership and a rapid diffusion.

The Reform of Agriculture

M. Lavoisier," a journalist wrote, "unlike his fellow chemists, did not have to seek the philosopher's stone, he simply found it in his office."[1] He did indeed belong to the financiers, a group made up of powerful individuals, involved in the king's affairs and managing the finances of the State while never neglecting their own.[2] But he deplored the sluggishness of bureaucracy and the arbitrariness of absolute power. His functions at the General Farm, his industrial activities, his experience as an important landowner had made him aware of the rigidities of society. He dreamed of a more liberal and modern administration that would set up a less burdensome tax system and efficient financial structures and encourage the creation of businesses. His new functions in the high administration of Agriculture and on the board of the Discount Bank would offer him new perspectives.

Committee on Agriculture Versus Society of Agriculture

Since 1783 Lavoisier had belonged to the Société d'Agriculture de Paris (Paris Society of Agriculture), created in 1761 by Henri Léonard Bertin, Controller-General of Finance, to encourage progress in agriculture. Its members came from what are now the departments of Seine, Seine-et-Oise, Seine-et-Marne, Eure-et-Loir, and Yonne. It soon consolidated its authority over the provincial societies and had offices in Paris, Beauvais, Meaux and Sens.

To thwart its hegemonic tendencies, Bertin had created within his ministry a committee responsible for proposing laws regarding agricultural policy. As a result of the efficacy of this committee; the Paris Society of Agriculture had progressively become inactive. In 1780 Bertin retired. After Necker's departure in 1781, François Bertier de Sauvigny, Intendant for the Paris region, tried to revive the Paris Society of Agriculture. "He was a magistrate who combined official ambition with a family tradition of enlightened, patrician agriculture, emphasizing stock-breeding and sylviculture. His father had been intendant of Paris before him and a member of Bertin's ministerial council. Besides the intendancy, Bertier was well placed at court, being superintendant of the queen's household."[3] He attracted to the society outstanding "improving" landowners, the duc de La Rochefoucauld-Liancourt, the duc de Charost, the duc d'Harcourt, the duc d'Ayen, and the marquis de Turbilly. He then invited members of the Academy of Science and other learned societies: Lavoisier, Henri Louis Duhamel du Monceau, Buffon, Antoine Laurent de Jussieu, Mathieu Tillet, Nicolas Desmarest, the naturalist Valmont de Bomare, the doctors Tenon and Petit, Claude Bourgelat, director of the veterinary school in Alfort, and General Jean Baptiste Vacquette de Gribeauval. He also invited Malesherbes, Louis Jean Marie Daubenton, the botanist André Thouin, the Abbé Alexandre Henri Tessier, the engineer Jean Rodolphe Perronet, Pierre Samuel Dupont, Antoine Fourcroy, and Félix Vicq d'Azyr to join. Pierre Marie Auguste Broussonnet was permanent secretary. The Society began to flourish once again. It revised its rules, published volumes of memoirs, recruited corresponding members from other countries, including Arthur Young, Sir Joseph Banks, Benjamin Franklin, the duc de Parma, and George Washington. It held weekly meetings on Thursdays at the Hôtel de Ville. Bertier de Sauvigny hoped to gain official recognition for the group, accompanied by a budget of 24,000 livres ($960,000) per year.

Calonne, the new Controller General of Finance was all the more favorable to the plan since he wanted to control the activities of the Society, too much directed, he felt, toward financial, social, and fiscal reforms, and limit them to strictly agricultural questions. Hence he supported the proposal in Parliament. But the plan was refused on the basis that the subsidy would profit essentially the treasurer and secretary of the Society and that it was more urgent to alleviate the countryside from the taxes and the corvée that was crushing it. Bertier had failed.

The exceptionally dry spring of 1785 shed a cruel light on the inadequacy of the services responsible for overseeing agriculture. Every day alarming reports arrived from provincial intendants announcing that farmers were going to be forced to slaughter more than half their livestock. The provincial Societies of Agriculture were proposing solutions. Calonne asked the Academy of Science to examine these proposals and then issue detailed instructions for what was to be done. Lavoisier hastily prepared a brochure entitled "Means of Compensating for the Scarcity of Fodder and of Increasing the Subsistence of Livestock." He advocated pruning trees, planting rutabagas, potatoes, beets, and corn, and converting fallow lands into meadows. Lavoisier's directive was sent to all the regional intendants and was published in the *Gazette de France* on June 7, 1785.

Calonne, pleased with this initial result, then decided to create within his ministry a permanent working group to deal with agricultural questions. Thus was born the Comité d'Administration de l'Agriculture, in short the Committee on Agriculture. Its director was Charles Bonaventure François Xavier Gravier de Vergennes, nephew of the Secretary of State for Foreign Affairs and then in charge of the Bureau des impositions (Taxation Office) at the Ministry of Finance. The scientific contingent included Lavoisier, Tillet, Darcet, and Poissonnier. Parmentier and Thouin had been approached, but had refused on Bertier de Sauvigny's orders. Consequently, Lavoisier needed help and explained:

M. Poissonnier for whose intelligence and good intentions I have incomparable esteem, will be absent for part of the summer. M. Darcet, a nice man in the best sense of the term and very learned in chemical matters, is neither a farmer nor an administrator, and he is going on a trip to Gascogne. M. Tillet, although industrious and enlightened, is already weakened by age and exhausted by hard work.[4]

Lavoisier suggested to Gravier de Vergennes that he should take on Pierre Samuel Dupont, who had been ennobled by the king in 1784 and thereafter called himself Du Pont, and Paul d'Albert de Lubert. The advice was followed and within a short time, the Committee on Agriculture became a true administrative service, exuberantly active. Between June 16, 1785 and September 18, 1787 it held sixty-nine meetings. Lavoisier missed only four.[5]

In a memoir on the organization of the work at the Committee, Lavoisier set up the operating rules and he wrote the minutes himself in a special register destined to serve as a guide to his successors. The difficult questions would be passed on to special committees or to the Academy of Science for study. Experimental cultivation would be carried out on enclosed fields of ten hectares, for example, on his property in Le Bourget. He even envisaged creating a farm for cattle breeding.

On July 7, 1785 he wrote a "Directive on the Penning of Woolbearing Animals" inspired by his own experience in sheep raising at Freschines, and there followed a series of directives on the best use of manures, how to compensate for the scarcity of fodder, and the cultivation of clover. To circulate these various instructions, Lavoisier dreamed of creating an agricultural journal. The Hoffmann printing method which, instead of movable characters used plates of one piece on which the characters were fused together, would reduce costs. With it, one could print only the number of copies necessary at a particular time, store the plates, and use them again in emergencies: droughts, heavy rains, late frosts, outbreaks of epizootic diseases. "Since the remedy would arrive just when the problem was beginning to show itself, the administration would be credited with having shown an enlightened clairvoyance that would have foreseen the needs of the people."[6]

To encourage the cultivation of rutabagas, he had seeds distributed to farmers, along with instructions as to how to choose the soils best adapted to them and how to prepare and sow them. But on the ground things were less simple. At Freschines, for example, the peasants would have liked to plant rutabagas, but the Intendant gave the seeds only to the poorest, those who paid less than 50 livres ($1,850) a year in taxes, and the Freschines peasants were too rich. In spite of the ban on importing seeds from other provinces, Lavoisier took it on himself to buy buckwheat for them in Sologne. The cost was less then 400 livres ($16,000), but he notified the Controller-General, afraid that the Intendant in Orléans would hear about the distributions and be offended that he had not been informed.[7]

The Committee on Agriculture was overloaded with activity. It circulated instructions written by Parmentier on the cultivation of potatoes and corn, prepared a pamphlet on wheat blight, analyzed a memoir on the use of peat ashes as fertilizer, tested a method for destroying weevils in grain by washing it. Lavoisier also got involved in less important questions: the best date for sowing oats, and the technique for cultivating *vesces* (peas and lentils) on fallow land.[8]

Lavoisier and Du Pont also proposed using State capital to create a bank for lending money to farmers at a reduced interest rate. It would buy from the owners of watermills the marshes and vast meadows flooded by the water reserves necessary for their functioning. Each mill, Lavoisier emphasized, produced 10,000 pounds of flour per year, but sacrificed 100,000 pounds of agricultural products. Canals would be built to dry out the inundated zones that would then be cultivated. The profits of this State society would be used to finance improvements in agriculture.

When the Committee was asked to take a stand on the meat trade, Lavoisier recommended a liberal solution. Certainly an official tariff had to be kept in Paris, so as to prevent the powerful profession of butchers from abusing its monopoly, but not everything should depend on the intervention of the State. To allow the prices to rise slightly in Paris and authorize ambulant butchers to sell there would attract meat from the country and create a healthy competition. It would also be a means, but Lavoisier did not say so, of increasing the taxes on goods coming into Paris, for which he was responsible.

But the rivalry between the Committee on Agriculture and the Society of Agriculture grew. Each of them wanted to create its own agricultural journal. When a circular on the destruction of maybugs was published by the Committee, their mutual hostility was greatly aggravated; Bertier wrote an ironic note denouncing the uneconomical character of the method recommended.

Du Pont replied sharply during the meeting of March 17, 1786 with a memoir on the difference between the Committee and the Society. The latter, he said, was only an academy, and could deal with only scientific and practical aspects of agriculture. Furthermore, its right to deal with them did not extend beyond the region of Paris. The Committee alone had the duty to demand an accounting of their work from all the Societies of Agriculture—the one in Paris as well—, to stimulate their competitive spirit, to point their research in the same direction, and to engage them in mutual cooperation. The Committee was a government department. It had the responsibility for "watching over the administration of benefits, reforming abuses, and improving the laws. These were not activities for an academy; it was necessary to probe too deeply into the wounds of the State. It was not as a scientist that the government acted in this assembly, but as master, benefactor, and father."[9]

The Committee also clashed with the provincial Societies of Agriculture, which refused to be ruled by it or cooperate in its surveys. Du Pont found a way to get around their obstinacy, thanks to his friend the Abbé Jean Laurent Lefebvre, Procurator General of the Order of Sainte-Geneviève. He simply took six hundred priors and parish priests belonging to the order as correspondents and sent them questionnaires and circulars.

In 1787 the Committee had twelve permanent members and nine hundred corresponding ones. Its influence was growing.[10] But its reformist propositions were disturbing and the finances of the State were at their lowest point. All of a sudden, it lost all its support. Vergennes was replaced by Blondel; Calonne was dismissed on April 9 and Etienne Loménie de Brienne succeeded him.

Thus Lavoisier had to give up his projects for the model farm, the agricultural journal, the publication of the *Atlas minéralogique de la France*, and the collection of plowing instruments. The very survival of the Committee was threatened and it ceased to function for three months. On July 31, 1787 the Committee received the new Controller General of Finance, Laurent de Villedeuil. To try to save the group, Lavoisier presented his important report on the "encouragement that must be given to agriculture," a true Physiocratic profession of faith:

Agriculture is the most important of all factories, and the value of its productions, according to conservative estimates, rises to more than 2.5 billion livres a year. It is this annual reproduction that provides for tax payments, the food and clothing of the people, and the export trade. Commerce and industry are dependent on materials that it furnishes. It is, consequently, the primary source, the almost unique source of all the national wealth.[11]

But, he continued, it would be difficult to obtain a 10 percent increase or an additional 250 million livres in agricultural production in France. Thus the mission of analyzing the agricultural situation, of defining a program of reforms, and finding the money to finance them should be entrusted to a reformed Committee on Agriculture, located within the office of the Controller General. Lavoisier listed nine obstacles to progress in agriculture. The two biggest of these stemmed from the very existence of two direct taxes, the *taille* and the *corvée*.[12]

In some regions the taille applied to landed property, but in most of the provinces it bore on individual incomes. Since the nobles were exempted from it by law, the commoners were the only ones to pay it. They complained loudly, saying that it was actually an incentive to discouragement since it hit hardest those trying to increase their income and capital. The corvée compelled farmers to leave their work in the fields to become roadmenders. Finally, "in some cantons, the *champarts*, the feudal and ecclesiastical *dîmes* (tithes), took more than half and sometimes the totality of the net product of cultivation."[13] Lavoisier made no mention of the other two direct taxes: the *capitation*, which affected only the commoners and was added to the taille; and the *vingtième* (twentieth) which was applied to income from buildings, trade, annuities, and feudal rights.

As for indirect taxes, he contested the collection methods more than the principle, deploring "the domestic intrusions connected with the duties for *aides*, salt and tobacco, visits that entail the invasion of privacy and, often, inhuman and indecent searches that bring desolation to families and tend to make odious the authority of the most human of kings."[14]

Lavoisier said not a word about *traites*, those duties imposed by domestic customs, which represented an essential part of the income of the General Farm and of which he himself controlled the collection in Paris.[15] The time had not yet come to question the entire fiscal system and to propose its complete overhaul. But he modified it when he could. In 1786, examining the revenue from taxes in the towns of Clermont-en-Argonne, Dun-sur-Meuse, and Stenay, he discovered that, when passing through these towns, Jews had to pay a special duty, called the *pied fourchu* or cloven hoof tax. It was unfair, insulting, costly—3 livres ($120) for travelers in carts or on horses and 30 sous for pedestrians—and anti-economical, because it diverted merchants from those regions. Lavoisier had this onerous duty abolished, and as a sign of gratitude the Jewish community in Metz sent him cakes on Passover. Madame Lavoisier would witness to the authenticity of this episode in a handwritten account.[16]

The other obstacles to the progress of agriculture concerned age-old practices. Peasants were forced to have their grain ground at the mill of the domain for a fee that amounted to about a sixth of their flour. There was the right of way which was opposed to enclosing fields and the destruction of fallow lands, and hence sacrificed the second hay crop, propagated epizootic diseases, and resulted in great damage to fields from the trampling of livestock. The mills had the custom of damming water that flooded a part of the meadows and converted grazing lands into marshes. Wheat exports were banned, a prohibitive law that limited the activity of cultivators and forbade them to produce more wheat than the nation consumed.[17] The result of all these constraints was economically disastrous:

Would you believe that a kingdom so fertile, endowed with an agriculture so important, which ought to be exporting products of all sorts, lacks hemp, linen, oil, wool, and livestock and that it obtains considerable amounts of them from outside its borders and hence is at the mercy of foreign countries for a large part of the agricultural products for which its soil is best suited?[18]

In spite of very insufficient means, the Committee on Agriculture had made excellent progress in two years, but it was essential to do more. Lavoisier proposed going back to a plan of Calonne's and creating a General Committee on Agriculture, Trade, and Finance, a kind of ministry made up of fourteen persons coming from the administration of finance, agriculture, commerce, and the General Farm. It would also incorporate the Department of Interior Navigation, responsible for the upkeep of rivers and forests within the royal lands, and would receive "a fixed sum of 30,000 livres ($1.2 million) per month."[19] The provinces would contribute financially in exchange for an increase in their resources and an advisory role concerning the use of funds.

This regionalization plan comprised an economic and social program: the struggle against the insalubrity of the countryside by draining of marshes, a new tax system and the creation of family enterprises, making it possible for agricultural laborers to work inside except for the periods of sowing and harvesting. This double activity would offer them the possibility of living in the country and leading a normal family life. It would also bring social peace. Finally, Lavoisier envisaged creating a State-subsidized system of mutual insurance against natural catastrophes such as hail, storms, floods, and epizootic diseases.

The General Committee would meet once a week to propose reforms, laws, instructions, and subsidies in conjunction with provincial representatives: intendants, learned societies, presidents of provincial assemblies and even of district assemblies. It would meet with the Controller General once a month and with the Garde des Sceaux twice a year to revise the laws.

The creation of such horizontal relationships would centralize the management of the quasi-totality of the economic activity of France in the hands of men accustomed to working together. The vertical relationships between the central power and the provinces would facilitate the efforts of the General Committee to develop agriculture, commerce, and economic life.

The wealth thus created would benefit individuals, as well as, through the taxes it would generate, the General Farm, the Royal Treasury, and the entire nation. But this physiocratic vision, seeking to reconcile individual interests with the general interest came too late in a country that had lost confidence in the central power and was dreaming only of controlling it by elected provincial assemblies.

Even if Lavoisier's proposals were not finally accepted, they gave new life to the Committee on Agriculture. Lavoisier began to "conceive the hope of being able to contribute to the national prosperity by acting on public opinion through writing and examples; by encouraging the large landowners, capitalists, and the prosperous to invest their surplus in land cultivation."[20]

But the Controllers General, Loménie de Brienne and Claude Guillaume Lambert, were concerned to see the Committee overstep its prerogatives by taking up political and economic questions. Claude François Lazowski, one of its non-conformist members, had greatly shocked the Assemblée des Notables by criticizing the territorial subsidy, a new tax project that he deemed absurd because it was proportional to each farmer's agricultural production and consequently the enemy of growth.

There was, too, the permanent hostility between the Committee and the Society of Agriculture. Looking for a site for his experimental farm, Lavoisier stumbled on something that was going to aggravate this hostility. He wanted to install the experimental farm at Maisons-Ville, on land that belonged to the Alfort veterinary school. But he discovered that some time before the land had been purchased on credit by Bertier de Sauvigny for a small down payment and a life annuity of 7,000 livres ($280,000) to the previous owner, without the Controller General's approval. Bertier de Sauvigny, who wanted to use the land for planting exotic fruit trees, resented Lavoisier's interference, and thanks to his powerful court connections could sabotage Lavoisier's project. The war between the Society and the Committee was not over, but it ceased temporarily in the summer of 1787, during the sitting of the Provincial Assembly of Orléans.

The "Provincial Assembly of Orléans"

In 1776 Turgot and Du Pont had conceived of a new form of regional representation, the provincial assemblies, to appease the hostility of public opinion toward the stifling administration of the intendants, agents of fiscal tyranny.

In 1778 Necker had created the first ones in Berry and Haute-Guyenne. Made up of local *notables* (prominent persons), these assemblies, where the representatives of the Third Estate would be equal in number to that of the two other orders combined, would constitute an initial attempt at having the French participate in the administration of their provinces. They would remain under the control of the intendants, however, and possess only limited authority. Yet they would decide on the allocation and levying of taxes, the construction and maintenance of roads, aid to commerce and creation of jobs, and the management of charity workshops. Necker's downfall in May 1781 had interrupted this attempt at decentralization.

In August 1786 this project appeared in Calonne's three-point reform plan: the creation of a uniform and more egalitarian tax system; the abolition of domestic customs and the ban on the grain trade, and the generalization of the advisory provincial assemblies. The Assemblée des Notables had accepted the plan, but requested that the distinction among the orders be maintained.

Loménie de Brienne, Controller General of Finances in April 1787, wanted to extend the provincial assemblies throughout the kingdom. The number of deputies from the Third Estate, doubled, would be equal to that of the Clergy and Nobility combined, and the voting would be done by the individual and not by order.

Lavoisier had been familiar with the idea of these provincial assemblies since the days when he was in close contact with Turgot and Du Pont. He was convinced that they were the last chance for a political reform. On September 4 he left Paris with his wife in his elegant dark blue English-style carriage, whose wheels were a handsome poppy red. The inside was lined with pearl gray cloth, bordered by blue, yellow, and beige braid.[21] They arrived in Orléans the following day.

The Provincial Assembly of Orléans, presided over by the duc de Luxembourg, had twenty-four members, twelve chosen by the king and the other twelve coopted by the first group. Lavoisier, designated as representative from Romorantin, sat with the Third Estate, even though he had inherited a title of nobility at his father's death in 1775.[22]

The first meeting, on September 6, defined the working methods. New members—the Abbé Sieyès, the Abbé Louis, the comte de Rochambeau, who had commanded the French troops in America, the baron de Montboissier, and the vicomte de Toulongeon—arrived on September 10. On September 12 it was announced that "M. le baron de Montboissier and M. de Lavoisier have been appointed to write the minutes."[23]

The fifth and sixth sessions, on September 13 and 14, were devoted to the budget of the Assembly and the nomination of members to a permanent committee responsible for writing memoirs on taxation, the major roads and public works, navigable rivers, population, agriculture, and trade. Then the Assembly adjourned.

Lavoisier returned hurriedly to present to the Paris Society of Agriculture on September 18 his memoir on "Results of Some Agricultural Experiments and Reflections on Their Relationship to Economics." He felt that the method he used at Freschines, based on exact calculations of costs and profits in operating a farm, could be extrapolated to the entire kingdom. A true science could then "furnish the economy with certain results on the division of territorial wealth."[24]

His professional experience had convinced him of the pressing need for a modernization of the fiscal system, something that at last was possible: "The wisdom and enlightenment that provincial assemblies will bring in the distribution of taxation, the solidity of the bases that they will adopt, will prevent similar errors, which alone suffice to oppose all agricultural progress."[25] Once again he proposed the creation of a General Committee on Agriculture to be composed of fourteen members: four representatives from the Royal Council of Finance, four from the Academy of Science, four from agricultural landowners, and two secretaries. But the Paris Society of Agriculture threatened to provoke serious difficulties if this new structure was created. Lavoisier and Du Pont were accused of being motivated by ambition, "of having relegated the Society to the domain of theoretical and academic discussions, whereas they, more clever, had reserved for themselves the merit of being practical, as well as the benefit of being able to act directly on the government."[26] The Society did not forgive what it considered a betrayal by its former members, and accused them of having access to financial advantages through the Committee. Therefore Lambert abandoned Lavoisier's plan and asked Cadet de Vaux to study the fusion of the two rival organizations.

On September 22 Lavoisier left Paris accompanied by Monge and Fourcroy to visit the Le Creusot forge. He returned on October 3 to discuss the transfer of the Hôtel-Dieu with Bailly, at the Hospital Commission.

On November 6 he presented to the Provincial Assembly of Orléans his *Instruction sur Agriculture*, destined to "furnish an initial foundation for the work of the provincial assembly on this crucial subject, until time and discussion have brought us broader knowledge."[27] In it he summed up his agronomical experience, confining himself to the purely technical aspect. It was clear that the government had asked him to avoid all financial, fiscal or statutory debate.

On November 11 he was back in Paris; the Academy of Science awarded its prize for the new dyeing techniques. On November 15 he returned to

Orléans for the second session of the Assembly. There were new royal recommendations, an official *grand-messe* and the creation of four committees:
Accounting; Taxes; Bridges and Roadways; Public Welfare and Agriculture.

Along with Sieyès and Rochambeau, Lavoisier was an active member of
the Committee for Public Welfare and Agriculture."The one who does everything, leads everybody, who always does his utmost is Lavoisier. His name
reappears at every instant."[28]

The first question to be studied was that of transforming the *vingtième*
into a new land tax, payable once a year by the province to the Royal Treasury. The new tax would be higher than the old one, 2.5 million livres instead
of 1.8 million, but fairer, because the nobles could no longer escape it and the
burden for the small landowners would be lightened.

Lavoisier and the deputies of the Third Estate, who had created a kind of
club at the Auberge de l'Epervier, favored this new arrangement. The clergy,
dispensed from taxation, also favored it; the Abbé Sieyès, Bishop of Chartres,
voted for it. The nobility were against it, except for the comte de Rochambeau who declared: "The nobility can gain the esteem of the province only
by embracing its interests and abandoning the advantages belonging to them
alone for those benefitting the nation."[29]

Finally, on November 30, the Assembly decided to propose to the king
a fixed sum of 2.3 million livres as the vingtième. To reduce collection costs,
it would itself see to the levying. The proposition was accepted. Another important question was the reform of the corvée. It was to be replaced by an
additional contribution to the taille, amounting to one-sixth of the original
payment. Lavoisier argued that, like the vingtième, it ought to be paid by
everybody. But opposition from the nobility and a few members of the Third
Estate forced him to withdraw his report and "wait for a time when minds
more accustomed to reflecting on the general welfare, could conceive that it
was noble to sacrifice a privilege, which was purely theoretical, for the well-
being of the most numerous class of the State."[30]

At the Commission of Public Welfare and Agriculture, Lavoisier presented a series of memoirs favoring agricultural progress, underlining the advantages of knowing all the demographic, geographic, and economic parame-
ters of a region, and proposed several creations:

A Discount Bank for the merchants of Orléans, Chartres, and Blois.
"Commerce in general, at least in most of the towns of the kingdom, is con-
strained by lack of capital. Thus, to increase capital is to spread and invigorate
trade. If the general funds of the province were entirely in the hands of its
administration, they could be employed usefully for itself and trade, to dis-

count merchants' bills of exchanges. In this respect, one would follow the rule established by the Discount Bank of Paris."[31]

An Insurance Fund would "insure the elderly and widows against poverty." In this establishment, a precursor of mutual insurance funds, "one would receive sums from people of all ages and conditions who would want to provide for themselves, their widows and children, whenever it was needed, a lifetime income of a sum to be determined according to a table set up for this purpose."[32] This plan, which he devised with the Abbé Jean Martin de Prades and the baron de Montboissier, was never realized. In the meantime, a financial company obtained for a period of fifteen years an exclusive privilege for a bank of savings and charity for the people.[33]

Charity Workshops to combat unemployment and begging were another priority. The able-bodied unemployed would be put to work: public works for men and spinning for women and children. Vagabonds would be sent to camps, the ill and infirm to hospitals. "The only means of reconciling the requirements of public order with the respect due to misery, suffering, misfortune, and poverty consists of opening workshops where individuals of all classes, sexes, and ages—as long as they are not ill or infirm—can find jobs that are proportionate to their strength and subsistence analogous to their needs."[34] He also suggested giving an allowance to unwed mothers so that their babies would not be abandoned in hospitals, "where undoubtedly they take a germ of corruption that destroys almost all of them."[35]

Lavoisier's inventive mind was filled with all sorts of plans: improving the navigation of the Loire by creating canals; drawing up a mineralogical map of the Orléanais on the same mode as the *Atlas minéralogique* that he had begun twenty years earlier with Guettard. He already had a part of the necessary elements and emphasized the advantages of such an atlas: "No one could propose building a road or canal without your being able to recognize, by simply consulting the map, the resources and facilities available for their construction, the nature of the material that could be used and the sites for establishing quarries or excavations. The same would be true for everything relating to the arts and manufacturing."[36]

The most important document he produced in that period was that of December 4–10, 1787, "On Agriculture and Trade in the Orléanais." In it, he took up his familiar ideas: agriculture in France was in a less flourishing state than in England. There each square mile produced 48,000 pounds, whereas in France the same surface yielded only 18,000 pounds. "The total consumption of England is almost double that of France, in proportion to the population and territory. But, if consumption is double, territorial production is necessarily double since, in a country that exports more than it imports, it is necessary that what is consumed every year be produced every year." [37]

In England agriculture had made rapid progress whereas it had remained almost stagnant in France. This difference was due not to a less fertile soil but to two economic factors: the taille and the excessively high interest rates. The taille was a true "incentive to discouragement." It resulted in capital being concentrated in towns where it was invested in commerce and speculation rather than being spent on improving agriculture. Agriculture, "almost the unique source of all wealth, has been left to the indigent citizens of the nation. It has not been the focus of any enterprising spirit or imaginative speculation, but on the contrary, it can be said that one has abandoned reality for the shadow." [38] Therefore it was essential to replace the taille by a unique and just tax.

As for the lack of capital, it prevented proprietors from making the necessary investments in their land and farmers from paying the annual operating expenses.

In England, a farm consisted only of the residence of the farmer, a stable for his horses, and a large hangar. There were no barns for storing harvests, granaries for fodder, cowsheds, or sheepfolds. The harvests were stacked in ricks around the farms. The livestock spent the entire year outside, even during the severe cold of winter, and were only the healthier and stronger for it. In France, on the contrary, farm buildings tied up an important amount of capital. The total income gained from the lease by the landowner represented an insufficient interest for the invested capital. Maintenance costs and taxes absorbed the greater part of his income. It was not surprising that he turned away from it. The farmer on his side did not invest enough in the agricultural material and operating costs for which he was responsible. A French farmer who exploited a three-plow farm (about 300 acres) invested in general less than 12,000 livres ($480,000) per year, or 40 livres ($1,600) per acre. In England, 5 pounds sterling ($3,000) was considered necessary to exploit the same surface. Thus the capital employed for cultivation in England was double, indeed, sometimes triple what it was in France. The result was that French agriculture suffered a two-fold imbalance; the investments in land and buildings were excessive and those in production inadequate. It was this inadequacy that conditioned the orientation of French agriculture toward wheat production, whereas in England it was turned toward livestock.

Agriculture in most of the French provinces, such as Beauce can be considered as one vast wheat factory. Livestock are only instruments used to cultivate or fertilize, and the benefit they provide is only slight. The English farming system is almost the reverse. Most farmers grow hardly more wheat than is necessary for feeding themselves and their animals and providing the necesssary straw. Wheat is produced for raising and feeding livestock, and it is toward their sale and exchange that all cultivation is directed.[39]

Lavoisier did not dare carry his analysis through to the end since he was forbidden to do so. He knew that to stimulate agriculture and trade, the first thing that had to be done was to change the fiscal system. He limited himself to recommending a concerted effort against wheat bunt; the creation of depots of good quality seeds; the increase in tillable land by draining marshes and cleaning rivers and streams; the improvement of flour and bread as well as grazing lands and herds; the development of industries for spinning wool, cotton, and hemp; and the encouragement of trade in livestock, grains, wood, wines from the Loire Valley, honey from the Gâtinais, and saffron.

An effort would also be made for the manufacturers: the Orléans sugar refineries; the factories making hats for Turkey; those in Olivet making painted cloth; those in Orléans making dyed fabrics; those in Vendôme making gloves; those in Châteaudun, Brou, and Authon making woolen blankets and white muslin; those in Blois making knives and thimbles; those in Montargis making paper; those in Châteaurenault making woolen cloth and serge; those in Pithiviers making knitted hosiery; the cutlery industry in Gien; and the makers of "billiard cloth and other woolen fabrics suitable for military uniforms" in Romorantin.[40] Finally, commercial exchanges had to be developed by profiting from the location of Orléans:

The Loire will soon open it up to communication with the two seas. The Mediterranean will provide it, by way of Marseille and the Rhône, all the commodities from the East and Provence. The Ocean will bring it the riches from our colonies, India, and the Dutch Spice Islands. The brandies from Aunis, Poitou, and Touraine reach it from the Vienne. [. . .] A large part of the wools from Sologne and Berry, as well as those from Spain, flow through Orléans, and it is in this town that the factories of Abbeville, Reims, and Sedan make their purchases.[41]

The description Lavoisier gave of the industrial activities of the region was not based on book knowledge but came from studies made in the field. Always looking for ways to develop economic activities in the region, he had investigated the possibility of creating a mill for spinning cotton. He had visited the one at Thieux, on M. de Montharan's property close to Essonne, employing fifty-two Indians brought from Pondichéry by M. de Suffren. He and his wife had visited the factory of MM. Michel and Boyetet, who made hats for the Turks. Madame Lavoisier had described in precise detail the methods by which "22,000 dozen" woolen hats were knitted and dyed and then sold in Marseille every year. She had given special emphasis to the socio-economic aspect: "The knitters earn 4 sous for each hat. They can easily make three per day, so that this work is more profitable for them than spinning hemp."[42] Next they had visited Jacques Constantin Périer's cotton mill, equipped with six machines brought from England, each one costing 12,000 livres. Madame Lavoisier had pointed out that the profitability of this factory, which was powered by men's muscles, was less than that of the one in l'Épine, near Essonne, which used water power.

As a realist, Lavoisier knew that he could not expect rapid change and that the reforms could be prepared only slowly. "The administration, in everything that touches its particular or domestic interests, must neither lead nor direct. It must be content to instruct and protect. It can sometimes give encouragement and rewards, but its most important role is to remove obstacles."[43]

At the closing session near the end of December, the provincial assembly set up an intermediary commission consisting of six members: Charles Victoire François d'Irumberri de Salaberry and the comte de Rouville for the nobility; Sieyès for the clergy; Lavoisier, Levassor du Bouchet, and Boesnier de l'Orme for the Third Estate. Lavoisier would return to Orléans in February 1788 to take part in its work. In the more intimate atmosphere of this intermediary committee, the debates often took a political turn, and one could see the beginning of the opposition between the highly placed civil servants of the ancien régime, like Lavoisier, partisans of progressive and limited reforms, and the out-and-out enemies of the privileged, such as Sieyès. "Several of his reflections are good," Lavoisier observed, "but they could have been presented a bit more moderately."[44]

Reassuringly, he wrote on February 20 to Valdec de Lessart, intendant of Finance: "Spirits are calm in the bailiwick of Blois and we are directed by good intentions and views. Attached as I am to M. Necker's person, and a zealous partisan of his administration, *as are all impartial people*, I hope that you will not doubt that I use the little ascendancy that I can obtain to serve simultaneously both the public welfare and the minister, whose interests happen to coincide at the moment."[45]

Except for the attack on corvées, which had displeased the nobility, all the memoirs Lavoisier had written were published in Orléans in 1788. The meetings continued until 1790, but participation was limited to members living in the region. Lavoisier no longer attended, and none of his plans would ever be realized. Another disappointment was being prepared for him in Paris. In May 1788 d'Ormesson, Breteuil, and Tarbé, wanting to end the war between the Committee on Agriculture and the Society of Agriculture, presented a compromise to Louis XVI, and soon thereafter a unique organization, the Royal Society of Agriculture, was created. It had a steering committee that brought together members of the former Committee—Lavoisier, Du Pont, Tillet, Desmarest, the Abbé Lefebvre—and loyal members of the Paris Society—Thouin, Broussonnet, and Marie François d'Ailly. The Paris Society had triumphed, but the abhorred Committee had penetrated its heart.

On July 18, three days after a violent hail storm that devastated harvests, the new Royal Society of Agriculture held its first meeting at the Hôtel de Ville. Parmentier and Lavoisier, at last brought together, studied the possible solutions and presented a number of measures for treating damaged trees and selecting seeds that could be sown at such a late date. The functioning of the young Royal Society was rather disorderly, however. Meetings were characterized by a certain confusion, since they were without any special order. Everybody spoke at once. Arthur Young, passing through Paris, was invited to suggest a subject for a prize of 1,200 livres offered by the Abbé Raynal. "Give it," he said, "in some way for the introduction of turnips." He was told that it was a hopeless undertaking. The government had attempted to get farmers to plant them, but always in vain. Rather pessimistic, Young noted:

I did not tell them that all hitherto done has been absolute folly; and that the right way to begin was to undo everything done. I am never present at any societies of agriculture, either in France or England, but I am much in doubt with myself whether, when best conducted, they do most good or mischief; that is, whether the benefits a national agriculture may, by great chance, owe to them, are not more than counterbalanced by the harm they effect, by turning the public attention to frivolous objects, instead of important ones, or dressing important ones in such a garb as to make them trifles? The only society that could be really useful would be that which, in the culture of a large farm, should exhibit a perfect example of good husbandry, for the use of such as would resort to it; consequently one that should consist solely of practical men; and then query whether many good cooks would not spoil a good dish.[46]

Lavoisier and the Chemical Industry

Lavoisier's frustrations occasioned by his lack of success in implementing his plans for agricultural reforms encouraged him to take a greater interest in politics. One might expect that a man like him, who had just launched chemistry on the road to modernity and who was such an efficient manager at the Gunpowder Administration, would have had an outstanding role in the development of the chemical industry in France. But actually this born organizer had no ambition for creating enterprises. His personal fortune and permanent contact with the world of deciders surely gave him opportunities. His management method based on exact accounts and balance sheets could have assured his success. And yet his numerous forays into the domain of applied chemistry remained sporadic, fragmented, and in the end unconnected with his theoretical conceptions. Although he had used his skills as an analyst at the Tobacco Commission to detect the presence of ashes thanks to the effervescence provoked by sulfuric acid, he had not succeeded in producing saltpeter by chemical synthesis from nitric acid at the Gunpowder Administration. His attempts to interest investors in the creation of industrial nitrate works had failed; the only profitable ones were those built by the Gunpowder Administration. Finally, the success he obtained there owed more to his administrative and management talents than to his scientific contributions. At the General Farm, he consistently put the interest of the company ahead of the development of chemical industries. John Holker in Rouen, Léonard Alban in Javel, and Jean Antoine Chaptal in Montpellier were even refused the saltpeter necessary for producing sulfuric acid. The importation of alum (hydrated double sulfate of potassium and aluminum) from Egypt, Spain, Ireland, and Scotland was consequently proportionately prolonged.

However, at the Committee on Agriculture, Lavoisier joined the efforts to slow down the importation of English cotton. At his instigation, the cultivation of linen and the creation of model spinning mills were encouraged. The price of thread being proportional to its thinness, he established the norms to be respected and set up a workshop in Paris, on the rue du Montparnasse, where could be woven, "along with the linen, a large number of stoles that had previously been made only in cotton or silk, and also satins, twills, ras de Saint-Cyr, basins, and all fabrics that were bound to have a large turnover."[47] They also made a sailcloth in twill that resisted the wind much better than ordinary canvas.

Using the process perfected by Berthollet in 1786, Lavoisier set up, close to the first workshop, a second one for bleaching linen with chlorine. Twenty stockholders divided the thirty shares issued at 300 livres ($12,000) each to form a new company. The Gunpowder Administration was to provide the chlorine that it extracted from salt, a byproduct of the refining of saltpeter, and at a preferential price: 12 sous per livre instead of 45. This experimental venture would have neither means nor time to reach the industrial level.

Other people went into the production of soda. In France, soda, which was necessary for making glass, soap, paper, and dyes, was extracted from the ashes of vegetable substances from the sea—kelp and salicorn—but the method produced hardly more than 15 percent of the sodium carbonate used and of the 25 million pounds consumed each year, 18 had to be imported.[48] Already in 1737 Duhamel du Monceau had suggested making soda from sea salt. In 1784 the Academy of Science took up the idea and proposed a competition. Guyton de Morveau, Jean Antoine Chaptal, and Jean Antoine Carny tested methods that, for the most part, employed sodium sulfate, which was transformed into carbonate by adding charcoal. In 1790 Hassenfratz in turn attempted, with Carny and Guyton de Morveau to find a way of manufacturing soda. He carried out various tests "in several laboratories and in particular the laboratory of M. Lavoisier." He kept the patron informed of his results, but could not "determine how much profit could be realized with his method."[49] One can suppose that Lavoisier wanted to know about the validity and profitability of the method before giving his financial support. Like the other potential investors, he remained deaf to the appeals launched by Hassenfratz in the *Journal de la Société de 1789*.

During this time Nicolas Leblanc was innovating by adding to the reaction chalk in precise proportions.[50] He obtained the prize of the Academy in 1789, and the patent in 1791, but the factory in Saint Denis would be swept away by the turns taken by the Revolution. Lavoisier would remain absent from these two projects that nevertheless illustrated his new chemistry.

Thus Lavoisier's attitude toward the great number of endeavors that announced the blossoming of industrial chemistry was ambiguous. His intellectual curiosity and pragmatism, his role as expert at the Academy of Science, his sincere desire to promote economic development should have been sufficient motives for multiple interventions. He dreamed of a modern France, one that would give the three major sectors of economic life, agriculture, commerce, and industry, their rightful place. Thanks to the wealth that would be created by them and a reformed tax system, the State would be able to aid regional development, create public services, and take over social assistance. Encoded data, statistics, and modern accounting methods would be the instruments of this policy.

But he preferred acting through committees and scientific, academic, or administrative authorities. Rather than being an individual entrepreneur, he was a technocrat, ready to launch industrial programs for the State. His personal domain was pure science, basic science, which was only fitting for an Academician. He left to his provincial colleagues, Guyton de Morveau and Chaptal, the task of applying the chemical revolution: the production of sulfuric acid, hydrochloric acid, sodium carbonate, hypochlorites.

He could give an expert evaluation of a project and appreciate its economic and social utility, but he did not go beyond the stage of the model and was rarely involved in its financing or realization. As a good State servant, he expected everything from it. But the Royal Treasury did not have the means for such a policy. In those days, the capitalists were timid and Lavoisier was no exception. His considerable fortune was invested primarily in Parisian real estate and agricultural land in Beauce; the rest was in stocks of the Discount Bank and the East India Company.

Even if Lavoisier's direct intervention remained limited, French industry would be greatly indebted to him. His contribution, both theoretical and technical, had four aspects. The first and most important one included the new chemistry, his method of chemical nomenclature, and the original bases of organic chemistry.

Second, he had also defined a new scientific approach, valid in many different fields: "Methodical, quantitative experimentation with repeated controls and precise measurements, were going to be systematically developed by his successors in their industrial efforts."[51]

Third, he played a significant role in technological progress: the precision scales, thermometers, barometers, aerometers, gasometers, calorimeters that he had made for his laboratory would become indispensable to future industrialists.[52]

His final contributions, the reform of weights and measures, the metric system, and decimal division, would complete this arsenal and ensure the development of chemical industry throughout the world.

13

A New Power

LOUIS XVI WAS NOT SO NAIVE. When he convened the Etats généraux (States General) on May 1, 1789, he had every intention of limiting their role to what it had always been: a means of obtaining financial resources.

The Parliament had requested that the States General be organized as they had been in 1614, in three distinct chambers, one for each order voting separately. But the Third Estate, representing more than 90 percent of the population, was no longer willing to be subjected to the other two orders. It was determined to make itself heard and obtain reforms. A generation of young people, who had experienced only declining profits and increasing unemployment since entering economic life, were demanding that Third Estate representation be doubled, that the vote be by head, and that the three orders deliberate in common. Its objective was to obtain civil, judicial, and fiscal equality for all, basic liberties, and representative government.

Philippe d'Orléans, Louis XVI's cousin, was orchestrating all this agitation. Grand Master of the Grand Lodge of Freemasonry in France since 1786, he was spending a part of his immense fortune to promote the installation of a constitutional monarchy, inspired by the English model, in France. The first political clubs began to be organized. Financiers, senior civil servants, scientists, and intellectuals met and exchanged ideas, hoping for a new world based on the thought of the Enlightenment. The Freemasons, who had almost six hundred lodges in France, exerted considerable influence on the clubs in Paris.[1]

Was Lavoisier a Freemason? There are reasons to believe he was, but there is no definite proof.[2] Whether or not he was inscribed in a lodge, it is certain that his political ideas evolved under the influence of Freemasonry. Almost all his friends belonged. Like them, he wanted a constitutional monarchy, a secular state, an efficient administration, a dynamic economy, and a more equitable tax system. He seemed to forget that he was one of the pillars of the unjust conservative system that was in force.

One of the first political clubs, the Societé des Trente (Society of Thirty) had been founded in September 1788 by Adrien Duport de Prélaville, a member of the Amis réunis lodge. This young advisor to the Paris Parlement was a zealous advocate of doubling the number of members in the Third Estate and of the common deliberation of the three orders. In his home, Lavoisier met Du Pont (de Nemours), the new name of Du Pont, who, when elected deputy from Nemours in May 1789, had added (de Nemours) to distinguish himself from another Du Pont (de Bigorre); later the parentheses would disappear; the marquis Marie Joseph de La Fayette, very much imbued with the ideals of the American Constitution, and his brother-in-law, the duc de Noailles; many of their friends, "American veterans" and Freemasons like the duc de Lauzun, the marquis de Latour-Maubourg, and the Lameth brothers.[3] The members met three times a week from seven to ten in the evening to discuss the forthcoming States General. A very efficient organization was set up. A propaganda committee financed trips to the provinces by "apostles," who distributed brochures and forms of wording for the Registers of Grievances. They spread the idea of a national assembly bringing together all the orders on an equal footing.

Although tinted with social ideology, Lavoisier's political position remained that of the upper middle class. His appetite for reform expressed the need for emancipation of the ruling class. Those who had savoir-faire and an enterprising spirit felt themselves held back by the conservative aristocrats, obstinate holders of a power they did not use in a dynamic way. Lavoisier and his friends wanted to have France evolve toward economic progress and free enterprise. Their model was England, which, following Necker's example, they were eager to imitate in agriculture, banking, and the parliamentary system. Thus one is not surprised to read what Lavoisier wrote regarding the States General: "This assembly should be composed of deputies from each order in a proportion more favorable to the Third Estate than is the case in the provincial assemblies, and voting should be done not by order but by head."[4]

Lavoisier was among the first to join the "Society of the Friends of Black People." Founded in 1788 by Brissot de Warville and Clavière, and presided over by Condorcet, its objective was the abolition of the slave trade and the emancipation of slaves. In spite of the interests of the General Farm in this trade through the East India Company, Lavoisier had let himself be convinced by the abolitionist arguments of his father-in-law, who had helped the Abbé Raynal write *Histoire philosophique et politique des deux Indes*. Among his fellow members were four colleagues from the General Farm: Gilbert Georges de Montcloux, Louis-Philippe Du Vaucel, Nicolas de Vismes de Saint-Alphonse, and Denis François Papillon de Sannois.[5] They soon numbered ninety-five, but their adversaries were much more numerous. They were all the shipowners in the large ports—Nantes, Bordeaux, Marseille, and Le Havre—who made a considerable profit from the trade: 223 livres for each slave, or in a single year an income of almost 7 million livres for each shipowner.

According to the baron d'Allarde, exportations toward the colonies and the slave trade represented a commerce of 80 million livres per year. France imported goods—sugar, coffee, cinnamon, pepper, cotton, indigo, and cochineal—worth 170 million livres from the Caribbean islands. A third sufficed for the national consumption; the rest was re-exported to other parts of Europe in exchange for wood, iron, and hemp. Thus France covered its own consumption, collected taxes on the goods consumed domestically, and, by trading the rest, supplied itself with indispensable raw materials. "In this regard, it is imperative that the colonies receive from the government the attention and encouragement necessary for providing the slaves needed for cultivation."[6]

To defend their interests, the colonists even created the Society of the French Colonists made up of shipowners, financiers, and a few deputies such as Pierre Victor Malouet, Antoine Pierre Joseph Barnave, and Jean Baptiste Mosneron de l'Aunay.

Necker felt that any reform was premature. The commercial rivalry with England left France little room to manoeuver. Besides, as the author of an anonymous pamphlet wrote, "as long as European nations continue to have their colonies cultivated by slaves, a nation whose possessions require many hands must avoid, as long as possible, depending on others to be supplied with the Negroes that it needs."[7]

The Memoir on the States General

During the summer of 1788, Lavoisier wrote a memoir for Necker on the convocation of the States General. Reviving the earlier plan of Turgot and Du Pont, he proposed a pyramid of elected representative assemblies, rising from districts to departments to provinces, in which vote would be by head and composition would be the same as that of provincial assemblies. On the question of quotas for each order, without going as far as demanding a representation proportional to the actual weight in the nation of the Third Estate, he expressed the wish that it might be less arbitrary.

These provincial assemblies, "once formed from members freely elected and delegated by communities, would be empowered to send representatives to the States General."[8] The assembly of elected deputies would be called the Assemblée nationale (National Assembly), and it would hold the legislative power. "This august assembly not only would have the right to levy or refuse taxation and to formulate complaints, but also to examine laws and possible reforms, and to make general regulations regarding legislation, the police and trade as well as taxation."[9]

The king would hold the executive power: "As the king alone has undivided executive power, he alone, after having obtained the necessary sanctions, can publish and implement the law, supervise its execution, and determine when it has been violated, and punish those responsible."[10] Before the States General the king would be expected to respect three indispensable preliminaries. First, he would have to promise to decree no order of imprisonment, exile, or even exclusion from the States General against any elected member. "Where force reigns, liberty ceases to exist, and where there is no liberty, there can be neither votes nor consent."[11] Second, everything done and said at the Assembly would be printed and published as it occurred; authors would have to sign their articles and could be taken to court for slander. Finally, the States General would be convened at regular dates, every three or five years.

Lavoisier felt that he was participating in an important reform and announced to his colleagues at the Provincial Assembly of Orléans that the hour of social justice had sounded. Certainly, he admitted, there would be protests—essentially dictated by interests—at the Court, but they would run up against the opinion of a vast majority, and "the nation is too enlightened today not to know that it has a duty to bring happinesss to the greatest number, and that if it is allowed to make exceptions of certain orders of citizens, especially in regard to taxation, it can only be in favor of the poor. The inequality of the tax burden can be tolerated only when it prejudices the wealthy."[12]

Lavoisier at the Discount Bank

On April 16, 1788 Lavoisier became a member of the board of directors of the Caisse d'Escompte (Discount Bank).[13] He would soon afterward serve as its president and play a decisive role in the conduct of French financial affairs.

This powerful private bank, created by Turgot in 1776, managed private fortunes, negotiated commercial bills of exchange, and above all advanced important sums to the Royal Treasury. It became the "bankers' bank" in 1778, when Necker urged the major Parisian banks to acquire more than a third of its capital. The banks Le Couteulx et cie; Tourton and Baur; Cottin; Vandenyver; Rilliet; Louis Julien et fils; Greffulhe and Montz (formerly Necker's bank) thus joined its board of directors and thanks to it, French and Genevan capitalists provided the royal coffers with the money needed not only for its current expenses and interests on debts, but also for its support of the American war for independence.

The Bank had the exclusive privilege of providing the mints in the kingdom with the gold and silver indispensable for making coins. Since 1787 one of its main functions had also been to issue banknotes, a thirty-year privilege the government had granted in exchange for an advance of 70 million livres. The Scottish banker John Law, who had taken charge of the French finances after the death of Louis XIV, had created in 1715 a central bank that could issue banknotes; but the bank had failed in 1720. In spite of the bad memories left by this bankruptcy, the banknotes of the Discount Bank, payable on presentation, had the confidence of the clients. The bank honored bills of exchange in cash or banknotes, and these banknotes had been circulating freely in increasing amounts: 20.5 million in 1781, 44.7 million in 1783, 99.2 million in 1786.

Because of its close ties with the Royal Treasury, the General Farm always had some of its men on the board of the Discount Bank. Thus, a private company was controlling the loans made to the government by a private bank. In 1787 Necker had had to deny that the Treasury was receiving funds from the Bank. The support the government showed it, he said, had no motive other than "encouraging trade, lowering interest rates and stimulating the circulation of currency."[14]

Things had changed a great deal since the early days of the Discount Bank. The *Compte rendu des finances*, published by Loménie de Brienne in March 1788, had revealed the Royal Treasury's deficit to be 160 million livres ($6.4 billion). Taxes were not coming in and all attempts to borrow money had been unsuccessful. Only a profound reform could save the country from disaster. An attentive observer such as Arthur Young saw the situation clearly and reported after a social event in Paris:

One opinion pervaded the whole company, that they were on the eve of some great revolution in the government; that everything pointed to it; the confusion in the finances great; with a deficit impossible to provide for without the meeting of the States General of the kingdom, yet no ideas formed of what would be the consequences of their meeting; no minister existing, or to be looked to, in or out of power, with such decisive talents as to promise any other remedy than palliative ones; a prince on the throne, with excellent dispositions, but without the resources of a mind that could govern in such a moment without ministers; a court buried in pleasure and dissipation, and adding to the distress, instead of endeavouring to be placed in a more independent situation; a great ferment amongst all ranks of men, who are eager for some change, without knowing what to look to, or to hope for; and a strong leaven of liberty, increasing every hour since the American Revolution; altogether form a combination of circumstances that promises ere long to ferment into motion, if some master hand, of very superior talent, and inflexible courage, be not found at the helm to guide events, instead of being driven by them." [15]

At the end of July the Treasury declared bankruptcy. Loménie de Brienne stopped payments in currency, which brought about a massive demand for reimbursement of the Discount Bank's notes. Very soon it could not cope and also stopped payments. On August 16 Brienne made the banknotes of the Discount Bank forced currency and convoked the States General for May 1, 1789.

One week later the King dismissed Brienne and reluctantly called on Necker for the second time. The announcement of these two decisions unleashed both great enthusiasm and new disturbances among the people. The jubilant crowd tried to force the inhabitants of the Palais Royal area to put candles in their windows as a sign of their approval and threw stones to break the panes of those who were recalcitrant. Lavoisier reported to Hassenfratz:

The guards, although in full force, tried to intervene, but they were driven back by the crowd. They withdrew to the Place de Grève and began to fire on the demonstrators who counterattacked with paving stones. The troops were finally forced to retreat altogether and the crowd set fire to several guardrooms. Yesterday the king gave responsibility to M. le Maréchal de Biron. A large number of French and Swiss soldiers has been sent in the different aeras of Paris, and last night the city has been quiet everywhere. [16]

When Necker returned at the end of August there remained only "400,000 francs, that is the funds needed to run the State for six hours, hopelessly sunk in the middle of the immense vacuum of the public coffers." [17] Necker re-established cash payments. As a result the stocks of the Discount Bank which had fallen to 3,550 livres per share, rose to 4,300. Nevertheless, Necker knew that he was facing a tense situation:

Every form of credit had been exhausted. And yet I had to find several million livres before the end of the week to meet specific commitments or expenses whose slightest delay would expose us to the most terrifying dangers. Therefore it was by tacking and using all the resources contained in a small circle that I managed to steer the fragile ship of State without having it break apart or run aground before the opening of the Etats généraux, a date that for me was like the first signal from a safe harbor. [18]

Necker turned to his usual partners, the directors of the Discount Bank. On September 4 he asked for an advance of 15 million livres. Even though the total amount of loans to the Royal Treasury surpassed what was authorized by law, the directors accepted, but on the condition that they "obtain from His Majesty his bond that would allow the Bank's directors to reassure the stockholders and also serve as a guarantee of repayment." [19] Regarding this condition, Louis XVI wrote in his own hand: "The present deliberation approved, and M. Necker will convey my satisfaction with it to the directors."[20]

On October 16 Necker asked for still another advance of 15 million livres. The directors once again accepted, on the same conditions. The total amount advanced to the Royal Treasury then came to 100 million livres. But even so, the financial situation of the Bank remained sound. At the end of the year, for a circulation of 102 million notes, the bank held 30 million livres in cash and 72 million in notes; 221 million bills of exchange were discounted and 6 million were in current accounts. The stockholders were receiving dividends of 7.5 percent. As a stockholder and director, Lavoisier had every reason to be satisfied. He hoped that the Discount Bank would be able to maintain payments, but he had not reckoned with Necker and his constant demands.

The Accident at Essonne

Meanwhile a new scientific success had occurred at the Arsenal laboratory. Berthollet had discovered the oxydizing properties of superoxygenated potassium muriate (potassium chlorate), and it was being envisaged as a replacement for saltpeter in making a gunpowder that would be even more powerful than the royal powder. The first laboratory tests had been extremely interesting, indicating that a mixture of sulfur, charcoal, and potassium chlorate could double the range of firearms.

Lavoisier decided to produce a large amount of this superoxygenated potassium muriate gunpowder and asked Berthollet to help him with the trials. On Saturday, October 26, 1788, accompanied by Madame Lavoisier, they set off for the gunpowder factory at Essonne, which employed sixty workers and produced 200,000 pounds of powder every year: gunpowder for cannons and rifles, explosives for mines, and poudre d'élite for hunting, destined for luxury firearms manufactured in Versailles. The old poudre royale, reserved for the king's hunts, was considered too dangerous and was no longer made. Since Lavoisier had become involved, production had made spectacular progress. In seven years that of saltpeter had gone from 1.5 million pounds to almost 4 million; the stock of gunpowder had risen to 5 million pounds. Thanks to a slightly modified composition (76 parts of saltpeter, 14 of sulfur, and 10 of charcoal), the gunpowder was definitely better. Its range had increased from 150 to 250 meters. France no longer had to import it, and the savings were estimated to be 28 million livres. Lavoisier had even been able to export large quantities of gunpowder to America. Reaching Essonne in the evening, the Lavoisiers and Berthollet went to bed early. The experiment

began at six o'clock the following morning. It was a Sunday, but numerous
visitors were on hand to observe the experiment, including Pierre Edme Le
Tors de Chessimont, the director of the factory, and Pierre de Chevrand, a
commissaire at the Gunpowder Administration. Only Eleuthère-Irénée Du
Pont, son of Pierre-Samuel, a student-chemist at Essonne and a protégé of
Lavoisier, was missing.

Lavoisier made certain that his instructions had been followed. Given
the risks involved for the foreseen production of 16 pounds of gunpowder,
he had requested an isolated mill, and reduced the number of workers, who
were protected by a partition of wooden beams. At seven o'clock, the workers
began to turn the crank that drove the foulons (crushers). Le Tors, Lavoisier and his wife, Berthollet, Chevrand and his sister, the master gunpowder
maker Aledin, and his apprentice Mallet stood facing the workers, on the un-
protected side. Although the precaution of moistening the powder had been
taken, it was not mixing well and stuck to the crushers. Using the tip of his
cane, Le Tors began to dislodge the heaps while joking about the effects an
explosion would produce. Lavoisier insisted that he not do this during the
crushing and pointed out that the protective partitions were useless if everyone stayed outside them. He then modified the proportions of the mixture
and asked that the ingredients for 20 pounds of gunpowder be prepared. But
the new preparation was just as adhesive. Le Tors continued his game which
he considered to be without danger since the mixture was incomplete. Lavoisier grew angry, pleaded with the observers to take refuge behind the beams,
and decided that the crushing would be suspended after every ten turns of the
mill so as to unstick the lumps and perfect the mixture.

At 8:00, a servant came to announce that breakfast was being served.
Only Mallet and Aledin stayed on, and they were warned not to mix the
powder when the mill was turning. While they were eating, Le Tors began to
worry about having left Aledin, the father of a family, in the mill. Would it
not have been better to entrust the task to an unmarried man? Lavoisier answered that if his instructions were respected, there would be no danger.

At 8:30, Le Tors and Mademoiselle de Chevrand returned directly to the
mill where the experiment was being carried out. The others stopped in an
empty mill to explain to Berthollet, who was new to the subject, the classical methods of fabrication. Suddenly there was a violent explosion. A thick
column of smoke arose. They hurried to the scene. The mill was in ruins,
the mortar in pieces. The explosion had thrown Le Tors and Mademoiselle
de Chevrand against a wall thirty feet away. The young woman had died immediately. Le Tors, one of whose legs had been blown off, had his right wrist
broken, a crushed thigh, and a blinded eye, and his scalp had been ripped
away. He survived only a few minutes. "The wall of beams behind which the

workers had been standing had resisted. They had experienced a great shock, but no wounds. The apprentice and the master gunpowder maker, who had been relieved of their post by M. Le Tors, had left a second before to go for something to eat."[21]

During the return to Paris, Berthollet blamed himself for having unwittingly caused the tragedy. But he remained no less convinced of the superiority of his gunpowder and hoped to find a safer method of producing it. Lavoisier was determined to pursue the trials in spite of the risks and he wrote a letter to Necker in that sense. Unlike the *Journal de Paris*, he did not ask himself whether "discoveries of this sort are more harmful than advantageous to humanity."[22]

As for Madame Lavoisier, she was pleased to receive a friendly letter from Franklin, writing from Philadelphia on October 23, 1788:

I have a long time been disabled from writing to my dear friend by a severe fit of the gout, or I should sooner have returned my thanks for her very kind present of the portrait which she has herself done me the honour to make of me. It is allowed by those who have seen it to have great merit as a picture in every respect; but what particularly endears it to me is the hand that drew it. Our English enemies, when they were in possession of this city and of my house, made a prisoner of my portrait, and carried it off with them, leaving that of its companion, my wife, by itself, a kind of widow: you have replaced the husband, and the lady seems to smile, as well pleased.[23]

The Blois Register of Grievances

On January 24, 1789 the letters convening the States General were sent out. The Assemblée des notables had granted the right to vote to all adult males having a residence and inscribed on the tax list. It had refused, however, to double the representation of the Third Estate. Louis XVI had not taken sides on the essential question of whether vote was to be by order or by head. The writing of the Registers of Grievances of the parishes and bailiwicks began.

A candidate for the Third Estate from Villefrancoeur, Lavoisier had made a slightly demagogic profession of political faith on March 4: " I declare that in accepting the noble post as your representative, I henceforth renounce all financial exemptions not shared by you; I will have myself included on the next roll for the taille for the farms I am exploiting in the parish of Villefrancoeur and Champigny; I will pay all the ancillary taxes included in the roll, even the representative right of the corvée, in proportion to the vingtièmes. Thus from now on there will be no financial distinction separating us; we shall all be brothers and friends."[24]

But he was not certain to win because in the parish assemblies discontent was running high. Apart from the State taxes, those who owned a patch of land were weighed down by the harsh measures of the landowners—in particular the commoners—who wanted by all means to make their land investments pay. Hence they burdened their farmers with corvées, and charged them inordinately for using the communal ovens, mills, and wine presses. In addition, the farmers had to pay indirect taxes (*cens* and *champarts*) as well as sales and inheritance taxes. The consolidation of properties had simply aggravated matters: small farms were increasingly rare. But it was they that gave employment to the most disadvantaged, the brassiers, who had only the strength in their arms (*bras*) for their survival. They had one or two animals that they led to graze on the communal lands, or on private land after the harvest, profiting from the right of "common grazing land." But this right was being threatened by the spreading practice of enclosing fields and properties. If it was abolished, they would have to sell the cow or two goats that had allowed them to survive. Thus there was a vast wave of discontent, difficult to control and potentially explosive.

On March 9, at the Palais de Justice of Blois, the Assembly for the election of the deputies at the States General was convened, at eight in the morning after the official Mass. The Assembly was presided over by Pierre Druillon, lieutenant-general of the bailiwick. Lavoisier's candidacy was contested from the beginning by Barthélémy Bellenoue-Villiers, bailiff of justice from Herbault, who cited two reasons: one, the parish of Villefrancoeur fell under the jurisdiction of Herbault, thus it was in the bailiwick of Tours and not of Blois; and, two, Lavoisier's status as noble and Farmer General was incompatible with that of a deputy of the Third Estate.

The lawyer from Blois, Jacques Samuel Dinocheau, was even more aggressive. Lavoisier explained later to his electors: "His speech was nothing more than a web of insults fit for inflaming passions, and had I not been extremely prudent, I do not know to what extremes the people might have gone in showing their opposition to me."[25]

The truth is that he had been caught unprepared. Less experienced in rural electoral meetings than in those held at the Academy, he replied with a legal-administrative argument that while undoubtedly pertinent was unsuitable, before beating a retreat. His friend Du Pont, because he was a recent member of the nobility, met similar difficulties at Nemours. He had proposed to the Third Estate delegates that they write the Register of Grievances from Chevannes together with the nobility. "It is not surprising," one of the delegates declared, "that such strange motions are made: there is a noble among us." The crowd was indignant and threatened to throw Du Pont out the window. At which point, he very opportunely threw his arms around a very portly man who, nonplused, demanded what Du Pont expected him to do. "Monsieur," Du Pont replied,"I am running for my life. I am about to be thrown from a window and I want you to serve as a mattress."[26] The crowd, delighted by the joke, cheered Du Pont, who immediately took control of the situation, justified himself, and was elected.

Lavoisier, beaten and greatly vexed, went back to Villefrancoeur to explain his defeat to the inhabitants. He could not contest the fact that he belonged to the nobility, albeit for only a short time, nor that he was a Farmer General. On the other hand, he was ready to prove that the village of Villefrancoeur did indeed belong to the bailiwick of Blois. The best proof, he argued, was that all the birth, marriage, and death certificates were registered there.

In fact, the debate concerned the château of Freschines, which, by a vagary, fell within the jurisdiction of Tours. Lavoisier tried by every means at hand to have the château and the village of Villefrancoeur recognized as belonging to the bailiwick of Blois, but it was too late. One after the other, two decisions went against him. Both the prosecuting attorney and the lieutenant-general of Blois confirmed that Villefrancoeur belonged to the bailiwick of Tours. Chevilly, intendant for the region of Orléans, appealed to Necker on March 23:

M. Lavoisier, Farmer General, is the generous citizen who offered the town of Blois 50,000 livres without interest to help purchase wheat in Nantes and Saumur. He wanted to remain anonymous and I respected his scrupulousness; his generosity is all the more praiseworthy since he has had reason to complain of the incivility of two lawyers who, through the most violent outbursts and insulting remarks against the Company to which he belongs, have succeeded in removing him from the Assembly of the Third Estate where he had presented himself as a deputy from his parish; since then, this parish has been recognized as not belonging to the bailiwick of Blois.[27]

In spite of Lavoisier's protests, added to those of Villefrancoeur's inhabitants, and all the recommendations coming from highly placed officials, nothing could be done. The lieutenant-general of Blois ratified the decision of the preliminary assembly. Lavoisier, forced to renounce his nomination to the Third Estate in Blois, then tried his chance on the side of the nobility. Its ninety-nine members, embarrassed by his being a Farmer General, refused his candidacy, but kept him as a recording secretary.[28] It was he who wrote, on March 28, the "Instructions Given by the Nobility of the Bailiwick of Blois to Its Deputies at the States General":

The goal of every social institution is to bring the greatest possible happiness to those who live under its laws. Happiness must not be reserved to a small number of men.

It belongs to all. It is not an exclusive privilege to be disputed, but a common right that must be preserved and shared, and public well-being is a source from which each person has the right to draw his own.[29]

The security of persons and the security of property are the two fertile principles that should preside over the new organization of society. For that it is sufficient to endow France with the permanent Constitution that has always been lacking. Constitutional monarchy would guarantee individual liberty, the abolition of privileges, equitable tax laws, the reorganization of the judicial system, the end of arbitrary police power, freedom of the press, and the right of elected representatives to vote the budget of the nation.

Individual liberty, the first and most sacred of human rights, was to belong to citizens of all orders and classes, without distinction or preference. And Lavoisier specified: "It is from personal liberty that is derived that of writing, printing, and publishing—with names of authors and printers—every kind of complaint and reflection relating to public and private affairs."[30]

There should be, he continued, absolute freedom of commerce and unrestricted circulation of grains and commodities; all duties collected within the kingdom should be eliminated and all customs barriers and tollgates transported to its frontiers with other countries, a rather surprising demand coming from the person responsible for collecting taxes on goods entering Paris. The freedom to work required the abolition of police regulations that imprisoned a host of artisans for minor faults, of exclusive privileges that hampered industry, of corporations and guilds that presented obstacles to the right to work, of manufacturing regulations, of numerous taxes that uselessly burdened industry without bringing anything to the State.

Equality in taxation was the second major demand: "Tax is a sharing of property. This sharing can only be voluntary, otherwise the right of property would be violated: hence the nation has an imprescriptible and inalienable right to consent to its taxes."[31] The tax paid by every citizen was to be proportional to the interest the citizen had in preserving his property, and was to be based on its value. Every property should be subjected to it: land, but also the incomes from royal pensions and remunerations from salaried employments. The nobility would abandon all the tax exemptions it had enjoyed until that time and pay taxes just like everybody else; the taille and corvée would be eliminated and all direct taxes would be transformed into a single one, the territorial tax. Taxes on salt, alcoholic drinks, and leathers would be reformed. The capitation, the exclusive right of bailiff-auctioneers to hold public sales in villages, registration fees, and taxes collected by the mail coach services, would be suppressed.

Justice was to be free and follow a simple procedure. All useless jurisdiction would be suppressed to the benefit of departmental courts. The location of these courts would be determined by what was convenient for citizens and not for the magistrates, "because the magistrates have been set up for the people and not the people for the magistrates."[32] Criminal laws, inspired by English jurisprudence, were to become more humane; the abuse of police regulations that could accuse citizens and send them to prison without proof or judgment would be abolished; the accused would be presumed innocent, benefit from legal counsel, and be able to appeal an initial judgment. The notarized minutes of court proceedings were to be kept in a public place where all citizens could consult them.

Agriculture was to be helped. Lavoisier recalled its backwardness in France in contrast to the English prosperity. The remedies? Decrease taxes, lower interest rates, remove the restrictions on the grain and commodities trade, encourage the purchase of communal ovens and mills, the draining of marshlands, the selection of livestock breeds, the creation of spinning and weaving workshops, the improvement of sanitary conditions and elementary education, and the standarization of weights and measures."[33] As for the royal forests and Domaines, it would be more economical to turn them over to the provincial administration. But selling them to meet the public debt would be dangerous: "A great nation, and especially a maritime nation like France, should regard its forests of tall trees as a national resource, essential to its defense, that should not leave the sovereign's hands."[34]

One of the most important tasks facing the States General was the establishment of the budget of the nation. Every effort to economize should be made and accounts should be carefully supervised. In case of a deficit, taxes should be increased only after having eliminated all nonindispensable expenditures. The Minister of Finance, and all the other ministers as well, should report to the States General on the use of funds paid into the National Treasury.

Here appear two ideas Lavoisier would later recall at the National Treasury. First, to reassure the creditors of the State—and the Discount Bank was the biggest of all—reimbursement of capital and interest payments on debts would no longer be the responsibility of the Royal Treasury but of a National Treasury. Second, each month a part of the revenues of the State would be placed there, guaranteeing that payments would always be made on time. "In this way, one will be able to say truthfully that the national debt has been consolidated."[35]

But the essential thing was not to identify the evils of French society or even to destroy them. It was rather to avoid their recurrence. And the only means for this was to give the country a Constitution. The States General, therefore, should not adjourn until a Constitution had been established. It was this body that held the legislative power, and it should meet at regular intervals—dates and locations should be fixed—and be completely independent of the executive power. Although it was up to the king to see that the law was carried out, he had no right to change or modify it without the approval of the nation.

As for the thorny question of whether voting was to be by order or by head, the nobility had difficulty reaching a decision. Finally it requested that vote by head be chosen when the nation as a whole was concerned, and vote by order be used on matters particular to each order. The deputies would receive "all powers, general and sufficient, to propose, establish, advise, and consent to everything that can concern the needs of the State, the reform of abuses, the establishment of a fixed and permanent order in all parts of the administration, the prosperity of the kingdom, and the good of each of its inhabitants." [36]

In spite of his convictions and talents as secretary-clerk, Lavoisier was not elected as a deputy. The representatives of the nobility preferred the Viscount Alexandre de Beauharnais and the chevalier Louis Jean de Phélines.[37] Lavoisier would be only an alternate. On his return from Blois, he had a letter from Louis XVI:

Your latest experiment, Monsieur, elicits all my admiration: this discovery proves that you have greatly enlarged the sphere of useful knowledge. Your experiments with inflammable gas show just how much you are contributing to this admirable science that progresses daily. The Queen and several other persons to whom I want to introduce this discovery will be in my office tomorrow evening at seven o'clock. Will you give me the pleasure of bringing me a copy of your *Traité des gaz inflammables*? You know, Monsieur, how deeply I esteem you.[38]

The authenticity of this letter is dubious. But if Lavoisier ever received it, one can imagine that he was delighted by the commentary and the invitation. Perhaps he asked himself whether the king had read very carefully the *Traité élémentaire de chimie*.

The Electors of Paris

Paris, however, was in a feverish state. The bookseller Nicolas Ruault wrote his brother, a priest in Evreux:

The commentaries on the States General grow by the hundreds every week. All Parisians seem to have become political authors who are just as prolific as the English in such matters. One now sees that they are not simply filled with idle curiosity, that their heads are not as light as one had been led to believe. You can rest assured that in the States General the Third Estate will prevail over the nobility and high clergy. If the latter do too much saber rattling, a way will be found to do without their votes.[39]

The royal decree of April 13, 1788, had divided Paris into sixteen districts and sixty sections. The Hôtel de Ville district was made up of the Saint-Jean en Grève, Saint-Gervais, Saint-Antoine Enfants trouvés, and Saint-Louis-de-la-Culture sections. This last one, to which Lavoisier belonged, included the Arsenals, the headquarters of the Gunpowder and Saltpeter Administration, the Célestins, Saint-Paul's church, and the port of Saint-Paul.

In April 1789 the first riots occurred in the faubourg Saint-Antoine. They were directed against Réveillon, the wallpaper manufacturer, who was a "patriot" very much in the public eye. It was said that he had declared that whereas a worker's salary was around 20 sous a day, 15 sous would be quite enough.

On April 22 the members of the nobility met at the Hotel de Ville to choose the electors who would represent them the next day at the general assembly of the three orders and elect the deputies from Paris. Lavoisier became one of the eight electors.[40] As usual, he took over the secretarial functions and wrote the "Instructions Given by the Nobility of the Hôtel de Ville to Its Deputies at the States General," which he signed along with the president, Rouette.

The Register included twenty-four articles. The nobility demanded the maintenance of the Catholic religion and the hereditary monarchy, but posed the principles of separation of powers. It claimed the imprescriptible right to individual liberty, protection of private property, freedom of the press, consolidation of the public debt, reform of civil and criminal laws, rapid and unbiased justice, abolition of special courts, and creation of an office of reconciliation. The mails were to be declared inviolable. The election of members of the municipality of Paris was to be free. The States General were to be convened at regular dates and be preceded by meetings of the provincial assemblies. All existing taxes were to be abolished and replaced by a new fiscal system; no tax or loan was to be levied without the approval of the States General. A "Declaration of the Rights of the Nation" was to be published and inscribed in all public registers. It should then be read in all the parishes of the kingdom every year on a particular holiday.

On May 3 the Assembly of Electors unanimously approved the Paris Registers of Grievances. An observation by Delavigne, an elector from the Third Estate, no doubt caught Lavoisier's eye: "The Farm has the grated tobacco prepared either in Paris or in its provincial factories. It is then put into barrels to facilitate its transport. *The amount of water added for the mouillage is 20 percent of the weight of the powdered tobacco.* This enormous quantity of water alters and spoils the tobacco. Being closed up, it goes moldy. On opening the barrels, one finds worms. Reduced to this state of decompositon, tobacco is a poison."[41]

This nasty affair still mobilized public opinion. Was this one of the reasons that Lavoisier was extremely reserved and did not announce his candidacy? Was it because the customs wall around Paris had made too much of a stir? Was he afraid that in Paris, as in Blois, he would encounter difficulties linked to his recent ennoblement and his functions as a Farmer General? Furthermore, could he be at the same time a candidate for deputy in Paris and an alternate in Blois? His case, however, was not isolated: three other electors, the comte Stanislas de Clermont-Tonnerre, Louis Henri Marthe Gouy d'Arsy, and Claude Louis de Saisseval, were also alternates. All three declared that they had accepted the positions only on the condition that they could become candidates elsewhere—in Paris, for example. As for Lavoisier, he was silent and said that he aspired to nothing.[42]

On May 20 the second stage of the elections by the college of the 407 electors from the Third Estate ended.[43] On May 25, three weeks late, the deputies from Paris joined their provincial colleagues in the States General at Versailles.

The States General

Louis XVI had opened the States General on May 5 before 1,139 still rather timid deputies. There were 291 from the clergy, 270 from the nobility, and 578 (of whom 200 were lawyers) from the Third Estate. Necker was persuaded that he could keep control of the financial and administrative reforms everyone was expecting. He knew that he could count on the most enlightened part of the Assembly. Of the deputies, 217 were Freemasons, and they had a great capacity to mobilize support. The intermixing favored by the lodges had contributed to the advent of a new social order, but plots and concerted actions were impossible among the numerous lodges with different, indeed sometimes opposing tendencies.[44]

Moreover, each participant's role was ambiguous. "Monsieur Necker," the king asked, "is it I who will be presenting the Constitution to the States General, or will they be presenting it to me?" Necker was somewhat at a loss for words in giving his answer. But he was all the more so when the same day the queen asked him "whether the States General would become the king's masters, or if the king would remain the nation's master?"[45]

Necker revealed to the deputies that the State had a deficit of 56 million livres. In reality it amounted to 80 million. The Discount Bank had been a good partner: in January 1789 it had advanced 25 million livres to the Royal Treasury and accepted 2 million in assignations (payment orders) on the Treasury instead of the interest due on the loan of 70 million livres in 1787. It had succeeded, however, in maintaining its reserves of gold and silver: 35 million in écus for a circulation of 103 million livres.

In April Necker had obtained a new loan of 12 million in banknotes. On May 15 he had asked for still another 12 million. "There is more than ever an intimate link between the interests of the Discount Bank and those of the Royal Treasury," he had said to the directors. "Look at the crisis in finances, Gentlemen, in grain supply, at the States General, and relieve me of that part of my worry that depends of you."[46]

On May 29 Lavoisier called a special meeting of the board of directors. He underlined the deplorable progression of the government debt and the risks it entailed. Making a new loan would be contrary to the statutes: currency was supposed to represent between a third and a quarter of the notes, and that limit had been reached. "In the present position, the funds on hand amount to only 29,500,000 livres, and the banknotes in circulation amount to 119,200,000 livres, which just about meets the stipulation of representing a quarter of the notes."[47]

The directors were worried. It was their money that was leaving the bank, endangering its very foundation. But they were in the habit of advancing money to the king, and had always ended up by recouping their outlay and even much more. Thus they agreed to make still another loan, because "of the necessity and indispensability" of the service demanded of them. And besides, they still had confidence in the royal signature. At their request, Louis XVI wrote at the bottom of the page on which their decision had been conveyed: "The conduct of the directors of the Discount Bank appears to me very wise, and I thank them for the confidence they have placed in me. I believe that present circumstances justify in every respect the new service that was asked of them by the director-general of my finances, and I shall see to it that their advance is repaid within six months."[48]

In the meantime, the Bank had become so accustomed to Necker's frequent injunctions that a clever forger, imitating the minister's signature, stole 150,000 livres from it, provoking much scornful laughter from the public.[49] But the value of public bills was falling every day. Bankruptcy was feared and there was general alarm. One read in the *Bulletin d'un Agent Secret*: "It has reached the point that the payment of notes from the Discount Bank has become very difficult. Necker, who is accused of having taken 65 million livres from it, has plunged prodigiously in the eyes of public opinion. There is grumbling coming from every direction. The orders and the Parliament are now against Necker, but private investors fear his departure."[50]

During this time, things were growing worse at the States General. "Treated as subjects when they wanted to be citizens, the representatives of the people refused to play merely walk-on parts in a drama that was taking place elsewhere. From May to June, they had held fast, demanding a common assembly where voting would be by head and not by order, and had urged others to join them. Suddenly history was racing out of control."[51]

On June 17 the deputies of the Third Estate declared themselves to be a National Assembly. On June 23 the King annulled their decision. "But when he was informed that the Third Estate refused to disperse even after his disciplinary speech at the royal session, he suddenly gave way, as he had so often given way before. 'Eh bien, foutre! Qu'ils restent!' he said wearily, oblivious of where such weakness might lead the kingdom."[52]

The reaction was not long in coming. Paris was on the verge of an uprising. The banks closed their doors. Soon after, the baron Pierre Victor de Bésenval, Minister of the Interior, learned that the people were preparing to attack the Discount Bank and the Royal Treasury. He requested instructions. On July 1 the maréchal duc de Broglie replied: "The King consents that you assemble all the forces on which you can rely to safeguard the Royal Treasury and the Discount Bank and that you confine yourself to defending these two positions whose importance you sense and which warrant our unique concentration, at a time when, unfortunately, we are in no condition to stave off everything."[53]

Louis XVI, feeling that things were going too far, was considering dismissing Necker and called up 30,000 to 40,000 troops to surround Paris. They were stationed at Versailles, Charenton, Vincennes, and Saint-Denis. Among them were ten regiments of Swiss and German mercenaries. "Firing Necker would deal a blow to public credit, and the Discount Bank could very well go bankrupt. The king will probably be forced to retreat from his plan," predicted the bailiff de Virieu.[54]

The deputies, no longer feeling safe in Versailles, demanded that the king send away the troops. He answered that he would keep them "close to Paris and Versailles so as to maintain public order and peace, and that he had the means to make everyone fulfill his duty."[55] In this case, he was deluding himself. In Paris the soldiers were no longer obeying their officers. Instead they strolled through the streets, gathered at the Palais Royal to hear the political orators, and swore allegiance to the Nation and the National Guard. Far from returning to their camp on the Champ de Mars, they were promising to fight for the people and not against them. Desertion was widespread. In the city, overrun by the unemployed, the price of bread reached an unheard-of level: 30 livres ($1,200) per setier.[56] Wheat flour rose to 50.

On July 11 the king did indeed dismiss Necker, and named the duc Victor François de Broglie as Minister of War. On the same day, the Assembly appointed a Finance Committee composed of sixty-two members. Disturbances broke out in Paris and Broglie warned Bésenval: "If there is a general uprising, it will be impossible for us to defend all of Paris. Hence you must limit yourself to the Stock Exchange, the Royal Treasury, the Bastille, and the Invalides."[57]

On July 12 Broglie once again instructed Bésenval: "M. Lavoisier, director of the Discount Bank, has told me that he fears that tomorrow great crowds will converge on the Discount Bank, and M. de Villedeuil thinks as I do that it is essential to prevent any disorder. I assured him that you would certainly do everything possible to do so and that the Discount Bank and the Royal Treasury were your principal objectives."[58] That was not enough to reassure Lavoisier. He proposed transferring the funds of the Discount Bank to the Bastille, but the suggestion was not followed.

On July 13 the stockbrokers decided to close the Exchange. Meanwhile, the National Assembly brushed aside any notion of official bankruptcy. In doing so, it was trying to reassure the creditors of the State, who were still supporting it, hoping to ensure that their money would be repaid. Thus, according to Rivarol's thesis, they contributed to the onset of the Revolution: 60,000 capitalists were looking to the States General not for a Constitution but for a financial guarantee. Worried about the consolidation of the public debt, their only hope was in the Assembly, and they used "the powerful means that a great amount of money, wide credit and extended contacts gave to support it."[59]

Moreover, three directors from the Discount Bank—Jean Boscary, Charles Nicolas Ducloz-Dufresnoy, and Tassin—were alternate deputies of the Third Estate in Paris. A fourth, Jean Barthélémy Le Couteulx de Canteleu, a famous banker, was a deputy from Rouen. André Daniel Laffon de Ladébat, future president of the Discount Bank, was a deputy from Gironde.

In Paris, everybody sensed that something momentous was about to happen. There were so many causes for discontent mixed with ambitions, intrigues, bitterness, and demands that even the abolition of every law and custom in force would hardly have sufficed to satisfy them. The intellectuals and writers had left for the country to seek peace and fresh air; therefore they were not on hand to give a faithful description of the revolution they had helped to provoke. A short distance away from the Bastille, near Lavoisier's Arsenal residence, lived one of his friends and colleagues from the Academy, Auguste Fougeroux de Bondaroy, a botanist and agronomist. A common interest in geology and chemistry had brought them together and over the years they had cosigned numerous reports, and had also repeated the experiments on the synthesis of water in the laboratory at Denainvilliers.[60]

In the month of July 1789, when heads were as hot as the cobblestones in the street, the two of them were in Paris, both witnesses and actors. One was at the Arsenal, the other in his house on the rue des Lions Saint-Paul. Thanks to Fougeroux, who kept a journal, Lavoisier's movements during those historic moments are better known to us.

The Assembly of the Parisian Electors

The situation in Paris was rather complex: the commanders of the royal troops were making their plans to enter Paris, while Bernard Jordan de Launay armed the Bastille for defending itself against the population in the surrounding quarter of Saint-Antoine. On Sunday July 12, at eleven in the evening, he had gunpowder stocks from the Arsenal transferred to the fortress, and 21,000 pounds were feverishly stored in the kitchen areas, in violation of all safety measures. The Paris crowd, stirred up by fear of the troop movements and anxiety over food shortages and unemployment, began to roam about the city. At the Invalides, the marquis de Sombreuil surrendered 32,000 rifles and several large cannons to the rioters without resisting. At the Hôtel de Breton-villiers, the headquarters of the General Farm, the clerks turned over to them the arms they had hidden.[61]

The 407 electors of the Third Estate seized power and installed themselves in the Hôtel de Ville, calling themselves the "Assembly of Parisian Electors." They declared their solidarity with the National Assembly and created a bourgeois militia of 12,000 men. On July 13 the electors from Saint-Louis-de-la-Culture appointed twelve commissioners, of whom one was Lavoisier, who were charged with maintaining order in their district.

On July 14, at six in the morning, Launay asked Clouet, Lavoisier's assistant at the Gunpower Administration, to have the gunpowder that had been stored near the kitchens in the Bastille transported to cellars. By ten the work was completed. Leaving the Bastille, Clouet, who was on a horse and dressed in formal clothes, was thought by the crowd to be Launay. He just missed being torn to pieces, and was saved only through the intervention of Charles Gaulard de Saudray, deputy commanding general of the National Guard.[62] In the afternoon, small groups coming from all parts of Paris and armed with rifles, pikes, swords, and spades, converged on the Bastille. The crowd wanted the surrender of the old prison which was more a symbol than a fortress. It held only seven men: four crooks, two madmen, and an accomplice of Damiens, the man who had tried to murder Louis XV in 1759. The garrison consisted of eighty-two veterans and thirty-two Swiss soldiers; the veterans were not very eager to fight. The governor, the marquis de Launay, wanted to set off the gunpowder magazine. But he was easily dissuaded by the veterans from doing so, and at five o'clock he surrendered.

At the same time, Lavoisier was on his way to the Hôtel de Ville for the meeting of the Assembly of Electors. His situation was ambiguous because he was serving both the royal power and its representatives, Bésenval and Launay, while being associated with the new power. The gunpowder he controlled was desired by both sides. He explained that, if the Arsenal had relinquished gunpowder to the Bastille, it was because "the commissioner could not disobey this order, but permission to keep in the warehouses the quantities of gunpowder necessary for a daily turnover of one week had been requested and obtained."[63] He asked "how much gunpowder would be needed by the new service on which the security and tranquility of the capital depended, and proposed to have additional supplies brought from Essone if it was thought necessary.[64]

By July 15 the victory of the new power was total. The King called back Necker and dismissed the troops concentrated around Paris. The astronomer Jean Sylvain Bailly was elected mayor of Paris and La Fayette was named commander of the National Guard. It was the two of them who welcomed Louis XVI in the capital on July 17 and had him wear the cockade, the official revolutionary symbol.[65] The King entered the Hôtel de Ville by passing under an archway of steel formed by the swords of electors who had thus borrowed the rite used for the entrance of an important visitor into a Masonic lodge.[66]

For the next five days, Lavoisier's whereabouts are unknown. It is hard to imagine that he went away immediately after that great victory.[67] Bailly was his colleague at the Academy and La Fayette a fellow member of the Society of Thirty, and he had very much looked forward to this political change. But perhaps he had imagined that it would be less tumultuous. In any case, he reappeared on July 20 at Versailles for a public relations operation. He had come with a few colleagues from the Discount Bank to pay homage to the National Assembly. The duc de La Rochefoucauld-Liancourt, who was presiding, saluted the "patriotism of a financial company that in the distressing times that have just shaken the capital, did not suspend payments."[68]

Their friends among the deputies also congratulated the bankers for having continued to assume their responsibilities in spite of the difficulties.

But Mirabeau, relentless in his struggle against "this egoistic and unfaithful institution," shouted, "A financier has come, in the name of his speculating company, to offer on credit all the necessary clarifications, somewhat like a swindler might come to inform Sainte Hermandad."[69]

A few days later, Lavoisier presented the financial situation of the Discount Bank to its shareholders: he suggested that, since the State owed it 70 million livres, the sum could serve to pay the patriotic contribution, a new tax that had to be improvised to supply the Treasury. But when the proposition was submitted to the National Assembly it was very badly received and provoked a violent outcry. There was absolutely no question of following his suggestion, since it did not bring in fresh money.

In Paris the disturbances grew worse. On July 22 the raging crowd hanged Louis Jean Bertier de Sauvigny, intendant of Paris, and Joseph François Foulon, his father-in-law, in the Place de Grève. The municipality being powerless to impose its authority, La Fayette and Bailly decided to resign their posts. This double decision was communicated to the Assembly of Electors by its president, Médéric Louis Elie Moreau de Saint-Méry. Lavoisier was one of the first to be informed, because he was at that moment meeting with the Food Commission, as he did every day to review the situation concerning the gunpowder supply for the National Guard. The districts sent emissaries to La Fayette urging him to reconsider his decision. Lavoisier and Monsure, designated as delegates from Saint-Louis-de-la-Culture, read in public a petition that "created quite a sensation with M. de La Fayette and the Assembly."[70] But La Fayette still hesitated. He wanted time to think it over, to seek advice, and he asked to withdraw to an adjoining room. But the Assembly and the crowd were opposed to his doing so. Finally, he left without giving an answer. It was only the following day that he agreed to return to his post.

Saint-Louis-de-la-Culture

The Assembly of Electors, which had temporarily governed the municipality, was dissolved and it was decided that the new administration would henceforth contain 120 representatives, two per district, elected by all men over twenty-five. When the polls in Saint-Louis-de-la-Culture opened on July 24 at nine in the morning, a considerable crowd had already gathered and were pressing to get in. Each person had a different opinion. Ten, then thirty names were proposed at the same time. Discussions went on until noon amid ever greater pandemonium and no decision could be reached. The curé from Saint

Paul, Pierre Louis Bossu, tried to restore order. It was finally agreed to elect the first twelve men on the list. Hardly had the decision been taken before the crowd insisted that new names be added. In the end, there were fifty. Lavoisier was among them, along with his friend Fougeroux de Bondaroy and four former fellow electors from the nobility of the IXe département: Nicolas Hugues Bizeau, Clément Nicolas Phélippe de Faronville, Nicolas Louis de Pinon, and André de Vouges de Chanteclair. There was also one of Lavoisier's enemies, in the person of a M. Gaudot, an employee of the General Farm, a customs officer at the Port Saint-Paul, who would soon afterward be accused of embezzlement and sent to prison.

M. de Rozoi proposed that July 17, the day when Louis XVI had visited Paris, "be, for future generations, a consoling day for true patriots, instructive for magistrates, terrifying for the agents of despotism, and glorious for kings."[71] But it was late, and everybody was in a hurry to get home for lunch. The fifty members took their oaths and the Assembly was adjourned at 2:20 p.m.

On Sunday July 26, the district committees met at the Hôtel de Ville and called themselves the "Assembly of the Representatives of the Commune de Paris." Bailly, La Fayette and Moreau de Saint-Méry were reinstated in their functions. But the newly elected representatives contested the participation of the former electors, who had been recruited on the basis of property qualifications. Called on to arbitrate between the former, moderate, power of the Assembly of Electors and the new, popular, power of the districts, incarnated in the Commune de Paris, Bailly emphasized the urgency of re-establishing order in the capital.

In the afternoon, the Committee for Saint-Louis-de-la-Culture created several offices for the military, the police, and municipal affairs, plus a special one for supervising the demolition of the Bastille, which had begun on July 14 and risked obstructing the sewer, known to be especially dangerous since three persons had been asphyxiated in it six years earlier. It was urgent to take protective measures. Lavoisier and Fougeroux de Bondaroy went to the spot, but could see nothing because of the milling crowd of the curious. They returned the next day, July 27, at nine and ordered Palloy, the entrepreneur in charge of the demolition, to suspend the destruction of the bastion bordering the sewer and to clear away the stones that had fallen into it.

Palloy asked who was going to pay him. Since there was no money to do so, a collection was organized. Some office members gave two or three *louis*. Lavoisier quickly understood that he should make a gesture and made four: personally, he gave 288 livres and then added 600 for the Gunpowder and Saltpeter Administration, 20,000 plus an additional 6,000 for the General Farm, and 12,000 on behalf of the directors of the Discount Bank. The inhabitants of the quarter would be solicited for the balance.

On July 28, however, he returned with his colleagues to the work site and discovered that his orders had been completely ignored. More than five hundred workers were in the process of tearing down the wall that overhung the sewer. But how could he hope to command obedience from 4,000 unemployed men from the neighborhood who were destroying the hated bastion with all their might? Bernard Poyet, the architect in charge, did promise, however, to have the stones removed from the ditch.

Feeling that the work was not being supervised carefully enough, Lavoisier went to see Pawlet, the commander of the Bastille, and insisted that a trench be dug at some distance from the bastion to divert the course of the sewer. That afternoon, another architect, Lucotte, proposed a means of destroying the Bastille. His method, faster and less costly than an explosion, would make it possible to preserve the materials for future use. The towers were to be shored up and then cut just above the foundations. Afterward, the wooden props would be burned and the towers would collapse. A heated discussion ensued. Lavoisier affirmed that this technique, used by the Romans and described by Vitruvius, could work. Its spectacular side would appeal to the observing Parisians. But Fougeroux opposed the plan. He felt that the undertaking would end "like the Abbé Miollan's balloon." On July 11, 1784 the Abbé Miollan had launched a Montgolfier balloon from the Luxembourg Garden. Far from flying from the garden, his balloon had pathetically caught fire before an enormous crowd of onlookers. Thereafter the expression referred to an undertaking that was disappointing or doomed to failure. Fougeroux said that the workers would never let Lucotte install his complicated arrangement, and that it would be very difficult to prop up the towers and cut their bases, which were eighteen feet thick. In any case, some of the stones would fall into the sewer. And, finally, the collapse of the towers would weaken the walls of the surrounding houses. Lavoisier, annoyed, suggested referring the matter to Bailly.

On July 29 another inventor, Cardon, proposed demolishing the fortress by using a lever ending in a sharp iron point. Introduced between the joints of the stones, it would be able to lift four rows at a time. But this plan, too, was considered unrealistic. While all this was being deliberated, however, the workers, who did not want to lose their salaries, continued with their pickaxes and the problem was soon solved.

At the Commune de Paris confusion reigned. Everyone was commanding, but no one was in charge. La Fayette, in particular, gave out orders without reflecting on their possible repercussions. To satisfy a greater number of candidates, he had just decided that the number of representatives of the Commune de Paris should be raised from 120 to 180. Similarly, by granting hunting rights to all Parisians, he virtually exhausted the stock of gunpowder at the Arsenal. Lavoisier was intending to have more gunpowder brought from Essone, but an unforeseen incident complicated the situation.

The Gunpowder Shipment

On August 5, at ten in the evening, a cluster of citizens rushed to the Hôtel de Ville to report that "something strange" was going on at the Port Saint-Paul. Ten thousand pounds of gunpowder from the Arsenal were being loaded on a boat. The whole quarter was in an uproar; they were convinced that this gunpowder was destined for the enemies of the Revolution and wanted to know whether the mayor and commanding general of the National Guard had given their approval. Since Bailly and La Fayette knew nothing about the matter, they ordered the gunpowder to be placed under guard until the following morning, then unloaded and returned to the warehouse at the Arsenal. In fact, Lavoisier subsequently explained, the entire affair was innocent and based on a misunderstanding. At the end of July, he had ordered 21,000 pounds of poudre de traite, used by slave traders, from the factories in Metz and Mézières.[72] This shipment of powder had to pass through Paris to be divided into two equal parts, one to be sent to Orléans, from which it would reach Nantes by way of the Loire; the other to be shipped down the Seine to Rouen.

But on July 29 the inhabitants of Château-Thierry, just outside Paris, noting the passage of a boat carrying gunpowder, had been persuaded that it was to be used by prince Lambesc's troops to attack Paris. They had stopped the boat and escorted it to the Port Saint-Paul. To put first things first, Lavoisier had ordered the powder transported to the Arsenal. But there, for reasons of security, it was impossible to stock more than 20,000 pounds. Hence this poudre de traite was taking up vital space and hampering expected deliveries.[73] Lavoisier had thus decided to send it to Essonne and have the boat return with 10,000 pounds of gunpowder urgently needed for the National Guard and the increased private demand, since everybody now had the right to hunt. He had asked the Hôtel de Ville for the necessary authorization, which had been signed by La Salle. But, actually, La Salle should not have signed. Named commanding general of the National Guard on July 14, he had held the post for only one day, having been replaced by La Fayette on July 15. Nevertheless, he had continued to sign orders that would later be contested.

On the morning of August 6, as the affair of the gunpowder shipment had begun to agitate the population, Lavoisier was at the Bastille discussing with the entrepreneurs the demolition costs that had risen to 23,892 livres and 7 sols. Poyet pointed out that it was urgent to organize an auction for selling the wood, iron, and lead that had been recuperated in the fortress, because it had become increasingly difficult to keep a watch over the depot, and thefts were occurring daily. At the same time, the committees from Saint-Louis and Saint-Gervais were amazed to note that the boat that had been brought from Château-Thierry was about to leave for Essonne. They were convinced that it contained not only gunpowder but also cannonballs, grapeshot, and rifles for suppressing the Paris revolution. Moreover, since they could hardly read, they mistook the words on the barrels, poudre de traite (slave traders' powder), for poudre de traître (traitors' powder).

Dusaulx, a Commune representative, noted that, above all, the citizens feared traitors to the revolutionary cause and plots from the royal court: "However hard we tried, we could never make the crowd understand that the barrels contained traders' powder. They insisted that it was traitors' powder."[74]

Passions rose, and the eight members of the National Guard who had been keeping watch over the boat were arrested and taken to the prison of the Hôtel de Ville, where they were threatened with hanging. A commander from Saint-Gervais came to ask the Commune to inspect the cargo of the boat. The president, Moreau de Saint-Méry, suggested that he get together with the other commissioners and help them unload the barrels. To calm the outrage of the people, he once again ordered the transfer of the gunpowder to the Arsenal.[75]

But the day was not yet over. Saint-Louis-de-la-Culture appointed two commissioners, Bichebois and Solomé, to oversee the unloading and delivery of the barrels to the Arsenal. The transfer took place amid an immense crowd of onlookers. Bichebois suggested opening several barrels to verify their contents. Two, then four, then six were opened and it was obvious that they contained gunpowder. But since Lavoisier had said that it was gunpowder of inferior quality, the crowd had concluded that he meant that it could not be used for fire-arms. A few ringleaders asked to make a test. They put a little powder into the chamber of a musket, and it ignited. They thus declared it to be of excellent quality and, shouting treason, seized Lavoisier and the senior Le Faucheux and took them off to the Hôtel de Ville. Along the way, many in the crowd were arguing for their immediate hanging, without bothering with a trial. But the two men were protected by the National Guard and reached the destination safe and sound. The danger had been real, but it was one "that the son of Le Faucheux voluntarily came to share with the courage of innocence," Lavoisier attested.[76]

At the Hôtel de Ville, the president quickly understood that a public debate was inevitable and that the crowd was going to insist on witnessing it, so he opened up the large hall. Without losing his calm, Lavoisier explained where the gunpowder came from, its nature, quality, and destination. He specified that everything had been done completely in the open, that authorization had been given in due form, and that his statements could be verified. The commissioners' report confirmed all this, but the suspicion was not entirely dissipated. The crowd persisted in seeing something peculiar in the transferral of the gunpowder and continued to make the wildest accusations. Fougeroux did not hide his emotion: "What times, what turmoil! What fears we had for an honest citizen! Dejection was general in our Assembly. All work stopped and we studied the face of each person who entered, dreading that we were about to learn the end of our colleague, M. Lavoisier, and the persons compromised in his misfortune."[77]

Finally, Lavoisier was declared innocent and the crowd gave up the idea of taking him to the Place de Grève as they had been planning to do. They then turned on La Salle, who took flight. Lavoisier left without being recognized and went back to his apartment, close to the Palais Royal, where on Wednesdays and Saturdays he was accustomed to discussing science and carrying out experiments in chemistry or physics with his colleagues from the Academy."[78] Night was falling and calm was gradually restored with the aid of troops. Bailly, returning from Versailles after midnight, found the Place de l'Hôtel de Ville perfectly quiet. The next day, the representatives of the Commune delivered an urgent message to Parisians: "Today our most ardent wish is nothing more than to see order restored in the capital; to see the rights of humanity respected; to see an end to these blindly committed excesses unworthy of a kind and generous nation."[79]

On the morning of August 8, coming back from Essonne, the boat carrying the gunpowder for hunting that had replaced the poudre de traite docked at the Port Saint-Paul. André Vouges de Chanteclair, deputy from the district of Saint-Louis-de-la-Culture, informed the Assembly. Representatives of the four districts went to oversee the unloading of the cargo and transferral, under escort, to the Arsenal warehouse. Lavoisier, along with six commissioners who had been designated by the Commune to make a detailed inventory of available munitions, was there to meet them.

At three o'clock, he very calmly went to the Academy of Science and resumed his usual activities. Fougeroux ran into him there. "This afternoon I was at the Academy where I saw M. Lavoisier who assured me that the night before, when he had been taken to the Hôtel de Ville, he had remained completely serene."[80] Nevertheless, Lavoisier was determined that his version of the events be known. At the Academy of Science and, the next day, at the Committee of Saint-Louis-de-la-Culture, he insisted on reading a statement of justification: "The slander," he said, "was refuted by a statement I made before five hundred persons, and its immediate circulation saved the lives of three patriots and the honor of the people of Paris who would have eternally reproached themselves for their death."[81] During the reading, the atmosphere was tense: "There were persons in that district, as everywhere else, who would have liked to see a negative interpretation of the conduct of Lavoisier and his associates in the affair," Fougeroux noted.[82]

Lavoisier asked the district to print his statement. He was told that he was free to print what he wanted, but that the district would not participate. He was reminded that he and his colleagues had been very lucky to get themselves out of a tight spot, and was advised to wait until things cooled down before publishing their justification.

On August 18, fearing the reaction of public opinion, the director of the Salon de Peinture asked Lavoisier to remove the large portrait consecrating the Lavoisier couple's glory, which had been painted by David the preceding year. "Paris and Helen," one of the artist's less compromising works, replaced it.

On September 18 the number of members in the Assembly of the Commune de Paris rose to three hundred, five for each of the sixty districts.[83] Among them were numerous Academicians, including Condorcet, Thouin, Jussieu, Cousin, Cassini, and Vandermonde. Lavoisier still represented the district of Saint-Louis-de-la Culture, but stayed in the background. He did not belong to the town council, nor did he take part in the major debates regarding the city's government. The newly formed Commune de Paris soon claimed to be directing the revolution throughout the country. On September 21 it asked Lavoisier to send 6,000 pounds of gunpowder to Orléans to aid in its defense. Lavoisier, who was eager to have the public forget about the unfortunate affair of the gunpowder shipment, rushed to carry out the order. He was even overly zealous and suggested that, henceforth, the powder destined for the National Guard be subjected to the same control as that supplied to the Army and Navy. And after consultation with the military committee and the National Guard, the Commune de Paris deemed the idea worthwhile.[84] The norms were set up by Condorcet, Vandermonde, and Lavoisier: three ounces of powder placed in a mortar ought to project a copper cannonball weighing sixty pounds to a distance of 90 toises (360 feet). During the verification, all the samples proved to have a greater range. Afterward the range would be mentioned on each barrel.

Siamese Elephants

The Commune de Paris asked Lavoisier to examine the financial state of the capital, which was not, to say the least, very sound. The revenue from the entries of cattle and alcohol had dropped by half. Expenditures, on the other hand, had soared to an extraordinary level because of the cost of supporting the soldiers and National Guard, protecting food convoys, demolishing the Bastille, assisting the poor, and compensating those wounded on July 14 as well as the families of those killed. The total outlay had already reached more than a million livres, whereas the gifts from wealthy benefactors represented only 750,000.[85] The generosity of the citizens began to be exhausted and the total amount of their contributions since July 14 was less than 600 livres.

But fashionable life continued in Paris. On September 25, Gouverneur Morris, future United States ambassador to France, met Madame Lavoisier at the Opera. At their first meeting in June, he had noted, "Madame appears to be an agreeable woman. She is tolerably handsome, but from her manner it would seem that she thinks her forte is the understanding rather than the person."[86] They had both enjoyed Vestris and Gardel's ballet, and he accompanied her back to the Arsenal. She offered him a cup of tea and confided in him. Morris reports: "When she told me she had no children, I jokingly chided her for her idleness, but she replied only that she had been unlucky."[87]

Lavoisier arrived late from the Hôtel de Ville, worried because the bakers were threatening to stop making bread unless one of their fellow bakers, who had just been arrested, was released. The matter was serious because public opinion was overheated, bread had already become scarce, and the bakers' shops were overrun. A day without bread would inevitably lead to new violence.

The Commune de Paris ceded to the bakers' demand and gave the order to all district presidents to do everything possible to persuade them to continue working. "Thus," Morris noted, "the new power is already being trampled on."[88]

On October 5 Morris was invited to lunch at the Arsenal. That time, it was Madame Lavoisier who was late. Her carriage had been stopped by women who were demonstrating because of the lack of bread and were on their way to Versailles to look for "the baker, the baker's wife and the baker's boy." She had been forced to get out and accompany them on foot for some time. Vandermonde also came to lunch that day. He kept insisting on the role of the Commune de Paris in the affairs of the nation and declared that Paris was supporting the entire kingdom. Morris, annoyed, replied: "Yes, Sir, exactly in the way that I feed the elephants in Siam."[89] Vandermonde did not reply. He was in a hurry to accompany his host to the Hôtel de Ville, where events were getting out of hand: six to seven thousand demonstrators had alrady left for Versailles. In the afternoon at five, La Fayette also left, followed by the National Guard and 20,000 Parisians armed with pikes and sickles. In Versailles there were turbulent scenes with considerable loss of life. The king ceded to all the demands and, on October 6, was installed in Paris at the Tuileries. The National Assembly declared itself inseparable from his person and came to join him in Paris.

Lavoisier continued to administer the Gunpowder and Saltpeter Administration, now under the control of the Commune de Paris. He had 15,000 pounds of gunpowder brought from Nancy to the warehouses of the Arsenal and sent 30,000 pounds of saltpeter to the gunpowder factory in Maromme, near Rouen. Within one year, he would ask for nine authorizations, accepted each time by a different administration. Then there was a new incident, when the town of Etampes blocked a convoy of 2,000 pounds of gunpowder destined for Orléans. Lavoisier, exasperated, wrote to Bailly: "It's about time that somebody convinced the town councils that gunpowder is not in the hands of the nation's enemies, but that, on the contrary, those who are in charge of producing and distributing it are second to none in their patriotism."[90]

14

An Economist in Action

HENCEFORTH LAVOISIER STEERED CLEAR of political affairs. His failure at the States General, the discretion of his interventions at the Commune de Paris, his distant relations with the National Assembly witnessed to his difficulty in speaking the language of politicians. They belonged to another world. A dialogue with them would have required more intuition and opening toward others on his part. His mind was too rational, his character too authoritarian to adapt themselves to tortuous and fragile political schemes. He was more at ease in the abstract world of figures and finance. His functions as director of the Discount Bank would lead him to play a decisive role in France's financial affairs.

The Nationalization of the Discount Bank

Since his return to power, Necker had been facing terrible difficulties. From October 1, 1788 to December 31, 1789, the cost of importing grains and flours to lower the price of bread and feed the unemployed had risen to more than 70 million livres; tax revenue was simply not coming in and everyone had lost confidence in the State. After the failure of two attempts at public borrowing, Necker was reduced to his usual expedient for bailing out the Royal Treasury: borrowing from the Discount Bank. But the stockholders needed persuading. They felt that they had already lent too much money to the king and were worried about the future. They demanded that the debt be reimbursed in some form. Necker felt that the only solution was to nationalize the Discount Bank and transform it into a State institution. He had first mentioned this plan in the National Assembly on August 27, 1789 and, aware of the deputies' mistrust, had tried to bring them together with the Bank:

It is of the utmost importance that the National Assembly very shortly get to know this institution much better, and that it appoint a committee made up of some of the

Bank's directors who, zealous for the public welfare, are in a position, through their knowledge, to guide the Assembly in choosing means to increase credit and the circulation of their bills. This same committee could also study various plans for setting up a State bank.[1]

But nobody listened, and the financial situation grew worse from day to day. On September 13 the State was on the point of suspending payments. At the last moment Necker reached an agreement with the Discount Bank's directors, more precisely with Lavoisier, and obtained a new advance of 12 million livres in bills and 200,000 in cash. Gratefully, he wrote to them: "I earnestly desire to be able to fulfill your hopes and remain worthy of the favorable opinion you have of me. I consider it my duty to assist whenever possible the well-known zeal of your Company for the public good and the King's glory."[2] But he could no longer, as before, arrange all this discreetly with the directors. The National Assembly was henceforth to exercise its right to inspect all transactions.

Mirabeau, who had his eye on Necker's post, was hoping for his failure and said so in plain language: "A too rapid financial regeneration would mean the death of the National Assembly, the disappearance of the Constitution, the ruin of all the plans of the reformers."[3] He demanded that the Discount Bank interrupt the forced circulation of its notes and ensure payment in cash. This measure would lead inevitably to its bankruptcy.

In normal times, the Bank honored the bills of exchange equally in cash or in banknotes; these were readily accepted, because they were convenient and reimbursable on presentation. The bank made its profit by accepting bills of exchange that produced interest for its banknotes that produced none. Had it been obliged to keep in cash a capital equal to that of the banknotes in circulation, it would have earned nothing. Its profit began only when the sum of the banknotes issued surpassed that of the currency on deposit. As Lavoisier explained, "the Bank was therefore constantly pulled by two opposing interests: on the one hand, it could make profits only as long as it increased the supply of its banknotes; on the other, if it issued too many, it risked not having sufficient cash for meeting all demands."[4]

It had been necessary to establish a rule for defining the minimal proportion between cash held by the bank and the banknotes in circulation. Lavoisier considered the balance upset when available liquid assets represented less than a third or a quarter of the banknotes. Below a third, discounting bills was slowed down, below a quarter, it was suspended; and the daily deposits of cash would soon reestablish the equilibrium. He insisted that to require the Discount Bank to honor banknotes in cash during a financial crisis and monetary instability was to court disaster. There were many who, following Mirabeau's example, saw this as a good solution: would it not be the financiers themselves who would bear the brunt? One deputy put it into words: "Since bankruptcy would fall only on the big Parisian capitalists and prominent citizens who are ruining the State with their excessive interests, I cannot see any great harm in it."[5]

The Bank's directors hardly saw things in this light. They demanded a hearing before the Finance Committee of the National Assembly, with which they attempted to justify themselves, protesting the obligation to pay in cash and abolish the banknotes.

On September 24 Necker proposed launching a *contribution patriotique* (patriotic levy), an obligatory borrowing equal to a quarter of each taxpayer's income and subsequently reimbursable. But that would be merely a stop gap. The only realistic solution was, he repeated, to nationalize the Discount Bank. A better way out of the financial crisis, suggested Du Pont de Nemours, would be for the government to take over the property of the Church. Necker's scheme of a patriotic levy would not work, he said, because only landed proprietors who received a net profit each year could pay the levy, and it was doubtful that even they could contribute one-fourth of their income. The Church received income of about 100 million livres from the tithes, which the state would take over. In addition the Church earned annual income from its lands, which Du Pont estimated at 60 million livres. Of course the churches would have to be maintained at government expense, the clergy paid their salaries, and the debt of the Church serviced.[6]

On October 17 La Fayette arranged an interview between Mirabeau and Necker in the hope that they could reach a compromise regarding this affair and govern together. The conversation lasted for five hours, but its only fruit was an excess of mutual antipathy. Necker considered Mirabeau dishonest, and the latter on leaving declared: "Just because Mr. Necker has one of the best minds in France, he thinks he is a genius; but his forte is limited to finance, and the State is not merely finance."[7] It was nevertheless difficult to ignore finance. On November 14 the deficit for 1789 was assessed at 90 million livres. If the 80 million deficit foreseen for 1790 was added, it would reach at least 170 million. And there was still the problem of getting people to pay their taxes and creating still another one to compensate for the decreased revenue caused by the abolition of the salt tax. To cover the deficit, there was no longer the recourse of borrowing from the public—the two recent attempts had failed—or of soliciting the Discount Bank, whose stockholders had refused to make another loan. Necker again proposed transforming the Discount Bank into a Banque de France (Figure 8), which would be governed by twenty-four

VUE DE LA BANQUE DE FRANCE,
Prise de la Rue Croix des Petits Champs.

Figure 8. The Banque de France. Bibliothèque des Arts Décoratifs, Paris.

directors controlled by commissioners appointed by the Assembly. The capital would be increased from 100 to 150 million livres by issuing 12,500 shares at 4,000 livres per share, payable in currency. That would bring the volume of banknotes in circulation to 240 million, of which 170 would immediately be lent to the State to cover the special expenses incurred in 1789 and 1790.

One of the advantages of this plan, on which Necker remained reserved, was the possibility of paying back the Discount Bank's shareholders for advances made to the Treasury before the Revolution. These reimbursements would be made by the *Caisse de l'Extraordinaire* (Special Bank), founded on funds from the patriotic tax and the sale of property that had belonged to the clergy and the Crown. The other advantage would be that the Royal Treasury could have a permanent assurance of advances from the new bank. Its banknotes, guaranteed by the nation, would be stamped with the French coat of arms and the words, "Garantie Nationale." To reimburse the National Bank, the Treasury would have only to draw written orders of payment, *rescriptions*, from the Special Bank.[8]

Mirabeau denounced the plan as unrealistic. Since it would be obligatory to cover the banknotes by keeping a third of their value in cash, as legal tender, at least 70 million livres would be necessary to guarantee 240 million banknotes. But the Discount Bank did not have 70 million. To find only 50 million, it would have to create 12,500 new shares at the artificial price of 4,000 livres per share. Who was going to buy them at such a price when the market price was only 3,700?[9]

Du Pont de Nemours underlined another inconvenience. "The annual gross national product of France is 4 billion livres. Of this amount, 2.5 billion are absorbed by cultivation and operating costs which include the maintenance of the farmers and others directly involved in productive labor. [. . .] Once these costs are subtracted from the gross national product, the net national product is no more than 1. 5 billion."[10]

Since half this amount was used to pay taxes, the money remaining in circulation was reduced to 750 million livres. To borrow 70 million would mean withdrawing almost 10 percent of this money, or more than the population could afford.[11] The revolutionary press denounced the plan born "from the greed and ambition" of the Discount Bank's directors. The Assembly, which wanted to remove the administration of finances from the king and Necker, distrusted the Bank. In spite of its inexperience, it had quickly understood that power belonged to the one who paid. The conversion of the Discount Bank into a State bank would ensure its stockholders "enormous profits and give them the fearsome advantage of controlling the destiny of the State, of making and unmaking its ministers, of having trade move in the direction that would be most advantageous to them and, finally, of placing the provinces at the mercy not of the city of Paris, but of a few Parisian bankers. Great power and great profit: these are the two objectives to which the Discount Bank's directors aspire."[12]

The Finance Committee wanted a true reform and a clear sharing of responsibility between the Assembly and royal power. The Assembly, representing legislative power, wanted full control of decisions concerning the finances of the State. It was no longer willing to allow the executive power, that is, the king and his Minister of Finance, to set the amount of fiscal receipts on the basis of expenditures. Thus the Assembly had to reinforce its control of the determination and implementation of the budget of the State. On November 16 it proposed the creation of two distinct administrations: a Caisse nationale, controlled by the Assembly and responsible for establishing the budget of expenses, and a Caisse d'administration, dependent on the Minister of Finance, that would manage the budget of the government. The discussion dragged on for three months.

On November 17 Lavoisier presided over the meeting of the board of di-

rectors of the Discount Bank and presented a financial report that was meant
to reassure shareholders. In spite of the loans to the State, he pointed out, the
situation remained sound. Bills representing 114 million livres were in circulation as compared to 102 million at the end of 1788. They were guaranteed
by the cash on deposit, bills of exchange, negotiable bills, the 70 million livres
placed as a guarantee at the Royal Treasury in 1787, and 60 million livres
worth of assignats due from the government. And he concluded, "Your position and that of the bills' holders are based on a perfect security." [13]

In fact, he knew full well that the 70 million livres serving as a guarantee in the Royal Treasury were virtually irretrievable, and that the 60 million
due from the government could at best be paid back only if it took out new
loans. He exhorted the stockholders to understand the present difficulties and
adopt a line of conduct acceptable to the hostile National Assembly. But the
stockholders were not fooled. None of their advice had been followed. The
financial practices of the Assembly were as alarming as ever. They demanded
solid guarantees before agreeing to new advances. The directors—Le Couteulx du Molay, Duruey, Cottin, Vandenyver—were charged with informing
Necker and the Finance Committee. The attacks resumed immediately. On
November 20 Mirabeau presented the Assembly with a motion criticizing the
Bank, its directors and their operations. He demanded that it cease to issue
banknotes and that its liquidation be begun. Banknote holders rushed to the
bank counters to be reimbursed, but their demands could not be met.

Lavoisier and his colleagues, indignant at having to support the financial and moral prejudices of unwarranted attacks, were equally worried by
the increasing number of fake banknotes in circulation. The Discount Bank
produced three sorts of banknotes: green (200 livres), blue (300), and white
(1000). On November 7 the police arrested three counterfeiters whose ring-
leader had in his residence cartons filled with banknotes on which the signatures, traced in pencil, had only to be gone over with ink. For that he had a
series of stoneware bottles containing different inks. Each bottle had a label
with the name of the corresponding banker. At the home of one accomplice
the police discovered a printing press and a considerable number of 1000
livre banknotes supposedly from the Bank. They had a slight odor of turpen-
tine and carried a false stamp: "Lo Compagnie" instead of "La Compagnie."
The words "Caisse d'Escompte," instead of being readable in filigree, were
printed outright. Interrogations, searches, and transfers took place. One of
the suspects escaped and was caught. The witnesses who were to testify withdrew. Time passed and the public lost interest, apart from the holders of fake
banknotes who published a brochure entitled "Should the Discount Bank Re-

imburse Its Counterfeit Banknotes?"[14] How could the Discount Bank do so, since it could not even reimburse the genuine ones?

On November 23 Lavoisier went to the National Assembly to plead the case of the Discount Bank. He distributed two documents designed to provide a background for his talk. The first, "On the Organization of Public Banks in General and of the Discount Bank in Particular," explained in sixteen pages how the Discount Bank worked. Lavoisier emphasized that the suspension of payments that had twice occurred was the government's fault much more than the Bank's. Only its concern for saving the State had forced the Bank to break its own rules. Instead of reproaching it, the deputies ought to be showing their gratitude. The creation of a great State bank would render still more important services. By lowering interest rates, it would favor the development of agriculture, trade, and industry. Lavoisier's plea then waxed lyrical:

It is up to the representatives of the nation alone to ensure this benefit, by taking the Discount Bank under their protection, by giving it a set constitution and establishing its credit on firm bases. It is only then that this institution having become national will be worthy of the power and splendor that a fortunate revolution promises the French Empire. It is only then that it can efficiently encourage commercial and agricultural undertakings, the establishment of an expansive manufacturing emulating those in England, the construction of canals and the undertaking of all kinds of public works. It is only then that it will stimulate throughout the country industry and activity, qualities natural to the French nation, but whose means have always been repressed by the existing form of government. It is only then that it will facilitate the circulation of currency in the provinces, the increase in tax revenue, the service of all banks, that it will simplify the accounting of the kingdom, that it will bring about considerable savings on receipts and expenses. In a word, it is only then that it will provide the nation simple means, adapted to the spirit of justice that guides its representatives, for diminishing the burden of the annual debt and facilitating loans at a very low interest rate whose yield will be used to support the more costly undertakings.[15]

The second document, "Address from the Shareholders of the Discount Bank to the Honorable Members of the National Assembly," urged the nomination of commissioners to control the bank statutes, management and operations. Lavoisier and his colleagues offered to "support by all their means, credit and capital, which amounts to 100 million livres, the establishment of a national bank."[16] The total assets of the Discount Bank, explained Lavoisier, amounted to 216 million livres: 159 owed by the government (70 as a deposit of guarantee, 89 advanced to the Treasury) and 57 in available funds. Since the banknotes in circulation totaled 114 million livres, the capital exceeded the total commitments by 102 million; of these 114 million in banknotes, 89 had been advanced to the Royal Treasury. It was definitely the incapacity of the government to reimburse its debt, and not inefficient management, that had led the Bank to suspend payments: "Let the Royal Treasury honor its commitments toward us and as of tomorrow we shall be ready to pay off all of ours."[17] Lavoisier repeated this several days later. Let the State's debt of 89 million livres be repaid to the Bank, "and immediately it will resume payments in cash and honor all its banknotes."[18]

The proposal to transform the Discount Bank into a national bank provoked passionate discussions and no less than six hundred speeches in the Assembly. They reflected, on the one hand the opposition between the financiers—French, Catholic, and bourgeois—and the bankers—Protestant and mostly foreign; on the other, the opposition between the provinces and Paris, and, in general, the hostility of the Assembly to the profits made by both the financiers and bankers. Among the most virulent adversaries were Mirabeau, the comte Adam Philippe de Custine, the marquis Gouy d'Arsy, the baron d'Allarde, and the baron de Cernon. A few deputies of the Third Estate, Regnault de Saint-Jean d'Angély, N. Lavenue, and Pierre Paul Bouchotte joined the main opponents. In their eyes, this combination contained "more vague hopes than specific resources, and too many possibilities for financial speculation."[19]

Du Pont de Nemours defended the Bank and his friend Lavoisier: "It is over a gaping and well-known abyss that the Discount Bank has risked its honor and fortune for the State. Like a lifeboat in the middle of stormy seas, it has saved the crew of a ship in danger of sinking. And that ship, which was France, has now safely arrived in the port of the National Assembly."[20] He recommended the adoption of Necker's plan, with the reservation that the privilege of the Bank not be exclusive and that the establishment of banks be free. He also suggested that the State undertake a major borrowing program.

Lavoisier made one last effort to convince the Assembly. Since it was impossible to find enough cash to meet the needs for the period ending with 1789 and beginning in 1790, it was necessary to create paper money. "Will it be paper money strictly speaking? Will it represent cash? Will it be with or without interest? Why not continue to use the paper of the Discount Bank which, at this moment, holds a kind of middle ground between paper money and banknotes representing cash? Such is the question submitted for the deliberation of the National Assembly."[21] He emphasized that, in public opinion, paper money was synonymous with failure or partial bankruptcy, but that, on the contrary, the paper money of the Discount Bank inspired confidence. It was used for all payments and did not depreciate. His final argument was perhaps not the most timely, given the mood of the Assembly: "I shall add one more reflection. The plan to be deliberated was proposed by a virtuous and upright minister (Necker), a friend of the nation, eager for its glory, whose motives cannot be questioned. He has pondered over banking and financial matters for a long time, making them his principal study, and he knows more about credit and monetary circulation than anybody else."[22]

During this time the financial crisis grew worse. Money was being hidden, the Treasury had run dry, and foreigners feared bankruptcy. The Paris market fell into total discredit. On November 27, before the mansion housing the Discount Bank, fighting broke out among holders of banknotes. On December 4 the duc Louis Marie Florent du Châtelet presented the conclusions of the commissioners, which brought out the constant interventions of Louis XVI and Necker in the affairs of the Bank, the imprudence of its directors that too readily ceded to them, their efforts to keep lending within limits, and the new infringements imposed by Necker.

François Louis Joseph de Laborde de Méréville then presented a competing proposal supported by Talleyrand, Joseph Barnave, and Adrien Duport de Prélaville. It was an old plan that had been elaborated by Isaac Panchaud and modified by Calonne. In it, a national bank would absorb the Discount Bank. Its capital of 300 million livres would be made up of the 100 million in stocks from the Discount Bank, 100 million in banknotes and 100 million in legal tender and royal bills of exchange. It would lend 250 million to the nation at the rate of 5 percent. A commission was appointed to compare the two projects.[23] On December 17 Jean Barthélémy Le Couteulx de Canteleu declared that the latter plan did not ensure immediate resources to the Treasury and would make the Assembly dependent on bankers. It would, he said, be better to keep the Discount Bank and find new resources: the sale of the property confiscated from the clergy would bring in 400 million livres and a special bank could issue *assignats* (banknotes) for an equal amount.

The Assembly still hesitated, caught between its distrust of the Discount Bank and its fear of a national bank that would be too strong and too close to executive power. Necker pressed the issue: "Today the banknotes in circulation represent 126 million livres and legal tender is being exhausted daily. There is general uncertainty and alarm, which are destructive to credit, and widespread unrest that could easily change into rebellion."[24]

In the end, the decrees adopted on December 19 and 21 were a compromise solution. The plan for a Banque de France was rejected. The Discount Bank would keep its status as a private bank, but it would be asked to double its capital by issuing 25,000 new shares, and to agree to lend the State still another 80 million. The directors succeeded in limiting the capital increase to one share for two. The debt of the State would be reimbursed by 170 million assignats, guaranteed by the sale of confiscated royal and clerical property, to be paid in sums of 10 million per month, beginning in January 1791.

In Paris, unemployment was rising, money was becoming scarce, business was stagnating. And the Discount Bank was being blamed for all these misfortunes. On January 10 the six major merchant organizations complained to the Commune de Paris about the lack of cash: "They can no longer buy new foodstuffs or bring them into Paris since their customers have paid them only in banknotes, which are unacceptable to their workers, their suppliers, or manufacturers. In this absolute dearth of cash, Paris will very soon lack all means of subsistence."[25] They asked the Commune de Paris to insist that the Discount Bank exchange at least 300,000 livres of banknotes against cash every day. The Commune appointed a commission and then, given the persistence of the complaints, added a second one, which summoned Lavoisier on February 17. During a stormy meeting, Lavoisier reminded his listeners that the Discount Bank had alone supported the Royal Treasury for the previous eighteen months, in a period threatened by famine, and that it had made possible considerable purchases of wheat from abroad.[26] Without it, he argued, the collapse of the Treasury would have been inevitable, all private fortunes would have been wiped out, industry and commerce paralyzed, and workers would therefore have lost their jobs. Furthermore, he pointed out, the National Assembly had confirmed its mission with its decrees issued in December.

Lavoisier, perhaps more attentive to the difficulties of the stockholders than to those of the population, regretted that a liquidation could not be envisaged because the government was insolvent. If a liquidation were possible, he declared, the directors would agree to it, "because the value of each share would then rise to 4,000 livres, whereas the present market value is below 3,500. They would thus realize a profit of 500 livres on each share, and moreover, they would be liberated from the daily sacrifices that they were being obliged to make to supply Paris with currency from abroad and rid themselves of shares that yielded little more than 5 percent, judging from the latest dividends."[27]

A representative of the Commune asked why the Bank did not resume its payments in cash. Lavoisier answered: "It has done everything it could to obtain currency. It has extracted everything possible in Spanish piasters and gold and silver coins from Spain and Holland."[28] Undoubtedly, family connections made the purchase of Spanish piasters easier. Le Couteulx de La Noraye, director of the Saint-Charles bank in Madrid, sold them to Lavoisier at the Discount Bank. Lavoisier lent them in turn to the State, represented by Le Couteulx de Canteleu, the financial expert of the Assembly; the Discount

Bank was reimbursed in assignats issued by Le Couteulx du Molay, a former director of the Discount Bank and at that time director of the Special Bank. Similarly, close friendly ties facilitated relations among Lavoisier and the four commissioners appointed by the Assembly to oversee the operations of the Discount Bank: Du Pont de Nemours, his step-son Jean Xavier Bureaux de Pusy, Pierre Claude Noël de Dellay d'Agier, and the duc de la Rochefoucauld. They all belonged to the Amis réunis lodge and saw each other regularly at the meetings of the Société de 1789.

The Society of 1789

In a letter of February 2, 1790 to Benjamin Franklin, Lavoisier began by bringing him up to date on the chemical revolution. He added:

As for the political revolution, we consider it an accomplished fact and, hence, irreversible. There still exists, however, the aristocratic party, although it is obviously the weakest and its efforts are futile; the democratic party has the greater advantage in numbers as well as in instruction, philosophy, and enlightenment. Those moderate persons who have kept their heads in this general effervescence think that circumstances have led us too far, that it is regrettable to have been forced to arm all citizens, that it is impolitic to place force in the hands of those who should be obeying it, and that it is to be feared that the new Constitution is going to procreate obstacles for the very people in favor of which it was written. We have reached the most crucial period, because at this moment municipalities are being formed throughout the kingdom. It seems that elections are taking place peacefully. The kingdom will be divided into eighty-three departments, the departments into districts, and each district into small cantons that will contain from two to four municipalities. But you will be able to get all the details from newspapers. We greatly regret that you are so far away from France at this time. Had you been here, you would have been our guide, and would have set the limits that we ought not to have overstepped."[29]

On February 5 Lavoisier took an oath of loyalty to the nation, the king, the law, and the Commune de Paris. "That meant trying to serve a great many masters whose interests and ideas were hard to reconcile. Perhaps this is why he decided to step aside and rejoin his friends in the more subdued atmosphere of the Society of 1789.[30] It was created on April 12, 1790 by Condorcet, La Fayette, Brissot de Warville, the duc de La Rochefoucauld-Liancourt, Talleyrand, Bailly, Mirabeau, Roederer, Le Chapelier, Du Pont de Nemours, and the Abbé Sieyès. "The Society was neither a sect nor a party, but a company of friends of mankind and, so to speak, purveyors of social truths."[31] In this group of physiocrats, all friends, who met to study social mathematics, Lavoisier hoped to find more serene ideological debates. But they were not

without ulterior motives because they were meant to counter the influence of
the Jacobins in the Assembly. Among the 413 members of the Society of 1789,
a large number were financiers:

At least fifty-five bankers, banker-merchants or stockbrokers, belonging to the major
Paris banks—the Le Couteulx, Vandenyver, Cottin and Jauge, Thélusson, Mallet, Greffulhe and Montz and many others—as well as numerous foreign bankers: the Dutch
Abbema and Walckiers, the English Boyd and Ker, and the Swiss Bontemps, Mallet,
and Haller. In 1790 there were seven of the twelve directors of the Discount Bank,
four Farmers General, six directors of state-owned companies, four Treasurers, as well
as several senior civil servants and many private speculators." [32]

The membership fee was very high, five louis d'or ($4,000), and members
were handpicked. At the inaugural banquet on May 12, 130 guests met in the
vast reception rooms of the Palais Royal. Enthusiastic toasts were made to
the Revolution, the city of Paris, the National Guard, French patriots, and the
United States. At the end of the dinner, the strollers in the garden began to
call for Bailly and La Fayette, who then greeted them from a window against
a background of military music and the cheers of the crowd. The same week,
in another banquet, presided over by Pierre Louis Roederer, a deputy in the
National Assembly, 190 guests celebrated the anniversary of the creation of
the Constituent Assembly.

But Lavoisier felt that a great deal of time had been lost in one year of
revolution, and he was eager to have things return to normal. "The situation
of public affairs in France for the past year," he wrote to Joseph Black on July 5,
"has slowed up scientific progress and distracted scientists from their most
cherished occupation. But it is to be hoped that peace and prosperity will replace those troubles that are inseparable from a great revolution." [33] Lavoisier
was referring to the conflict between the part of public opinion supporting
the king and the part in favor of the Assembly. In the major French cities,
the National Guard had organized "federations", which were invited to take
part in a great celebration in Paris on July 14, 1790. Lavoisier, like numerous
Parisians, was host to provincial delegates and accompanied them to the fête
de la Fédération on the Champ de Mars. Necker attended with his daughter
Germaine, the future Madame de Staël, who later wrote:

The spectators were exhilarated; it seemed to them that the king and liberty had become completely compatible. A limited monarchy had always been the wish of France
and the last movement inspiring a truly national enthusiasm could be seen at the 1790
celebration. However, persons capable of reflection were far from being swept away
by the general optimism. I observed deep anxiety in my father's face. At a time when
people believed they were celebrating a victory, he had already sensed perhaps that
there were no resources left. [34]

The festivities went on for several days. On July 15 there was dancing on the Pont-Neuf festooned with greenery in honor of Henri IV. The curious spilled over onto the embankments to watch the water jousts between argumentative bargemen. In the evenings of July 18 and 19 there was dancing on the Place de la Bastille, which had been decorated with flowers, greasy poles, and civic emblems. The Champs-Elysées were lit up, and a Montgolfier balloon was launched from the Champ de Mars.

While this popular merrymaking was taking place, Lavoisier, in the quiet of his study, was writing again to Black: "Since the revolution taking place in France is naturally bound to render superfluous some of those who were attached to the former administration, it is possible that one of the first uses I shall make of my new freedom will be to travel, especially to England and Edinburgh, to see you there, to listen to you, and to profit from your instruction and advice."[35]

This sudden desire for a sabbatical year, completely out of character for a man who had never left France, expressed a deep-seated anxiety. However, Black's answer a few weeks later, on October 24, 1790, brought Lavoisier immense satisfaction. The great Scottish chemist had been won over to his new theory and commented:

And how could it be otherwise? Your numerous experiments, carried out on a large scale and so well conceived, were conducted with such care and scrupulous attention to all circumstances that nothing can be more satisfying than the proofs you achieved. The system that you have based on facts is so intimately connected to them, so simple and intelligible, that it is bound to gain increasing approval, and it will be adopted by a great number of chemists who had grown accustomed to the old system.[36]

Reflections on Assignats

The reasons for anxiety were certainly not lacking. The social and financial situations in France were disastrous. The government was in debt beyond the acceptable limits. The Finance Committee of the Assembly had estimated the total debt at more than 4.2 billion livres: 1.9 for the *dette exigible* (short-term debt) and 2.3 for the *dette constituée* (long-term debt). The long-term debt was well defined and consolidated; it was reimbursable in life annuities and nobody in the Assembly questioned the obligation of its annual payment. The short-term debt, on the other hand, was made of anticipations, assignations, and other urgent advances to the Royal Treasury by the financiers and bankers; it was considered by the Assembly as expensive, disastrous, and immoral. Nevertheless, to refuse to repay it would mean the end of all credit. Finally, in the budget for 1790 which reached 610 million livres, 250 were needed for paying interests on the debt (89.5 for the short-term debt, 164 for the long-term debt), and 360 were allocated for current expenses.

To meet such needs, it would be necessary to bring in 610 million livres in taxes, an amount never collected under the ancien régime. Tax revenue had plummeted. The various farms that had produced 153 million livres in taxes in 1788, had provided only 18 million in 1790. Prices were soaring and money was becoming more scarce. The Finance Committee of the Assembly decided that the issuing of paper money was inevitable. On July 25 Necker pleaded with the deputies to keep the assignats for their true function, the payment of special expenses and the short-term debt. Mirabeau replied:

The first issuing of 400 million livres in assignats was only a temporary remedy and not a complete cure; as time passes it quickly brings back the same needs, and these needs bring the same distress. As long as we do not establish, on a recognizably solid basis, a vast operation, a broad overall policy that will place us above events, we shall be forever hostages to fortune. I shudder to think that within two months we shall have exhausted our assignats. Once they are gone, what will we have to support us? Nothing! I can already see the Minister of Finance coming dolefully to present us with a new certificate of ruin. Good heavens, is this what is called financial expertise? [37]

There was, Mirabeau continued, a simple means of reducing the burden: reimburse the short-term debt by selling national property, which represented approximately the same value of 2 billion livres. Thus the revenue needed each year would be reduced by 89.5 million, the amount of interest being paid on this debt. But the more reasonable deputies were opposed to issuing more assignats. Lebrun, a member of the Finance Committee protested:

If you want to renege on the commitments of the State, at least do it loyally. You will be throwing a billion livres in paper money at your creditors, but they have neither bread nor cash! Therefore your paper must be transformable into bread and cash. With this plan, everything in the government would be changed into paper. But can employees and soldiers be paid with paper? Is it with paper that we are going to send out ships that are waiting to be armed? It is being argued that these clever operations will save the revolution. I say to you that they will kill both the revolution and the National Assembly.[38]

On August 27 Necker added his confirmation that creating an enormous mass of paper money would have disastrous consequences: "Don't be misled; apart from the speculators, the great majority of citizens would be affected in some way or other by this vast undertaking which, by upsetting all relationships, changing all prices, and introducing the wildest fluctuations, would shatter all fortunes and create an even more dangerous commotion."[39]

The deputies responded with sarcasms. "I was surprised," declared Gouy d'Arsy, "to see the Minister of Finance, who up to now has presented no plan of his own, has offered only half-way measures and useless palliatives—his only solution has been more taxes and a monstrous alliance with the Discount Bank—that this minister, I repeat, came to attack the one general plan that had been put forward."[40]

In fact, two plans had been proposed. Talleyrand's would use money from the sale of national property to settle all the financial claims of the short-term debt, without converting it into paper money. Mirabeau's would immediately create assignats worth 2 billion livres and use them as paper money for reimbursing the debt; they would later be gradually withdrawn from circulation as the national property was sold. Two days later, at the Society of 1789, Lavoisier, in his "Reflections on Assignats and the Liquidation of the Short-Term Debt," explained that the former plan was insufficient and the latter dangerous. His was based on the same principle, the sale of national property: "At this time when a part of the revenues of the State is not coming in, when the Public Treasury, in addition to the current expenses and interest for which it is responsible, has been forced to deal with an awesome outstanding debt, the State, as you well know, Gentlemen, has no recourse other than to sell national property."[41]

But the important step was to determine the value of national property. Since the income from the former ecclesiastical property was 200 million livres a year, one could theoretically, on the basis of a habitual revenue of 5 percent, evaluate the capital at 4 billion livres. But the disappearance of tithes, which made up half the revenue of the clergy, the exemption from customs, and the protective measures for forests had considerably reduced the profitability of these holdings. Hence their value had to be reduced by two-thirds and placed at 1.3 billion. The same reduction would have to apply to the confiscated royal property, whose value was no more than 500 million. In all, the worth of the national property did not surpass 1.8 billion. And even so, the totality of this sum was not available. The Assembly had already created assignats worth 400 million, guaranteed by national property. It still had to reimburse 250 million livres of advances on the tax revenue for 1790 and foresee a deficit of 100 million on the tax revenue for 1791. Once these 750 million were deducted, there would remain only 1.05 billion. Capital was melting like snow in the sun. Lavoisier warned:

You will be frightened, Gentlemen, to see that a capital that was 4 billion when the nation took possession of it, has been reduced to 1 billion in such a short time, and perhaps you will regret that a moment of enthusiasm committed the Assembly to renouncing the tithe whose redemption would have contributed so effectively to the reestablishment of business and the extinction of the public debt.[42]

In any case, he continued, it would be useless to create 2 billion livres of assignats because the Finance Committee had exaggerated the figure of the short-term debt, which actually did not surpass 1.2 billion. Furthermore, it would be dangerous to issue more assignats because that would mean doubling the money supply, which totaled 2 billion. The result would be the doubling of prices of national products and money would lose half its value. In fact, he admitted that the process would perhaps not be quite so drastic, because the national property would serve as a partial guarantee of this increase in the money supply, but a generalized inflation would nevertheless be inevitable. "All the merchandise, foodstuffs, movable, and real estate of the kingdom, all salaries and manpower costs would increase by 25 percent. Not only would we no longer export anything, but our neighbors, whose labor costs would not have experienced the same increase, would inundate our provinces with their merchandise to the point of completely ruining our trade."[43]

In summary, "only the smallest possible number of assignats should be put into circulation, and only as required by circumstances. Issuing more than 800 million would entail the greatest risk, and the issuing should be done successively and slowly."[44]

Lavoisier's paper was published by the *Journal de la Société de 1789*, created by Condorcet and printed by Du Pont de Nemours. The journal contained essentially papers on economics, constitutional law, and international politics, and it was read by influential people and deputies. Lavoisier's intervention obtained some immediate success. The Assembly decided that the total worth of assignats in circulation should rise to 1.2 billion livres; 800 million would be added to the 400 already issued in December 1789, with the uncertain guarantee of the yield from the sale of national property. But during the year 1790 the borrowing of the State from the Discount Bank accelerated: 20 million in April, 20 in May, 50 in June, 45 in July, 40 in August and 40 in September. The Discount Bank was reimbursed with assignats issued by the Special Bank. The moderate political world was losing control of events, and panic prevailed over financial technique.

Paper money brought about a speculative spirit that had its comical side. Certain former nuns were dealing in blond wigs, still another was selling men's shoes; an herb seller could make 20,000 livres in one day and then tuck them all in her wallet. The imagination lost itself in regions of fabulous wealth. Everybody was transformed into a trader, spoke only in terms of millions of livres, and the smallest exchange took on the air of an important transaction. What was remarkable in all this was that the intelligent man held on to his assignats and the stupid one got rid of them. The latter came out better; less carried away by the fictional increase of his wealth, he accumulated merchandise, saying to himself that it would always be worth something.[45]

The deputies were deaf to all warnings about the dangers of too many assignats. They ignored Du Pont's famous memoir, "The Effects of Assignats on the Price of Bread," just as they did the protests of Talleyrand, Allarde, Boislandry, Forbonnais, Condorcet, Lavoisier, and those of the provincial towns, not to mention the hostility of peasants.[46] All efforts were in vain. Discouraged, Necker resigned on September 3, 1790 and left France amid general indifference. On September 25 Du Pont tried once more to explain to the Assembly the inconveniences of assignats and their effect on the price of commodities and merchandise:

M. Lavoisier, alternate deputy from the bailiwick of Blois, backed up by the authority of Hume and Smith, and, still more, of reason, has proven beyond a doubt that, if the amount of cash in circulation were suddenly doubled, the prices of our goods would double. The necessary balance of payments between nations would be reestablished only after much of our currency had flowed out to foreign countries. He has also shown that since silver is the only currency to which all nations attach an equal value, and hence it can be used anywhere, we could not establish an overabundance of two types of currency, one real, the other fictitious, without having the more valuable one, the convertible silver, flow to foreign countries until our exaggerated prices fell.[47]

Eager to escape the habitual criticism that he was an overly systematic physiocrat, Du Pont specified that his speech had nothing to do with a philosophical system but was the fruit of experience. He took as an example the paper money created in the United States of America ten years earlier, reminding the deputies of the National Assembly: "You have seen how, in spite of all the efforts of Congress, Paine, Adams, Washington, and Franklin, this paper depreciated to the point that with it a pair of boots cost thirty-six thousand francs, and that, a little later, a supper for four friends, which would have cost ten écus in coin, cost fifty thousand écus in paper money."[48]

Neither Du Pont's eloquence nor Lavoisier's demonstration was able to prevent massive issuing of assignats. Originally devised as a means of paying the short-term debt, they would become legal tender and replace all other forms of money. Lavoisier had failed to protect the interests of the Discount Bank. The short-term debt would never be reimbursed. Indirect taxes had been abolished and the General Farm itself was in danger of total elimination. Increasingly skeptical of political action, Lavoisier took refuge in his scientific work and activities of a social nature. The world was becoming incomprehensible for the cold theoretician who felt himself increasingly isolated. The

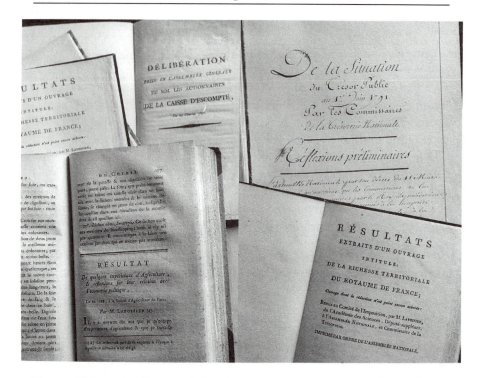

Figure 9. Title pages of Lavoisier's best-known works in economics. Private collection.

Society of 1789 began to lose its members, discouraged by the austere financial discussions and the attacks from the Jacobin press. Mirabeau joined the
Jacobin Club, whose influence in the Assembly was constantly growing. The
last members left. Even Condorcet took his distance, and the fifteenth and
final issue of his *Journal de la Société de 1789* appeared on September 15.

The last one to leave, in January 1791, was Lavoisier, who had continued
to serve as secretary: "To deserve well of humanity and pay tribute to his
country," he said, "it is not indispensable for a person to be called to public
and prominent functions that assist in the organization and regeneration of
empires. The physicist, too, can, in the silence of his laboratory, carry out the
functions of a patriot."[49]

The Territorial Wealth of the Kingdom of France

But Lavoisier's reputation as a financial expert and economist pursued him. The Comité des Impositions (Taxation Committee) of the National Assembly called on him to establish the bases for the new tax system.[50] Under Roederer's proposal, the Taxation Committee had first created a stamp tax. Then Roederer tried to destroy the monopoly of the General Farm on the cultivation, manufacture, and sale of tobacco. Only a few privileged provinces (Flandres, Artois, Hainault, Cambrésis, Alsace, Franche-Comté) had a right to cultivate tobacco. Roederer favoured a plan calling for the free cultivation and manufacture of tobacco and the creation of a state-owned company replacing the Farm and selling tobacco imported from America. Du Pont de Nemours and the Farmers General Desmarest and Delahante had done their best to protect the monopoly that every year generated revenues of over 30 million livres for the Royal Treasury. Lavoisier himself had written a memoir describing the views of the General Farm in this regard.[51] He explained that the state-owned company would not bring the same amount of revenue to the State and that the suppression of the monopoly would create "a major problem with fraud on the part of the employees of the company itself."[52]

Finally, Mirabeau made a counter-proposal suggested by Lavoisier: a new tobacco monopoly would take away, with compensation, from the former privileged provinces their rights to cultivate tobacco and would guarantee to the State revenues of 30 million livres. Roederer denied Mirabeau's figures and insisted on the difficult situation that would be created in Alsace for the 6,000 workers employed by the tobacco manufacturers of Strasbourg. On February 12, 1791 the Assembly voted 382 to 360 in favor of the Taxation Committee. "The tax monopoly was dead, and the pro-monopoly forces and the American interests were defeated."[53] From that moment, Roederer sought the total abolition of the General Farm. "You will be able," he said to the Assembly, "from the 1st of April to terminate the appointments of the Farmers General and régisseurs. [. . .] The rendering of accounts ought not to be a means of prolonging their appointments."[54]

Those who were advocating a radical reform of the financial system and the destruction of the General Farm now dominated the Taxation Committee. Direct taxes—the *contribution foncière*, tax on land and buildings; the *contribution mobilière*, which combined a personal tax, a sumptuary tax and a tax on rent; and the *contribution des patentes*, tax on commercial income—had become the principal source of revenue of the State.

The deputies estimated that the tax on land and buildings would represent 80 percent of the resources of the State, but they did not know precisely what the national income was. The estimations varied considerably, ranging from 2.5 billion livres according to Du Pont de Nemours to 4 billion according to the Ecclesiastical Committee of the Assembly, in charge of the confiscated clerical property. Jean François Tolosan estimated it at 3 billion (2 billion from agriculture, 700 million from manufacturing and the colonies, and 300 million from real estate revenues).

To know the precise figures, it would be necessary to determine each farmer's net income and then multiply it by their number. But there was no national cadaster, or land registry, giving an accurate description of each farmer's property. The law of November 23, 1790 required municipalities to provide information on this subject, but they had no means of gathering it. Even with this information, the calculation of each farmer's net revenue would require several steps: evaluating the yields of the harvests, and then subtracting the interest paid on loans, the maintenance costs for buildings, equipment and animals, the salaries of the workers, and the rent paid to the landowner.

To simplify matters, the deputies decided that each farmer's net revenue would be considered as equal to the rent he paid, and the tax to be levied would equal a sixth of this income. But they still did not know how much that would bring to the coffers of the State. The advice of a man like Lavoisier, an expert respected for his precision and known for his economic studies, would be invaluable. On March 15, 1791, in the middle of the tobacco monopoly discussions, he went to the Assembly to help the Taxation Committee assess the national revenue. He presented the results extracted from a work entitled *De la Richesse territoriale du Royaume de France* (On the Territorial Wealth of the Kingdom of France), which marked a milestone in the history of economic science and national statistics and accounting.

It was seven years earlier, in 1784, when he had been working with the Committee on Agriculture, that he and Du Pont had begun a methodical study of the demography and the national production of France. "Since then," he told the committee, "I have sought to give more scope to this work, to gather more concrete information, to increase the means of verification, to devise methods for calculating consumption and production, as we did for calculating the population."[55] He applied the same quantitative approach to socio-economic questions that he used in scientific studies:

The kind of combinations and calculations whose examples I have tried to give here are the basis for all economics. This science, like almost all others, began through metaphysical discussions and reasoning. Its theory has advanced, but the practical science is in its infancy. The result is that the politician lacks the facts on which to base his speculations.[56]

Lavoisier began by defining the national revenue as equal to the sum of the farmers' net incomes.[57] Like the physiocrats, he based his method of national accounting essentially on agriculture since it was the most important source of wealth, but like Smith, he also considered trade and industry as real sources of wealth. Since the agricultural revenue was not directly available, it had to be calculated. To get it, he called on three types of aggregates inspired by the physiocrats: the territorial yield in kind, the territorial income in money, and the net income.

The territorial yield in kind was "the sum of all the production of the soil, of everything that grows from the earth and depends on it, whether for the use of man or animals."[58] The territorial income in money was the portion of the preceding that could be converted into money, that is, the territorial product stripped of its double uses. For example, there was double use when the prices of both straw and wheat were counted in the production of a farm. The straw had no commercial value, and should be included in the value of wheat. Similarly, the fodder and oats eaten by the work horses had no commercial value and were to be integrated into the value of wheat. The net income was what remained of the territorial revenue in money after subtracting all expenses and costs connected with an agricultural exploitation, in particular, the feeding and maintenance of workers.

Lavoisier insisted that the only way to calculate the territorial revenue precisely and equitably so that the State took its legitimate part without hindering economic development would be to have a bureau of statistics. Since none existed, indirect methods had to be used. Confident as always in the law of conservation of matter, he estimated that the annual gross national product could be determined from the annual national consumption: "There is an equation, an equality, between what is produced and what is consumed; thus, to know what is produced, it suffices to know what is consumed, and vice versa."[59]

The calculation of annual consumption rested on a second principle: "The total consumption of a kingdom is equal to the average consumption of individuals, multiplied by their number."[60] Lavoisier estimated the population of the kingdom at 25 million. In fact, it was closer to 28 million, and France was at that time the most populous country in Europe.[61] Individual consumption was easier to estimate for a Farmer General: "The annual consumption of wheat, rye, and barley, used as human nutrition throughout the kingdom, reaches 11 billion 667 pounds. When one adds what is used for sowing—2 billion 333 million pounds—the total consumption of wheat, rye, and barley comes to 14 billion pounds a year."[62] To those expenses had to be added those for meat, clothing, lodging, and heat. Lavoisier estimated that, in total, an adult male's annual consumption amounted to 250 livres per year.

In a rural household composed of a husband, wife and three young children, the father's consumption can be estimated at 251 livres, the mother's at 167 livres, 6 sous, 8 deniers and that of the three children at a sum equivalent to the mother's. Hence a total of 585 livres, 13 sous, 4 deniers for the family and roughly 117 livres, 2 sous, 8 deniers per person. To cover these expenses, the couple have to earn at least 38 sous, 3 deniers every day, including holidays and Sundays. This income is not achieved by the poorest families and is far less than that of the richest. It could be considered the average consumption of all the inhabitants of the kingdom, but since poor citizens far outnumber the comfortably off, the sum is still a bit above the average expenditure. It is quite remarkable that, after so much research and calculation, one reaches the precise result indicated by M. Quesnay in *La Philosophie rurale*, a result that gave rise to Voltaire's brilliant brochure entitled *L'homme aux quarante écus* ["The Man with Forty Ecus"]. This pamphlet is a masterpiece of both intellectual depth and humor. For the philosopher, it is a complete treatise on economics. For the masses it is a highly amusing tale. Voltaire, the supreme genius, found a way to bring himself down to everybody's level. Nevertheless, in this work, Voltaire supposed the inhabitants of France to be a little better off than they were, especially at the time he was writing it. Perhaps he did not include very young children. However that may be, according to my calculation, the average consumption of the inhabitants of France comes to 110 livres per person. By multiplying this sum by the number of the inhabitants of the kingdom, that is by 25 million, one would reach a figure of 2 billion, 750 million for the total consumption of France.[63]

It then remained to ascertain that the production figures—surface multiplied by yield—were equal to those of the national consumption. The balance sheet method was applied here as it was in chemistry: nothing was lost, nothing was created. Lavoisier estimated the area of France to be about 105 million arpents or 536,235 km2. Of these, only 65 million arpents or 332,000 km2 were sown with cereal crops; the rest were covered with forests, vineyards, meadows, moors, uncultivated land, roads, rivers, and so forth.

Finally, the annual gross product, the real income of the kingdom, stripped of all double uses, was about 2 billion, 750 million. The figures tallied well, but this was not the net product. To calculate it, it was necessary to deduct the cultivation costs, the consumption of all who contributed to it, and agricultural expenses. And this amounted to a bit more than half the gross product. The net product or taxable national income was on average around 1.2 billion livres. It varied according to the price of wheat. "It goes beyond 1.2 billion when the price of wheat is two sous per pound; it does not surpass 1.05 billion when the price falls to 1 sou, 6 deniers. Thus it is impossible that the property tax, set at a sixth of the taxable net revenue by the National Assembly, could bring in more than 180 million livres."[64] The urban property tax represented 30 million livres. "Thus the property tax from all the kingdom, based on the proportions decreed by the National Assembly, would reach scarcely more than 210 million."[65]

The members of the Taxation Committee, who had estimated the needs of the State at 600 million livres, were greatly disappointed. To improve the tax yield, Lavoisier suggested increasing the rate to a fifth rather than a sixth of the net income. But the Committee rejected his recommendation. Two days later, the Assembly assessed the taxable national income at 1.8 billion livres and refused to change the tax rate; 300 million livres was expected. Lavoisier's calculations had been denied. Roederer emphasized nevertheless that his study "contained many details of great interest; if the National Assembly printed it, it would be making a great gift to political calculators and all citizens."[66]

The small brochure of 48 pages, eventually printed in 1791, aroused the keen interest of the public because of its economic data and of its revelation of the weak demographic importance of the nobility as compared to that of the Third Estate. Everybody could see that "the former nobles, including the ennobled, formed only 3 percent of the population of the kingdom and their number—including men, women, and children—was only 83,000 of whom only 18,323 were in a condition to bear arms," Lavoisier wrote. "One sees that the other classes of society, habitually grouped under the heading of the Third Estate, could provide, on the contrary, contingents of 5,500,000 for bearing arms."[67] For the deputies it was scandalous that so few men held so much wealth, power, and means for political action.

The importance and originality of this economic study are recognized today. In it, Lavoisier emerges as a rigorous practician of political arithmetic and the precursor of national statistics. He recommended the creation of a central statistical service,

a public institution where the results of the balance of agriculture, commerce, and population would be combined, where the overall situation of the kingdom—its resources in men, production, industry, and accumulated capital could be depicted in a condensed table. To form this major institution that exists in no other nation, that can exist only in France, the National Assembly has only to want to do it. The present organization of the kingdom seems to lend itself to this kind of research.[68]

The idea was not entirely new. In 1784 Necker had already envisaged an institution that would make a census of the major economic data of the

nation: population, finances of the State, foreign investment, taxes, exports
and imports, hospitals and homes for old people, roads, operations of the Discount Bank, and State-owned pawnshops. To such an institution, he wanted

to entrust instructive research on the scope of the major products consumed, the relationship of the amount of seeds planted and the yield of the soil in different parts of
the kingdom, the determination of the number of acres in cultivation and variations in
labor costs. He wanted it to determine the number of nobles and compare their privileges with those of the commoners, to find out how many ecclesiastics and Protestants
the kingdom contained, to study the progress of luxury in the preeminent cities and
the decreased life expectancy in several dangerous professions. He also wanted it to
look into the interest of foreigners and specific nations in public funds, the state and
occupation of beggars or unfortunate persons cared for in the various charitable institutions, and many other equally interesting subjects.[69]

Thus Lavoisier, along with Quesnay, can be considered a precursor of
national accounting. What he proposed was indeed a statistical depiction of
the economy of a country, within a coherent framework, in the form of an en-
semble of aggregates. "There is a means of bringing a much greater degree of
clarity to this work. It would consist of forming, for an ordinary year, the account or general assessment of all the production of the kingdom. Each kind
of produce would have its particular section. Agriculture would be considered
as the domain of a single individual, who would be responsible for collecting
statistics regarding its production and would have to justify their use."[70] It
would be considered an economic whole, with a column for receipts, including the totality of production, and one for expenses, including all the costs.
The same method would be used for trade and industry. Lavoisier specified:
"To this general account in kind would be added a general account in money
which would interact with all the others."[71] This material balance joined to
a financial one was definitely the foreshadowing of a national accounting.[72]
Aware of the innovative character of his proposition, Lavoisier wrote:

A work of this kind would contain within a few pages the entire science of economics,
or rather that science would cease to be one, because its results would be so clear, so
palpable, the different questions raised would be so easy to resolve, that there could
no longer be any differences of opinion.[73]

Lavoisier drew his information from authors who had preceded him:
Alexis Paucton, the Abbé Jean Joseph d'Expilly, Louis Messance, who used
data from Jean Baptiste de La Michodière, and Jean Baptiste Moheau. But
much information also came from his experience as a landowner in Freschines and Le Bourget, his participation in the socio-economic studies for
the Academy of Science on prisons, hospitals, slaughterhouses, and urbanism

in Paris and, above all, from his perfect knowledge of the custom duties collected at the entries to Paris, since he was responsible for them.[74] But he was not a mere specialist of political arithmetic. He formulated the principle of equality of uses and resources by type of production, an innate idea with this advocate of balance sheets. For him statistics and accounting were complementary, and O. Arkhipoff comments: "The French Revolution, which had made general statistics possible, could equally found the national accounting, thanks to the genius of one man, Lavoisier."[75]

Lavoisier had his brochure printed by Du Pont.[76] Like all deputies in the Constituent Assembly, Du Pont had declared himself not "re-eligible," and found himself out of a job in September 1791. Lavoisier lent him 71,000 livres to help him buy the printing house belonging to Lamelle at the Hôtel Bretonvilliers on the Isle Saint-Louis. Du Pont had acquired a good knowledge of printing while publishing, in close collaboration with P. F. Didot, the *Éphémérides du citoyen*. Slightly over-confident as usual, Du Pont wrote in the pamphlet distributed to prospective clients: "I shall charge high prices for those who have taste and appreciate typographical perfection. I shall work well and at the lowest prices for those who seek only truths and ideas in books. I shall work rapidly for everybody. I am happy to end up where Franklin began, and in no way humiliated by the fact that an entire lifetime separates us."[77]

But Du Pont did not really have the penchant for business. Eleuthère-Irenée, who had left Essonne when Lavoisier ceased to be a régisseur in 1791, did most of the work in spite of his inexperience. The father preferred to talk politics and idealize the role he had played in the Constituent Assembly: "Perfectly independent, frank and proud as liberty, my only interest was the Constitution, the complete establishment of the rights of man and citizen, the restoration of financial stability, justice, humanity, respect for the laws we had made and the reign of order and peace."[78]

Lavoisier also gave him the job of publishing the memoirs presented at the Academy of Science. The collaboration was sometimes a little difficult. The volume with papers for 1788 did not sell well, and it was soon apparent that scarcely half the volume for 1789 had been set and that only two sheets of the 1790 collection had been printed. Thus there was a considerable delay in getting out the memoirs for 1792. Lavoisier could not resist the temptation of giving Du Pont a piece of advice on his marketing methods: "It is in your interest to let it be known as soon as possible that you are publishing them and you can hope for a quick turnover only if you accustom French and foreign bookstores as well as scientists to address themselves to you. Perhaps it would be a good idea to put an announcement in the more widely circulated newspapers."[79]

The Abolition of the General Farm

On March 2 the Allarde Law, retroactive to July 14, 1789, did away with corporations and guilds, tollgates, the salt tax, the tobacco monopoly, and domestic customs duties. Liberalism was the order of the day. And on March 20
the National Assembly abolished the General Farm. *Le Père Duchesne*, an ex-
tremist newspaper headed by Jacques René Hébert, expressed the popular
satisfaction:

How I would like to be at the headquarters of the General Farm to contemplate the
fat mugs of all those financiers sitting around their green baize when they hear about
the decree of the Assembly. What grimaces all those jackasses will make on realizing
that they will be forced to part with their beautiful palaces, their handsome country
houses, and fine furnishings. [. . .] But those jackasses are undoubtedly going to imitate the other aristocrats and try to carry away their plunder to a foreign country. I
therefore urge all citizens to meet in their sections and oblige these people to give an
accounting of their past conduct and to turn over all that they have acquired by theft
and banditry.[80]

In this climate of hate, certain former employees of the General Farm
stood out by their virulence. They demanded to be reimbursed for what they
had paid into the pension fund of the Farm, created in 1774 at Lavoisier's
instigation, considering that they had been exploited: "Our adversaries are
afraid of providing the documents that they obstinately refuse to give us,
documents that are all the more interesting because they would bring millions to the National Treasury."[81]

The Assembly entrusted the liquidation of the General Farm and the rendering of the accounts to six Farmers: Clément de Laâge de Bellefaye, Alexandre Victor de Saint-Amand, François Puissant de La Villeguérie, Guillaume
Couturier, Jacques Joseph de La Perrière, and Jacques Delahante, aided by
three assistant Farmers: François Jean Vente, Alphonse de Vismes de Saint-
Alphonse, and Etienne Marie Delahante.[82]

The commission could not establish definitive accounts before receiving
the individual accounts of the tax collectors; but precisely these collectors
were busy selling for the government the stocks of salt and tobacco stored in
the graneries and warehouses of the Gabelles. And they could not establish
their accounts until all bills had been paid.

Lavoisier did not participate in this work, but he became a candidate for
an administrative post in the national customs, and to his great disappointment, he did not succeed. He then sought to become an administrator of the
new Paris tollgate taxes, thereafter to be collected by the State. On April 7,
with this end in view, he wrote a memoir to Louis XVI that reflected his per-

sistence. He pointed out his different services over the years, the risks he had run at the time of the accident at Essonne and the gunpowder affair at the Port Saint-Paul, his responsibilities at the Discount Bank, the General Farm and Paris tollgates, and the studies done for the National Assembly and the Taxation Committee.

In these circumstances, the Sire Lavoisier, confident in His Majesty's justice and goodness, dares to ask to be assured of one of the two posts of director that will very shortly be created for the Paris tollgate taxes. He asks it as one having grown old in this work, all of whose details he knows in depth. In requesting this post, he does not wish to replace anyone or harm anyone. He is simply asking to keep a position that he held for a long time and that he still holds, to which no one has a more incontestable right than he, especially since M. de Saint-Cristau has been appointed to one of the posts of director of National Customs.

Nota bene: the Taxation Committee had insisted most urgently that the Sire Lavoisier be appointed to one of the directorships of National Customs; and he was bitterly disappointed to learn that he had been struck from the list presented to the King. This is still another consideration that could persuade His Majesty to use this opportunity to rectify the disappointment that *this removal from the list has caused both the Taxation Committee and the Sire Lavoisier*.[83]

In the rough copy, Lavoisier made a significant change in the final sentence: he had at first mentioned only the disappointment of the "Sire Lavoisier," but to give his request more weight he had added the "Taxation Committee." In spite of his relentlessness, his request was rejected. But he had not yet had his last word.

15

French Finances

THE NATIONAL ASSEMBLY WAS DETERMINED to remove the control of public finances from executive power and to create a separate executive power which "assumed responsibility for borrowing, taxing, and spending, processes hitherto managed by the great corps of venal financiers."[1] A minimum of coordination between these two executive powers was nevertheless needed. On March 6, 1790, Necker had proposed the creation of an office for administering the Public Treasury, which would work with both the Minister of Finance and the Finance Committee of the Assembly. The members of this office, Treasury Commissioners, would be chosen from the deputies and appointed by the king. "This office would fix all daily expenses and modes of payment. It would oversee all receipts and, in a word, direct all the activity of the Treasury, without exception or restriction."[2]

In order to mark the separation of powers and shield the deputies from the attraction of the Royal Court, the Assembly had forbidden its members to accept government jobs. Necker, greatly affected by this refusal as he was by the little attention they paid to his warnings about the dangers of issuing more assignats, as we know, slipped away in September and left France.

The Assembly then took control of the Public Treasury and on December 20, Roederer forbade all interference by the executive in financial matters. "Principles would be compromised if the government were allowed to administer finances."[3] And he specified what he meant by declaring: "The Treasury is not royal, it is national."[4]

The Assembly replaced the Controller General of Finance by a Minister of Public Taxation with limited powers, responsible only for establishing the tax base and collecting taxes; deprived of all economic, commercial and financial data, he could neither foresee nor control their yield. Economic activities were transferred to the new Interior Ministry, and foreign trade to the Ministry of Foreign Affairs. Along with the General Farm and the corps of financiers, the old fiscal system had entirely disappeared.

The National Treasury

On March 27, 1791 the Assembly took over the direction of the Public Treasury and appointed the six commissioners under its control. They could not belong to any ministerial department; they were placed "under the regular supervision of the legislators; and three deputies would sit in on their deliberations and verify the funds and records. The annual salary of the commissioners was to be 15,000 livres.[5] Three deputies were to participate in their deliberations and inspect their books. Thus the legislative power would be in charge of the finances of the State. The Assembly had under its orders an actual ministry that controlled all the others, since it had the exclusive right to authorize payments and left the king no freedom in the use of public monies.

A decree of April 7 named the first six commissioners: Jean de Vaines for the Public Revenue Office; Antoine Pierre Dutremblay for Marine Expenditures; Daniel Etienne Rouillé de l'Estang for War Expenditures; Lavoisier for Miscellaneous Expenditures: clergy, civil list, foreign affairs, bridges and roads, the national gendarmerie, academies; Condorcet for the Debt; Barthélemy Huber, Necker's friend, for Central Accounting. Etienne Clavière, who had been hoping for Huber's post, accused him of being a schemer and speculator and of having gone bankrupt in England. Huber resigned in May and François Pierre Cornut de La Fontaine, who had been first clerk of finances at the Royal Treasury, replaced him. These six commissioners made up the Comité de Trésorerie (Treasury Committee), whose offices were on the rue Vivienne and the rue Neuve des Petits Champs.[6] The members were to take turns serving as president for a month at a time.

The accumulation of posts being highly unpopular, Lavoisier, who had held five at the height of his career in 1788, feared that his new functions would cause him to lose the directorship of the Gunpowder and Saltpeter Administration, where one of the four positions had already been abolished. Furthermore, he had just been subjected to an attack from his old enemy Marat in *L'Ami du peuple*, the journal of the partisans of the left:

I denounce to you the coryphaeus—the leader of the chorus—of the charlatans, Master Lavoisier, son of a land-grabber, apprentice-chemist, pupil of the Genevan stock-jobber Necker, a Farmer General, Commissioner for Gunpower and Saltpeter, director of the Discount Bank, secretary to the king, member of the Academy of Science, intimate of Vauvilliers, unfaithful administrator of the Paris Food Commission, and the greatest schemer of our times. Would you believe that this little gentleman who enjoys an income of 40,000 livres and whose only claim to public recognition is that he imprisoned Paris by cutting off the fresh air with a wall that cost the poor people 33 million livres and that he moved gunpowder from the Arsenal into the Bastille on the night of July 12 and 13, is engaged in a devilish intrigue to get himself elected as administrator of the department of Paris?[7]

Lavoisier could have done without this publicity. In any case, he thought it would be wise to refuse the salary from the Treasury, so as to make the point that his main job, the one he wanted to keep, was at the Arsenal. He informed Louis Hardouin Tarbé, the new minister of Public Taxation, of this fact. Then, moved by a strange inspiration, he showed remarkable tactlessness, given the general opinion in which he was held, by publishing an open letter in *Le Moniteur* on April 9:

By resigning from the king's service, by dedicating myself to difficult functions that may surpass my strength, in a word, by renouncing a way of life I was accustomed to leading, I believe I can give the greatest proof possible of my devotion to the nation. As the reward for this sacrifice, I ask only to be allowed to carry out the new functions entrusted to me without pay. My remuneration as the head of the Gunpowder Administration, precisely because it is modest, suits my way of life, my tastes and needs. And at a time when so many good citizens are losing their jobs, I could never, for anything in the world, consent to accept two salaries.[8]

Lavoisier was immediately set upon by the violently antirevolutionary periodical of the *Ultras* (Extreme Royalists), the *Actes des Apôtres*:

O, generous Lavoisier, your pathetic letter,
I must admit, brought me close to tears;
You have won our hearts
By describing your heroic conduct.
What an astonishing example of moderation!
To be content with an income of a hundred thousand écus,
Which you have earned, Heaven knows! And then
To give your time to your country for nothing.
What a tempting example.
Ah! What a pity I cannot follow it, alas!
Between ourselves, I see that Necker is your model,
Like him, you want no salary;
But also, like him, you know perfectly well
Just how far you can dip into the new funds.
Our adored master, following his subjects' wishes,
Could place his confidence in no one better than you;
The misfortunes of France all vanish
When you condescend to give in to the King's entreaties,
And Heaven allows us to renew our hope.
Your equal in virtue, the worthy Condorcet,
Since he is no longer noble, has had his eye on fortune:
Blasé to honors, glory is too ordinary for him;

It is only an illusion, he needs something concrete.
It is all very well to be inscribed in the temple of Memory,
But the one of Wealth also has its merit:
The Academician, to give his glory a rest,
Now transforms himself into a big financier.
There you are then, both of you, pillars of France!
You are going to stuff yourselves with bills, with assignats;
You will be the croupiers of the head of Finance,
Perhaps even of the deputies at the National Assembly.
Friends, certainly in our times,
You are what we must call great men;
Therefore, you are sure to have your tomb
Beside the coffin of the famous Mirabeau;
And to prove it to you, we must urge the passage of a major decree,
Which is that no later than tomorrow, both of you, dead or not,
Be solemnly placed in his funerary vault.[9]

Following this piece of humorous poetry came a commentary which was even more severe and paradoxically resembled Marat's accusations:

The aforementioned Lavoisier assures us in his letter that while a mass of decent people are dying of hunger and have no salaries, he cannot reconcile himself to receiving two, that is, to being paid by both the Royal Treasury and the Gunpowder Administration. His modesty leads him to prefer the salary of the latter because it is lower, and meagerness is what suits him best. The Revolution has produced strange miracles! Because the learned financier did not think this way before. Not only did he find it entirely just to receive two salaries for more than twenty years from the Farms and the Gunpowder Administration, for very ordinary services, but he did not disdain to rob from genuine scientists at the Academy of Science an allowance of a thousand écus per year, which he definitely decided to savor, despite his repugnance for money. But he had to have it so as to prove that he was a true colleague of his fellow Academicians. In this beautiful century in which virtue inspires everything, produces everything, overturns everything, how worthy it would be of M. Lavoisier's sublime generosity to turn over to his generous nation, to this good people among whom he has been so fortunate to be born, everything he has received in excess, since he has been earning a double, triple and even quadruple salary! Because he is also at the Discount Bank.[10]

Even Brissot de Warville, a moderate Girondin and founder of the Société des Amis des Noirs, had already published an attack against Lavoisier which had overtones of an indictment:

Farmer General and Academician, two titles for the encouragement of despotism; besides he is the author of the plan for constructing a wall around Paris. Hooted down in Blois when he presented himself for the elections, he received only charitable votes. Lavoisier became a chemist; he would have become an alchemist if he had followed only his inextinguishable thirst for gold. But he and his associates have found surer means of satisfying that thirst through the excessive moistening of tobacco and the speculative and monopolistic purchase of grains. France owes them eight to ten famines.[11]

Nevertheless Lavoisier asked Brissot to publish the open letter in his periodical, *Le Patriote Français*: "M. Lavoisier would have liked to be better known by M. Brissot-Warville, who would then have spared him the epithets which he did not deserve. He hopes that his conduct at all times and under all circumstances will always prove that nobody is more firmly attached to the principles of the revolution than he is."[12]

Brissot refused to publish the letter, arguing that a civil servant did not have the right to refuse a salary. If the practice spread, he said, all civil service offices would end up in the hands of the wealthy. In his *Mémoires*, Brissot relates the reasons which led him to reject Lavoisier's letter:

It is true, I did not think very much of his administrative and financial knowledge; or rather, I regarded him as belonging to that class of people who are naturally opposed to the public interest. I did not approve of his nomination as alternate deputy to the National Assembly and still less of that as administrator of the Treasury. Lavoisier, the Farmer General and president of that Discount Bank, the superior officers of which had for a long time tried to get control of the finances of the State, and who, in the interest of their notes, had all written against the assignats, seemed to me out of place in the administration of the Treasury and unable to vote freely against ministers to whom he was subordinated. I attacked his nomination.[13]

Lavoisier did not react. As throughout his life when fate went against him, his character led him to control his emotions, to abstract and shelter himself from the outside world by taking refuge in cerebral activity. The work at the Treasury provided such an opportunity. But, learning that a reorganization was taking place at the Arsenal, he wrote to Tarbé to save his post:

I am counting on the oral assurance you gave me, in the king's name, that my right to a post at the Gunpowder Administration will not be suspended and that I will have it as soon as one of the three posts becomes vacant. I also count on the assurance you gave me that I can keep my apartment there in which I installed myself at my own expense and where I have invested a considerable amount in laboratories, offices and instruments connected with the sciences I pursue.[14]

Tarbé agreed and answered:

I thought, Monsieur, that it would be possible to reconcile these diverse interests on the one hand by asking you to remain for the time being at the National Treasury where your knowledge and experience can be of such great use, and on the other by keeping open the possibility of your occupying one of the administrative posts at the

Arsenal as soon as it becomes vacant. This possibility and the certainty of the help your knowledge can give to the improvement of the Gunpowder Administration would justify your keeping the apartment, which is not intended for any public use.[15]

Given Lavoisier's unremitting effort to defend his interests, it might be assumed that his personal finances were meager. But this was far from the case. His tax return for 1791 declared a total income of 37,500 livres ($1.4 million). 27,500 livres came from his investments in property: 11,000 from his farm at Freschines, 11,000 from two houses in Paris on the rue des Bons Enfants and rue Saint-Honoré, and 5,500 from the house and farm at Le Bourget.[16] From the Gunpowder Administration came 10,000 livres: 4,000 as a fixed salary and 6,000 in bonuses.[17] He made no mention of either his salary from the Academy or his remuneration and income as director of the Discount Bank. Under the heading "lifestyle Information," he listed six servants: a chambermaid, cook, coachman, and three footmen.

The Situation of the National Treasury as of June 1, 1791

The National Treasury Commissioners took up their functions officially on April 14, 1791, and sent a declaration of allegiance, written by Condorcet, to the Assembly:

Having the responsibility of guarding the deposit of taxes that the will of the people has dedicated to the maintenance of rights, we shall watch over this treasure of freedom, which from now on will be used only for preserving or defending it. As faithful enforcers of the decrees of the National Assembly, they alone will rule our conduct. The limit they have set for us will always be sacred and we solemnly swear never to forget that these gifts from the people, deposited in the common treasury, have not ceased to belong to it, and must be spent only for it and at the wish of its representatives, the only judges of its needs and sole interpreter of its will. We shall never lose sight of the fact that the certitude of good order in the National Treasury is the only means of inspiring men to endure the hardships imposed by taxation, and of perpetuating that confidence in the public faith that the courageous justice of the National Assembly was able to create amid a revolution and maintain in spite of all the storms. We consider the habitual and immediate supervision that it will exercise over us as an honorable encouragement. We shall put our whole hearts into showing ourselves to be constantly occupied with dissipating that obscurity and complication which produce disorder by providing the means of dissimulating it. We adhere wholeheartedly to the maxim that *the only useful action is the just one, and the only honest one is the one that can be made public.*
 For a free people, financial difficulties are the first step toward corruption, which is only a disguised slavery. The monster of inequality feeds itself on those lost riches that avid hands amass. It is with the gold of nations that the treacherous forge their chains, that tyranny purchases its weapons, and the thankless tasks of our functions will be

ennobled in our eyes by the idea that the guardians of public funds are also soldiers of freedom. We request the Assembly, by its own decrees, to call the institution destined to oversee all receipts and expenditures, the National Treasury. It will remind all citizens of the sacred foundation on which their confidence should rest.[18]

The new designation was adopted and the six new officials set to work with zeal. "The duties involved in my post as National Treasury Commissioner leave me little time," Lavoisier wrote to Nicolas Charles Parisis, his cousin and real estate agent, on April 25, 1791.[19] The commissioners immediately initiated a complete audit of the books of the Treasury', examining the organization of services, working methods, the state of the various files, the financial situation, and the functions and salaries of the employees.

They found a situation that would be unthinkable today. At that time, France had no national accounting, no annual budget, no forecasting, no monitoring of receipts and expenditures. Everything operated according to the wishes of the king, who was the only one to authorize any outlays. The role of the Controller General of Finance had been to obtain, by whatever means he could, the wherewithal to cover expenses over which he had no control. The Abbé Terray had resolved the problem by periodic bankruptcies. Turgot had tried to slow down royal spending. Necker had managed the deficit by repeated borrowing. Calonne and Brienne had been unable to imagine other methods. No one had succeeded in undertaking a fundamental reform of the fiscal system.

In 1788 the budget had reached approximately 630 million livres. Of the receipts, 32.5 percent came from indirect taxes, 24.6 percent from direct taxes, 21.4 percent from borrowing, 8 percent from royal property rents, 2.6 percent from lotteries. Of this budget, 51 percent went for paying the debt, and 49 percent for public expenditures: 17 percent for the War Ministry, 7.2 percent for the Navy and Colonies, 6 percent for Finance, 5.7 percent for Royal Household, 3 percent for Justice and Police, 2.3 percent for Foreign Affairs, 2 percent for Education and Public Welfare, and 6 percent for assistance to cities and states. The deficit had been growing every year, in spite of regular increases in taxes.[20]

By 1791 the king had essentially lost all power in financial matters, but the National Assembly and its Finance Committee were showing the same casualness as he had in the management of the funds of the State. The reorganization of the Treasury dated only from March 1788. After the scandalous bankruptcies of the General Treasurers of the Marine and War Ministries, Baudard de Saint-James and Mégret de Sérilly respectively, Loménie de Brienne had abolished the posts of Treasurers for those departments as well as for the Royal Household, Miscellaneous Expenditures and, Bridges and Roads. He had replaced them by a single administrator assisted by five clerks. A unique fund provided liquid assets to the auxiliary funds in charge of actual payment. They had been reduced to three after the Royal Household had been replaced by a civil list. Thus, even before the revolution, Loménie de Brienne had carried out a fundamental reorganization of the financial administration and created the National Treasury. Private financiers and bankers were no longer in charge of state finances; they had been replaced by salaried administrators. As stated by Brienne himself:

It happened that since some treasurers of the different funds did not always separate their own affairs from those entrusted to them, the disorder overtaking their private fortunes redounded on our Royal Treasury. These losses resulted from advances made to them or the confusion of bills and the difficulty of distinguishing those connected with our service, and also from debts which it was often impossible to recover in their entirety in spite of the precautions taken by the law.[21]

The ideas of the six commissioners, the fruit of numerous meetings, were summarized in an important handwritten document "On the Situation of the Public Treasury as of June 1, 1791."[22] Their most urgent task, they specified, was to make a general inventory of public funds, "to find out what exists, by studying the relationship with the former order and, by a thorough examination, to guard against the innovative spirit that wants to change everything and the spirit of routine that sees nothing to improve."[23] They drew up a complete organization chart describing the functions of more than 500 civil servants working in thirty offices. The bill for their wages reached 1,464,220 livres, not counting the salaries of the senior civil servants or the costs of paper, printing, firewood, lighting, and transport of currency. The principal causes that had contributed to complicating the operations of the nation's finances, the commissioners declared, were all inherent in the ancien régime. They should disappear in the new order being established by the National Assembly.

The first cause stemmed from the fact that the Controller General of Finance had been answerable only to the king, the only person who could authorize public expenditures. The cleverness of the ministers had "consisted of knowing how to cover up their incompetence, their liberalities and plundering by orders signed by the king."[24]

The second cause was linked with the presence of royal treasurers and cashiers. The former, guarantors of moral responsibility, had to answer for the good or bad use of funds. The latter, given the material responsibility, vouched for the actual presence in the funds of the sums that were supposed to be there. The treasurers could be abolished with no problem, explained the

Treasury Commissioners, since the moral responsibility had been entrusted to them by the National Assembly. There was little risk that six men of good reputation, jointly responsible and checking on each other, could undertake an embezzlement scheme. Moreover, they would need the assurance of their subordinates' complicity. But such complicity would become completely impossible if accounts were published and known to the public. Besides, following the English model, the Assembly had created its own Treasury Committee. It was up to it to exercise this moral responsibility. As for the cashiers, the problem was different because of the material responsibility incumbant on them. Entrusting them with funds needed for weekly, indeed daily payments was unavoidable. The ideal would have been to require them to post a security bond, but their salaries did not allow it. Nevertheless, an organization could not be founded on the postulate that all cashiers were honest. On the contrary, one had to start from the opposite hypothesis.

A third difficulty was linked to the antiquated accounting system. Even though the legitimacy and reality of all payments were established by records, numerous verifications, and expense accounts provided by the administration of the Treasury, all documents had to be signed by the treasurer, the only Treasury official accredited by the Accounting Office. Hence there was a double accounting, but the latter was the only legal one in the eyes of the law. Moreover, the presentation of accounts destined for the Royal Council of Finances did not meet the approval of the Accounting Office. Thus all the work had to be repeated, the genuine accounts made into voluminous ones; the sums had to be written out in full, and records of expenses detailed. The result was mountains of files and increasing costs, offering no additional guarantees: "These outmoded forms, devised at a time when people scarcely knew how to write, let alone count, these relics of ignorance and barbarism, that the esprit de corps has so religiously preserved, and whose particular interests have so cruelly aggravated the burden, will undoubtedly disappear permanently in the new order being established." [25]

A fourth source of difficulty was the impossibility of reforming the methods "whether it was because routine had set in and obstructed all innovation, or because the flood of matters perpetually being renewed did not allow the various employees the time to think about ways of improving them. It was impossible for the senior civil servants to make, even in their own offices, the changes that appeared to them most important." [26] When the National Assembly had wanted precise information from the administration of finance, it had been easier to create a Central Accounting Office than to have the old structures evolve. Afterward, it was possible to clarify the expenditures in a detailed fashion and respond rapidly to the questions of the Assembly.

Another cause for the perpetuation of confusion in ideas and responsibilities was, as Lavoisier pointed out, the imprecise language used by civil servants. He wanted to invent a new one and create a new method of financial nomenclature similar to the one he had devised for chemistry. For example, the word *comptabilité*, accounting, had been used for all paying operations. Thereafter one would use the word "verification" for the control of the actual payments and the word "accounting" for the control of their validity.

Lavoisier proposed a number of new ideas. First, the Treasury should open an account at the Discount Bank. This idea had already been included in his plan for creating a Banque de France. To give the Discount Bank the status of a state organism was for him the surest means of immediately securing qualified personnel and, secondly, of facilitating the reimbursement of the debt to the stockholders. He pointed out:

Everybody knows that the Discount Bank has funds of 140 million livres. All of this money, of which more than 60 million are in the hands of the nation, has been especially earmarked as a guarantee of the cashiers' honest management [. . .] The book-keeping is such that each cashier's situation can be established at any time. Exactly what has been deposited and withdrawn, and how much remains, whether in deniers or bills, can be ascertained immediately. This service is provided without charge by the banks, which are thus indemnified by the use of funds that it supplies them and by the opportunity it gives to put their bills in circulation. There is no reason why the Public Treasury, just like any individual, should not have its accounts at the Discount Bank."[27]

Afterward the National Treasury would have only one *caisse* left, the one for Receipts, entrusted to a single cashier. Every day the Treasury would deposit in the Discount Bank the sums necessary for payments. The process would be simple, economical, and reliable. It would eliminate the need for an auxiliary fund especially for expenditures, as well as concerns about moral and material responsibility. Everything was already prepared for the change, and the clients would only have to cross the street since the two institutions were so near each other. Necker had left Paris more than six months earlier, but several of the commissioners, including Lavoisier, remained linked to him through their interests and common goals, one of which was giving the Discount Bank the status of a state agency, since it was felt to be the surest means of guaranteeing the considerable sums advanced by it to the now defunct Royal Treasury and ensuring their management by the National Treasury. "It was more than two years ago," Lavoisier emphasized, "that the bases of this plan for organizing the Public Treasury were presented to M. Necker, a good judge of such matters, who discussed and approved them and who was waiting for favorable circumstances for their execution."[28]

Public opinion and the deputies of the National Assembly were much too hostile to the Discount Bank to accept this strange idea of having the State's funds managed by a private bank, and the plan was eventually rejected.

Lavoisier's second recommendation was that the commissioners should make use of a statistical office "to prepare in advance all the calculations that can facilitate the legislatures' work and help them judge any proposed financial deals. The same objective would not be filled by consulting figures at the last moment. All the elements of calculation have to be discussed, all the data have to be determined beforehand. These preliminary preparations should extend to all parts of political arithmetic."[29]

This statistical office would provide tables showing receipts and expenditures, projected calculations on the extinguishment of the debt, exchange rates, and banking transactions. If an office of this kind had existed, he pointed out, the Constituent Assembly would have lost less time and made better financial choices. "It would have had, in those first months it was convening, precise information on a wide range of subjects, the lack of which has already cost it long and difficult efforts and will continue to do so."[30]

But, Condorcet emphasized, the office could have an even larger role. It would not limit itself to data relating to financial administration, but would cover "all aspects of political statistics, because everything is interconnected. All information on population, trade, and territorial production gathered in different sectors of the administration would be brought together in this office. Discussed, combined, subjected to calculation, this information would after a few years present, in the simplest of forms, an immense collection of political facts useful to all branches of public administration."[31] This statistical office, which also resembled the one Necker was dreaming of in 1784, can be seen as the precursor of France's present *Institut National de la Statistique et des Etudes Economiques* (INSEE).

Third, Lavoisier felt, the Treasury should have modern accounting methods. One ledger would give the daily balance of receipts and expenditures; another would give the same information for the month, trimester, and year; and a third would compare receipts within a year with expenditures; finally, there should be an internal accounting of sums collected and paid out, making it possible to check on the administration's efficiency. He recommended using double entry book-keeping in all the receipts and expenditures offices, with a methodical presentation of all the headings. A central office would combine all the accounts in its books. In this way, all operations could be verified every day; errors would be almost impossible and always easy to recognize and correct:

It is the ledgers in the central office that will show the general accounts of the National Treasury, the statements that should reveal the financial situation at all times with more or less detail. One of them will naturally contain tables showing what had been collected and paid out for every year and will be distributed so that the receipts and outlays of any one year can be compared, article by article, with those of other years. It will cover ten consecutive years. Tables of this type do not yet exist in any country, and yet they are the only means of winning the trust of a nation in its own affairs.[32]

Finally Lavoisier proposed again a statistical representation of the economy of the country in the form of a group of aggregates. Each type of activity—agriculture, commerce, and industry—would have its own section. This made up a rough blueprint, already foretold in the "Territorial Wealth of the Kingdom of France," of a national accounting.

Since the National Assembly had been unable to define specifically their responsibilities, the Commissioners then proceeded to do it themselves. They were to control all receipts and expenditures, but their task was to be limited strictly to one of control. They were not to interfere in execution. Their responsibility was collective and they were independent of both executive and legislative power. Their functions, they felt, ought to be ensured for a minimal duration which had not been specified by the decree. Finally, they considered it impossible to reduce the operating costs of the Treasury. To do so, they would have had either to reduce the salaries of the directors or the number of employees. The former alternative would have risked demotivating the directors; the latter would have led to delays and accounting errors. The safety of the State's finances, they said, the necessity of preventing abuse, and that of establishing confidence had to take precedence over everything else. The Commissioners belonged to the elite who, until then, had directed the revolution. They could still believe that they were going to create an ideal world:

By devoting ourselves to the duty that the National Assembly has assigned us, we have never lost sight of this truth, borne out by the history of all who have enjoyed a free constitution, that it is the misuse of the public funds that has always struck the first blows against liberty. We must seek to prevent abuses and not simply to curb them, because they are in themselves means of impunity. The corruption born of these abuses has always produced servitude. In a country where the obscure and vicious administration of public finances makes it easy for some power or other to buy men, there are soon only the oppressers who buy, the deceitful who sell themselves, and the cowardly who pay.[33]

James Hall witnessed the Lavoisiers' progressive views in this period. He recalled having dined with them in May at the home of the Terray family: "All that family are violent aristocrats. Monsieur and Madame Lavoisier, who were there, battled for the other side of the question. Monsieur Terray and Monsieur Lavoisier got into a warm dispute about the new and old system of taxes and of government. Monsieur Lavoisier spoke with perfect reason and truth, tho' with a degree of heat; this I was glad to see in him as his manner is generally rather shy and as till lately he has not spoken out fully out about the revolution." [34]

Important political events were brewing with the opening of the campaign for elections to the National Assembly on May 27. Condorcet was a parliamentary candidate. He had left the Treasury, declaring that it did not have the necessary independence from executive power since the Commissioners and the members of the Accounting Office were appointed by the king and could be dismissed by him. "Therefore, the alternative is to choose these public servants by national elections or else abandon the nation's Treasury to ministerial extravagance that would open up a new source of corruption, and make the rebirth of confidence out of the question." [35] His predictions did not materialize, but the situation led the Commissioners to go beyond their status and exercise considerable power. On June 21 the king fled from Paris with all his family. They were arrested in Varennes and brought back to the capital. Republican posters inspired by Thomas Paine and Condorcet appeared on the walls of the city. Other posters, dictated by La Fayette, replied. The debate over the deposition of the king sparked a quarrel between the partisans of an Orléanist regency and the various republican tendencies. Lavoisier seemed to be undecided. On June 28 he entertained James Hall at dinner, along with Du Pont de Nemours, Achille Pierre Dionis du Séjour, Jean Antoine Cousin, Armand Seguin and Jean Baptiste Meusnier. All the talk was about current events. After dinner the party broke up into small groups and James Hall reported:

We noticed the great wavering of almost every individual in the company, except M. Dupont, about royalty; he was clearly for republicanism and said that all that had been hitherto done by the Assembly was in that same spirit and that the introduction of the king into the constitution was a mere mask. The rest of the company, in particular M. Lavoisier, who is generally very steady, varied back and forwards several times. This appears to me to arise from the fact that they are now for the first time agitating in their minds the comparison between a republic and a monarchy; the subject is vast and admits of many views; as a man proceeds in his investigation, the most contradictory conclusions follow one another very rapidly in his mind.[36]

On July 11 Lavoisier represented the Academy of Science at the solemn ceremony in which Voltaire's ashes were transferred to the Panthéon. Among the onlookers there were many wearing red caps, the Roman emblem of freed slaves and a rallying sign for ardent republicans. In the procession, Lavoisier was saying to himself that the same crowd that was acclaiming the dead Voltaire would have shouted him down as an aristocrat had he been alive. Rather pessimistic, he remarked to Hall "that some years hence there would be a period in which the generation would be ignorant owing to the breach made in all the education in the kingdom by the revolution."[37]

On July 17 a group of demonstrators gathered at the Champs de Mars and laid on the altar, elevated three days before for the Fête de la Fédération, a petition demanding the institution of a Republic. The National Assembly asked Bailly to disperse them. When the crowd did not break up, La Fayette ordered the National Guard to fire and fifty people were killed. The Constituent Assembly had only two more months of existence. The National Treasury from that moment became a closed impenetrable world. The constant changes of political personnel protected it from the major upheavals of the Revolution and gave it a complete independence regarding both executive and legislative power. In theory, its true master was the legislative power, represented by the Finance Committee and three members of the Assembly. But the Constituents who had instituted it hardly had the time to oversee its activities. Not being re-eligible, they were thereafter absent. Their successors, deputies elected to the Legislative Assembly on September 27, 1791, were too ignorant in financial matters to control the institution they had inherited. Condorcet was the only one of the Assembly's 746 members to understand the exact role of the National Treasury, its means and responsibilities. As for executive power, it was precisely dependent on the Treasury since the ministers could make no expenditures without the previous authorization of the Commissioners. This is how a large part of the personnel of the Treasury, made up of men from the old régime, came through the Revolution without mishap, ensuring continuity from Louis XVI to Bonaparte. Thus, six months after their nomination, the Treasury Commissioners were led to play a determining role in France's financial affairs and to abandon the sound rules made for calmer times. Their responsibilities became enormous.

They controlled all receipts. Direct taxes paid to 544 district collectors in the 83 departments of the country were turned over to the Ministry of Public Taxation. The money was then conveyed to the Treasury Commissioners.

They controlled all expenditures. At the end of each year, an Assembly decree fixed the budget of each ministry for the following year. This budget was paid on a monthly basis and a *Registre de prospectus* (Register of Forecasts) printed the authorized amount that could be spent. At the beginning of each month, the ministers sent statements, divided into weeks, which for every expenditure indicated to which category it belonged, where it was paid, and to whom. The Central Accounting Office checked the statements. No payment could be authorized if the corresponding expenditure was not included in the Register of Forecasts. Once the checking had been done and the approval of at least three Commissioners given, the cashier was authorized to pay. If an expenditure appeared dubious, the Commissioners had to refer it to the Finance Committee. Overspending and fraud were impossible.

Lavoisier dealt with Miscellaneous Expenditures. "He made payments to or for the administration of (1) police, commerce, transport, mines, food supplies (*subsistances*) and stud farms; (2) the postal system and *messageries*; (3) the royal *loteries*; (4) the Paris guard and the *maréchaussée* of the Ile de France; (5) the *turcies et levées* or building and maintenance of dikes along the Loire and some of its tributaries; (6) royal buildings; (7) Paris streets; (8) the roads and bridges service; and (9) the payments to the corporation of arts and trades (*arts et métiers*)."[38]

To these, had been added at the beginning of the revolution, the expenditures of the Church, the Mint, and the Royal Household.[39] Thus Lavoisier regularly transferred to the king the amounts needed for the civil list, 25 million livres per year, or 685,000 livres ($27 million) every ten days. This function exposed him to certain suspicions: was he not providing the king with ammunition and Spanish gold? Therefore he came to be identified even more with the camp of the wealthy and the counter-revolutionaries.

The Commissioners centralized all financial accounting. They received all information, and did double entry book-keeping that included all the data from the Treasury, the district tax collectors, and the individual taxpayers. "Lavoisier set up an accounting system that was so strict and simple," Fourcroy wrote, "that it was possible to know the exact state of public funds at the end of each day."[40]

The Commissioners paid pensions and interest on the debt, controlled the reimbursements of the Special Bank, ensured the exchange of assignats and bought currency.

From its establishment, the Treasury had to defend the value of the French currency, threatened by fears of war. It first carried out arbitrage on precious metals and commercial paper, then once war broke out (1792), it struggled against the flight of currency to foreign countries, blocking a certain amount for the indispensable payment of troops. It had to re-use requisitioned copper, silver and gold, and finally, for each payment made abroad, it had to play on the differences among European monies and the rate at which bills of exchange were accepted. Rapidly, its operations affected practically all economic activity, civil and military supplies and what remained of banking exchanges.[41]

The Commissioners made constant efforts to find money, at first through the banks in Paris, Dunkirk, Lille, and Douai, and later directly from English, Belgian, and Dutch banks. Thus they obtained the millions needed for maintaining the armies. At the same time, they negotiated bills of exchange on the principal markets, bought up assignats in massive quantities, helped

foreigners or émigrés to get their money out of France, participated in clandestine and profitable arbitrage with the banks of Boyd and Ker, Greffulhe
and Montz, and Mallet and Perrégaux, and thus found themselves at the center of a monetary market of European dimension.

A secretary coordinated the various services of the National Treasury by
keeping archives, recording deliberations, taking care of correspondence, and
preparing the statutory documents. The post was given to a young lawyer,
Nicolas Grouvelle. Every day he wrote a financial statement, and every fifteen
days a general account of receipts and outlays was sent to both the Assembly and the executive power. Each month the Commissioners and the chief
cashier, Garat, sent the Finance Committee a statement of receipts and expenditures, which was subsequently printed and published.

The National Treasury had become a state within a State, and Lavoisier
was its brilliant spokesman.

The Financial State of France as of January 1, 1792

In November 1791 Lavoisier presented to the National Assembly the financial position of the nation based on estimates of expenditures. He had been
strongly advised to revise upwards the figures contained in his first study on
national income. But flexibility and diplomacy were not his strong points,
and he made few concessions in his report:

At a time when everything is exaggerated, both good and evil, when everyone sees
things through a glass that either magnifies or reduces them, distances or brings them
closer, when no one sees things in their true perspective or place, I felt that it would
be useful to consider our situation dispassionately and apply strict arithemetic calculation to the State's finances. [. . .] This report will be as cool as reason. I would have
preferred to present merely statements and figures, with all types of arguments eliminated, because facts never deceive us; it is our judgment that leads us astray.[42]

He recalled his earlier conclusion that land taxes, fixed at a sixth of the
national income, could bring in no more than 200 million livres, and property taxes no more than 30. Thus only 230 million livres in receipts could be
counted on for 1791. And for 1792 he foresaw 280 million, only half of which
would be collected during the year.

What were the budgetary forecasts for 1792? The total receipts, he said,
would reach 482 million livres: 140 for the 1792 land and property taxes; 175
for the overdue taxes from 1791; 320 for the overdue taxes from 1790. Stamp
duties and registration fees for 1792 would bring in 60 million, customs 15,
the lotteries 6, trading licenses 12, mail services 14, forests 10 and the patri-

otic tax 30. The 60 million livres of income from national property were not included in the total.

Expenditures were expected to reach 708 million: 606 for ordinary needs and 102 for special ones: the budgets of the Ministries of War and Marine, judicial functions, the printing of assignats, the Weights and Measures Commission, the purchase of currency abroad and exchange losses, exceptional assistance to the city of Paris, and a reserve for unforeseen expenses.

The estimated deficit for 1792 was thus 226 million livres, plus 40 million carried over from 1791. To make up for this total deficit of 266 million, the Special Bank would have to be called on. But it was already having to underwrite the short-term debt, which was 240 million livres for 1792. Hence it would have to provide a total of 506 million. "It would therefore be possible to meet all the needs for 1792 by issuing assignats to the value of 506 million livres, which, added to the 1400 millions' worth that will be circulating by the first of the year, would make a total of 1,906 million."[43]

But, ever prudent, Lavoisier asked for an extra 200 million livres for "things to be settled," without specifying their nature. Could this have been the remainder of a debt to the Discount Bank? He wound up with a figure of 700 million livres. He also suggested increasing the number of five-livre assignats, which were much in demand since the general climate of distrust had caused gold and silver money to disappear from circulation. In the middle of this financial and fiscal statement, the economist reappeared:

It cannot be denied that the more or less extensive issuing of assignats has a definite influence on exchange rates. But it would be a great mistake to believe that this lowering of exchange rates was entirely to our disadvantage. If, on the one hand, it hinders the importation of foreign goods, on the other it fosters the export of the products of our industry. Besides, the lowering of the exchange rate does not depend solely on the unpopularity of assignats. It also stems from the fact that we have a considerable outstanding debt with other countries. [. . .] As long as this is true, the result will be beneficial to the export of national products, a kind of bonus for our trade and industry. Our manufacturers will work to pay off our debt and, in exchange for their efforts, they will imperceptibly extract the metals we lack; the balance which has been upset will be restored and the financial crisis itself will become a means of prosperity.[44]

This return to Forbonnais's theories and arguments developed twenty years earlier in his *Eloge de Colbert*, was no doubt more an expression of Lavoisier's desire to adapt himself to a hostile audience than a sincere conviction of the benefits of issuing assignats. The creation of more assignats had appeared to him calamitous not long before, but here he was ready to issue 700 million worth, bringing the total to 2.5 billion. If their circulation became excessive, he said, a borrowing of 4 percent would be launched to slow it down. It was surely a utopian remedy. Who would accept such low interest in an inflationary period?

Then he returned to the subject of the value of the national property. It had been assessed at 3.5 billion livres, and the calculations on the settlement of the short-term and long-term debts had been based on this hypothesis. But, he warned, its precipitate sale plus the inadequate money supply in circulation would make it impossible to reach this figure. "It is highly doubtful that the yield from the sale of national property would bring in more than 3 billion."[45]

Therefore there would be a deficit, and a portion of the assignats would not be guaranteed. Fifteen months earlier, speaking to the Society of 1789, he had estimated the deficit at only 1 billion. Inflation could of course explain part of this difference, but also he could be suspected of manipulating figures according to the circumstances. He showed more rigor regarding expenditures for 1792, which should remain fixed at 708 million. It would suffice to increase taxes by raising the land tax rate to a fifth of the income. He said in conclusion:

The re-establishment of financial stability is possible, as long as the deputies assume their responsibilities. Because I dare to make the sad prediction that if the taxes decreed for 1791 have not been fully collected within a few months; that if in six months at most the fiscal system for 1792 has not been decreed and activated, then no human force will be able to save the country from a terrible catastrophe, from which the old régime, with all its abuses, nevertheless spared us the horror. [. . .] Make no mistake about it, the Revolution will be truly completed, the Constitution achieved only when we shall have solidly established a revenue sufficient for meeting public expenditures.[46]

His financial plan would not be applied. The young Legislative Assembly had sat for only two months. Its deputies did not have the financial experience and lucidity necessary for understanding the gravity of his warning. The taxes did not come in, the issuing of assignats accelerated, and there began to be talk of war.

Farewell to Finance

The political situation bequeathed by the Constituent Assembly was far from healthy. The king's flight to Varennes had broken up the ranks of the monarchists, who had attempted to reorganize themselves within the club known as the *Feuillants*. The liberal revolution had slid out of control. On September 19, 1791 Bailly had resigned as mayor of Paris. La Fayette had left the National Guard, hoping to replace him, but it was Jerôme Pétion de Villeneuve who had been elected mayor on November 14. New clubs and revolutionary news-

papers continued to sprout up. The poor and unemployed looted the food
convoys and ransacked shops. The less well off Parisians armed themselves
with pikes. Threats of war with Austria grew. The prudent began to stand
aloof. On January 14, 1792 Talleyrand judiciously got himself sent on a diplomatic mission to London.

At the same time, Lavoisier began distancing himself from the financial
world. He left the Discount Bank in January 1792. In appreciation for his services, the stockholders made haste to have engraved a large gold medal dating
from 1776. On the edge was written in large rather crude letters: "To M.
Lavoisier, from the General Assembly of Stockholders, January 21, 1792."[47]

After his departure the Discount Bank attempted to redress its financial
situation. But wild speculation, the fall in value of the assignat and a succession of bankruptcies jeopardized its success. The exchange rate for 100 livres in
assignats was only 63 livres, 5 sous in currency. When the Convention on August 24, 1793, decreed the abolition of the Discount Bank, the stockholders
would lose 90 percent of their investment, as a result of the devaluation of
the assignats. Many of them would also lose their lives under the blade of the
guillotine. Sébastian Mercier judged them harshly:

The Discount Bank has the right to claim its place among the principal causes that led
to the Revolution. [. . .] It was this institution that produced the mixed generation
of speculators, princes, courtisans, magistrates, military men, financiers, lawyers and
brokers. The great amount of fictitious currency paid out in the capital caused this imprudent and unthinking youth surrounding the throne to imagine that it was at the
head of an inexhaustible nation, forever enslaved. It dreamt only of having a good
time, believing itself to be absolute and not wanting to be controlled by anything. It
presumed that it could even dispense with dignity, that magic virtue of royal courts.[48]

The Bank however, had rendered real services during its seventeen years
of existence: it had discounted bills of exchange representing 4 billion livres,
lent 265 million livres to the government, and provided more than 200 million
livres in currency to the Mint.[49] Its liquidation, entrusted to Laffon-Ladébat,
would be completed only under the Empire. The Banque de France would replace it, opening its doors on 1 ventôse An VIII (February 20, 1800); it would
be instituted by the laws of 24 germinal An XI and of April 22, 1806.

In February 1792, a few days after leaving the Discount Bank, Lavoisier
also left the National Treasury. His direct assistant, Philippe Pierre François
Gislain, had accused him of drawing more than one salary, asking: "Should it
not be necessary for an Academician receiving a salary from that institution
as well as one from the administration to choose between them?"[50]

Lavoisier, who had already had to give up his post at the Gunpowder and

Saltpeter Administration, had finally decided to accept the salary from the National Treasury, but Gislain now refused to pay it and declared that "unless there is a law that officially states it, no claim of this kind will be recognized by this department."[51] Lavoisier's colleagues at the National Treasury, rather embarrassed, replied:

You know that it does not depend on us, regardless of our opinion, to decide on payments. You will conclude that it is indispensable that you obtain a law. Moreover, we will add that there are decrees for the War section that are even stricter than the one in Miscellaneous Expenditures. For example, the veteran loses his pension once he returns to service. We greatly regret that given our situation it is impossible to do what would be in the interest of the Academy and particularly of our colleague.[52]

Lavoisier, Savalette de Langes, and Rouillé de l'Estang then decided to consult the authorities. And when Gislain received the answer, he commented: "We strongly suspect that these observations are all to the advantage of the learned party that the Treasury Committee made both judges and litigants in their own cause."[53]

During this time, Louis XVI, who had chosen to adopt the worst possible course of action in order to attain his own ends, called to the government the Jacobin ministers, close to the *Montagnard* extremists. At the Ministry of Finance, Etienne Clavière replaced Tarbé, a Necker man, his enemy and rival. Lavoisier, close to the *Feuillants*, representatives of the capitalist bourgeoisie favorable to a constitutional monarchy, could not envisage working with Clavière and left the National Treasury in February. Two of his colleagues, Jean de Vaisnes and Rouillé de l'Etang, soon followed him.

But only a few months later, on June 12, Louis XVI dismissed Clavière and two other Jacobin ministers, Jean Marie Roland and Joseph Servan, and tried to form a moderate government by calling on unknown *Feuillants*. He offered the Ministry of War to Pierre Auguste Lajard, Foreign Affairs to La Garde de Chambonas, the Interior to Antoine René Terrier de Monciel, and Finance to Charles Gilloton de Beaulieu. Jean Lacoste remained at the Ministry of Marine and Antoine Duranthon at Justice. He offered Lavoisier the Ministry of Public Taxation, a post that in other times would have delighted him. But after three days of reflection, Lavoisier turned it down:

Sire, it is not from a fainthearted fear of which I am incapable or from lack of concern for the nation or, I confess, from a sense of inadequacy, that I am constrainted to refuse the mark of confidence with which Your Majesty has honored me in asking me to become Minister of Public Taxation. During the time that I was associated with the National Treasury and had the good fortune to work with Your Majesty, I witnessed your patriotic feelings, your great solicitude for the happiness of the people, your inflexibly strict principles and unshakeable integrity, and, for that reason, I sense more keenly that I can express what I am losing by refusing your kindness. But, Sire, it is the duty of an honest man and citizen to accept such a position only if he has the hope of fulfilling its obligations to their fullest extent. I am neither a Jacobin nor a Feuillant. I belong to no society or club. Being accustomed to weighing everything on the scales of my own conscience and reason, I would never consent to allowing any party to determine my opinions.[54]

Lavoisier declared that he remained faithful to a conservative and liberal vision that was no longer acceptable in that period of clashing extremes. He could envisage a ministerial function only within a constitutional framework, and he clearly saw that the Legislative Assembly had gone beyond the limits set by the Constitution. What could a constitutional minister do? Being unable to act according to his principles and his conscience, he would appeal in vain to the law. His resistance would be seen as a crime and he would perish, victim of his duty.

On the other hand, Lavoisier knew too well that the Ministry of Finance no longer held any power; its mission was limited to collecting taxes. He knew what he was talking about, since at the National Treasury, which depended on legislative power, he and his colleagues had controlled the totality of France's financial affairs. He knew that the post he was being offered was an empty shell and that any steps he might take there would be destined to failure. Events proved him right. Five days later, on June 20, a crowd of rioters invaded the Tuileries and attempted to force the king to recall the Jacobin ministers. In spite of their threats, the king refused. Nevertheless, everybody understood that the decisive struggle had begun. The moderate elements, close to the Feuillants, were going to make one last effort to slow down the seizure of power by the people. And in this attempt to restore order Lavoisier would appear to be an enemy of the Revolution.

Overthrow of the Monarchy

On July 11 the Assembly proclaimed that the country was in danger of invasion. Pierre Victurnien Vergniaud and then Brissot de Warville denounced the king's alliance with Austria and demanded his deposition. On July 28 Brunswick's manifesto promising to destroy Paris if the king's person was harmed, was spread throughout the city. Two days later, the patriots from Marseilles entered the capital singing Rouget de Lisle's anthem, which from that time would be known as the "Marseillaise." The following day, July 31, the Mauconseil section of the Commune de Paris declared at the Assembly that it "no longer recognized Louis XVI as king of the French," and urged other sections to join it.[55] On August 3 Pétion, supported by Carra, declared that forty-seven of the forty-eight sections of Paris were also demanding deposition.

On August 5 the Assembly, as it did every Sunday, devoted its session to petitions from the sections. The Bibliothèque section disassociated itself from Mauconseil and defended the king. Collot d'Herbois contested its representativeness, arguing that it was divided into two parties, "one respectable, containing a large number of patriots who are denigrated by the name of sans-culottes, and the other corrupt, composed of financiers, stockbrokers, and speculators. It was from this latter nest of counter-revolution on the rue Vivienne that the disruptive support for the king was coming."[56]

He could have said the same thing for the Arsenal section. It had met on August 2 and asked Lavoisier and Grillot to draw up a petition against the king's deposition. Three days later the delegation, led by Lavoisier and made up of Gunpowder Administration employees, members of the legal profession, and tax officials, went to the Assembly. They read a declaration condemning the maneuvers of the factious who sought to mislead the Assembly by presenting deposition as the wish of the entire population instead of the scheme of a handful of citizens. Lavoisier and his delegation insisted that the Constitution be respected:

If this important question of the king's deposition is one of the cases foreseen by the Constitution, then decide on it as legislators. Decide, we entreat you, and we shall respect your decision. But until it has been rendered, we prohibit any attack on constituted power. We shall respect this power because we have sworn to uphold it and we are loyal to our oaths. [. . .] Members of the Legislature, the citizens of the Arsenal section have felt that they owed to themselves and all of France this candid statement of their principles: a sincere attachment to the Constitution and laws and an inviolable respect for all constituted authority. Down with despots, down with every kind of seditionary. This is our profession of faith.[57]

But on August 8 the Jacobins regained control of the Arsenal section and disavowed Lavoisier's text:

On Sunday, an insolent coalition of persons profiting from the old order of things, slandered the Arsenal section. [. . .] It was essential to their plan that they attack, with their poisoned but fortunately powerless breath, the wish pronounced by the great majority of sections. [. . .] This majority cannot be contradicted except by men such as these on whom our section spews forth the scorn and opprobrium with which it was covered for a short time by their intrigues.[58]

On August 9 the Assembly was still incapable of arbitrating the debate on the king's deposition. The Théâtre-français section, the Quinze-vingts section, and 28 others formed a revolutionary Municipal Assembly, took control of the Commune de Paris and attacked the Royal Palace of the Tuileries.

On August 10 "the populace murdered several hundred persons including members of the Swiss Guards and the Palace domestic staff and groups of gentlemen loyal to the king. Those Feuillants and other political moderates who did not hide, as did Roederer, Du Pont de Nemours, and hundreds of others, were killed along with the rest, their bodies plundered, stripped, mutilated, and their heads hacked off and paraded about on pikes."[59] The insurrectionary Commune de Paris deposed Louis XVI, who took refuge in the Logograph's lodge at the Assembly. The monarchy had come to an end.

The next day, the Academy of Science held its regular meeting. Twenty-two Academicians, including Lavoisier, were present, but for the first time since the beginning of the Revolution, no scientific paper was on the program. One reads in the minutes:

M. Fourcroy announced to the Academy that the Society of Medicine had struck from its membership list several émigrés who were generally recognized as counter-revolutionaries. He proposed that the Academy do the same for certain of its members known for their lack of public spiritedness. To this end, members' names would be read and certain ones would be removed. Several persons remarked that the Academy had no right to exclude any of its members, and that their principles and political opinions were not the business of the Academy since the progress of science was its unique goal. Moreover it was said that the National Assembly was on the point of reorganizing the Academy and that it would exercise the right, which it alone could have, of removing from the Academy anyone it deemed should be excluded.[60]

As the list was read, only a few changes of address were indicated. The minutes mentioned no names. Later Fourcroy returned to the attack. His proposition was once again evaded, but not without embarrassment, by his colleagues' unanimous vote. It was, however, only a postponement.

On August 13 the members of the royal family, were transferred to the Conciergerie prison. The Assembly delegated executive power to a temporary council composed of Danton, Clavière, Servan, Lebrun, Roland, and Monge.

Return to the Gunpowder Administration

Clavière, at that time Minister of the Interior, asked Lavoisier to return to his old job at the Gunpowder Administration to replace his three former colleagues: Clouet was absent, the senior Le Faucheux too old, and his son on tour. Lavoisier refused a post as director, again fearing the problem of two salaries, but agreed to take over for the time needed to relaunch production. The Administration was supposed to have a permanent stock of 4 million pounds of powder, but the considerable supplies demanded by the Minister of War had almost exhausted its reserves.[61]

Saltpeter was lacking. Lavoisier obtained an exceptional budget of 600,000 livres, and restored the right of the saltpeter men to take soil, plaster, rubble, and demolition material without paying. However, "no searches were to be made in private residences without the permission of the citizens."[62] He perfected techniques for assaying saltpeter.[63] In fact, the quality indicated by the saltpeter men was in general different from that observed by the Administration after refining by heat. Endless conflicts had ensued. He had discovered that a part of saltpeter evaporated after the prolonged boiling necessary for its refinement. A loss of 30 percent of the weight of saltpeter from its crude state to the product refined by three re-crystallizations would be accepted by the Administration. The price of crude saltpeter would be increased by as much. In fact, he advised replacing refining by heat by washing in cold water. Another reason justified the price increase. "Since assignats were losing 30 to 40 percent of their value in the provinces and this loss was increasing daily, the costs of fabrication were increased in approximately the same proportion, and yet the price of saltpeter had remained the same."[64]

On August 15 Lavoisier left the Arsenal. There was still work to be done on the apartment into which he intended to move at 243 Boulevard de la Madeleine in the mansion of the banker Le Couteulx de La Noraye, so he went to live with one of his former colleagues at the General Farm, Jean Baptiste Boullongne de Magnanville, at 18 rue Mirabeau.[65] He also rented a pied-à-terre in Saint-Cloud, on the rue du Calvaire, where he could take refuge in case of trouble.[66] Three days after his departure, the commissioners of the Piques section burst into the warehouses of the Arsenal, arrested both the Le Faucheux, and carried them off to the La Force Prison. The father committed suicide; the son was freed five days later by order of the National Assembly. The position of director was then offered to Fourcroy, who accepted and resigned soon after; it was later offered to Louis Pierre Dufourny, who accepted.

Under the influence of the Commune de Paris, mob violence spread throughout the city. During the five days from September 2 to 7, more than a thousand people, accused of plots and conspiracy with the Austrians and Prussians, were massacred in the prisons. Lavoisier, who felt himself in danger, was in a hurry to leave Paris. Power had descended to the streets and he hoped to find some peace in the country. On September 10 he went to the

Police Superintendant for the Place Vendôme section to get a passport for his trip to Freschines. The passport mentioned: "We certify that M. Antoine Laurent Lavoisier of the Academy of Science, native of Paris, department of Paris—aged 49, 5 ft., 4 in. tall, with brown hair and eyebrows, brown eyes, long nose, small mouth, round chin, normal forehead, thin face—residing at 18 rue Mirabeau, which belongs to this section, has stated to us that he intends to go to Blois, in the department of Loir-et-Cher."[67] But the controller of the Gunpowder Administration insisted on receiving the accounts before Lavoisier's departure. "I shall return at the beginning of October," he replied, "and I shall consult with you and the directors, who will no doubt have been chosen by that time, so as to speed up as much as possible the work on the accounts of the Administration. Nobody is more interested in this matter than I."[68] Before leaving, he dismissed Masselot, his faithful servant, and gave him a horse; but he still had to prove that the animal was disabled, because otherwise it would have been needed by the Army.

I the undersigned Antoine Laurent Lavoisier certify to all whom it may concern that the said Louis Antoine Masselot has served me for twenty years as butler, that during all that time I had only praise for his punctuality and loyalty, that it is with regret that I have to let him go because of changes in my fortune, and that as proof of my satisfaction with his service I have given him a horse, recognized as disabled by the commissioners of the municipality, for his use during his trip. Paris, September 13, 1792, the fourth year of liberty, the first of equality.[69]

Last Autumn at Freschines

Reaching his farm on September 15, Lavoisier stayed there almost two months. The rumors of public life reached him only in mutted form. Nevertheless, events were rushing forward in Paris. Danton, Robespierre, and Collot d'Herbois were sitting at the Convention, which had succeeded the Legislative Assembly. The Victory of Valmy took place on September 20, when the French Army, commanded by General François Christophe Kellermann, drove back the attack of the Prussions led by duc Guillaume Ferdinand de Brunswick. For the first time, according to official history, a French army of the people, made up of volunteers inspired by national feeling and using artillery intensively, had conquered. Even if numerous witnesses confirmed the version of Franco-Prussian negotiations before the battle, the symbolic significance of the event was considerable.[70] The first gesture of the Convention, on September 21, was to abolish royalty. The Republic was proclaimed the next day and a decree ordered that all public articles be dated "Year 1 of the French Republic."

At Freschines Lavoisier tried to join the villagers' celebration: "Today, October 14, 1792, first year of the French Republic, just after Vespers had been sung in this parish," the municipal register specified, "the tree of Liberty was planted in the public square of this village, just in front of the Church's entrance, by the citizen Lavoisier and his wife, owners of the property of Freschines, who also provided the tree. They afterward gave 60 livres to our national guard to be used in drinking to their health."[71] But the gift turned out to be on the skimpy side. The autumn was warm and the peasants' thirst intense. An extra 24 livres were needed to pay for the supper. The mayor, his deputy assistant, and clerk were ready to charge the sum to the 1793 budget. But their accounting devices turned out to be unnecessary as the municipal records attest: "The twenty-four livres were paid back to me by the citizen Lavoisier."[72]

These minor embarrassments did not prevent the couple from savoring the charm of late autumn in the Cisse Valley. The grounds around the château were well-kept. The trees had begun to give shade and the alley of lindens that led from the château to the stable was splendid. Each morning, in the golden light of the rising sun, Lavoisier's eyes could linger over the sculpted coat of arms on the stone and brick façade of the stable. The arms had been acquired by his father along with the title of nobility and in 1789 had caused his electoral disappointment, "azure with a silver chevron, charged with three ermine tips, accompanied by two commanding silver stars and a rampant lion; support two lions; a crown of count."[73] Uncertain, he was asking himself if he should not have this aristocratic symbol destroyed, but the sculpture was so refined that he could not bear to see it pounded into bits. November called him back to Paris for the reopening of the Academy of Science.

16

The Chemistry of Life

AT THE END OF 1790 Lavoisier had decided to renounce all political activity and confine himself to the role of financial consultant to the National Assembly. He resumed his scientific work, which, since the beginning of the revolution, he had in practice delegated to his new assistants, Hassenfratz and Seguin. For the first time, he was envisaging medical applications for his research. "The scientist," he wrote, "can hope to diminish the mass of evils that afflict the human species, to increase its enjoyment and well-being and even if the new routes he is opening up could prolong the average life of men by a few years, or even a few days, he, too, could aspire to the glorious title of 'benefactor of humanity.'"[1]

In the previous 20 years he had devoted numerous studies to public health, including the ventilation of theaters, projects to supply drinking water to Paris, and methods for draining liquid wastes and reducing accidents provoked by carbon monoxide. He had even written that the atmosphere could carry pathogenic agents.

He had been only thirty when, on February 20, 1773, he set forth in his laboratory notebook the famous research program whose goal was to investigate "the air that fixes itself to or is released from bodies." At that point he was not trying to penetrate the mysteries of the chemistry of life, but, more modestly, was studying fixed air (carbon dioxide), that gas with which Priestley was claiming he could treat scurvy. He wanted to find a general theory comprising the five circumstances in which air is fixed or released: combustion, calcination, chemical combinations, respiration, vegetation. Never deviating from this path, he had redefined the notion of element and eliminated phlogiston, established the nature of air and water, and explained the role of oxygen in oxidations, combustions, and calcination. These contributions are usually considered as the main features of the chemical revolution. His oxygen theory of acids was too rigid since it could not take into account hydrochloric acid, sulfurated hydrogen and hydrocyanic acid. But the role of oxygen in the formation of the oxy-acids had nonetheless been clearly shown.

But in the process Lavoisier had progressively adopted the viewpoint of a physiologist and understood the links between mineral chemistry and the mechanisms of animal and vegetable life. He had come to study living organisms following a chemical analogy that proved to be extremely fruitful for biological research. His work, initially focused on respiration, gradually evolved toward a much more comprehensive analysis of nutrition and energetic metabolism in man and led him to a most original insight as to the essential role of the liver in organic syntheses. He eventually developed an overall theory regarding the cycle of the three kingdoms of nature and the chemistry of living organisms.

The Physiology of Respiration

Everybody knows today that the physiology of respiration is one of the most complex of the vital processes, the junction where pulmonary ventilation, blood circulation, transport of blood gases, nutrition, cellular life, and its chemical reactions meet. It is in fact responsible, under the brain's control, for the living being's acido-basic, thermic, and metabolic equilibria.

For twenty years Lavoisier had been encountering animal respiration at each stage of his research. Already in May 1777 he had published his "Experiments on Animal Respiration and the Changes That Occur When Air Passes Through the Lungs," later complemented by a "Memoir on the Combustion of Candles in Atmospheric Air and in Eminently Breathable Air." On June 18, 1783 he developed these ideas in the "Memoir on Heat," written with Laplace. In February 1785, at the Royal Academy of Medicine, he presented a memoir on "the changes that occur in air in the various circumstances bringing men together in groups." Finally, on November 17, 1790, he and Armand Seguin tried, in "The First Memoir on Animal Respiration," to make a synthesis of what they had learned about the subject.

The role of respiration, he said, is not to cool the blood, as the ancients believed: "Respiration is only a slow combustion of carbon and hydrogen, similar in every way to that which takes place in a lamp or lighted candle and, from this viewpoint, breathing animals are actual combustible bodies that are burning and wasting away."[2] Atmospheric air furnished oxygen and caloric. The blood, basic substance of the living being, provided the fuel. On leaving the lungs, the exhaled air contained less oxygen than the air inhaled.

This combustion generated carbonic gas and water. This combustion was the source of animal heat, he continued:

Since vital air cannot be converted into carbonic acid except by an addition of carbon, and cannot be converted into water except by an addition of hydrogen, and the double combination cannot occur unless the vital air loses a part of its specific caloric, the result is that the effect of respiration is to extract from the blood a portion of carbon and hydrogen and to replace it with a portion of its specific caloric. During circulation, the caloric is distributed with the blood throughout the animal system, and maintains that almost constant temperature observed in all breathing animals.[3]

Nourishment should restore the losses of the organism, otherwise "very soon the lamp would run out of oil and the animal would perish, just as a lamp goes out when it lacks fuel."[4]

Nitrogen is not a respiratory gas, he pointed out. It enters the lungs and comes out unchanged. Moreover, it can be replaced by hydrogen: "We placed guinea-pigs under glass bell jars filled with a mixture of vital air and pure hydrogen gas, essentially in the same proportions in volume as those existing between vital air and nitrogen in atmospheric air. They remained there a long time without appearing to suffer. [. . .] The hydrogen gas did not seem to have diminished and it came out of their lungs relatively unchanged."[5]

The variation in oxygen concentration in the gas breathed does not change its consumption by the organism.

It is known that the purer the air in which combustion occurs, the faster the combustion. Thus, for example, within a given time, much more charcoal, or any other fuel, is consumed in vital air than in atmospheric air. It had always been thought that the same was true for respiration, that it ought to accelerate in vital air, and then release— either in the lungs or the circulatory system—a greater quantity of caloric. But the experiment has destroyed all these assumptions that were based only on analogy.[6]

A relationship exists between the mechanical work carried out by a living being and the measurable biochemical phenomena that are its driving force. To reach that conclusion, Lavoisier had to estimate the cost of these gaseous exchanges and the effect that rest, digestion and muscular activity had on them. The calorimeter, invented with Laplace, allowed him to measure the heat released by an animal, to compare it with that released by the combustion of charcoal and thus to determine the animal's expenditure of energy.

In 1790 he was trying to measure animal and then human consumption of oxygen. A guinea-pig consumed 50 cubic inches per hour. (An inch equals 2.7 centimeters, a cubic inch approximately 20 milliliters). When it came time to perform calorimetric tests on a human being, Seguin volunteered his services (Figures 10, 11). He dressed himself in a special suit made of taffeta

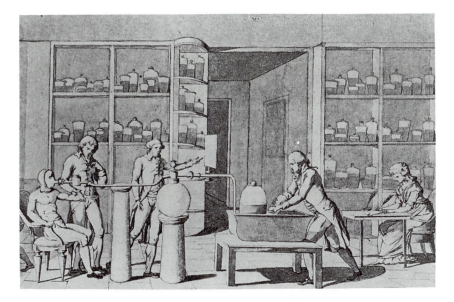

Figure 10. Experiments on the physiology of respiration at rest. Lavoisier, standing, center, manipulates the pneumatic trough providing oxygen to Seguin, seated in repose at the left. Mme Lavoisier, seated at right, keeps the laboratory record. Drawing by Mme Lavoisier. Private collection.

coated with elastic rubber, through which no air or humidity could penetrate. It was closed above the head by a strong ligature. A tube stuck around his lips with putty allowed him to breathe. His consumption of oxygen was measured in different situations. Inactive and on an empty stomach, at an ambient temperature of 26 degrees on a mercury thermometer (32.5° C), he consumed 1210 cubic inches of oxygen per hour—or 400 ml per minute.

Thus was born the notion of inescapable basic expenditure, linked to minimal physiological activity, independent of all exterior stimulation. It was the future basal metabolism. During digestion the consumption increased to 1800 or 1900 cubic inches. It also increased with lowered temperatures and during muscular exercise. If the two factors were combined, consumption could triple. Therefore it adapted to the individual's needs, and the body temperature remained constant. "In the same memoir, the authors proposed two biometric laws, perhaps the first to be enunciated: on the one hand, the correlation between the heart rate and the energy consumed during exercise, and on the other, between oxygen consumption and the respiratory and heart rates. The data of modern physiology have shown these laws to be exact."[7]

Lavoisier dans son laboratoire

Figure 11. Experiments on the physiology of respiration during work. Seguin, seated, center, is working a foot treadle. Lavoisier, standing at left, gives orders to an assistant. Drawing by Mme Lavoisier. Private collection.

The locus of this combustion remained unknown to Lavoisier. He asked himself whether the carbonic gas was formed "in the lungs or during circulation, by the combination of the oxygen of atmospheric air with the carbon of blood."[8] He was not, however, too far from the right hypothesis: "It is possible that a part of this carbonic acid is formed by digestion, that it is introduced into the circulation with the chyle, in a word, that reaching the lungs, it is discharged from the blood as the oxygen combines with it through a superior affinity."[9]

Concerning the changes in the color of blood as it passes through the lungs, Seguin expressed in Lavoisier's name a highly contestable opinion: "It can be concluded, along with M. Lavoisier and Dr. Crawford, that the change in blood color results from its combination with hydrogen. In passing through the lungs, the blood leaves a part of the hydrogen it contains, and then acquires its bright red color."[10] Hassenfratz attributed the same opinion to him in almost the same terms.[11] The master's silence might pass for agreement. But it reveals especially that, absorbed by finances and politics, Lavoisier was supervising his disciples less closely. Seguin played an increasingly important role in the continuation of the work, to the point of almost escaping Lavoisier's control. It was he who carried out in the Arsenal laboratory a number of experiments to which Lavoisier's contribution was only a theoretical interpretation. But this meant that he lost the benefit of his usual method which entailed constant confrontation of the hypothesis with the results, and vice versa, until perfect agreement was reached.

On April 9, 1791 it was Seguin who presented the elements of the future "Second Memoir on Respiration" to the Academy.[12] Essentially he gave the details of the experiments on the guinea-pig described in the first memoir and emphasized the point noted by Lavoisier, that the consumption of oxygen remained constant regardless of the amounts available.

On May 4, 1791, according to the minutes of the Academy, Lavoisier gave a reading of this second memoir.[13] Undoubtedly dissatisfied with the content, he asked Seguin for modifications. Two years later, the written report was still unfinished and the definitive text appeared only in 1814 in the *Annales de Chimie*.[14]

The Physiology of Perspiration

Lavoisier had identified the biological regulators whose equilibrium ensured the state of health: respiration, which brought the combustion agent, oxygen, and nutrition, which provided the fuels, hydrogen and carbon. The production of heat resulting from this combustion constituted thermogenesis. It had to be counterbalanced by a mechanism of thermolysis, or loss of heat from the body, perspiration, which continuously drew water from the organism and combined it with caloric to transform it into vapor. The loss of caloric led to a cooling that maintained the constant temperature of the body. "It is not only by the pores of the skin that this aqueous emanation takes place," Lavoisier specified. "A considerable quantity of humidity is also exhaled by the lungs at each expiration."[15]

The input/output method and the use of scales were as always much in evidence. To determine the weight of water lost through perspiration, it sufficed to determine the total weight loss of an individual in a given time and then to subtract from it the amount of water lost by respiration. On May 11, 1791 Lavoisier described to the Academicians the extremely sensitive and accurate scale he had used to conduct the experiments with Seguin and to weigh him with the minute margin of error of 18 grains for 125 pounds.[16]

In the "First Memoir on Animal Perspiration," he analyzed the respective roles of perspiration through the skin, pulmonary perspiration, and respiration. To break down the water loss connected with each of these three phenomena was not easy. "The means we used," he said, "although simple in theory, presented extreme difficulties in practice."[17] We are today forced to admit that they had not been surmounted.

Seguin had once again put on his airtight suit that permitted him to breathe through a tube attached around his mouth. Lavoisier measured the initial amount of air available, as well as the amount of water and carbonic gas exhaled. By weighing Seguin nude before and after the experiments, he determined the total weight loss due to the three combined factors. By weighing him dressed in the special suit at the beginning and end of the experiment, he eliminated the loss of water by cutaneous perspiration, which remained in the garment, and could then calculate by subtraction the loss of weight linked with the two pulmonary factors.

It remained to separate what, during respiration, stemmed in theory from the water loss formed by hydrogen combustion and what was due to pulmonary perspiration. But the authors lost control of both the experimental protocol and the physiological theory. The complexity of the hydroelectrolytic exchanges in the lungs far surpassed what they could imagine.

Moreover, Seguin, who carried out the subsequent tests virtually on his own, showed more imagination than scientific rigor. He was weighed four times a day, and sometimes he had to remain motionless for hours so as to determine his weight loss when he was inactive. Each day he weighed his liquid and solid intake and his faeces. He spent long hours in a bathtub filled with water or with his body covered in oil in order to disassociate the invisible perspiration from his sweat. His brother and friends also participated in the tests. He even used patients hospitalized for venereal diseases and treated by baths of corrosive sublimate or bichloride of mercury. Although the experiments lasted eleven months, they brought little new scientific information. The authors admitted this in the conclusion: "We repeat once again, to avoid all ambiguity, these results are exact only in a supposition that seems probable to us. It is one of the solutions to an unspecified problem that we shall resolve in a more rigorous way by the process of elimination and new experiments."[18]

In 1791 Lavoisier had been successively elected National Treasury Commissioner, member of the Committee on Weights and Measures, Treasurer of the Academy of Science, and member of the Advisory Board for Arts and Trades. This highly talented man, who had been able to hold ten jobs at once, began to be overwhelmed, to the detriment of his personal research.

In presenting the "Second Memoir on Perspiration" at the Academy on February 22, 1792, he announced that the work had been done by Seguin alone, and that the experiments described were entirely Seguin's.[19] One suspects that he was keeping his distance from his young assistant whose theories had begun to trouble him.

For this research, Seguin had continued to wear an airtight suit, but the first one had been replaced by one made of rubber coated leather. To separate the effects of perspiration from those of respiration, the air in the garment was pumped out, causing the suit to adhere to the body, which prevented cutaneous perspiration. The experiments confirmed the role of cutaneous perspiration in the maintenance of homeothermia: it was its evaporation that kept the body temperature at its normal level. But the theory again became confused. Seguin believed that he had observed with the skin as with the lungs a multitude of complicated effects among which was "a filtration of viscous humor [. . .] that separates itself from the blood by excessively fine networks and is then dissolved in the air of respiration."[20] He even imagined that the skin had exhaling vessels that released water and inhaling ones that absorbed it. For want of experimental results, and always more at ease in the domain of political ideas, Seguin went on to philosophize on social inequalities:

This evenness of temperature which the wealthy man obtains with so much effort by combining the productions of two hemispheres—Indian silk and Spanish wool—by using a multitude of men to weave precious fabrics, is reached by the poor man in a much less complicated way, one that makes him dependent on no one: Nature simply accelerates his respiration in proportion to his needs.[21]

Lavoisier had no doubt reread Seguin's text and been rather alarmed. Prudent, he added: "Although we are still far from our goal, we shall pause for awhile before continuing this vast undertaking. By gathering our strength and ideas, by reinforcing ourselves with the knowledge passed on to us by the men of genius and learned medical doctors surrounding us, we are preparing to undertake the task we have set for ourselves with renewed courage."[22]

Lavoisier would not take up the subject again. In eighteen years of study and reflection, he had covered the essential questions: the role of pulmonary ventilation; its relationship to the circulation of the blood; the analogy between respiration and combustion; the mechanism of animal heat and homeothermia; the regulation of the respiratory function and its relationship to perspiration and nutrition.

The Animal Machine

Many questions remained unanswered. More than a century would pass before it was established that respiration is intended to produce the energy necessary for the maintenance and development of living structures; that this energy comes from oxidation, in the cells and tissues, of three classes of organic substances: carbohydrates, lipids, and proteins; that the site of this oxidation is a microscopic body at the center of the cell, the mitochondrion; and that this mitochondrion consumes oxygen harnessed by the lungs from the atmospheric air and conveyed to the tissues by hemoglobin and produces carbonic gas, carried from the tissues to the lungs by the blood and then exhaled into the atmospheric air. Therefore there are two intermediaries between the air and the cells of the tissues: first, the red cells that fix and release large quantities of oxygen and carbonic gas and transport these gases from the tissues to the lungs; second, the pulmonary ventilation that ensures a constant interchange between the lungs and the atmosphere.[23]

Nevertheless, the link established by Lavoisier between respiration, perspiration, body heat, and nutrition foreshadowed the modern concept of biological energetics:

The animal machine is governed principally by three main regulators; respiration, which consumes hydrogen and carbon and provides caloric; perspiration, which increases or decreases, depending on whether more or less caloric is needed; and finally, digestion, which restores to the blood what it has lost through respiration and perspiration.[24]

He had guessed that the blood transported the carbon necessary for the combustion reaction with oxygen, but it was not until Claude Bernard's work that it was understood how carbon reached the interior of the organism.[25] Carbohydrates, absorbed by the intestine and carried to the liver by the portal vein, are the real fuel that oxygen burns: combustion takes place not in the lungs but rather in all the tissues of the organism, and the blood regulates this functional whole.

Lavoisier could foresee the day when one could know more about animal chemistry, as he wrote to Vincenzo Dandolo, his Italian translator: "These two memoirs on respiration that I am sending you are a relatively good beginning to understanding animal physiology, but as far as digestion and the formation of chyle and blood are concerned, everything remains to be done. I have a few ideas and intend to carry out some experiments."[26]

One of these ideas was that it could be possible to establish the energetic costs of any human activity, including intellectual ones. For example, "the efforts required of someone giving a speech or playing a musical instrument. One might even evaluate the mechanical energy spent by a philosopher who is thinking, a scholar who is writing, or a musician who is composing."[27] He had understood that the functions of the organism are subjected to a regulating system that permits the individual to adapt to all circumstances:

Is he inactive or resting? Then circulation as well as respiration is slowed down. He uses less air. His lungs exhale less carbon and hydrogen and consequently he needs less food. Does he have to work hard? Respiration accelerates, he consumes more air and loses more hydrogen and carbon. Consequently, he needs to restore his strength more often, especially by nutrition.[28]

The end of 1790 was approaching and politics had permeated everything. Seguin, who had helped write the report, had used the occasion to deplore social inequalities:

By what fatality is it that the poor man, who lives from the work of his hands, who is obliged to use all the strength that nature has given him in order to survive, consumes more energy than the idle man, whereas the latter has less need to regenerate his forces? Why, by a shocking contrast, should the rich man enjoy an abundance that he does not physically need and that would seem to be intended for the working man? Let us beware, however, of maligning nature and accusing it of faults that undoubtedly stem from our social institutions and which, perhaps, are inseparable from them. Let us simply be eternally grateful to philosophy and humanity which are joining forces to promise us sound institutions that will tend to equalize fortunes, increase the wages of labor and assure it its just reward, and to present to all classes of society, and especially to the destitute, more enjoyment and good fortune.[29]

The Physiology of Nutrition

Trying to reach a better understanding of the physiology of nutrition, Lavoisier proposed to the Academy on July 28, 1792, the subject for a prize to be awarded in 1794: 5,000 livres would be given to the best study on *animalization*, that is, the organic synthesis of animal tissues after the absorption of food. He recalled that the first phases of the physiology of digestion were already well known: the successive action of saliva in the mouth, of gastric juices in the stomach, of bile and pancreatic juices that converted nourishment into chyle. "One part is absorbed in the blood to compensate for the losses that are constantly taking place through respiration and perspiration; and in the end Nature rejects in the form of excrements, all the material it cannot use."[30]

Here too the balance sheet method had to apply: the total receipts should be equal to the total expenditures: "Animals that are in good health and fully grown constantly return each day, when digestion has finished, to the same weight they had the day before in similar circumstances. Thus, the sum of matter equal to what is received in the intestines is consumed and expended by perspiration, respiration or by the various excretions."[31]

The document brings to light Lavoisier's early comprehension of the metabolic role of the liver:

The Academy, willing to explore in methodical order all the characteristics of animal-ization, has decided to start by one of the principal, and has selected the role of the liver and bile. [. . .] Until now, scientists have limited themselves to the functions of bile in the digestion. But recent discoveries concerning the nature of this fluid and its colouring matter, the stones of the gall bladder, the parenchyma of the liver and its oily compsition, demand the attention of the physicians. It is easy to foresee that other than the secretion of bile, or rather that through the secretion of bile, an organ as im-portant in size, connections, and vascular structure as the liver fills a whole system of functions, the extent of which science has not yet grasped.[32]

The prize of the Academy of Science would go to the competitor who could shed at least some new light on the essential points: the anatomy of the liver and gall bladder; a comparative analysis of the bile in different animal species; a chemical study of the parenchyma of the liver; a study of the blood of the portal vein and its comparison with the blood of other regions of the body; a definition of the functions of the liver and bile and their relationship to other functions; the major illnesses of the hepatic and biliary systems in man and animals. In his commentaries, Lavoisier provided a glimpse of his own hypotheses on the importance of hepatic functions in anabolism:

By proposing this subject and emphasizing all its difficulties, the Academy realizes that it will require chemical research based in particular on the recently acquired analytical means of chemistry. It feels and hopes that this work will oblige those who undertake it to determine the nature of the blood of the portal vein, and to contrast it with the arterial and venous blood of other regions. [. . .] It is time to take up the complicated questions presented by the phenomena of animal economy, and it is from the joint efforts of physics, anatomy and chemistry that we can hope to find answers.[33]

But it is clear that Lavoisier's aim was not only to understand the physi-ology of nutrition or even the mechanism of tissue anabolism. He was will-ing to take up "the complicated questions" of animal physiology and he was among the first to foresee the value of a chemical approach to these ques-tions. He had definitely begun another scientific revolution, that of biology, to which Claude Bernard would bear witness:

If, starting from the fact pointed out by Lavoisier, we have now come down to the experimental analysis of vital functions, we shall see that in all tissues and organs, it is oxygen that is always both the stimulator of physico-chemical phenomena and the condition of the functional activity of organized matter. Oxygen penetrates animals by the respiratory surface, and circulation spreads life in all the organs and organic elements by distributing the oxygen dissolved in the arterial blood.[34]

Nature's Three Kingdoms

It remained for Lavoisier to devise a comprehensive system regulating the chemical exchanges among Nature's three kingdoms, and he did it in 1792. Prior to his work, it was thought that the living world consisted of only two kingdoms: the vegetable, destined to develop nutriments, and the animal, which drew its required energy from the nourishment provided by the former. In his *Chymie expérimentale et raisonnée*, Antoine Baumé wrote:

I consider nature a vast chemical laboratory in which all kinds of compositions and decompositions are formed. Vegetation is the basic instrument the Creator uses to set all of nature in motion. Vegetables are organized bodies that grow on the dry areas of the globe and within its waters. Their function is to combine immediately the four elements (water, earth, air and fire) and to serve as food for animals. Nature uses both kingdoms to form all existing combustible matter.[35]

And Claude Bernard, describing these views of the past in his *Leçons sur les phénomènes de la vie communs aux animaux et aux végétaux*, comments:

In living beings, the phenomena of destruction or vital combustion were absolutely separated from the phenomena of reduction or organic synthesis. The role of vital creation had been assigned to the vegetable kingdom, whereas organic destruction had been reserved for the animal one. The animal organism was incapable of forming any of the principles of which it is made up—fat, albumin, fibrin, starch, sugar; they were all provided by the vegetable kingdom and animal nutrition was hardly more than the placing in them of materials uniquely developed by plants.[36]

But Lavoisier's vision was much more modern than Baumé's. In the *Traité élémentaire de Chimie*, in 1789, he had explained how he had been led to invent the technique for analyzing organic bodies by combustion, a discovery that earned him a place among the founders of organic chemistry. As far back as 1774 he had noted that fire, rather than separating the components of plants, destroyed them completely. Certainly fire revealed that oak was a combination of water, acids, and oils whose residue was charcoal, itself decomposable into earth and fixed alkali. But the analysis needed to be pushed further.[37] In July 1777 he had learned that Bergman had obtained saccharin and oxalic acid through distillation, by having nitric acid react on sugar. But his attempt to repeat the experiment had failed. Instead of oxalic acid, he had obtained nitric acid, water, and a coal-like residue. In February 1779 heating sugar more slowly, he had succeeded in synthesizing oxalic acid and, departing from this unique example, extended his general theory of acids to organic acids.

But above all he had understood that intense heat decomposed the sugar into hydrogen and carbon. In combining with the oxygen of nitric acid, carbon formed carbonic gas and hydrogen formed water. In measuring the quantities of carbonic gas and water produced by the combustion of an organic substance, one could deduce the amount of carbon and hydrogen it contained. This was the principle of organic analysis.

He had then analyzed spirits of wine, olive oil, and wax in the same way and had seen that vegetable matter resulted from the combination of oxygen, hydrogen, and carbon.[38] "The elements for all the acids of this kingdom are hydrogen and carbon, sometimes hydrogen, carbon and phosphorus, the whole combined with a more or less considerable amount of oxygen. The vegetable kingdom also has oxides that are formed from the same double or triple, but less oxygenated, elements."[39]

In another text, Lavoisier specified that all these remarks were applicable to animal substances as well: "These substances are also the result of a triple combination of oxygen, hydrogen, and carbon. They do not contain, already formed, water, carbonic acid, or oil, but simply all their elements. The least degree of heat, as long as it is slightly higher than boiling water, suffices for uniting oxygen and hydrogen, and hydrogen and carbon, and for forming oil and water. But also the phenomena become more complicated, because there exists, as M. Berthollet has shown, a fourth principle in animal matter, nitrogen, which, with hydrogen, forms volatile alkali or ammonia."[40]

The way in which he described alcoholic—or, in his own words, "winey" —fermentation was a decisive step in his understanding of vegetable and animal chemistry. It was in this text that he formulated the principle of the conservation of matter and, for the first time, designated a chemical reaction by an equation:

Nothing is created, neither in the processes of art nor of nature, and in principle it can be stated that in every process there is an equal quantity of matter before and after it has taken place, that the quality and quantity of the principles are the same, and that there are only changes, modifications. All the art of experimentation in chemistry is based on this principle. In every experiment, one is obliged to suppose a real equality or equation between the principles of the bodies one is examining and those that are obtained from them through analysis. Thus since raisin must gives carbonic acid gas and alcohol, I can say that raisin must = carbonic acid + alcohol. [. . .] The effects of the winey fermentation are thus reduced to separating into two parts the sugar, which is an oxide; and then oxygenating one part at the expense of the other to form carbonic acid, and deoxygenating the other part in favor of the first so as to form a combustible substance, which is an alcohol. All this occurs in such a way that if it were possible to recombine the two substances—alcohol and carbonic acid—one could reconstitute the sugar.[41]

This then is the definition of organic synthesis. The meaning of Lavoisier's text goes well beyond that of the simple weight equation that has habitually been attributed to it. He makes very clear that it is not a matter of quantitative equality, but of an identity of nature between constituent elements: "the quality and quantity of the principles are the same, there are only changes, modifications."[42] He was now ready to describe the general cycle of living matter:

Vegetation draws from air, water and the mineral kingdom the material necessary for its organization; animals nourish themselves with vegetables or other animals that have themselves been nourished by vegetation. Subsequently, fermentation, putrefaction, and combustion perpetually return to the atmosphere and mineral kingdom the principles that vegetable and animal life have borrowed from them. What are the processes used by nature to achieve this marvelous circulation among the three kingdoms?[43]

Already in 1789, he had answered the question and written in the *Traité élémentaire de chimie*:

We have seen how a small number of simple substances, or at least not yet decomposed substances, such as nitrogen, sulphur, phosphorus, carbon, the muriatic radical and hydrogen, form, when combined with oxygen, all the oxides and acids composing the vegetable and animal kingdoms: we have admired the simplicity of the means by which Nature multiplies properties and forms.[44]

Now, in 1792, he could go further and write in the subject for the prize of the Academy:

The cause and mechanism of these phenomena have up to now been enveloped in an almost inpenetrable veil. One suspects, however, that since putrefaction and combustion are the means that nature employs to give the mineral kingdom the material it has taken from it to form plants and animals, then vegetation and animal development must be processes that are just the opposite of combustion and putrefaction."[45]

Lavoisier's contributions were more conceptual than practical and he could bring only a few experimental answers to these major scientific questions. The appropriate means did not exist and, in any case, he had lost the taste for laboratory work. Ambition, multiple activities, and, soon, personal cares would lead him to delegate his scientific work. The days of basic research had passed, along with his involvement in public finances. The changing times were now demanding socially useful activities: assistance to artisans, reflections on public education, and the creation of the metric system.

He left to his contemporaries, in particular to Fourcroy and Vauquelin, the job of identifying new organic substances. For his part, he had undertaken the exploration of vegetable and animal chemistry in a very original and personal fashion. He had invented the method of analysis by combustion, showed that compound radicals combine with oxygen to form oxides (such as sugar or alcohol) and acids (such as oxalic acid or acetic acid), and established the quantitative composition of several organic substances.[46] He would not have the time to go further, but although limited and brief, his incursion into these disciplines would greatly modify their evolution. As F. L. Holmes writes: "While Lavoisier contributed the key to future analyses of the elementary composition of organic compounds, his contemporaries contributed the foundations for the isolation and identification of those compounds upon which the elementary analyses could then be performed. The organic chemistry which matured during the next half century rested as heavily on the one as the other."[47]

But the exploration of such a vast domain was unattainable for him and he urged all the scientific community to investigate the genesis of plant and animal substances. The study of plants was passed on to his colleagues at the Academy: Jussieu, Berthollet, Thouin, Desfontaines, and Fourcroy worked with him at the *Jardin des Plantes*. Seguin and Hassenfratz joined them, but a difference of opinion soon divided the two younger men. Hassenfratz argued that vegetation was nourished exclusively by humus. All carbon reached it by its roots, which absorbed it from organic wastes contained in the soil: "Of all ways of explaining the increase of carbon in plants by the act of vegetation, the one most compatible with the facts observed is based on the dissolving of carbon in water, its subsequent absorption by the roots of the plants and its deposit within the plants; thus carbon dissolved in water is one of the nutritive substances of the plants.[48] It was only in 1840 that his theory was refuted by Liebig. According to Seguin, since carbonic acid is formed during vegetal combustion, there had to be a decomposition of carbonic acid at the moment of their synthesis.

To arbitrate the debate, in the spring of 1792 Lavoisier devised a kind of photosynthesis. If wood or some plant matter was burned in a bell jar filled with oxygen, the plant substance was converted into CO_2 and H_2O. Thus by removing the oxygen from carbonic acid and water, one should be able to re-form a plant compound. "Although we do not have the technical means of performing this marvel, it is not unlikely—and analysis leads us to believe it—that it is the step nature takes for forming plants."[49]

Thus ended Lavoisier's foray into the study of the chemistry of life. After William Harvey, he may be considered the first major figure in modern biology. Very conscious of the decisive advances he had brought about, in 1792 he would claim as his property "the first ideas concerning the composition of vegetable and animal substances."[50]

Even though he was unable to give the experimental demonstration of organic syntheses, Lavoisier's merit was to have initiated a new approach to the study of living organisms, one based on the analysis of their physico-chemical mechanisms. A particularly fertile path was cleared for the development of biochemistry. After having reformed, organized and endowed the language of mineral chemistry, he had invented organic chemistry and understood that, basically, nothing separated the two. He had explored the principal functions of animal life and worked as a physiologist: at first concentrating on the study of respiration, he had evolved toward a comprehensive approach to nutrition and energetic metabolism in man. By an innovative intuition, he had sensed the essential role of the liver in the organic syntheses. Finally, he had developed an overall theory of the cycle of the three kingdoms of Nature and the chemistry of life. Alone, Lavoisier had covered a conceptual itinerary that would take official science almost a century to open up. Certainly, he drew on the heritage of concepts laboriously developed by those who preceded him. But his physico-chemical approach to the phenomena of life would be of major heuristic value to his successors, François Magendie and, especially, Claude Bernard.

In the Service of the Arts and Trades

THE NATIONAL ASSEMBLY HAD BECOME used to consulting scientists about all sorts of subjects and then having them share in its action, just as the king's ministers had done in the past. The Academicians gave advice on hospitals, the monetary system, savings banks, the new republican calendar, steam engines, the oiled taffeta used for soldiers' coats, and water storage on warships. And when the artisans needed guidance, they gladly provided it.

But gradually, alongside the increasingly controversial Academy of Science, there cropped up a whole range of organizations specializing in advising and encouraging the applied arts. Among them were the Bureau de consultation des Arts et Métiers (Advisory Board for Arts and Trades), the Lycée des Arts, and the Commission des Poids et Mesures (Commission on Weights and Measures).

Excluded from political and financial responsibility from the beginning of 1792, Lavoisier was called on to be part of these new structures.

The Advisory Board for Arts and Trades

From January 1792 Lavoisier belonged to the Advisory Board for Arts and Trades, which was created by the National Assembly to give both concrete assistance and general encouragement to artisans.[1]

One of the major complaints of the artisans was the great difficulty they encountered in having their inventions recognized by the Academy of Science and approved by letters-patent which protected their intellectual property. They felt very resentful toward the Academy. "What a lot of trouble, obstacles, distress, and disgust always await those who dare present themselves to our administration as creators of inventions useful to mankind," wrote the chevalier Stanislas de Boufflers when presenting to the Constituent National Assembly his *Rapport sur la propriété des auteurs de découvertes et d'inventions en tout genre d'industrie, le 30 Décembre 1790.*[2]

Lavoisier had long looked favorably on the applied sciences, and saw a means of saving the Academy of Science through its closer cooperation with artisans. "The Academy," he wrote, "is a free court, open to anyone who presents inventions to be judged. [. . .] This court is useful to those who consult it, because they find in the commissioners assigned to them enlightened guides who regard it as their duty to help them with their advice and to modify or correct their discoveries whenever they are able."[3] Since for him the Advisory Board for Arts and Trades posed a threat to the Academy of Science, it was important that members of the latter be in the majority. Even though little is known about Lavoisier's personal role in creating the board, it can be assumed that the choice of its members provoked a considerable power struggle. "The Commerce Committee as well as M. de Boufflers experienced repeated difficulties, were hampered by numerous obstructions; all the resources of academic intrigue were studied and constantly used, one after the other. Ground was ceded foot by foot, inch by inch."[4]

In the end, fifteen of the members of the Board came from the Academy of Science: Lavoisier, Le Roy, Bossut, Desmarets, Borda, Vandermonde, Coulomb, Berthollet, Meusnier, Brisson, Périer, Rochon, Duhamel du Monceau, Lagrange, and Laplace. Fifteen came from learned societies: Bourru and Jumelin from the Faculty of Medicine, Louis from the Academy of Surgery, Hallé from the Royal Society of Medicine, Parmentier from the Society of Agriculture, Pelletier from the Society of Natural History, Hassenfratz from the Society of the Annales de Chimie, Silvestre from the Société Philomatique, Servières, Trouville, Guiraut and Leblanc from the Société des Artistes Inventeurs, Droz and Calippe from the Société du Point Central, Lucotte from the Society of United Artisans. Later they would be joined by Baumé, Fourcroy, and Cousin from the Academy of Science, Desaudray from the Lycée des Arts, Dumas, a doctor, Desault, a surgeon, Millin, a naturalist.

Dating from November 19, 1791 the thirty unpaid members met regularly at the Louvre to write reports on such diverse subjects as breadmaking, the publication of the "Arts and Trades Collection," the best method for printing assignats, and projects for educational reform. With a budget of 300,000 livres, they brought new scientific techniques to the attention of the government, helped artisans to apply them, and gave financial help to those needing it.[5]

Bread had become increasingly scarce and expensive in Paris and bakeries were besieged from daybreak. Happy the citizen who after waiting in line from three to four hours managed to buy bread and then get back to his home without being manhandled or maimed by the hungry crowd. In the general atmosphere of suspicion, it was important to prevent bakers from cheating and to know precisely how much bread they could make with the flour alloted to them. Nicolas Desmarest received a prize for having calculated that "the sack containing 320 pounds of flour normally gives 104 to 105 four-pound loaves."[6]

The Academy of Science had begun, a century earlier, a collection of works describing the Arts and Trades. The original in-folio volumes, illustrated with numerous engraved plates, gave a meticulous description of the seventy leading craft industries in France. Duhamel du Monceau, the editor, had contributed his famous "General Treatise on Fishing." Fougeroux de Bondaroy had written on the skills of the slate-quarry worker, the cooper, the cutler and the producers of fine leathers gilded with gold or silver. Jacques François had explained the art of distilling aqua fortis. It was also possible to consult the collection for the methods used by pinmakers, papermakers, printers, bookbinders, gilders, and mirrormakers and to learn how painters and makers of harpsichords and fake pearls went about their work.

Initially 250 volumes had been foreseen. The competition of a Swiss pirate in-quarto edition, the absence of government aid, and the *Encyclopédie* appearance had slowed and eventually preempted sale of the collection twenty years earlier. Lavoisier considered bringing out a new edition, but eventually dropped the project because more pressing matters were calling.

At the beginning of 1793, responding to a request from the Comité des Monnaies (Currency Committee), the Advisory Board asked him to head a special commission for solving the problem of counterfeit assignats. Although in his eyes the expedient of the assignats was contributing to the deterioration of the financial situation of France, Lavoisier could appreciate the importance of the technical and industrial aspects of this unprecedented monetary phenomenon. Drawing on his experience at the Discount Bank, he spent three months studying the problem and defining new printing methods. Assignats should be stamped with easily identifiable characteristic marks and the greatest number possible of unrelated techniques should be used. For each technique, the best—and most difficult to copy—craftsmen should be employed. All assignats ought to be perfectly identical.

He investigated the best ingredients for the paper: was it preferable to use white or ecru rags, hemp, or unbleached linen? He asked for samples from all the manufacturers, among them Étienne Alexandre Jacques Anisson-Duperron, whose factory was near Montargis; La Garde the elder, whose workshop was in the Marais; La Garde the younger, who worked at Courtalin en Brie; the brothers Didot from Essonne; François Johannot; the brothers Montgolfier in Annonay; and Henri Villermain in Angoulême.[7]

He compared quality, strength and prices of the different products, and asked each of the seven competitors to produce a special kind of paper to be used for a particular denomination of assignat. He examined the ways the paper was colored, the techniques for engraving and producing watermarks, the inks, and the typography. To speed up the printing, he recommended polytypage, which, thanks to steel plates, made it possible to print up to 20,000 completely identical proofs. "This method," he wrote, "is the simplest, quickest, and cheapest of those that can be used to provide assignats of the same sum with the rigorous identity that will discourage counterfeiters and facilitate means of verification."[8]

Therefore, while condemning the monetary device of assignats, Lavoisier became the best technician for facilitating their circulation. From December 21, 1789 to February 19, 1796, the date on which their production ceased, the State issued assignats for a total value of 45 billion livres. But in 1796, their true value represented only 1 percent of their nominal value.

Four hundred artisans presented their dossiers to the Advisory Board for Arts and Trades. "From Nicolas Leblanc's crystallization of aluminum sulfate to the transparent tableau created by the drafttsman Carmontelle, the range of the applied science represented was very broad. Of particular interest were spinning and weaving, agriculture, construction, water conveyance, metallurgy, chronometry, paper-making, engraving, heating systems, physics, transport, dyeing, and dressings, as well as the making of arms."[9]

Lavoisier co-signed six experts' reports. He had his last contact with the Board when he was preparing for his trial: on April 18, 1794 he asked for an attestation of his services to science. At no time was he able to play a role in granting patents. Patent claims were handled by the minister of the Interior, who was advised by a Bureau Consultatif des Arts et Manufactures, which is not be confused with the Bureau de Consultation des Arts et Métiers. The latter, a creation of the Convention, disappeared when it did.

The Meter, Universal Standard of Measurement

Since 1790 Lavoisier had been occupied with another reform of major importance, the unification of the weights and measures system. He had often deplored the incredible diversity of units of measure as a great detriment to trade. The value of the toise (6 feet), the foot, the inch, the line (3.175 mm), the ell, the pound, and the hogshead of grain varied from one province, one town and even one parish to another.

For quite some time he had been using the decimal system for his personal work, and had recommended that his colleagues in chemistry do the same, "while waiting for the day when men will come together to adopt a single standard for weights and measures."[10]

On May 8, 1790 the National Assembly had assigned the Academy of Science the task of creating an international system of weights and measures based on a universally accepted unit. The unit had to be taken in nature, so that all nations could have recourse to it in case of loss or alteration of standards. The reformers were looking beyond the borders of France, and hoping to set up an international committee. But the English refused their invitation outright, the Spanish went no further than sending an observer, and the United States of America showed only circumspect interest. Berlin, Vienna, and Moscow remained completely silent.

The commission, composed of Lavoisier, Condorcet, Borda, Lagrange, and Tillet—soon joined by Laplace and Monge—gave itself a triple objective. It proposed to choose a universal physical standard as a basic unit of measure, to adopt decimal division, and to combine all units of measurement into a coherent system.

The simplest step would have been to take as a basic unit the length of the pendulum ticking seconds at a given latitude. Lavoisier rejected the idea, arguing that the second was not a natural unit but only an arbitrary fraction of a true one, the day. Moreover, the choice of latitude could be challenged by other countries. He also rejected the measure of the quarter-circle of the equator as too difficult to realize. There remained the measure of an arc of the meridian. Already realized in 1740 by the Abbé de La Caille and Cassini de Thury, it could be easily taken up again thanks to Borda's new graduated circle, capable of measuring angles with an excellent precision. "One of the secret motives for giving preference to the quarter-circle of the meridian was the desire to establish as quickly as possible the reputation of the graduated circle," wrote Jean-Baptiste Delambre.[11]

There were other reasons: First, Laplace had an interest in the improvement of geodetic data, writes Charles C. Gillispie:

He had obtained the expressions since called Laplace's functions in a memoir of 1785. They permit comparing the value for the force of gravity measured by timing the pendulum with that calculated from the inverse square law of attraction. The comparison could be made at any point where geodetic measurements—in this case along the meridian—permitted calculation of the radius of the earth. The pendulum alone gave only one side of the equation.[12]

Second, a new survey would cover the same ground that the abbé La Caille had traversed in 1749 in measuring the meridian from Dunkirk to Perpignan:

Extending his chain of triangles to Barcelona would anchor both ends at sea level, while redoing them would either confirm or improve their accuracy. The new chain would then constitute a grid that could be laid conformably over the Cassini map of France, which had been fleshed out, so to say, on the skeleton, or rather the back-bone, of the La Caille triangulation, and only just completed, except for Brittany. The cartographers who in 1791 partitioned the country into 83 departments and the de-partments into cantons and districts worked their task on its 170-odd sheets. Now, with its triangles perfected, with the church steeples that had served as observation points identified and repaired if need be, it might serve as the framework within which to fit the finer, more intricate, and more contentious detail of land registry and assess-ment—a national cadastre.[13]

On March 30, 1791 the Assembly adopted the Academy's plan, which was that the unit of length would be equal to the ten millionth part of the quadrant of the meridian of the earth. Once the unit of length was defined, it would be easy to deduce the unit of capacity by cubing it. And this unit of capacity would make it possible to define the unit of weight, explained Talley-rand, "by using an ingenious process of M. Lavoisier, who has determined with the greatest exactitude the weight of a cubic foot of water distilled at the temperature of 14.4 degrees on the Réaumur thermometer, or 18 degrees centigrade."[14]

The work began in May 1792. First of all, the necessary instruments, which had no equivalents, had to be fabricated. Nicolas Fortin and Fourché were asked to provide the temporary standards; Mercklein and Kutsch the comparators; Laurenz J. Jecker, Tourroude and François Philippe Charpen-tier various instruments; Marc Étienne Jannetti, the famous caster of bells from Marseille, was to mold the platinum for the permanent standards. For the geodesic measures, Etienne Lenoir made quarter-circles. For the measure-ment of the bases, Borda knew that the greatest source of inaccuracy in previ-ous surveys was the expansion or contraction of measuring rods with rise or fall in temperature. With Lenoir, he designed rules of an altogether new type:

Borda's solution exhibited, as did the principle of his repeating circle, the elegance of accepting a problem rather than the ingenuity of circumventing its effect. His rules were to be made of platinum, the least expansible of metal. He enclosed the platinum strip, almost as flexible as a piece of wire, in a snug sleeve of copper six inches shorter. The platinum core and the copper casing were attached at one end. The other end of each was free to move according to the coefficient of expansion of the metal. As the day grew warmer, the surveyor could read the extent to which the copper crept along the platinum off a scale on the platinum strip which, together with a vernier on the copper sleeve, made the device in effect a thermometer, indicating the temperature at any moment by the excess of the dilation of the copper over the platinum. He could then reduce the differential expansion of the two to the absolute expansion of the platinum. The measuring rods would thus be self-correcting for variations in tempera-ture. Each was equipped with a coupling to attach it to the next so that they might be laid precisely end to end.[15]

The construction of the rules was very difficult because platinum melts only at very high temperatures. Lavoisier and Seguin had to construct several porcelain ovens, fed first by oxygen alone, then by oxygen and hydrogen, because the extreme heat had caused them to explode. But Lavoisier finally succeeded in melting more than a hundred pounds of platinum for the rulers, the balls of the pendulums, and the cylinders.

Pierre François André Méchain and Jean-Baptiste Delambre were responsible for surveying the length of the meridian arc from Dunkirk to Barcelona. The distance between these two cities represented more than a tenth of the arc to be measured, which was sufficient. "This arc offered, in addition to its large expanse, the advantage of having its two extreme points at sea level, of crossing the mean parallel and following the meridian already traced in France. This provided a way of using already completed work to verify what we were planning to do."[16]

Méchain left for Spain, Delambre for the Paris suburbs and then for Dunkirk. Each had four assistants and two carriages, one of which was reserved for instruments, drawn by four post horses. They encountered enormous obstacles, were repeatedly arrested, and had great difficulty in receiving the funds Lavoisier sent them.

They carried out the linear measurements on the surface and the geodetic calculations according to the triangulation principle. They picked out groups of three points along the axis of the meridian, each visible to the other, such as towers, châteaux, or steeples, defining a succession of triangles. They used Borda's circle to determine the angles. They measured a single side, or the base of each triangle. They could then calculate the length of the two other sides using trigonometry and mark their results on the map. Their strange maneuvers caused them regularly to be taken for spies, and they found themselves in prison more than once.

Lavoisier, both secretary and treasurer of the group, managed the budget of 300,000 livres which was to cover salaries, travel expenses, and the fabrication of instruments. It was he who reported on the progress of the work to two members of the National Assembly: Claude Antoine Prieur, deputy from the Côte d'Or and a member of the Committee of Public Safety, and Louis François Antoine Arbogast. The meetings between these two men and the Committee took place at his home, but relationships were not easy. There was often talk of politics and the debates were heated. Prieur, vehemently antimonarchist, often found himself alone against all the others. The force of his arguments did not always compensate for his numerical disadvantage. "He had a deep resentment against Lavoisier especially," Delambre recalled, "and those of his colleagues, such as Borda and Coulomb, who showed themselves most ardent, witty, and biting in disputes."[17]

Lavoisier managed nevertheless to get the twenty-eight men working for the committee excused from the general requisition for weapons production. He was constantly appealing to the National Treasury for the funds voted by the Assembly, and wrote letter after letter to Laffon-Ladébat, deputy and spokesman for the budget. The members of the Convention, which above all was seeking to resolve a practical problem, had little understanding of the sophisticated operations of the Commission on Weights and Measures. They felt that things had been needlessly complicated and wanted to simplify the project so as to move faster. Lavoisier protested, arguing that this "would substitute a limited and narrow idea for one of the most beautiful and vast conceptions of the human mind. It would mean preferring a local and particular measure to a general system, which includes geography, navigational skills, surveying, weights, currency, and measurements of solids and liquids. In a word, it would mean losing, perhaps forever, the inestimable advantage of eliminating all calculation problems by the use of decimal divisions."[18]

At the end of September 1792 Fourcroy, who had just been elected fourth substitute deputy to the Convention, was appointed by the Public Education Committee, of which he was a member, to follow the affair closely. A member of the Jacobin Club, he shared the role of Assembly secretary with eleven colleagues. He also belonged to the Committee of Public Safety and the administration of the department of Paris. So many honors had turned his head a bit, causing him to overdo his sans-culotte convictions. He still met Lavoisier at the Advisory Board for the Arts and Trades, at the Lycée and the Academy, and, although he was afraid of compromising himself, he nevertheless helped Lavoisier when he could do so without taking a risk. "How far have you advanced with Weights and Measures?" was his constant question. On November 25, 1792 Lavoisier announced that the work was well on its way. Soon the only thing left to do would be "making the standards that will be sent to different countries and perhaps also to those learned societies in Europe who, by their prestige, could contribute most to spreading their use."[19] The Abbé Henri Baptiste Grégoire, who was presiding over the meeting, complimented the "respected scientists." "You will have the glory," he said, "of having discovered for the entire world this stable unit and beneficial truth that is going to become a new link between nations. It is one of the most useful conquests of equality."[20]

During the month of January 1793, Lavoisier and the Abbé Juste Haüy worked together to define the unit of weight, the grave—the future kilogram; starting with the unit of capacity, they determined the weight of the cubic decimeter of distilled water at the temperature of melting ice. Brisson, Vandermonde and Tillet, shortly afterwards replaced by Berthollet, collected all the measures of length, capacity and weight used in France at the Church of Sainte-Geneviève (the present Panthéon), and compared them to the new units. At the Paris Observatory, Borda and Cassini calculated the number of oscillations for a pendulum measuring one meter. Later they went to Bordeaux, at 45° latitude and sea level, to measure the length of the pendulum ticking seconds and they had compared the number of oscillations of the two pendulums within a day. Throughout the last week of May and the first week of June 1793 Lavoisier, Borda, and Lenoir installed the rules for the measurement of the bases in the garden of the house at 243 boulevard de la Madeleine where Lavoisier had recently moved. There they labored together on the difficult task of calibrating these fine instruments.

Up to that point, Lavoisier had spent 150,000 livres, or half of the foreseen budget. The definitive budget would depend on the number of standards to be sent to the departments. All the standards had to be made of platinum and he had bought more than 560 marcs (140 kilograms) for a total cost of 40,000 livres ($1.6 million)."[21]

Lavoisier warned the Convention that it had one final step to take to perfect its work: "No matter how perfect the metric system may be, it will have been adopted in vain, the monetary divisions of the system will have been linked in vain and this work will lose the greatest part of its utility, if the accounting books continue to be divided into 240 parts, that is into 20 sous and the sou into 12 pennies."[22] The following day, he proposed to the Currency Committee that they too should apply the decimal system and divide livres into ten décimes and each décime into ten centimes.[23]

The Lycée des Arts

In 1781 a private school for adults had been created in Paris by Pilâtre de Rozier. Known as the Musée de Monsieur, it gave courses in science. For ten years it had been teaching mathematics, physics, and chemistry to 650 subscribers, each of whom paid 3 louis per year. On June 14, 1785 Pilâtre and another aeronaut, Romain, met their death in an attempt to cross the Channel. Their balloon caught fire or exploded after leaving the French coast near Calais. After Pilâtre's death, the Musée de Monsieur changed its name to "the Lycée" and the numerous Academicians who taught there, in particular Fourcroy and Lavoisier, became stockholders. But Republican sympathizers had begun to drop out because the ideas expressed there were too conservative, and a part of its aristocratic clientele had already left France. In the autumn of 1792 the Lycée was experiencing financial difficulties and asked the Convention for help. The latter gave 10,000 livres but recalled "with regret that certain members of the Lycée have indulged in exaggerated statements and exhibited principles contrary to the public interest." In the future, it warned, they "ought to join the fortunes and interests of patriotism and the Lycée in their views and means."[24]

Thereafter, the administrators decided that the Lycée would be called the Lycée républicain. But otherwise nothing indicated that the advice of the Convention was going to be followed and Lavoisier felt it wiser to distance himself. In 1788 he had joined the Société Philomatique, a group of young people interested in science who had gathered around Augustin François Silvestre.[25] Soon afterward, its membership included most of the Academicians, who, threatened with the closing of the Academy, were seeking to re-group themselves.

Silvestre, who was secretary for the Advisory Board for Arts and Trades, urged them to create another private society with a more republican inspiration, which would be called the Lycée des Arts, the word "arts" referring to artisans and manufacturers and hence emphasizing the desire to be useful to the public.

The great debate at the time was what was going to prevail, science or the technical arts. As Servières wrote:

The harmful disfavor that some people are trying to cast on science stems more from ignorance than from dishonesty. [. . .] It would be absurd to separate science from applied science. That would be as ridiculous as the fable of the limbs and the stomach of the body. But, at the same time, I do not want science to affect a superiority that could make it odious, just as Cato became too austere through virtue. Science and the technical arts must always have equal rights.[26]

The Lycée des Arts was installed in the middle of the garden of the Palais-Egalité, formerly the Palais-Royal, in the building called "the Circus," which had the form of a tent. Decorated inside by a colonnade and covered on the outside by lattice work, it was reached by a gothic reception room at the end of which a landscape in trompe l'oeil led to the lecture hall capable of accommodating four hundred people. To the sides there were a café, reading room, exhibition hall and large galleries.[27] All the professors were friends.[28] They were to be paid 24 livres for each lecture, but because of treasury difficulties, no one had yet been paid in November, 1793.[29]

The promoters of the Lycée des Arts had their office at 35, impasse de la Corderie. They had a preliminary statement printed and distributed to prospective investors or participants, describing their enterprise:

Their intention is to create in Paris, the center of taste and talents, a kind of free and primary assembly of artisans, so that in the future these valuable men will be judged exclusively by their peers, and thus be spared the slow and abusive forms of academic censure. They must be reminded constantly of their dignity, of the unique standard of common usefulness. The Lycée des Arts should prepare for them rewards all the more flattering because they will be bestowed by general esteem alone. [. . .] According to the rules, the professors are to distance themselves absolutely from the Academic aristocracy, banish the sluggish and narrow educational forms prevalent in the private schools, and lead minds to consider the sciences only in their useful relationship to the Arts and Trades.[30]

On April 7, 1793 at Lavoisier's request, Fourcroy, accompanied by four deputies from the Convention, came to preside over the inaugural meeting. All the members of the Public Education Committee were also there. Fourcroy pointed out:

Under the old régime, the men in power patronized the sciences and technical arts for their personal satisfaction and vanity. Now, their justification is the public good. This is surely proof that the Revolution is not harmful to scientific progress, as some of its detractors have tried to make people believe. [. . .] Have we not made advantageous discoveries and kept up our research in astronomy, natural history, mineralogy, chemistry and physics? [. . .] The mechanical and chemical arts, linked to the sciences by practice and theory and rapidly progressing toward perfection, are perhaps of all human occupations, those for which the French Revolution has been most favorable. [. . .] A host of new factories have been created on the outskirts of Paris and in neighboring departments. Their objective is in particular the production of mineral acids, the salts most useful in the technical arts, the bleaching of cloth using Berthollet's method, the preparation of tallow, whale blubber and oils, the breaking down of sea salt for extracting soda, the smoothing of silk, the production of gelatin from bones and flesh of animals, various dressing of hides and bristles, the spinning of cotton and wool, etc.[31]

Without naming Lavoisier, the orator insisted on the new voluntary societies that were contributing to the progress and encouragement of the technical arts: the Commune des Arts, the Point Central des Arts et Métiers, the Society of Inventions and Discoveries, the Advisory Board for Arts and Trades, "created by a beneficial law, uniquely French, that rewards inventors with recompenses whose value is doubled by the fact that they have been judged by their peers."[32]

On May 4 Lavoisier advised the directors of the the Lycée républicain to adapt their teaching to the times and create, as had been done at the Lycée des Arts, courses in economics, agriculture, history, geography and mechanics; and to establish a central society of arts and sciences that would organize public meetings every two or three months. To reassure them about their own future, he declared that if the Lycée des Arts failed, they would have to gather up the pieces and keep afloat everything that could be useful to the advancement of the sciences and technical arts, to the progress of national education, and the prosperity of its establishment."[33]

On May 5 Lavoisier presented at the Lycée des Arts a report co-authored with Fourcroy describing Berthollet's method of bleaching linen with chlorine. Berthollet had not yet received any recompense for his discovery, but the Lycée des Arts, he pointed out, was correcting this oversight by awarding him a civic crown. Its financial state did not permit it to do more because subscribers were few, the profits of the shops and restaurants were meager and the shopkeepers were behind in paying their rents.

The Lycée des Arts also had other responsibilities: a showroom where newly invented machines could be purchased, a credit system for artisans, and the publishing of the *Journal du Lycée des Arts*, which would print more than a hundred fifty reports on useful inventions signed by Fourcroy, Lalande, Lavoisier, Parcieux and Vicq d'Azyr.

On Sunday May 9 before a large audience, Lavoisier presented a résumé of the latest activities of the Academy of Science. A prize had been awarded to Guyton de Morveau for the first two volumes of the *Dictionnaire de chimie, pharmacie and métallurgie* contained in the *Encyclopédie méthodique*. Another award had been given to the younger Duhamel for his report on the exploitation of French coal mines and a third had gone to Charles Gilbert Romme, brother of the Convention deputy and professor of hydrography at Rochefort, for his "Memoir on the Resistance of Fluids."

Four new prizes were announced for 1794 and 1795: 400 livres would be awarded to the person finding a way of reducing the leeway of warships under sail; 2,160 livres were being offered for the most efficient and safest method of cleaning out wells and cesspools; and 3,240 livres would go to the best study on steam engines; the most important prize of 5,000 livres was intended for a pocket watch that could be used for determining longitudes at sea. The dial was to conform to the new decimal system: the day divided into ten hours, the hour into a hundred minutes, and the minute into a hundred seconds.

In the development of nautical chronometers, the French were far behind the English. The one invented by John Harrison, tested during a voyage to Jamaica, had varied only 5 seconds on the outward trip and 5 minutes during the entire journey, which had lasted two months. Harrison had been handsomely rewarded by a prize of 20,000 English pounds. Prudently, the Academy was limiting the competition to French artisans, a decision that Lavoisier contested:

Thus, even in the century of enlightenment and equality, even in the eyes of one of the best learned societies in Europe, there still exists a difference among the men who cover the face of the earth. There still exist national distinctions between scientists and

artisans! No doubt, and it must be believed for the honor of philosophy, citizens natu-
ralized in France, those who have made it their adopted country, are not included in
this ban. But the Academy has not yet clarified this point.[34]

Ferdinand Berthoud would win the prize in a hard fought competition
with Pierre Le Roy and Claude Etienne Janvier; the latter's son, Antide Janvier, was a famous maker of watches with decimal dials.

Lavoisier next took up the recent discoveries: Baumé had found a way of
producing silk as white as that imported from China at great expense; Laplace
had studied the expansion of glass, metals, and fluid for the Commission on
Weights and Measures; Williams, of Philadelphia, had established a law of
variation in the temperature of sea water so precise that it allowed ship cap-
tains to estimate the distance separating them from the coast.

Finally, someone had suggested creating a Savings Bank for the people.
"Up to now, propositions of this kind have almost always hidden financial
speculations," commented Lavoisier, who had remained rather bitter after seeing his plan from the days of the Assemblée de l'Orléanais taken up by speculators. "It was not really to help the poor that they wanted to accumulate
their savings, but rather to convert a part of them into capital for their own
business investments."[35] The new plan, Lavoisier explained, was genuinely directed toward social usefulness: "The industrious artisan can place his savings
more profitably there than elsewhere. For a modest sum, a husband can assure his wife's subsistence. Parents can protect their children from the horrors
of indigence. The public good and mores will surely benefit from it."[36]

As for the comte Jean François de La Pérouse, who had set out to sail
around the world, there had been no news since Jean Baptiste Barthélémy de
Lesseps had brought back his letters describing the Kamschatka Peninsula in
1787. The Minister of Marine Affairs had asked Louis Marie Antoine Milet-
Mureau to gather all notes, reports, letters or observations concerning the
voyage and to prepare them for publication.[37]

On Sunday, July 7 Lavoisier presented a clarification of the work done
on the reform of weights and measures, a "monument erected to the glory
of the French Revolution." He announced the imminent conclusion of the
work, and ended by the prophetic assertion of the durability of the reform:
"Experience has taught," he said, "that these kinds of monuments last longer
than those in marble and bronze."[38]

The Cultural Revolution

Lavoisier had emphasized the outstanding role played by the Academy of Science in the reform because heavy threats were weighing on the institution.

Paris was actually in full cultural revolution. Everybody was contesting the academic science allegedly monopolized by mandarins and proclaiming that modern science should above all be useful to the people. In *La Science sans-culottisée*, Henri Decremps demanded the abolition of Latin, Greek, mathematics, and algebra, which, he said, made science inaccessible to the people. Scientists, he argued, must be treated like nobles: only the "good ones" must be kept, that is, those who are ready to serve political power and devote themselves to social objectives. Jean Paul Marat, greatly frustrated at not having been elected to the Academy of Science, described it ironically in Letter X of *Les charlatans modernes*:

A collection of vain men, very proud to meet twice a week to chatter idly about fleurs-de-lys [the monarchist symbol]; they are like automatons accustomed to following certain formulas and applying them blindly, just like a horse who, in turning a mill, makes a certain number of circles before stopping [. . .] The Academy of Science has met 11,409 times, published 380 eulogies, given 3,956 "approvals" for new processes ranging from concoctions of rouge, hair cream, corn plasters and anti-bug ointments to the most advantageous forms for toupees, wigs, and enema-nozzles for syringes as well as a thousand other subjects of similar importance. It is divided into several classes, each one believing itself to be superior to all the others. In their public and private meetings, these classes unfailingly show each other signs of boredom and disdain. What a pleasure it is to see the mathematicians yawn, cough, spit, and snigger when a chemistry paper is being read, and the chemists snigger, spit, cough, and yawn when a mathematics paper is presented.[39]

In this climate of repudiation of official science, presented as elitist and sterile, the abolition of the academies seemed imminent. Their defenders were forced to act in roundabout ways which were described in 1803 by Jean Baptiste Biot:

The Convention was divided in two parts which, under the same appearances, were moving toward clashing goals. One half, composed of ignorant and ferocious men, dominated by sheer force. The other, more enlightened, defended themselves by their shrewdness. The former, uneasy holders of absolute power, and ready to risk everything to keep it, wanted to crush the talents and learning that made them aware of their humiliating inferiority. The others, although speaking the same language, acted in the opposite sense. They were trying to save the sciences and technical arts by covering them with their enemies' coat. But in order to keep their influence, they were obliged never to expose themselves. They used their means only with the greatest reserve; and this rapprochement explains both the good they did, the evil they prevented, and the misfortunes they were unable to stop.[40]

On June 2, 1793, at the climax of the struggle that had endured for two years, the 267 Montagnards eliminated the 136 Girondins (29 were arrested, the others fled). The former, led by Maximilien de Robespierre, Georges Danton, Jean Paul Marat, and their friends, then became the sole masters of

France. On June 29 they had the Convention adopt the Constitution of the Year 1, which established a crushing pre-eminence of legislative power, the power of the Convention, over executive power.

On July 13 Marat was assassinated by the great-grand niece of Pierre Corneille, Charlotte Corday, who had been manipulated by the Girondins. Condemned to death on July 17 by the Revolutionary Tribunal, she was executed that very day on the Place de la Révolution. Her gesture would have disastrous consequences for the political situation and radicalize the members of the Convention. Not content to have Marat embalmed on July 15, to give him a grandiose funeral the following day, to commission David to paint his portrait, and to organize a veritable cult to his memory, the Jacobin Club demanded a few weeks later, on August 30, that the Reign of Terror be established. Adopted by the Convention on September 5, it went into effect on September 17 with the "loi des suspects." Under it, all partisans of the monarchy or federalism, all émigrés, former nobles, and relatives of émigrés who had not shown their support for the Revolution, all civil servants dismissed by the Convention and those not possessing a "certificate of civic virtue" or unable to justify their means of existence or perform their civic duties were considered "suspect."

Lavoisier, as a member of the National Guard, had been obliged to participate in "Marat's funeral." There he was, with his gun on his shoulder, parading before Marat's half-naked body, which David, the organizer of the ceremony, had dressed in Roman style. What a revenge for the man who had been rejected by the Academy of Science because of Lavoisier to have him pay the last tribute to his dead body! But for Lavoisier it was an occasion to realize that persecution of aristocrats, the wealthy, the émigrés, and a host of others was going to become fanatical.

Bread was in short supply, all foodstuffs were scarce, and taxes were rising. Even the time limit for making tax declarations had been shortened. Thus Lavoisier was in a rush to make an accurate declaration of his property. In addition to the 1,000 hectares of wheat fields in Freschines and the farm at Le Bourget inherited from his father, he now owned to the north of Viller-Cotterêts, the region from which his family had come, more than 800 hectares of land that had been confiscated from the clergy and sold as national property. The purchase, for which Charles Antoine Parisis, his business agent in Villers-Cotterêts, had served as the intermediary, had been made for a total price of 1,228,375 livres ($45.5 million).

The recent acquisitions were spread out over three departments—Aine, Oise, and Seine-et-Oise—and Lavoisier had not yet had the time to visit them. "Therefore," he wrote to Parisis, "would you please make extracts of my assessed income in the registers of each of the parishes where I own property. The law allows only fifteen days for making declarations, hence there is no time to lose."[41]

In the meantime he was not overlooking concerns for everyday life: "I do not know if beans have become as scarce where you are as they are in the Paris area. In the destitute state in which we shall find ourselves this winter as far as food is concerned, it is essential that you send us the beans due to me as rent."[42]

Treasurer of the Royal Academy of Science since 1792, he was continuously asking for funds, with the same energy that he applied to claiming his beans, from Joseph Dominique Garat, Minister of the Interior, from the Treasury Commissioners, and the Committee on Public Education represented by Arbogast and Lakanal.[43]

Through the Committee on Public Education, he had managed to temper somewhat the hostility of the Finance Committee toward the Academicians, whom they regarded as opponents. He had obtained two decrees, one authorizing the Academy to appoint new members to vacant places and the other re-establishing the payment of salaries. He advanced funds for the activities of the Academy from his personal accounts and constantly struggled against vexing police measures. The Minister of the Interior had taken it into his head to ask the Academicians for certificates of residence. On June 12 Lavoisier reminded him that, according to the terms of the law decreed by the Convention, it was to the Academy's treasurer alone that those drawing salaries had to justify their residence. "Allow us to point out to you, Citizen, that the only thing that the Minister of the Interior appears to have the right to require in this matter, is that the department certify that none of the Academicians included on the payroll of the Academy figures among the émigrés."[44]

The Academicians multiplied their demonstrations of civic virtue. They studied means of preserving biscuits and vegetables at sea, a new model for a cannon and cannonballs, the possibility of setting up a row of cannons on the same carriage. And they gave patriotic gifts—a sum of 11,845 livres and a gold ingot worth 12,000 livres. They even asked that the tapestries decorating the meeting hall be removed because they presented "attributes that ought to be banished from a republican government."

To illustrate the social usefulness of the Academy, Lavoisier, backed by Félix Vicq d'Azyr, proposed to Joseph Lakanal that it absorb the Society of Medicine. "Since medicine can strictly speaking be considered neither an applied art nor a purely speculative science, why not create a Bureau de consultation pour les régles de Salubrité (Advisory Board of Health)?"[45]

This board, composed of thirty-six members—twenty-four generalists and twelve surgeons—would include the members of the Academy in the classes of anatomy, chemistry, natural history, and botany. The group would meet twice weekly at the Academy, maintain a regular correspondence with departmental health officers, and combat endemic and epizootic diseases.[46]

In July 1793, under the title "Summary of the Work of the Academy of Science," Lavoisier wrote a report that appeared without his name. He summarized the work done by the Academy for the creation of the metric system and emphasized that the results were there to see, the units already defined. The linear unit of measure was the mètre, which equaled 0,513243 toise of the Academy. The unit of surface was the are; the unit of capacity the pinte, a thousandth part of the barrel or cubic palme; and the unit of weight was the grave, the equivalent of 2 pounds, 5 gros, and 49 grains of the marc's weight.

Thus from this time forward the national Convention can pass on to the French nation and to people throughout the world, the inestimable benefit of universal units of measurement and rely on the zeal Academy to carry this great work to the highest degree of perfection possible.[47]

Lavoisier's efforts on behalf of the Academy had not been fruitless. On August 1 the Convention renewed its vote of confidence in the Academy and adopted the temporary system of standardization of measures based on the mètre, are, pinte, and grave. It also made it responsible for overseeing the execution of the decree and consulted it on the standard of gold and silver coins. Nevertheless, disturbing incidents were becoming more frequent and the situation grew so precarious that even the title of Academician became an insult and those who held it did not dare to call themselves anything other than artisans. Vandermonde was arrested and accused of corruption in furnishing supplies to the army. Lavoisier, Lagrange, Borda, and Haüy immediately wrote to the Committee on Public Education to request his liberation.[48] Monge and Berthollet supported them. The referees, Romme and Fourcroy, lent a sympathetic ear to their colleagues and Vandermonde was freed three days later. To avoid the repetition of such incidents, Lavoisier tried to obtain for those Academicians responsible for weights and measures the status of "Convention representatives," since they were under its orders. He did not succeed, but for twelve of them he managed to get safe-conducts that he asked the Convention to stamp "so that they can be recognized as such."[49]

But the animosity toward the academies remained just as sharp. The Convention asked for a report from the Committee on Public Education. The Abbé Grégoire wrote it, making every effort to save the Academy of Science and his friend Lavoisier, who had become increasingly worried by the passionate tone of the debate. "We are in a position," he said," where it is just as dangerous to do something as to do nothing."[50] Finally, the two men agreed on a plan for a decree of seven articles that would save the essential roles of the academies. The first article proclaimed that "all academies and literary societies licensed and endowed by the nation are abolished." But the following ones attenuated its severity. The Academy of Science was to remain temporarily in charge of the work given to it by the Convention. It would continue to enjoy its attributions. In the meantime, the Committee on Public Education would present a plan for a new society destined for the advancement of the arts and applied science. Moreover, citizens would retain the right to meet in voluntary societies so as to contribute to the progress of knowledge. The scenario had been well set up and Grégoire thought that he would be able to placate the relentless adversaries of the Academy while creating a new institution that would fulfill the same functions. He explained:

To preserve both men and things, we had to appear to give in to circumstances and ourselves propose the abolition of all the academies except for those of Science and Surgery and the Societies of Medicine and Agriculture. The others were ordered to present policy plans more in line with the principles of liberty and which, consequently would sully neither the title of protector—since it is the law alone that should protect—nor honorary titles, since it is the man and not the place that must count in societies. I spoke with Lavoisier about this plan and he approved it.[51]

The Abolition of the Academies

On August 8 the abbé Grégoire presented to the Convention an indictment of the most reactionary aspects of the academies, in order to defend what he judged to be the essential and, in an allusive way, his friend Lavoisier:

The Academy of Science, which has always been made up of the most outstanding Europeans, has described more than four hundred machines and published one hundred thirty volume which are among the most noble monuments to the human mind. It continues with admirable activity the work you have given it on the silver of the abolished churches, the assay of gold and silver coins, the production of saltpeter and the measurement of a degree of the meridian, research that needs still another year to be completed. You have just adopted its work on weights and measures. It is presently involved in the production of new standards and the adaptation of the new measures to those which until now have been used in the various regions of France. We do not reproach those Academicians dedicated to the cultivation of science for their esprit de corps, which is to societies what egoism is to individuals. We would be dishonored if our scientists were reduced to carrying their talents and our shame to foreign shores. Note that all the technical arts, all the sciences are interconnected, from the branch to Kepler's astronomical rules, to the most abstract depths of calculation and physical astronomy by which our scientists have enlarged the mass of knowledge that we owe to Newton's genius, to the most sublime chemical research, because it was again the Academy of Science that regenerated chemistry and presented to an astonished Europe the only theory that has been supported by nature.[52]

But, speaking just after Grégoire, David made a fanatical attack on the Academy of Painting and Sculpture, with which he had an old score to settle, and for good measure he condemned them all.

Let them be closed forever, these schools of flattery and servility. [. . .] If you speak of one Academy, you speak of them all. The same spirit, the same men are found in all of them. [. . .] In the name of humanity and justice, for the love of art, and especially for your love of youth, let us destroy, annihilate, these pernicious academies. They can no longer exist in a free regime. As an Academician I have done my duty. Now it is up to you to give your verdict! [53]

In a few sentences, David simply swept away Grégoire's reasonable propositions and obtained the abolition of all academies and learned societies. "Having been unable to convince the Convention to preserve certain societies, in particular the Academy of Science," Grégoire wrote," we foresaw that persecution would be directed against the scientists in a painful future."[54]

The Lycée des Arts remained the last chance. On Sunday August 11 Lavoisier met his colleagues there, and, with his customary stubbornness, he attempted to muster energies:

During this deplorable interval that is going to exist between the period of important work done by learned societies and the time when the links with it, once completely cut, can be retied, this establishment acquires new interest and merits a more favorable attention since it has become the main meeting place of those famous men whose long years of research, service, and experience can never go unrecognized and whose usefulness it is all the easier to appreciate when we contemplate their small number, not only in France, but in the entire world.[55]

Since the law forbade it, the Academy could no longer meet, but its members could come together in a "voluntary and open society for the advancement of science." This is the way the work of Vicq d'Azyr on anatomy, the publication of René Louis Desfontaines's voyage, the printing of Desmarest's mineralogical maps, the work in chemistry of Fourcroy, Sage, and Berthollet, and the standardization of weights and measures would be carried out. Furthermore, numerous artisans charged with making machines, scales, standards, and platinum rulers would set to work and earn a living. Henceforth Lavoisier's efforts would be concentrated in this direction. He would be constantly boosting friends and pleading their causes to the political authorities.

It was once again Lakanal who, bypassing the Committee on Public Education, wrested from the Convention on August 14 a decree allowing Academicians to meet and receive their salaries:

The task I gave myself for the cause of the Academy of Science was very difficult. First, because the Academy had been abolished, and then the Finance Committee, made up, it must be said, of decent citizens, was inflexible when I asked for funds for the scientists, the Academicians. What rebuffs I suffered! The opinion had been spread that Academicians were all opposed to the new order of things and unfortunately there was some truth in this supposition.[56]

Three days later, Lavoisier, who had convoked his colleagues to meet at the Academy found the door closed. Between 5 and 9 in the morning seals had been placed on all the rooms. The reason was that, in the interval, still another decree had been issued. David and Romme had personally overseen its execution. Patiently, Lavoisier asked the Committee on Public Education to arbitrate: "The time has come, Citizen Representatives, for the Convention to bring a halt to this uncertainty that leaves the sciences in a state of stagnation and holds up important work that the Convention itself has the greatest interest in seeing completed."[57]

The Temporary Commission on Weights and Measures

It was true that the Convention was impatient to see the weights and measures project finished. To get out of the deadlock, Fourcroy proposed appointing a new committee of Academicians. Lakanal opposed the idea since the decree of August 14 had confirmed the mission of the scientists of the Academy and nothing guaranteed that the same ones would be reappointed. The discussions continued for several days. Finally, on September 9 Lavoisier and Fourcroy managed to get the Convention to accept a "Temporary Commission on Weights and Measures" composed of twelve members: ten came from the Academy and were already involved in the project. They were Lavoisier, Borda, Haüy, Coulomb, Berthollet, Delambre, and Monge. Fourcroy and Arbogast represented the Committee on Public Education of the Convention.[58]

Lavoisier was elected treasurer at the first meeting. The various procedures, letters, interventions, and conversations were multiplied during these days of crisis. Lavoisier and Fourcroy met almost constantly. Even if their political convictions separated them, they remained linked by their long scientific collaboration. Numerous written traces witness to their friendly cooperation, in particular in the choice of the new premises of the commission. Lavoisier selected the rooms in the old Louvre that had been used by the Academy of Architecture, the Academy of Inscriptions and the Académie française. The working sessions were to take place on the second, fifth and eighth day of each decade at very precisely 7 decimal hours, "that is, according to the old clock, at 48 minutes past four in the afternoon."

He tried to cope with every emergency: the "grave" standard for the Currency Committee, the new experiments on the fusion of platinum, the accounts of the Commission on Weights and Measures, a report on the Academy of Science requested by Fourcroy, a convocation of the Advisory Board for Arts and Trades, the financial difficulties of the Lycée. For this last problem, he and Silvestre decided to approach the Committee on Public Education. But times had certainly changed. Not only did they obtain nothing, but Fourcroy was very severe: "The stability of the Lycée," he said, "no longer depends on its finances but rather on its regeneration. Unless it is profoundly overhauled and renewed, it is on the brink of being destroyed by the very persons from whom it expects help."[59]

Fourcroy insisted on a purge to get rid of the counter-revolutionaries, the emigrés, and all those whom public opinion rejected. But, on the other hand, he said, those who "by their civic virtues, by their love of the sciences and applied arts, by their zeal for the interests of this institution have seemed worthy of being called to make up the Lycée républicain a new and regenerated institution," would be protected.[60] Regenerating institutions and reforming public education were certainly objectives capable of mobilizing Lavoisier.

Reflections on Public Education

From the first days of the Revolution, Lavoisier had participated in the debate on public education. His experience in training chemists, saltpeter men and gunpowder technicians, as well as agents for the General Farm and tobacco manufacturers, had developed his pedagogical ideas and the courses at the Lycée des Arts gave him the opportunity to put them into practice. Certain of them were his own, many had come from Condillac, his intellectual mentor. Also, Talleyrand and Condorcet had become his contemporary guides. Lavoisier's ideas on teaching and education were impregnated with the spirit of the Enlightenment and left no room for religion. Did he become anticlerical at the Collège Mazarin, or later in the clubs? It is difficult to say.

Under the old régime, France had numerous universities, hundreds of secondary schools, and thousands of elementary schools set up by both private initiative and local religious authorities. But public opinion, the clergy, and teachers had long been urging reforms that actually had more to do with an outlook than a reorganization. "In 1789, education was no doubt vicious, but it was organized."[61]

The initial reforms of the Constituent Assembly led to the rapid disintegration of the system: the abolition of privileges, feudal rights, and tithes reduced the resources of the schools. Then the confiscation and subsequent sale of clerical property had resulted in the disappearance of numerous educational premises. Soon afterward were added difficulties with personnel: the abolition of religious orders, the civil constitution of the clergy, the obligatory oath of loyalty and the law on non-juring priests eliminated a great number of teachers.

Shortly before the Constituent Assembly had adjourned, Talleyrand had presented his "Report on Public Education," in which he wrote that to improve the mediocre teaching in traditional schools, a new educational system would be necessary. Education should be open to all and universal, and the individual should be able to study whatever he wished. The freedom to teach was not to be the exclusive privilege of any one class. Nevertheless he felt that the teaching profession should remain subject to the king's authority as represented by commissioners and inspectors, a proposal that led to violent criticism and the eventual rejection of the plan.

On September 3, 1792, the Constituent Assembly had decided to organize "a system of public education available to all citizens, free as to choice of subjects indispensable to all men, and whose establishment would be distributed gradually according to the divisions of the kingdom."[62]

A month later, almost immediately after being elected, the Legislative Assembly had created a Committee on Public Education that had asked Talleyrand to publish his report. For the first text he had called on Laplace, Monge, Condorcet, Vicq d'Azyr, and La Harpe for advice. Before submitting the second version, he asked Lavoisier to give his criticism within eight days: "I would be most grateful if you would show great severity and tell me frankly what you find displeasing in this lengthy work."[63]

Lavoisier, punctilious as always, had immediately sent Talleyrand a long text criticizing the clerical educational system.[64] "Education, as it exists in almost all of Europe," he wrote, "was set up not to produce citizens, but priests, monks, and theologians. The spirit of the Church has always loathed any innovation, and because the first Christians spoke and prayed in Latin, because most of the Church Fathers wrote in Latin, it was concluded that regardless of the country, or changes that might occur in the vernacular of that country, it was necessary to pray in Latin until the end of time. The result has been that the entire European educational system finds itself entirely focused on teaching Latin."[65]

The only disciplines taught, he continued, were metaphysics, moral philosophy, and theology:

This is how everything that might tend to destroy errors and prejudices was kept in the hands of those who had an interest in propagating them. This epoch, consisting of sixteen centuries, has been almost entirely lost for reason and philosophy. The progress of the human mind has been entirely suspended and, often, there have even been regressions. It will be forever a blot on the history of humanity and it forces us to consider just how great those who have overturned these antique monuments of ignorance and barbarism will be in the eyes of posterity.[66]

Lavoisier recommended the establishment of a simplified and practical educational system. The purpose of both rural and urban elementary schools would be to form men and citizens. The district schools were to produce literate citizens. Reading and writing would not be obligatory in rural areas, but, on the other hand, children should be taught how to count. The school terms would last no longer than six months, each would deal with only one subject at a time so that "the chain of ideas that make up science is never broken or interrupted."[67]

The recruitment and training of teachers would be slow and difficult, he predicted, because in France pedagogy was still in its infancy and the logic of sciences little known. The only good elementary courses still existing were in the mathematical sciences. Thus it was essential to create an institute in the capital that would be responsible for supervising public education. It would print pedagogical works and arrange competitive examinations for teachers. In the beginning the supply of candidates would be inferior to the demand, but this situation would quickly be corrected "because one of the laws of nature is that where there are public functions to be filled, people emerge to exercise them."[68]

The professors would receive a modest salary, plus a bonus based on the number of regular pupils. Anyone "who does not have the support of public opinion, will find his classroom empty. All teachers will want to please, whether through their choice of subject matter or through its presentation."[69]

In this case, Lavoisier was applying to education the liberal ideas of the

Physiocrats, persuaded that "even without close attention and supervision, the flaws of the new system will correct themselves as long as administrators let things run their course."[70]

In the end, Talleyrand used none of Lavoisier's comments and his second report was identical to the first. The beginning of his long career as a diplomat had distracted him from the subject. But other people in Paris continued to study the problem. During 1791 Condorcet published five papers on the subject. Elected president of the Committee on Public Education, he had presented his "Report on the General Organization of Public Education" to the Assembly on April 20, 1792.[71] Individual talents are unequal, he admitted, but men have equal rights and the role of public education is to restore equality of opportunity. It must form responsible citizens, capable not simply of admiring completed legislation, but of judging and correcting it. Education should be as equal, universal, and complete as possible. All men can then provide for their needs, assure their natural well-being, know and exercise their rights, and fulfill their duties.

Condorcet proposed a dual education system. Alongside the private schools there would be public ones, including elementary and secondary schools, instituts, and lycées, which would be free and accessible to all.

Elementary schools (31,000) would be opened for boys and girls from the ages of six to eleven in each village of four hundred inhabitants. Every Sunday, the teacher would explain to them the Constitution and the Declaration of The Rights of Man and of The Citizen, not as heaven sent tablets to be worshipped, but as fruits of human reason.

Secondary schools (500) would be created in the towns with more than 4,000 inhabitants. They would introduce the pupils to mathematics, natural history, chemistry as applied to the technical arts and courses in moral philosophy and the social sciences.

On the departmental level, 114 instituts would offer a still more complete education. They would enroll 80,000 male students from 15 to 18 years old for a four-year program. Nothing was planned for girls at this level.

Finally, 9 Lycées in the major towns of France would train the teachers.

A National Society of Arts and Sciences, at the summit of the structure, would supervise and direct general education, improve teaching methods, encourage useful discoveries, and keep up a regular correspondence with learned societies in foreign countries. This autonomous assembly of scholars would replace the academies, and its members would be divided into four sections: mathematics and the physical sciences; the moral and political sciences; the applied sciences; literature and the fine arts.

This education would be free, secular and apolitical. No religious teaching could be acceptable within the framework of public education. "Each religion must be taught in its places of worship by its own ministers."[72]

The rule was to apply to political opinion as well. "Since the first condition of all education is to teach only truths, the schools that public authorities provide for the purpose must be as independent as possible from all political authority."[73]

Condorcet, convinced that knowledge could transform society, had radicalized Talleyrand's plan. The free education implicit in the latter, was explicitly proclaimed at all levels. Equality was demanded as society's end, and education was declared to be the means for achieving it. The teacher's independence was to be absolute, his role was not to teach "a new catechism for children," a dogma, but to form free citizens.

On April 20, 1792 the day on which he presented his plan for reorganizing public education, a political event stole the show from Condorcet. Louis XVI had just announced to the Assembly the declaration of war on Austria. Presented rapidly and incompletely amid general distraction, the plan was neither discussed nor adopted. The Assembly simply had it printed.

In the days that followed, other plans were successively proposed by Lakanal, the Abbé Sieyès, and Pierre Claude François Daunou. All of them were rejected as being hierarchical and elitist. "We are still being asked to believe," Pierre Joseph Cambon shouted, "that the only way to make a good shoe is in an academy with a compass in hand, but the only place to make shoes is in a cobbler's shop."[74]

At the Lycée des Arts and at the Advisory Board for Arts and Trades, Lavoisier was taking more interest in the special problem of technical training for artisans. He agreed with Hassenfratz, who felt that the most "essential part of public education, its potential contribution to national industry through special training in the Arts and Trades," was being neglected. He protested:

This useful education is being replaced by celebrations [. . .] But even though we are a trading, manufacturing, and agricultural people, we are surrounded by industrious populations. We must beware that our neighbors organize their industry more efficiently and destroy our factories and trade while we are busy organizing celebrations. It is not with celebrations that the English have managed to acquire a great supremacy in the political equilibrium of Europe. It is not with celebrations that the United States of America have become a flourishing nation. It is by giving their industry all the development it can possibly absorb.[75]

The "Petition on Public Education" sent by Lavoisier to the Convention on July 7, 1793 on behalf of the Lycée des Arts, proposed joining elementary education with a technical training adapted to the needs of farmers, artisans, and manufacturers. It would then be possible, he said, to give a new boost to national industry, to invigorate trade, and to permit France to compete with its neighbors and become the wealthiest country in Europe. To accomplish this, France had to produce goods at competitive prices. "Now, we can achieve the same production at lower costs by improving the applied science, technical skills, and agriculture and by developing the physical and moral qualities of workers, farmers, and artisans."[76] Professional training would be easy to organize. In the districts, 2,500 technical training schools for adults could be set up. Practical courses for artisans, workers, and farmers could be given in the evenings and in particular on holidays and Sundays. The first professors for these schools would be trained by the Lycée des Arts.

The petition was well received by the president of the Convention, Jean Bon de Saint-André. Even David spoke up for the idea during the session of Saturday, July 13, 1793. At his request, the petition was passed on to the Committee on Public Education to be added to the general report.

The Advisory Board for Arts and Trades also claimed a special competence in the matter. Placed between the sciences and the applied science, it could understand how discoveries were made and how they were spread. Having reflected on what could contribute to the applied science and to the perfection of human mind, the members expressed surprise that "in all the plans presented for the establishment of a national public education system, the applied science seem to have been entirely overlooked.[77]

They appointed a committee to develop a plan for the education of artisans. It included Lavoisier, Desaudray, Hassenfratz, Fourcroy, and Borda who hastily drew up a paper on Public Education for Artisans: "In its reflections, the Advisory Board intends to pursue only one aspect of public education, the one relating to the practical arts. It leaves to others the task of convincing the Convention of the importance of literature and the fine arts."[78]

A hundred copies of the brochure were printed by Du Pont de Nemours and kept ready for distribution. But on July 13, 1793 Robespierre personally defended a Spartan plan for education developed by Michel Le Peletier de Saint-Fargeau. It foresaw placing all children from six to twelve years of age in Maisons d'égalité, for a free and compulsory education. The program was simple. The children were to be "taught to read, write, count, and measure. They are also to be instructed in moral principles, given a summary knowledge of the Constitution, and basic ideas of domestic and rural economics. Their memory is to be developed by engraving it with the most beautiful features of free peoples and the French Revolution. This then is the essential for every citizen, the education due to all."[79]

Agricultural work would complete the program. If a Maison d'égalité did not have enough land for cultivation, the children would be taken on the roads to spread gravel. Hoping to combat this extreme plan as well as to revive the one for substituting a National Society of the Arts for the Academy of Science, then on the eve of its disappearance, Lavoisier had the idea of enlarging the scope of his two texts on technical education and making a general proposal for public instruction. Bearing the stamp of several of its predecessors, the new text was entitled "Reflections on Public Education."[80] Lavoisier borrowed from Condillac the psychological data on how knowledge is acquired and then derived his own pedagogical method.

Man is born with senses and faculties, but with no ideas. His brain is a tabula rasa that has received no impressions, but is prepared to receive them. These impressions, communicated to him by the senses, are called sensations. But although all our ideas reach us exclusively by the senses, it is by the exercise of our faculties that we learn to know the properties of bodies surrounding us. The result is that the newly born child is obliged to learn to do everything with the help of his senses. It is a true course in physical knowledge. This formation of children's first ideas is something worthy of philosophers' meditation. An attentive observation leaves no doubt that the child learns about the properties of bodies by passing from the known to the unknown, by following a successive method that resembles the one used by geometers. In this series of experiments, he has no need for expensive instruments. The instruments he uses are simply all the bodies surrounding him.[81]

From the moment of his birth, Lavoisier explained, a child discovers optics and perspective. The child learns to estimate distances, the effects of weight and falling bodies. Then comes mechanics. The stick becomes a lever, the ball bounces, the channel dug along a stream teaches the laws of the equilibrium of fluids. The child learns to work with wood using the hammer, nail, knife, axe, and saw. Similarly he becomes familiar with the tools of the blacksmith and locksmith. The knowledge of plants, flowers, fruits, seeds, soils, and fertilizers, easily acquired in the country, leads to agriculture.

At the age of six, according to Lavoisier's plan, the children would attend an elementary school, free and open to all regardless of social class. There they would be taught to read, write, and count and be exposed to some natural history, historical tales, and examples of patriotism and charity. Subsequently, the boys would learn to use the ruler and compass, to measure surfaces and survey fields, to estimate solids. The notions of length, width, and depth would then easily lead up to the concepts of surface and volume in practical geometry. The study of thermometry, the observation of the mercury column of the barometer would teach the bases of experimental physics.

When by exercising their senses children have acquired a sufficient sum of ideas and knowledge, they can then be taught the elementary principles of moral philosophy.

Their teachers will explain to them the rights and duties of man, the end he sets for himself in society; how property is established and transmitted. They will be given, as much as possible, some notions of trade and how to set up a business or other operation, and how to keep accounts.[82]

Concerning the education of girls, one can imagine that Lavoisier did not consult his wife; she would probably not have approved of the program reserved to them:

They will learn the arts that they have been exclusively destined to exercise; they will be taught everything concerning needlework, spinning, and knitting. They will be instructed in food preparation, household management, caring for the sick, and the physical education of children. The principles of moral philosophy will also be developed for them and they will be given some notions of history and local geography. In a word, they will be given the basic principles of what makes up the beautiful in the arts of taste and the basic amenities of life.[83]

At the age of eleven, the children would go to schools of arts and applied science, technical schools that could be established by citizens in the principal towns of the districts. Two choices would then be open to them. One course, leading toward public service, would be focused on the study of languages and literature. The other, leading to jobs in applied science, was, Lavoisier pointed out, the special concern of the Advisory Board. All arts needed draftsmen and that would be the first common training. Mechanical arts would be differentiated from chemical ones. The former, using machines, would rely on theoretical mechanics and graphic geometry: the use of the ruler and compass and the measurement of surfaces would lead to rules of perspective, essential for stonecarving and carpentry. For the chemical arts, one would progress from the description of natural substances to their different reactions: combustions, decombustions, dissolutions, crystallizations, precipitations, and fermentations.

The third level would be that of the Instituts nationaux, or Schools of Arts and Applied Science, established in the principal departmental towns. There would be five in Paris, two each in Bordeaux and Lyon, and one in each of the others. They would offer four major disciplines: languages, literature and fine arts; moral and political sciences; mathematics, physics and chemistry; and applied science, with particular reference to medicine, surgery, obstetrics, pharmacy, hygiene, and agriculture. Each one would be endowed with a library and laboratories with instruments and materials for studying physics, astronomy, and natural history. There would be models of various machines, and both botanical and agricultural gardens. The directors of these institutions would regularly hold public meetings where papers on the most recent discoveries could be read.

In the twelve most important towns in France, national universities would be created. The one in Paris would be divided into six institutions. At the Bibliothèque Nationale, one would study ancient and modern languages, literature and the art of thinking, reasoning and writing; at the Louvre, the fine arts; at the Collège Mazarin, mathematics, physics, chemistry, metallurgy and geometry; at the National Observatory, astronomy; at the Jardin des Plantes, natural history, botany and mineralogy; at the School of Surgery, human and veterinary medicine, anatomy, obstetrics, materia medica, and pharmacy.

Finally, four "National Societies for the Advancement of the Sciences and the Arts and for the Improvement of the Human Mind" would teach the physical sciences and mathematics, applied science, moral and political sciences, and literature and fine arts. Although similar to those imagined by Condorcet, they were no longer to be brought together in a unique structure responsible for supervising all of national education. There were two reasons for this. One was the repeated rejection of whatever was considered to be an elitist central structure and the other was Lavoisier's desire to use them as substitutes for the threatened academies.

During several working sessions, the plan was revised, and in the end it differed from the one written by Condorcet only by the greater place allocated to technical training. More than a borrowing, the proposed plan was a tribute to Condorcet who, under arrest since July 8 for complicity with the Girondins, was being hidden by Madame Vernet and could no longer express himself.

But the economic ideas that were found in the conclusion were certainly Lavoisier's:

We must organize public education in all its aspects, and hence stimulate the arts, sciences, industry, and trade. Just consider the way all nations, our rivals, seek ways to compensate for what is lacking to them in strength, population, and territorial wealth! A nation that does not participate in this general evolution, a nation in which science and applied science remain stagnant will soon be completely outstripped by its competitors. It will gradually lose all its means of competing. Its trade, strength, and wealth will fall into foreign hands and it will become prey to whoever wants to invade it.[84]

Lavoisier, Fourcroy, and Borda, in full agreement, decided to submit the plan to the Convention on Sunday, September 22. The next day three handwritten copies were hurriedly sent to the president. In the meantime Du Pont printed 2,000 copies destined for the members of the Convention, the 48 sections of the Commune de Paris, the 83 departments, and the Lycée des Arts.

But they were not sent. On October 17 the Convention passed the "Law of Suspects" which began the Reign of Terror. Lavoisier decided to wait for a more opportune time. He did receive some encouragement however from the Committee on Public Education, which awarded him with an "honorable mention," and from the society of the "Point central des Arts et Métiers," which promised its support.

On November 4 the Advisory Board was still awaiting favorable circumstances. Lavoisier had only three more weeks of freedom. It was the commencement of a dark period whose excesses Fourcroy would later denounce:

To block incessantly by frivolous objections the plans for education proposed within these walls, to present an educational plan that was unworkable in the circumstances in which the Republic found itself, with the result that there was no education at all, and at the same time to destroy all public establishments without replacing them; in a word, to annihilate everything and everyone useful to education, this is a rough sketch of the vast plot hatched with the most dangerous and perfidious skill by out and out conspirators.[85]

France would have to wait for two more years and the Daunou law of 3 brumaire An IV (October 1795) before it had a general law for public education.

18

The Arrest

The Rendering of the Farm's Accounts

B UT THE THREAD OF DESTINY became more tangled: the General Farm had not been forgotten. Lavoisier had resigned from his office shortly before its abolition in June 1791. But as a former shareholder he was collectively responsible for the actions of his five colleagues, Laâge, Puissant, Couturier, La Perrière, and Delahante, who were in charge of liquidating the Farm's accounts. They argued that they had still not received the definitive records from the tax collectors, but were selling the stocks of salt and tobacco in the warehouses of the Farm and settling litigation connected with the abolition of the tollgates around Paris. Roederer had charged that they were trying to prolong the situation: "By immediately suppressing the warehouses," he said, "you will deny the General Farms all pretext for delay in rendering its accounts. As long as the warehouses remain, the warehousemen will want to perpetuate their existence."[1]

The Farmers were also having to deal with disgruntled former employees who had received no redundancy payments and hence had brought a series of legal actions against them.[2] "Of the 25,000 to 30,000 claims for pensions or assistance, there are still only 7,000 that have been settled," wrote Clavière, "and of the 3,500 pensions granted, no more than 330 have been liquidated. What remains to be done is overwhelming, especially when one thinks of the growing impatience intensified by anxiety and all the complaints embittered by need."[3]

Former officers at the Paris tollgates were also denouncing the management of their pension fund. They accused the Farm of having misappropriated 3 million livres of contributions that had not been returned to them, and offered to share the money, once retrieved, with the State.[4]

The Farmers replied with a justificatory memoir, prompting still another pamphlet from the employees: "Ah! If it were possible to leaf through the ledgers turned over to the government by the Farm, what heretofore unknown mysteries would be revealed! Beware, all you who have bled the poor and deceived the best of kings."[5]

Clerks, tobacco graters, invalids, coal transporters, a horde of former wage earners attacked the Farmers, accusing them of obstructing the investigation: "Our adversaries are afraid to have their documents seen and they categorically refuse to turn them over to us. These papers are all the more interesting since they would bring in millions to the National Treasury."[6]

The decisions of the courts were invariably favorable to the plaintiffs and a sum of almost 20 million livres had already been awarded. The Convention began to worry. It definitely wanted for its own funds the 300 to 400 million livres that were supposedly in the coffers of the Farm. As early as December 31, 1792 Clavière had expressed surprise that eighteen months after the abolition of the General Farm, the liquidation committee had not completed its work. The Committee on Public Safety decided to hand the matter over to the Finance Committee.

On February 25, 1793 Jean Louis Carra, deputy from Saône-et-Loire and founder with Mercier of the *Annales Patriotiques*, demanded the creation of a special justice committee to investigate the crimes and abuses perpetrated by the General Farm since 1740, and to examine all contracts signed with the king, determine the legitimacy of its profits, and order restitution if necessary: "Legislators, there is no time to lose," Carra shouted passionately, "all those plunderers of public monies, those leeches of the people, those execrable speculators are going to rush to sell their property in France and take flight, carrying to your enemies the rest of the public fortune if you yourselves do not make haste to stop them."[7]

But his speech had no immediate follow-up. The struggle between the Montagnards and the Girondins dominated the scene, and temporarily relegated the Farmers General to the background. Before long, however, the subject of the liquidation of the General Farm's accounts cropped up again. The Farmers, increasingly uneasy, met with an attorney at their former headquarters on the rue de Grenelle Saint-Honoré. "We discussed the state of affairs," Etienne Marie Delahante wrote, "and there was no hiding the fact that it was very critical. We decided to choose ten or twelve of our group to follow the matter closely from day to day, and we immediately nominated them."[8]

At the end of May, they formed a deputation to explain their case to Clavière, the minister of finance, who, suspect as a Girondin, was scarcely in a position to help them. "When we arrived at the minister's office," wrote Delahante, "he sent a message saying that he would see us right away, but we had to wait quite a long time. And then when he finally did appear, he was flanked by two men, each carrying a bare sword, who never left his side."[9]

In fact, on June 2, impelled by the sans-culottes, the Convention voted to arrest the twenty-nine Girondist deputies and the ministers, Clavière and Lebrun. Maximilien de Robespierre recorded in his notebook: "The present uprising has to continue until the measures necessary for saving the Republic have been taken. The people must unite with the Convention, which must use them. The sans-culottes should be given arms and their anger incited; we have to light their way. Their republican enthusiasm must be fired by every possible means."[10]

On June 5, before the *Comité de Comptabilité* (Accounting Committee) of the Convention, Louis Marie Bon de Montaut, deputy from Gers, accused the Farmers in charge of liquidating the accounts of stalling tactics .

On September 5 the sans-culottes invaded the Convention. Under their pressure, the Reign of Terror was made the order of the day, and it was decreed that all personal papers belonging to former Farmers General and bankers be placed under seal. The Convention ordered the dissolution of the group of liquidators, the transfer of all available funds to the Public Treasury, and the affixing of seals "on all their offices and papers collected at the headquarters of the Farm as well as on papers they may have in their homes."[11]

On September 10 two commissaires from the Piques section, Bernard Datègre and Bonaventure Dussard, went to no. 243 boulevard de la Madeleine to search Lavoisier's personal papers. Romme and Foucroy, representing the Committee on Public Education, accompanied them to recover instruments used for the weights and measures project. They found nothing suspicious except a packet of letters in English from Franklin, Priestley, Black, and Wedgwood and a letter in Italian from Spallanzani. The letters were seized to be sent to the Committee on Public Education.[12] Fearing that a malicious hand might add compromising documents, Lavoisier asked to apply his personal seal "so that the package containing the aforementioned correspondence can be opened only by the committee. It is not from distrust that he requests this precaution, but from a sense of order."[13] As a result of the action of the Convention, 20 million livres in assignats and 9,000 livres in cash were taken from the headquarters of the Farm before seals were affixed.

Despairing over the political and financial situation, Lavoisier decided to devote all his time to the sciences and to revising the *Elements of Chemistry*, going back over his and his colleagues' work. He would not have had the time a few months earlier: "Then it was still possible to hope to be useful in administrative circles," he wrote to his English translator Robert Kerr, "but now that France is racked by conflicts, it has become extremely difficult to do any good, and you have to be either very ambitious or completely crazy to aspire to high positions."[14]

In September 1793, while Lavoisier with Fourcroy's help was installing the Temporary Commission on Weights and Measures and preparing his plan for public education, the position of the Farmers General became critical. The Farm's accounts were still unsettled. The files were no longer accessible and the liquidation committee had been abolished. On September 24, through Nicolas Delamare, a member of the Finance Committee, the Farmers asked the Convention to release their papers and promised to present the totality of the accounts before April 1, 1794. The proposition was accepted. But as their spokesman was coming down from the platform, another member of the Finance Committee was moving up to it. Antoine Dupin, deputy from Aisne and former supernumerary controller at the General Farm, began to speak, claiming to know all about the misappropriation of funds by the Farmers and insisting that their accounts be checked by five independent auditors, supervised by two members of the Convention. Caught off guard, Delamare could only register his protest and "the sires Gaudot, de Vernon, Jacquart, Mathey, and de Châteauneuf were appointed to verify the accounts and administration of the former Farmers General. MM. Dupin and Jac, members of the Convention, were appointed to supervise the auditors and assist them in their task."[15]

Even though Dupin's motion was perfectly legitimate, his rancor against his former employers no doubt played a part in it. A friend of Bertrand Barère de Vieuzac, Georges Couthon, and Pierre Lebas, he was well known in Paris for the luxurious and refined parties he hosted in his splendid mansion, accompanied by his mistress, Madame de Bonnefoi. He was going to play a determining role in the trial of the Farmers General. His associate, Jac, a deputy from Gard, was only a minor figure. The five auditors were also former employees of the Farm. Gaudot had been a tollgate official at the Port Saint-Paul. "He had talent, but he was still better known for his lack of scruples and his nastiness."[16] Condemned and imprisoned in 1789 for taking 500,000 livres from the cash-box of the Farm and falsifying the books, he had escaped prison on August 10, 1792 by presenting himself as a patriot and victim of the Farmers General. Vernon, former director of the salt and tobacco taxes in Paris, had always been well treated at the Farm, but Gaudot bribed him. Jacquart and Mathey, rather ordinary types, had been chief clerks. Guillaume, called Châteauneuf, had been deputy chief clerk in the Correspondence Office. Their task was to examine all the accounts concerning the Laurent David, Salzard, and Mager leases, to denounce any abuses found, and to furnish proof of embezzlement. Their work was to be submitted to the Accounting Office, and their bonuses would be proportional to the sums they would bring to the coffers of the State.[17]

On September 28 the Convention authorized removing the seals from the Farmers' personal papers and Lavoisier received a "certificate of civic virtue" from Baillie, secretary-clerk of the Piques section: "I hasten to send you the report relating to the removal of the seals that had been affixed on your papers. Everything in it praises your public-spiritedness and is susceptible to dissipating any trace of suspicion."[18]

It was precisely this document Fourcroy was counting on to justify keeping Lavoisier on among the founders of the Lycée républicain. As for the letters that had been taken from boulevard de la Madeleine, Fourcroy made it his business to see that they were returned, and that was the end of the matter.[19]

A day later the Convention decreed the maximum general price regarding basic foodstuffs and wages. Persons known to possess some commodity or other were to be subject to constant requisitions. Simple prudence advised one to anticipate them. The clerk of the Piques section took note of such a gesture by Lavoisier:

The 400 livres in assignats and the sum that the 200 pounds of crystallized sugar you offered have been earmarked for the war effort. You had left it up to the committee to decide how the money was to be used and it considered that this was the most urgent need. I take the occasion to inform you that the sale of the sugar will take place next Thursday. Therefore, you can send it to this section at that time."[20]

But gifts in money or in kind were not sufficient. It was also necessary to give of oneself and participate in funerals, civic processions, and various other ceremonies dedicated to the cult of the martyrs of liberty. On October 8 Lavoisier was called by the national guard for the unveiling of the busts of Marat and Le Peletier. On October 15, in accordance with the law, he informed his section of the provisions he had on hand for his personal consumption. He specified that his declaration differed from that given in August: a part of the fabric had been used for making curtains and he had made a gift to the committee of the Piques section of everything that was not absolutely indispensable to him. The list of what remained was impressive and appetizing:

4 barrels of flour; 100 lbs. of rice; 20 lbs. of table oil and approximately 180 lbs. of fuel oil; 40 lbs. of Orléans sugar; 70 lbs. of candy sugar, similar to that given as a patriotic gift to the section [a discreet reminder!]; 200 lbs. of tallow candles; 110 lbs. of beeswax candles; 160 lbs. of coffee; 300 lbs. of salt; 8 hogsheads [8,000 liters!] of wine; 39 bottles of brandy; 26 bottles of liqueur; 100 ells of household cloth, cotton,

and muslin; several Indian remnants; a few remnants of flannelette and wool destined principally for clothing poor children in the country.[21]

In retrospect one is somewhat surprised that he was so anxious to recover the beans paid to him as rent from his properties. But it must be said that the occasions for more or less spontaneous gifts, in kind or money, were on the increase. Thus on October 24 "the citizen Lavoisier, residing on the boulevard de la Madeleine, contributed a sum of 100 livres [$4,000] to charity. It will be used to cover the costs of the war in the department of Vendée."[22] This curious act of charity would be his last gesture as a free man.

A Lost Opportunity

It was 4 frimaire An II (November 24, 1793).[23] François Louis Bourdon, a Convention deputy from Oise, exclaimed during a discussion concerning finances: "This is the hundredth time we have discussed the accounts of the Farmers General. I demand that those public leeches be arrested and that if their accounts are not presented in a month, then the Convention must turn them over to the sword of the law."[24] His proposal was approved by a show of hands. Nobody pointed out that the new expiration date differed from the one agreed to two months earlier. But it is true that the Constituent Assembly had itself set the deadline as the preceding January 1.

The Convention immediately decreed that "all the former collectors for the Ministry of Finance and the Farmers General who had signed the David, Salzard, and Mager leases would be placed under arrest in the same premises, that their papers would be transported there and that if their accounts were not presented in a month the Convention would pronounce against them whatever justice required"[25]

The *Père Duchesne* was jubilant: "I have a great urge to put on my Sunday clothes and go and congratulate those Gentlemen, the Farmers General. Gentlemen Jackasses, I would say, you did well to build your superb palaces and châteaux when you did, because if you had to start over again, you could no longer steal enough to build a cottage."[26]

The summonses were issued by the Police Department and served without delay. That very day, nineteen former Farmers General were arrested and taken to the Port Libre Prison, formerly the Port Royal Convent, where they found several former tax collectors from the Ministry of Finance and ex-administrators of State property.[27] "Shiver my timbers, there they are, brought down at last, those Farmers General who grew rich only by ruining poor people!" exulted the *Père Duchesne*.[28]

However, when the police went to the Arsenal and then to Lavoisier's home to arrest him, they did not find him. On that particular day he was on duty with the National Guard. Alerted, he did not return home, but wandered about Paris for some time before finding a refuge with a M. Lucas, the former usher of the Academy. Later he moved to the old premises of the Academy in the Louvre, staying there for four days during which he took every possible step to avoid being arrested. He was hoping that his work on weights and measures, for which he had the support of the Committee on Public Education, would save him from the common fate of the Farmers General. In the worst of hypotheses, he thought, he would lose his fortune. If that were to happen, he had already decided to become a pharmacist, the profession, in fact, that conformed most closely to his tastes and aptitudes.[29] Thus on November 25 he wrote to the Committee on Public Education:

Lavoisier, of the former Academy of Sciences, left the General Farm almost three years ago. Called at that time to a post as National Treasury Commissioner, he had a major role in organizing the present Treasury. He is now a member of the National Committee on Weights and Measures. It is well known that he was never involved in the general affairs of the Farm, which were conducted by a small committee, appointed by the Minister of Finance; and besides, his published works attest to the fact that he has always been principally engaged in scientific pursuits. He does not belong to the group of commissioners who were named to execute the decree regarding the rendering of the General Farm's accounts. Therefore he cannot be held responsible for the delay for which these commissioners are reproached. Hence he does not believe that he can be included in the law that ordered the Farmers General to be placed under arrest until the accounts are rendered.

In this state of doubt, he requests that the National Convention inform him if it intended that he should participate in the preparation of the Farm's accounts, a task for which he does not believe himself qualified, or if he might continue to fulfill his functions at the Committee of Weights and Measures for which he has worked with such enthusiasm and, if it may be said, with some usefulness.[30]

The following day, he asked for the arbitration of the Comité de Sûreté générale (Committee of General Security), in charge of police matters and circumspectly hostile to Maximilien de Robespierre, who had begun to rule despotically not only the Committee of Public Safety, but the nation as well:

Lavoisier, of the former Academy of Science, has been charged, by the decrees of the National Convention, to help establish new measures adopted by the National Convention. On the other hand, a newly issued decree orders that former Farmers General be imprisoned to work on their accounts. He is prepared to give himself up, but he thinks that prior to such a step he should be informed of which of these decrees he ought to obey. The Committee of General Security could reconcile the execution of the two decrees if, temporarily, it ordered that Lavoisier remain under arrest, guarded by two of his sans-culotte brothers. He wishes to point out that it has been more than three years since he left the General Farm and that his person and all his fortune guarantee his moral and physical responsibility.[31]

There was no response. Lavoisier panicked, consulted his wife, father-in-law, and a few friends, and, instead of fleeing like some of his colleagues, decided to give himself up. This choice may seem surprising. It is probable that Paulze, a rather rigid and legalistic man, refused the idea of flight for himself, and that Madame Lavoisier insisted that her husband stay near him. In any case, Lavoisier was too respectful of the order to evade it. Furthermore, he was confident that the court could be easily convinced that the dealings of the General Farm were perfectly legal. Some of his colleagues were more lucid, and Étienne Marie Delahante recorded:

When we spoke among ourselves about the nomination of the commissioners, several former Farmers General confidently insisted that since the administration of the General Farm had always been entirely in order, there was no reason to fear that it could be justly accused of abuses. But I did not share their confidence. I foresaw that the commissioners would accuse us of fictional abuses, that we would not be allowed to defend ourselves against the charges, and would be judged guilty of these alleged corrupt practices; thus we would be doomed.[32]

The Port-Libre Prison

Thus on 8 frimaire An II (November 28), accompanied by his father-in-law, Lavoisier presented himself to the officer at Port-Libre prison, commonly called "la Bourbe" (the Bog). The clerk laconically inscribed his arrival in the prison register: "From 8 frimaire, Lavoisier, former Farmer General. Grounds: for the rendering of accounts. By order of the police."[33]

The prison held two hundred inmates, of whom 27 had been Farmers General and another 27 tax collectors at the Ministry of Finance. The former were housed in the main three-story building with a view of the Observatory and the rue d'Enfer. Each floor contained 32 cells separated by a wide corridor at the end of which stood a big stove. Lavoisier and Paulze were in a cell with two beds on the second floor. They ate at the end of the hallway in the salon, a spacious room in which six tables for 16 persons were set up for meals. Food and other detention costs had to be paid for by the prisoners. One of the prisoners, Philippe E. Coissin, drew a picture of their way of life at the Port-Libre prison:

We gave 30 sous a day for those who had no means to feed themselves, and bread for all, at the expense of the rich who gave according to their resources. The expenses at the prison were handled by a perfectly organized interior administration. A treasurer collected the money and authorized all the expenditures for firewood, water, lighting, stoves, tables, chairs, and other small furniture in the cells. Everything had to be paid for by the wealthy. We were even made to buy a dog to guard us, for which we were charged 240 livres. The expenses for the guard, which reached daily 150 livres, had to be added.[34]

The two sexes were separated. The ladies were in another part of the prison separated by a wicket. All prisoners came together at the end of the day, and Coissin remembers:

In the evening, we met in the salon in the middle of which we set up a large table. Each prisoner brought his or her own candle. The men sat around the table. Some of them had books, others wrote. It was a veritable reading room. Everyone was extremely silent. Those who congregated near the stove to warm themselves were careful to speak in low voices. The women gathered round a small table and engaged in feminine activities. Some embroidered, others knitted. Then arrived an improvised light supper. Everyone rushed to set up the tables and suddenly gaity replaced the silence, causing us to forget that we were in prison. And, in fact, nothing could have resembled one less. There were neither bars nor bolts. The doors were closed only by simple latches. There was good society, excellent conversation, and special consideration for the women. We might have been simply an extended family having come together for a visit in a vast château.[35]

Even class distinctions became blurred:

Although a few people did not appear to be advocates of equality, this minor disparity was overcome by the solidarity that reigned among the prisoners. Because the prohibition to communicate had been lifted from the first day, the sans-culottes prisoners spoke freely with the other inmates, came to our concerts, and lectures and were not the least embellishment of our salon. However, at nine o'clock, we had to go back to our cells for roll call. We parted with regret, but always with the hope of seeing each other the following day. [. . .] After roll call, we could meet again, either around the stove or in our rooms. The men and women who had acquaintances in surrounding buildings could go and spend the rest of the night with them there, armed, however, with cards signed by the concierge. These small pleasures made the absence of freedom more bearable.[36]

The prison life of the Farmers General organized itself in a not altogether disagreeable way. "From the beginning," Delahante wrote, "we managed to have ourselves served quite good dinners; however, we soon realized that we could harm our cause by eating too well, and we decided to spend no more than 40 sous per person. Our society was soon enhanced by several ladies, and the greatest harmony always reigned among the prisoners. We would even have led a rather pleasant existence if we had not had to struggle against worries about the future."[37] Their worries, alas, were justified. On 10 frimaire (November 30), Louis Marie Bon de Montaut opposed Dupin's motion to free the former tax collectors of the Ministry of Finance who had handed over their accounts. "These men have robbed the nation," he vociferated, "it is to the nation and not to other thieves appointed by our former despots that they must render their accounts."[38] Even if their case differed from that of the Farmers General, the incident revealed the extent of the hatred that pursued the financiers of the old régime. To their anxiety about the future was added petty harassment by the jailers:

One day a chicken fricassee was delivered from the outside. One of the guards grabbed a drumstick and would have eaten it if he had not been seen by the kitchen boy who protested that his master would be accused of not having sent it. Then, after having sucked it, he tossed it back in the pan, saying that he had only wanted to see if the sauce was good. When plums or fruits were delivered, another jailer always began by tasting them, and if he found them good, he offered them round to his comrades, who accepted them and thus diminished the treats that were brought to us and that we obtained only with great difficulty and at excessively high prices.[39]

On the same day that Montaut had vented his hostility to financiers, Lavoisier received a reply to the letter he had addressed to his colleagues at the Advisory Board for Arts and Trades to notify them that he could not attend their next meeting. He had proposed that he resign as president to avoid compromising them. Cousin, Borda, Coulomb, Hallé, Lagrange, Laplace, Parmentier, Servières, Silvestre, and Jean Baptiste Hermand de Trouville refused his resignation and tried to reassure him. "The Convention felt it had to made a broad gesture that touches you only by its generality. But, Citizen, when, like you, one is sure of one's patriotism, of which one has unceasingly given proofs by complete dedication of the most distinguished talents to the nation, one ought not to worry. The Board desires that your new occupations do not force you to interrupt all correspondence with it."[40]

Even if they pretended to believe that their president was the object of a purely administrative measure and would soon be back among them, they were not so naive as to ignore his dangerous position. They hoped that the letter would serve at least as a testimony to his patriotism and devoted service to the nation. That was just about all they could do.

Lavoisier was also waiting impatiently for a reply from the Commission on Weights and Measures, confirming that his participation in its work was indispensable. He was counting on Borda and Haüy, a non-juring priest, who owed his life to him since Lavoisier had obtained his release from prison just before the massacres. The same day he wrote a letter to his wife:

The prisoners, my dear, are affected agreeably or disagreeably by the least details concerning them. Much distress was caused by the Convention's passing to the order of the day after Montaut's comments. This morning, your papa, Deville, and I were given a heated room and this minor event has kept us busy. We are no longer thinking about our problems, but rather about arranging the room, putting up boards. Baudry is sawing, nailing, and building, and I hope that we shall be reasonably settled by this evening. Unfortunately, I see already that our room is going to be the general meeting place. Hence, no more quiet.

I am beginning to lead the kind of life that is suitable to the circumstances in which I find myself. Yesterday afternoon, I worked for two and a half hours. [. . .] Furthermore, we are in perfect health and lack for nothing. I am waiting for the decrees that you have to collect. I beg you not to burden yourself with useless efforts and to look after your health. Everything suggests that this affair is going to be drawn out over a long period. Our address is: first floor hall, number 23, room at the end. We need a shovel, a pair of tongs, matches and a common bellows.[41]

After giving the doorkeeper a generous tip, his wife obtained the authorization to visit him and send him indispensable objects and food. She went to great pains to increase the prisoners' comforts and help them collect the essentials for their defense. Ever since they had been in prison, the Farmers had been discussing the strategy to adopt in presenting their case:

A few young people suggested that we offer to abandon our fortunes, and one of them even showed us the plan he had drawn up in a letter he proposed sending to the Convention. The idea was so unreasonable that it was rejected by all sensible people. It was on the contrary decided that we should write to say that it was impossible for us to work on the accounts as long as we were separated from our papers and clerks, and to request that we be permitted to move to the headquarters of the Farm where we would promise to stay until the accounts were settled.[42]

The petition, written by Delahante, stated that "the former Farmers General, held in the building once known as Port Royal, request to be transferred to the headquarters of the Farm where they can communicate with their clerks and have access to all the papers necessary for settling their accounts and satisfying the Convention's wishes."[43] On 19 frimaire (December 9) Lavoisier wrote to Fourcroy and asked him to support this request:

Citizen Representative, the circumstances in which I find myself do not allow me to hope to keep the appointment for arranging the transport of the safe of the Academy. However, the safe contains more than 50,000 livres in cash as well as assignats. [. . .] There is a special procedure for opening it, and as far as I am aware, I am the only one who knows it. But, to go to the Museum for this purpose, I will need a special authorization from the Committee of General Security. I could profit from the occasion to give you the remaining memoirs relating to the former Academy, a general survey of the funds it received while I held the office of treasurer, of what was spent and what remains. All these documents are ready. It is extremely important for me to be able to confer with you. I am sending you, Citizen, the copy of a petition that the former Farmers General have addressed to the National Convention. It is limited to a few simple and obviously just requests. I hope that you will read and support it, whether as deputy or as member of the societies of the peoples. Fraternal greetings.[44]

On 27 frimaire (December 17), Madame Lavoisier had a distinctly unpleasant experience. As the result of a decision by the Committee of General Security to affix seals on the property of all former Farmers General "both in their Paris residences and those located in the country," four members of the Piques section came to sequester her furniture and other belongings in the apartment on the boulevard de la Madeleine. There followed a most embarrassing interrogation:

We asked the Citizen Lavoisier if she had any silver. She answered that she had taken it all to the Mint. We then asked if she had a country house and she replied that she did not. But we commissaires later learned that her husband, the Citizen Lavoisier, owns a very large property called Freschines, located at Villefrancoeur, in the department of Loir-et-Cher, three leagues from Blois. Consequently, we returned to ask her for an explanation. She replied that she had thought we were referring to a country cottage near Paris that her husband had previously sold. She added that the proof that she was not trying to deceive us was that her husband had listed all his property in his tax declaration. For this reason we suspended our investigation.[45]

But the commissaires were not content to do their work halfway, and after all they set off to Freschines to see for themselves. Arriving there on 11 nivôse (December 31), they discovered that it was a vast estate with an annual income of from 25,000 to 30,000 livres. They dutifully affixed seals on all the rooms, except for the dining room, where they found only a table and two chairs. The silver had disappeared. From the initial livestock, there remained only 8 workhorses, 29 cows and goats, 8 pigs, and 270 sheep. The rest had been stolen. Everything was placed under the guard of two men, lodged in the kitchen and paid 5 livres per day.

At Port-Libre during this time, Lavoisier was worrying about Marie-Anne's health and wrote to her:

My dear one, you are giving yourself a lot of trouble, exhausting yourself both physically and emotionally, and, alas, I cannot share your burden. Do be careful that your health is not affected. That would be the greatest of misfortunes. I have had a long and successful career, and have enjoyed a happy existence ever since I can remember. You have contributed and continue to contribute to that happiness every day by the signs of affection you show me. I shall leave behind me memories of esteem and consideration. Thus, my task is accomplished. But you, on the other hand, still have a long life ahead of you. Do not jeopardize it. I thought I noticed yesterday that you were sad.

Why be so, since I am resigned to everything and I consider as won all that I shall not lose. Besides, we can still hope to be together again and, in the meantime, your visits provide me with some pleasant interludes.

Do not forget our assignats *à face royale*.[46] However, the matter is not urgent, since we still have ten days to exchange them. We need sugar, but I think we have enough to last until tomorrow evening. Your papa will write the next letter. If you have the chance to send a few bottles of table wine, it would be a great help to your papa who until now has been footing the bill for all the wine. Deville provides grapes and pears in abundance.[47]

The same day he learned that the petition written by Borda and Haüy had been left with the Committee of General Security. It stated that the Commission on Weights and Measures considered Lavoisier's presence indispensable for continuing the work of verifying the standards. The studies being done on the determination of weights and the expansion of metals had been brought to a halt by his absence and no one could replace him. "It is urgent that this citizen be able to return to the important work that he has always performed with as much fervor as accomplishment."[48]

The Committee of General Security refused, "given that Citizen Lavoisier is included on the list of former Farmers General placed under arrest in execution of the decree of the National Convention."[49] And to cut short any new attempt to free him, the Committee of Public Safety,

considering just how important it is for the improvement of public morale that government officials delegate functions and responsibilities only to those men who have proved themselves worthy of confidence by their republican virtues and abhorence of kings, and after having consulted with the members of the Committee on Public Education, has decided that as of today Borda, Lavoisier, Laplace, Coulomb, Brisson, and Delambre will cease to be members of the Commission on Weights and Measures.[50]

On the first of nivôse (December 21) the Currency Committee attempted in its turn to appeal to the Committee of Public Safety: "To weigh the new coins, we need special scales, whose construction is extremely delicate. And yet their fabrication has just been suspended as a result of Citizen Lavoisier's arrest. Take whatever steps you deem appropriate in regard to this citizen, but he must be allowed to work in his laboratory."[51]

This appeal had no more success than the preceding ones. However, the request of the Farmers General to be transferred to the former headquarters of the Farm was accepted, and on 5 nivôse (December 25) a long stream of carriages arrived at the prison to transport the prisoners. "They said good bye to everybody, generously tipped the concierge for his services, and left behind 4,000 livres to purchase mattresses for the infirmary and aid indigent citizens. They were generally missed."[52] Lavoisier left behind curtains, a backgammon table, candelabra, a mattress, and personal effects he had been forbidden to take.[53]

Return to the Offices of the Farm

The cortege of fourteen carriages, each carrying two prisoners escorted by two gendarmes, left Port-Libre and reached the rue de Grenelle Saint-Honoré at nightfall. On that Christmas night it was very cold. The auditors of the accounts had transformed the mansion into a prison by installing heavy oak doors, beamed partitions and iron bars on the windows. The building, which had been conceived for offices, offered little comfort. Most of the prisoners slept on mattresses placed directly on the floor. Lavoisier shared a small room with his father-in-law. The price for "room and board" was set at 5 livres per day, payable in assignats. Certain prisoners whose property had been sequestered had to borrow money to pay. After several days, seven more colleagues were brought to join them. Another, Mercier, was transferred to the Madelonnettes. Sannois slipped away and was not pursued.

The rendering of the accounts was at last about to begin. Delahante took charge and divided up the tasks according to capacities and priority. The schedule then became as strict as it had been in the times of the splendor of the Farm. The working day began at nine o'clock, with a meeting to bring everyone up to date on how things were progressing. From 9:30 to 2:00 each person examined the subject for which he was responsible. There was a break for lunch and rest, and from 5:00 to 8:00 another period of individual work. Before supper, a joint meeting was held with the division heads. At ten o'clock, they all retired to their rooms. But even so, the work dragged on. Saint-Amand, Paulze, and Lavoisier brought together the most qualified among them to discuss details concerning the salt tax or tobacco. Delahante reported:

It was in these small groups of eight or nine that we were first informed of the charges that the so-called auditors were going to bring against us. They all bore the stamp of either the most complete ignorance or dishonesty, and we had no doubt that, if we were able to have our answers heard, they could easily be refuted. But we were very much afraid that the charges would be ruled on without ever having been officially communicated to us. Consequently, we thought that it would be a good idea to try to refute them in a memoir. M. Lavoisier wanted very much to write it and the task could not have been given to a more skillful hand.[54]

Before anything, Lavoisier, complying with the law of September 3, began by writing his declaration of personal income for 1793. The instructions were certainly more precise and restrictive than they had been in 1791, because the statement was much more detailed.

The total income from real estate, essentially rural properties and farms, was 105,607 livres:

in the department of Loir-et-Cher:	24,082 livres
in the department of Aisne:	40,978 livres
in the department of Oise:	4,899 livres
in the department of Seine-et-Oise:	20,778 livres
in Paris, for a house on rue de Bons Enfants:	6,000 livres
in the district of Saint-Denis:	8,870 livres

Lavoisier had indeed become a major landowner. Other than his estates in Freschines and Le Bourget, he owned "several tracts of land in the communes of La Courneuve, Grandmesnil, Drancy, Dugny, and Bonneuil, which he had inherited from his aunt, Constance Punctis, and several fields that he had bought in Clichy-la-Garenne."[55]

He had also acquired important nationalized property in the departments of Aisne, Oise and Seine-et-Oise for an investment of 1,282, 375 livres.[56] A part of these holdings had been purchased for him by his cousin, Nicolas Charles Parisis, in the canton of Villers-Cotterêts: "The four farms of Lessard, l'Epine, La Place and Soulmont alone represent a total surface of 1,574 arpents, or almost 800 hectares."[57]

He also owned two farms in Seine-et-Oise and Oise: Motière and Pesleine respectively. His last purchase by auction, dated October 10, 1792, concerned a piece of land at Taillefontaine for which he paid 6,025 livres.[58]

To his declaration, he added his other income reaching 16,030 livres:

life annuities:	5,000 livres
43 shares in the Discount Bank	3,600 livres
122 shares in the new East India Company	4,880 livres
interest on the debt of Irénée Du Pont de Nemours	2,550 livres[59]

His total revenue for 1793 thus reached the considerable figure of 121,637 livres ($4.5 million). But it is also true that assignats had already lost 25 percent of their initial value. However Lavoisier was too well informed to have kept assignats.

He also prepared a file for his personal defense that he wanted to be complete and capable of warding off even the most unforeseen accusations. On January 7, 1794 he obtained the authorization to go to his home to get some documents. The commissaires Philippon and Moutonnet, who had only just returned from Freschines, accompanied him. The seals affixed on the door to

the left in the entrance hall were removed and Lavoisier recovered his "memoirs in physics and chemistry yet to be printed, various documents relating
to his declaration for the national loan and several handwritten registers of
laboratory experiments."[60] In fact, he was also working on all his scientific
memoirs, which he hoped to have printed in eight volumes.

The one document still lacking in the file for his defense reached him on
January 10 in good order: "I the undersigned, secretary-general of the department, certify that the citizen Antoine Laurent Lavoisier, former member of
the Academy of Science, residing at number 243 boulevard de la Madeleine,
municipality of Paris, is not included on the list of émigrés arrested up to now
by the directory."[61]

The task of the collective defense of the Farmers General was laborious in a different way, because the accusations had not been precisely stated.
Dupin was hardly of any help to them. As Lavoisier wrote: "The Farmers
General have learned that a report concerning them has been printed, that it
contains some serious charges of which they have only vague ideas; that it
contains other charges about which they have not the slightest notion, that
the discussions are to begin within a few days and the members of the Finance
Committee themselves desire information and enlightenment."[62]

Replies to Charges

Lavoisier's written refutation was printed in a brochure of 42 pages entitled
"Response to the Charges Made Against the Former Farmers General":

The impossibility of making a sufficient number of handwritten copies in their defense
during the brief interval remaining has forced them to resort to printing, not for influ-
encing public opinion, for which these remarks are not intended, but for establishing
definitive facts, for producing authentic written proof that can serve as a basis for the
verdict that the National Convention must pronounce.[63]

The text, undated and without the name of either author or printer, was
to have included 47 pages of written documentation, notably financial tables,
but Ballard, the printer, was unable to provide them because their composition would have been very difficult and he had to meet a deadline.

Lavoisier had developed a long argument, very technical and backed by
figures, divided into eleven rebuttals to the presumed charges. The auditors
having in fact refused to pass them on, the Farmers had learned of them only
through family and friends. Only the first charge had been officially formulated by Dupin on 28 brumaire (November 18):

I urge you, Citizens, to tell us according to what law you divided among yourselves, and before any division with the government: (1) during the Laurent David lease,10 percent of 60 million livres; (2) 6 percent of 33,600,000 livres, the amount of your *fonds d'avance* [capital investment]. Your written comments must be presented within three days. We warn you that if you do not have what we have asked for within that time, we shall consider your silence as a confession of illegal distribution of funds.[64]

To put it plainly, they were suspected of unlawfully taking an excessive interest of 10 percent and 6 percent on their capital investment, whereas, according to the terms of the lease, they were entitled to only 4 percent for the funds advanced to the King. Thus a reimbursement of 53,068,526 livres was being demanded. On the one hand, the charge mixed clauses from two different leases; on the other, it played on a confusion of terms that was probably intentional: the word avances (advances) designated both the capital that strictly speaking belonged to the Farm and the payments made "in advance" to the Royal Treasury. Delahante specified:

The advances of the Farmers General were capital funds, the funds needed for operating the Farm, made up of the 1,500,000 francs that each Farmer General had to pay on entering the company. The deduction, before all profit sharing, of 10 percent interest on the first 60 million and 6 percent on 33,600,000 livres formed the principal fixed remuneration for the Farmers General. It was not only positively stipulated in the two leases in question, as in all the previous ones, but it was one of the principal bases of the contract. Another article of the contract stipulated, it is true, the rate of 4 percent for the advances made by the Farm. In spite of the use of the same word, there was no connection between the advances of the Farmers General and the advances made to the Treasury. The Farm did not make its payments at the times set by the contract, but rather as the money came in. It settled its payment orders as they were presented to it. It kept what in present accounting terms one would call the current account of the Treasury, which it credited with the amount of the lease and which it debited from the payments. But since neither the terms current account nor those of debit and credit were known at the time, and since the Farm was always "in advance" with the Treasury, this account was called the "compte d'avances" and it was its interest rate that had been set at 4 percent.[65]

The argumentation was correct and the practice perfectly legal. One can nevertheless question the contestable practice that existed before Necker: the capital of the Farm represented 93 million livres, of which 72 were a genuine advance to the government, the balance being destined to reimburse the value of material, saltworks, and tobacco manufactures to the owners of the previous lease.

To dispose of these important sums, the new Farmers took out loans from family or friends, or their bankers. But they incorporated the interest, set at 10 percent for 60 million and 6 percent on the rest, into the expenses of the Farm. They deducted the repayment of the interest from the income of the Farm before determining the profit and its subsequent division between the Royal Treasury and the Farm. In other words, it was the Royal Treasury that was paying, by failing to earn, the interests on the loans taken out by the Farmers for the acquisition of the lease of the Farm.

The shrewdness and dishonesty of Dupin consisted in recalling schemes that had not been used in recent years, of creating an inextricable amalgam between different kinds of "advances," thus profiting from the tribunal's ignorance in financial matters to shore up a weak case. The rebuttals written by Lavoisier had a technocratic character that even today makes them very difficult for nonspecialists. Certainly they were no better understood by the readers of the time.

The second charge against the General Farmers—not made known in writing—focused on "the exchange of the 3/10 for a share in the profits." Dupin was alluding to a clause, imposed by the Abbé Terray, Controller General in 1770, in the Alaterre lease: all the profits of the Farm were to be subjected to a set deduction of 3/10 for the State. It was the beginning of a profit sharing between the State and the General Farm. In 1774 the Farmers had managed to replace the fixed deduction of 3/10 by a variable deduction inversely proportional to profits: 5/10 up to 4 million, 4/10 from 4 to 8 million, 3/10 from 8 to 12 million and 2/10 beyond. Lavoisier justified this new clause by saying that it brought to the nation "during the David lease an extraordinary sum of more than 17 million livres on which it could not have counted."[66]

The third and fourth accusations were serious in quite another way in the eyes of public opinion: "(1) What registered law authorized you to sell in your offices grated tobacco at 3 livres 12 sous per pound? (2) On what regulation did you base yourself to introduce a certain quantity of water into your grated tobacco, and what was this quantity per quintal [100 kilograms]?"[67] In fact, the General Farm was accused of having increased the weight of the tobacco by 14 percent through the addition of water, and it was being asked to reimburse the State 29,963,496 livres for this fraud.

Lavoisier, as we know, had always opposed the excessive moistening of tobacco, a practice engaged in by both dealers and manufacturers. Once again, he showed, using available figures, that in the fabrication of grated tobacco it was necessary to add water equivalent to from 14 to 18 percent of its weight. But, he pointed out, the amount of water to be considered was not what was added during the processing, since most of it evaporated, but what remained when the tobacco was sold to the consumer. He argued that it never went beyond 3 percent, that is 6 lbs, 8 ounces, $1\frac{3}{4}$ gros per 100 kilograms of tobacco. And the price for this extra weight was not collected by the Farm, since, for every order of 16 ounces, it always added without charge an extra ounce of tobacco, or the exact equivalent of the weight of water.

Since 1786, the proportion of water had even been reduced to 2.5 percent. At the same time, the quality of the tobacco had been improved by the elimination of rotting leaves and large stalks. On the other hand, since the abolition of the monopoly of the Farm, tobacco manufactures had been created in Paris and the provinces. They were free to choose their processing methods and had no constraints other than satisfying their customers' taste. And yet, Lavoisier specified, "they have all adopted the methods formerly used by the Farm. All of them have almost exclusively gone into the production of grated tobacco and fabricated only very few "carrots."[68]

The fifth accusation argued that the Farmers paid their leases to the Treasury with scandalous delays, and that the funds they kept in the interim were used for speculation. It was said that they owed the sum of 10,136,022 livres in overdue interest. The Farmers, Lavoisier explained, always paid in advance of the dates specified on the leases and legally they were not overdue. But what they were being reproached for was not paying the sums just as soon as they were received. In fact, he pointed out, the dates on the receipts given by the Treasury were always several months later than the payments because the accounts had to be verified beforehand. "How could one possibly imagine," Lavoisier underlined, "that a government constantly hounded by obligations, which always knew the situation of the funds of the Farm, and almost always exhausted its monies to the last sou, would have left substantial funds at the disposition of the former Farmers General?"[69] The argument was clever, but Dupin produced documents seeming to confirm delays in payment.

The sixth charge accused the Farmers of having used, between 1789 and 1791, the funds of the nation to settle its own debts, whereas officially the Farm had not existed since July 1, 1789, given the retroactive decree of March 27, 1791. Lavoisier replied that "the former Farmers General were thus under state control for 21 months during which they thought they were still independent. They cannot be blamed for not having foreseen an event that depended neither on their power nor will."[70]

The seventh accusation concerned "the deduction before dividing profits of a sum of 1,250,000 livres, during the Salzard lease." Lavoisier easily showed that a sum of the same amount had been paid to the Treasury during the Salzard lease on November 20, 1787, since the profits had to be shared equally between it and the Farm. He could not refrain from a touch of humor: "More direct communication of the kind frequently offered by the Farmers General to the Citizen Auditors, could have prevented this and similar errors. It is a pity that they did not take advantage of it.[71]

The eighth accusation referred to a violation of the Stamp Law which dated from after the abolition of the Farm. The other charges, all minor, focused on indemnities, bonuses, and gifts considered abusive, taking deductions before dividing profits, and unjustified or excessive expenses.

Nicolas François de Mollien, a former employee of the Farm, arrested at the same time as his employers, was witness to their efforts to prepare a defense that was as clear and precise as a report they would have written earlier for the Ministry of Finance:

They did not leave a single objection unanswered, a single calculation unrefuted, a single justification undocumented. And since the charge against them could not take on a revolutionary color, they were, in spite of circumstances, awaiting the verdict with serenity. Even after four years of revolution, these decent men had no better understanding of the spirit of the verdicts being issued in those times and the thrust of political passions. Nothing proves more clearly just how much they were cut off from all the extreme parties.[72]

A month after their return to the headquarters of the Farm, on 7 pluviôse (January 27, 1794), they were ready to submit their accounts to the Finance Committee. There was nevertheless one point on which the Farmers did not have a completely clear conscience. At the time of the abolition of the Farm in 1791, 48 million livres had been given by the National Assembly as a reimbursement for their warehouses and tobacco factories. In going over their books they found that the value of these facilities was only 26.5 million livres. On Lavoisier's advice, they offered to reimburse 21.5 million. The auditors, however, took all the credit for this repayment, saying that it had resulted from their investigation alone. Could the Farmers General really plead that it had been an honest mistake? It seems that it would be difficult to make an error of such magnitude, one that was double the amount justified.

In all, the Farmers General were accused of the embezzlement and squandering of a sum totaling 107,603, 862 livres or, if one added the previously mentioned 21.5 million, as Dupin insisted, 130 million livres.

Lavoisier continued to work on his personal defense. He had been somewhat disappointed by the initial response of his colleagues at the Advisory Board for Arts and Trades, and had asked them on 29 germinal An II (April 18, 1794) for an attestation of his competence and loyal services:

The time is approaching, at least I hope it is, when returning to the work from which it might have been hoped I would never be distracted, I shall be able to resume my collaboration with you. Desiring at this time to be able to give an exact reckoning of my conduct since the beginning of the revolution, I take the liberty of calling on you to testify in my behalf: I would like to have, in the form of a certificate or an extract from the minutes of the Board, or in whatever manner you deem appropriate, your confirmation that, after having contributed to the advancement of human knowledge by important discoveries in physics and chemistry, discoveries that have influenced the progress of applied science, and that are described in numerous memoirs included in the collection of the former Academy of Science, I was appointed to the Advisory Board at the time of its formation, that I regularly attended its meetings, and that I sought to make myself useful and fulfill the goal of the Board by informing it of the merit of artisans entitled to national rewards. I would also like to ask the special committee, appointed in the beginning of 1793 at the request of the Currency Committee of the Convention to advise it on ways of improving the fabrication of assignats so as to make counterfeiting more difficult, to certify that during the more than three months of activity of the committee, I contributed to its work with zeal and effectiveness. Since our reports were made directly to the committee of the Convention, bypassing the Advisory Board, this certificate, I realize, can only be given individually by those who worked with me, unless you think it is suitable to include everything in one document. As I recall, the group was made up of the Citizens Trouville, Desmarets, Berthollet, and myself.

If giving this attestation in the form of a certificate seems strange to you, perhaps you could write it as a report that could be given at an Advisory Board meeting and end with a preamble and pronouncement. This would not be the first time that you have appointed people to describe specific work done by the members of the Board and encourage their rights to public recognition. May I flatter myself that you place me in this category? I am asking you to certify nothing but facts, and I even beg you to avoid presenting them in a way that could reflect the friendship or confidence which you have so often shown me. Fraternal greetings.[73]

The members of the Board, who met on April 22 and were presided over by Lagrange, sent the requested attestation.

The Advisory Board for Arts and Trades, after having heard the report of its committee members on the request and contributions of Citizen Lavoisier, considering the number and importance of this citizen's discoveries, the great and useful revolution that they have helped to bring about in chemistry, the light they have shed on the nature of many substances of which we knew little before, and on the major phenomena of vegetation and the animal system, and the advantages that have resulted for almost all of the applied arts related to chemistry, such as dyeing, the analysis and exploitation of mines, etc., and that the vote of the majority of European scientists has raised Citizen Lavoisier to a distinguished rank among those who have brought honor to France, considering also that Citizen Lavoisier has enthusiastically and regularly shared the commitment of the Advisory Board to bringing useful artisans the rewards due to their talents, the Board has resolved that this testimony of its esteem will be recorded in its minutes and that an extract will be sent to Citizen Lavoisier.[74]

Lavoisier also received the support of the agents from the Gunpowder and Saltpeter Administration, Le Faucheux and Jacques Pierre Champy, who tried to gain time for him by saying that he should be asked to write a report on his former management of the Administration.

Cadet and Baumé sent him a certificate stating that he had always opposed the excessive moistening of tobacco, something they had been able to confirm during their official investigation in 1784.[75]

These interventions belie the claim that Lavoisier was simply abandoned by his colleagues and that nothing was done to try to save him. It is no less true, however, that the four men, Monge, Hassenfratz, Guyton de Morveau, and Fourcroy, who were best placed to rescue him, since they belonged to the majority of the Convention, did not speak up in his favor.

Therefore, feeling that above all he had to rely on himself, Lavoisier undertook to write an autobiographical note, more than a little disingenuous, since he insisted essentially on his activities as servant of the State and ardent republican.

He recalled his activity during twenty-five years at the Academy of Science, given concrete expression by eighty memoirs, and his membership in "almost all the academies of Europe." Undoubtedly he wanted to underline the discredit that would redound on France over any harm to his person.

He also insisted on his agricultural experiments in Freschines, their high cost—120,000 livres—and on the benefits that they had brought to the town of Orléans and its surroundings: "During the winter of 1788 to 1789, he had made an interest free loan of 50,000 livres to the city of Blois and one of 6,000 to Romorantin to feed the inhabitants, stock the markets with wheat, and lower the prices of foodstuffs. Always constant in his principles, for the past ten years, in times of distress, he had made weekly shipments of wheat to the market in Blois, and sold it below the prevailing prices."[76]

There was no mention of the General Farm, the Gunpowder and Saltpeter Administration or the Discount Bank. His prudence is understandable but very naive given that he was a public figure to which the press had devoted so many not necessarily favorable articles.

On the other hand, he did emphasize his political career, which was modest: elector in Paris in 1789 and alternate deputy of the nobility in Blois at the Constituent Assembly, representative of the temporary Commune de Paris and member of the National Guard.

His greatest assets remained his career as administrator and civil servant: consultant to the Committee on Public Health and the Currency Committee, author of a work on the territorial wealth of France, National Treasury Commissioner, member of the Advisory Board for Arts and Trades, and director of the Commission on Weights and Measures.

Finally, he wrote, "on every occasion, he has borne arms for the defense of liberty, notably on August 10, 1792, when he was enlisted to stand guard at the gunpowder warehouse of the Arsenal, and on May 31, 1793, when he was a member of the battalion of the Piques section posted at the Place de la Révolution."[77] Even though it was a modest military experience, it had a symbolic value.

Was he hoping to disarm his enemies? The members of the Convention were not his personal enemies but enemies of the Farm. They wanted to destroy a contemptible institution and seize the immense fortune it supposedly had. The Farmers General made a great mistake by furnishing them with a pretext. In March 1791 the Assembly had set January 1, 1793 as the date for rendering their accounts. The deadline had not been respected and that was the legal grounds for their arrest.

Lavoisier had a perfect understanding of the political situation. It was neither blindness nor pride that kept him in his country at a time when he could justifiably have felt himself threatened. He knew that the social group to which he belonged, that of the financiers, was the object of suspicions and that public opinion was ready to believe the worst about it. He chose to differentiate himself from the Farmers General and said that he no longer had any connection with them. Thanks to Fourcroy and the Commission on Weights and Measures, he believed that he had succeeded in his reconversion as a specialist in education and applied science. But the facts were obstinate. Whether he wanted it or not, he was always associated with that rich and odious institution which the revolutionary power was determined to bring down, and hence he was exposed to the same dangers as its other members. Farmer General, administrator in both the tobacco and gunpowder monopolies, director of the Discount Bank and National Treasury Commissioner, he represented that elite caste of financiers involved in the management of public funds. After the Revolution he had attempted to assume that role in government no longer as a private capitalist, but as a senior civil servant. But common opinion could not be bothered with such subtle distinctions and the Convention needed money too desperately to weigh them closely. The Farmers General made up a detested and affluent social group. To attack its members was to do justice and help bail out the State from its financial difficulties. Wealth alone had become sufficient for attracting the attention of revolutionary justice. It also justified its rigor, and in facing it a wealthy defendant did not have the slight chance of salvation that the poor one sometimes retained. To condemn the rich to death and confiscate their property was referred to, alluding to the location of the guillotine, as "minting coins on the Place de la Révolution." At such a time, it was surely a serious error to think that it would suffice to present a sound financial statement in order to escape danger.

Lavoisier's second error was to think that his value as a scientist and expert in socially useful techniques would protect him. How, he reasoned, could a scientist, known throughout Europe, who had placed his talents in the service of great causes such as the reforms of weights and measures, public education, and the training of artisans, fail to have his case separated from that of the other Farmers General?

It is undoubtedly in this double error of analysis that the explanation for Lavoisier's blindness can be found. We know from his letters that he had envisaged going to spend a kind of sabbatical year in Scotland, working with Black. Why did he give up such a wise plan? Why did he not try simply to fade into the background? He had sold to his colleague Coulomb a part of his property in Blésois, the Thoisy farm, and Coulomb and Borda were able to take refuge there during the most difficult moments of the Reign of Terror.

But was Lavoisier, who loved order and discipline, who insisted that all proofs had to be based on numbers, sensitive enough to the current mood to size up his standing with the public and his life expectancy?

The Trial

WHILE DUPIN WAS PREPARING his report on the accounts of the General Farm for the Finance and Accounting Committees, the prisoners' families and friends were multiplying their efforts to help them. A former director of the legal department of the Farm, Féval, tried twice to meet with the committees, hoping to learn the specific charges, but they refused to see him. Their deliberations were to remain secret. Pierre Loysel, former director of the Saint-Gobain factory and member of the Convention, also sought to intervene in their behalf, but had no success.

It was then that a unique chance arose. Lavoisier's friend Pluvinet, the pharmacist on the rue des Lombards who supplied him with laboratory reagents, was the cousin of Madame Dupin, the deputy's sister-in-law. This pretty woman of easy virtue often accompanied Madame de Mailly to the lively parties given by Barère. Both Antoine Fouquier-Tinville, public prosecutor, and Marie Joseph Chénier were vying for her favors. Using this connection, Pluvinet devised a plan:

He informed his cousin of what he was trying to do, and convinced her to make a concentrated effort to persuade Dupin to help Lavoisier. She succeeded in getting his ear, but he complained that Madame Lavoisier had not deigned to approach him and had sent only aristocrats instead. The lady persevered, however, and assured him that Madame Lavoisier would call on him. She obtained his promise that Lavoisier's case would be considered separately, that he would have him transferred to another prison, and that during the move, he could try to escape. In a word, Dupin agreed to cooperate and to make his report as little unfavorable to him as he possibly could. Pluvinet then informed Madame Lavoisier that Dupin was well disposed to aid her husband, and advised her to profit from the circumstances by going to see him at once and offering her thanks.

Madame Lavoisier went to the court reporter's office where Pluvinet was also waiting, but she did not bother to greet the pharmacist. As soon as she was in Dupin's office, she assumed a proud and imposing attitude and announced that she had not come to humble herself to the point of soliciting the pity of a Jacobin for Lavoisier. She insisted that her husband was innocent and that only villains could accuse him.

Dupin, taken aback by such rude remarks, tried to answer, but Madame Lavoisier interrupted him, continued her tirade and heaped abuse on all the deputies who had anything to do with the case of the Farmers General. She said that she only wanted justice and was not asking for mercy, that Lavoisier would consider himself dishonored to have his case separated from that of his colleagues; that people wanted to destroy them so as to lay hands on their fortunes, but that, if they perished, they would die innocent. [. . .] Undoubtedly, Madame Lavoisier was speaking the truth, but was that a time to be so truthful? Dupin, outraged by this misplaced dignity, dismissed Madame Lavoisier and was subsequently deaf to all entreaties made on Lavoisier's behalf.[1]

What might Dupin have done, had Madame Lavoisier behaved differently? She might have been able to persuade him of her husband's innocence by reasonable arguments, she might have softened his rigor by her feminine charms, or she might have tried to bribe him. Dupin could in fact have saved Lavoisier. It would have sufficed, without dismissing his case completely, simply to detach it from the others. The Convention was attacking the institution of the Farm rather than the persons of the Farmers General. Certain interventions were successful without forcing the Convention to renounce its principles. Fourteen Farmers General were never arrested. Jean François Verdun was freed before the trial and three young assistants were released during the proceedings as a result of mediations. But could Madame Lavoisier have envisaged saving her husband without saving her father? Such a dilemma was perhaps too tortuous for her to answer.

Dupin's Accusations

Dupin sent an initial report of 187 pages to the two committees in charge of the case. It evoked the main charges mentioned earlier, discussed Lavoisier's memoir in his defense, and confirmed the presumed debt of 107 or so million livres for the last three of the Farm's leases.[2]

Of the ninety-five Farmers General who were "debtors" to the State, forty-five were already dead, but their heirs were liable to payment, in proportion to the years of membership, just as were the surviving Farmers. Since he had been a member titulaire for 9 years and 9 months, Lavoisier was required to pay 1,204,345 livres 10 sous plus 470,000 livres for the period when he was Baudon's assistant.

After two entire sessions spent in examining Dupin's report, the committees concluded that it should be presented to the Convention. On 16 floréal (May 5), in a new report of 24 pages, Dupin "revealed the abuses of authority, exactions, and embezzlements of all sorts that the Farmers General allowed themselves and that justified considerable claims."[3]

The auditors, he pointed out, had worked with the tireless zeal, perfect conscience, and impartiality appropriate to the people's representatives. All the Farmers General were guilty of misuse and misappropriation of funds; furthermore, he called the attention of the Convention "to a crime of an entirely different nature which, motivated by a sordid desire for profits, had had immoral, impolitic and disastrous effects. This was the grating of tobacco in the factories of the General Farm. From the moment they were granted the right to pulverize tobacco, the most revolting violations set in."[4]

He admitted that certain Farmers General had been opposed to the excessive moistening of tobacco. "They were Verdun, Neveu, Montcloux, Dauteroche, Paulze, and others."[5] Lavoisier was not included, although he had been named in the auditors' initial report. Dupin then returned to the liquidation of the accounts of the Farm, still pending, and concluded with the particularly grave accusation of conspiracy against the Republic: "If the former Farmers General had not been impatiently awaiting the return of the old Régime, would they have postponed obeying your decrees for two years instead of getting down to the business of settling their accounts?[6]

Since the enactment of the law of suspects, the charge of conspiracy against the Republic imposed appearance before the Revolutionary Tribunal and almost automatically led to the death sentence with confiscation of property. At 4:30 in the afternoon of the same day, the decree distraining the Revolutionary Tribunal, competent court of law since March 10, 1793, was voted and adopted. Dupin had written up the decree. "The National Convention sends the former Farmers General involved in the David, Salzard, and Mager leases to the Revolutionary Tribunal to be judged in conformity with the law. The National Convention reserves for itself the right to rule on restitutions, indemnities, fines, and confiscations due to the Nation and to bring action against the former Farmers General and all who were croupiers, pensioners, heirs, donees or eligible parties, during the David, Salzard, and Mager leases."[7]

A woman who had been present when the vote was taken went directly to the headquarters of the Farm to inform the prisoners. The first one she met was Lavoisier, who took it upon himself to notify his colleagues. Immediately understanding that their fate was sealed, they burned their personal papers and began writing to their families. Mollien and Boullongne, who had obtained opium for a collective suicide, offered some to Lavoisier. He replied:

I do not feel any more attachment to life than you. Mine has already been sacrificed. The final moments awaiting us will be painful no doubt, but we would not be assured of avoiding them by the means you are proposing: asphyxia might serve us better. But why go out to meet death? Could it be because it is humiliating to receive it by another's order, and especially an unjust one? In this case, the very excess of injustice erases the shame. We can all look confidently at both our private life and the judgment that will be made on it perhaps within a few months. Our judges are neither on the tribunal that summoned us, nor in the population that will insult us. A plague is ravaging France. It has the advantage of striking its victims with a single blow. It is close at hand, but it is not impossible that it will halt before reaching a few of us at least. To kill ourselves would be to absolve the fanatics who have unleashed this plague. Let us think of those who have preceded us, and try not to leave a less good example to those who will follow.[8]

The Conciergerie

Fouquier-Tinville lost no time in writing up the indictment and sending the order to transfer the Farmers General to the Conciergerie. At seven in the evening, several members of the Commune de Paris, draped in tricolored scarves and accompanied by mounted gendarmes and four large covered wagons, arrived at the headquarters of the Farm.

Nécard, the concierge, proceeded to round up the prisoners while the representatives of the Commune drank and joked in the lodge. Assembling everyone took more than an hour. The guards, who during four months of shared life had become friendly with the prisoners, held back their tears. Thirty-two Farmers General were led by groups of four to the wagons. They remained silent. Nicolas François Mollien, the young employee who had been arrested along with the Farmers, was the thirty-third on the list. But as he was awaiting his turn, the concierge pushed him back into the mansion and whispered, "Stay there. You have no business here."[9]

It was already nightfall when the wagons began to move, surrounded by a double row of gendarmes on horseback. A cluster of men on foot, carrying torches, lit the procession as it made its way from the rue de Grenelle Saint-Honoré to the Conciergerie, passing over the Pont Neuf. The journey was slow and cumbersome and ended only at eleven in the evening. After the formalities of registration, the prisoners were locked in cells. A few had trestle beds, without mattresses or blankets. The others slept on benches or on the floor.

The following morning, 17 floréal (May 6), the guards opened the doors and gathered the men in the hall that Marie-Antoinette had occupied. They spent the entire day waiting. In the morning, a delegation from the Lycée des Arts led by Desaudray came to present Lavoisier with a metal crown decorated with small gilded stars as a token of esteem.[10] A watercolor of the period depicts the scene and Lakanal testified: "When the blood of the innocent was being shed in overflowing torrents, the Lycée des Arts dared to remind hearts of humanity. It publicly consoled and adopted the victim's children. It crowned Lavoisier when he was in chains."[11]

Delahante, thanks to the protection of his relative, Judge Dobsent, had obtained three rooms which he gave in the evening to his closest friends and the eldest members of the group. Lavoisier, Paulze, and Nicolas Deville de Noailly took the smallest one. The others shared six pairs of sheets, a few mattresses and blankets. They lay down completely dressed, but found it hard to fall asleep: the biting fleas and the noise of rats fighting in the courtyard kept them awake until daybreak.

The Interrogation

On 18 floréal (May 7), at 6:30 in the morning, they were told that they would soon be called for an interrogation. An hour later, the gendarmes arrived, and after searching them, led them up a narrow, dark staircase to the clerk's office, located to the side of the Revolutionary Tribunal, under the arches of the Conciergerie. They were then questioned one by one by the same Dobsent. The clerk Nenot wrote the report concerning Lavoisier:

Interrogation by Claude Emmanuel Dobsent, judge of the Revolutionary Tribunal, in the presence of Fouquier-Tinville, public prosecutor, of Antoine Laurent Lavoisier, fifty years old, born in Paris, former Farmer General and member of the former Academy of Science, residing in Paris on the boulevard de la Madeleine, in the Piques section;

when asked to name the departments for which he was responsible, he replied that he had been in charge of only the departments of Lorraine and Evêchés and the domain of Flanders;

he was again asked if he had been guilty of misappropriation of government funds, exactions and fraudulent practices toward the people. He replied that when he had learned of certain abuses, particularly in regard to tobacco, he had denounced them, which he could prove by authentic documents;

he was asked if he had chosen an attorney to defend him. He answered that he did not know one; then the Citizen Sézille was assigned to him.

Read and signed with ourselves and the court clerk. Dobsent, Lavoisier, A. Q. Fouquier and Nenot.[12]

And that was all. These formalities finished, the prisoners were returned to their cells. Since their assignats had been taken, they were unable to buy their dinner. Just as they were getting ready to ask for the bread that was distributed to indigent prisoners, the concierge's wife came to serve them a delicious meal accompanied by excellent wines. They never knew who the generous donor was, but they had in the meantime learned that they were to appear before the Revolutionary Tribunal the following day, and they set about writing a few words of farewell to their families.

Curiously it was to his cousin Augez de Villers that Lavoisier addressed his last letter, as far as we know:

I have had a reasonably long and especially a very happy career, and I believe that I will be remembered with a few regrets, perhaps with a little glory. What more could I have desired? The events by which I am surrounded are probably going to spare me the inconvenience of old age. I shall die intact, which is still another advantage that I must count among the many I have enjoyed. If I experience a few painful feelings, it is for not having done more for my family, for having been stripped of everything and finding myself unable to give to it or you any token of my affection and gratitude. It is therefore true that to avoid a sinister end and the imputation of guilt it does not suffice to exercise all the social virtues, render important services to the country, and pursue a career devoted to the progress of the arts and human knowledge. I am writing to you today because tomorrow it may no longer be allowed, and in these final moments it is a great consolation to be thinking of you and the people who are dear to me. Remember me to those who care for me and share this letter with them. It is likely to be the last one that I shall write to you.[13]

This apparent serenity was belied by a hastily scribbled note for Fouquier-Tinville which revealed a genuine anxiety:

Citizen, when I went up to the Chambre du Conseil at noon for the interrogation, they took from me a bundle of papers essential for my personal defense. I have only very little time to go over them and prepare myself for what I must explain tomorrow at the Tribunal. Be so good, Citizen, as to order that they be returned to me.[14]

This note never received an answer. The Farmers spent the rest of the afternoon in discussion. Would they be judged the following day? Some of them were still in doubt when the bell summoned the prisoners to retire to their cells.

The Indictment

They had been in their cells almost an hour and a half when a clerk arrived with a batch of papers which he said were for them. Delahante recounted:

We were called one by one and handed a single sheet. It was filled on both sides with a very fine penmanship that was difficult to read. But after deciphering only a few words, we realized that it contained the indictment against us. Eager to know the grounds for the charges, each of us was scanning his sheet to try to find the important points. We were making a great effort to read the writing when from the courtyard someone shouted that we should put out our lights. We extinguished all the candles except one, which we tried to hide, but we soon realized that it could be seen from the courtyard, which was that night lit by terracotta lamps. A guard was making his rounds, seeming to confirm the rumor that Madame Elisabeth [Louis XVI's sister] had been brought to the Conciergerie earlier that evening. Consequently, we were forced to wait for the dawn before trying and discover what the specific accusations were.[15]

With the coming of daylight, the defendants were able to make out the charges:

Indictment drawn up by Antoine Quentin Fouquier-Tinville, public prosecutor of the Revolutionary Tribunal against [there followed the names, ages and addresses of the thirty-two defendants] all former Farmers General implicated in the David, Salzard, and Mager leases:

1. For having taken 10 percent interest, instead of limiting themselves during the David lease to drawing the interest of 4 percent that the court registered lease granted them on the 72 million livres of loans reimbursable by year and by one sixth, and for having made, through attributions introduced in the operating costs, non-allotted profits, whose capital increased in their hands.

2. For having misappropriated public funds by introducing into tobacco, after its processing, water in proportion to a seventh of its weight, and then having the public pay for the water as though it were tobacco, a practice as dangerous for the consumer's health as it was harmful to his interests.

3. For having broken the terms of the lease which subjected them to paying monthly the product of taxes that had been granted to them under State control.

4. For having violated the government's rights by substituting for the tenth established by the edict of 1764 and the ruling of February 4, 1770 on the profits resulting from the lease, the clauses of the ruling of February 21, 1774.

5. For having solicited and obtained an indemnity for the withdrawal of a part of the collection that had been entrusted to them, when it is obvious that this withdrawal had cost them nothing.

6. For having kept funds coming from profits which should have been paid to the Public Treasury, at the moment when they divided up the share belonging to them.

7. For having granted special gratifications to persons who had no claim to them and moreover having ordered expenditures contrary to established principles and by this means having disposed of what rightfully belonged to the government.

8. Finally, for having liquidated the debit side of accounts concerning their administration with money coming from the national administration.
16 floréal An II.[16]

The Revolutionary Tribunal

On 19 floréal An II (Thursday, May 8, 1794), the prisoners were called just after daybreak. Fifteen minutes later, they were led to the court clerk of the Conciergerie, searched, and stripped of all the personal belongings, watches, and jewelry that had not been taken when they entered. In the long list of objects given to the clerk Wolff by the concierge Richard was "a silver watch, in the name of Berthoud, n° 2433, and a small gold key, that he declared as belonging to Lavoisier."[17]

At this point the Farmer General Verdun, whose daughter had married Jean Nicolas Billaud-Varenne, a friend of Robespierre, was suddenly released. The thirty-one remaining defendants were taken into a room adjoining the Tribunal. There they found four citizens dressed in black who were the officially appointed lawyers. One of them, Claude François Chauveau-Lagarde, was famous for having defended Charlotte Corday, Queen Marie-Antoinette, and Madame Élisabeth; the others, Guesde, Guyot-Desherbiers, and La Fleutrie, were completely unknown, as was Sézille, who was to have represented Lavoisier but who never showed up. They began to look over the file, but after fifteen minutes they were told that the Tribunal was opening its session.

It was ten o'clock when the defendants were led into the "Salle de la Liberté." On a platform about 50 centimeters high sat the president, Jean-Baptiste Coffinhal, flanked by two assessors, the judges Étienne Foucault and François Joseph Denizot. All of them were wearing black robes, white ties, and hats with feathers. On the table in front of them stood a bottle of wine and a glass. Behind them, on the wall lit by two oil lamps, were the busts of Brutus, Marat, and Le Peletier surrounding the Declaration of the Rights of Man and of the Citizen, To the right of the president, somewhat in the background, sat Claude Royer, deputy public prosecutor.[18] Below the judges sat the court clerk, Anne Ducray.

The defendants were seated on tiers, to the right of the Tribunal, and surrounded by gendarmes. To the left, on a bench, were the seven members of the jury: Leroy, the former Marquis de Montfabert, called Dix-Août (August 10); Pigeot, a barber; Renaudin, a musical instrument maker; Klispis, a jeweler; Gravier, a vinegar merchant; Auvray, a stagecoach employee; and Desboissaux.

Facing the judges were the four defense attorneys. In the back of the hall, behind a balustrade, a large crowd of onlookers were squeezed into the remaining space. Their constant chatter interspersed with the cries of the children made it difficult to hear what was being said.

Coffinhal opened the proceedings by calling each of the defendants and asking him if he was a noble and what he had done since the beginning of the Revolution. This took an hour and a half, during which the judges and jurors amused themselves by making fun of the defendants' answers. The session recessed at 11:30 and was resumed at noon. The clerk then read the indictment. That done, Delahante relates:

The president declared that the arguments were going to begin. Royer, public prosecutor, rose and asked that the Farmers General respond to his question. In all likeli-
hood, he himself did not know what he was saying, but it is certain that none of us
understood. The president called on M. Sanlot to answer it. M. Sanlot reminded him
that he had just stated that he had been merely an assistant in the General Farm and
that it had been more than ten years since he had left his post, which meant that he
had no knowledge of its administration and could say nothing about the charges in
the indictment that had just been read.[19]

Cross-examined in his turn, Delaâge became flustered, said that the
Farmers General had discussed all the the acts of which they were accused in
a memoir and referred the questioner to this memoir. Coffinhal then turned
toward Alexandre Victor de Saint-Amand: "Let us see if Mr. de Saint-Amand,
who ruled the General Farm so despotically, will be in a better state to give ex-
planations."[20] Saint-Amand had not understood Royer's question and asked
if it could be repeated.

Royer rose: "Since my first question seems obscure, I shall let it drop,
but I ask Mr. de Saint-Amand to explain why, when it came time to take out
a new lease, the Farmers General gave the Minister only false inventories of
the products of the preceding one, which made it impossible for him to set
the new lease's cost at what it should have been.[21]

Saint-Amand replied that the costs of the leases were not calculated on
the figures furnished by the Farmers General, but on those from the office of
the Minister of Finance, based on the collectors' accounts. The Farmers General, from their side, proceeded in the same way so as to be able to discuss the
value of the leases.

Coffinhal interrupted and threatened that the defendants would be
judged "without stopping" if they continued to stall for time. He instructed
them to answer the questions by yes or no.

Saint-Amand objected "that no negative response would have sufficed to
clear the Farmers General of the charges against them, whereas the explanation he had just given obviously proved not only that they had not submitted
false inventories, but that they had not even been in the position to give one,
since it was on the basis of the Minister's own figures that the price of the
leases was determined."[22]

Then suddenly Royer jumped up from his chair, ordered silence, and
read a decree issued that very day:

The National Convention, considering that the assistants of the former Farmers General, who were in no way implicated in he David, Mager, and Salzard leases, and hence
should not have been included in the law of 16 floréal which sent the citizens Farmers
General to the Revolutionary Tribunal, has concluded that the citizens Delahante,

Delaâge de Bellefaye, and Sanlot, assistants, should be immediately removed from the proceedings and returned to the prisons where they were being held.[23]

Gendarmes came to take away the three men, pallid and trembling with emotion. The decree saving them had been obtained in extremis by Dobsent. After appealing in vain to Fouquier-Tinville, he had managed to get Dupin to write it and have it signed by the Convention's president. It was one o'clock when Royer began his closing argument for the prosecution. The *Bulletin du Tribunal Révolutionnaire* analyzed it this way:

The public prosecutor summed up this case in a few words. Going over the different forms of exactions and misappropriations of funds of which the so called former Farmers General are accused, he proved their guilt succinctly and convincingly. He concluded that the extent of the crimes of these vampires knew no bounds, that they called for revenge, that the immorality of these men was engraved in public opinion, and that they had been the perpetual authors of all the evils from which France had been suffering for a long time.[24]

The defense lawyers then presented their arguments, but the Tribunal, the jury, and the public, all impatient for the verdict, scarcely listened to them.

Jean Noël Hallé, in the name of the Advisory Board for Arts and Trades, had sent the judges a long report detailing the services Lavoisier had rendered to the Republic, but Coffinhal had refused to acknowledge it. Legend has it that he commented, "The Republic has no need of scientists; justice must follow its course." It is now known that the statement is apocryphal. Certainly, public opinion tended to confuse scientists and academicians with aristocrats and counter-revolutionaries; however, it was not Lavoisier's trial that was being held, but that of the Farmers General without distinction of person. The jury, like the judges, was persuaded that they were guilty of crimes. The bias against them had been growing for a long time. The scandal of the tobacco moistening had outraged all France. The judicial and financial subtleties and the dry reports had not enlightened anyone.

"The Revolutionary Tribunal, being a special criminal court, had no powers to deal with any of the offenses with which the Farmers General were charged, but only with counter-revolutionary activity."[25] Thus Coffinhal, in his instructions to the jury, could not pose the question in the context suggested by Dupin's report. He had to refer to counter-revolutionary activity in complicity with the foreigner, which was punishable by death:

Did there exist a conspiracy against the French people tending to favor, by all possible means, the success of the enemies of France? In particular, did they amass financial means by various kinds of exactions and misappropriation of funds belonging to the French people; by mixing with tobacco not only water but other ingredients harmful to the health of those citizens using it; by collecting 6 or 10 percent interest on different guaranties as well as on the capital investment necessary for the exploitation of the General Farm; by holding funds that should have been paid directly to the National Treasury, and by pillaging and stealing from the people and the National Treasury, so as to deprive the Nation of the immense sums necessary for the war of the Republic against the coalition of despots and to hand over these sums to these despots?[26]

The response of the jury was not recorded in the court report. Only Coffinhal's signature is found in the space provided for its inscription. He pronounced the verdict:

The declaration of the jury is that there constantly existed a conspiracy against the French people, tending to favor, by all possible means, the success of the enemies of France; that Clément Delaâge, Louis Balthazar Dangé-Bagneux, Jacques Paulze, Antoine Laurent Lavoisier, François Puissant, Alexandre Victor Saint-Amand, Gilbert Georges Montcloux, Adam François Parcelle Saint-Cristau, Jean Baptiste Boullongne, Louis Marie Lebas de Courmont, Charles René Parseval Frileuse, Nicolas Jacques Papillon d'Auteroche, Jean Germain Maubert-Neuilly, Jacques Joseph Brac La Perrière, Claude François Rougeot, François Joseph Vente, Denis Henri Fabus-Vernand, Nicolas Deville, Clément Cugnot-l'Epinay, Louis Adrien Prévost d'Arlincourt, Jérôme François Hector Saleure de Grizien, Etienne Marin Delahaye, François Marie Ménage-Pressigny, Guillaume Couturier, Louis Philippe Duvaucel, Alexandre Philibert Pierre Parseval, Jean François Didelot, Jean Louis Loiseau-Bérenger, ex-nobles and former Farmers General are all convicted of being the authors of or acomplices in this conspiracy,

after having heard the public prosecutor on the application of the law, the tribunal condemns the above named to the death sentence, in conformity with Article 4 of Section One of the first title of part Two of the penal code which has been read and which is thus worded: "Every ruse, every secret agreement with the enemies of France that tends to facilitate their entry into the dependencies of the French Empire, or turns over to them towns, fortresses, ports, ships, warehouses, or arsenals belonging to France or provides aid to them in the form of soldiers, money, provisions, or ammunition or encourages in any way whatsoever the incursion of their weapons on French territory or their use against our land or sea forces, or undermines the loyalty of officers, soldiers, or other citizens toward the French nation, will be punished by death,"

declares the property of the condemned as acquired by the Republic in conformity with Article 2 of Title 2 of the law of last March 10, to the exceptions brought by the aforementioned law, and orders that at the public prosecutor's request, the present sentence be executed within 24 hours at the Place de la Révolution of this city and printed, posted, and published throughout the Republic. Signed: Coffinhal, Denizot, Foucault, Ducray.[27]

Across the cover of the file containing the documents relating to the trial of the Farmers General was written in large letters a macabre and chilling title: "Delaâge, Bagneux, Paulze, Lavoisier, and others, all Farmers General. Sentenced 19 floréal. DEATH."

The verdict had been foreseeable, the condemnation certain. Neverthe-less all the legal forms had been respected.

The Execution

The sentence pronounced, the men were returned to the Conciergerie. The bailiff Nappier notified the concierge, Richard, of the sentence and gave him 28 individual discharge forms.[28] The condemned men were soon thereafter crammed into wagons to be taken to the Place de la Révolution. The munici-pal officers, on horseback with sabres in hand, cleared a passageway through the dense crowd. The procession passed along the Quai de l'Horloge, over the Pont au Change, and followed the Quai de la Mégisserie before reaching the Louvre. Looking across the Seine, Lavoisier could see the Collège Mazarin where he had spent his early years. The Farmers, jolted by the cobblestones, remained silent. Papillon d'Auteroche, observing the crowds angrily shaking their fists and thinking of his confiscated property, remarked: "What grieves me most is to have such unpleasant heirs."[29]

When they reached the Place de la Révolution, it was five in the evening and still fully light. With hands tied behind their backs, they stepped down from their wagons to the foot of the guillotine, and then climbed up a steep stairway in the order of their inscription on the indictment. Paulze was third in line, Lavoisier fourth.

A witness, Cheverny, wrote: "Everybody knew about the barbarous exe-cution of these decent men. M. de Lavoisier, summoned the night before to present the balanced accounts, was condemned along with the others. He pre-pared them for death. They met their ends with great dignity. But the poor M. de Boullongne was led to the scaffold in a pitiful state."[30]

It took only thirty-five minutes to execute twenty-eight Farmers Gen-eral. The execution over, Eustache Nappier, the bailiff of the Revolutionary Tribunal, impassively filled out the printed form for the report.[31] Fréron's newspaper, l'Orateur du peuple, rejoiced: "The blood that inundated the Place recalled the purple beds where a short while ago they were leading their luxurious life."[32]

The employees stacked the bodies on the wagons, while the heads were collected in a large wicker basket. The procession, escorted by horsemen from the Parisian Guard, took the streets of la Madeleine, l'Arcade, and la Pologne, crossed the rue Saint-Lazare, and followed the rue du Rocher and the rue des Errancis. It left the city by the elegant Mousseaux tollgate of the General Farm (presently a part of the Parc Monceau) and entered the new graveyard that had been created when the Madeleine Cemetary had been closed on 14 ventôse An II (March 4, 1794). Large common graves had been dug on a wasteland called Errancis, which means "maimed person."

These graves were used for the 943 victims who were guillotined at the Place de la Revolution between March 25 and June 9, 1794. In addition to the Farmers General, they also buried Madame Elisabeth, Danton, Fabre d'Eglantine, and Camille and Lucile Desmoulins.[33] After 9 thermidor (July 27, 1794), they were joined by Robespierre, Saint-Just, Fouquier-Tinville, and 176 others. When the boulevard de Courcelles was built in 1859, the remains of the victims were transported to the Catacombs, and today there exists no trace of the "Cemetery of the Errancis." The site corresponds to the Place Prosper Goubaux, between the Metro station of Villiers and the intersection of the rues du Rocher et de Monceau.

Could Lavoisier Have Been Saved?

The day after Lavoisier's execution, a disillusioned Lagrange commented: "It took them only an instant to cut off that head but it is unlikely that a hundred years will suffice to reproduce a similar one."[34]

Could Lavoisier have been saved? Undoubtedly. And in the first place, by himself. Some opportune mission abroad or a trip to a distant province planned before the Reign of Terror would have allowed him to wait for less troubled times. But flight was not easy to organize and it was repugnant to his self-esteem. He who knew so well how to decide for others did not know how to negotiate for himself. A little less pride and rigidity, a little more intuition and subtlety, indeed a good dose of cynicism, would have certainly allowed him to extricate himself. This masterly calculator was in the end naive, and it is this surprising trait that makes his case all the more moving.

His execution was the result of enormous misunderstandings. The first one was to imagine that it would suffice to break off obvious contacts with the General Farm to escape its destiny. A second was to believe that the corrected errors in the accounts of the Farm furnished to Dupin would justify dropping the case. A third was to misjudge the mentality of the members of the Convention, who were incapable of reconciling the positions of the Committee on Public Education, which was trying to save an irreplaceable scientist, and that of the Committee of Public Safety, which was determined to destroy the former Farmers General.

Furthermore, his wife might have shown herself more skillful in dealing with Dupin. The successful steps taken in favor of the assistants prove that such an outcome was possible in Lavoisier's case as well. Of the 45 Farmers General involved in the last lease, 18 escaped death. There remained, of course, bribery, a widely used recourse to which Dupin, Fouquier-Tinville, and Coffinhal were not insensitive.[35]

But Lavoisier would have needed far better public relations agents than the proud Marie Anne. It is surely to the credit of our times to have understood that individuals as well as institutions must develop favorable relationships with the public to endure in times of crisis. In spite of the danger to which they exposed themselves, Lavoisier's friends and former assistants made attempts to help, as long as they viewed him as a scientist and colleague. But when the trial of the Farmers General began they turned away, not only because of the personal risks, but because they were convinced that the charges against the Farm were valid. Hence they did not feel they had the recognized authority or right to intervene.

Borda, Haüy, Desaudray, and Hallé all did what they could, as did the colleagues at the Lycée des Arts and the Advisory Board for Arts and Trades. It was his former collaborators, close to power, who were the most disappointing. Guyton de Morveau felt his own life threatened. Four days after Lavoisier's execution, he got himself sent on a mission with General Jourdan to launch the *Entreprenant*, an observation balloon. Called back to Paris in the first days of thermidor (July 19), he took his time in returning and left the Army of the North only ten days later. He arrived four days after Robespierre's fall to learn that his name had been on his final list of suspects.

Hassenfratz and Monge were fervent Jacobins, regular attendants at the meetings of the club, elected to hold office and preside over its deliberations. Even after successive purges, they "emerged pure from the crucible of trials." But they kept their distance. As for Berthollet, in spite of his close ties with Monge and Fourcroy, he held no political post and had no influence.

In their eyes, Lavoisier probably shared responsibility for the crimes imputed to the Farmers General. They had neither desire nor capacity to question the judgment of a power in which they were participating. Perhaps in the end, they did not consider his scientific contribution as unique and irreplaceable: men of science like him and treated as equals, they felt themselves to be just as much as he the fathers of the new chemistry. Also they had not forgotten that the day when they had dared to speak of the "theory of the French chemists," Lavoisier had claimed it exclusively, not without a certain meanness of spirit: "This theory is not, as I have heard it said, 'the theory of the French chemists', it is mine. . . ."[36]

As for the specific role of Fourcroy, a great debate divides historians. Did he or did he not intervene to save Lavoisier? According to some, he was

ruthlessly ambitious and fanatical and did nothing. This was the theory of
Dr. Sacombe, his contemporary: "If a man is so cowardly as to keep silent
when, with a single word, he could save a great man's life, then he ought to
know at least how to expiate his silence."[37] According to others, he risked his
life to do all that was humanly possible in a period when everyone was afraid
for himself, in particular after the law of suspects of September 1793.

At the time of the trial, Fourcroy was a member of the Convention and
his revolutionary convictions were intact. Political success had led him to take
extremists positions. At the Jacobin Club, he declared that he taught medicine only to "feed his sans-culotte father and sisters," but such a statement was
largely self-serving.

In fact, as we have seen, Fourcroy worked through the Commission on
Weights and Measures to protect Lavoisier. And when his colleague was arrested and sentenced, he undertook, according to his student André Laugier,
incredibly audacious steps to save him:

This is a fact that unfortunately is too little known and to which MM. Carnot and
Prieur de La Côte d'Or can bear witness. A day or so before Lavoisier was slaughtered,
M. de Fourcroy, although he had no right to do so, dared to enter the Assembly hall
where the Committee of Public Safety was meeting. He spoke in favor of Lavoisier
and explained with the passion so natural to him what a dreadful loss for the sciences
the death of this great chemist would be. Since Robespierre, then the president of the
committee, did not answer, no one else ventured to speak, and M. de Fourcroy was
obliged to leave without anyone seeming to pay the slightest attention to what he had
said. Hardly was he outside the door when the president complained of his gall, men-
acing Fourcroy, and so terrified Prieur de La Côte d'Or that he ran after Fourcroy and
urged him not to do anything more if he wanted to save his own head.[38]

"I made efforts for the unfortunate Lavoisier," Fourcroy wrote, "but I
failed, although a few hopes were held out. His fate was decided along with
that of all the Farmers General."[39] Contemporaries Georges Cuvier, Antoine
Claire Thibaudeau, and Eugène Chevreul came to Fourcroy's defense. Not
only, they said, did he have great respect and friendship for Lavoisier, but
he had tried to help him insofar as he was able. Certainly he was behind the
purge of the Lycée where Lavoisier taught, and then that of the Academy of
Science, but paradoxically that was intended to save him. In the end, Fourcroy admitted that he had felt his own life in danger:

Think back to those dreadful times when Lavoisier perished along with so many other
illustrious martyrs to liberty, knowledge, talents, and virtue. Think back to those
times, so deplorable and distressing for the history of our revolution, when we had to
hide our tears in our hearts so as not to betray our sensitivity to tyranny; when, for
the dominant horde, the slightest signs of compassion and pity were admissions of

complicity with those it had pronounced guilty; when terror created a vast distance between people, even friends; when it isolated families from each other, even within their own homes; when the least word, the slightest indication of solicitude for the unfortunate who were preceding you on the road to death were considered crimes and conspiracies. Reread those fatal pages of our history and reply to those who dredge up from those horrible sacrifices, perfidious doubts, or still more criminal slanders against men who supposedly had some power or influence to stop these executions. From the tyrant's viewpoint, did not these men, by their works and lives completely dedicated to public service, merit the same fate as Lavoisier? Were they not already under the shadow of arrest? Would their blood not have been mixed with that of the illustrious victim in just a few more days? Had not the judge-executioner proclaimed that the republic had no need of scientists, and that a single intelligent man sufficed to run its affairs? [40]

Although Fourcroy seemed to support the apocryphal statement that "the Republic had no need of scientists," it is essential to keep in mind that it was not scientists but the Farmers General who were being judged. Lavoisier died because he was one of them. In this context, Fourcroy could do nothing for him.

Scientists Under the Reign of Terror

Besides, the attitude of the Convention and the Committee of Public Safety in regard to scientists can at first sight appear contradictory. Some were condemned to death, others saved their heads by keeping a low profile. Still others took over vitally important functions for the young Republic. The different fates can be explained by the political path followed by each man. Scientists did not make up a homogeneous class, distinct from the rest of society, even if they sometimes gave that illusion. Just like other citizens, they had their individual political opinions, ambitions, and friendships. In the critical period of the Reign of Terror, they were forced to choose their camp. Seven scientists perished as victims of their political opinions and not as men of science.

The duc de La Rochefoucauld d'Enville, honorary member of the Academy of Science, patron of scientists and a true friend of liberty, did not appear before the Revolutionary Tribunal. Condemned to death by the instigators of the "people's movement" of August 10, 1792, which led to the collapse of monarchy, he left Paris to seek refuge in Forges. Arrested and brought to Gisors, he was lynched by a mob on September 14.

Jean Sylvain Bailly was the first victim of the Reign of Terror. An outstanding astronomer and Academician, he presided over the 1789 meeting in the Jeu de Paume when the members of the Third Estate swore not to adjourn before giving France a Constitution. Soon afterwards he became mayor of Paris. Ambitious and naive, he, along with La Fayette, had immense prestige at the beginning of the Revolution. But the decision to fire on the demonstrators at the Champs de Mars in July, 1791 ended all that. He was condemned to death by the Revolutionary Tribunal and guillotined on November 10, 1793.

The baron Philippe Frédéric de Dietrich, chemist and metallurgist and associate member of the Academy of Science, was mayor of Strasbourg. It was in his house that Rouget de l'Isle composed the Marseillaise. On the day after, August 10, 1792, he asked the Assembly to guarantee the inviolability of royal authority and to punish the inciters of riots. Placed on the list of suspects, he fled to Switzerland but later returned to France. Initially acquitted by a provincial court, he was denounced as an émigré, condemned by the Revolutionary Tribunal, and guillotined on December 28, 1793.

Condorcet's destiny was just as tragic. Deputy at the Legislative Assembly and then at the Convention, he sought to reconcile the Girondins and the Montagnards and refused to vote for the death of Louis XVI. In 1792 he developed a constitutional plan that Robespierre and Marat attacked as being aristocratic. The Committee of Public Safety proposed another, which the Convention adopted without debate. However, Condorcet criticized it vehemently and urged citizens to vote against it. Accused of high treason, he hid out in Paris for nine months during which he wrote his *Esquisse d'un tableau historique des progrès de l'esprit humain*. He finally fled the capital, was arrested in Clamart and taken to the prison in Bourg-Egalité (formerly Bourg-la-Reine). The following morning, April 8, 1794, the jailer found him dead in his cell. Whether he committed suicide or died of a heart attack was never known.

Jean Baptiste Gaspard Bochart de Saron, astronomer and mathematician, was in 1789 the first president of the Parlement de Paris. He had a magnificent collection of astronomical instruments that he lent to his colleagues. Of a timorous nature, he asked his bookbinder to disemblazon all the books in his library and remove the fleurs de lys from the hands of his clocks. But he did sign a protest against the suppression of Parliament which resulted in his being brought before the Revolutionary Tribunal and guillotined on April 20, 1794.

Chrétien Guillaume de Lamoignon de Malesherbes, botanist and honorary member of the Academy of Science, was arrested in June 1793 for having served as defense lawyer for Louis XVI when he was tried by the Convention. He was guillotined on April 22, 1794.

The seventh and not the least was Lavoisier.

Numerous scientists tried to make themselves forgotten during the revolutionary crisis, but none of them emigrated. Baumé, Bayen, Borda, Coulomb,

Cadet, Brisson, and Parmentier took refuge in the country. Cadet de Gassi-court quietly taught chemistry at the Lycée des Arts. Charles, the inventor of the hydrogen balloon, and Cassini, director of the Paris Observatory, managed to save their lives. The astronomers Lalande, Laplace, Delambre, the mineralogists Haüy, Sage, Dolomieu, Desmarest, the mathematicians Bossut, Legendre, Fourier, and the Montgolfier brothers also succeeded in fading into the background. None of them were considered to be fervent enough republicans to be associated with the mobilization of scientists.

Dionis du Séjour and Vicq d'Azyr, crushed by fear, died just after thermidor. Daubenton, listed in the census as a shepherd because in 1782 he had published a work entitled "Instructions for Shepherds and Owners of Flocks," continued his circumspect research at the Museum of Natural History. Seguin abandoned chemistry and took up making shoes for the army, thanks to a patent for his method of waterproofing leather. He amassed a huge fortune, which resulted in his being arrested several times under the Empire.

Chaptal's case was special: a respected chemist and manufacturer in Montpellier, he had supported the Girondins. Considered suspect under the Reign of Terror, he was arrested in 1793 by orders coming from Paris. But he was released after ten days and went to hide in the Cévennes. In December 1793, Carnot and Prieur de La Côte d'Or called him to Paris to replace Lavoisier, who had just been arrested, at the Gunpowder and Saltpeter Administration. He preferred, however, to stay in the Midi as gunpowder and saltpeter inspector. On March 23, 1794 Carnot insisted on his presence in Paris and made him director of the saltpeter refinery in Saint-Germain-des-Prés and the Grenelle gunpowder manufacture. Denounced on three different occasions, he was saved by the Committee of Public Safety.

Other scientists were preparing for the future. The necessity for organizing the defense of the country, for providing soldiers with gunpowder and weapons, brought out the eminent place of science and applied science: Carnot, Guyton de Morveau, Fourcroy, Berthollet, Monge, Hassenfratz, Carny, Chappe, Meusnier, Dufourny, Périer, Pluvinet, Conté, and Vandermonde were going to demonstrate that the Republic needed scientists. The imagination and enthusiasm of these men would work wonders in the dramatic crisis that France endured in the An II.

La Citoyenne Lavo

A MONTH AFTER LAVOISIER'S EXECUTION, the loi de prairial (June 10, 1794) installed the grande Terreur, removing the suspects' last means of defense, since moral presumption of guilt had eliminated the need for witnesses. "The law gives slandered patriots patriotic juries to defend them; it does not do the same for conspirators."[1] Between that time and 9 thermidor, or in forty-seven days, the Revolutionary Tribunal sentenced 1,376 people to death. Another 7,321 filled the prisons of the capital. Of the 130 million livres the Farmers General owed to the State, according to Dupin, only slightly more than 67 had been recovered. The balance was to be paid by their heirs.[2] Living alone, Madame Lavoisier led an increasingly precarious existence. Her father and husband were dead, her brother was in hiding, and her property had been seized.

The Confiscation of Property

Soon after the executions, bailiffs had arrived at the boulevard de la Madeleine to make an inventory of all the books, furniture, objets d'art, and scientific instruments. They left behind a thick handwritten document of 178 pages.[3] Everything described in it was to be confiscated and handed over to the institutions of the State. On May 30, the Citizens Quinquet and Le Roy, pharmacists, came to confiscate:

from the physics laboratory a pair of copper scales with iron beams and brackets, a Riché hygrometer, a Fontana eudiometer, an electric machine, a copper conductor, electric chimes, two electrometers, a copper exciter, a Leyden jar, two tableaux magiques, an electric stool [. . .] from the first chemistry laboratory, 14 sifters, a stoneware fountain with two faucets, 64 glass containers, flasks, tanks and retorts, 146 plain glass bottles with inverted necks, 35 flasks of various sizes [. . .] from the second chemistry laboratory, a terracotta furnace, a copper still with pewter basin, 10 furnace grills, 2 tripods, 2 bellows, several flasks containing coal tar, fuming nitrous acid, mercury, 47 plain glass vessels, 130 flasks, 7 pounds of cloves.[4]

On June 10 Citizen Jean Baptiste Trouville, director of the fleet of car-riages of the Republic, seized "a bright blue English style diligence, spring-born, lined in light grey wool with blue, canary yellow, and beige braid, having red wheels and steel trim; and a dark blue English style vis-à-vis car-riage, also spring-born, having a narrow white border, with gilded arms, upholstered in blue and white starred Utrecht velvet, with the same braid, having grey wheels and gilded trim."[5]

At the request of the Committee on Public Education, Berthollet came to make a list of the chemical instruments; he was accompanied by an expert, Nicolas Leblanc, who had created in Saint-Denis the first artificial soda fac-tory in France.[6]

Leblanc returned four times in November to make the appraisal, assisted by two agents from the Domaine national, a glass merchant and an apothe-cary. They began by bringing up from the cellar all the glass which they had found "in piles and ill-assorted": 2,145 retorts, cucurbits, tanks, stills, pelicans; 3,129 jars; 549 flasks containing crystallized saltpeter, sulfuric acid, muriatic acid, nitric acid, potassium, diaphoretic antimony, manganese, phosphorus, bismuth, platinum, and so forth. The total was appraised at 7,267 livres 16 sols.

For the instruments used in physics experiments, Leblanc had the help of Lenoir and Fortin, who appraised Megnié's big gazometer and its acces-sories at 8,000 livres.[7] The instruments used for combustion of oils and wine spirits and fermentation tests were valued at 1,600 livres; the two calorimeters with tin lamps at 600; the large pneumatic machine with two cylinders built by Fortin at 800; two large balloons for weighing air at 100, a large labora-tory scale at 150; twenty thermometers at 60; a Moissy barometer "mounted in mahogany but in poor condition, air has entered the tube," at 100.[8] And so it continued for several pages: electric machines, Papin machines, compasses, sextants, astrolabes, barometers and precision scales, a mass of costly instru-ments. There was a total of 125 articles estimated to be worth 20,327 livres.[9]

Pluvinet had the mineralogical collection moved to the Central School for Public Works, the future Ecole Polytechnique. Geoffroy Saint-Hilaire took nine bottles of liquid mercury and two of red mercury oxide to the Museum of Natural History. The Committee of Public Safety kept for itself Lavoisier's library, his two desks, one with a roll top, and six armchairs.[10]

Thus all the furniture, including the Pannier marquetry clock, the paint-ings, bibelots, statues, and silver, gradually disappeared. Madame Lavoisier wandered about in empty rooms with the sole company of the faithful Mas-selot, who had come back to serve and assist her. Nothing remained of the pretty decoration installed only a few months earlier.

In the large reception room on the ground floor, only the slightly lighter rectangles on the wood paneling were left as reminders of the missing paintings: Coypel's "Love as Teacher," Suis's "Death of Cédécia's Children," and Girodet's "Coriolan's Departure for Exile."

The bookcases were empty except for the catalogue listing the 560 volumes that had been removed. The eight headings were a digest of Lavoisier's life, tastes, and works: mineralogy and metallurgy; chemistry; physics; natural history; mathematics; geography; collections.

Madame Lavoisier installed herself in the small living room on the ground floor that gave onto a miniscule garden. Her only furniture was a modest painted wooden bed mounted on casters and covered with white twill, three wicker chairs, and a pair of chipped porcelain vases. The pair of Louis XVI mahogany chests of drawers, adorned with gilded bronze and topped with white marble, the small mahogany chiffonier, the six armchairs covered in crimson velvet, and the Zimmerman pianoforte had vanished along with everything else.

She knew that she was going to be arrested, but she did not have the heart to flee. Besides, where could she have gone? Freschines, confiscated with its furniture, books, and harvests, was soon going to be sold at auction. She had only two faithful friends remaining, the Du Pont de Nemours: Pierre Samuel and his son Eleuthère Irénée. They insisted that she take refuge on their property at Bois des Fossés, but she hesitated and constantly put off departure. This delay can be explained by the ambiguity of her relationship with Pierre Samuel.

Du Pont de Nemours, Suitor and Debtor

Pierre Samuel, who dared not leave the country to return to Paris, was devastated by the loss of his friend Lavoisier. On December 22, 1792, he had paid tribute to the Lavoisiers by dedicating to them his last book, a work of moral and political philosophy entitled *La philosophie de l'univers*:

I saw this virtuous citizen, one of the most enlightened, gentlest and wisest men who ever existed, one of those who had most constantly and effectively served the nation and mankind, and who served them up to the last moments of his life, perish in the most unjust, the most tyrannical, the most cruel way. I will never cease to mourn him. He was an outstanding scientist, particularly trained to apply to the physical sciences the rigorous method and precise analysis by which the truth is grasped. His widow, today the unhappiest of women, was the worthy companion, the valuable collaborator in all his work.[11]

A more tender feeling was mixed with his compassion for Marie Anne. Still in love with her, but now rejected, he complained of feminine fickleness.

He had attributed to Arimane, the evil spirit in his *Philosophie de l'univers*, the diabolical idea of endowing women with vanity and coquetry. He had her say:

Even the most virtuous and faithful of women will be pleased by tributes from those whom they have no intention of rewarding with their love. Even their refusals will be appealing, because they will be disguised in declarations of esteem or friendship. They will say, "Do not hope," believing perhaps that they have destroyed all hope. But the captivating charm of their voice, the pride with which, thanks to my attentions, the perfect victim will be consumed, will reply: "You must still hope." And the very gentleness of the feminine character will seem to confirm that admonition by a remarkable succession of kindnesses, attentions, and considerations that women consider as simple and appropriate consolations, but in which they will nevertheless have the secret pleasure of prolonging their power. Thus they will mislead, either intentionally or unwittingly, the lover whom they have decided to reject. They will consequently profoundly disturb and often even crush the happiness of the ones they had chosen to console by kindness.[12]

This quite transparent lesson was addressed to Marie Anne. Besides, Arimane could very well be an anagram for Marie Anne. In the letters Pierre Samuel wrote daily to his son, alone in Paris, he was constantly asking for news of her. So as not the attract the attention of the police, who monitored correspondence closely, he designated her by rather naive code names: "my cousin from the boulevard," "the citizen," or "Citizen Lavo." He urged his son to assure her that she was expected at Bois des Fossés, that everything was ready for her arrival.

On 5 prairial (May 24) Eleuthère Irénée wrote to his father: "I have seen Citizen Lavo several times. She was kind enough to come to me, since I could not go to her. I shall see her again when I return. It is likely that I shall then bring her with me to the country for a few days. Prepare a room."[13]

But Marie Anne continued to procrastinate and eventually refused outright, fearing that her former lover was harboring illusions. On 26 prairial (June 14) she was arrested by order of the Committee of General Security and taken to a prison in the rue Neuve des Capucines, only a short distance from where she lived. Six days later, Pierre Samuel was arrested at Bois des Fossés, taken to Paris, and detained at another prison, la Force. In most of the forty-nine letters he sent to his son while he was being held, he asked for news of his friend.

On 22 messidor (July 10) Eleuthère Irénée announced, in coded language, that Madame Lavoisier had been arrested: "The citizen about whom our good friend asks for news has met with a very great tribulation. Faure goes to see her often and we hope that she will be happily extricated in a few days."[14]

On 8 thermidor (July 26) Pierre Samuel expressed his growing concern:

"I am terribly eager for news of my cousin who to my great delight had been contemplating settling in our commune when she last came to visit."[15] The following day came Robespierre's downfall, but nothing changed in the prisoners' life.

On 15 thermidor (August 2) Le Couteulx de la Noraye, in whose mansion Madame Lavoisier had her apartment, was also arrested and taken to la Force. He was accused of misappropriating public funds when he was director of the water company. The news he brought to Pierre Samuel from the outside was most alarming. According to him, Madame Lavoisier was about to be condemned to death.

On 16 thermidor (August 3) Pierre Samuel, who was beside himself with anxiety, begged his son for details: "Tell the citizen if it is my cousin who lives on the boulevard whose news you give me, because it is about her in particular that I want to hear."[16]

On 17 thermidor (August 4) a reassuring letter arrived and he replied with obvious relief: "Give my fondest greetings to my cousin of whom you speak and whose improved health makes me feel extremely joyful. Because Le Couteulx de la Noraye, who is here, had passed on to me, as certain and concrete, dismaying news, which had broken my heart and shattered my courage."[17]

But Pierre Samuel was still not certain that he had fully understood and he returned to the subject: "The citizen has forgotten if it is my cousin from the boulevard, who recently visited Bois des Fossés whom you have seen and who is doing well. Repeat it to him and to me."[18]

At the same time, Madame Lavoisier was taking her fate in hand. On 24 thermidor (August 11) she wrote to the revolutionary committee of her residential section:

Citizens, you have already demanded the release of several citizens from your section held in different prisons. Shall I be the only one not to benefit from your justice? I have nevertheless every claim on it. I belong to the sans-culottes. I have no fortune. I have been detained by order of the Committee of General Security, but my arrest warrant contains no motive, and, in all good conscience, I cannot conceive of one. My opinions are well known. I have always had republican principles in my heart and have openly professed them. The seals affixed on my papers during last August and the subsequent report that was made are proof of this.

Misfortune has few friends. Among the small number of those who are interested in me, some are prevented from helping because of their own problems, others are simply in no position to do so. To whom can I address myself if not to the revolutionary committee of my section, so that justice be done by me, or at least that I be given the means of responding to the charges against me, if they exist? Therefore, Citizens, I now regard you as my protectors. Thus I dare to ask you to intercede with the

Committee of General Security for my release, or at least to determine the reasons for which I am being held.[19]

The secretary of the "surveillance committee" faithfully recopied information contained in Citizen Lavoisier's file into the register of the section:

Presumed income while her husband was alive, 25,000 livres. Present income, 2,000 livres. Her relations and connections are unknown to the committee. But it can be assumed that, collaborating daily with her husband in his work, she was involved only with what related to their domestic occupations. This woman's opinions and character are unknown to the committee. According to her, she is a patriot, but that is difficult to know. The committee nevertheless declares that it is not aware of anything against the above-mentioned Citizen Lavoisier and refers the matter to the Committee of General Security, which having ordered the arrest, must know the reasons for it.[20]

On 25 thermidor (August 12) Du Pont asked his son to deliver an affectionate message: "Give my devoted greetings to my cousin who is responsible for my having written those wise, strong, and pious ideas. I do not write to her directly because I do not wish either to tire or worry her. But she knows what I think and what she means to me."[21]

The Committee of General Security reached a decision on 30 thermidor (August 17): "Citizen Lavoisier will be immediately released and will lodge an appeal with the Administration of National Property to have the seals removed from the objects that may belong to her in the house she inhabited with Citizen Lavoisier, her husband."[22] She had spent sixty-five days in prison.

On 3 fructidor (August 20) Pierre Samuel again sent a doting message: "A thousand, ten thousand wishes to my cousin from the boulevard, whom I dare not fatigue with my letters although I have a great yearning to write to her often."[23]

On 6 fructidor (August 23) Eleuthère Irénée, who was doing everything possible to get his father released, was terribly upset to have missed seeing Le Couteulx de la Noraye, who had just been freed and had returned to the boulevard de la Madeleine: "I was visiting our cousin when he left his apartment. I ran after him but in vain."[24] There was a severe response from Pierre Samuel:

You must not regret having missed seeing the citizen who lives in the same building as our cousin, given that he is a man who always promises more than he can deliver and never tells the truth. [. . .] Now, answer my question about our cousin. Was she really arrested or was she only threatened? In the former case, how were you able to see her? As for the justice rendered her, I am not surprised, and I hope she will be rendered even more. You know that even though she gave me, gives me and is bound to give me still much grief, she has so many virtues, such reason and merit that she shares my heart even with you, my beloved child. Therefore, everything that interests her interests me more than I can say. And that neighbor, the liar I mentioned at the beginning of the letter, told me so many contradictory things about her that, although I took all he said with a grain of salt, I desire more information.[25]

More than simply a faithful friend's solicitude, these words are permeated by the nostalgia of a distant lover. Now a widower, the prisoner did not cease to dream of the woman he had known rich, beautiful, and happy, but who was then living from Masselot's charity. Dupin in fact had withdrawn her last source of income on September 24. But it was obvious that she wanted to maintain only quasi-filial relations with Pierre Samuel. She was 36, he was 55 and not very attractive: bald and stooped, he already looked like an old man.[26] Could he hope that she would accept his impassioned declarations?[27] He did not hide his disappointment from his son:

Although she seeks to express affection for me and to ask for the continuation of mine "for my daughter," she is far from diminishing the pain she causes me. She asks me to postpone all explanation until we see each other again, a time I can scarcely hope for or any longer desire. But remaining greatly distressed for her, and myself wounded to the bottom of my heart, I still think that I should suspend all resolution and keep myself open to indulgence for an old and unhappy friend, who was especially commended to me by her dying husband, my closest friend.

There was no great merit in being attached to her when she had beauty, health, wealth, credit, ideas, a superior intelligence and reason. But now that all this has been lost or singularly diminished, that she is being wronged and suffering misfortunes, then simultaneously I should do my duty and pay the debts of our long friendship. I shall fulfill this duty as far as possible and much further than is convenient for my happiness to which, since she offers me only her friendship, she can no longer contribute, other than by the opportunity she gives me to master myself, to forgive, and to do good. Because the sore may heal, but the scar will remain.[28]

The correspondence continued, with Citizen Lavoisier occupying a large place in it, and the complaints of the former lover were always just as fervid. On 2 brumaire (October 23), he wrote: "I have almost come to a decision concerning her and have informed her of it. I shall be fair, obliging, generous, indulgent, honest and free and, if I can be, happy. But I dare not answer for that: she had all my heart and she has broken it."[29]

Between them there were not only disappointed feelings but also problems of money. Madame Lavoisier was asking to be reimbursed the 71,000 livres lent by her husband in June 1791 for setting up the printing plant in the Hôtel de Bretonvilliers. With interest, the debt would come to 88,000 livres ($3.5 million), which Pierre Samuel was simply unable to pay. In April 1795 he sent three letters to his son, one after the other:

Put all pressure on Faure for settling the account with Citizen Lavoisier. That is more important to our business and to my peace of mind than I can say. On one point, she is right to be angry with us. [. . .] And that we are in the wrong in this respect is deeply distressing to me. Exert pressure on Faure every day, without fail, to settle the account. [. . .] It is one of our most important tasks, and the one which personally interests me most.[30]

Faure might very well do his utmost to comply with instructions, but there was simply no money for reimbursing her. Du Pont envisaged selling his printing office, which he estimated to be worth 50,000 livres, or his property at Bois des Fossés. But times were hardly favorable, since there were no buyers. The printing plant would not be sold until May 21, 1799 and brought only 25,000 livres. The debt would eventually be paid by the sale of Bois des Fossés on June 28, 1815.

Dupin's Indictment

More inflexible than ever, Madame Lavoisier decided to obtain the restoration of her husband's property as well as that belonging specifically to her. On December 10, 1794 the Abbé Morellet published *Le cri des familles* (The Cry of the Families), a brochure that stirred public opinion in favor of the widows and children of the executed Farmers General. He argued that the confiscated property should be returned to the heirs. The pamphlet had such a success that there were three printings in fifteen days. At the same time, court proceedings were started:

The families petitioned the Convention to send the Farmers' accounts and the auditors' statement to the office of the Accounting Commissioners whose report, according to the law, should have preceded Dupin's. This petition was supported by a series of papers, written by the famous jurisconsult, M. Antoine Roy, in response to diverse charges by the auditors, and addressed to the Legislation Committee, which had recently been set up to receive complaints and conduct investigations into the claims that were surging up everywhere against the tyrannical acts committed during the Reign of Terror. One of the papers, entitled "Denunciation of Dupin," asked for revenge.[31]

A current of opinion supported by François Antoine de Boissy d'Anglas and Jean Denis de Lanjuinais began to take shape in the Convention. Feeling himself threatened, Dupin counterattacked:

You will recall, citizens, to what point the public had been aroused against the former Farmers General, the ranting of Cambon, who announced that the Farmers General would cough up at least 300 million, Montaut's harangues that provoked their imprisonment, and those of several other deputies who caused the vaults of this room to ring with their virulent speeches against those collectors of public monies. The most odious terms were heaped on them. Pamphlets, newspaper articles, and diatribes spread profusely and galvanized opinion. Every means of corruption that could attract and blind men was used to damn the Farmers in the public's mind. Soon, all those who over the years had gained their livelihood and that of their families from the salaries of the General Farm, became the most zealous persecutors, the most relentless enemies of their former benefactors. [. . .] Such outbursts were always the precursors of some vast operation. In this case, the idea had been conceived by Robespierre and his accomplices on the Committee of Public Safety, then thrown out to the Jacobins, in whose vile den it was welcomed before being spread and patronized in every corner of the Republic by the thousand voices that that famous club had under its orders and that the ringleaders often exploited to propagate their doctrine, which was destructive to every principle of morality, honor, and humanity.

This particular operation, proposed several times by Bon de Montaut, was the expropriation of the property of the Farmers General. The various squanderings of Robespierre and his henchmen had made these monsters realize the necessity to *battre monnaie* (mint coins), as it was called by their faction. In their delirium, the plan's initiators had greatly exaggerated the Farmers' fortunes, and it took no great effort of genius to conceive that in sacrificing the Farmers they would enrich the Public Treasury, into which they were dipping shamelessly. But to sacrifice these citizens, it was necessary to instigate a persecution so widespread that the Convention itself would find that it had no choice but to obey what was called the voice of the people or the national will, but which was in fact only the result of a financial scheme dreamt up by Robespierre and his minions. You have no doubt observed this kind of approach in several circumstances, but there is no example where it was more clearly demonstrated than in the case of the Farmers General.[32]

Adopting a noble stance, Dupin claimed that he had taken risks to help the accused prepare their defense, that it was even alleged that he had sold himself to them. He then went on to declare bombastically: "I had braved calumny, could have faced death, but dishonor and infamy were beyond my strength."[33] He pointed out the lack of legality in the verdict pronounced:

Did the Farmers General actually stand trial? Does the confiscation resulting from condemnation apply to them? Are their families on the contrary not justified in considering this confiscation invalid? The question will not be difficult to answer. I feel inexpressibly distressed in saying to you that the decree issued by the National Convention on the basis of my report, on behalf of the committees that ordered it, was the tocsin of death for the Farmers General. They should have been informed of the different counts of the indictment and had the chance to discuss them. They should have been shown all the documentation and then questioned about it. Nothing of this sort was done: they should have been heard, but they were not. They were sent to death without ever being tried.[34]

And he concluded bravely by reading the text of a proposed decree favorable to the Farmers' heirs: "All sequestration placed on their property and on that of their heirs, representatives, assistants and others will be removed and converted into a simple apposition of seals on the buildings until the accounts of the General Farm have been settled."[35]

The Deputy Lecointre sought to block the move by objecting that to order the review of a single verdict would be to open all of them to reconsideration. Nevertheless, on June 6, 1795 the Convention decided to return to the heirs all the property that had belonged to the executed Farmers General. But Dupin's speech to the Convention had suddenly drawn public attention in his direction, and a series of attacks on him began, the first ones appearing in *L'orateur du peuple* on June 5 and 24.

On July 9 and 25, 1795 Madame Lavoisier, along with Delahaye's widow and the sons of Papillon d'Auteroche and Montcloux, launched a campaign to see that justice was done by the new Legislation Committee. In a brochure printed by Du Pont and using Dupin's own arguments against him, Madame Lavoisier accused him of the murder of the Farmers General:

He admits in the speech he made to the Tribune on 16 floréal, the anniversary of his crime, that the Robespierre faction wanted to MINT COINS [page 4]; *that the sacrifice of the Farmers General was the result of a financial scheme carefully devised by Robespierre and his accomplices* [page 5]; *that the review of the matter by the committees was felt to be taking too much time and frustrated the impatience of those who, having speculated on the fortunes of the victims they had designated, wanted them to be sentenced without examination and in a revolutionary way* [pages 5 and 6]. He himself took charge of cutting short, evading and violating the procedures prescribed by the decrees of the Convention, of expediting and implementing the *revolutionary measures, the assassination strategem* ordered by Robespierre and his accomplices.[36]

She underlined the irregularities of the trial and Dupin's behavior:

On 18 floréal, the day before the verdict, Dupin, even more rushed than the Tribunal, used the authority of the Committee of General Security to make an inventory of the valuable furniture, personal effects, and papers left by the Farmers General, who had not yet been condemned, who in fact never were condemned because there is no statement to this effect from the jury and, consequently, no sentence. This capital point was made during Fouquier-Tinville's trial, and Dupin admitted it to the Convention when he spoke on 16 floréal. But these procedural details mattered little to him. He did not wait for the day of the murder or of the sentencing to dispose of the plunder. He had the power given to him the night before. And whether to leave less trace of his infamy or to be rewarded for it, he added the functions of bailiff-auctioneer to those of jailer, which he had already attributed to himself during the victims' detention.[37]

Later in "A Supplement to the Denunciation of Dupin," she specified
that he had purely and simply stolen the money and assignats that had been in
the wallets of the Farmers General. Dupin, resorting to rather hollow words,
argued that he had had no power and had done everything possible to give
the accused the means for defending themselves:

The bloody law of 22 prairial had not yet been enacted. At that time, nothing ordered
sentencing men without their testimony and I doubt if any of my colleagues would
have dared say any more than I did in my report to the National Convention, so as
to influence favorably the Tribunal before which I was obliged to send the accused,
in conformity with the decision of the three combined committees, which was ratified by the entire Convention. Today I am being accused of having sent the Farmers
General to their death. Then I was accused of having sold myself to them. Today I
am accused of having rushed through the report. Then I was accused of having done
everything to slow it up. I am now charged with having instigated the decree that
brought them before the court, whereas I was only the spokeman of the three committees and the entire Convention supported the decree. And what has been proven
since, and shows that the true murderers of the Farmers General had no need of anything else—whether the decisions of the Convention and the committees or the advice
of the latter's spokeman—is that they all counted for nothing. The fact is that the indictment of the Farmers General had been drawn up by Fouquier-Tinville before the
report was made, before the decree was issued, and their death had already been decided on by the Committee of Public Safety.[38]

Madame Lavoisier, in a "Second Supplement to the Denunciation Presented Against Dupin," destroyed his arguments one by one and demanded
that Dupin be tried. The debates dragged on. Finally, on August 13, 1795,
Dupin was arrested and stripped of his mandate as a representative of the
people. He energetically defended himself from the accusation of theft in his
"Report to the French People."[39] Nevertheless he was tried and convicted,
but he was released from prison as a result of an amnesty on October 26. He
would thereafter occupy a modest post as a collector of indirect taxes.

At the same time, assisted by Antoine Roy, Madame Lavoisier began the
long and laborious process of recovering her property. "The Commission of
Public Works, the Mining Bureau, the Archives, the Office of Public Education, the Museum, the Temporary Commission of the Arts, the Committee
of Public Safety, and all official institutions, one after the other, returned to
her the objects earlier assigned to them, and, successively, furniture, books,
maps and plans, paintings, musical instruments and scientific material were
returned to the apartment on the Boulevard de la Madeleine."[40]

On October 21, 1795 Geoffroy Saint-Hilaire, secretary of the Museum,
offered, not without some embarrassment, to return the four bottles of mercury weighing 80 pounds and two flasks of red mercuric sulfide.[41] Marie Anne

did not bother to respond until January 23, 1796, and then with only a laconic note: "Citizen Lavoisier reclaims 80 lbs of liquid mercury and 2 flasks of red mercuric sulfide taken from her to be transported to the Museum of Natural History and which are now in the possession of Citizen Geoffroy, representative of this institution."

On November 21 Oudry, secretary general of the Temporary Commission of the Arts, returned "twelve Holland registers." Six of them had been used for secretarial purposes, he specified, "the other six are intact and all have been returned to Citizen Paulze Lavoisier."[42]

With a relentless and faultless determination, she recovered all the objects that had been seized several months earlier. In April 1796 she obtained the official restoration of all her husband's property and could at last enjoy its income. To her faithful servant Masselot she immediately made a gift of land located in Batignolles, and she gave the Abbé Morellet 100 gold louis.

Tribute to Lavoisier

Public opinion also began to redress the wrongs and to render justice to Lavoisier. The first publication dedicated to his life and work appeared as early as 1795. It was written by the astronomer Jérôme Lalande: "Lavoisier was tall, with graceful and fine facial features. Of a gentle, sociable and obliging character, his activity extended to all aspects of life. His credit, reputation and fortune and his position at the Treasury gave him a preponderance of which he profited only to do good, but which nevertheless did not fail to make some people jealous. I prefer to think that they did not contribute to his death."[43]

Lalande produced an archetypical synthesis of Lavoisier's scientific work that has been a reference for biographers for the past two centuries:

Lavoisier made it known that air was composed of two fluids, one breathable, the other mephitic; that the breathable part was itself composed of an oxygen principle susceptible to being fixed in bodies, and that this principle combined with metals during their calcination and with combustible bodies during their combustion; that, in the former case, the compound formed was a calx or metallic oxide; that in the latter, it was an acid, differing according to the nature of the body that had been burned. From this came the entire theory of combustion, of acidification, and the separation of bodies found in nature into combustible and incombustible or burned bodies. From this also came the recognition of fixed air, now known as carbonic acid, because it results from the combustion of carbon, because it is composed of carbon and oxygen.[44]

On October 22, 1795 the Lycée des Arts organized an expiatory ceremony. Jean-Baptiste Bouillon-Lagrange, Jean Darcet, and Michel Jean Jérôme

Dizé presented a "Report on the Progress in Chemistry and What It Owes to the Work of the Deceased Lavoisier." The authors referred to Lalande's text and recalled Lavoisier's discovery of a method of organic analysis by combustion. They made mention of the *Atlas minéralogique de la France*, the agronomical experiments, the contributions to improved techniques of dyeing and bleaching, the gunpowder and saltpeter production, the studies on paper making, the conversion of iron into steel, the fusion of platinum, and the new system of weights and meaures.[45]

On the other hand, they said nothing about his career as a financier and economist, a subject that was doubtless difficult to bring up. After the speeches, as the hall resounded with songs of praise and was redolent with just-released perfume, there suddenly arose two pyramids, 25 feet high, topped by busts of Lavoisier and Pierre Joseph Desault, former chief surgeon at the Hôtel-Dieu, crowned with laural wreaths. At the base of the pyramid dedicated to Lavoisier was written:

Lavoisier, victim of tyranny,
Respected friend of the arts,
Still lives through his genius,
And continues to serve humanity.[46]

On August 2, 1796 the Lycée organized a second "Funeral Service in Honor of Lavoisier." Those in charge of the decoration showed great imagination. On the frontispiece of the entrance door was written "To the Immortal Lavoisier." In the first rooms could be seen the replicas of the tombs of Voltaire and Rousseau, covered with garlands, greenery, and flowers. Facing the stairway was a pyramid 8 meters high, surrounded by freshly cut poplars. At the base of the pyramid a door adorned with white marble caryatids simulated the entry to a tomb. On the pediment was written "Respect the Dead." Passing through the door, one entered a large hall whose walls were draped with black crepe strewn with ermine and supported by garlands. Twenty funeral lamps were set on columns. Each of them had an escutcheon with the title of one of Lavoisier's discoveries. The room was lit by an enormous center light decorated with flowers and cypress branches. Before a large curtain were the simulated tombs of Pierre Joseph Desault, Félix Vicq d'Azyr, and the astronomer Alexandre Guy Pingré.

Three thousand people attended the ceremony. The men were dressed in black and the women wore white with crowns of roses on their heads. It opened with a long speech by Abbé François Valentin Mulot, a constitutional priest and repentant Jacobin, on "The respect due to the dead." Next, Fourcroy gave an impassioned "Eulogy to Lavoisier" and attempted to defend himself from the charge that he had done nothing to save his master. He even declared that Lavoisier was the father of the "new chemical doctrine, which belongs to him exclusively."[47] His glory, he said, had nothing to fear from his collaborators: "He borrowed almost nothing from the witnesses of his work or even his collaborators and after he had conceived the necessity and plan for the great revolution he had been contemplating for several years, he called on his colleagues only to help him execute it. It was he alone who initiated, pursued and achieved it."[48]

Desaudray recited verses on "The Immortality of the Soul." Laïs and Chenard performed a hierodrama entitled "The Death of Lavoisier." In the final scene, the statue of Liberty "laid on his forehead the immortal crown awarded to genius," and a hundred choristers burst into song:

Let us hallow the benefits that come from useful talents;
Let us open to Lavoisier the splendors of history;
To sanctify his genius forever,
Let a momument be erected to his memory.[49]

It does not seem that Madame Lavoisier was present at this spectacle. She had broken off all relations with those students and friends of her husband who, like Fourcroy, Hassenfratz, and Guyton de Morveau, had sat on the Convention's benches and been unable to save him. But the evening was so successful that a second performance was given the following week.

The End of a Great Love

In *La philosophie de l'univers*, addressing the Lavoisiers, Pierre Samuel Du Pont de Nemours had written:

The bases and general disposition of the metaphysical world are little known; parts of it are impossible to know, but others are accessible. They lie in the middle of a misty ocean, like a chain of islands that can be followed, because they are connected underneath like mountains, and are a skeletal framework of the globe like all archipelagos. To reach these islands, after plotting their coves and capes, two vessels have been given to us. One is called *Observation* and the other *Profound Thought*. You are Argonauts, accustomed to steering them. I sail with you.[50]

But the navigation had been difficult. Du Pont had been elected in December 1795 to membership in the National Institute of Sciences and Arts—the Institute of France—a reconstitution of the suppressed Academies. He was then chosen in late October 1795 to sit in the Council of Elders where for two years he advocated physiocratic views. Arrested in the anti-royalist coup d'état of 18 fructidor, he spent only twenty-four hours at La Force prison but during his absence the print shop was ransacked and the presses damaged. These misfortunes convinced him that he could no longer hope for a political career in France. At the end of an V, he obtained an appointment "to a post as traveling scientist charged with investigating all aspects of human knowledge in foreign countries."[51] He notified his son, consul in Charleston, South Carolina: "My first journey will be to the United States of America. Irénée will come along as my secretary. If you already have a leave to come to Europe or have the intention of asking for it, do not be in any great hurry. Wait for us."[52]

Pierre Samuel had decided to follow in the footsteps of Talleyrand, who had made a great deal of money in the United States by speculating on land in Pennsylvania and New York, on behalf of Dutch and Swiss bankers. More ambitious, however, his plan combined investment in property with trade in commodities and agricultural exploitation. Collecting the funds for all this took more than two years and left him the time to write Madame Lavoisier several apologetic farewell letters, although on September 26, 1795 he had married Madame Poivre, the widow of an administrator in Réunion and Mauritius.

On October 23, 1798 he wrote Marie Anne a letter tinged with nostalgia which gives a valuable indication concerning the liaison between them since it situates the beginning in 1781:

It is the riches remaining to us that are a pleasure to weigh, that must be made use of, that it is heartwarming to treasure. If we had never seen each other, each of us would now find it most agreeable to discover in the midst of the world as it is someone who had as much intelligence, education, common sense, wisdom, determination, morality, and the habit of good company as we both possess. And we would certainly become good companions. Why should twenty-two years of acquaintance and seventeen of intimacy and lasting esteem spoil that possibility? Did I not write the *Philosophy of the Universe* for you? It is a rather handsome bill of exchange, although drawn at the end of my credit. But you will no doubt honor it. As for me, I cannot help it, I could never be lacking in friendship or a tender and indulgent attitude toward you.[53]

The actual departure would take place a year later. Leaving Paris on September 8, Du Pont, overwhelmed with emotion, wrote an admirable letter that he neither signed nor sent but kept on his person for a long time, as can be seen by the frayed folds of the paper:

I leave my country, weeping that I can serve it only from afar, although I know that I am one of the men who best comprehends its affairs. But no one understands my language anymore. Here I could neither influence any authority nor exercise it. I would perish fruitless, whether from misery, abandon, murder by the Jacobins or hanging by the aristocrats. If you could have continued to love me, I would have patiently accepted that destiny because a single evening with you around the fire, or a single morning on the rue Lenoir would have been compensation for both my eyes and heart. But your tenderness ceased when I first held public office. Something changed between the Constituent and Legislative Assemblies. For three years, you repeatedly wounded my heart with pin pricks, and then you broke it absolutely by going to Franche-Comté. Desperate, furious, and then a little calmer, I deluded myself into thinking that I could be saved by a very affectionate friendship. But I found it more than cold, almost nonexistant in fact. The only time I recognized its accent was in your last letter. [. . .] Why did it have to come so late? As for myself, I was excessively angry with you. My heart was overwhelmed with rage. Then I worked on myself to try and understand your viewpoint and cooled down. I have never ceased for one minute to love you more than my life. A single word from you opens and penetrates my soul. I cannot help myself. It moves me to the very fiber of my being. I belonged to you, my dear young lady, as I have belonged to no one else. And it seems to me that I was a blessing to you. [. . .] But you deemed otherwise. You grew tired of my affection. You spared me no cruelty. You outraged my self-esteem as well as my love for you, both very sensitive, both very susceptible. [. . .] It is not impossible that I shall succeed, I would wager that I have about one in four chances of it. And then I shall again honor our friendship. Because, my dear lady, your name will always be linked with mine. I have bound our reputations to each other by my *Philosophy of the Universe*, that solid and brilliant fruit of my regrets and tears. You will be renowned for yourself, for your knowledge, reason, varied talents, and beauty of which David's painting and your own will preserve the lively and touching features. You will also be renowned for your clever and virtuous husband of whom you were so worthy.[54]

Du Pont was to sail from La Rochelle on October 1, 1799 on the *American Eagle*. The diligence taking him there passed through Blois. His heart was so thrown into turmoil that he might have been a very young man. He asked at the post house if Madame Lavoisier was still at Freschines and learned that she had just left. He scanned the road anxiously. Would their carriages not cross each other? He lamented:

Ah, my dear, it is all your fault, your unique and stubborn fault. During this trip I have been doing some sad reading: the posthumous works of d'Alembert. In them, I discover that Mademoiselle de Lespinasse was unfaithful to him, abandoned him, deceived him and treated him dreadfully. And did not Madame de Warens leave and deceive Jean Jacques and eventuallly dump him for a wigmaker? Madame du Châtelet left Voltaire and was unfaithful to him, having a child with Saint-Lambert. Is it then a fatality going back as far as Eve in the earthly paradise? If that were the case, reason and justice would say that one must calm down and make allowances. But before that can happen, love must be somewhat weakened. In its full bloom, it is as merciless, exclusive and arrogant as Satan. It is possible that later, tempered by logic and long reflection, it can become tender and moderate, even a rather mild Eros. It is that love that I must carry to America.[55]

The last letter from France was written on September 16, just before sailing:

It would surely seem that love, whether with one nuance or the other, is the only relationship that can exist between us. I have learned that you are not made for friendship. You have none of its effusions, interest, consolations, advice, caresses, chatter, or sweet silence. When your tenderness ceases, so does everything else. You become cold, hard, quarrelsome, and a disagreeable expression arrives spontaneoulsy on your lips. [. . .] Then why did I love you? Why does your image pursue me? Why would I pay any price for the happiness of knowing that I had not ceased to please you? It is because you are so reasonable, intelligent, and wise. It is because in talking with you (and you converse well only with your lover, friends only seal your lips), I could truly confer with an intelligence; it is because you are very beautiful, having the kind of looks that exert great power over me; it is because for a long time I believed that you loved me above all others and I cannot imagine how such a feeling, and the proofs you gave me of it, could be destroyed. Finally, it is because I am indebted to you for the happiest moments of my life, and we must not let all that become sterile just because recent times have been so terribly unhappy.[56]

If Madame Lavoisier had renounced neither love nor happiness in 1799, she no longer saw them in the person of Pierre Samuel. He was 60, she was 40. Certainly she had become rather stout, but she was still attractive. Her keen mind, dynamism, and fortune were powerful assets. And she knew it.

The Lavoisier Mills

In the end, Pierre Samuel left for America with his two sons and stepdaughter, Madame Bureaux de Puzy. After a difficult crossing, he arrived on January 1, 1800 in New York, where he found his wife who had preceded him. The difficulties of getting settled and his financial problems did not make him forget Madame Lavoisier.

In February 1801 he wrote to Philippe Nicolas Harmand, head clerk at the National Treasury: "Apart from an absence of kindness, which however I experienced in earlier times, she is a woman of the highest élite. No one has more intelligence, aptitude, and talent for all kinds of work. No one has such a sure and vigorous judgment as long as scornful passions do not lead it astray. She has a masculine soul in the body of a woman who was beautiful for a long time."[57]

In 1802, at Jefferson's request, he returned to France to participate in the negotiations for the purchase of the Louisiana Territory by the United States. Finally Bonaparte agreed to sell it for 17 million francs. This personal success persuaded Pierre Samuel to stay in France.

In the meantime, Eleuthère Irénée had taken the major decision to create a powder works in America, where the only good gunpowder came from

England. The local fabrication was still using methods from the time of Louis XIV. The young Du Pont had learned modern procedures from Lavoisier at Essonne. After a brief trip to France in 1802 to obtain material and recruit experienced collaborators, he found the ideal site for his powder works on the Brandywine Creek near Wilmington, Delaware.

When it came time to choose the new company's name, the discussion was lively. Pierre Samuel recommended "Eleutherian Mills"; Victor suggested "E.-I. Du Pont de Nemours Gunpowder Manufacture"; Bauduy, Eleuthère Irénée's associate, would have preferred "Du Pont, Bauduy and Company". Eleuthère Irénée thought that he had come up with the best idea: "I finally chose "Lavoisier Mills," which showed my gratitude to the person whose kindness toward me was the primary cause of my undertaking. I hope that Madame Lavoisier will not disapprove of my giving this name to an important and well equipped factory, founded on her husband's principles and discoveries, and which would not exist without all he did for me." [58]

But Pierre Samuel, perhaps after having consulted Madame Lavoisier, refused and, in the end, the firm took the name of "Du Pont de Nemours and Company." After a difficult beginning, it developed rapidly. The accrued profits for the years 1803 to 1809 were $45,000. The profits for 1811 alone reached the same figure. The War of 1812 greatly accelerated its earnings. When Eleuthère Irénée died in 1834, the business was already very prosperous. With the following decades it experienced a prodigiously rapid growth. In the twentieth century, two world wars and the conquest of nuclear energy also contributed to its expansion. The company whose motto is "Better living through chemistry" is today one of the largest chemical firms in the world.

The *Mémoires de Chimie*

In 1792 Lavoisier had begun to envisage publishing his complete works in eight volumes. He had even worked on this project while he was in prison, at Port-Libre and later at the former headquarters of the Farm. While he was detained, his wife brought him proofs of the first notebooks printed by Eleuthère Irénée. From his country house in Bois des Fossés, where he was hiding from the police, Pierre Samuel wrote almost every day to his son. He gave very precise instructions on how to keep spaces in the margins by using a lead plate, which would allow for adding titles after proofs were corrected. But Eleuthère Irénée knew more about making gunpowder than about printing; and it is precisely the titles in the margin that contain the greatest number of printing errors.

In 1796 Madame Lavoisier asked Armand Seguin to help her go over the texts and write a preface to them. Seguin, who had acquired a fortune by supplying shoes to the army thanks to his special process for tanning leather, wrote a text in which he not only overestimated his own contribution but treated Lavoisier's "judges" with great tact. Appalled, Marie Anne got rid of him. In 1803, with the help of Pierre Samuel Du Pont, she composed a brief introduction to the *Mémoires de Chimie*:

> In 1792 M. Lavoisier decided to bring together all of his memoirs read at the Academy over a twenty-year period. He wanted the collection to be a kind of history of modern chemistry. To make this history more interesting and complete, he intended to include memoirs of those scientists who, having adopted his system, had carried out experiments reinforcing it. This corpus was to have been made up of eight volumes. Europe knows why the project could not be finished. We have found almost all of the first volume, all of the second, and a few pages of the fourth. Several scientists have expressed the desire that they be published. We hesitated for a long time. It is difficult not to fear publishing work that was left unfinished by a man who justly enjoyed an outstanding reputation. Now that he is no longer here, the judgment of those who esteem him must become especially severe, and publish only what can add to the glory of a beloved and revered being. We might have stood firm and refused to bring out these fragments, if they did not contain (p. 78 of volume two) memoirs of M. Lavoisier that claim, on the basis of facts he presents there, the new chemical theory as belonging to him.
>
> It is therefore a duty toward him to establish scientific opinion on this truth. We ask your indulgence for the errors that may have crept into some other parts of the collection. It will be granted, we trust, when it is known that most of the proofs were read during the final moments of the author's life; and that, although he was aware that his murder was being planned, M. Lavoisier calmly and courageously continued to apply himself to a work that he believed would be useful to the sciences, giving a great example of the serenity that wisdom and virtue can preserve in the midst of even the most horrible misfortunes.[59]

The *Mémoires de Chimie*, whose printing had been begun by Du Pont more than ten years earlier in 1793, appeared in two volumes without a title page or publisher's name. There was no index or table of contents and there were numerous errors which Madame Lavoisier failed to modify or correct. There was still a long way to go before completing the anticipated eight volumes.

Volume I, as had been foreseen by Lavoisier, contained fourteen memoirs, of which four had been written with Laplace. Six among them, previously unpublished, concerned caloric, its definition, and its effects on solid and liquid bodies and aeriform fluids; the states of matter; heat and calorimetry; and the analysis of atmospheric air. Volume II contained fourteen of Lavoisier's memoirs, of which five were previously unpublished, and six of Seguin's texts. Its subject was the analysis of air and its constituents; the formation of acids and oxides, nitric acid, and carbonic acid; and the analysis and synthesis of water. Volume III was missing. Volume IV was represented by five memoirs on respiration, nutrition, and animal heat, written by Seguin. Volumes V, VI, VII, and VIII were completely missing.

The work was not sold but offered to institutions and illustrious scientists such as Jean Baptiste Joseph Delambre, Georges Cuvier, Gaspard Riche de Prony, Joseph Louis de Lagrange, Pierre Simon de Laplace, Claude Louis Berthollet, François Arago, Jean Baptiste Biot, and Alexandre von Humboldt, who were all frequent guests at Madame Lavoisier's hôtel particulier on the rue d'Anjou Saint-Honoré (today the rue Lavoisier). "Libraries can possess no more touching monument," wrote Cuvier. "These final lines of a man of genius, writing still although already in the shadow of the scaffold; these mutilated volumes, these talks interrupted in the middle of a sentence, whose continuation is forever lost, are reminders of all that those terrible times, to which we allude, produced in horror and terror."[60]

Comtesse de Rumford

In 1805, when she was 47, Madame Lavoisier married Benjamin Thomson, an American from Massachusetts and loyalist colonel in the English army, who had become Count Rumford in 1791 by the grace of the Bavarian elector who rewarded him for his efforts to improve living conditions of the poor in Munich. This scientist had made himself known by his work on light, his demonstration of the mechanical nature of heat, and his studies on the rational use of nourishment and fuels, which had practical applications: inexpensive soups and fireplaces designed to recover heat. In 1801 he became smitten by Marie Anne:

I met this amiable lady in Paris. I think that she would see no obstacle to marrying me and I would be making a very good match. A childless widow who never had children, she is about my age, in good health and very sociable. Her personal fortune is considerable and reputation excellent. She lives in elegant style, and is hostess to the greatest philosophers and the most eminent scientists and writers in Paris. And above all, she is kindness itself. Furthermore, she is extremely intelligent (in the English sense of the word). In short, she is another Lady Palmerston. She was very beautiful in her youth and, even now, at 46 or 48, she is still quite handsome, of medium height, but rather "en bon point" than slender. She is extremely lively and writes admirably well.[61]

Rumford wooed her insistently for four years, writing her almost three hundred letters in which there alternated expressions of admiration, passion, a lover's wounded pride, and even lyricism: "I can imagine nothing sweeter than to live with you, work with you all day, and then fall asleep in your arms."[62]

Like Lavoisier before him, he shared his scientific theories with her. She was used to conversing with scientists, independent, mocking, and authoritarian, and she proved difficult to win.

Rumford himself did not have an easy character. Cuvier, while paying tribute to his talents as a scientist and philanthropist, drew an uncompromising portrait of him:

He would have been utterly charming if his affability had equaled his zeal for being useful to the public. But it must be said that his conversation and his entire bearing were permeated with a most extraordinary attitude in a man so constantly well treated by others and who had done so much good for them: it was as though he had rendered all his services to his fellow men without ever liking or even respecting them. In his person, he was from all points of view and every imaginable aspect, the very epitome of order. His needs, pleasures, and work were calculated in the same way as his experiments. He drank only water, and ate only grilled or roasted meat, because boiled beef, he said, is a little less nourishing per volume. In short, he allowed himself nothing superfluous, not even a step or a word, and it was in the strictest sense that he interpreted the word superfluous.[63]

In 1803 Madame Lavoisier spent three months in Munich with her suitor. In October of the same year he came to join her in Paris in her charming house surrounded by an English garden in the most elegant section of the city. The marriage took place on October 22, 1805. François Auguste de Frénilly, a memorialist with a caustic pen, repeated the gossip concerning the couple:

M. de Rumford, chemist-philanthropist and escapee from Pennsylvania, after having built fireplaces in London, organized kitchens in Munich, and filled Europe with inexpensive soups, had just appeared on the Paris scene with that halo of glory that is brought only from afar. A man of some fifty years, he was tall with a rather noble bearing, dry and rigid like an American, condescending and arrogant like a Republican, and recently grafted with a title and decoration from Bavaria. But he had no worldly fortune other than his ribbon, his noble appellation, his furnaces, and his soups. Madame de Lavoisier saw the count and said: "He's the man for me." Unfortunately for her, the count did not say: "She's the woman for me." He let himself be attracted, then irritated, then adored, and set off again for Germany. I would have done the same thing. But for him to neglect such a fortune simply because the heroine was ugly, old, and enormously stout would have been so fantastic that no one in Paris would have believed it.[64]

Very quickly they noticed that they were not made for each other. Disputes, even in public, were frequent. M. de Rumford liked the quiet of his laboratory and his rose gardens. She preferred to entertain her friends. Neither of them wanted to make a concession. One day when Madame Lavoisier had invited friends whom Rumford did not like, he forbade the porter to let them in, and they were forced to speak with their hostess through the gate. Revenge was not long in coming: she poured boiling water over his beloved roses.

This stormy union lasted only four years. After long and difficult haggling, Rumford finally listened to reason and in 1809 an amicable separation was arranged, in exchange for a sum that contemporaries estimated at between 300,000 and 400,000 francs.[65]

The Old Turk

"After that," wrote Guizot, "for the next twenty-seven years, no event, one might say, no incident, would disturb Madame de Rumford in her noble and pleasant way of life. She devoted herself entirely to her friends and the people she entertained with a rather singular mixture of rudeness and courtesy. She was always very good company and showed a great understanding of the world, although her language could be brusque and she was subject to authoritarian whims."[66]

She entertained on Mondays, Tuesdays, and Fridays. Although her guests were highly dissimilar, they all belonged to the best society, and came with great pleasure to hear excellent concerts given by the most celebrated performers of the day. Among her friends were the scientists already mentioned, and members of Paris high society such as the duc de Broglie, the duc de Plaisance, the duc de Cadore, the duc d'Albuféra, Monsieur and Madame de Rémusat, Lady Edgeworth, and Lord Holland.

Under the Empire, Madame de Rumford's home had, in addition to its general pleasantness, a particualr merit: what was felt and discussed there was not official; a certain freedom of thought and language reigned. And yet it was completely devoid of hostility or political design. It was uniquely freedom of thought, the habit of having one's own opinions and expressing them exactly as one pleases, without worrying about whether authority might hear about them or what it might do if it did. It was therefore a most valuable merit, more precious than one can imagine today. You have to have lived under the vacuum pump to appreciate the luxury of being able to breath.[67]

A frequent guest, who occupied a special place and maintained friendly and at last serene relations with Madame Lavoisier, was Pierre Samuel Du Pont. After the successful negotiations for the Louisiana Purchase, he had remained in Paris, regularly attending the meetings of the Academy of Moral and Political Sciences.

Exiled in 1815 during the Hundred Days when Napoleon was attempting to organize a constitutional monarchy, he left France again and wrote Madame Lavoisier one final love letter:

My dear daughter, In France I had the choice between adversities that were hard to bear, or misconduct to which it would have been impossible for me to stoop. I hope therefore that your noble and courageous friendship will not disapprove of the decision I have made. By taking it, I am losing (and for me this is by far the most distressing loss) your kind company, but it might well have been removed from me in any case had I stayed. I carry with me the inviolable and tender affection that I have devoted to you for thirty-four years. It reminds me of both the happiest and bitterest circumstances of my life. Contrary winds only strengthen the roots of trees. No matter where I am and for as long as I live, you will have an intimate friend, one who has tried his best to make himself worthy of your goodness. He is not yet at the end of this effort. He still looks forward to glory and public service.[68]

Du Pont died two years later in Wilmington, from a chill caught while helping to put out a fire at his son's powder works. Madame Lavoisier saw the friends of her youth gradually disappear and she lived more and more alone. "That poor woman with her philosophy, her liberalism, her mustaches, and her cabriolet interested no one," commented Frénilly. "But the love affairs of this widow who was over forty-five, provided a quite comical subject for reflection."[69] George Sand met Madame Lavoisier one day at Couterets: "Madame de Rumford, widow of a scientist known by imbeciles like me for his soups and fireplaces, has just arrived with her very pretty young niece."[70] In his correspondence, Prosper Mérimée mentions "Madame de Rumford and her hundred fifty kilograms of plain flesh."[71]

The most picturesque account on Madame Lavoisier is the one left by Adrien Delahante, grandson of the Farmer General, drawn from the calls he and his brother paid on her:

We came to the rue d'Anjou and stopped before a semicircular wall with a wrought iron gate leading into the vast garden surrounding the house. The porter let us in, however, through a small side door pierced in the wall's corner. Just as we entered the alley of trees, a loud bell rang to announce our arrival. Then, feeling increasingly uneasy, our hearts began to beat faster. But there was no turning back, and by the time we reached the front hall we had bravely gotten hold of ourselves. An elderly footman, bald and dressed in old-fashioned French-style livery, greeted us with a kind smile. He led us through the winter garden, which ran alongside the house, to the door of the *salon* into which he ushered us with an intimidating solemnity.

The first thing that struck the eye, to the right on a panel, was David's large full-length portrait of Monsieur and Madame Lavoisier. Monsieur Lavoisier, dressed in Louis XVI style, was seated at a table holding chemical instruments. Behind her husband, leaning on the back of his chair, stood the young Madame Lavoisier with powdered hair and dressed all in white. We moved toward the fireplace while admiring this magnificent painting and came to a halt before a love seat in the depths of which, wound up into a ball, could be seen a kind of old Turk.

This old Turk was all that remained of the beautiful young woman depicted by David: it was Madame de Rumford, with her aged, masculine face, coiffed and rigged out in the most bizarre way. She greeted us in her abrupt manner, which was not unkind, asked us to sit down, and began asking us questions about our studies and pastimes. The conversation could not have interested her very much. It would often happen that after a few minutes she would suddenly get up from the love seat and go and stand with her back to the fireplace, just like a man. She would then pull up her skirts from behind as high as her garters and leisurely warm her enormous calves. Shortly afterwards she would dismiss us politley, and we did not have to be told twice! She often gave elegant balls that we enjoyed more than the visits, in spite of her active surveillance and the severity with which she chased us away from the buffet to have us dance the quadrille.[72]

On February 10, 1836 Marie Anne Pierrette Paulze Lavoisier de Rumford, who had known eight different forms of government—Louis XV, Louis XVI, the Revolution, the Directoire, the Empire, Louis XVIII, Charles X, and Louis-Philippe—and seven constitutions, died suddenly at the age of seventy-eight.

Notes

Prologue

1. Lavoisier, *Correspondance*, vol. V, p. 135. Letter from Hassenfratz to Madame Lavoisier, February 20, 1788, Archives de l'Académie des Sciences, Lavoisier Collection, dation Chabrol.

2. It is very difficult to establish the precise equivalent in current francs or dollars. The costs of certain services and goods have risen, others have fallen; some goods and services have been replaced by others. E. Faure writes: "To reach the most valid comparison possible, it is necessary to modify the first coefficient, that of prices, by a second one, that of the overall improvement of living standards or, what amounts to the same thing, the rise of the average income of Frenchmen." *La disgrâce de Turgot* (Paris: Gallimard, 1961), p. 62. According to Faure, the monetary multiplying coefficient between 1789 and 1958 is 2,000. Since Faure calculated in old francs, this coefficient must first be divided by 100 to obtain new francs, then multiplied by 10 to compensate for the monetary erosion between 1961 and 1996. Thus the multiplying coefficient for comparing monetary values in francs between 1789 and 1996 is 200.

J. Fourastié, in *Prix de vente et prix de revient* (Paris: Domat-Monchrestien, 1949) defines a method based on the hourly salary of a laborer and ends up with the same conversion coefficient of 220.

J.C. Toutain estimates the gross annual income per capita in 1789 at 220 francs ("Le produit intérieur brut de la France de 1789 à 1982," *Economies et Sociétés* 21 [May 1987]:76). In a personal communication, he specifies: "The gross domestic product per capita is today 100,000 francs of which the State takes and spends 45,000 francs, almost half, whereas in 1789, the State took almost nothing. The minimum salary per year is also around 50,000 francs, without considering the indirect income represented by collective consumption (roads, social security system, etc.) that would double the individual income. Thus, the multiplier of the available individual income between 1789 and 1996 would be 200. But whether one uses the minimum salary or the gross domestic product per person, the fact remains that today one does not buy the same thing with 40,000 francs as was bought with 200 francs in 1789."

See also J.-P. Poirier, *Lavoisier, théoricien et praticien de l'économie*, Thesis for the degree of Doctor of Philosophy (Economics) at the Université Panthéon-Assas, Paris (Lille: Atelier national de reproduction des thèses, 1992), pp. 16–17:

The coefficient of 200 for the French franc gives more or less satisfying results depending on the nature of the goods considered: 1) The daily salary of a laborer in 1789 was 20 sous (1 franc), that of a journeyman mason 40 sous (2 francs), that of a carpenter or locksmith 50 sous (2.50 francs), following Georges Rudé, *The Crowd in the French Revolution* (London: Oxford University Press, 1967). That corresponds today to 200 francs per day for an unskilled laborer and 400 to 500 francs for a skilled one. 2) The price of a loaf of bread weighing four livres, around 10 sous in 1789, is 20 francs today, whereas it should reach 100 francs. It is true that the productivity of land planted to wheat has increased more than tenfold. 3) Turgot, who received an annual salary of 80,000 livres, would today receive 16 million francs, or 3.2 million dollars. 4) The large *Encyclopédie* in its beautiful original folio edition cost 980 francs when it appeared, or almost 200,000 current francs, which is precisely the price asked today by a rare book-dealer. 5) The Lavoisier's portrait, for which David was paid 7,000 livres, would cost $280,000 today, a high price, but one in the range of those received by currently recognized painters. Political circumstances prevented the portrait from being shown at the 1789 Salon. Today it is the pride of the French Collections at the Metropolitan Museum of Art in New York.

Thus to transform 1789 livres into 1996 francs the multiplying coefficient is 200. To obtain the equivalent in 1996 dollars, the result is divided by 5 when the dollar is at 5 francs. More simply, 1789 livres can be transformed into 1996 dollars by multiplying by 40.

Chapter 1: Youth

1. On February 23, 1741, the notaire of Châtelet registered "the sale by Jacques Waroquier to Jean Antoine Lavoisier, his nephew and lawyer at the Parlement, of the station and hereditary duties as prosecutor as well as his office with its furniture." L. Velluz, *Vie de Lavoisier* (Paris: Plon, 1966), p. 27.

2. Today rue Pecquay, connecting rue des Blanc-Manteaux with rue Rambuteau.

3. Today rue de Vauvilliers, between rue Saint-Honoré and rue Coquillière.

4. Today the building, located on the Quai Conti, houses the Institut de France.

5. L. S. Mercier, *Tableau de Paris* (Paris: Pagnerre et Lecou, 1853), p. 269.

6. He left "a fortune of 137,000 livres divided among three inheritors." E. Grimaux, *Lavoisier, 1743–1794* (Paris: Alcan, 1888), p. 3.

7. Archives de l'Académie des Sciences, Lavoisier Collection, ms. 1259.

8. Ibid.

9. R. Taton, *Enseignement et diffusion des sciences en France au XVIIIe siècle* (Paris: Herrmann, 1986), p. 144.

10. Abbé Carlier, "Discours historique sur la vie et les écrits de feu M. l'abbé de La Caille," in La Caille, *Journal historique du voyage au Cap de Bonne Espérance* (Paris: Guillyn, 1763), p. 22.

11. Archives de l'Académie des Sciences, Lavoisier Collection, ms. 1259.

12. "Having arrived at philosophy, he developed such a taste for the sciences that he decided to devote himself to them entirely." G. Cuvier, in L. G. Michaud, ed., *Biographie universelle* (Paris: Michaud, 1819), vol. 23, p. 461.

13. Lavoisier, *Correspondance*, letter from M. de Troncq, Rennes, March 28, 1762, fasc. 1, p. 2.

14. E. Grimaux, *Lavoisier, 1743–1794*, p. 12.

15. *Mémoire qui renferme des observations minéralogiques faites dans plusieurs en-*

droits des provinces qui avoisinent la Champagne. Ière partie: Du Valois. Lavoisier Collection, Courtesy of the Rare and Manuscript Collections, Cornell University Library.

16. Lavoisier, "Observations d'Histoire naturelle sur les environs de Villers-Cotterêts," *Oeuvres*, vol. V., pp. 48–52, and "Observations d'Histoire naturelle de Lisy, la Ferté-sous-Jouarre et Meaux," pp. 84–90.

17. Archives de l'Académie des Sciences, Lavoisier Collection, note from September 17–23, 1763, ms. 419.

18. *Oeuvres*, vol. IV, p. 4.

19. J. E. Guettard, *Mémoire sur les Ardoisières d'Angers, 1758*, in H. Guerlac, "A Note on Lavoisier's Scientific Education," *Isis* 47 (1956): 215.

20. G. F. Rouelle, *Prospectus du cours d'expériences chymiques* (Paris: 1759), 4 pages in-octavo.

21. "Cours de Rouelle rédigé par M. Diderot, communiqué par M. Basile, demeurant rue des Marmousets." Archives de l'Académie des Sciences, Lavoisier Collection, dation Chabrol.

22. "Sur la manière d'enseigner la chimie." Archives de l'Académie des Sciences, Lavoisier Collection, ms. 1259, quoted by B. Bensaude-Vincent in "A View of the Chemical Revolution Through Contemporary Textbooks: Lavoisier, Fourcroy, and Chaptal," *British Journal for the History of Science* 23 (1990): 435–60.

23. Quoted by Daumas in *Lavoisier* (Paris: Gallimard, 1941), p. 25.

24. G. F. Rouelle, *Prospectus du cours d'expériences chymiques*, p. 2.

25. G. F. Rouelle, *Cours de chymie*, manuscript in 6 volumes in folio, Introduction, vol. 1, pp. 27–28. Joachim Becher (1635–1682), physician, chemist, and mineralogist had hesitated as to whether there were two, three, four, or even five elements: air, water, and three sorts of earth (vitrifiable, inflammable, and mercurial). The inflammable earth would become the phlogiston of his student, Georg Ernst Stahl.

26. Lavoisier, quoted by R. Siegfried in "Lavoisier's View of the Gaseous State and Its Early Application to Pneumatic Chemistry," *Isis* 63 (1972): 62.

27. G. E. Stahl,*Traité du soufre*, translated from the German by Baron d'Holbach (Paris: P. F. Didot, 1766), p. 55.

28. F. Hoefer, *Histoire de la chimie* (Paris: Didot, 1869), vol. II, pp. 399–400.

29. Archives de l'Académie des Sciences, Lavoisier Collection, ms. 1259.

30. "Certificat de résidence du 10 mai du l'an second de la R. F." Archives de l'Académie de Sciences, Lavoisier Collection, ms. 1715. Before the Revolution, 1 French foot = 12 inches = 0.324 meter.

31. Graphological analysis done by H. Ogier du Terrail from a manuscript signed by Lavoisier.

32. *Oeuvres*, vol. III, p. 84.

33. "He will signal his passage with flames."

34. *L'Avant-Coureur*, Wednesday, April 9, 1766, p. 248. The report on the various ways of improving the lighting of the streets in large cities was not published in Lavoisier's life time.

35. *Histoire de l'Académie Royale des Sciences de 1782* (Paris: Imprimerie Royale, 1785), pp. 1–2.

36. The Academy of Science had twelve honorary members: the comte de Maurepas, Henri Léonard Jean Baptiste Bertin, the comte Louis Phélipeaux de Saint-Florentin, and Jean Baptiste Machault, all ministers; the Field Marshal duc de Riche-

lieu, the comte Yves Marie Desmarets de Maillebois, Chrétien Guillaume de Lamoignon de Malesherbes, the cardinal de Luynes, the marquis de Paulmy d'Argenson,
Daniel Trudaine, the marquis de Courtanvaux, and the king. There were eighteen pensionnaires: the geometricians, Mairan, Fontaine des Bertins, d'Alembert; the astronomers, Cassini de Thury, Lemonnier, Maraldi; the engineers, Nollet, Vaucanson, Montigny; the anatomists, Morand, Daubenton, Hérissan; the botanists, Jussieu, Duhamel
du Monceau, Guettard; the chemists, La Condamine, Bourdelin, Malouin. There were
twelve associate members and twelve assistant ones. Each "class" included three salaried members, two associates, and two assistants. The Academy also accepted free
associates and foreign associates such as Morgagni, Bernoulli, Van Swieten, Haller,
Euler and Linné. Finally, there were the Permanent Secretary, Grandjean de Fouchy,
and the Treasurer, Buffon. Only honorary members and the pensionnaires had the
right to vote.

37. *Oeuvres*, vol. III, p. 111.

38. Ibid., p. 112.

39. Ibid., p. 111.

40. *Mémoires de mathématiques et de physique*, more commonly called *Mémoires
des savants étrangers* (Paris: Imprimerie Royale, 1768), pp. 341–57.

41. *Mémoires de mathématiques et de physique*, vol. V, Preface, p. xiv. The problem tackled was more difficult than he thought, and the solubility of gypsum in water
would not be clarified until 1901, by Hullet.

42. *Oeuvres*, vol. III, pp. 123–24.

43. Ibid., p. 135.

44. *Correspondance*, fasc. I, p. 10.

45. Ibid.

46. A thousand écus represented 6,000 livres: thus three salaried members at
2,000 livres each, plus the unpaid two associates and two assistants.

47. *Oeuvres*, vol. III, p. 109.

48. Archives de l'Académie des Sciences, Lavoisier Collection, ms. 1259.

49. *Oeuvres*, vol. V, p. 233.

50. Ibid., p. 229.

51. R. Rappaport, "Lavoisier's Theory of the Earth," *British Journal for the History of Science* 23 (1973): 252.

52. *Oeuvres*, vol. V, p. 215.

53. Ibid., p. 216.

54. These objects can be seen in the Lavoisier Collection, Rare and Manuscript
Collections, Cornell University Library.

55. *Correspondance*, fasc. I, p. 17.

56. Ibid., p. 30. As curator of the duc d'Orléans's Natural History Collection,
Guettard lived in the Palais Royal.

57. Ibid., pp. 56–57.

58. Ibid., p. 51.

59. Ibid., p. 65.

60. Ibid., p. 73.

61. Ibid., p. 63.

62. Ibid, p. 66.

63. Ibid., pp. 70–71.

64. Ibid., p. 94.

65. M. Beretta, "Lavoisier as a Reader of Chemical Literature," *Revue d'Histoire des Sciences* 48 (1995): 76.

66. *Correspondance*, fasc. I, p. 87.

67. *Oeuvres*, vol. III, p. 146.

Chapter 2: Farmer General and Academician

1. 340,000 livres were paid in cash; the surplus was paid by Lavoisier's father in the form of drafts whose 5 percent interest was paid in advance.

2. The *gabelle*, or salt tax, was the heaviest and most unpopular. Each year it brought 60 million livres to the State and 17 million to the Farm. *Aides* were taxes on tobacco, alcoholic drinks, playing cards, meats, oils, and soaps. Taxes were also collected from the obligatory stamping of gold, silver, leather goods, iron, and paper. *Traites* were the customs duties collected at 1,600 tollgates along France's borders and at entries into towns; the Farm also collected duties on goods coming into Paris and those coming from the *domaine d'Occident* (America). The direct taxes—the *taille*, the poll tax, and the twentieth part—were collected for the king by *receveurs généraux* from the Finance Ministry. Other direct taxes such as the *champart*, a tax on wheat, and the *cens*, a tax for the use of roads, were paid to the nobility; the tithe was paid to the Church.

3. A. Delahante, *Une famille de finance au XVIIIe siècle* (Paris: Hetzel, 1881), vol. I, p. 288.

4. N. F. Mollien, *Mémoires d'un ministre du Trésor public* (Paris: Fournier, 1898), vol. I, p. 105.

5. J. Paulze, Archives Nationales, 129 A P, no. 6, pp. 113–29, quoted in Y. Durand, *Les fermiers généraux au XVIIIe siècle* (Paris: Presses Universitaires de France, 1971), p. 120.

6. Its use was described for the first time in *La chanson des pilotes*, by shipowner Jean Ango. Jacques Cartier referred to it in *Bref Récit*. In 1558, André Thévet, monk and naturalist, a native of Angoulême, described the plant in *Les singularités de la France antarctique*. He brought back from his trip to Brazil some grains of *pétun* that he succeeded in acclimating in Charente and called *herbe angoumoisine*. Jean Nicot, ambassador of Catherine de Médici, launched the fashion, which spread with incredible rapidity. Colbert understood that the exclusive privilege of selling tobacco, reserved for the king, would be an important source of income, and in 1674 he created an indirect and ad hoc tax. The General Farm obtained the rights to collect this tax in 1727. Without any great increase in expenses, it could use for this purpose the personnel available for collecting *traites* and the salt tax.

7. *Correspondance*, fasc. I, pp. 145–47.

8. Ibid., p. 164.

9. *Oeuvres*, vol. VI, p. 589.

10. Lavoisier, letter of June 22, 1778, quoted by A. Delahante, *Une famille de finance*, vol. I, pp. 338–39.

11. *Correspondance*, fasc. I, p. 178.

12. Ibid., p. 204.

13. Ibid., p. 195.

14. Ibid., p. 219.

15. D. I. Duveen and H. P. Klickstein, *A Bibliography of the Works of Lavoisier* (London: Dawson, 1944), p. 237.

16. Guettard and Monnet, *Atlas minéralogique de la France* (Paris: Dupain-Triel, 1778), p. 2.

17. "Notice sur la vie et les ouvrages de Lavoisier," *Magasin Encyclopédique* V (1795): 174–88.

18. M. C. Sahut, Conservateur au département des Peintures, Musée du Louvre. Personal communication. Plan in Louis Hautecoeur, *Histoire du Louvre* (Paris: Editions de l'Illustration, 1928), p. 70.

19. Diderot–d'Alembert, *Encyclopédie ou dictionnaire raisonné des sciences, des arts et des métiers* (Paris: 1753), vol. III, p. 409. Gabriel François Venel, a physician from Montpellier and Inspector-General of Mineral Waters, was responsible along with his friend Pierre Bayen, pharmacist and chemist, for analyzing all mineral waters in France. "He is better known for what he promised the sciences than for what he actually did for them," Antoine Fourcroy wrote severely in *Dictionnaire de Chimie, Encyclopédie Méthodique* (1795), vol. III, p. 262.

20. Voltaire, *L'homme aux quarante écus* (Paris: Editions de la Couronne, 1946), pp. 12–13.

21. Voltaire, *Correspondance* (Paris: Gallimard, la Pléiade Collection, 1985), vol. IX, p. 521.

22. Voltaire, quoted by E. Durand in *A. Deparcieux, notice biographique* (Paris: Brabo-Alais, 1904), p. 85.

23. *Oeuvres*, vol. III, p. 220.

24. Ibid., pp. 148–49.

25. 1 livre = 16 ounces = 489.51 grams; 1 ounce = 8 *gros* = 30.59 grams; 1 *gros* = 7 grains = 3.824 grams; 1 grain = 0.053 grams.

26. *Oeuvres*, vol. III, p. 145.

27. J. B. Dumas, *Leçons de philosophie chimique* (Paris: Gauthier-Villars, 1937), p. 80.

28. *Oeuvres*, vol. II, p. 25.

29. *Observations sur la physique* (1771), vol. I, p. 79.

30. J. B. Gough, "Lavoisier's Mémoirs on the Nature of Water and Their Place in the Chemical Revolution," *Ambix* 20 (1983): p. 97.

31. E. Saigey, *Les Sciences au XVIIIᵉ siècle* (Paris: Germer Baillière, 1873), p. 138.

32. W. A. Smeaton, "L'Avant Coureur," *Annals of Science* 13 (1957): 224.

33. *Oeuvres*, vol. IV, p. 44.

34. *Correspondance*, fasc. II, p. 391.

35. *Observations sur la physique*. (June 1772), vol. II, p. 231.

36. *Oeuvres*, vol. IV, p. 418.

37. *Oeuvres*, vol. VI, p. 80.

38. *Oeuvres*, vol. IV, p. 224.

39. *Oeuvres*, vol. III, p. 250.

40. H. Thirion, *La vie privée des financiers au XVIIIᵉ siècle* (Paris: Plon, 1895), p. 151.

41. J. B. Auget de Montyon, *Particularités et observations sur les ministres des finances de France les plus célèbres, depuis 1660 jusqu'en 1791*. (Paris: Le Normant, 1812), 155.

42. P. de Bachaumont, *Mémoires secrets pour servir à l'histoire de la république des lettres en France* (London: 1777–1789), vol. X, p. 200.

43. These objects are a part of the Lavoisier Collection, Rare and Manuscript Collections, Cornell University Library.

44. E. Grimaux, *Lavoisier 1743-1794*. (Paris: Alcan, 1888), p. 36.

45. Ibid., p. 37.

46. D. Hume, "Essai sur le commerce," in E. Daire and G. de Molinari, eds., *Mélanges d'économie politique* (Paris: Guillaumin, 1847), vol. I, p. 16.

47. Ibid., Introduction, p. vi.

48. Lavoisier, *Reading Notes*, October 3, 1772, 42 pages, Archives de l'Académie des Sciences, Lavoisier Collection, dation Chabrol, card 280, file 6.

49. *Oeuvres*, vol. VI, pp. 112–13.

50. Ibid., p. 117.

51. Ibid., p 118.

52. Ibid., pp. 122–23, quoted by A. Donovan, *Antoine Lavoisier: Science, Administration, and Revolution*. (Oxford and Cambridge, Mass.: Blackwell, 1993), p. 128.

53. R. Stourm, *Les finances de l'ancien régime et de la Révolution* (Paris: Guillaumin, 1885), vol. I, p. 37.

54. J. Necker, *Sur l'administration de M. Necker, par lui-même* (Paris: Hôtel de Thou, 1791), p. 6.

55. *Mémoire de M. Necker, en réponse à celui de M. l'abbé Morellet sur la Cie des Indes* (Paris: 1769), pp. 20–21.

56. H. Lüthy, *La banque protestante en France, de la révocation de l'édit de Nantes à la Révolution* (Paris: SEVPEN, 1961), vol. II, pp. 370–71.

57. Marquis de Ségur, *Louis XVI et Necker. Au couchant de la monarchie* (Paris: Calmann-Lévy, 1914), p. 24.

58. R. Stourm, *Les finances de l'ancien régime*, p. 38.

59. J. Necker, *Eloge de Jean Baptiste Colbert* (Paris: Demonville, 1776), pp. 64–100.

60. Ibid., p. 39.

61. Ibid., p. 48.

Chapter 3: Fixed Air and Pneumatic Chemistry

1. E. H. de Grouchy and P. Cottin, *Journal inédit du duc de Croÿ, 1718-1784* (Paris: Flammarion, 1906–1907), vol. III, p. 20.

2. *Oeuvres*, vol. II, p. 41.

3. J. E. Guettard, "Voyage fait en 1760 à la suite de M. le Marquis de Paulmy, Ambassadeur de France auprès du Roi de Pologne," Archives de l'Académie des Sciences, p. 118, quoted by H. Guerlac, *Lavoisier: The Crucial Year* (Ithaca, N.Y.: Cornell University Press, 1961), p. 81.

4. *Introduction aux observations sur la physique, sur l'histoire naturelle et sur les arts*, extracts from two papers by Darcet, vol. I, pp. 108–23.

5. Ibid., vol. I, p. 120.

6. P. J. Macquer, *Dictionnaire de chymie* (Paris: Didot, 1778), vol. I, p. 494.

7. Ibid., p. 498.

8. Ibid., p. 499.

9. Ibid., p. 497.

10. Ibid., p. 498.

11. *Oeuvres*, vol. II, p. 50.

12. P. J. Macquer, *Dictionnaire de chymie*, vol. I, p. 500.

13. Ibid., p. 501.

14. *Oeuvres*, vol. II, p. 56.

15. Ibid., p. 56.

16. João Jacinto de Magalhàes had left the monastery at Coimbra where he was studying sciences in 1755 and spent the next nine years in Paris, where he gallicized his name. At Daniel Trudaine's request, he settled in London in 1764. Like Trudaine's other special envoys—Gabriel Jars, Jean Baptiste Duhamel, and Nicolas Desmarest—his mission was to send scientific, technical, and industrial information to Paris. He was responsible for dispatching many scientific articles, books, and instruments, to the continent.

17. J. P. Brissot de Warville, *Journal du Lycée de Londres* 1 (1784): 194, note 1.

18. J. Keir, *The First Part of a Dictionary of Chemistry* (London: Elliott and Kay, 1777), vol. I, pp. iii–iv.

19. J. Priestley, *Experiments and Observations on Different Kinds of Air* (London: J. Johnson, 1774), vol. I, pp. 53–54.

20. B. Franklin, quoted in J. Priestley, *Experiments and Observations on Different Kinds of Air*, vol. I, pp. 94–95.

21. J. Priestley, *Experiments and Observations on Different Kinds of Air*, vol. I, p. 29.

22. Letter from Magellan to Macquer, March 20, 1772, *Journal de Hardy*, Bibliothéque Nationale, ms. 12306, 18.

23. A. F. Fourcroy would later say that Priestley's observations "contained a great many discoveries and new comments, and still more, the germs of discoveries; but, it must be admitted, these discoveries truly had no connection, no coherence, and they could not yet form any real theory or body of doctrine." *Dictionnaire de Chimie, Encyclopédie méthodique* (1795), vol. III, p. 384.

24. *Observations sur la physique* (April 1772), pp. 85–86.

25. *Correspondance*, fasc. II, p. 368.

26. *Opuscules physiques et chymiques*, p. 1.

27. N. Lémery, *Cours de chymie* (Paris: 1730), p. 299.

28. *Oeuvres*, vol. III, p. 265.

29. P. J. Macquer, *Dictionnaire de chymie* (1st ed., 1766) vol. I, p. 397–98. Quoted by Guerlac, *Lavoisier: The Crucial Year*, p. 91.

30. *Oeuvres*, vol. III, 266.

31. *Opuscules physiques et chymiques*, pp. 1–2.

32. Ibid., p. 1.

33. "From the Dutch *ghoast*, which means esprit; in English *ghost* and in German *geist*." Ibid., p. 5.

34. S. Hales, *Vegetable Staticks: or An Account of some Statical Experiments on the-*

Sap in Vegetables: Being an Essay towards a Natural History of Vegetation. (London: W. and J. Innys, 1727), p. iv.

35. Ibid., p. 313.

36. *Oeuvres*, vol. II, p. 7.

37. *Opuscules physiques et chymiques*, pp. 25–26.

38. J. Black, *Experiments upon Magnesia Alba, Quick-lime and other Alcaline Substances* (Edinburgh: William Creech, 1777), p. 30.

39. D. MacBride, *Experimental Essays on Medical and Philosophical Subjects* (London: A. Millar and T. Cadell, 1767), p. 59.

40. J. Priestley, *Experiments and Observations on Different Kinds of Air*, vol. I, p. 102.

41. A. Fourcroy, *Dictionnaire de Chimie, Encyclopédie méthodique* (1795), vol. III, p. 365.

42. *Oeuvres*, vol. III, p. 262.

43. Ibid., p. 266.

44. Ibid., p. 275.

45. Ibid., p. 276.

46. Ibid., p. 320.

Chapter 4: The Calcination of Metals

1. "Expériences de l'augmentation du poids de certaines matières par la calcination," *Mémoires de l'Académie des Sciences* 1 (1667): 5.

2. L. Béraut, *Dissertation sur la cause de l'augmentation de poids que certaines matières acquièrent dans leur calcination, qui a remporté le prix au jugement de l'Académie Royale des Belles Lettres, Sciences et Arts* (Bordeaux: Pierre Brun, 1747), 36 pages.

3. Guyton de Morveau, "Dissertation sur le phlogistique considéré comme corps grave et par rapport aux changements de pesanteur qu'il produit sur les corps auxquels il s'unit," in *Digressions académiques, ou Essais sur quelques sujets de physique, de chymie et d'histoire naturelle* (Dijon: Frantin, 1772). The report had been presented at the Académie de Dijon in December 1770.

4. A. Baumé, *Chymie expérimentale et raisonnée* (Paris: Didot, 1774), Foreword, p. xxii.

5. *Procès Verbaux de l'Académie Royale des Sciences* 91 (1772), fol. 35 verso.

6. *Correspondance*, fasc. II, p. 405.

7. Condorcet, *Oeuvres complètes*, edited by A. Condorcet-O'Connor and M. F. Arago (Paris: Didot Frères, 1847–1849), vol. II, p. 39.

8. Unpublished letter (1772) from Condorcet to "M. de Morveau, Procureur général au Parlement de Dijon," reproduced on page 49 of the catalogue for the auction held at the Hôtel Drouot, Paris on December 6 and 7, 1995 by MM. Laurin, Guilloux, Buffetaud, Tailleur.

9. Diderot and d'Alembert, *Encyclopédie* (1779), vol. XIII, p. 596, article entitled "Expansibilité."

10. C. Henry, *Correspondance inédite de Condorcet et de Turgot, 1770–1779* (Geneva: Slatkine, 1970), p. 58.

11. Ibid., p. 59.

12. Ibid., p. 112.

13. Ibid., pp. 61–62.

14. The process for preparing phosphorus, long a secret, was known in France from 1692, thanks to Guillaume Homberg who got it from Johann Kunckel in Dresden. The rather complicated method entailed evaporating the residue of putrefied and distilled human urine in the presence of three times the amount of very fine white sand. Robert Boyle used the same process, whose secret he had got from Johann Daniel Krafft, another German from Dresden, who had bought it for 200 *thalers* from Hennig Brand in Hamburg. In 1737, Jean Hellot presented to the Paris Academy of Science a much simpler method perfected by Macquer and Rouelle. In 1743, Andreas Sigismund Marggraf, a German chemist, published in the *Memoirs of the Berlin Academy* "a new and very good process for obtaining more easily, quickly and cheaply than before a good quantity of phosphorus." But the final stage of the distillation of urine was accompanied by a loss of phosphorus in the form of a reddish brown deposit on the neck of the retort. Pierre François Mitouard improved the yield by washing this residue in distilled water and obtained an excellent phosphorus.

15. *Oeuvres*, vol. IV, p. 142.

16. Archives de l'Académie des Sciences, Lavoisier Collection, small notebook entitled "Analyse de différentes eaux," p. 38.

17. "Mémoire sur l'acide du phosphore et sur ses combinaisons avec différentes substances salines, terreuses et métalliques," Archives de l'Académie des Sciences, Lavoisier Collection, ms. 1308 D.

18. In fact, this method is unsuitable for producing sulfuric acid, because a great part of the sulfurous anhydride formed during combustion is lost in the atmosphere. J. R. Partington emphasizes that no one has ever been able to explain what Lavoisier really did. Stahl had carried out the same experiment and obtained a weight of sulfuric acid inferior to that of the sulfur consumed. Moreover, this is what had led him to attribute a negative weight to the phlogiston. See J. R. Partington, *A History of Chemistry* (London: Macmillan, 1962), vol. III, p. 385.

19. Archives de l'Académie des Sciences, Lavoisier Collection, ms. 1303.

20. "I realized then that the property of increasing weight by calcination, which is simply a slower combustion, was not particular to metals, as had been thought, but that it was a general law in nature to which a large number of solid and liquid bodies could be subjected." Ibid.

21. Litharge is PbO, and not Pb_3O_4, which is minium.

22. *Correspondance*, fasc. II, p. 389.

23. *Oeuvres*, vol. II, p. 103.

24. J. B. Bucquet, "Expériences physico-chimiques sur l'air qui se dégage des corps dans le temps de leur décomposition et qu'on connait sous le nom vulgaire d'air fixé," *Mémoires de mathématique et de physique présentés à l'Académie Royale des Sciences par divers savants* 7 (1773/1776): 1–17.

25. *Oeuvres*, vol. I, p. 550.

26. Ibid., p. 543.

27. Ibid., pp. 545–46.

28. A. F. Fourcroy,*Dictionnaire de chimie*, vol. III, p. 386.

29. A. Baumé, quoted in A. F. Fourcroy, *Dictionnaire de chimie*, vol. III, p. 387.

30. "So you are going to choose a chemist," Turgot wrote. "In such matters, the Academy has sometimes chosen the worst. After its stupidity in rejecting Rouelle and Darcet for Sage, it should have elected them, in spite of their decision never to present themselves again. This redress was their due, and the Academy would have had men who would have been to its credit. Baumé has remained a man of merit." C. Henry, *Correspondance*, pp. 123–24.

31. For a number of years this plan of action was erroneously dated February 20, 1772.

32. Lavoisier quoted by M. Berthelot, "Introduction du premier registre de laboratoire," *La révolution chimique: Lavoisier* Paris: Alcan, 1890), pp. 46–49.

33. Ibid.

34. Ibid, pp. 233–34.

35. Archives de l'Académie des Sciences, Lavoisier Collection, ms. 170.

36. M. Berthelot, *La r130volution chimique: Lavoisier*, pp. 235–36.

37. Ibid., p. 236.

38. Handwritten letter from Trudaine de Montigny to Lavoisier, August 2, 1773. Archives de l'Académie des Sciences, Lavoisier Collection, dation Chabrol, 2, file 3.

39. Lavoisier, *Opuscules physiques et chymiques*, Introduction, pp. iii–v.

40. "Théorie de M. Black sur l'air fixe ou fixé contenu dans les terres calcaires et sur les phénomènes que produit en elles la privation de ce même air," in *Opuscules physiques et chymiques*, p. 37.

41. Ibid., pp. 254–55.

42. Ibid., p. 293.

43. Ibid., p. 373.

Chapter 5: The Oxygen Dispute

1. *Oeuvres*, vol. III, p. 315.

2. Potassium hydroxide.

3. H. Faure, *Pierre Bayen, chimiste* (Châlons-sur-Marne: J. L. Le Roy, 1865), pp. 15–16.

4. P. Bayen, *Observations sur la physique, sur l'histoire naturelle et sur les arts*, vol. III (1774), pp. 129–45. 129–45.

5. Ibid.

6. *Oeuvres*, vol. IV, p. 190.

7. A. Fourcroy, *Dictionnaire de chimie*, vol. III, p. 457.

8. J. Priestley, *Experiments and Observations on Different Kinds of Air, 1775* (London: J. Johnson, 1775), vol. II, p. 34.

9. Priestley obtained nitrous air (nitric oxide) by treating copper with diluted nitric acid. "This gas cannot be breathed; it turns red on contact with atmospheric air, it is not precipitated by limewater and in the presence of hydrogen gives off a green flame. Finally, at its formation, it absorbs a fifth of the available atmospheric air; the more tainted the air, the more it is absorbed." In 1772, Priestley measured the "goodness" of air by mixing a known volume of air with nitrous air (nitric oxide) over water and noting the contraction due to the removal of oxygen and solution of the resulting

higher oxides of nitrogen in the water. J. R. Partington, *A Short History of Chemistry*, 3rd ed. (New York: Dover, 1960), p. 115.

10. J. Priestley, *Experiments and Observations on Different Kinds of Air* (1775), vol. II, p. 36.

11. Ibid.

12. J. Priestley,*The Doctrine of Phlogiston Established* (Northumberland: for the author, 1800), p. 32.

13. J. Priestley, *Experiments and Observations on Different Kinds of Air* (1775), vol. II, p. 40.

14. Ibid., p. 45.

15. Ibid., p. 102.

16. Handwritten letter from January 19, 1768, quoted in Daumas, *Lavoisier*, p. 94.

17. J. B. Dumas, *Leçons de philosophie chimique* (Paris: Gauthier-Villars, 1937), p. 58.

18. C. W. Scheele, *Traité chimique de l'air et du feu*, translated by baron de Dietrich (Paris: rue et Hôtel Serpente, 1781), p. 104.

19. Ibid., pp. 184–85.

20. *Correspondance*, fasc. II, pp. 435–36.

21. C. W. Scheele, *Traité chimique de l'air et du feu*, pp. 100–101.

22. E. Grimaux, "Une lettre inédite de Scheele à Lavoisier, " *Revue générale des sciences pures et appliquées* 1 (1890): 1–2; Uno Bocklund, "A Lost Letter from Scheele to Lavoisier," *Lychnos* (1957): 39–62; A. R. Butler, "Lavoisier: A Letter from Sweden," *Chemistry in Britain* (July 1984): 618.

23. Letter from C. W. Scheele to Lavoisier, sent from Uppsala on September 30, 1774. Archives de l'Académie des Sciences, Lavoisier Collection, dation Chabrol, carton 2, file 3.

24. *Oeuvres*, vol. II, p. 120.

25. Lavoisier, "Sur la calcination des métaux dans les vaisseaux fermés, et sur la cause de l'augmentation de poids qu'ils acquièrent pendant cette opération," *Observations sur la physique*, vol. IV (1774), p. 451.

26. G. F. Cigna, *Mélanges de philosophie et de mathématiques de la Société royale de Turin*, vol. alter (1760–1761), p. 176. Quoted by Lavoisier in *Observations sur la physique*, vol. IV (1774), p. 453.

27. "Dissertation de M. Cigna sur les causes de l'extinction de la lumière d'une bougie et de la mort des animaux renfermés dans un espace plein d'air," *Introduction aux observations sur la physique, sur l'histoire naturelle et sur les arts*, vol. II (1772), p. 97.

28. Ibid., translated by H. Guerlac in *Lavoisier: The Crucial Year*, p. 169.

29. *Observations sur la physique*, vol. IV (1774), p. 452. Quoted in *Correspondance*, fasc. II, p. 465.

30. See chapter 2, no. 25.

31. The Third Laboratory Register, p. 62, quoted in Berthelot, *La révolution chimique, Lavoisier*, pp. 264–67.

32. *Correspondance*, fasc. II, p. 477.

33. "Mémoire sur la nature du principe qui se combine avec les métaux pendant leur calcination et qui en augmente le poids, lu à la rentrée de l'Académie le 26 avril par M. Lavoisier," *Observations sur la physique*, vol. V (1775), pp. 429–33.

34. Ibid.

35. J. Priestley, *Experiments and Observations on Different Kinds of Air*, vol. II, p. 320.

36. *Observations sur la physique*, vol. V (1775), p. 429.

37. Magellan wrote to Lavoisier: "I send regularly to M. Trudaine, Dr. Priestley's worksheets, that is the pages from his second volume on the new discoveries of different types of air, and I have no doubt that he will pass them on to you as they arrive." *Correspondance*, fasc. II, p. 506.

38. E. C. Genêt, *Scribblings for my Memoires*, portfolio I, ms. 9, Library of Congress, Division of Manuscripts, Washington. Quoted in T. D. Phillips, "Lavoisier and Priestley," *Isis* 46 (1955): 53.

39. A. Fourcroy, *Dictionnaire de chimie*, vol. III, p. 457.

40. In 1798 Lamétherie attacked: "Lavoisier did not mention Bayen, because he was not a member of the Academy, a common practice." *Journal de Physique* III (floréal An VI, 1798): 392. In 1809 he did it again, clearly accusing him of plagiarism: "Lavoisier, wanting to appropriate Bayen's discovery (because Bayen did not belong to the Academy) on the revivification of red precipitate or mercury oxide, without the addition of charcoal, and all that Bayen had said against the phlogiston theory and that of Cavendish on the composition of water, never speaks of these excellent experiments. I protested for them, and he never forgave me." *Journal de Physique* LXIX (1809): 63.

41. J. Rey, *Essays sur la recherche de la cause pour laquelle l'étain et le plomb augmentent de poids quand on les calcine* (Bazas, 1630), chap. XVI, p. 98 (BN: 8° Rés. ms. 158). *Nouvelle édition, revue sur l'exemplaire original et augmentée sur les manuscrits de la Bibliothèque du Roy et des Minimes des Paris*, with notes by Mr Gobet (Paris: Ruault, 1777), p. 66.

42. J. Rey, *Essays sur la recherche*, p. 115. *Nouvelle édition*, p. 83.

43. *Observations sur la physique*, vol. V (1775), p. 48.

44. *Oeuvres*, vol. II, p. 629.

45. *Oeuvres*, vol. II, p. 97.

46. Quoted in J. R. Partington, *A History of Chemistry*, vol. III, p. 633.

47. *Oeuvres*, vol. II, p. 100.

48. M. Berthelot, *La révolution chimique, Lavoisier*, p. 60.

49. It was in September 1774, when Scheele left Uppsala for the small town of Koping, that Scheele told Lavoisier about his own method for producing oxygen from silver nitrate. "The letter leaving Upsala on September 30 reached Paris after seventeen days, about the time of the dinner with Priestley." A. R. Butler, "Lavoisier: A Letter from Sweden," *Chemistry in Britain*, p. 619.

50. G. Cuvier, *Rapport historique sur les progrès des sciences naturelles depuis 1789 et sur leur état actuel* (Paris: Verdière et Ladrange, 1828), p. 66.

Chapter 6: The Turgot Years

1. Condorcet, *Oeuvres complètes*, vol. I, "Letter to Voltaire, July 22, 1774."

2. Dupont was elected in 1789 deputy from the bailiwick of Nemours, and afterward called himself "Du Pont de Nemours."

3. A. R. J. Turgot, *Oeuvres*, ed. Eugène Daire (Paris: Guillaumin, 1844), vol. I, p. 171.

4. *Oeuvres*, vol. VI, pp. 125–86. "Calculs des produits des différent baux de la ferme générale, avec des détails très particuliers sur les frais de régie du bail de Laurent David."

5. N. F. Mollien, *Mémoires d'un ministre du Trésor public, 1780-1815* (Paris: Fournier, 1845), vol. I, p. 68.

6. The case arose twice in the period 1691–1697. The lease called Pierre Pointeau had left a deficit of 50 million livres ($2 billion). The Farmers-General had been obliged to advance it by taking out loans, and for their trouble the king had given them a bonus of 800,000 livres ($32 million), which represented 20,000 livres ($800,000) per person for six years. E. Grimaux, *Lavoisier, 1743-1794*, p. 66.

7. Archives Nationales, 129 ap 17, *Memoires Affaires générales*, vol. II, p. 180.

8. *Oeuvres*, vol. VI, p. 158.

9. N. F. Mollien, *Mémoires d'un ministre du Trésor*, vol. I, pp. 67–68. He spoke of francs because he was writing in 1845, but he was referring to the livres of 1774.

10. *Oeuvres*, vol. VI, p. 158.

11. é. Grimaux, *Lavoisier, 1743-1794*, p. 68.

12. J. B. Coquereau, *Memoires de l'abbé Terray* (London: 1776), p. 180 (B.N., 8° Lf 7622).

13. A. Delahante, *Une famille de finance au XVIIIe siècle* (Paris: Hetzel, 1881), vol. I, p. 243.

14. P. S. Dupont, *Mémoires sur la vie et les ouvrages de M. Turgot* (Philadelphia, 1782), part two, p. 192.

15. Ibid., p. 26.

16. A. Delahante, *Une famille de finance au XVIIIe siècle*, p. 244.

17. P. S. Dupont, *Mémoires sur la vie et les ouvrages de M. Turgot*, p. 28.

18. M. Dez, "Mémoire sur la théorie du jaugeage," *Mémoires de mathématique et de physique, savants étrangers* (Paris: Moutard, 1776), vol. VII, p. 388.

19. *Encyclopédie*, supplément III, vol. III, p. 507.

20. A. Birembaut, "Quelques aspects de la personnalité de Lavoisier," *Extrait des actes du congrés de Luxembourg, 72e session de l'Association Française pour l'Avancement des Sciences*, July 1953, p. 54, and C. Henry, *Correspondance inédite*, p. 273.

21. P. S. Dupont, *Mémoires sur la vie et les ouvrages de M. Turgot*, p. 82.

22. M. Daumas, *Lavoisier*, p. 144.

23. *Oeuvres*, vol. V, p. 97.

24. P. S. Dupont, *Mémoires sur la vie et les ouvrages de M. Turgot*, p. 77.

25. England imported its saltpeter from India, Prussia produced 150,000 pounds and Sweden between 200,000 and 600,000 pounds.

26. *Oeuvres*, vol. V, p. 695.

27. Ibid.

28. Archives de l'Académie des Sciences, Lavoisier Collection, ms. no. 685.

29. P. S. Dupont, *Mémoires sur la vie et les ouvrages de M. Turgot*, p. 84.

30. *Oeuvres*, vol. V, p. 704.

31. P. S. Dupont, *Mémoires sur la vie et les ouvrages de M. Turgot*, p. 81.

32. "Histoire de ce qui s'est passé relativement au prix proposé sur la formation

du salpêtre," *Mémoires de mathématiques et de physique, Savants étrangers*, vol. XI, p. 11.

33. M. Chevrand, "Observations sur les moyens d'augmenter la récolte du salpêtre en France," *Mémoires de mathématiques et de physique*, pp. 326–27.

34. In 1599 the duc de Sully, Grand Maître de l'Artillerie, had created an extraordinarily luxurious group of residences, workshops, warehouses and foundries at the Arsenal. Henry IV was a regular visitor and it was on his way there that he was assassinated by François Ravaillac on May 14, 1610. Sully's construction was almost entirely destroyed by a fire in 1716, but was reconstructed between 1716 and 1729 by the architect Germain Boffrand, according to the original layout. Only one room containing the magnificent seventeenth century decoration has survived. It was Marshal de La Meilleraye's bedroom whose paneling with a gold background was painted by Noel Quillerier.

35. Note written by Madame Lavoisier, quoted by G. Cuvier, "Lavoisier," in L. G. Michaud, *Biographie universelle*, vol. 23, p. 462.

36. Quoted in A. Birembaut in " L'Académie royale des Sciences en 1780 vue par l'astronome suédois Lexell 1740–1784," *Revue d'Histoire des Sciences et de Leurs Applications* 10 (1957): 161.

37. *Correspondance*, fasc. II, pp. 502–503.

38. Also, the number of chemists increased. Most of them, like the Rouelle brothers, Bayen, Baumé, Macquer, Parmentier, Pelletier, Proust, Vauquelin, Brongniart, Cadet de Gassicourt, Demachy, Sage, Quinquet, Mitouard, and Venel, came from pharmacies. Others, like Baron, d'Arcet, Tillet, Gibelin, Marat, and Fourcroy were doctors. But there were also lawyers like Lavoisier himself and Guyton de Morveau, and aristocrats like Chaptal and Duhamel du Monceau. And there was also an ecclesiastic, the Abbé Rozier.

39. F. Quesnay, *Dialogue sur les artisans*, in C. Gide and C. Rist, eds., *Histoire des doctrines économiques depuis les physiocrates jusqu'à nos jours* (Paris: Recueil Sirey, 1926), p. 12.

40. P. S. Dupont, *Journal d'agriculture, du commerce et des finances*, June 1766.

41. E. Daire and G. de Molinari, *Mélanges d'économie politique* (Paris: Guillaumin, 1847), vol. I, p. 445.

42. E. Faure, *La disgrace de Turgot* (Paris: Gallimard, 1961), p. 216.

43. *Journal de l'Abbé de Véri* (Paris: Editions Jules Tallandier, 1928), vol. I, p. 445.

Chapter 7: The New Chemistry

1. F. L. Holmes, "Lavoisier's Conceptual Passage," in *The Chemical Revolution: Essays in Reinterpretation*, ed. A. Donovan *Osiris* 2d ser. 4 (1988): 91.

2. R. Descartes, *Discours de la méthode* (Paris: Collection 10/18, 1985), p. 82.

3. J. Mayow, *Tractatus primus de respiratione* (Leyde, 1671), p. 12.

4. Quoted in R. Flandrois in "Influence des travaux de Lavoisier sur l'évolution de la physiologie respiratoire," *Revue Lyvonnaise de Médecine* (1965): 900.

5. *Opuscules physiques et chymiques*, p. 304.

6. *Observations sur la physique* vol. V, (1775), pp. 429–33.

7. "Expériences sur la décomposition de l'air dans le poumon et sur un des principaux usages de la respiration dans l'économie animale,"Archives de l'Académie des Sciences, ms. 1349, pp. 6–7.

8. Lavoisier, *Cahier de laboratoire* no. IV, quoted by Berthelot, *La révolution chimique, Lavoisier*, p. 272.

9. *Oeuvres*, vol. II, p. 176.

10. Ibid., p. 177.

11. *Oeuvres*, vol. V, p. 276.

12. Ibid., p. 278.

13. Ibid.

14. *Oeuvres*, vol. II, p. 129.

15. Ibid., p. 251.

16. M. Crosland, "Chemistry and the Chemical Revolution," in *The Ferment of Knowledge*, ed. George S. Rousseau and Roy Porter eds., (Cambridge: Cambridge University Press, 1980), pp. 408–9.

17. *Oeuvres*, vol. II, p. 228.

18. *Correspondance*, fasc. III, p. 565. Letter to Thomas Henry.

19. H. Guerlac, *Antoine Laurent Lavoisier, Chemist and Revolutionary* (New York: Scribner's, 1973), p. 105.

20. *Oeuvres*, vol. II, p. 228.

21. Y. G. Dorfman, *Lavuaze*, 2nd ed. (Moscow: Academy of Sciences, 1962), pp. 136–40.

22. H. M. Leicester, "Boyle, Lomonosov, Lavoisier and the Corpuscular Theory of Matter," *Isis* 58 (1967): 243.

23. "Notice abrégée de plusieurs Mémoires rédigés en commun par MM. Bucquet et Lavoisier et sur lesquels ils prient l'Académie de leur donner date avant sa séparation." Archives de l'Académie des Sciences, Lavoisier Collection, file 363.

24. L. G. Michaud, *Biographie universelle.*, vol. 23, p. 462.

25. 24 livres ($960)

26. J. P. Marat, *Recherches physiques sur le feu* (Paris: Cl. Ant. Jombert, 1780), p. 15.

27. B. G. Sage, *Analyse chimique et concordance des trois règnes* (Paris: Imprimerie Royale, 1786), vol. I, p. 117, quoted in Claude A. Lopez, *Benjamin Franklin and the French Revolution* (Philadelphia: American Philosophical Society, 1990), p. 9.

28. G. Walter, *Marat* (Paris: Albin Michel, 1933), p. 63.

29. Ibid., p. 64.

30. Ibid., pp. 64–65.

31. J. P. Marat, *Recherches physiques sur le feu*, p. 97.

32. *Oeuvres*, vol. IV, p. 360.

33. E. Grimaux, *Lavoisier, 1743–1794*, p. 122.

34. P. J. Macquer, *Dictionnaire de chymie*, 1778, vol. I, pp. 348–49.

35. Ibid., p. 349.

36. Ibid., pp. 349–52.

37. J. M. Raymond-Latour, *Souvenirs d'un oisif* (Lyon and Paris: Ayné Fils and Isidore Person, 1836), pp. 159–60.

38. Ch. Charles Gillispie, *The Edge of Objectivity: An Essay in the History of Scientific Ideas* (Princeton, N.J.: Princeton University Press, 1960), p. 205.

Chapter 8: The First Necker Ministry

1. *Correspondance*, fasc. III, p. 606.
2. A. Delahante, *Une famille de finance au XVIIIe siècle*, vol. I, p. 329.
3. Ibid., p. 333.
4. Ibid., p. 335.
5. Ibid., p. 336.
6. Ibid., p. 338.
7. Ibid., p. 338–39.
8. Refining techniques were improved. But methods for determining the raw saltpeter content in pure saltpeter and for dissolving impurities without attacking the saltpeter were still lacking. In 1785 Guyton de Morveau and Riffaut des Hêtres proposed one, but it was only in 1820 that a reliable method was found.
9. *Oeuvres*, vol. V, p. 448.
10. Duc de La Rochefoucauld, "Mémoire sur la génération du salpêtre dans la craie," *Mémoires de mathématiques et de physique, Savants étrangers*, vol. XI, p. 610.
11. *Oeuvres*, vol. V, pp. 599–600. Lavoisier certainly stayed several days in Angoulême. He described a quarry producing millstone that was hard and had good cleavage "between Angoulême and the Montbron mill," and "going from the faubourg de l'Houmeau to the cannon forge a bit further along," he noted a kind of bluish stone at the base of the river's banks. And there still exists in Saint Savinien a rue Nitrière which leads from the old saltpeter quarry to the Charente. The saltpeter was taken to the river to be loaded on gabbarts or barges.
12. "Rapport fait le 6 août 1789 à l'assemblée des représentants de la Commune [. . .] par un de Messieurs les Régisseurs des Poudres," in *Actes de la Commune de Paris pendant la Révolution*, ed. S. Lacroix (Paris: 1894), Vol. I, pp. 106–16. The details that follow are taken from the same document.
13. 70 to 80 toises =136 to 155 meters or 420 to 480 feet.115 to 130 toises = 224 to 263 meters or 690 to 780 feet.
14. *Oeuvres*, vol. V, p. 700.
15. *Correspondance*, fasc. III, p. 623.
16. "Histoire de ce qui s'est passé relativement au prix proposé sur la formation du salpêtre," *Mémoires de mathématique et de physique*, Savants étrangers vol. 11, p. 10.
17. *Correspondance*, fasc. IV, p. 202.
18. *Annales de Chimie* XV (Paris: Rue Serpente: 1792): 315.
19. On March 21, 1778 he bought from Field Marshal comte de Rochambeau the properties of Champrenault, located in the parish of Villefrancoeur, and Champigny in Beauce, near Chapelle Vendômoise, including, other than the buildings, 127 hectares of land, for 45,000 livres ($1.8 million) paid as an annual income of 2,250 livres ($90,000). On March 26 he purchased from Jean-Baptiste Bégon the property of Freschines, including a house and outbuildings, two sharecropping farms, the land belonging to the Grand et Petit Défait, la Salle, la Vallée, Ramay Villebouzon, la Pelletière, la Coutonnerie, la Prévôte and la Pigeonnière, or a total of 694 hectares for 229,075 livres ($9 million) of which 135,000 livres were paid in cash, and the remaining 100,000 livres were to be paid as an annual income of 5,000 livres ($200,000). On February 11, 1780

he purchased from Pierre Petit, a ploughman, various parcels of land for 1,324 livres ($53,000). Mademoiselle Punctis died in January 1781, leaving all her fortune to her nephew. The inheritance allowed him to increase his landholdings by a bit more. On October 28, 1781 he bought from Michel Daubichon, a lawyer at the Parlement, the land and sharecropping farm known as Bordy in the commune of Saint Léonard for the sum of 11,324 livres ($453,000). On June 9, 1784 he bought from François Pierre Petit, squire, the property of Thoisy, which included a château and its outbuildings, and four sharecropping farms, all of it representing 335 hectares of cultivated lands, vineyards, meadows and forest, for 100,000 livres ($4 million) of which 40,000 ($1.6 million) were paid in cash, the rest being paid as annual and perpetual income of 3000 livres ($120,000). Finally, on August 7, 1784 he bought the fief of Villanteuil, consisting of honorary, seigneurial dues without any land, for an annual and perpetual payment of 450 livres ($18,000). Of this entire domain, 1,129 hectares were wheatgrowing land that had cost him 389,000 livres, or an average cost of 345 livres ($13,800) per hectare. G. Diot, "Lavoisier à Villefrancoeur, Champigny et Freschines," *Bulletin de la Section Culturelle du Syndicat d'Initiative de la Vallée de la Cisse* 2 (1974): 52. Today the value of the land would be approximately five times less.

20. *Annales de Chimie* XV: 303.

21. Ibid., p. 304.

22. Ibid., p.310.

23. Ibid., p. 312.

24. Ibid., p. 313.

25. Ibid., p. 316.

26. *Annales de chimie* XV: 309.

27. Ch. C. Gillispie, "Notice biographique de Lavoisier par Mme Lavoisier," *Revue d'Histoire des Sciences et de Leurs Applications* 9 (1956): 59.

28. A. Dupré, *Extrait du Journal de Loir-et-Cher*, 17 et 19 novembre 1867, p. 10.

29. M. Beretta, *Bibliotheca Lavoisieriana: The Catalogue of the Library of Antoine Laurent Lavoisier* (Firenze: Leo S. Olschki, Biblioteca di Nuncius, 1995), p. 65.

30. A. Cauchie, "Le domaine de Freschines sous Lavoisier," *Mémoires de la Société des Sciences et Lettres du Loir-et-Cher* 14, 2 (30 juin 1900): 60.

31. Letter from P. S. Du Pont de Nemours to Madame Lavoisier, October 23, 1798, Manuscript Department, MS Fr 80, by permission of the Houghton Library, Harvard University, See chapter 20.

32. Letter from P. S. Du Pont de Nemours to Madame Lavoisier, April 1815, Manuscript department, MS Fr 80, by permission of the Houghton Library, Harvard University, Cambridge, MA 02138.

33. P. S. Du Pont, quoted in P. Jolly, *Dupont de Nemours: Apostle of Liberty and the Promised Land* (Wilmington, Del.: Brandywine Publishing Company, 1977), p. 57.

34. Quoted in D. McKie, *Antoine Lavoisier, Scientist, Economist, Social Reformer*, (London: Constable, 1952), p. 70

35. F. A. de Frénilly, *Souvenirs* (Paris: Plon Nourrit, 1908), p. 11.

36. Linguet, *Annales politiques, civiles et littéraires* (London: 1777), vol. III, pp. 258–59.

37. J. Necker, *Eloge de Colbert* (Paris: Demonville, 1786), 2nd ed., note p. 66.

38. J. Necker, *Sur la législation et le commerce des grains* (Paris: Pissot, 1775), vol. I, pp. 224–25.

39. Ibid., p. 98.

40. Located at the corner of the present rue de l'Ecole de Médecine and rue Dubois.

41. *Edit* from August 26, 1777.

42. *Oeuvres*, vol. III, p. 462.

43. Ibid., pp. 466–67.

44. The present Quai Morland.

45. *Oeuvres*, vol. III p. 497.

46. *Encyclopèdie*, article "Hôpital."

47. L. S. Mercier, *Tableau de Paris*, vol. III, p. 226.

48. Quoted in R. Escholier, *Hôtel-Dieu* (Lyon: Ciba Laboratories, 1938), p. 41.

49. *Oeuvres*, vol. III, p. 91.

50. Ibid. p. 98.

51. This would provoke long debates with the lampmakers over who had invented the parabolic lamps. In 1806, the Société de Genève would conclude in a report written by Benjamin Thomson Rumford, Guyton de Morveau, Gaspard Monge and Jacques Alexandre Charles: "In a century as enlightened as ours, it is very difficult to claim exclusive ownership of an idea. The most sublime conceptions have germinated simultaneously in so many minds, and hardly have they dawned before everyone starts to shout that it was his idea too. But they all lay claim to these ideas in vain, because they are so to speak the century's property and like the river's waters return to the ocean from which they came." Quoted in *Oeuvres*, vol. III, p. 105.

52. An exchange of correspondance between Madame Necker and Lavoisier can be consulted at Archives de l'Académie des Sciences, Lavoisier Collection, dation Chabrol, carton no. 1, file 36.

53. J. Necker, *Sur l'administration de M. Necker, par lui-même* (Paris: 1791), p. 16.

54. C. G. de Vergennes, *Observations remises à Louis XVI et par ses ordres, le 3 mai 1781*, in J.-L. Giraud Soulavie, *Mémoires historiques et politiques du règne de Louis XVI, depuis son mariage jusqu'à sa mort* (Paris: Treuttel et Würtz, An, 1801), vol. IV, p. 153.

Chapter 9: The Crowning Achievement of the Chemical Revolution

1. H. Guerlac, *Memoir on Heat*, translation of *Mémoire sur la chaleur*, (New York: Neale Watson Academic Publications, 1982), Introduction, p. xii.

2. R. Hahn, "Lavoisier et ses collaborateurs: une équipe au travail," in Christiane Demeulenaere-Douyère, ed., *Il y a 200 ans Lavoisier*, Actes du Colloque organisé à l'occasion du Bicentenaire de la mort d'Antoine-Laurent de Lavoisier, Paris-Blois, 3–6 mai 1994 (Paris: Technique et Documentation Lavoisier, 1995), p. 60.

3. *Correspondance*, fasc. III, p. 714. A second postscript mentioned the inoculation against smallpox of Madame Lavoisier, who, as a modern woman, was one of the first in France to test the method. It emerges from the final lines that she was not always easy to get along with: "Shall I dare ask you to give my regards to Madame de Lavoisier and express to her my concern for her inoculation's success? Because of this interest, I beg her to forgive me for the advice I gave her yesterday, which was to forgo the meeting next Saturday at M. de Viller's. She did not consider it good advice, but

it seemed to me, and it still does, that in her present circumstances, she cannot be too cautious." Ibid.

4. *Oeuvres*, vol. II, pp. 287–88.

5. Not without excusing himself for the neologism: "I admit that by combining two denominations, one derived from Latin, the other from Greek, I am exposing myself to criticism, justified up to a point. But I believed that in scientific matters one could allow oneself less purity of language to obtain greater purity of ideas." *Traité élémentaire de chimie*, vol. II, p. 68. Condillac would, no doubt, have disapproved this lack of respect for the major principles of the future *Méthode de nomenclature chimique*. However, the problem was difficult since the word *thermomètre*, etymologically correct, already indicated something else.

6. *Oeuvres*, vol. II, p. 331.

7. Published in August of the same year 1783 as a fifty-page brochure in four parts, it was reprinted in 1784 in the *Mémoires de l'Académie Royale des Sciences* (1780): 355–408. Lavoisier always in a hurry, succeeded in having this memoir published in the 1780 volume printed with a four-year delay.

8. *Oeuvres*, vol. II, p. 331.

9. Ibid., pp. 331–32.

10. V.A. Eyles, "The Evolution of a Chemist," *Annals of Science* 19 (1963): 167.

11. Ibid., pp. 169–70.

12. *Oeuvres*, vol. II, pp. 332–33.

13. H. Guerlac, *Memoir on Heat*, Introduction, p. xvii.

14. P. J. Macquer, *Dictionnaire de chymie* (1778), vol. II, p. 314.

15. M. Daumas, *Lavoisier, théoricien et expérimentateur* (Paris: Presses Universitaires de France, 1955), p. 144.

16. *The writings of Benjamin Franklin, Collected and Edited with a Life and Introduction*, ed. Albert Henry Smyth (New York: Macmillan, 1905–1907), vol. 8, p. 314.

17. Letter from Priestley to Lavoisier, dated July 10, 1782., Archives de l'Académie des Sciences, Lavoisier Collection, dation Chabrol, carton 2, file 3, sheet 68.

18. He had also noted that an electric spark, crossing atmospheric air enriched by enough oxygen to combine with the totality of the nitrogen present, produced a small gas bubble that was impossible to decompose. A century later, Baron Rayleigh and Sir William Ramsay would show that this residual bubble was an inert gas, argon. D. McKie, *Antoine Lavoisier* (London: Constable, 1952), p. 124.

19. *Oeuvres*, vol. II, p. 338.

20. Lavoisier, Laboratory Register VIII, folio 63, in Berthelot, *La révolution chimique, Lavoisier*, p. 293.

21. *Oeuvres*, vol. II, p. 339.

22. Ibid., p. 335.

23. Ibid., p. 339.

24. Ibid., p. 344.

25. Ibid., p. 345. In fact, he indicated: "A few drops of humidity that I had constantly found in the container in all the reductions of calces and lead that I had done, made me suspect that independently of the fixed elastic fluid, there existed a portion of water in the minium, that it separated from it during the reduction and that it was probably the cause of the weight loss I had observed." *Opuscules physiques et chymiques*, p. 269.

26. *Oeuvres*, vol. III, p. 719.

27. P. L. Clément, *Les Montgolfières* (Paris: Tardy, 1982), pp. 32–33.

28. *Oeuvres*, vol. III, p. 726.

29. Ibid., p. 727.

30. Ch. C. Gillispie, *The Montgolfier Brothers and the Invention of Aviation* (Princeton, N.J.: Princeton University Press, 1983), p. 88.

31. *Oeuvres*, vol. III, p. 730.

32. Ibid., p. 731.

33. *Benjamin Franklin: His Life as He Wrote it*, ed. Esmond Wright (London: Folio Society, 1989), p. 236.

34. P. L. Clément, *Les Montgolfières* , p. 70.

35. *Oeuvres*, vol. III, p. 734.

36. Ibid.

37. Ibid., pp. 734–35.

38. *Correspondance*, fasc. IV, p. 10.

39. Ibid., p. 10. Letter from Meusnier to M. de Baer, Swedish minister.

40. "Procès verbal de l'expérience aérostatique de l'Académie de Dijon," Archives de l'Académie des Sciences, Lavoisier Collection, 1442–47.

41. *A Scientific Correspondence During the Chemical Revolution: Louis Bernard Guyton de Morveau and Richard Kirwan, 1782–1802*, ed. E. Grison, M. Goupil, and P. Bret (Berkeley: University of California Office for History of Science and Technology, 1994), p. 81.

42. A. Young, *Travels During the years 1787, 1788 and 1789* (London: W. Richardson, 1794), vol. I, pp. 78–79.

43. *Oeuvres*, vol. V, p. 333.

44. Ibid., p. 334.

45. "Développement des dernières expériences sur la décomposition et la recomposition de l'eau." Extract from the *Journal Polytype*, February 26, 1786. Lavoisier is certainly the author of this text, which appears in the *Mémoires de Chimie*, vol. II, pp. 219–20 and in *Oeuvres*, vol. V, p. 320.

46. M. Berthelot, *La révolution chimique, Lavoisier*, p. 122.

47. G. Darboux, *éloges et discours académiques* (Paris: Librairie scientifique A. Hermann et Fils, 1912), p. 236.

48. *Oeuvres*, vol. II, p. 683.

49. We know today that the atmosphere is composed of 21 percent oxygen, 78 percent nitrogen, 0.9 percent argon, and 0.03 percent CO_2.

50. *Oeuvres*, vol. II, p. 687.

51. Ibid.

Chapter 10: A Senior Civil Servant

1. Marc and Muriel Vigié, *L'herbe à Nicot* (Paris: Fayard, 1989), p. 196.

2. *Oeuvres*, vol. III, p. 501.

3. Ibid., p. 506.

4. Ibid., p. 514

5. Ibid., p. 509.

6. Ibid.,p. 527.

7. The hypochondrium is the upper part of the abdomen.

8. N. F. de Neufchâteau, *Le Conservateur, ou Recueil de morceaux inédits d'histoire, de politique, de littérature et de philosophie* (Paris: An XII,1799), pp. 146–55, quoted in Duveen and Klickstein, "Benjamin Franklin (1706–1790) and Antoine Laurent Lavoisier (1743–1794)," Part III, *Annals of Science* 13 (1957): 43–44.

9. *Rapport des Commissaires chargés par le Roi de l'examen du magnétisme animal* (Paris: Imprimerie Royale, 1784), p. 64.

10. Ch. Deslon, *Supplément aux deux rapports de MM. les commissaires de l'Académie et de la Faculté de Médecine, et de la Société royale de Médecine* (Amsterdam-Paris: 1784), pp. 79–80.

11. A. L. de Jussieu, "Rapport de l'un des Commissaires chargés par le Roi de l'examen du magnétisme animal," in C. Burdin and F. Dubois, eds., *Histoire académique du magnétisme animal* (Paris: Baillière, 1841).

12. J. P. Brissot, *De la vérité, ou méditations sur les moyens de parvenir à la vérité dans toutes les connaissances humaines* (Neuchâtel: 1782), pp. 165–66.

13. J. P. Marat, *Les charlatans modernes ou Lettres sur le charlatanisme académique* (Paris: Imprimerie de Marat, 1791), letter IV, p. 13, note.

14. Condorcet Bibliothèque de l'Institut de France, ms. 876, pp. 95–96. Quoted in K. M. Baker, *Condorcet: raison et politique* (Paris: Hermann, 1988), p. 102.

15. Quoted in A. Birembaut, "L'Académie royale des Sciences en 1780 vue par l'astronome suédois Lexell 1740–1784n," *Revue d'Histoire des Sciences et de Leurs Applications* 10 (1957): 162.

16. *Oeuvres*, vol. IV, p. 567.

17. The committee was composed of the duc d'Ayen and the duc de La Rochefoucauld, the President de Saron, Bailly, who was supernumerary, Grandjean de Fouchy, Tillet, and the most senior pensionnaires of each class: Abbé Bossut, Lemonnier, Daubenton, Cadet, and Adanson.

18. *Oeuvres*, vol. IV, p. 569.

19. Ibid., p. 573.

20. Ibid., p. 575. It was from the Chaillot foundry, the first in France, that, after the Revolution, would come the first steam engines based on Watt's model.

21. *Oeuvres*, vol. III, p. 603.

22. Ibid., p. 636.

23. Ibid., p. 647.

24. Ibid., p. 668.

25. Ibid., p. 701.

26. F. Bellec, *La généreuse et tragique expédition de La Pérouse* (Rennes: Editions Ouest-France, 1985), p. 66.

27. *Oeuvres*, vol. IV, p. 729.

28. Ibid., p. 759.

29. J. Dunmore and M. de Brossard, *Le voyage de La Pérouse, 1785–1788* (Paris: Imprimerie Nationale, 1985), vol. I, p. 46.

30. A. Delahante, *Une famille de finance au XVIIIe siècle*, vol. I, p. 343.

31. F. Métra, *Gazette anecdotique du règne de Louis XVI: portefeuille d'un talon rouge* (Paris: Rouveyre, 1881), p. 180.

32. "Mémoire de Vergennes pour le Roi, 31 août 1776," in Henri Doniol, *Histoire de la participation de la France à l'établissement des Etats-Unis d'Amérique* (Paris: Imprimerie Nationale, 1886–1898), vol. I, p. 571.

33. J. R. Dull, *Franklin the Diplomat: The French Mission*, Transactions of the American Philosophical Society 72, part I (Philadelphia: American Philosophical Society, 1982), p. 50.

34. P. J. Cambon, "Rapport à la Convention du 3 germinal An II," quoted in René Stourm, *Les finances de l'Ancien Régime et de la Révolution* (Paris: Guillaumin, 1885), vol. 2, p. 205.

35. F. Aftalion, *L'économie de la Révolution française* (Paris: Hachette, collection Pluriel, 1987), p. 38.

36. J. F. Bosher, *The French Revolution* (New York-London: W. W. Norton, 1988), p. 95. Bosher refers to F. Braesch, in *Finances et monnaies révolutionnaires* (Paris: La maison du livre français, 1936), fasc. 2, p. 202.

37. Duc de Lévis, *Souvenirs et portraits, 1780–1789* (Paris: Beaupré, 1815), p. 77.

38. Archives de l'Académie des Sciences, Lavoisier Collection, ms. 12586.

39. Marc Vigié and Muriel Vigié, *L'herbe à Nicot*, p. 476.

40. *Rapport des Commissaires réviseurs des trois compagnies de Finances aux Représentants du Peuple chargés de surveiller leurs travaux, et lu aux Comités des Finances et de la Comptabilité.* (Paris: Convention nationale, 16 floréal An II, 5 mai 1794), Item 20, p. 131.

41. M. de Lescure, *Correspondance secrète sur Louis XVI, Marie-Antoinette, la Cour et la Ville* (Paris: Plon, 1866), vol. I, p. 551.

42. A. Delahante, *Une famille de finance au XVIIIᵉ siècle*, vol. I, p. 360.

43. F. Metra, *Correspondance secrète sur Louis XVI*, vol. XVIII, p. 68, quoted in A. Delahante, *Une famille de finance au XVIIIᵉ siècle*, vol. I, p. 378.

44. H. Thirion, *La vie des financiers au XVIIIᵉ siècle*, p. 457.

45. Ibid., p. 456.

46. L. S. Mercier, *Le nouveau Paris* (Paris: Fuchs, Pougens, Cramer, 1797), vol. VI, pp. 177–79.

47. M. de Lescure, *Correspondance secrète sur Louis XVI*, vol. 1, pp. 579–80.

48. *Réclamation d'un citoyen contre la nouvelle enceinte de Paris, élevée par les fermiers généraux* (no place, no publisher: 1787). J. A. Dulaure, the author, recounted: "This very brief brochure, attributed to the comte de Mirabeau, caused a great to-do and provoked the greatest vigilance from the police. It should be added that several libraries selling it were searched at night by the police who took several copies. One financier, I was told, offered 20,000 francs to anyone who could discover the author. The brochure sold for 3 livres ($120). A certain Guerbaer, then a book peddler and police spy, today a book printer on the Pont-Neuf selling only aristocratic works, had taken on the responsibility for printing and distributing it. I had every reason to believe that once he had made enough profit, he would himself denounce the author to the police. I got nothing from it. It had been written in two nights and printed in one." Document in the L. Scheler Collection, quoted in L. Scheler, *Lavoisier et le principe chimique* (Paris: Seghers, 1964), p. 193.

49. L. S. Mercier, *Le nouveau Paris*, vol. VI, pp. 177–79.

50. J. P. Poirier, *Lavoisier, théoricien et praticien de l'économie*, p. 115.

51. *Oeuvres*, vol. III, p. 585.

52. Ibid., p. 598.
53. Ibid., p. 591.

Chapter 11: The Tools of Communication

1. Quoted in V.A. Eyles, "The Evolution of a Chemist," *Annals of Science* 19 (1963): 167.

2. These reservations were expressed by Priestley, Bewley, Cavendish, Kirwan, and Westrumb in England; Bergman and Scheele in Sweden; Crell, Wieglieb, Hermbstadt, and Kaerstem in Germany; Van Marum, Deiman, Van Troostwijk, Nieuwland, and Bondt in Holland; the Chevalier Landriani in Italy; Lamétherie, Chaptal, Macquer, and even Lavoisier's close associates Fourcroy, Berthollet, and Guyton de Morveau in France.

3. *Oeuvres*, vol. II, pp. 623–24.

4. Ibid., p. 640.

5. Ibid., p. 655.

6. R. Kirwan, *An Essay on Phlogiston and the Constitution of Acids*, A New Edition (London: J. Johnson, 1789), pp. 3–4.

7. Ibid., p. 6.

8. Ibid., p. 8.

9. Berthollet had observed that when chlorine was mixed with water and exposed to the sun, oxygen was discharged, and that chlorine dissolved metals without effervescence. From this he deduced, incorrectly, that chlorine was a compound body, capable at some times of transferring its oxygen to metals and at others of releasing it.

10. M. Van Marum, *Journal physique de mon séjour à Paris en 1785*, quoted by H. A. M. Snelders in "The New Chemistry in the Netherlands," *Osiris* 2nd ser. 4 (1988): 127.

11. Guyton de Morveau, *Dictionnaire de chimie* (1786), vol. I, p. 29.

12. Ibid., vol. I, p. 626.

13. A. Young, *Travels During the Years 1787, 1788, and 1789* (London: W. Richardson, 1794), vol. I, p. 166.

14. Ibid., p. 167.

15. *A Scientific Correspondence During the Chemical Revolution: Louis Bernard Guyton de Morveau and Richard Kirwan, 1782–1802*, p. 153.

16. Ibid.

17. Van Marum, *Life and Work* (Haarlem: H. D. Tjeenk Willink and Zoon; Leyden: Noordhoff International Publishing, 1969–1976), vol. 6, pp. 193–286. Quoted in Snelders, "The New Chemistry in the Netherlands," 128.

18. R. Kirwan, *An Essay on Phlogiston*, p. 22.

19. A. Young, *Travels During the Years 1787, 1788, and 1789*, vol. I, p. 163.

20. Ibid., p.165. Madame Picardet's ability to discuss agreeable subjects would lead her to marry Guyton de Morveau in 1798.

21. Ibid.

22. Ibid., pp. 165–66.

23. W. Nicholson, in R. Kirwan, *An Essay on Phlogiston*, p. xi.

24. Guyton de Morveau, "Sur les dénominations chymiques, la nécessité d'en perfectionner le système, et les règles pour y parvenir," *Observations sur la Physique* 19 (1782): 370–82.

25. Guyton de Morveau, "Sur l'utilité d'un cours public de chimie dans la ville de Dijon," memoir read at the Dijon Academy of Science on November 17, 1774, p. 11.

26. Guyton de Morveau, "Sur les dénominations chymiques, la nécessité d'en perfectionner le système et les règles pour y parvenir," *Observations sur la Physique* 19 (1782): 373.

27. Ibid., p. 374.

28. Ibid.

29. *Méthode de nomenclature chimique* (Paris: Cuchet, 1787), p. 26.

30. Ibid., pp. 6–8.

31. Condillac, "Discours préliminaire," *Oeuvres choisies* (Paris: 1796), p. 26.

32. D. Duveen and R. Hahn, "A Note on Some Lavoisieriana in the *Journal de Paris*," *Isis* 51 (1960): 64.

33. Ibid.

34. Ibid., p. 65.

35. Quoted in M. Daumas, *Lavoisier, théoricien et expérimentateur*, pp. 60–61.

36. G. Cuvier, *Recueil des éloges historiques lus dans les séances publiques de l'Institut royal de France* (Strasbourg and Paris: Levrault, 1819), vol. II, pp. 17–18.

37. *Oeuvres*, vol. VI, pp. 97–98.

38. Ibid., p. 618.

39. *Méthode de nomenclature chimique*, pp. 13–14.

40. Oxygen "which engenders acids"; hydrogen "which engenders water"; azote "unsuited to life."

41. The word barite comes from the Greek word meaning "heavy."

42. The word potassium comies from the German *pot asche*, ashes from a pot.

43. *Dictionnaire de chimie*, *"Nomenclature"* (Paris: Agasse, 1808), vol. V, p. 256.

44. *Méthode de nomenclature chimique*, p. 17.

45. M. Beretta, *The Enlightenment of Matter: The Definition of Chemistry from Agricola to Lavoisier* (Canton, Mass.: SHP, Watson, 1993), p. 203.

46. "La chimica di Lavoisier [. . .] e divenuta una scienza fisico-quantitativa del mutamento chimico," F. Abbri, *Le terre, l'acqua e le arie: la rivoluzione chimica del Settecento* (Bologna: Il Mulino, 1984), p. 385

47. *Oeuvres*, vol. V, p. 377.

48. D. Duveen and H. Klickstein, *A Bibliography of the Works of A. L. Lavoisier* (London: Dawson and Weil, 1954), pp. 124–25.

49. Quoted in R. Halleux, "La révolution lavoisienne en Belgique," in *Lavoisier et la révolution chimique*, p. 295.

50. J. C. de La Métherie, "Essai sur la nomenclature chimique," *Observations sur la Physique* 31 (1787): 277.

51. *A Scientific Correspondence During the Chemical Revolution: Louis Bernard Guyton de Morveau and Richard Kirwan, 1782-1802*, p. 34.

52. B. Bensaude-Vincent, "A propos de la Méthode de Nomenclature chimique, Esquisse historique, suivie du texte de 1787," *Cahiers d'Histoire et de Philosophie des Sciences* 6 (1983): 1 F.

53. Letter dated September 1, 1787, quoted in E. Grimaux, *Lavoisier, 1743–1794*, p. 372.

54. *Les Annales de Chimie ou Recueil de mémoires concernant la chimie et les arts qui en dépendent* were published by Cuchet located on the rue Serpente. Each volume, made up of 20 sheets of 16 pages or a total of three 320 pages, cost 960 livres ($38,000), of which 160 went to Adet, who was responsible for correcting the proofs. The authors received 32 livres ($1280) per sheet.

55. M. Crosland, *In the Shadow of Lavoisier: The* Annales de Chimie *and the Establishment of a New Science* (Oxford: British Society for the History of Science, 1994), pp. 76–77.

56. *Oeuvres*, vol. II, p. 104.

57. Lavoisier, *Elements of Chemistry in a new systematic order, containing all the modern discoveries*, translated by Robert Kerr (Edinburgh, 1790; reprint New York: Dover, 1965), pp. xviii–xix.

58. Ibid., p. xxxiii.

59. Ibid., Introduction by D. McKie, p. xxix.

60. Ibid.

61. Ibid., Preface of the Author, p. xviii.

62. Ibid., p. xxi.

63. Ibid., p. 177.

64. Ibid., p. 172.

65. The second printing of the first edition would indeed consist of two volumes but Cuchet, anxious to use up his stock, simply printed the title pages for each volume, while the pagination remained continuous (vol. I, pp. 1–322; vol. II, pp. 323–653). The second edition had three versions: the first was printed in three volumes by Cuchet in 1789; the second in two volumes was a pirate edition printed by Boiste and contained slight variations; the plates, redrawn, were no longer signed by Madame Lavoisier. The third version, consisting of two volumes, was brought out by Boiste in 1793. The format was smaller, the paper lighter and of inferior quality. The editing, on the other hand, was more meticulous and the original plates were reproduced. The third edition was published by Deterville in 1801.

66. Letter from Lavoisier to B. Franklin, February 2, 1790, Archives de l'Académie des Sciences, Lavoisier Collection, dation Chabrol, ms., carton 1, files 42 and 22 B.

67. Marat, *Les charlatans modernes*, letter XI, p. 36.

68. Lavoisier, quoted in L. Scheler, *Lavoisier et la Révolution française: le Lycée des Arts* (Paris: Hermann, 1956), p. 55.

69. Ibid., p. 32.

70. I. Bernard Cohen, *Revolution in Science* (Cambridge Mass: Belknap Press of Harvard University Press, 1985), p. 229.

71. N. Wise, "Mediations: Enlightenment Balancing Acts, or the Technologies of Rationalism," in Paul Horwich, ed., *World Changes: Thomas Kuhn and the Nature of Science* (Cambridge Mass.: Bradford Books, MIT Press, 1992), p. 249.

Chapter 12: The Reform of Agriculture

1. H. Thirion, *La vie privée des financiers au XVIIIe siècle* (Paris: Plon, 1896), p. 431.

2. Forty Farmers General, twenty-five Directors General of the Aides et Droits réunis, and twenty-five Administrators General of the Domaines.

3. C. C. Gillispie, *Science and Polity in France at the End of the Old Regime* (Princeton, N.J.: Princeton University Press, 1980), p. 377.

4. *Correspondance*, fasc. IV, p. 130.

5. On August 4 and December 27, 1785 and August 14, 1787 he was at Freschines. On September 11, 1787 he was attending the Provincial Assembly of Orléans.

6. *Oeuvres*, vol. VI, p. 229.

7. Archives de l'Académie des Sciences, Lavoisier Collection, ms. 1610.

8. He was undoubtedly the anonymous author of other brochures. On this point see M. Lenglen "Lavoisier agronome," reprint from *Bulletin des Engrais* (November 30, 1936): 58.

9. Ibid., p. 30.

10. The Royal Almanac of 1787 listed its members, presided over by Gravier de Vergennes: Tillet, Poissonnier, Lavoisier, Darcet, Du Pont, the duc de La Rochefoucauld-Liancourt, Lefebvre, Courtois de Minut, Cheyssac, Le Hoc, Lazowski, and Lubert.

11. Quoted in G. Schelle and E. Grimaux, *Lavoisier, statistique agricole et projets de réformes* (Paris: Guillaumin, 1894), pp. 6–7.

12. The direct taxes were the *taille*, the *corvée*, the *capitation*, and the *vingtième*.

13. *Oeuvres*, vol. VI, p. 218.

14. Ibid.

15. Indirect taxes included *gabelles* (salt taxes), *aides*, and *traites*.

16. "The Jewish community in Metz gave him an honorable testimony of gratitude for having removed from them the obligation to pay a toll that was both persecutory and ignonimous." Madame Lavoisier, quoted in G. Michaud, *Biographie universelle*, vol. 23, p. 465.

17. *Oeuvres*, vol. VI, p. 219.

18. Ibid.

19. Ibid., p. 221.

20. *Oeuvres*, vol. II, p. 822.

21. Archives Nationales, Etude Gondouin, XCIX 1754.

22. The senior Lavoisier had bought in 1772 the office of Conseiller-secrétaire du Roi, Maison, Finance et Couronne de France, which conferred a hereditary title of nobility.

23. *Procès-verbal des séances de l'Assemblée Provinciale de l'Orléanais, tenue à Orléans, le 6 septembre 1787* (Orléans: Imprimerie Couret de Villeneuve, 1787), p. 54.

24. "Résultat de quelques expériences d'agriculture et réflexions sur leur relation avec l'économie politique," *Annales de Chimie* 15 (1792) 312.

25. *Oeuvres*, vol. II, p. 819.

26. L. Passy, *Histoire de la Société Nationale d'Agriculture de France*, quoted in M. Lenglen, "Lavoisier agronome," p. 31.

27. *Oeuvres*, vol. VI, p. 204.

28. L. de Lavergne, "Les assemblées provinciales en France," *Revue des Deux Mondes* (1861): 694.

29. Madame Lavoisier, *Voyage d'Orléans pendant l'Assemblée provinciale depuis le 17 Novembre 1787 jusqu'au 22 Décembre de la même année*, ms., Madame Lavoisier's handwriting, private collection.

30. Ibid.

31. *Oeuvres*, vol. VI, p. 241.

32. Ibid., p. 246.

33. Lavoisier wrote to the Abbé de Prades: "We were overtaken by speed regarding the plan we had made to establish a bank of savings and charity for the people, and while we were deliberating on how to set it up on solid bases and according to the wisest principles, a financial company obtained the exclusive privilege for fifteen years. Since then, the company has published a very broad prospectus to which it has joined tables. The objective of the privilege accorded was an establishment so similar to the one we had proposed and which had been described in a work printed by M de La Roque that he has publicly claimed in a printed memoir that has just appeared. He explains that if he did not solicit this privilege, it was not because it was not as easy for him as for anybody else to form a company, but because he had not believed that an object of charity ought to become an object of financial speculation, and that it seemed preferable to him to give the profits to hospitals. [. . .] It seems to me that in these circumstance, we can only be mere spectators of the fight. [. . .] If, moreover, the bank is set up, if the capital and the provinces can benefit from it, in a word, if it is formed on equitable bases, then it little matters who does it." Quoted in Grimaux, *Lavoisier, 1743–1794*, p. 180.

34. *Oeuvres*, vol. VI, pp. 250–51.

35. Ibid., p. 284.

36. Ibid., p. 255.

37. Ibid., p. 256.

38. Ibid., pp. 256–57.

39. Ibid., p. 260.

40. Ibid., p. 279.

41. Ibid., p. 280.

42. Madame Lavoisier, *Voyage d'Orléans pendant l'Assemblée provinciale*.

43. *Oeuvres*, vol. VI, p. 262.

44. Bibliothèque d'Orléans, Lavoisier Collection, 3, quoted in J. D. Bredin, *Sieyès, la clé de la Révolution française* (Paris: Edidions de Fallois, 1988), p. 70.

45. He had written: "like all the most enlightened people in France," but he crossed out the phrase, judging it imprudent or excessive, Archives de l'Académie des Sciences, Lavoisier Collection, dation Chabrol, carton 1, file 6.

46. A. Young, *Travels During the Years 1787, 1788, 1789*, vol. 1, p. 120.

47. H. Pigeonneau and A. de Foville, *L'administration de l'agriculture au Contrôle Général des Finances* (Paris: Guillaumin, 1882), p. 310.

48. Sodium carbonate, to be distinguished from sodium hydroxide or caustic soda; the use of the same term, soda, for the two substances is an abuse of the language.

49. E. Grison, "Hassenfratz, Carny et Lavoisier dans la compétition pour la fabrication de la soude artificielle en 1790," *History and Technology* 10 (1993): 179–97.

50. His patent, dated September 25, 1791, described first the formation of sodium sulfate from sea salt and sulfuric acid, then the production of sodium carbonate by heating sodium sulfate with charcoal and chalk (calcium carbonate).

51. B. Bensaude-Vincent, *Lavoisier: Mémoire d'une révolution* (Paris: Flammarion, 1993), p. 340.

52. B. Bensaude-Vincent and I. Stengers, *Histoire de la chimie* (Paris: Editions La Découverte, 1993), p. 121.

Chapter 13: A New Power

1. N. Deschamps, *Les sociétés secrètes et la Société* (Paris: Oudin, 1880), vol. 2, pp. 138–39. La Loge de la Candeur, to which belonged Choderlos de Laclos, Merlin de Douai, Talleyrand-Périgord, Custine, Noailles, Brissot, Montmorency-Laval, Latouche-Tréville, La Fayette, the Lameth brothers, Sillery, the Marquis de Lusignan, and the Prince de Broglie, had the objective of establishing a constitutional monarchy and replacing Louis XVI by his cousin, the duc d'Orléans. La Loge des Neuf Soeurs was more radical. It brought together the deputies from the Grand Orient, the Abbé Sieyès, Bailly, Pétion, Guillotin, Condorcet, Camille Desmoulins, Lacépède, Fourcroy, Millin, Chénier, Franklin, Mercier, and Lalande, who dreamed of republican equality and democracy. Les Amis Réunis held even more extreme positions and advocated the abolition of privileges and the equality of all citizens. In it could be found the Abbé Sieyès, d'Espagnac, Condorcet, Barnave, Le Chapelier, Duport de Prélaville, the Lameth brothers, the vicomte de Beauharnais, the duc de La Rochefoucauld-Liancourt, Du Pont (de Nemours), Bureaux de Pusy, husband of his step-daughter, Robespierre, Cabanis, Volney, the Abbé Grégoire, Chamfort, Delley d'Agier, the baron d'Allarde, Beaumarchais, Roederer, and Le Coulteux de La Noraye. Chénier, Fourcroy, La Mettrie, Laclos, Marat, Mercier, Saint-Just, and Babeuf would join them later.

2. His name did not appear on the lists established on the basis of the Masonic Collection in the Bibliothèque nationale, according to A. Le Bihan, *Francs-Maçons Parisiens du Grand Orient de France, fin du XVIIIe siècle* (Paris: Presses Universitaires de France, 1966) and *Francs-Maçons et ateliers parisiens de la Grande Loge de France au XVIIIe siècle* (Paris: Presses Universitaires de France, 1973). However, his heir Madame de Chazelles possessed in 1950 "two aprons and other Masonic symbols having belonged to her illustrious ancestor. [. . .] Lavoisier expressed his obedience by placing in certain of his signatures three dots within the lower circle of the first letter of his name." L. Lomuller, "Lavoisier financier," *Chimie et Industrie* 63, 4 (April 1950): 420–24. Dujarric de la Rivière confirms this fact: "Lavoisier was a Freemason, and we had the opportunity of seeing his Masonic symbols at the Museum in Saint-Cosme-de-Vair, in the home of Madame de Chazelles." *E.I. Du Pont de Nemours, élève de Lavoisier* (Paris: Librairie des Champs-Elysées, 1954), p. 25. Maître E. Ader, auctioneer, sold as "having belonged to the famous physicist Lavoisier two aprons in painted silk with symbols and a Freemasonry cord. End of the XVIIIe century." Catalogue from the sale *Souvenirs de Lavoisier*, 114, Hôtel Drouot, March 7, 1956. Nevertheless, a doubt remains concerning the origin of these symbols found after Madame Lavoisier's death: they could have belonged to M. de Rumford.

3. Among the members were also the ducs de Luynes, de La Rochefoucauld-Liancourt, d'Aumont, de Richelieu, de Montmorency-Luxembourg, and d'Aiguillon, the Marshal de Beauvau, the comte de Castellane, Duval d'Eprémesnil, the prince de Ligne, Clavière, Savalette de Langes, Le Peletier de Saint-Fargeau, the lawyer Target, Le Chapelier, Roederer, Talleyrand, the Abbé Sieyès, Sillery, and Biron. The society, made up mostly of Freemasons, also had sympathizers: the two Trudaines, Duport-Dutertre, the Abbé Louis, Huguet de Semonville, Saint-Just, Lacretelle, and the friends of the banker Kornmann: Bergasse, Brissot, Carra, and Gorsas.

4. *Oeuvres*, vol. VI, p. 334.

5. Also belonging were La Fayette, the Abbé Sieyès, Carra, Le Peletier de Saint-

Fargeau, the Lameth brothers, the duc de La Rochefoucauld, Lacépède, the Abbé Grégoire, and the elder Mirabeau.

6. Baron d'Allarde, deputy from Saint-Pierre le Moutier, *Motion sur un nouveau régime des finances* (Versailles: Baudouin, 1789), pp. 28–29.

7. Quoted in J. Vidalenc, "Le traite des nègres en France au début de la Révolution française, 1789–1793," *Annales de l'Histoire de la Révolution Française*, p. 56. On March 8, 1790 the Assembly granted the rights of citizens to the Blacks, but said nothing about the slave trade and gave the colonists the guarantees they had asked for. In Martinique the slaves rebelled. That insurrection and the loss of Santo Domingo in 1791 would deal a fatal blow to French trade. Imports would subsequently come only from the Antilles and Mauritius.

8. *Oeuvres*, vol. VI, p. 330.

9. Ibid., p. 321.

10. Ibid., p. 321.

11. Ibid., p. 322.

12. Quoted in E. Grimaux, *Lavoisier, 1743–1794*, p. 192.

13. The *Almanach Royal* of 1788 listed his fellow directors as Le Normand, Lambert, Tassin, Pache de Montguyon, Rilliet, Siau, Taillepied de Bondi, Julien, Le Couteulx de la Noraye, Duruey, Grand, and Cottin.

14. J. Necker, *Compte rendu au Roi au mois de janvier 1787* (Paris: Imprimerie Royale, 1781), p. 24.

15. A. Young, *Travels During the Years 1787, 1788 and 1789*, vol. I, p. 80.

16. *Correspondance*, vol. 5, p. 208. Letter from Lavoisier to J. H. Hassenfratz, August 31, 1788.

17. P. S. Du Pont de Nemours, *Discours devant l'Assemblée Nationale sur les Banques en général* (Paris: Baudouin, November 1789), p. 30.

18. J. Necker, *Sur l'administration de M. Necker, par lui-même* (Paris: Hôtel de Thou, 1791), pp. 28–29.

19. *Délibérations des Administrateurs de la Caisse d'Escompte des 4 septembre, 16 octobre 1788 et 29 mai 1789* (Paris: Imprimerie de Clousier, 1789), p. 7.

20. Lavoisier, *Rapport sur la Caisse d'Escompte fait à l'Assemblée Nationale, le 4 décembre, par ses Commissaires, et imprimé par son ordre* (undated [1789]), p. 19.

21. *Journal de Paris*, October 31, 1788, quoted in Fourcroy, *Dictionnaire de chimie*, vol. 3, note p. 607.

22. Ibid.

23. B. Franklin, quoted in D. McKie, *Antoine Lavoisier: Scientist, Economist, Social Reformer* (London: Constable, 1952), p. 70.

24. Lavoisier, *Adresse de remerciements aux habitants de la paroisse de Villefrancoeur* (Bailliage de Blois, s.l., 4 mars 1789), p. 2.

25. "Déliberation des habitants de la paroisse de Villefrancoeur du 3 avril 1789," Archives nationales, C 16, plaquette 32, document 22.

26. P. Jolly, *Du Pont de Nemours, soldat de la liberte* (Paris: Presses Universitaires de France, 1956), p. 72.

27. Letter from M. de Chevilly, *intendant de la généralité d'Orléans*, to Mr. Necker, March 23, 1789, Archives Nationales, B A /22, file 2.

28. "In Blois, M. de Lavoisier was excluded because he was a Farmer General." *Correspondance secrète sur Louis XVI, Marie-Antoinette, la Cour et la ville*, (Paris: Plon, 1866), vol. II, p. 340.

29. *Oeuvres*, vol. VI, p. 335.

30. Ibid., pp. 336–37.

31. Ibid., p. 338.

32. Ibid., p. 342.

33. Ibid., p. 351.

34. Ibid., p. 344.

35. Ibid., pp. 346–47.

36. Ibid., p. 362.

37. Husband of Joséphine Tascher de La Pagerie and a general in Custine's army, he would be condemned by the Revolutionary Tribunal and guillotined on June 23, 1794. His widow would marry Napoleon Bonaparte.

38. C. Kunstler, *Les rois de France: la politique de nos rois* (Paris: Fayard, 1942), p. 327.

39. N. Ruault, *Gazette d'un Parisien sous la Révolution: lettres à son frère, 1783–1796* (Paris: Librairie Académique Perrin, 1976), letter of February 24, 1789, p.126.

40. Along with Faronville, Pinon, Vouges de Chanteclair, Drouyn de Vaudeuil, Musnier de Plaigne, Charnois, and Bizeau.

41. Delavigne, "Observations pour MM. les Commissaires à la rédaction du Cahier de Paris, May 2, 1789, "Archives nationales, B A /64, A 1.

42. C.L. Chassin, *Les élections et les Cahiers de Paris en 1789* (Paris: Jouhaust et Signaux, Noblet, Maison Quantin, 1888), vol. IV, p. 354.

43. The electoral rule stating that elections for the Third Estate would take place in two degrees had stirred up great discontent in the capital where, also, in order to vote, one had to satisfy one of the following conditions: the possession of an office or rank or the payment of a direct tax (capitation) of 6 livres ($200), a relatively high sum at the time. There were only 50,000 voters for about 600,000 inhabitants. The Parisians resented this discrimination.

44. P. Lamarque, *Les Francs-Maçons aux Etats généraux de 1789 et à l'Assemblée nationale* (Paris: Edimaf, 1981). According to F. G. Hourtoulle, "of a total of 1,336 deputies having actually participated at the Assemblée Nationale Constituante, there were 319 who were definitely Freemasons, and 13 others who might have been." *Franc-Maçonnerie et Révolution* (Paris: Carrère, 1989), p. 98.

45. *Correspondance secrète*, vol. II, p. 352.

46. *Déliberations des administrateurs de la Caisse d'Escompte des 4 septembre, 16 octobre 1788 et 28 mai 1789* (Paris: Imprimerie de Clousier, 1789), p. 16.

47. Ibid.

48. Ibid., p. 20.

49. Archives du Ministère des Affaires Etrangères, Collection "France," T. 1405, May 8, 1789; *Journal de Hardy*, Bibliothèque Nationale, ms. 2573, quoted in R. Bigo, *Caisse d'Escompte, 1773–1795* (Paris: Presses Universitaires de France, 1927), note 134.

50. Archives du Ministère des Affaires Etrangères, Collection "France," T. 1405, May-June 1789, p. 239.

51. F. Mitterand, "Discours prononcé à Versailles pour le deux centième anniversaire du serment du Jeu de Paume," *Le Monde*, June 20, 1989.

52. J. F. Bosher, *The French Revolution* (New York: W. W. Norton, 1988), p. 131.

53. Archives Nationales, B B/30, n° 161.

54. Grouchy and Guillois, *La Révolution française racontée par un diplomate étranger* (Paris: Flammarion, no date), p. 112.

55. L. Scheler, *Lavoisier et la Révolution française, Part II, "Le journal de Fougeroux de Bondaroy"* (Paris: Hermann, 1956–60), p. 26.

56. Or 12 bushels of 13 liters, or 156 liters.

57. R. Bigo, *La Caisse d'Escompte et les origines de la Banque de France* (Paris: Presses Universitaires de France, 1927), p. 142.

58. P. V. Bésenval, *Mémoires* (Paris: Baudouin, 1921), vol. II, p. 363.

59. C.E. de Ferrières, *Mémoires* (Paris: 1799), vol. I, pp. 71–72.

60. Fougeroux de Bondaroy was the author of numerous memoirs dealing with such subjects as charcoal, petroleum, sulfur, vitrifiable substances, the dissolving of phosphorus in urine, the decomposition of sea salt, the formation of ice. In the collection entitled *Descriptions des Arts et Métiers*, published by the Académie Royale des Sciences, he wrote four monographs on the cutlery industry, cooperage, the production of gilded or silvered leathers, and the art of extracting slate from quarries. In 1766 he had published a small work, the fruit of a trip to Naples, where he had gone to visit the recently discovered ruins of Pompei and Herculanum.

61. During the night of July 7 to 8, the Farmers General had withdrawn the rifles and bayonets from the brigades responsible for guarding the tollgates, pretending that they needed overhauling. But the last thing the employees sent to collect them intended to do was to turn over their crop to the arquebusier of the Farm. L. Scheler, *Lavoisier et la Révolution française, Part II*, p. 110.

62. Gaulard de Saudray, who was wounded during the clash, was awarded a "certificate of good conduct" by the committee at the Hôtel de Ville. See *Annales parisiennes, politiques et critiques mais véritables* (Paris: Knapen fils, 1789), pp. 91–96.

63. *Oeuvres*, vol. V, p. 720.

64. Ibid., p. 721.

65. In which the colors of Paris, red and blue, surrounded the royal white.

66. E. Grimaux, *Lavoisier 1743–1794*, p. 200.

67. Could his heirs, through misguided zeal, have destroyed every trace of his participation?

68. *Suite du procès-verbal de l'Assemblée nationale du lundi 20 juillet 1789* (Paris: Baudouin, 1789).

69. Mirabeau, *Dix-neuvième lettre à ses commettants*, quoted in R. Bigo, *La Caisse d'Escompte et les origines de la Banque de France*, p. 146. The "Sainte Hermandad," a Spanish institution founded in the fifteenth century to combat banditry, was the equivalent of the French gendarmerie.

70. M. de Rozoi, *Discours prononcé à l'Assemblée Générale du District de Saint-Louis de la Culture*, Paris, July 24, 1789. Bibliothèque Nationale, Lb 40 348.

71. Ibid.

72. "Rapport fait le 6 août 1789 à l'assemblée des représentants de la Commune [. . .] par un de Messieurs les Régisseurs des Poudres," in *Actes de la Commune de Paris pendant la Révolution*, vol. I, pp. 106–16. The details that follow were taken from the same document.

73. On August 6 there remained only a thousand pounds of fine powder, 400 of poudre royale, 240 of regular gunpowder, and not an ounce of the explosive powder needed by quarries every day.

74. J. Dusaulx, *De l'insurrection parisienne et de la prise de la Bastille* (Paris: 1790), p. 246.

75. "Extrait du procès-verbal des représentants de la Commune de Paris du jeudi 6 août 1789," in *Actes de la Commune de Paris pendant la Révolution*, vol. I, pp. 106–16.

76. *Oeuvres*, vol. V, p. 718.

77. L. Scheler, *Lavoisier et la Révolution française, Part II*, p. 126.

78. Ibid., pp. 127–28.

79. *Actes de la Commune de Paris pendant la Révolution*, vol. 1, pp. 106–16.

80. L. Scheler, *Lavoisier et la Révolution française, Part II*, p. 132.

81. *Oeuvres*, vol. V., p. 721.

82. L. Scheler, *Lavoisier et la Révolution française, Part II*, p. 137.

83. On July 25 the Assemblée des représentants de districts, with a total membership of a 120, had replaced the Assemblée des électeurs de Paris. On August 5, 60 others had been named. And then on September 18 the Commune de Paris added 120 more, bringing the total number to 300. Lavoisier was among those elected in the last election.

84. *Actes de la Commune de Paris pendant la Révolution*, vol. 2, pp. 37–38.

85. 115,000 livres advanced by the Royal Treasury, 214,000 livres representing the value of the wheat given by the government, and about 300,000 livres from voluntary contributions. The notary profession, the canons of Notre-Dame, and the directors of the Discount Bank each gave 12,000 livres; the Farmers General made two gifts of 20,000 and 6,000 respectively; the king's secretaries, 15,000; the Count de Provence, 5,400; the Archbishop of Paris, 20,000; less important donations came from the universities, theaters and individuals.

86. G. Morris, *A Diary of the French Revolution* (Boston: Houghton Mifflin, 1939), vol. I, p. 109.

87. Ibid., p. 230.

88. Ibid.

89. Ibid., p. 243.

90. Letter to Bailly on October 25, 1789, quoted in E. Grimaux, *Lavoisier, 1743–1794*, p. 94.

Chapter 14: An Economist in Action

1. *Rapport de M. Necker, Premier Ministre des Finances, lu à l'Assemblée Nationale le 27 août 1789* (Paris: Imprimerie Royale, 1789), pp. 9–10.

2. Necker, Handwritten letter, Versailles, September 13, 1788, private collection.

3. Quoted in R. Bigo, *La Caisse d'Escompte*, p. 139.

4. Lavoisier, *De l'organisation des banques publiques en général, et de la Caisse d'Escompte en particulier* (Paris: Clousier, 1789), p. 6.

5. Quoted in F. Aftalion, *L'économie de la Révolution française* (Paris: Hachette, 1987), p. 84.

6. R. D. Harris, *Necker and the Revolution of 1789* (Lanham-New York-London: University Press of America, 1986), p. 658.

7. Duc de Lévis, *Souvenirs et portraits (1780-1789)* (Paris: L. Beaupré, 1815), p. 213.

8. M. Bruguière, *Gestionnaires et profiteurs de la Révolution* (Paris: Orban, 1986), p. 61.

9. Mirabeau, November 20, 1789, in Méjan, *Collection complète des travaux de M. Mirabeau*, vol. II, pp. 487–88.

10. P. S. Du Pont de Nemours, *Discours sur l'état et les ressources des finances, prononcé à l'Assemblée nationale le 24 septembre 1789* (Versailles: Baudouin, 1789), pp. 9–10

11. "In fact, the obligatory borrowing was only of very little help to the Treasury since its yield, limited to 32 million livres, was not entirely collected until 1792." F. Aftalion, *L'économie de la Révolution française*, p. 85.

12. E. Loustallot, *Les Révolutions de Paris*, n° 23, December 1789, quoted in J. Egret, *Necker, ministre de Louis XVI* (Paris: H. Champion, 1975), p. 383.

13. *Discours prononcé à l'Assemblée générale des Actionnaires de la Caisse d'Escompte le 17 novembre 1789* (Paris: Clousier, 1789).

14. Two of the counterfeiters, Champclos and Grandmaison, were killed in the Abbaye Prison during the unrest of September 1792. Other affairs would have a more rapid conclusion: the culprits were sent to the galleys or hung on the Place de Grève.

15. Lavoisier, *De l'organisation des banques*, pp.15–16.

16. Lavoisier, *Adresse des actionnaires de la Caisse d'Escompte à Nosseigneurs de l'Assemblée nationale* (Paris: Baudouin, 1789), p. 4.

17. Ibid., p. 8.

18. Lavoisier, *Observations sur la position actuelle de la Caisse d'Escompte* (Paris: Clousier, 1789), p. 17.

19. E. L. Bailly, *Mémoires*, vol. II, p. 284.

20. P. S. Du Pont, *Discours prononcé à l'Assemblée nationale sur les banques en général, sur la Caisse d'Escompte en particulier, et sur le projet du Premier ministre des Finances, relativement à cette dernière* (Paris: Baudouin, 1789), p. 31.

21. Lavoisier, *Réponse à quelques objections relatives à la Caisse d'Escompte* (Paris: Clousier, undated), pp. 27–29.

22. Ibid.

23. It included Le Couteulx de Canteleu, Le Couteulx du Molay, Pierre Hubert Anson, Du Pont de Nemours, Laborde de Méréville, d'Ailly, Jacques Antoine de Cazalès, the Abbé Maury, the marquis de Montesquiou, Talleyrand, and the baron d'Allarde. The duc du Châtelet, Mirabeau, and Roederer were substitutes.

24. Quoted in M. Marion, *Histoire financière de la France depuis 1715* (Paris: Rousseau et Cie, 1919), vol. II, pp. 64–65.

25. Ibid., p. 101.

26. Lavoisier, *Observations adressées à MM. les représentants de la Commune de Paris par l'administration de la Caisse d'Escompte* (Paris: Clousier, 1790), pp. 3–4.

27. Ibid., pp. 19–20.

28. Ibid., p. 20.

29. Letter from Lavoisier to B. Franklin, dated February 2, 1790, Archives de l'Académie des Sciences, Lavoisier Collection, dation Chabrol, carton l, files 42 and 22 B, quoted by Duveen and Klickstein, "Benjamin Franklin (1706–1790) and Antoine Laurent Lavoisier (1743–1794), Part III," *Annals of Science* 13 (1957): 37–38.

30. L. Scheler points out that the Society of 1789 or Club of 1789 should not be confused with "Le Club," an association founded in 1782 and to which Lavoisier belonged until 1784. Le Club held its meetings in the Arcades of the Palais Royal, passage de Beaujolais, n. 82. Its members came mainly from the nobility, and it still existed in 1789.

31. Condorcet, *Prospectus du Journal de la Société de 1789* (Paris: Lejay, 1790), p. 3.

32. K. M. Baker, *Condorcet: From Natural Philosophy to Social Mathematics* (Chicago: University of Chicago Press, 1975), pp. 272–85.

33. Quoted in L. Velluz, *Vie de Lavoisier* (Paris: Plon, 1966), p. 132.

34. G. de Staël, *Considerations sur les principaux événements de la Révolution française* (Paris: Delaunay, Bossange et Masson, 1818), p. 378.

35. Letter to Black, July 24, 1790, Archives de l'Académie des Sciences, Lavoisier Collection, 1225–18. The same letter was sent to Banks, Blagden, Hall, Henry, Priestley, and Watt, but only the one addressed to Black referred to his "instruction and advice."

36. "Copie d'une lettre de Mr Joseph Black à Mr Lavoisier," *Annales de Chimie* 8 (janvier 1791): 226–27.

37. R. Stourm, *Les finances de l'ancien régime et de la Révolution* (Paris: Guillaumin, 1885), vol. II, p. 280.

38. Ibid., p. 279.

39. J. Necker, *Mémoire adressé à l'Assemblée Nationale, le 27 août 1790, par le Premier Ministre des Finances* (Paris: Imprimerie Royale, 1790), p. 11.

40. R. Stourm, *Les finances de l'ancien régime et de la Révolution*, vol. II, p. 281.

41. *Oeuvres*, vol. VI, p. 364–65.

42. Ibid., p. 367.

43. Ibid., p. 372.

44. Ibid., p. 381. *Réflexions sur les assignats et sur la liquidation de la dette exigible ou arriérée* (Paris: Clousier, 1790), was printed as a 35-page brochure, for the Assembly. It was complemented by another 32-page brochure entitled *Addition aux observations de M. Lavoisier, député suppléant au bailliage de Blois, sur la liquidation de la dette exigible ou arriérée* (Paris: Clousier, undated).

45. L. S. Mercier, *Le Tableau de Paris*, vol. III, chap. LXXX, p. 37.

46. The Commune of Angoulême showed remarkable lucidity: "The issuing of 2 billion livres of assignats appears to us to be a fatal presage, a most reprehensible disappointment, both a physical and moral evil, and the greatest of calamities. Those wise and proud colonists—the Americans—who taught us to know and conquer our rights, and to use them, withstood the rigors of war and seasons and chased away the tyrants; but they could not back their paper money." *Délibération du conseil de la Commune d'Angoulême*, Bibliothèque Nationale, Lb. 39, 4157.

47. *Opinion de M. Du Pont, député de Nemours, sur le projet de créer pour dix-neuf cents millions d'assignats-monnaie, sans intérêt, exposée à l'Assemblée nationale le 25 septembre 1790* (Paris: Baudouin, 1790), pp. 19–20.

48. Ibid., p. 31.

49. *Oeuvres*, vol. II, p. 703.

50. The members of the Comité des Impositions, named on January 21, 1790, were: the duc de La Rochefoucauld, Du Pont, Talleyrand, Roederer, Luc Jacques Edouard Dauchy, Joseph François Auguste Monneron, Marie Joseph Jary, Duport de Prélaville, the baron d'Allarde, Laborde de Mereville, the comte Joseph Defermon des Chapellières.

51. Lavoisier, "Observations sur la constitution et le régime de la Ferme," Archives Nationales: 29 A P 85, quoted in Jacob Price, *France and the Chesapeake: A History of the French Tobacco Monopoly, 1674–1791, and of Its Relationship to the British and*

American Tobacco Trades (Ann Arbor: University of Michigan Press, 1973), vol. 2, pp. 809–10.

52. K. Margerison, "P.-L. Roederer: Political Thought and Practice During the French Revolution," *Transactions of the American Philosophical Society* 73 (1983): 47.

53. Ibid, p. 52.

54. *Archives parlementaires de 1787 à 1860*, ed. M. J. Mavidal and M. E. Laurent (Paris, Paul Dupont, 1879), 1ᵉ ser., vol. XXIII, p. 670.

55. *Oeuvres*, vol. VI, p. 404.

56. Ibid., p. 405.

57. The term "national revenue" came from Forbonnais, who used it in 1767 in his *Principes et observations économiques*.

58. *Oeuvres*, vol. VI, p. 406.

59. Ibid., p. 408.

60. Ibid.

61. 12.6 million men and 12.4 million women. But he had underestimated. The census carried out between July 1790 and May 1791 counted 27 million inhabitants. J. C. Perrot, *Lavoisier: de la richesse territoriale du royaume de France* (Paris: éditions du C.T.H.S., 1988), pp. 83–85.

62. *Oeuvres*, vol. VI, p. 409. Wheat production in France for 1994 was 60 billion tons, or ten times greater.

63. Ibid., pp. 413–14.

64. Ibid., pp. 416–17.

65. Ibid.

66. Quoted in Lenglen, "Lavoisier agronome," *Bulletin des Engrais* (Paris, Nov. 30, 1936), p. 89.

67. *Oeuvres*, vol. VI, p. 409.

68. Ibid., p. 405.

69. Ibid., pp. 357–58.

70. Ibid., p. 415.

71. Ibid.

72. G. Klotz, "Réforme fiscale, physiocratie et statistique: le cas Lavoisier," *Idées économiques sous la Révolution (1789–1794)* (Lyon: Presses Universitaires, 1989), p. 132.

73. *Oeuvres*, vol. VI, pp. 415–16.

74. Numerous evaluations of territorial production had already been done by Alexis Jean Pierre Paucton, the abbé Jean Joseph d'Expilly, Claude François Lazowski, and Jean François Tolosan who worked from information provided by intendants and parish priests.

75. O. Arkhipoff, "A propos d'un Bicentenaire: Lavoisier, De la Richesse Territoriale du Royaume de France," *Journal de la Société de Statistique de Paris* 1 (1990): 37.

76. It would be reprinted in 1796, 1810, 1819, 1847, 1886, 1893, and 1988. The most complete edition was the one printed in 1893 (*Oeuvres*, vol. VI) which was the first to include the previously unpublished figures on population, horses and livestock, area of the kingdom, consumption, taxable net income, and a "General Account of the Products of the Kingdom, Divided by Sections," giving values, balanced in production and use for oats, fodders, straw, wheat and rye, livestock, forests, vineyards, and silk.

77. Quoted in R. Dujarric de La Rivière, *E. I. Du Pont de Nemours, élève de Lavoisier* (Paris: Librairie des Champs Elysées, 1954), p. 79.

78. *Imprimerie de Dupont, député de Nemours à l'Assemblée Nationale*, notice, Paris, June 8, 1791. Du Pont, like most aristocrats during this period, renounced his particle and wrote again his name Dupont.

79. Quoted in R. Dujarric de La Rivière, *E. I. Du Pont de Nemours, élève de Lavoisier*, p. 79.

80. *Le Véritable Père Duchesne*, n° 33, pp. 5–6.

81. *Supplique à Nosseigneurs les Etats généraux adressée par les commis des Fermes du département de Paris*, in E. Grimaux, *Lavoisier, 1743-1794*, p. 256.

82. A. Delahante, *Une famille de finance au XVIIIe*, vol. II, p. 218.

83. Archives de l'Académie des Sciences, Lavoisier Collection, ms. 1674, underlined by author.

Chapter 15: French Finances

1. J. F. Bosher, *The French Revolution*, p. 244.

2. *Histoire parlementaire de la Révolution française*, ed. J. B. Buchez and P. C. Roux (Paris: Paulin, 1834), vol. IV, pp. 472–73.

3. P. L. Roederer, quoted in R. Stourm, *Les finances de l'Ancien régime et de la Révolution* (Paris: Guillaumin, 1885), vol. II, 285.

4. P. L. Roederer, Archives Nationales, ms. 29 A P 82.

5. Mr. Gaudin, duc de Gaëte, *Mémoires, souvenirs, opinions et écrits* (Paris: Baudouin, 1826), vol. I, p. 27.

6. At the site where the Bibliothèque Nationale now stands.

7. *L'Ami du peuple*, n. 353, Thursday January 27, 1791, p. 5. Jean François Vauvilliers, a Greek scholar, deputy substitute to the Estates General, was in charge of the Paris Food Commission. His name had appeared in the king's record of secret accounts, the "Red Book," as having received 5,000 livres.

8. Lavoisier, *Le Moniteur*, Saturday, April 9, 1791.

9. *Actes des Apôtres*, 1791, n. 256, pp. 10–12. Bibliothèque Nationale, 8°, Lc2, 273.

10. Ibid.. The journalist forgot in his commentary Lavoisier's position at the Committee on Agriculture.

11. J. P. Brissot de Warville, *Mémoires* (Paris: Ladvocat, 1830–32), vol. IV, pp. 20–21.

12. Letter from Lavoisier to Brissot de Warville, quoted in D. Duveen, "Antoine Laurent Lavoisier and the French Revolution," *Journal of Chemical Education* 31 (1954): 65.

13. J. P. Brissot de Warville, *Mémoires*, vol. II, p. 11.

14. Quoted in E. Grimaux, *Lavoisier, 1743-1794*, p. 210.

15. Archives de l'Académie des Sciences, Lavoisier Collection, ms. 1701.

16. Ibid., 1712.

17. Ibid., 1713.

18. *Archives parlementaires de 1787 à 1860*, 1e ser., vol. XXV, p. 76.

19. Archives de l'Académie des Sciences, Lavoisier Collection, new acquisitions, 1990.

20. See F. Braesch, *Finances et monnaies révolutionnaires* (Paris: La Maison du Livre Français, 1936).

21. *édit du Roi portant suppression de tous les offices de gardes du trésor royal,*(March 1788), 8 p., Bibliothèque Nationale, 27 d 12 (10).

22. *De la situation du trésor public au 1er juin 1791*, by the National Treasury Commissioners, ms. in fol. of 237 p., coming from Lavoisier's personal library and bearing his ex-libris, private collection.

23. Ibid., p. 3.

24. Ibid.,p. 125.

25. Ibid., p. 6.

26. Ibid., p. 127.

27. Ibid., pp. 131–32.

28. Ibid., p. 133.

29. Ibid., pp. 146–47, 164–65.

30. Ibid., p. 147.

31. Condorcet, *Sur l'administration des finances*, handwritten note for the Treasury Committee, Bibliothèque de l'Institut de France, ms. 865, fol. 72. Other fragments of this note can be found in folios 134–37.

32. *De la situation du trésor public au 1er juin 1791*, p. 176.

33. *De la situation du trésor public au 1er juin 1791*, p. 184.

34. J. Hall, quoted in V. A. Eyles, "The Evolution of a Chemist," *Annals of Science* 19 (1963): 179.

35. Condorcet, *Oeuvres* (Paris: Didot, 1847), vol. XII, pp. 98–101.

36. J. Hall, ms. 6332, folios 23–24, Department of Manuscripts, Courtesy of the National Library of Scotland, Edinburgh. Quoted in J. A. Chaldecott, "Scientific Activities in Paris in 1791," *Annals of Science* 24 (1968): 32.

37. J. Hall, ms. 6330, folios 162–64, Department of Manuscripts, Courtesy of the National Library of Scotland, Edinburgh. Quoted in J. A. Chaldecott, "Scientific Activities in Paris in 1791," p. 31.

38. J. F. Bosher, *French Finances, 1771–1795: From Business to Bureaucracy* (London-New York: Cambridge University Press, 1970), p. 208.

39. *Almanach royal de 1792*, p. 247.

40. A. F. Fourcroy, *Notice sur la vie et les travaux de Lavoisier*, p. 42.

41. M. Bruguière, *Gestionnaires et profiteurs de la Révolution* (Paris: Orban, 1986), p. 66.

42. *Oeuvres*, vol. VI, p. 464.

43. Ibid., p. 500.

44. Ibid., p. 503.

45. Ibid., p. 511.

46. Ibid.

47. Lavoisier Collection, Rare and Manuscript Collections, Cornell University Library.

48. L. S. Mercier, *Le tableau de Paris*, vol. 1, p. 45.

49. R. Bigo, *La Caisse d'Escompte et les origines de la Banque de Fance* (Paris: Presses Universitaires de France, 1927), p. 220.

50. L. Scheler, *Lavoisier et le principe chimique*, pp. 116–17.

51. P.P.F. Gislain, *Necessité pour les fonctionnaires publics qui jouissent de deux traite-*

ments de se restreindre à un seul, Paris, February 6, 1793, Archives de l'Académie des Sciences, Lavoisier Collection, 1201.

52. Letter from Condorcet, La Fontaine, Gaudin, de Vaines, National Treasury Commissioners, to Lavoisier, Archives de l'Académie des Sciences, Lavoisier Collection, 1201.

53. *Protestation de Gislain, payeur principal des dépenses diverses de la Trésorie nationale; suivie du rapport fait à la société populaire de la section de la Montagne de Paris* (Paris: Laurens, 19 ventôse an III).

54. Archives de l'Académie des Sciences, Lavoisier Collection, 1725.

55. *Le Moniteur*, August 6, 1792, p. 327.

56. Collot d'Herbois, quoted in Mortimer-Ternaux, *Histoire de la Terreur, 1792–1794* (Paris: Michel Lévy, 1862), vol. II, p. 186.

57. Ibid., pp. 401–2, partially reported in the supplement of the *Journal de Paris*, August 6, 1792.

58. Ibid., p. 405.

59. J. F. Bosher, *The French Revolution*, p. 178.

60. J. Bertrand, *L'Académie des Sciences et les Académiciens de 1666 à 1793* (Paris: 1869), quoted in G. Barthélemy, *Les savants sous la Révolution* (Paris: Cénomane, 1989), pp. 218–19.

61. *Oeuvres*, vol. V., p. 735.

62. Ibid., p. 739.

63. Mémoire sur les différentes méthodes proposées pour déterminer le titre ou la qualité du salpêtre brut," *Annales de Chimie*, Paris XV (December 1792): 224–67; XVI (January 1793): 1–39.

64. *Oeuvres*, vol. V, p. 735.

65. D. Duveen, "Antoine Laurent Lavoisier (1743–1794): A Note Regarding his Domicile During the French Revolution," *Isis* 42 (1951): 233. Contrary to what Duveen writes, the certificate is signed not Boullonque but Boullongne.

66. Ibid., p. 234.

67. Ibid., p. 233

68. Lavoisier, unpublished handwritten letter dated August 31, 1792, private collection.

69. Lavoisier Collection, Rare and Manuscript Collections, Cornell University Library.

70. "Some negotiations were brewing," wrote a French officer, eyewitness in the Prussian camp, "and subsequent events proved it by the outcome of the battle of Valmy, where I was, commanded by Kellermann. The cannon killed only a few men because no one came close enough to it; and a few days later, the Prussians withdrew." D. J. Malabiou de Boisredon, *Mémoires et journal de guerre*, ms. in folio of 151 p., in C. Guérin and D. Courvoisier, *Dix livres choisis* (Paris: Librairie Giraud-Badin, 1991).

71. G. Diot, "Lavoisier à Villefrancoeur, Champigny et Freschines," *Bulletin de la Section Culturelle du Syndicat d'Initiatives de la Vallée de la Cisse* 2 (1974): 59.

72. Ibid.

73. P. Lemay, "Généalogie. Blason. Ex-Libris. Cachets de Lavoisier," *Bulletin de la Société Française d'Histoire de la Médecine* 28 (1934): 195–96.

Chapter 16: The Chemistry of Life

1. *Oeuvres*, vol. II, p. 703."*Premier mémoire sur la respiration des animaux*," November 17, 1790.

2. *Oeuvres*, vol. II, p. 691.

3. Ibid., p. 692.

4. Ibid., p. 691.

5. Ibid., p. 695.

6. Ibid., p. 694.

7. P. Dejours, "Lavoisier physiologiste," in C. Demeulenaere-Douyère, ed., *Il y a 200 ans Lavoisier*, p. 14.

8. *Oeuvres*, vol. II, p. 702.

9. Ibid.

10. A. S. Seguin, "Second mémoire sur le calorique," *Annales de Chimie* V (1790): 267.

11. J. H. Hassenfratz, "Sur la combinaison de l'oxygène avec le carbone et l'hydrogène du sang, sur la dissolution de l'oxygène dans le sang, et sur la manière dont le calorique se dégage," *Annales de Chimie* IX (1791): 261–62.

12. Lavoisier and Seguin, "Second mémoire sur la respiration,"*Annales de Chimie* XCI (1814): 318.

13. *Procès-verbaux des séances de l'Académie des Sciences* (1791): 333, quoted in M. Daumas, *Lavoisier*, p. 64.

14. E. Grimaux, *Lavoisier, 1743–1794*, p. 357.

15. *Oeuvres*, vol. II, p. 706.

16. *Procès-verbaux* (1791): 336, quoted in M. Daumas, *Lavoisier*, p. 64.

17. *Oeuvres*, vol. II, p. 709.

18. Ibid., p. 712.

19. *Procès-verbaux* (1792), quoted in M. Daumas, *Lavoisier*, p. 65. Daumas specified that it was the memoir published by Seguin in *Annales de Chimie* XC (1814): 5.

20. *Oeuvres*, Vol. V, p.379.

21. Ibid., p. 388.

22. Ibid., p. 380.

23. The red cell is in a paradoxical situation: "Rich in oxygen, it is incapable of using it directly. It is deprived of the mitochrondrial system, thus the chain of respiratory cytochromes, and the enzymes of the Krebs cycle. Its principal source of energy is the anaerobic pathway of Embden-Meyerhof glycolysis." H. Wajcman, B. Lantz and R. Girot, *Les maladies du globule rouge* (Paris: Editions I.N.S.E.R.M./Médecine-Sciences, Flammarion, 1992), p. 45.

24. *Oeuvres*, vol. II, p. 700.

25. F. L. Holmes, *Lavoisier and the Chemistry of Life* (Madison-London: University of Wisconsin Press, 1985), p. 157.

26. Lavoisier, letter to Vincenzo Dandolo, dated 13 November, 1791. Archives de l'Académie des Sciences, Lavoisier Collection, dation Chabrol.

27. *Oeuvres*, vol. II, p. 697.

28. Ibid., pp. 699–700.

29. Ibid., pp. 698–99.

30. Ibid., p. 34.

31. Ibid.

32. *Oeuvres*, vol. VI, p. 35.

33. Ibid., pp. 35–36. The prize was never awarded, since in January 1794 the Academy was abolished for several months.

34. Cl. Bernard, *La science expérimentale* (Paris: Baillière, 1878), pp. 122–23.

35. A. Baumé, *Chymie expérimentale et raisonnée* (Paris: Didot, 1774), vol. I, p. xj.

36. Cl. Bernard, *Leçons sur les phénomènes de la vie communs aux animaux et aux végétaux* (Paris: Baillière, 1878), vol. I, p. 136.

37. "We still do not know 1° what is the quality of that immense amount of air that is released during distillation: it is probably a combination of fixed and inflammable air; 2° the nature of the oil: it appears that it can be reduced to air and water by combustion, but we know nothing more; 3° what charcoal is; we know, of course, that when it burns it converts the surrounding air into fixed air; but we do not know if it itself gives fixed air, what is released during combustion and the relationship of what remains with the original weight of charcoal." Lavoisier's Laboratory Note Book, quoted in M. Berthelot, *La révolution chimique: Lavoisier*, p. 260.

38. *Oeuvres*, vol. II, p. 588.

39. *Traité élémentaire de chimie*, vol. I, pp. 124–125.

40. *Oeuvres*, vol. II, pp. 664–66.

41. *Traité élémentaire de chimie*, vol. I, pp. 141 and 150.

42. Ibid., pp. 140–141.

43. *Oeuvres*, vol. VI, p. 33.

44. *Traité élémentaire de chimie*, vol. I, p. 162.

45. *Oeuvres*, tome VI, p. 33.

46. J. R. Partington, *A History of Chemistry*, vol. III, p. 468.

47. F. L. Holmes, *Lavoisier and the Chemistry of Life*, p. 409.

48. J. H. Hassenfratz, "Sur la nutrition des végétaux, troisième mémoire," *Annales de Chimie* 14 (1792): 63–64.

49. *Rapport de Lavoisier à l'Académie des Sciences à propos des mémoires sur la végétation présentés par Hassenfratz le 25 février 1792 et par Seguin le 7 mars 1792*. Quoted in M. Lenglen in "Lavoisier agronome," *Bulletin des Engrais* (November 30, 1936): 96. Things are more complicated. At first, luminous energy provokes a photolysis of water: $4 H_2O + energy = 4H^+ + 4 OH^-$. At the same time, the active light of the chlorophyll pigments synthesizes the molecules of A.T.P., accumulators of energy. Then comes a chemical reaction that can occur without light: $CO_2 + 4 H^+ = 1/6 C_6H_{12}O_6 + H_2O$ and $4 OH^- = 2 H_2O + O_2$. The ratio CO_2 / O_2 is equal to 1.

50. *Mémoires de Chimie*, ed. Madame Lavoisier (Paris: Du Pont, 1803), vol. 2, p. 87, and *Oeuvres*, vol. II, p. 104.

Chapter 17: In the Service of the Arts and Trades

1. General Morin, "Note sur le bureau de consultation des Arts et Métiers." *Annales du Conservatoire Impérial des Arts et Métiers* VIII (1867–1868): 5–16.

2. S. de Boufflers, quoted in Regnault, *De la législation et de la jurisprudence concernant les brevets d'invention* (Paris: 1825), pp. 16–17.

3. *Oeuvres*, vol. IV, pp. 619–20.

4. *Journal des Sciences, Arts et Métiers* 1(1792): 5, quoted in D. De Place, "Le Bureau de Consultation pour les Arts, Paris 1791–1796," *History and Technology* 5 (1988): 140–41.

5. It was the prefiguration of the present *Agence Nationale pour la Valorisation des Applications de la Recherche*. (ANVAR).

6. R. Taton, *Enseignement et diffusion des sciences en France au XVIIIe siècle* (Paris: Hermann, 1986), p. 504.

7. *Oeuvres*, vol. IV, pp. 629–38, 669–712; vol. VI, pp. 706–10.

8. *Oeuvres*, vol. VI, p. 709.

9. D. De Place, "Le Bureau de Consultation pour les Arts, Paris 1791–1796," *History and Technology* 5 (1988): 149–50.

10. *Oeuvres*, vol. I, p. 249.

11. J. B. Delambre, quoted in Bigourdan, *Le système métrique des poids et mesures*, p. 20.

12. Ch. C. Gillispie, "The Rationale of the Metric System," *Science and Enlightenment Conference* (University of California Los Angeles, February 23, 1996): 6.

13. Ibid., p. 10.

14. Ch. M. de Talleyrand-Périgord, *Proposition faite à l'Assemblée nationale sur les Poids et Mesures* (Paris, 1790).

15. Ch. C. Gillispie, personal communication, April 2, 1996.

16. S. A. Tarbé, *Manuel pratique des poids et mesures, des monnaies et du calcul décimal* (Paris, 1799).

17. J. B. J. Delambre, *Histoire de la Mesure de la Terre*, in G. Kersaint, *A.F. de Fourcroy, sa vie et son oeuvre* (Paris: éditions du Museum National d'Histoire Naturelle, 1966), ser. D, vol. II, p. 64.

18. Archives de l'Académie des Sciences, Lavoisier Collection, ms. 144.

19. J. C. de Borda, quoted in E. Grimaux, *Lavoisier, 1743–1794*, p. 228.

20. Ibid.

21. The marc was equal to 8 ounces or 244.75 grams. Lavoisier had bought from Bréguet in January, "28 marcs of platinum at 9 livres per ounce, which comes to a sum of 2,016 livres." Ibid., p. 679.

22. *Oeuvres*, vol. VI, p. 703.

23. Loysel, the president of the committee, and Frécine, would use Lavoisier's text, without giving him credit, in the *Précis historique sur l'uniformité des poids et mesures*.

24. Quoted in G. Kersaint, *A. F. de Fourcroy, sa vie et son oeuvre*, p. 47.

25. The sciences in favor were natural history, anatomy, physics, chemistry, medicine, mechanical arts, rural economics, trade, and mathematics. *Notice sur l'Institution de la Société Philomatique*, printed by the "citoyens Du Pont" publishers for the Academy of Sciences, rue Helvétius, n° 57," Archives de l'Académie des Sciences, Lavoisier Collection, no. 162–63.

26. C. U. Servières, "Projection de quelques idées générales qui pourraient entrer dans l'introduction au projet de décret concernant l'Instruction Publique," September 6, 1793, Archives de l'Académie des Sciences, Lavoisier Collection, dation Chabrol, 5, file 83.

27. The courses were divided into eight sections: economics and commerce; rural economics; mathematics and its applications; general physics (natural history,

zoology, botany, mineralogy, anatomy, physiology, medicine, and chemistry); experimental physics; fine arts; literature; technology (arts and applied science, manufacturing). Archives de l'Académie des Sciences, Lavoisier Collection, dation Chabrol, 5, file 84.

28. Berthollet, from the Commission on Currency and the Commission on Agriculture and Arts, Berthoud watch-maker, Boissy d'Anglas representing the people, Brongniart from the Society of Natural History, Coquebert from the Société Philomatique, Darcet professor of chemistry, Daubenton professor at the école des Ponts et Chaussées, Desault professor of surgery, Fourcroy representative of the people, professor of chemistry, Hassenfratz member of the Commune de Paris and the Advisory Board for Arts and Trades, Jussieu of the Société du Muséum du Jardin des Plantes, Lavoisier, Leblanc, Le Roy, chemists, Lamarck, Millin, Parmentier, naturalists, Ventenat, professor of botany.

29. A. Birembaut, "A propos d'une publication récente sur Lavoisier et le Lycée des Arts," *Revue d'histoire des sciences et de leurs applications* 11 (1958): 269.

30. Officially registered on August 12, 1792, the Lycée des Arts (whose administrative offices were at 35, impasse de la Corderie) had as its founders Pierre Gervais, decorative artist, and Charles Gaulard de Saudray, member of the Advisory Board for Applied Arts and Crafts. It was the latter (see chap. 14) who had saved Clouet from the Parisian crowd on July 14, 1789. L. Scheler, *Lavoisier et la Révolution française*, vol. I, pp. 13–14.

31. A. F. Fourcroy, "Discours sur l'état actuel des Sciences et des Arts dans la République française," delivered Sunday April 7, 1793, *Journal du Lycée des Arts* I (September 1795): 47–68.

32. Ibid., p. 67.

33. *Oeuvres*, vol. VI, p. 569.

34. L. Scheler, *Lavoisier et la Révolution française*, vol. I, p. 32.

35. Ibid., pp. 35–36.

36. Ibid., p. 36.

37. Milet-Mureau would publish in 1797 the *Voyage de La Pérouse autour du monde* in 4 in 4° volumes, with an atlas in folio.

38. L. Scheler, *Lavoisier et la Révolution française*, vol. I, p. 50.

39. J. P. Marat, *Les charlatans modernes ou lettres sur le charlatanisme académique*, letter X (Paris: Imprimerie de Marat, 1791), Bibliothèque National, Z.P. 1. 406.

40. J. B. Biot, *Essai sur l'histoire générale des sciences pendant la Révolution française* (Paris: 1803), quoted in J. P. Legrand and M. Le Goff, *L'activité des savants pendant la Révolution française* (Paris: 1989), pp. 194–95.

41. E. J. Holmyard, "An Unpublished Letter of Lavoisier," *Nature* 130 (July 16, 1932): 97.

42. Ibid.

43. The Committee on Public Education was made up of Romme, David, Daunou, M.-J. Chénier, Arbogast, Sieyès, Condorcet, Bourdon, Grégoire, Guyton de Morveau, and Fourcroy.

44. Lavoisier, autographed letter signed June 12, 1793, cosigned by d'Arcet, president, Laplace, vice-president, and Bovy, acting as secretary. *Catalogue de Livres et Autographes* (Paris: Librairie Les Neuf Muses, 1991), n. 124.

45. Archives de l'Académie des Sciences, Lavoisier Collection, file 1008.

46. *Exposé sommaire des travaux de Joseph Lakanal* (Paris: Firmin Didot, 1838), pp. 206–7.

47. L. Scheler, *Lavoisier et la Révolution française*, vol. I, p. 64.

48. Archives Nationales, F/ 17/ 1135, n. 30.

49. Ibid., n. 32.

50. Quoted in J. Bertrand, *L'Académie des Sciences et les académiciens*, p. 432.

51. Abbé Grégoire, *Mémoires ecclésiastiques, politiques et littéraires* (Paris: Editions de Santé, 1989), p. 62.

52. Abbé Grégoire, "Discours à la Convention, 8 août 1793," in *Archives Parlementaires de 1787 à 1860* (Paris: CNRS, 1965), ser. 1.

53. Quoted in M.C. Sahut and R. Michel, *David, l'art et le politique* (Paris: Gallimard, La Découverte, 1989), pp. 158–59.

54. Abbé Grégoire, *Mémoires ecclésiastiques, politiques et littéraires*, pp. 62–63.

55. *Journal du Lycée des Arts* 12 (August 25, 1793): 2–4.

56. *Exposé sommaire des travaux de Joseph Lakanal* , p. 224.

57. Archives Nationales, F 17, 1336 dr 5, p. 148.

58. Meusnier and Tillet were dead. Condorcet, who had been sought by the police since July 8, 1793, was hiding in a friend's house on the rue Servandoni.

59. Quoted in G. Kersaint, *A. F. de Fourcroy, sa vie et son oeuvre*, p. 48.

60. Ibid.

61. Daunou, *Moniteur* dated 2 brumaire, An IV, Archives Nationales.

62. O. Gréard, *La législation de l'instruction primaire en France depuis 1789 jusqu'à nos jours* (Paris: 1889), vol. I, p. 3.

63. J. Guillaume, "Lavoisier anticlérical et révolutionnaire," *Révolution française*, 1907, p. 409.

64. The handwritten copy has been preserved, but is incomplete. Of a total of 16 pages, only pages 1 and 2, and 9 through 16 remain.

65. J. Guillaume, *Procés verbaux du Comité d'Instruction publique de la Convention nationale* (Paris: 1894), vol. II, Introduction, lviii–lix. This text is little known because Grimaux had kept it in his possession so as not to offend Lavoisier's heirs, who were embarrassed by the anticlerical opinions of their ancestor. J. Guillaume obtained the permission to publish it in 1894.

66. Ibid., lix.

67. Ibid., p. 413.

68. Ibid., p. 414.

69. Ibid.

70. Ibid., p. 415.

71. Condorcet, *Oeuvres*, vol. VII, p. 451.

72. Ibid., p. 483.

73. Ibid., p. 451.

74. Quoted in E. Allain, *L'oeuvre scolaire de la Révolution, 1789–1802* (Paris: 1891), p. 33.

75. J. Guillaume, *Procés verbaux du Comité d'Instruction publique de la Convention* , pp. 525–80.

76. "Petition presentée à la Convention nationale sur l'Instruction publique par le Directoire du Lycée des Arts," *Journal du Lycée des Arts* ll (July 15, 1793): 1–4.

77. *Oeuvres*, vol. IV, p. 649.

78. *Réflexions sur l'Instruction publique, présentées à la Convention nationale par le bureau de consultation des Arts et Métiers*, printed by Du Pont "père et fils, imprimeurs de l'Académie des Sciences," pp. 12 and 20.

79. M. Le Peletier de Saint-Fargeau, *Plan d'éducation nationale*, read at the Convention on July 13, 1793 (Paris: Baudouin, undated)

80. *Réflexions sur l'Instruction publique*. Only the *projet de décret* is included in Lavoisier's *Oeuvres*, vol. IV, pp. 649–68. Both the *Réflexions* and the *projet de Décret* can be found in *Oeuvres*, vol. VI, pp. 516–58. The Lavoisier Collection in the Archives de l'Academie des Sciences now contains five important manuscripts, very much revised and corrected, entitled *Projet de Décret sur l'Education publique proposé à la Convention nationale par le bureau de consultation des Arts et Métiers*, dation Chabrol, 5, files 77–81.

81. *Réflexions sur l'Instruction publique*, pp. 1–2.

82. *Oeuvres*, vol. VI, p. 539.

83. Ibid., p. 526.

84. Ibid., pp. 530–31.

85. A. Fourcroy, *Rapport et projet de décret du 7 vendémiaire, An II* (printed by the Comité de Salut Public, October 7, 1793), pp. 1–3.

Chapter 18: The Arrest

1. *Archives parlementaires de 1787 à 1860*, ed. M. J. Mavidal and M. E. Laurent, 1st ser., vol. 23, p. 670. Quoted in K. Margerison, *P.-L. Roederer: Political Thought and Practice During the French Revolution*, Transactions of the American Philosophical Society 73, part 1 (Philadelphia: American Philosophical Society, 1983), p. 52.

2. A. Delahante, *Une famille de finance au XVIII* siècle*, vol. II, pp. 218–19.

3. *Mémoire lu par le citoyen Clavière, Ministre des Contributions publiques, à la Convention nationale, le 5 octobre 1792* (Paris: 1792), p. 8.

4. *Hommage à la nation du tiers d'une somme de plusieurs millions offert par les commis des Fermes du Roi aux entrées de la capitale à prélever sur les fonds de leurs caisses de pension, 1789*. Archives Nationales, AD IX 532, no. 9.

5. *Mémoire pour les commis des Fermes du Roi, 6 janvier 1790*. Archives Nationales, AD IX 532.

6. *Avis intéressant aux citoyens patriotes ou contrepoison des libelles et anonymes répandus par les agents des Fermiers Généraux contre les employés, 1791*, Bibliothèque de la Ville de Paris.

7. *Le Moniteur* 60 (March 1, 1793): 580.

8. A. Delahante, *Une famille de finance au XVIII* siècle*, vol. II, p. 240.

9. Ibid., p. 234. On the subject of Clavière's misappropriation of funds, see also O. Blanc, *La corruption sous la Terreur, 1792-1794* (Paris: Laffont, 1992), pp. 77–79.

10. Robespierre, quoted in Jean Massin, *Almanach de la Révolution française* (Paris: Club Français du Livre, 1963), p. 220.

11. A. Delahante, *Une famille de finance au XVIII* siècle*, vol. II, p. 232.

12. Archives Nationales, carton du comité d'Instruction publique, F/17/1326, folder 18. Of the 21 letters seized, 17 remain today.

13. *Procès verbal de perquisition et d'apposition de scellés*, Archives Nationales, F/7/1757.

14. Letter of January 6, 1793 quoted in Duveen and Klickstein, *A Bibliography of the Works of Antoine Laurent Lavoisier* (London: Dawson and Sons, 1954), p. 186.

15. A. Delahante, *Une famille de finance au XVIIIe siècle*, vol. II, pp. 241–42.

16. Ibid., p. 242.

17. E. Grimaux, *Lavoisier, 1743–1794*, p. 264.

18. Ibid., p. 263.

19. Lavoisier Collection. Rare and Manuscript Collections, Cornell University Library.

20. Ibid.

21. bid.

22. Ibid.

23. The Convention had adopted the Republican Calendar, which began October 7 or 16 vendémiaire An II.

24. E. Grimaux, *Lavoisier, 1743–1794*, p. 266.

25. H. Thirion, *La vie privée des financiers au XVIIIe siècle* (Paris: Plon, 1895), p. 481.

26. *Je suis le véritable Père Duchesne* 28 (1793): 3.

27. The building is today the Port Royal Maternity Hospital, and is located at 121–123, boulevard de Port-Royal.

28. *Je suis le véritable Père Duchesne* 33 (1793): 1–2.

29. J. J. Lalande, "Notice sur Lavoisier, " *Magasin Encyclopédique*, vol. V, p. 174.

30. Archives Nationales, F 17 1135.

31. Archives Nationales, F 7 4770.

32. A. Delahante, *Une famille de finance au XVIIIe siècle*, vol. II, p. 243.

33. Archives de la Préfecture de Police, quoted in Grimaux, *Lavoisier, 1743–1794*, p. 270.

34. Coissin, *Tableau des prisons de Paris sous le règne de Robespierre* (Paris: Chez Michel, 1795), p. 68.

35. Ibid., pp. 69–70.

36. Ibid., pp. 71–72.

37. A. Delahante, *Une famille de finance au XVIIIe siècle*, vol. II, p. 268.

38. E. Grimaux, *Lavoisier, 1743–1794*, pp. 273–74.

39. Coissin, *Tableau des prisons de Paris sous le règne de Robespierre*, p. 76.

40. Lavoisier Collection, Courtesy of the Rare and Manuscript Collections, Cornell University Library.

41. Archives de l'Académie des Sciences, Lavoisier Collection, dation Chabrol, 1, file II.

42. A. Delahante, *Une famille de finance au XVIIIe siècle*, vol. II, pp. 268–69.

43. *Le Moniteur Universel* 74 (14 frimaire An II): 573.

44. D. Duveen, *Notes and Records of the Royal Society* 13, 1 (June 1958): 59–60.

45. Archives Nationales, F 7 4770.

46. A recent decree by the Convention had stipulated replacing all assignats with symbols of the ancien régime by ones with republican designs.

47. Quoted in R. Dujarric de la Rivière and M. Chabrier, *La vie et l'œuvre de Lavoisier*, p. 95.

48. Archives Nationales, F 7 4770.

49. Ibid.

50. Quoted in M. Daumas, *Lavoisier*, p. 220. The members of the Public Education Committee responsible for supervising the weights and measures project were Fourcroy, Grégoire, Romme, Arbogast and Guyton de Morveau.

51. E. Grimaux, *Lavoisier, 1743–1794*, p. 276.

52. Coissin, *Tableau des prisons de Paris sous le règne de Robespierre*, p. 88.

53. Archives de la Ville de Paris, DQ 10.III. DR 2263.

54. A. Delahante,*Une famille de finance au XVIIIe siècle*, vol. II, pp. 272–73.

55. L. Scheler, *Lavoisier et le principe chimique*, pp. 145–46.

56. Archives Nationales, Etude Gondouin, XCIX, 7 prairial An IV.

57. *Plans des fermes et domaines appartenant à Madame Lavoisier dans le canton de Villers-Cotterêts, levés par Choisy, notaire et arpenteur à Villers-Cotterêts en 1792*, Ms. L. Scheler collection.

58. L. Scheler, *Lavoisier et le principe chimique* (Paris: Seghers, 1964), p. 199.

59. *Déclaration de revenus pour 1793*, accession 18, Hagley Museum and L ibrary, Wilmington, Delaware.

60. Archives Nationales, F 7 4770.

61. Lavoisier Collection, Courtesy of the Rare and Manuscript Collections, Cornell University Library.

62. *Oeuvres*, vol. VI, p. 571.

63. Ibid..

64. Ibid., p. 575.

65. A. Delahante,*Une famille de finance au XVIIIe siècle*, vol. II, pp. 474–75.

66. *Oeuvres*, vol. VI, p. 583.

67. Ibid.

68. Ibid., p. 598.

69. Ibid;, p. 600.

70. Ibid., p. 602.

71. Ibid., p. 604.

72. F. N. Mollien, *Mémoires d'un ministre du Trésor public, 1780–1815*, vol. I, pp. 148–62.

73. *Oeuvres*, vol. IV, pp. 713–14.

74. Ibid., pp. 714–15.

75. Cadet de Gassicourt accused explicitly the "barbarous forethought" of the Committee of General Security, which had spirited away all the supporting documents in the affair. Archives de l'Académie des Sciences, Lavoisier Collection, 1727.

76. *Notice de ce que Lavoisier, ci-devant commissaire de la Trésorerie nationale, de la ci-devant Académie des Sciences, membre du bureau de consultation des Arts et Métiers, cultivateur dans le district de Blois, département du Loir et Cher, a fait pour la Révolution*:

Lavoisier, member of almost all the Academies of Europe, has in the main dedicated his life to work relating to physics and chemistry. During the twenty-five years that he was a member of the Academy of Science, he had printed in its Collection more than eighty memoirs of which many contained important discoveries for the arts, sciences and humanity. To this end he dedicated a part of his fortune. For more than fifteen years he was also engaged in costly agricultural experiments for which he spent more than 120,000 livres. He intends to publish shortly a book on this subject. He did not wait for the Revolution to declare his principles concerning liberty and equality. In 1787, he was a member of the Assemblée provinciale d'Orléans, where he was a constant and courageous defender of the interests of the people. The entire town of Orléans can witness to this fact. During the winter of 1778 to 1779, he lent without interest to the city of Blois fifty thousand livres and six thousand to the town of Romorantin to feed the people, stock the wheat markets and lower the price of foodstuffs. Unwavering in his principles, for the past ten years, in times of distress, he sent each week to the market at Blois wheat that he sold at below prevailing prices. He was électeur in 1789. Député suppléant at the Constituent Assembly in the same year. Temporarary representative of the Commune de Paris at the end of 1789 and the beginning of 1790. Active in the national guard from the first moments of the Revolution. The Constituent Assembly ordered by decree the printing of a work he did on the national wealth, the surface area of the French territory, its population and territorial production. He was a consultant to the Committee on Health and to the Currency Committee. He was appointed National Treasury Commissioner in 1791, and helped to set up the present Treasury. He served in this post for one and a half year and left only after having completely accomplished the job he had been asked to do. In 1791 he was appointed a member of the Advisory Board for Arts and Trades established by decree by the legislative Assembly to attribute national rewards for deserving and indigent artisans. In 1793 he was asked by the Currency Committee to contribute to a general plan for the fabrication and revision of assignats and to devise a method to make their counterfeiting impossible. From 1790 to 1793 he was responsible for all operations relating to the establishment of the new measures decreed by the national representation. Finally, on all occasions, he has borne arms for the defense of liberty, in particular on August 10, 1792, when he was enlisted to stand guard at the gunpowder warehouse of the Arsenal, and on May 31, 1793, when he was a member of the battalion of the Piques section posted at the Place de la Révolution." (Archives de l'Académie des Sciences, Lavoisier Collection, 1724)

77. Ibid.

Chapter 19: The Trial

1. Cadet de Gassicourt, Archives de l'Académie des Sciences, Lavoisier Collection, file 1030.

2. *Rapport des commissaires réviseurs des trois compagnies de finances aux représentants du peuple chargés de surveiller leurs travaux, et lu aux comités des Finances et de Comptabilité par Motet, Châteauneuf, Jaquart, Gaudot, Vernon, Imprimé par ordre de la Conventional nationale, avec des pièces justificatives* (Paris, 1794), 187 p.

3. A. Dupin, *Rapport fait au nom des Comités de Sûreté générale, des Finances et de l'Examen des Comptes réunis à la Commission sur l'administration des fermiers généraux, 16 floréal An II*, p. 2.

4. Ibid., p. 16.

5. Ibid., p. 20.

6. Ibid., pp. 22–23.

7. Ibid., p. 24.

8. F. N. Mollien, *Mémoires d'un ministre du Trésor public*, vol. I, pp. 167–68.

9. Ibid., p. 169.

10. J. Gaulard Desaudray, *La mort de Lavoisier, hyerodrame* (Paris: Imprimerie de la Feuille du Cultivateur, AnIV, 1796), p. 3.

11. J. Lakanal, "Rapport sur le Lycée des Arts," *Journal du Lycée des Arts* 11 (4 vendémiaire An IV).

12. A. Tuetey, *Répertoire général des sources manuscrites de l'histoire de Paris pendant la Révolution française* (Paris: Imprimerie Nouvelle, 1914), vol. 11, p. 415, ref. 1412, and Archives Nationales, W/362, no. 785. Transferred to modern section.

13. *Journal du Lycée des Arts* 3 (1795): 229–30.

14. Archives Nationales, W 1 A, 193.

15. A. Delahante,*Une famille de finances au XVIIIᵉ siècle*, vol. II, pp. 302–3.

16. A. Tuetey, *Répertoire général des sources*, p. 452, ref. 1582, and Archives Nationales, W 362, no. 785.

17. Ibid., p. 454, ref. 1588, and Archives Nationales, W 534.

18. Fouquier-Tinville had three deputies: Fleuriot-Lescot, Gribeauval, and Gilbert Liendon. Usually Liendon is cited as having replaced Fouquier-Tinville for the trial of the Farmers General, but Delahante categorically designates Claude Royer, former parish priest at Châlons-sur-Saône.

19. A. Delahante, *Une famille de finances au XVIIIᵉ siècle*, vol. II, p. 310.

20. Ibid.

21. Ibid., p. 311.

22. Ibid., p. 312.

23. A. Tuetey, *Répertoire général des sources*, vol. 11, p. 406, ref. 1380, and Archives Nationales, W 362, no. 785.

24. *Bulletin du Tribunal Révolutionnaire*, part 4, no. 78 to 81.

25. D. McKie, *Antoine Lavoisier: Scientist, Economist, Social Reformer* (London: Constable, 1952), p. 306.

26. A. Tuetey, *Répertoire général des sources*, vol. 11, p. 453, ref. 1584, and Archives Nationales, W 362, no. 785.

27. Archives Nationales, W 362 no. 785.

28. Ibid.

29. *Les Mémoires de Sanson*, quoted in H. Thirion, *La vie privée des financiers au XVIIIᵉ siècle* (Paris: Plon, 1895), p. 503.

30. H. Thirion, *La vie privée des financiers au XVIIIᵉ siècle*, p. 504.

31. Archives Nationales, W 527.

32. Quoted in E. Grimaux, *Lavoisier, 1743-1794*, p. 306. It was impossible for us, as it was for him, to find this quote in the *Orateur du peuple*.

33. Y. de Sainte-Agnès, *Guide du Paris révolutionnaire* (Paris: Perrin, 1989), p. 101. 32 Farmers General were judged in the session of 19 floréal An II. Four of them—Verdun, Farmer General, and three assistants, Delahante, Sanlot, and Delaâge junior—escaped death. Mollien, a simple clerk, did not stand trial. Thus 28 Farmers General were condemned to death and executed. Another 6 would be arrested and condemned later. Of the 45 Farmers General participating in the last lease, 11 escaped the guillotine: Verdun, Legendre de Luçay, Papillon de Sannois, Saleure de Grizien junior, Moncloux junior, Doazan, Saint-Alphonse, Paulze junior, Pignon, Veymerange, and Augeard.

34. J. B. Delambre, "Eloge de Lagrange," *Les Mémoires de l'Institut.* (1812); 14.

35. See O. Blanc, *La corruption sous la Terreur* (Paris: Laffont, 1992), pp. 174–85.

36. *Oeuvres*, vol. II, p. 104.

37. Dr. Sacombe, *Appel à l'Institut national du jugement surpris à sa classe des Sciences Physiques et Mathématiques par Fourcroy et ses amis* (Paris: An VIII), p. 45.

38. A. Laugier, Bibliothèque de l'Institut de France, Cuvier Collection, Catalogue Deherain, 191.2, quoted in G. Kersaint, *Antoine François de Fourcroy, sa vie, son oeuvre*, p. 73.

39. M. Daumas, "Justification de l'attitude de Fourcroy pendant la Terreur," *Revue d'Histoire des Sciences et de Leurs Applications* 11 (1958): 274.

40. *Notice sur la vie et les travaux de Lavoisier*, read 15 thermidor An IV at the Lycée des Arts, Archives de l'Académie des Sciences, Lavoisier Collection, file 1732, pp. 44–45.

Chapter 20: La Citoyenne Lavo

1. J. Massin, *Almanach de la Révolution française* (Paris: Club Français du Livre, 1963), p. 302.

2. The value of the assignat fell sharply during the summer of 1794, and was worth no more than 40 percent of its face value. Thus, to transform 1794 livres into 1996 dollars, sums must be multiplied by 16 and not by 40. The debt can be estimated as being equivalent to a billion dollars in 1996.

3. *Inventaire des biens saisis au domicile de Lavoisier, 243, boulevard de la Madeleine*, Lavoisier Collection. Courtesy of the Rare and Manuscript Collections, Cornell University Library.

4. Archives Nationales, Etude Gondouin, germinal à prairial an IV, XCIX 754.

5. Ibid.

6. Archives Nationales, F 17 1337 A, file 5 (51).

7. For the details and understanding of this capital and valuable instrument, as well as of the following four, Lavoisier's *Eléments de chymie* should be consulted." Archives Nationales, Etude Gondouin, XCIX 754 (no. 8).

8. Ibid.

9. Ibid.

10. Archives Nationales, F 17 4757.

11. P. S. Du Pont de Nemours, *La philosophie de l'univers* (Paris: Goujon, fructidor an VII), 3rd ed., publisher's introduction.

12. Ibid., pp. 29–30.

13. R. Dujarric de la Rivière, *E.I. Du Pont de Nemours, élève de Lavoisier* (Paris: Librairie des Champs-Elysées, 1954), p. 216.

14. Ibid., p. 217.

15. G. Chinard, *Lettres de Du Pont de Nemours écrites de la prison de la Force* (Paris: A. Margraff, 1929), p. 29.

16. R. Dujarric de la Rivière, *E.I. Du Pont de Nemours, élève de Lavoisier*, p. 217.

17. G. Chinard, *Lettres de Du Pont de Nemours*, p. 49.

18. Ibid., p. 51.

19. Archives Nationales, F 7 4770, file 2.

20. Ibid.

21. G. Chinard, *Lettres de Du Pont de Nemours*, p. 65.

22. Archives Nationales, F 7 4770, file 2 (Documents 12, 14, 15, 18).

23. G. Chinard, *Lettres de Du Pont de Nemours*, p. 87.

24. M. Bouloiseau, *Bourgeoisie et Révolution: les Du Pont de Nemours* (Paris: Bibliothèque Nationale, 1972), p. 216.

25. G. Chinard, *Lettres de Du Pont de Nemours*, pp. 94–95.

26. "Mr Dupont with his bent back and bald head, seemed much older than he was. A member of the Conseil des Cinq-Cents suggested to Chénier that he speak in favor of this old man, which he did, treating him as an octogenarian from whom there was nothing to be feared; but he was not placed on the list. The truth is that he was not yet sixty years old." Monchanin, *Notice sur la vie de Du Pont de Nemours* (Paris: Delaunay, 1818), pp. 36–37.

27. Ambrose Saricks stresses that there had been an intimate amorous relationship, in *Pierre-Samuel Du Pont de Nemours* (Lawrence: University of Kansas Press, 1965), note 9, p. 417.

28. R. Dujarric de la Rivière, *E.I. Du Pont de Nemours, élève de Lavoisier*, p. 222.

29. Ibid., p. 225.

30. Ibid., pp. 228–29.

31. A. Delahante, *Une famille de finance au XVIIIᵉ siècle*, vol. II, pp. 470–71.

32. A. Dupin, *Motion d'ordre et exposé fidèle de tout ce qui s'est passé dans l'affaire des Fermiers Généraux, assassinés par la faction Robespierre et ses complices, le 19 floréal, an troisième de la République, par le Tribunal révolutionnaire* (Paris: Imprimerie Nationale, floréal an II) pp. 3–4.

33. Ibid., pp. 7–8.

34. Ibid., p. 9.

35. Ibid., p. 12.

36. Madame Lavoisier, *Dénonciation présentée au Comité de Législation de la Convention Nationale contre le représentant du peuple Dupin*, p. 8.

37. Ibid., p. 14.

38. A. Dupin, *Réponse à la dénonciation présentée par les veuves et les enfants des ci-devant Fermiers-généraux*, 44 pages (Paris: Imprimerie Nationale, 1795), pp. 1–2.

39. Archives Nationales, AD IX 533.

40. L. Scheler, *Lavoisier et le principe chimique*, pp. 143–44.

41. Archives Nationales, F 17 1076, no. 14.

42. Ibid., no. 8.

43. J. J. Lalande, *Magasin Encyclopédique*, 1795, vol. V, p. 174.

44. Ibid., pp. 179–83.

45. In 1775, Lavoisier had participated in two evaluations of the quality of steel produced by two factories. *Oeuvres*, vol. IV, pp. 210–20. On September 22, 1787 he visited the Creusot ironworks with Monge and Fourcroy.

46. *Journal du Lycée des Arts* 3 (1795): 203.

47. A. Fourcroy, *Notice sur la vie et les travaux de Lavoisier, précédée d'un discours sur les funérailles, et suivie d'une ode sur l'immortalité de l'âme*, read 15 thermidor, an IV at the Lycée des Arts (Paris: Imprimerie de la Feuille du Cultivateur, An IV), p. 36, and Archives de l'Académie des Sciences, Lavoisier Collection, 1731.

48. Ibid.

49. Ibid.

50. P. S. Du Pont de Nemours, *La philosophie de l'univers*, pp. 39–41.

51. M. Bouloiseau, *Bourgeoisie et Révolution: les Du Pont de Nemours*, p. 137.

52. Letter from Pierre Samuel to Victor Du Pont de Nemours, September 20, 1797, Winterthur Manuscripts, GR 2, Box 3, Hagley Museum and Library, Wilmington, Delaware.

53. P. S. Du Pont, October 23, 1798, Manuscript Department, Fr 80, by permission of the Houghton Library, Harvard University.

54. P. S. Du Pont, letter written 22 fructidor An VII (September 8, 1799), Longwood Manuscripts, GR 1, Box 1, Hagley Museum and Library, Wilmington, Delaware.

55. P. S. Du Pont, October 1, 1799, Manuscript Department, Fr 80, by permission of the Houghton Library, Harvard University.

56. P. S. Du Pont, September 16, 1799, Manuscript Department, Fr 80, by permission of the Houghton Library, Harvard University.

57. L. Scheler, *Lavoisier et le principe chimique*, p. 147.

58. B. G. Du Pont, *Correspondence of Pierre and Irénée du Pont* (Wilmington: University of Delaware Press, 1926).

59. Madame Lavoisier, Preface to the *Mémoires de Chimie* (Paris: 1803).

60. G. Cuvier, in L. G. Michaud, *Biographie universelle* (Paris: Michaud, 1819), vol. 23, p. 465.

61. Quoted in D. Duveen, "Madame Lavoisier, 1758–1836," *Chymia* (1953): 21.

62. Quoted in S. Blatin, "Un amour physique et chimique," *Historia* 356 (July 1976): 105.

63. G. Cuvier, *Recueil des éloges historiques*, vol. II, pp. 190–251.

64. A. F. de Frénilly, *Souvenirs* (Paris: Plon, Nourrit, 1908), p. 282.

65. Or about 1.5 million dollars in 1996. Rumford died in 1814. On his tomb in the Auteuil Cemetary is written: "Celebrated physicist, enlightened philosopher, his discoveries on light and heat have brought fame to his name. His works to improve the fate of the poor will always be cherished by the friends of humanity."

66. F. Guizot, "La comtesse de Rumford," in *Mélanges biographiques et littéraires* (Paris: Lévy Frères, 1868), pp. 82–83.

67. Ibid., p. 83.

68. P. S. Du Pont, March 31, 1815, Manuscript Department, Fr 80, by permission of the Houghton Library, Harvard University.

69. A. F. de Frénilly, *Souvenirs*, p. 284.

70. G. Sand, *Histoire de ma vie: oeuvres autobiographiques* (Paris: Gallimard, 1971), vol. 2, p. 66.

71. P. Mérimée, *Correspondance*, vol. XVI, p. 57.

72. A. Delahante, *Une famille de finance au XVIIIᵉ siècle*, pp. 546–49.

Bibliography

I. Works of Antoine-Laurent Lavoisier

MANUSCRIPTS

Archives de l'Académie des Sciences. The Lavoisier Collection contains more than 2,000 documents in 40 cartons, including 13 laboratory registers, manuscripts, letters, and scientific, political, and economic papers.

Archives Nationales. Documents concerning Lavoisier's property and legacy, the General Farm and the trial of the Farmers General.

Bibliothèque Municipale de Clermont-Ferrand. 3 cartons of correspondence.

Bibliothèque Municipale d'Orléans. 1 carton of documents concerning the Assemblée provinciale de l'Orléanais.

Archives départementales du Loir et Cher, Blois. Documents concerning the States General in the Blésois.

Cornell University Library, Ithaca, N. Y. The Lavoisier Collection includes 324 manuscripts related to science, public administration, and politics, and 1,288 titles of printed material: more than 90 percent of the 705 entries in the standard *Bibliography of the Works of Antoine Laurent Lavoisier, 1743-1794* by Denis I. Duveen and Herbert S. Klickstein, and 430 titles from the original library of Lavoisier and his wife.

MANUSCRIPTS OF MARIE ANNE LAVOISIER (NÉE PAULZE)

Hagley Museum and Library, Wilmington, Delaware. Correspondence between Madame Lavoisier and P. S. Du Pont de Nemours and others.

Houghton Library, Harvard University, Cambridge, Massachusetts. Correspondence between P. S. Du Pont de Nemours and Madame Lavoisier.

COLLECTED WORKS

Oeuvres de Lavoisier publiées par les soins du Ministère de l'Instruction publique. 6 vols. Vols. 1–4, ed. J. B. Dumas, vols. 5–6, ed. E. Grimaux. Paris: Imprimerie Nationale, 1864–1893.

Correspondance (vol. 7 of *Oeuvres*), collected and annotated by René Fric, fasc. I (1768–1769), fasc. II (1770–1775), fasc. III (1776–1783), Paris: Albin Michel, 1955–1957–1964; under the auspices of Lavoisier Committee of the Academy of Science, Introduction by Michelle Goupil, fasc. IV (1784–1786), Paris: Belin, 1986, vol. V (1787–1788), Paris: Académie des Sciences,1993.

Duveen, Denis I. and Herbert S. Klickstein. *A Bibliography of the Works of Antoine Laurent Lavoisier, 1743–1794*. London: Dawson and Sons and E. Weil, 1954.

———. *Supplement* by D.I. Duveen. London: Dawson of Pall Mall, 1965.

———. *Catalogue of Printed Works by and Memorabilia of Antoine-Laurent de Lavoisier, 1743–1794*. Exhibited at the Grolier Club, New York, 1952.

Bret, Patrice. "Trois décennies d'études Lavoisiennes: Supplément aux bibliographies de Duveen." *Revue d'Histoire des Sciences* 48 (1995): 169–97.

More than one hundred of Lavoisier's contributions to periodical works can be found in the *Mémoires de l'Académie Royale des Sciences*, the *Observations sur la Physique, sur l'Histoire Naturelle et sur les Arts*, the *Annales de Chimie*, and the *Histoire de la Société Royale de Médecine*.

SEPARATE WORKS

Opuscules physiques et chymiques. Paris: Durand-Didot-Esprit, 1774.

Instructions sur le blanchissage des toiles de chanvre et de lin. Undated (1779).

Nouveau prix extraordinaire proposé par l'Académie Royale des Sciences pour l'année 1784.

"Instruction sur le parcage des bêtes à laine." In *Tableau de l'administration de la ville de Toulouse pour l'année 1785*. Toulouse: Imprimerie de Maître Jean Florent Daour, 1785.

Procès verbal des séances de l'Assemblée provinciale de l'Orléanais tenu à Orléans le 6 septembre 1797. Orléans: Imprimerie de Couret de Villeneuve, 1787.

Mémoire sur les impositions lu à l'Assemblée provinciale de l'Orléanais. 1788.

Traité élémentaire de chimie présenté dans un ordre nouveau et d'après les découvertes récentes, avec Figures. 2 vols. Paris: Cuchet,1789.

Instructions données par la noblesse du bailliage de Blois [. . .] , 28 mars 1789.

Adresse de remerciements aux habitants de la paroisse deVillefrancoeur, bailliage de Blois. 1789.

Rapport sur la Caisse d'Escompte fait à l'Assemblée Nationale, le 4 décembre, par ses Commissaires, et imprimé par son ordre. Undated (1789). This report incorporates "Délibération des administrateurs de la Caisse d'Escompte du 4 septembre 1788"; "IIe délibération des administrateurs de la Caisse d'Escompte du 16 octobre 1788"; and "Délibération extraordinaire des administrateurs de la Caisse d'Escompte du 29 mai 1789."

De l'organisation des banques publiques en général, et de la Caisse d'Escompte en particulier. Paris: Clousier, 1789.

Discours prononcé à l'Assemblée générale des Actionnaires de la Caisse d'Escompte le 17 nov.1789. Paris: Clousier, 1789.

Adresse des actionnaires de la Caisse d'Escompte à Nosseigneurs de l'Assemblée nationale, 20 novembre 1789. Paris: Baudouin, 1789.

Observations sur la position actuelle de la Caisse d'Escompte. Paris: Clousier, 1789.

Observations adressées à MM. les représentants de la Commune de Paris par l'administration de la Caisse d'Escompte, 17 février 1790. Paris: Clousier, 1790.

Réflexions sur les assignats et sur la liquidation de la dette exigible ou arriérée, 29 août 1790. Paris: Clousier, 1790.

Addition aux observations de M. Lavoisier, député suppléant au bailliage de Blois, sur la liquidation de la dette exigible ou arriérée. Paris: Clousier, undated (1790).

Réponse à quelques objections relatives à la Caisse d'Escompte. Paris: Clousier, undated (1790).

Mémoire de la Régie des Poudres. Paris: Clousier, 1791.

Mémoire sur la vente des tabacs appartenant à la nation, 1791. Archives Nationales, 29 AP 85.

Observations sur la motion faite par M. Osselin, le 17 février 1791, à la Société des Amis de la Constitution, relativement à la Régie des Poudres et Salpêtres. Paris: Clousier, 1791.

Résultats extraits d'un ouvrage intitulé De la Richesse territoriale du Royaume de France. Paris: Imprimerie Nationale, 1791.

De l'état des finances de la France au 1er janvier 1792. Paris: Du Pont, 1791.

Programme du prix proposé par l'Académie sur la nutrition pour 1794. Paris: Du Pont, 1792.

Réflexions sur l'Instruction publique. Paris: Du Pont père et fils, 1793.

Réponses aux inculpations faites contre les ci-devant Fermiers généraux. Paris: 1794.

Mémoires de Chimie, ed. Madame Lavoisier. 2 vols. Paris: Du Pont,1803.

COLLECTIVE WORKS

Commissaires nommés par l'Académie pour le jugement du prix du salpêtre. *Recueil de mémoires et d'observations sur la formation et sur la fabrication du salpêtre.* Paris: Lacombe, 1776.

Régisseurs généraux des Poudres et Salpêtres. *Instruction sur l'établissement des nitrières et sur la fabrication du salpêtre.* Paris: Imprimerie Royale, 1777.

———. *Observations sur le travail des eaux-mères de salpêtre et sur celui des eaux d'atelier.* Paris: Imprimerie Royale, 1778.

———. *L'art de fabriquer le salin et la potasse.* Paris: Imprimerie Royale, 1779.

[Lavoisier,] Guettard et Monnet. *Atlas minéralogique de la France.* Paris: undated (1780).

Lavoisier et de La Place. *Mémoire sur la chaleur lu à l'Académie Royale des Sciences le 28 juin 1783.* Paris: Imprimerie Royale, 1783.

Rapport des Commissaires chargés par le Roi de l'examen du magnétisme animal. Paris: Imprimerie Royale, 1784.

Recueil de mémoires et de pièces sur la formation et la fabrication du salpêtre. Paris: Imprimerie de Moutard, 1786.

Rapport des Commissaires chargés par l'Académie de l'examen du projet d'un nouvel Hôtel-Dieu. Paris: Imprimerie Royale, 1786.

MM. de Morveau, Lavoisier, Berthollet et de Fourcroy. *Méthode de nomenclature chimique. On y a joint un nouveau système de caractères chimiques, adaptés à cette nomenclature, par MM. Hassenfratz et Adet.* Paris: Cuchet, 1787.

MM. de Morveau, Lavoisier, de La Place, Monge, Berthollet et de Fourcroy. *Essai sur le phlogistique et sur la constitution des acides, traduit de l'anglais de M. Kirwan, avec des notes.* Paris: Rue et Hôtel Serpente, 1788.

Commissaires de la Trésorerie Nationale. *États des recettes et des dépenses faites à la Trésorerie Nationale, juillet, août, septembre 1791.* Paris: Imprimerie Nationale, 1791.

―――. *De la situation du Trésor public au premier Juin 1791, par les Commissaires de la Trésorerie Nationale.* Manuscript in folio, 237 p., coming from Lavoisier's personal library and bearing his ex-libris. Listed as Nb in Catalogue de livres faisant partie de la bibliothèque de feu Madame Lavoisier, comtesse de Rumford. 2 vols. Paris: 1836. Private collection.

MM. Morveau, Lavoisier, Monge, Berthollet, de Fourcroy, de Dietrich, Hassenfratz, Adet. *Annales de Chimie: recueil de Mémoires concernant la chimie et les arts qui en dépendent.* 18 vols. Paris: Rue Serpente; London: Chez J. de Boffe, 1789–1793.

II. Studies on Lavoisier

Abbri, Ferdinando. *Le terre, l'acqua e le arie: la rivoluzione chimica del Settecento.* Bologna: Il Mulino, 1984.

―――. *A. L. Lavoisier, Memorie Scientifiche.* Roma-Napoli: Theoria, 1986.

―――. "L'immagine di Lavoisier nella cultura italiana." In *Seminario internazionale per il bicentenario della scomparsa di Antoine Laurent Lavoisier (1743–1794)*, pp. 219–30.

―――. "Science and Politics in the Italian Reception of Lavoisier's Nomenclature." In Bensaude-Vincent et al., *Lavoisier in European Context: Negotiating a New Language for Chemistry*, pp. 249–65.

Abbri, Ferdinando and Marco Beretta. "Bibliography of the *Méthode de nomenclature chimique* and of the *Traité élémentaire de chimie* and Their European Translations (1787–1800)." In Bensaude-Vincent et al., *Lavoisier in European Context: Negotiating a New Language for Chemistry*, pp. 279–91.

Abrahams, Harold J. "Lavoisier's Proposals for French Education." *Journal of Chemical Education* 31 (1954): 403–16.

―――. "A Summary of Lavoisier's Proposals for Training in Science and Medicine." *Bulletin of the History of Medicine* 32 (1958): 389–407.

―――. "Lavoisier and His Contemporaries Debate the Supply of Water for Paris." *Bulletin of the New York Academy of Medicine* 5 (1981): 355–91.

Amiable, René. "La Révolution française et les Poudriers, Lavoisier, Carny et les autres." *L'Armement* (December 1989).

―――. "Lavoisier et la révolution poudrière." In *Lavoisier et la révolution chimique: Actes du colloque tenu à l'occasion du bicentenaire de la publication du "Traité élémentaire de chimie," 4–5 décembre 1989.* Palaiseau: SABIX-École Polytechnique, 1992, pp. 239–52.

Anastasi, Auguste. "Inventaire du laboratoire de Lavoisier." In *Nicolas Leblanc, sa vie ses travaux et l'histoire de la soude artificielle.* Paris: Hachette, 1884.

Anderson, Wilda C. "The Rhetoric of Scientific Language: An Example from Lavoisier." *MLN* 96 (1981): 746–70.

―――. *Between the Library and the Laboratory: The Language of Chemistry in the Eighteenth Century.* Baltimore: Johns Hopkins University Press, 1984.

Baker, Keith M. and William A. Smeaton. "The Origins and the Authorship of the Educational Proposals Published in 1793 by the Bureau de Consultation des Arts et Métiers and Generally Ascribed to Lavoisier." *Annals of Science* 21 (1965): 33–46.

Basu, Prajit K. "Similarities and Dissimilarities Between Joseph Priestley and Antoine

Lavoisier's Chemical Belief." *Studies in the History and Philosophy of Science* 23 (1992): 445–69.

———. "Scientific Explanation in the History of Chemistry: The Priestley-Lavoisier Debate." *Dissertation Abstracts International* 53 (1993): 3937-A.

Belin, Pierre. "Un collaborateur d'Antoine-Laurent Lavoisier à l'Hôtel de l'Arsenal: Jean-Baptiste Meusnier (1754–1793)." In Goupil et al., eds., *Lavoisier et la révolution chimique*. Palaiseau: SABIX-École Polytechnique, 1992, pp. 263–93.

Bensaude-Vincent, Bernadette. "A Founder Myth of the History of Science? The Lavoisier Case." In Loren Graham, Wolf Lepenies, and Peter Weingart, eds., *Functions and Uses of Disciplinary Histories*. Dordrecht: Reidel, 1983, pp. 53–78.

———. "Une mythologie révolutionnaire dans la chimie française." *Annals of Science* 40 (1983): 189–96.

———. "Lavoisier, une révolution scientifique." In Michel Serres, ed., *Eléments d'Histoire des Sciences*. Paris: Bordas, 1989, pp. 363–85.

———. "A View of Chemical Revolution Through Contemporary Textbooks: Lavoisier, Fourcroy and Chaptal." *British Journal for the Philosophy of Science* 23 (1990): 435–60.

———. "The Balance Between Chemistry and Politics." *Eighteenth Century Theory and Interpretation* 33 (1992): 217–37.

———. *Lavoisier: Mémoire d'une révolution*. Paris: Flammarion, 1994.

———. "Eaux et mesures. Eclairages sur l'itinéraire intellectuel du jeune Lavoisier." *Revue d'Histoire des Sciences* 48 (1995): 49–69.

———. "Introductory Essay: A Geographical History of Eighteenth Century Chemistry." In Bensaude-Vincent et al., *Lavoisier in European Context: Negotiating a New Language for Chemistry*, pp. 1–17.

Bensaude-Vincent, Bernadette and F. Abbri, eds. *Lavoisier in European Context: Negotiating a New Language for Chemistry*. Nantucket, Mass.: Science History Publications, 1996.

Beretta, Marco. "A.-L. Lavoisier en Italie (1774–1800)." In *Echanges d'influences scientifiques et techniques entre pays européens de 1780 à 1830. Actes du 114e Congrès national des sociétés savantes (Paris, 3–9 avril 1989)*. Paris: Editions du CTHS, 1990, pp. 125–45.

———. "The Historiography of Chemistry in the 18th Century: A Preliminary Survey and Bibliography." *Ambix* 39 (1992): 1–10.

———. "Torbern, Bergman in France: An Unpublished Letter by Lavoisier to Guyton de Morveau." *Lychnos* (1992): 167–170.

———. "Chemists in the Storm: Lavoisier, Priestley and the French Revolution." *Nuncius* 8, 1 (1993): 75–104.

———. *The Enlightenment of Matter: the Definition of Chemistry from Agricola to Lavoisier*. Nantucket, Mass.: Science History Publications,, 1993.

———. "Lavoisier and His New Biographers." *Lychnos* (1994): 153–60.

———. *A New Course in Chemistry: Lavoisier's First Chemical Papers*. Firenze: Leo S. Olshki, Biblioteca di Nuncius, 13, 1994.

———. *Bibliotheca Lavoisieriana: The Catalogue of the Library of Antoine Laurent Lavoisier*. Firenze: Leo S. Olschki, Biblioteca di Nuncius, 16, 1995.

———. "Lavoisier as a Reader of Chemical Literature." *Revue d'Histoire des Sciences* 48 (1995): 71–96.

———. "Italian Translations of the Methode de Nomenclature Chimique and the Traité Elémentaire de Chimie: The Case of Vincenzo Dandolo." In Bensaude-Vincent et al., *Lavoisier in European Context: Negotiating a New Language for Chemistry*, pp. 225–47.

Berthelot, Marcelin. *Notice historique sur Lavoisier.* Paris: Firmin Didot, 1889.

———. *La révolution chimique, Lavoisier: ouvrage suivi de notice et extraits des régistres inédits de laboratoire de Lavoisier.* Paris: Alcan, 1890.

———. "Sur les registres de laboratoire de Lavoisier." *Comptes Rendus de l'Académie des Sciences* 135 (1902): 549–57.

Bertrand, Gabriel. "Lavoisier et la découverte de l'oxygène." *Archives Internationales d'Histoire des Sciences* 3 (1950): 307–15.

Besnier, Charles. "L'oeuvre et la vie de Lavoisier." *L'information Scientifique* 1 (1960).

Bicentenaire de la publication du Traité élémentaire de chimie par Lavoisier. Actes du Symposium organisé à Louvain-la-Neuve in April 1989. *Revue des Questions Scientifiques* 160 (1989): 145–219.

Birembaut, Arthur. "A propos des biographies de Lavoisier." In *Actes du VIIe Congrès International d'Histoire des Sciences* (Jerusalem). Paris: Hermann, 1953, pp.216–20.

———. "Quelques aspects de la personnalité de Lavoisier." In Association Française pour l'Avancement des Sciences, ed., *Actes du Congrès de Luxembourg, 72e session.* Luxembourg, Bourg-Bourger,1953, pp. 539–42.

———. "La correspondance de Lavoisier." *Annales de l'Histoire de la Révolution Française* (1957): 340–51.

———. "A propos d'une publication récente sur Lavoisier et le Lycée des Arts." *Revue d'Histoire des Sciences* 11 (1958): 267–74.

———. "Les deux déterminations de l'unité de masse du système métrique." *Revue d'Histoire des Sciences* 12 (1959): 25–54.

———. "Lavoisier: 1743-1794." *Encyclopedia Universalis* 1965.

Boklund, Uno. "A Lost Letter from Scheele to Lavoisier." *Lychnos* (1957): 39–62.

Bouis, R. "Un écho d'une réclamation de Lavoisier en 1793." *Annales de l'Histoire de la Révolution Française* 139 (1955): 168–69.

Bret, Patrice. "Une tentative d'exploitation militaire de la recherche en chimie: Berthollet et la poudre au muriate oxygéné de potasse (1787-1794)." In M. Goupil et al., *Lavoisier et la révolution chimique*, pp. 195–238.

———. "La Régie des Poudres et Salpêtres (1775–1792)." In Lavoisier, *Correspondance*, vol. V (1787–1788), Annexe III. Paris: Académie des Sciences,1993, pp. 259–67.

Butler, Anthony R. "Lavoisier, a Letter from Sweden." *Chemistry in Britain* 20 (1984): 617–19.

Carmichael, Emmett B. "Antoine-Laurent Lavoisier." *Alabama Journal of Medicine and Allied Sciences* 10 (1973): 328–39.

Carozzi, Alberto V. "Lavoisier's Fundamental Contribution to Stratigraphy." *Ohio Journal of Science* 65 (1965): 71–85.

Chaldecott, J. A. "The Bulk Fusion of Platinum: Early Experiments by Lavoisier and Seguin." *Platinum Metals Review* 14 (1970): 24–48.

Chavanne, Albert. "Les aspects juridiques du procès de Lavoisier." *Revue Lyonnaise de Médecine* 14 (1965): 303–7.

Chertok, Léon and Isabelle Stengers. *Le coeur et la raison: l'hypnose en question de Lavoisier à Lacan.* Paris: Payot, 1989.

Cohen, I. Bernard. *From Leonardo to Lavoisier, 1450–1800*. New YorK: Scribner, 1980.

———. *Revolution in Science*, Cambridge, Mass. and London: Harvard University Press, 1985.

Commémoration du bicentenaire de la naissance de Lavoisier. Paris: Masson, 1945.

Conant, James Bryant. "The Overthrow of the Phlogiston Theory: The Chemical Revolution of 1775–1789." In J.B. Conant and L. K. Nash, eds., *Harvard Case Histories in Experimental Science*. Cambridge, Mass.: Harvard University Press, 1957, vol. 1, pp. 65–115.

Court, Susan. "The *Annales de Chimie*, 1789–1815." *Ambix* 19 (1972): 113–28.

Courte, Pierre. "Aperçu sur l'œuvre géologique de Lavoisier." *Annales de la Société Géologique du Nord* 69 (1949): 369–75.

Courty, Pr. "Influence des travaux de Lavoisier sur l'évolution de la chimie." *Revue Lyonnaise de Médecine* (1965): 75–85.

Crosland, Maurice P. *Les héritiers de Lavoisier*. Paris: Palais de la Découverte, 1968.

———. "Lavoisier's Theory of Acidity." *Isis* 64 (1973): 306–25.

———. "Chemistry and the Chemical Revolution." In G. S. Rousseau and Roy Porter eds., *The Ferment of Knowledge: Studies in the Historiography of Eighteenth Century Science*. Cambridge: Cambridge University Press, 1980, pp. 389–416.

———. "Lavoisier le mal aimé." *La Recherche* 14 (1983): 785–91.

———. "The Successors of Lavoisier." *Revue des Questions Scientifiques* 160 (1989): 205–19.

———. *In the Shadow of Lavoisier: The* Annales de Chimie *and the Establishment of a New Science*." Oxford: British Society for the History of Science, 1994.

Culotta, Charles A. *A History of Respiratory Theory: Lavoisier to Paul Bert (1777–1780)*. Thesis, University of Wisconsin, 1968.

———. "On the Color of Blood from Lavoisier to Hoppe-Seyler, 1777–1864: A Theoretical Dilemma." *Episteme* 4 (1970): 219–33.

———. *Respiration and the Lavoisier Tradition: Theory and Modification, 1777–1850*. Transactions of the American Philosophical Society 63 pt. 2. Philadelphia: American Philosophical Society, 1972.

Daumas, Maurice. *Lavoisier*. Paris: Gallimard, 1941.

———. "Les appareils d'expérimentation de Lavoisier." *Chymia* 3 (1950): 45–62.

———. "L'élaboration du Traité de chimie de Lavoisier." *Archives Internationales d'Histoire des Sciences* 29 (1950): 570–90.

———. "Polémiques au sujet des priorités de Lavoisier." *Revue d'Histoire des Sciences* 3 (1950): 133–55.

———. *Lavoisier, théoricien et expérimentateur*. Paris: Presses Universitaires de France, 1955.

———. "Lavoisier et ses historiens." *Archives Internationales d'Histoire des Sciences* 10 (1957): 19–23.

———. "Justification de l'attitude de Fourcroy pendant la Terreur." *Revue d'Histoire des Sciences* 11 (1958): 273–74.

Daumas, Maurice and Denis I. Duveen. "Lavoisier's Relatively Unknown Large-Scale Decomposition and Synthesis of Water, February 27 and 28, 1785." *Chymia* 5 (1959): 113–29.

Davis, Kenneth S. *The Cautionary Scientists: Priestley, Lavoisier, and the Founding of Modern Chemistry*, New York: Putnam, 1966.

———. "Boyle's Conception of Element Compared with That of Lavoisier." *Isis* 16 (1931): 82–91.

Débats et chantiers actuels autour de Lavoisier et de la révolution chimique. Centre International de Synthèse, ed. *Revue d'Histoire des Sciences* 48 (1995).

Decour, Philippe. "L'aventure scientifique: Lavoisier et la Révolution." *Archives Internationales Claude Bernard* 7 (1974).

Delhez, Robert. "Révolution chimique et Révolution française: le discours préliminaire au *Traité élémentaire de chimie* de Lavoisier." *Revue des Questions Scientifiques* 143 (1972): 3–26.

Dejours, Pierre. "Lavoisier physiologiste." In Demeulenaere-Douyère, ed., *Il y a 200 ans Lavoisier*. Actes du Colloque organisé à l'occasion du Bicentenaire de la mort d'Antoine-Laurent de Lavoisier par l'Académie des Sciences et l'Académie d'Agriculture de France. Paris-Blois, 3–6 May 1994. Paris: Technique et Documentation Lavoisier, 1995, pp. 11–18.

Demeulenaere-Douyère, Christiane, ed. *Il y a 200 ans Lavoisier*. Actes du Colloque organisé à l'occasion du Bicentenaire de la mort d'Antoine-Laurent de Lavoisier par l'Académie des Sciences et l'Académie d'Agriculture de France. Paris-Blois, 3–6 May 1994. Paris: Technique et Documentation Lavoisier, 1995.

Déré, Anne Claire. "La réception de la nomenclature réformée par le corps médical français." In Bensaude-Vincent et al., *Lavoisier in European Context: Negotiating a New Language for Chemistry*, pp. 207–24.

Desaudray, Charles. *La mort de Lavoisier, hyérodrame*. Paris: Imprimerie de la Feuille du Cultivateur, An IV, 1796.

Diot, Georges. "Lavoisier à Villefrancoeur (1778–1794)." *Bulletin de la Section Culturelle du Syndicat d'Initiatives de la Vallée de la Cisse* 2 (1974): 51–61.

Dommanget, M. "Lavoisier à Crépy en Valois et Villers Cotterêts." *Annales de l'Histoire de la Révolution Française* 33 (1961): 267–69.

Donovan, Arthur L. "Scottish Responses to the New Chemistry of Lavoisier." In Roseann Runt, ed., *Studies in Eighteenth-Century Culture*, vol. 9. Madison: University of Wisconsin Press, 1979, pp. 237–49.

———, ed. *The Chemical Revolution: Essays in Reinterpretation*. Special issue, *Osiris* 2d. ser. (1988).

———. "Lavoisier and the Origins of Modern Chemistry." In Donovan, ed., *The Chemical Revolution*, pp. 214–31.

———. "Buffon, Lavoisier, and the Transformation of French Chemistry." In J. Gayon, ed., *Actes du colloque international Buffon 88*. Paris: Vrin, 1992, pp. 387–95.

———. "Lavoisier's Two Publics." *Transactions of the International Congress on the Enlightenment* 8 (1992): 1181–3.

———. "Newton and Lavoisier: From Chemistry as a Branch of Natural Philosophy to Chemistry as a Positive Science." In Paul Theerman and Adele F. Seeff, eds., *Action and Reaction*. Newark: University of Delaware Press, 1993, pp. 255–76.

———. *Antoine Lavoisier: Science, Administration, and Revolution*, Oxford and Cambridge Mass.: Blackwell Science Biographies, 1993.

———. "The New Nomenclature Among the Scots: Assessing Novel Chemical Claims in a Culture Under Strain." In Bensaude-Vincent et al., *Lavoisier in European Context: Negotiating a New Language for Chemistry*, pp. 113–22.

Dujarric de la Rivière, René. *Lavoisier économiste*. Paris: Masson, 1949.

———. *E.I. Du Pont de Nemours, élève de Lavoisier*. Paris: Librairie des Champs Élysées, 1954.

———. *Dames de la Révolution*, Périgueux: Fanlac, 1963.

Dujarric de la Rivière, René and Madeleine Chabrier. *La vie et l'œuvre de Lavoisier d'après ses écrits*. Paris: Albin Michel, 1959.

Duncan, Alistair M. "Some Theoretical Aspects of Eighteenth Century Tables of Affinity." *Annals of Science* 18 (1962): 177–94, 217–32.

———. "The Function of Affinity Tables and Lavoisier's List of Elements." *Ambix* 17 (1970): 28–42.

Duveen, Denis I. "Antoine Lavoisier's *Traité Élémentaire de Chimie*, a Bibliographical Note." *Isis* 41 (1950): 168–71.

———. "An Unpublished Report on the Waterproofing of Shoe Leather by Lavoisier and Hassenfratz." *Annals of Science* 8 (1952): 162–64.

———. "Antoine-Laurent Lavoisier 1743–1794: A Note Regarding His Domicile During the French Revolution." *Isis* 42 (1951): 233–34.

———. "Madame Lavoisier." *Chymia* 4 (1953): 13–29.

———. "Lavoisier." *Scientific American* 194 (1956): 85–94.

———. "Antoine-Laurent Lavoisier and the French Revolution." *Journal of Chemical Education*, part I, 31 (1954): 60–65; part II, 34 (1957): 502–3; part III, 35 (1958): 233–34; part IV, 35 (1958): 470–71.

———. "Antoine-Laurent Lavoisier 1743–1794." In Eduard Farber, ed., *Great Chemists*. New York-London: Interscience Publishers, 1961, pp. 261–81.

Duveen, Denis I. and Roger Hahn. "A Note on Some Lavoisiereana in the *Journal de Paris*." *Isis* 51 (1960): 64–66.

———. "Deux lettres de Laplace à Lavoisier." *Revue d'Histoire des Sciences* 21 (1968): 337–42.

Duveen, Denis I. and Herbert S. Klickstein. "Two Early American Eulogies on Lavoisier." *Journal of History of Medicine* 8 (1953): 442–44.

———. "A Letter from Berthollet to Blagden Relating to the Experiments for a Large Scale Synthesis of Water Carried Out by Lavoisier and Meusnié in 1785." *Annals of Science* 10 (1954): 58–62.

———. "Medallic Portraiture of Antoine-Laurent Lavoisier." *Journal of Chemical Education* 31 (1954): 308–9.

———. "Antoine-Laurent Lavoisier (1743–1794) and Christopher Columbus (1446–1506)." *Annals of Science* 10 (1954): 63–68.

———. "Le journal politype des Sciences et des Arts." *Papers of the Bibliographical Society of America* 48 (1954): 402–10.

———. "Antoine-Laurent Lavoisier's Contributions to Medicine and Public Health." *Bulletin of the History of Medicine* 29 (1955): 164–79.

———. "A Letter from Guyton de Morveau to Macquart Relating to Lavoisier's Attack Against the Phlogiston Theory (1778); Morveau's Conversion to Lavoisier's Doctrines in 1787." *Osiris* 12 (1956): 342–67.

———. "Benjamin Franklin, 1706–1790, and Antoine-Laurent Lavoisier, 1743–1794." *Annals of Science* part I, 11 (1955): 103–28; part II, 11 (1955): 271–309; part III, 13 (1957): 30–46.

———. "Some New Facts Relating to the Arrest of Antoine-Laurent Lavoisier." *Isis* 49 (1958): 347–48.

———. "Pour une collaboration des historiens de Lavoisier." Remarks on the Proposal of Maurice Daumas. *Actes du VIIIe Congrès International d'Histoire des Sciences.* Paris: Hermann, 1958, pp. 531–36.

Duveen, Denis I. and Lucien Scheler. "Des illustrations inédites pour les Mémoires de chimie." *Revue d'Histoire des Sciences* 12 (1959): 345–53.

Edelstein, S. M. "The Chemical Revolution in America from the Pages of the Medical Repository." *Chymia* 5 (1959): 155–79.

Exposition au Palais de la Découverte, à l'occasion du deuxième centenaire de la naissance de Lavoisier. Paris: November1943.

Eyles, V. A. "The Evolution of a Chemist, Sir James Hall, 1761–1832, and His Relations with Joseph Black, Antoine Lavoisier, and Other Scientists of the Period." *Annals of Science* 19 (1963): 153–82.

Fauque, Danielle. "Lavoisier deux cents ans après: A propos des ouvrages du Bicentenaire." *Revue d'Histoire des Sciences* 48 (1995): 143–68.

Flandrois, A. "Influence des travaux de Lavoisier sur l'évolution de la physiologie respiratoire." *Revue Lyonnaise de Médecine* (1965): 87–92.

Foregger, Richard. "Respiration Experiments of Lavoisier." *Archives Internationales d'Histoire des Sciences* 13 (1960): 103–6.

Fourcroy, Antoine François de. *Notice sur la vie et les travaux de Lavoisier.* Paris: Imprimerie de la Feuille du Cultivateur, 1796.

French, Sydney J. "The Chemical Revolution: The Second Phase." *Journal of Chemical Education* 27 (1950): 83–8.

———. *Torch and Crucible: The Life and Death of Antoine Lavoisier.* Princeton, N. J.: Princeton University Press, 1941.

———. "The Du Ponts and the Lavoisiers: A Bit of Untold History with an Accent on America." *Journal of Chemical Education* 56 (1979): 781–93.

Fric, René. "Une lettre inédite de Lavoisier à B. Franklin." *Bulletin d'Histoire des Sciences d'Auvergne* 9 (1924): 145–52.

———. "Contribution à l'étude de l'évolution des idées de Lavoisier sur la nature de l'air et sur la calcination des métaux." *Archives Internationales d'Histoire des Sciences* 12 (1959): 137–68.

Fromont, H. *Essai sur l'administration de l'Assemblée provinciale de la généralité d'Orléans, 1787–1790.* Paris 1907.

Fulton, John F., Denis I. Duveen and Herbert S. Klickstein. "Antoine-Laurent Lavoisier's Reflexions sur les effets de l'éther nitreux dans l'économie animale." *Journal of the History of Medicine and Allied Sciences* 8 (1953): 318–23.

Gago, Ramon and Juan Carrillo. "A Bibliographical Study of the Reception of Lavoisier's Work in Spain: Addenda to a Bibliography by Duveen and Klickstein." *Ambix* 27 (1980): 19–25.

Gago, Ramon. "The New Chemistry in Spain." In Donovan, ed., *The Chemical Revolution*, pp. 169–92.

Gillispie, Charles C. "Notice biographique de Lavoisier par Madame Lavoisier." *Revue d'Histoire des Sciences* 9 (1956): 52–61.

Gough, Jerry B. "Lavoisier's Early Career in Science: An Examination of New Evidence." *British Journal for the History of Science* 4 (1968): 52–57.

———. "Nouvelle contribution à l'étude de l'évolution des idées de Lavoisier sur la nature de l'air et sur la calcination des métaux." *Archives Internationales d'Histoire des Sciences* 22 (1969): 267–75.

———. *The Foundations of Modern Chemistry: The Origin and Development of the Concept of the Gaseous State and Its Role in the Chemical Revolution of the Eighteenth Century.* Thesis, Cornell University, 1971. Ann Arbor: University of Michigan Microfilms, 1972.

———. "The Origins of Lavoisier's Theory of the Gaseous State." In Harry Woolf, ed.,*The Analytic Spirit: Essays on the History of Science in Honor of Henry Guerlac,* Ithaca, N. Y.: Cornell University Press, 1981, pp. 15–39.

———. "Some Early References to Revolutions in Chemistry." *Ambix* 29 (1982): 106–9.

———. "Lavoisier's Memoirs on the Nature of Water and Their Place in the Chemical Revolution." *Ambix* 30 (1983): 89–106.

———. "Lavoisier and the Fulfillment of the Stahlian Revolution,." In Donovan, ed., *The Chemical Revolution,* pp.15–33.

Gould, Stephen Jay. "The Passion of Antoine Lavoisier." *Annals of the Museum of Natural History* 98, 6 (1989): 16–22.

Goupil, Michelle. "La correspondance de Lavoisier." *Revue des Questions Scientifiques* 160 (1989): 191–203.

———. "Diffusion de la chimie française en Europe occidentale à travers la correspondance de Lavoisier." In *Échanges d'influences scientifiques et techniques entre pays européens de 1780 à 1830: Actes du 114e Congrès des sociétés savante, 3–9 avril 1989.* Paris: Editions du CTHS, 1990, pp.147–60.

———. "La description des Arts et Métiers." In Lavoisier, *Correspondance,* vol. V (1787–1788), Annexe V. Paris: Académie des Sciences, 1993, pp. 277–86.

———. "Claude Louis Berthollet, collaborateur et continuateur de Lavoisier." In M. Goupil, et al., *Lavoisier et la révolution chimique,* pp. 35–53.

——— et al., eds. *Lavoisier et la révolution chimique: Actes du colloque tenu à l'occasion du bicentenaire de la publication du "Traité élémentaire de chimie", 4–5 décembre 1989.* Palaiseau: SABIX-École Polytechnique, 1992.

Grave, E. "Une lettre inédite de Lavoisier au duc de Larochefoucauld." *Bulletin de la Société d'Histoire de la Pharmacie* 1 (1913): 59–61.

Greenbaum Louis S. O. "The Humanitarianism of Antoine-Laurent Lavoisier." *Studies on Voltaire and the Eighteenth Century* 88 (1972): 651–75.

Grimaux, Édouard. "Mort de Lavoisier." *Revue des Deux Mondes* 79 (1887): 884–930.

———. *Lavoisier, 1743-1794, d'après sa correspondance.* Paris: Alcan, 1888.

Grison, Emmanuel. "Hassenfratz et Lavoisier." In M. Goupil. et al., *Lavoisier et la révolution chimique,* pp. 51–62.

Guerlac, Henry. "Lavoisier and His Biographers." *Isis* 45 (1954): 51–62.

———. "A Note on Lavoisier's Scientific Education." *Isis* 47 (1956): 211–16.

———. "The Origin of Lavoisier's Work on Combustion." *Archives Internationales d'Histoire des Sciences* 12 (1959): 113–35.

———. "A Lost Memoir of Lavoisier." *Isis* 50 (1959): 125–29.

———. *Lavoisier, the Crucial Year: The Background and Origin of His First Experiments on Combustion in 1772.* Ithaca N. Y.: Cornell University Press, 1961.

———. "A Curious Lavoisier Episode." *Chymia* 7 (1961): 103–8.

———. "Laplace's Collaboration with Lavoisier." *Actes du XIIe Congrès International de l'Histoire des Sciences* 12 (1968): 31–36.

———. "Lavoisier, Antoine-Laurent." In Charles C. Gillispie, ed., *Dictionary of Scientific Biography.* New York: Scribner, 1970–80, 8: 66–91. Published as Henry

Guerlac, *Antoine-Laurent Lavoisier: Chemist and Revolutionary*. New York: Scribner, 1975.

———. "The Chemical Revolution: A Word from Monsieur Fourcroy." *Ambix* 23 (1976): 1–4.

———. "Chemistry as a Branch of Physics: Laplace's Collaboration with Lavoisier." *Historical Papers in Physical Sciences* 7 (1976): 193–276.

———. "The Lavoisier Papers: A Checkered History." *Archives Internationales d'Histoire des Sciences* 29 (1979): 95–100.

Guillaume, James. "Lavoisier anticlérical et révolutionnaire." *Cahiers de la Révolution Française* 26 (1907): 403–23; *Études Révolutionnaires* (1908): 354–79.

———. "Les idées de Lavoisier sur l'instruction sociale de l'enfance." *L'École Rénovée* 1 (1909): 23–30.

Guizot, François. "Madame de Rumford (1758–1836)." In Guizot, *Mélanges biographiques et littéraires*. Paris: Michel Lévy, 1868, pp. 49–88.

Hahn, Roger. "Fourcroy Advocate of Lavoisier?" *Archives Internationales d'Histoire des Sciences* 12 (1959): 285–86.

Halleux, R. "A propos des précurseurs de Lavoisier." *Revue des Questions Scientifiques* 160 (1989): 155–67

———. "La révolution lavoisienne en Belgique." In M. Goupil et al., *Lavoisier et la révolution chimique*, pp. 295–311.

Hahn, Roger. "Lavoisier et ses collaborateurs: une équipe au travail." In Demeulenaere-Douyère, ed., *Il y a 200 ans Lavoisier*, pp. 55–63.

Hartley, H. "Antoine-Laurent Lavoisier, 26 August 1743–8 May 1794." *Proceedings of the Royal Society*. 189 A (1947): 427–56.

Hartog, Philip. J. "The Newer Views of Priestley and Lavoisier." *Annals of Science* 5 (1941): 1–56.

Hollister, S. C. *Antoine-Laurent Lavoisier*. Ithaca, N. Y.: Cornell University Library, 1963.

Holmes, Frederic Lawrence. "Lavoisier and Krebs: The Individual Scientist in the Near and Deeper Past." *Isis* 75 (1984): 131–42.

———. *Lavoisier and the Chemistry of Life*, Madison-London: University of Wisconsin Press, 1985.

———. "Lavoisier's Conceptual Passage." In Donovan, ed., *The Chemical Revolution*, pp. 82–92.

———. "The Chemical Revolution." In Holmes, *Eighteenth Century Chemistry as an Investigative Entreprise*. Berkeley: University of California Office for History of Science and Technology, 1989.

———. "The Boundaries of Lavoisier's Chemical Revolution." *Revue d'Histoire des Sciences* 48 (1995): 9–48.

Holmyard, E. J. "An Unpublished Letter of Lavoisier." *Nature* (July 16, 1932): 97.

Houllevigne, L. "Lavoisier agronome." *Temps* 3 (1937).

Hunt, Leslie B. "The First Real Melting of Platinum: Lavoisier's Ultimate Success with Oxygen." *Platinum Metals Review* 26 (1982): 79–86.

Jacques, Jean. "Lavoisier et ses historiens français." *Revue des Questions Scientifiques* 160 (1989): 169–89.

Jennings, Richard. "Lavoisier's Views on Phlogiston and the Matter of Fire Before About 1770." *Ambix* 27 (1981): 206–9.

Kawashima, Keiko. "Image de Mme Lavoisier à travers les trois biographies de Lavoisier." *Kagakushi* 19 (1992): 188–204.

Kersaint, Georges. "Fourcroy a-t-il fait des démarches pour sauver Lavoisier?" *Revue Générale des Sciences* 65 (1958): 27–31.

———. "Lavoisier, Fourcroy et le scrutin épuratoire du Lycée de la rue de Valois." *Bulletin de la Société Chimique de France* 27 (1958): 259–60.

———. "A propos d'un article de Lucien Scheler sur une lettre de Fourcroy à Lavoisier." *Revue d'Histoire des Sciences* 16 (1963): 83–84.

Klooster, H. S. Van. "Franklin and Lavoisier." *Journal of Chemical Education* 23 (1946): 107–9.

Knight, David. "Crossing the Channel with the New Language." In Bensaude-Vincent et al., *Lavoisier in European Context: Negotiating a New Language for Chemistry*, pp. 143–54.

Kohler, Robert. E., Jr. "The Origin of Lavoisier's First Experiments on Combustion." *Isis* 63 (1972): 349–55.

Kremer, Richard. "Defending Lavoisier: The French Academic Prize Competition of 1821." *History and Philosophy of the Life Sciences* 8 (1986): 41–65.

Kritsman, Victor A. "Lavoisier's Contribution to the Appearance of Structural Concepts in Chemistry." *Janus* 73 (1986–1990): 29–37.

Lalande, J. J. Le François de. "Notice sur la vie et les ouvrages de Lavoisier." *Magasin Encyclopédique* 5–6 (1795): 174–88.

Langins, Janis. "Hydrogen Production for Ballooning During the French Revolution: An Early Example of Chemical Process Development." *Annals of Science* 40 (1983): 531–58.

"Lavoisier." *Vie des savants Illustres du XVIIIᵉ siècle*. Paris: Hachette, 1870, pp. 444–89.

Lavoisier and the Chemical Revolution: A Special Bicentennial Issue, ed. William B. Jensen. *Bulletin for the History of Chemistry* 5 (1989).

"Lavoisier." In *Les Cahiers de Science et Vie*. Special issue, no.14. Paris, April 1993.

Le Chatelier, Henri. *Lavoisier (Antoine-Laurent) [. . .] Traité élémentaire de chimie*. Paris: 1937.

Le Grand, Homer E. "Lavoisier's Oxygen Theory of Acidity." *Annals of Science* 29 (1973): 1–18.

———. "The Conversion of C. L. Berthollet to Lavoisier's Chemistry." *Ambix* 22 (1975): 58–70.

Leicester, Henry M. "The Spread of Lavoisier's Theory in Russia." *Chymia* 5 (1959): 138–44.

———. "Boyle, Lomonosov, Lavoisier, and the Corpuscular Theory of Matter." *Isis* 58 (1967): 240–44.

Lemay, P. "Lavoisier, iconographie française." *Bulletin de la Société Française d'Histoire de la Médecine* 28 (1934): 146–50.

———. "Les habitations de Lavoisier." *Bulletin de la Société Française d'Histoire de la Médecine* 28 (1934): 156–60.

———. "Généalogie, blason, ex libris, cachets de Lavoisier." *Bulletin de la Société Française d'Histoire de la Médecine* 28 (1934): 194–198.

———. "Jean Rey, précurseur de Torricelli, Pascal et Lavoisier." *Bulletin de la Société Française d'Histoire de la Médecine* 32 (1938): 148–63.

————. "La Pompe Funèbre de Lavoisier au Lycée des Arts." *Revue d'Histoire de la Pharmacie* 46 (1958): 230–37.

Lenglen, M. "Lavoisier agronome." Conférence faite à la réunion annuelle des directeurs des stations agronomiques et des laboratoires agricoles, 30 novembre 1936." *Bulletin des Engrais* (1936).

Leroux, Lucien and Désiré Leroux. *Lavoisier*. Nobles Vies, Grandes Oeuvres 12. Paris: Plon, 1928.

Levere, Trevor H. "Martinus van Marum (1750–1837): The Introduction of Lavoisier's Chemistry into the Low Countries." *Janus* 53 (1966): 115–34.

————. "Lavoisier, Language, Instruments and the Chemical Revolution." In Trevor H. Levere and William R. Shea, eds., *Nature, Experiments and the Sciences*. Dordrecht: Kluwer, 1990, pp. 207–23.

Levin, A. "Venel, Lavoisier, Fourcroy, Cabanis and the Idea of Scientific Revolution: The French Political Context and the General Patterns of the Conceptualization of Scientific Change." *History of Science* 22 (1984): 303–20.

LLana, James W. "A Contribution of Natural History to the Chemical Revolution in France." *Ambix* 32 (1985): 71–91.

Lodwig, T. H. and William A. Smeaton. "The Ice Calorimeter of Lavoisier and Laplace and Some of Its Critics, *Annals of Science* 31 (1975): 1–18.

Lomüller, L. "Lavoisier financier." *Chimie et Industrie* 63 (1950): 420–24.

Lopez, Claude A. "Saltpeter, Tin, and Gunpowder: Addenda to the Correspondence of Lavoisier and Franklin." *Annals of Science* 16 (1960): 83–94.

Lundgren, Anders. "The New Chemistry in Sweden." In Donovan, ed., *The Chemical Revolution*, pp. 146–68.

Marcus, Rebecca B. *Antoine Lavoisier and the Revolution in Chemistry*. New York: Watts, 1964.

Mauskopf, Seymour H. "Gunpowder and the Chemical Revolution." In Donovan, ed., *The Chemical Revolution*, pp. 93–118.

————. "Lavoisier and the Improvement of Gunpowder Production." *Revue d'Histoire des Sciences* 48 (1995): 95–124.

McDonald, E. "The Collaboration of Bucquet and Lavoisier." *Ambix* 13 (1965): 74–84.

McEvoy, John G. "Continuity and Discontinuity in the Chemical Revolution." In Donovan, ed., *The Chemical Revolution*, pp. 195–213.

————. "Priestley Responds to Lavoisier's Nomenclature: Language, Liberty, and Chemistry in the English Enlightenment." In Bensaude-Vincent et al., *Lavoisier in European Context: Negotiating a New Language for Chemistry*, pp. 123–42.

McKie, Douglas. "Lavoisier's Three Notes on Combustion, 1772." *Archeion* 14 (1932): 15–30.

————. *Antoine Lavoisier, the Father of Modern Chemisttry*. London: Victor Gollanez, 1935.

————. "Antoine-Laurent Lavoisier, 1743–1794." *Notes and Records of the Royal Society* 7 (1949): 1–41.

————. *Antoine Lavoisier: Scientist, Economist, Social Reformer*, London: Constable; New York: Schuman, 1952.

————. "On Some Pre-Publication Copies for Lavoisier's Traité (1789)." *Ambix* 9 (1961): 37–46.

————. *Antoine Lavoisier: Elements of Chemistry*, New York: Dover, 1965.

Meldrum, Andrew Norman. "Lavoisier's Work on the Nature of Water and the Supposed Transmutation of Water into Earth, 1768–1773." *Archeion* 14 (1932): 246–47.

———. "Lavoisier's Three Notes on Combustion." *Archeion* 14 (1932): 15–30.

———. "Lavoisier's Early Work in Science, 1763–1771." Part 1, *Isis* 19 (1933): 330–63; part 2, *Isis* 20 (1934): 396–425.

Melhado, Evan N. "Chemistry, Physics and the Chemical Revolution." *Isis* 76 (1985): 195–211.

———. "Towards an Understanding of the Chemical Revolution." *Knowledge and Society: Studies in the Sociology of Science Past and Present* 8 (1990): 123–37.

Metzger, Hélène. "Introduction à l'étude du rôle de Lavoisier dans l'histoire de la chimie." *Archeion* 14 (1932): 31–50.

———. *La philosophie de la matière chez Lavoisier*. Actualités Scientifiques et Industrielles. Paris: Hermann, 1935.

Mieli, Aldo. "Le rôle de Lavoisier dans l'histoire des sciences." *Archeion* 14 (1932): 51–56.

———. "Una Lettera di A. Lavoisier a J. Black." *Archeion* 25 (1943): 238–39.

Milne-Edwards, A. *Lavoisier: la chaleur et la respiration, 1770–1789*. Paris: G. Masson, 1892.

Morris, Robert J. "Lavoisier on Fire and Air: The Memoir of July 1772." *Isis* 60 (1969): 374–77. Guerlac's Reply, pp. 381–82.

———. "Lavoisier and the Caloric Theory." *British Journal for the History of Science* 6 (1972): 1–38.

Mousson-Lanauze. "Le Dr Jean Rey, précurseur de Lavoisier." *Bulletin de la Société Française d'Histoire de la Médecine* 16 (1922): 433–40.

Mulot. *Discours sur les funérailles et le respect dû aux morts*. Paris: Imprimerie de la Feuille du Cultivateur, 1796.

Musgrave, Alan. "Why did Oxygen Supplant Phlogiston?" In Colin Howson, ed., *Research Programs in the Chemical Revolution: Method and Appraisal in the Physical Sciences*, Cambridge: Cambridge University Press, 1976, pp. 181–209.

Partington, James R. "Lavoisier's Memoir on the Composition of Nitric Acid." *Annals of Science* 9 (1953): 96–98.

———. "The Discovery of Oxygen." *Journal of Chemical Education* 39 (1962): 123–25.

Perrin, Carleton Everett. "Prelude to Lavoisier's Theory of Calcination: Some Observations on Mercurius Calcinatus per se." *Ambix* 16 (1969): 140–51.

———. "Early Opposition to the Phlogiston Theory: Two Anonymous Attacks." *British Journal for the History of Science* 5 (1970): 128–44.

———. "Lavoisier's Table of Elements: A Reappraisal." *Ambix* 20 (1973): 95–105.

———. "Lavoisier, Monge and the Synthesis of Water: A Case of Pure Coïncidence?" *British Journal for the History of Science* 6 (1973): 424–28.

———. "A Reluctant Catalyst: Joseph Black and the Edinburgh Reception of Lavoisier's Chemistry." *Ambix* 29 (1982): 141–46.

———. "Did Lavoisier Report to the Academy of Sciences on His Own Book?" *Isis* 75 (1984): 343–48.

———. "Of Theory Shifts and Industrial Innovations: The Relations of J. A. C. Chaptal and A. L. Lavoisier." *Annals of Science* 43 (1986): 511–42.

———. "Lavoisier's Thoughts on Calcination and Combustion, 1772–1773." *Isis* 77 (1986): 6 47–66.

———. "Revolution or Reform. The Chemical Revolution and Eighteenth Century Concepts of Scientific Change." *History of Science* 25 (1987): 395–424.

———. "The Chemical Revolution: Shifts in Guiding Assumptions." In Arthur L. Donovan et al. eds., *Scrutinizing Science: Empirical Studies of Scientific Change*. Dordrecht: Kluwer, 1988, pp. 105–24.

———. "Research Traditions, Lavoisier, and the Chemical Revolution." In Donovan, ed., *The Chemical Revolution*, pp. 53–81.

———. "The Lavoisier-Bucquet Collaboration: A Conjecture." *Ambix* 36 (1989): 5–13.

———. "Document, Text and Myth: Lavoisier's Crucial Year Revisited." *British Journal for the History of Science* 22 (1989): 3–25.

———. "Chemistry as Peer of Physics: A Response to Donovan and Melhado on Lavoisier." *Isis* 81 (1990): 259–70.

Perrot, Jean-Claude. *Lavoisier: de la richesse territoriale du Royaume de France*. Paris: Editions du C.T.H.S, 1988.

———. "Les comptabilités économiques de Lavoisier." In Demeulenaere-Douyère, ed., *Il y a 200 ans Lavoisier*, pp. 95–110.

Phillips, T.D. "Lavoisier and Priestley." *Isis* 46 (1955): 53.

Poirier, Jean-Pierre. *Lavoisier, théoricien et praticien de l'économie*. Thèse de doctorat en sciences économiques de l'Université Panthéon-Assas, Paris, 1992.

———. *Antoine-Laurent de Lavoisier,1743-1794*. Paris: Pygmalion-Gérard Watelet, 1993.

———. "Marat et l'Académie des Sciences: le différent avec Lavoisier." In Jean Bernard, Jean François Lemaire and Jean Pierre Poirier, eds., *Marat, homme de science?* Paris: Les Empêcheurs de Penser en Rond, 1993, pp. 35–63.

———. "Antoine-Laurent de Lavoisier (1743–1794): industriel sous l'Ancien Régime." *L'Industrie Nationale* n.s. 1 (1993): 7–10.

———. "Antoine-Laurent Lavoisier, 1743–1794." Catalogue de l'exposition *Il y a 200 ans Lavoisier*, Chapelle de la Sorbonne, January-February 1994. Paris: Académie des Science, 1994, pp. 5–19. Also in *La Vie des Sciences. Comptes Rendus de l'Académie des Sciences* ser. gen. 11, 3 (1994): 197–221.

———. "Lavoisier et les idées de bienfaisance." Musée des Arts et Métiers, *La Revue* 6 (1994): 6–16.

———. "Le couple Lavoisier sous l'oeil de David." Musée des Arts et Métiers, *La Revue* 6 (1994): 26–29.

———. "Lavoisier et l'industrie chimique en France." *L'Actualité Chimique* 2 (March–April 1994): 40–43.

———. "Madame Lavoisier." *L'Actualité Chimique* 2 (March–April 1994): 44–47.

———. "Lavoisier: Fermier-général, banquier et commissaire de la Trésorerie Nationale." In Demeulenaere-Douyère, ed., *Il y a 200 ans Lavoisier*, pp. 111–34.

———. "Lavoisier recaudador general, banquero y comisario de la tesoreria general." In Patricia Aceves Pastrana, ed., *Las ciencias quimicas y biologicas en la formacion de un Mundo Nuevo*. México: Universidad Autonóma Metropolitana Unidad Xochimilco, 1995, pp. 31–47.

————. "How Du Pont Almost Began as Lavoisier Mills." *Chemical Heritage* 13, 1 (1995), pp.2–3.

————. "Lavoisier précurseur de Claude Bernard." *Histoire des Sciences Médicales* 30 (1996): 19–28.

Rappaport, Rhoda. "Biography and Portrait, Antoine-Laurent Lavoisier." *Journal of Nutrition* 79 (1963): 1–8.

————. "Lavoisier's Geologic Activities 1763–1792." *Isis* 58 (1967): 375–84.

————. "The Early Disputes Between Lavoisier and Monnet, 1779–1781." *British Journal for the History of Science* 4 (1969): 233–44.

————. "The Geological Atlas of Guettard, Lavoisier, and Monnet: Conflicting Views of the Nature of Geology." In Cecil J. Schneer, ed., *Toward a History of Geology*, Proceedings of the New Hampshire Interdisciplinary Conference on the History of Geology, 1967. Cambridge, Mass.: MIT Press, 1969.

————. "Lavoisier's Theory of the Earth." *British Journal for the History of Science* 6 (1973): 247–60.

Raymond-Latour, Jean Michel. *Souvenirs d'un oisif.* 2 vols. Lyon et Paris: Ayné Fils et Isidore Person, 1836. (BN: Microfiche Ln 27 17068).

Richet, Charles. "Lavoisier et la chaleur animale." *Revue Scientifique* 34 (1884): 141–46.

Riedman, Sarah Regal. *Antoine-Laurent Lavoisier, Scientist and Citizen.* Reissue, London: Abelard-Schuman, 1967.

Roberts, Lissa. "A Word and the World: The Significance of Naming the Calorimeter." *Isis* 82 (1991): 199–222.

————. "Condillac, Lavoisier, and the Instrumentalization of Science." *Eighteenth Century Theory and Interpretation* 33 (1992): 252–71.

————. "Science Dynamics: The Dutch Meat the "New" Chemistry." In Bensaude-Vincent et al., *Lavoisier in European Context: Negotiating a New Language for Chemistry*, pp. 87–112.

Rosenthal, M. J. "Lavoisier et son influence sur les progrès de la physiologie." *Revue Scientifique* 47 (1891): 33–42.

Salzberg, Hugh W. "Lavoisier and the Chemical Revolution." Chapter 12 in Salzberg, *From Caveman to Chemist: Circumstances and Achievements.* Washington, D. C.: American Chemical Society, 1991.

Savoie, Philippe. "Lavoisier et l'Assemblée Provinciale de l'Orléanais." In Lavoisier, *Correspondance*, vol. V (1787–1788), Annexe VII. Paris: Académie des Sciences, 1993, pp. 291–93.

Scheler, Lucien. *Lavoisier et la Révolution française.* Part I: *Le lycée des Arts*; part II: *Le journal de Fourgeroux de Bondaroy.* Paris: Hermann, 1956–1960.

————. "Note sur un portrait inconnu de Lavoisier." *Revue d'Histoire des Sciences* 14 (1961): 10–12.

————. "Antoine-Laurent Lavoisier et Michel Adanson, rédacteurs de programmes des prix à l'Académie des Sciences." *Revue d'Histoire des Sciences* 14 (1961): 257–84.

————. "Antoine-Laurent Lavoisier et le *Journal d'Histoire naturelle*." *Revue d'Histoire des Sciences* 14 (1961): 1–9.

————. "A propos d'une lettre de Fourcroy à Lavoisier du 3 septembre 1793." *Revue d'Histoire des Sciences* 15 (1962): 43–50.

————. *Lavoisier et le principe chimique* (Paris: Seghers, 1964).

———. "Lavoisier et la Régie des Poudres." *Revue d'Histoire des Sciences* 29 (1976): 194–222.

———. "Deux lettres inédites de Madame Lavoisier." *Revue d'Histoire des Sciences* 38 (1985): 121–30.

Scheler, Lucien and William A. Smeaton. "An Account of Lavoisier's Reconciliation with the Church a Short Time Before His Death." *Annals of Science* 14 (1958): 148–53.

Schelle, Gustave et Édouard Grimaux. *Lavoisier: statistique agricole et projets de réformes.* Paris. Guillaumin, 1894.

Sellier, François. "Un précurseur sans disciples: Lavoisier." *Économie Appliquée* (1948): 641–58.

Seminario internazionale per il bicentenario della scomparsa di Antoine Laurent Lavoisier (1743–1794). Roma, 20 ottobre 1994. Memorie di Scienze Fisiche e Naturali, vol. 112. Rendiconti della Accademia nazionale delle scienze detta dei XL, ser. 5, vol. 18 (1996).

Shimao, Eikoh. "The Reception of Lavoisier's Chemistry in Japan." *Isis* 63 (1972): 309–20.

Siegfried, Robert. "An Attempt in the United States to Resolve the Differences Between the Oxygen and the Phlogiston Theories." *Isis* 46 (1955): 327–36.

———. "Lavoisier's View of the Gaseous State and Its Early Application to Pneumatic Chemistry." *Isis* 63 (1972): 59–78.

———. "Lavoisier's Table of Simple Substances, Its Origin and Interpretation." *Ambix* 29 (1982): 29–48.

———. "Lavoisier and the Phlogistic Connection." *Ambix* 36 (1989): 31–40.

———. "The Chemical Revolution in the History of Chemistry." In Donovan, ed., *The Chemical Revolution*, pp. 34–52.

Siegfried, Robert and Betty J. Dobbs. "Composition: A Neglected Aspect of "The Chemical Revolution." *Annals of Science* 24 (1968): 275–93.

Smeaton, William A. "The Contributions of P. J. Macquer, P. O. Bergman, and L. B. Guyton de Morveau to the Reform of Chemical Nomenclature." *Annals of Science* 10 (1954): 87–106.

———. "The Early Years of the *Lycée* and the *Lycée des Arts*: A Chapter in the Lives of A. L. Lavoisier and A. F. de Fourcroy." *Annals of Science* 11 (1955): 257–67.

———. "Lavoisier's Membership of the *Société Royale d'Agriculture* and the *Comité d'Agriculture*." *Annals of Science* 12 (1956): 267–77.

———. "Lavoisier's Membership in the *Société Royale de Médecine*." *Annals of Science* 12 (1956): 228–44.

———. "*L'Avant-coureur*, the Journal in Which Some of Lavoisier's Earliest Research was Reported." *Annals of Science* 13 (1957): 219–34.

———. "Lavoisier's Membership in the Assembly of Representatives of the Commune of Paris: 1789–1790." *Annals of Science* 13 (1957): 235–48.

———. "New Light on Lavoisier: The Research of the Last Ten Years." *History of Science* 2 (1963): 51–69.

———. "Some Large Burning Lenses and Their Use by Eighteenth Century French and British Chemists." *Annals of Science* 44 (1987): 205–76.

———. "M. et Mme. Lavoisier in 1789: The Chemical Revolution and the French Revolution." *Ambix* 36 (1989): 1–4.

———. "Mme. Lavoisier, P. S. and E.I. Du Pont de Nemours and the Publication of Lavoisier's *Mémoires de Chimie.*" *Ambix* 36 (1989): 22–30.

Snelders, H. A. M. "The New Chemistry in the Netherlands." In Donovan, ed., *The Chemical Revolution*, pp. 121–45.

Stephenson, O. W. "The Supply of Gunpowder in 1776." *American Historical Review* 30 (1925): 271–81.

Storrs, F. C. "Lavoisier's Technical Reports, 1768–1794." *Annals of Science* 22 (1966): 251–75; 24 (1968): 179–97.

Szabadvary, Ferenc. *Antoine-Laurent Lavoisier: The Investigator and His Times, 1743–1794.* Cincinnati, Ohio: University of Cincinnati, 1977.

Thomson, Thomas. "Biographical Account of Monsieur Lavoisier." *Annals of Philosophy* 2 (1813): 81–92.

Toulmin, Stephen E. "Crucial Experiments: Priestley and Lavoisier." *Journal of the History of Ideas* 18 (1957): 205–220.

Truchot, Pierre. "Les instruments de Lavoisier: Relation d'une visite à la Canière (Puy de Dôme) où se trouvent réunis les appareils ayant servi à Lavoisier." *Annales de Chimie et de Physique* 18 (1879): 289–319.

Valentin, Michel. "Lavoisier et le travail des hommes." *Travail Humain* 42, 1 (1979): 105–12.

———. L'ergonomie à la fin du XVIIIe siècle." In Valentin *Travail des hommes.* Paris: Docis, 1978, pp. 124–58.

———. "Lavoisier et le problème méphitique des fosses d'aisance." In Lavoisier, *Correspondance*, vol. V (1787–1788), Annexe VI. Paris: Académie des Sciences, 1993, pp. 287–90.

———. "Lavoisier et les projets de reconstruction de l'Hôtel-Dieu." In Lavoisier, *Correspondance*, vol. V (1787–1788), Annexe II. Paris: Académie des Sciences, 1993, pp. 253–58.

Velluz, Léon. *Vie de Lavoisier.* Paris: Plon, 1966.

Vergnaud, Marguerite. "Science et progrès d'après Lavoisier." *Cahiers Internationaux de Sociologie* 15 (1953): 174–86.

———. "Un savant pendant la Révolution." *Archives Internationales de Sociologie* 17 (1954): 123–39.

Vergnaud, Marguerite and Denis I. Duveen. "L'explication de la mort de Lavoisier." *Archives Internationales d'Histoire des Sciences* 9 (1954): 43–50.

Viel, Claude. "Guyton-Morveau, père de la Nomenclature chimique." In Goupil et al., *Lavoisier et la révolution chimique*, pp. 129–70.

Voisin, M. E. "Lavoisier cultivateur vendômois." *Bulletin de la Société Archéologique de Blois* (April 1969): 71–74.

Yoshida, A. "Une nouvelle interprétation de la genèse des expériences de Lavoisier sur la combustion en 1773." *Historia Scientiarium* 36 (1984): 83–94.

III. Works of General History, Economic History,
and History of Science

Aftalion, Florin. *L'économie de la Révolution française.* Paris: Hachette, 1987.

Aftalion, Fred. *Histoire de la chimie.* Paris: Masson, 1988. English. *A History of the*

International Chemical Industry, trans. Otto Theodor Benfey. Philadelphia: University of Pennsylvania Press, 1991.

Albury, William Randall. *The Logic of Condillac and the Structure of French Chemical and Biological Theory, 1780–1801*. Baltimore: Johns Hopkins University Press, 1972.

Allain, Eugène. *L'oeuvre scolaire de la Révolution 1789–1802*. Paris, 1891.

Ameller, Michel, André Passeron, and Marie Renault. *1789–1989: L'Assemblée Nationale*. Paris: Hachette, 1989.

Arkhipoff, Oleg. "A propos d'un bicentenaire: Lavoisier. 'De la richesse du royaume de France'." *Journal de la Société de Statistique de Paris* 1 (1990): 37–55.

———. "Une révolution dans la Révolution: Condorcet, Lavoisier et Peuchet. La pensée économique pendant la Révolution française." Actes du colloque international de Vizille, 6–8 septembre 1989, *Économie et Sociétés* 24 (1990): 363–70.

Aubry, Paul. *Monge: le savant ami de Napoléon Bonaparte, 1746–1818*. Paris: Gauthier-Villars, 1954.

Augeard, J. M. *Mémoires secrets, 1760–1800*. Paris: Plon, 1866.

Aulard, François Alphonse. *La société des Jacobins: Recueil de documents pour l'histoire du Club des Jacobins de Paris*. Paris: Jouaust-Noble-Quantin, 1889.

———. *L'histoire politique de la Révolution française*. Paris: Colin, 1901.

Bachaumont, Louis Petit de. *Mémoires secrets pour servir à l'histoire de la république des lettres en France depuis 1762 jusqu'à nos jours*. 36 vols. London: John Adamson, 1781–1789. Reprint Westmead, Hants.: Gregg International, 1980.

Badinter, Élisabeth et Robert Badinter. *Condorcet. (1743–1794): Un intellectuel en politique*. Paris: Fayard, 1988.

Bailly, Jean Sylvain and Honoré, baron Duveyrier. *Procès verbal des séances de délibération de l'assemblée générale des électeurs de Paris*. 3 vols. Paris: Baudouin, 1790.

Bailly, Jean Sylvain. *Mémoires*. 3 vols. Paris: Levrault-Schoell, 1804.

Baker, Keith M. "Les débuts de Condorcet au secrétariat de l'Académie Royale des Sciences (1773–1776)." *Revue d'Histoire des Sciences* 20 (1967): 229–80.

———. "Political and Social Science in Eighteenth-Century France: The Société de 1789." In John Francis Bosher, ed., *French Government and Society, 1500–1850*. London: Athlone Press of the University of London, 1973, pp. 208–30.

———. *Condorcet: From Natural Philosophy to Social Mathematics*. Chicago: University of Chicago Press, 1975.

———. *Condorcet: raison et politique*. Paris: Hermann, 1988.

Banque de France. *Notice historique sur la Caisse d'Escompte*. Paris. Archives de la Banque de France.

Barthélemy, Guy. *Les Savants sous la Révolution*. Le Mans: Cénomane, 1988.

Baudeau, Abbé. "Explication du tableau économique." In *Ephémérides 1767–1768*. Paris: Delalain, 1776.

Baumé, Antoine. *Chymie expérimentale et raisonnée*. 4 vols. Paris: Didot, 1774.

Béaud, M. "Le Bureau de la balance du commerce, 1781–1791." *Revue d'Histoire de l'Économie et des Sociétés* 3 (1964): 357–77.

Beer, John. "Eighteenth Century Theories on the Process of Dyeing." *Isis* 51 (1960): 21–30.

Bekerman, Gérard. *La comptabilité nationale: histoire, concepts, critique*. Paris: Presses Universitaires de France, 1985.

Bensaude-Vincent, Bernadette and Isabelle Stengers. *Histoire de la chimie.* Paris: La Découverte, 1993.

Béraud, P. L. *Dissertation sur la cause de l'augmentation de poids que certaines matières acquièrent dans la calcination.* Bordeaux: Brun, 1741.

Bertrand, J. *L'Académie des Sciences et les académiciens de 1666 à 1793.* Paris: J. Hetzel, 1869.

Bésenval, Pierre Victor, baron de. *Mémoires.* 4 vols. Paris: chez F. Buisson, 1805–1807.

Beugnot, J. C. *Mémoires, 1783–1815.* Paris: E. Dentu,1866.

Bigo, Robert. *La Caisse d'Escompte (1776–1793) et les origines de la Banque de France.* Thèse. Paris: 1927.

———. *Les bases historiques de la finance moderne.* Paris: A. Colin, 1933.

Biot, Jean Baptiste. *Essai sur l'histoire générale des sciences pendant la Révolution française.* Paris: Duprat, An XI (1803).

Birembaut, Arthur. "L'Académie Royale des Sciences en 1780 vue par l'astronome suédois Lexell,1740–1784." *Revue d'Histoire des Sciences* 10 (1957): 148–66.

Black, Joseph. *Experiment upon Magnesia Alba, Quick Lime, and Some other Alcaline Substances.* 1755. Alambic Club reprints, 1. Edinburgh: William F. Clay, 1898.

Blanc, Olivier. *La corruption sous la Terreur.* Paris: Laffont, 1992.

Blanqui, Auguste. *Histoire de l'économie politique en Europe depuis les anciens jusqu'à nos jours.* 2 vols. Paris: Guillaumin, 1842.

Bloch, Camille. *Procès-verbaux du comité des Finances de l'Assemblée Constitutuante.* Rennes: Oberthur, 1922.

Bluche, François. *La vie quotidienne en France au temps de la Révolution (1788–1795).* Paris: Hachette, 1983.

Boas, Marie (Hall). *Robert Boyle and Seventeenth Century Chemistry.* Cambridge: Cambridge University Press, 1958.

———. "The History of the Concept of Element." In D. S. L. Cardwell, ed., *John Dalton and the Progress of Science: Papers presented to a Congress of Historians.* New York: Barnes and Noble, 1968, pp. 21–39.

Boiteau, Paul. *Etat de la France en 1789.* Paris: Guillaumin, 889.

Boklund, Uno, ed. *Karl Wilhelm Scheele: His Work and Life.* Stockholm, 1961.

Bosher, John Francis. "Jacques Necker et l'État moderne." *Bulletin de la Société Historique du Canada.* (1963).

———. *French Finances, 1770–1795: From Business to Bureaucracy.* Cambridge: Cambridge University Press, 1970.

———. *The French Revolution.* New York-London: W. W. Norton, 1988.

———, ed. *French Government and Society, 1500–1850.* London: Athlone Press of the University of London, 1973.

Bouchary, Jean. *Le marché des changes à Paris à la fin du XVIIIe siècle (1778–1800).* Paris: Hartmann, 1937.

———. *Les compagnies financières à Paris à la fin du XVIIIe siècle.* 3 vols. Paris: Rivière, 1940–1942.

———. *Les manieurs d'argent à Paris à la fin du XVIIIe siècle,* 3 vols. Paris: Rivière, 1939–1943.

———. *L'eau à Paris à la fin du XVIIIe siècle: la Compagnie des eaux de Paris et l'entreprise de l'Yvette.* Paris: Rivière, 1946.

———. *Les faux-monnayeurs sous la Révolution française.* Paris: Rivière, 1946.

Bouloiseau, Marc. *Bourgeoisie et Révolution: les Du Pont de Nemours*. Paris: Bibliothèque Nationale, 1972.

Bourde, André J. *The Influence of England on the French Agronomes, 1750–1789*. Cambridge: Cambridge University Press, 1953.

———. *Agronomie et agronomes en France au XVIIIe siècle*. 3 vols. Paris: SEVPEN, 1967.

Bourquin, Marie-Hélène and Emmanuel Hepp. *Aspects de la contrebande au XVIIIe siècle*. Paris: Presses Universitaires de France, 1969.

Bouyer, Christian. *Les hommes d'argent: histoire des grandes fortunes de France du XVIIIe siècle à 1914*. Paris: Olivier Orban, 1990.

Braesch, Frédéric 1911—*La Commune de 1792: histoire de Paris du 20 juin au 2 décembre 1792*. Paris: Hachette, 1911.

———. *Finances et monnaie révolutionnaires, recherche, études et documents*. 2 vols. Vol. I, *Les exercices budgétaires 1790 et 1791 d'après les comptes du Trésor*. Nancy: 1934. Vol. II, *Les recettes et les dépenses du Trésor pendant l'année 1789*. Paris: La Maison du Livre Français, 1936.

———. *1789, L'année cruciale*. Paris: Gallimard, 1941.

Braudel, Fernand and Ernest Labrousse. *Histoire économique et sociale de la France, 1660–1789*. 3 vols. Paris: Presses Universitairs de France, 1970–1976.

Bredin, Jean-Denis. *Sieyès, la clé de la Révolution française*. Paris: Editions de Fallois, 1988.

Brissot de Warville, Jacques-Pierre. *Mémoires*. 4 vols. Paris: Ladvocat, 1830–1832.

Bruguière, Michel. *Gestionnaires et profiteurs de la Révolution*. Paris: Olivier Orban, 1986.

———. *Pour une renaissance de l'histoire financière, XVIIIe–XXe siècles*. Comité pour l'histoire économique et financière de la France. Paris: Ministère des Finances, 1992.

Buchez, J. B. and P. C. Roux-Lavergne *Histoire parlementaire de la Révolution française ou Journal des Assemblées nationales depuis 1789 jusqu'en 1815*. Paris: Paulin, 1934.

Butterfield, Herbert. *The Origins of Modern Science, 1300–1800*. New York: Collier, 1962.

Cambon, Joseph. *Rapport sur le compte des recettes et dépenses de la nation depuis le 1er mai 1789 jusqu'au 1er septembre 1793, qui a été présenté par les Commissaires de la Trésorerie Nationale, fait au nom du Comité des finances à la séance du 3 germinal An II*. Bibliothèque Nationale: 8° Le 38 736.

Campardon. *Tribunal révolutionnaire de Paris*. 2 vols. Paris: Plon, 1866.

Carré, H. "Le premier ministre Necker, 1776–1781." *Bulletin de la Société d'Histoire de la Révolution Française* (February 1903).

Castelnau, Jacques Thomas. *Marat, l'ami du peuple? 1744–1793*. Corbeil: Chez Crété, 1939.

Cavendish, Henry. *Experiments on Air*. Alembic Club Reprints, 3, Edinburgh: William F. Clay, 1895.

Chaldecott, J. A. "Scientific Activities in Paris in 1791." *Annals of Science* 24 (1968): 21–52.

Challamel, Augustin. *Les clubs contre-révolutionnaires*. Paris: Cerf, 1895. Reprint New York: AMS Press, 1974.

Challamel, Augustin and Wilhelm Tenin. *Les Français sous la Révolution*. Paris: Challamel, undated.

Chambon, receveur général des finances. *Traité général du commerce de l'Amérique.* 2 vols. Amsterdam: Marc-Michel Rey, 1783.

Chaptal, Jean Antoine. *Éléments de Chymie.* Paris: Deterville, 1795.

Chapuisat, Édouard. *Necker, 1732–1804.* Paris: 1938.

Charavay, E. *Assemblée électorale de Paris: 2 septembre 1792–17 frimaire An II.* 2 vols. Paris: Cerf, 1890–1925. Reprint New York: AMS Press, 1974.

Chassin, Charles Louis. *Les élections de Paris en 1789*: 4 vols. Paris: Jouhaust et Sigaux-Noblet-Maison Quantin, 1888–1889.

Chaussinand-Nogaret, Guy—*Gens de finance au XVIIIe siècle.* Paris: Bordas, 1972. Reprint. Paris: Complexe, 1993.

Chevallier, Pierre. *Histoire de la franc-maçonnerie française*, 3 vols. Paris: Fayard, 1974.

Christie, John R. R. and J. V. Golenski. "The Spreading of the World." *History of Science* 20 (1982): 235–66.

Clavreuil, Bernard. *La marche des sciences pendant la Révolution.* Paris: Librairie Thomas-Scheler, 1989.

Clément, Pierre and Alfred Lemoine. *MM. de Silhouette, Bouret, les derniers fermiers généraux.* Paris: Didier, 1872.

Clément, Pierre Louis. *Les Montgolfières, leur invention, leur évolution du XVIIIe siècle à nos jours.* Paris: Tardy, 1982.

Coissin, Philippe E. *Almanach des prisons. Tableau des prisons de Paris, sous le règne de Robespierre, pour faire suite à l'Almanach des prisons. Second tableau des prisons sous le règne de Robespierre.* Paris: Michel, An III (1795).

Collection complète de tous les ouvrages pour et contre M. Necker avec des notes critiques, politiques et secrètes. 3 vols. Utrecht, 1781.

Condillac, Etienne Bonnot, Abbé de. *Le commerce et le gouvernement considérés relativement l'un à l'autre.* Paris: Jombert and Cellot, 1776.

———. *Oeuvres choisies.* 2 vols. Paris: 1796.

Condorcet, J. A. N. Caritat de. *Oeuvres complètes*, ed. A. Condorcet O'Connor and M. F. Arago, 12 vols. Paris: Didot Frères, 1847–1849.

———. *Esquisse d'un tableau historique des progrès de l'esprit humain.* Paris: Agasse, An III (1795).

———. *Arithmétique politique: textes rares ou inédits, 1767–1789*, ed. Bernard Bru and Pierre Crépel. Paris: Institut National d'Etudes Démographiques, 1994.

Coquereau, Jean Baptiste Louis. *Mémoires de l'Abbé Terrai, Controlleur-Général des Finances.* London, 1776.

Cormeré, baron Mahy de. *Mémoire sur les finances et le crédit.* Paris: Chez l'auteur, 1789.

———. *Recherches et considérations nouvelles sur les finances.* 2 vols. London, 1789.

Crosland, Maurice P. *Historical Studies in the Language of Chemistry* Cambridge; Mass.: Harvard University Press, 1962.

———. "The Development of Chemistry in the Eighteenth Century." *Studies on Voltaire and the Eighteenth Century* 24 (1963): 369–441.

———. *The Society of Arcueil: A View of French Science at the Time of Napoléon I.* Cambridge, Mass.: Harvard University Press, 1967.

Crouzet, François. *La grande inflation: la monnaie en France de Louis XVI à Napoléon.* Paris: Fayard, 1993.

Custine, comte de. *Réflexions sur la proposition du premier ministre des Finances de sanc-*

tionner comme caisse nationale la Caisse d'Escompte appartenant à des capitalistes. Paris: Baudouin, 1789.

Cuvier, Georges. *Recueil des éloges historiques lus dans les séances publiques de l'Institut Royal de France.* 3 vols. Strasbourg: Levrault, 1819–1827.

———. *Rapport historique sur les progrès des sciences naturelles depuis 1789, et sur leur état actuel.* Paris: Verdière et Lagrange, 1828.

Dagognet, François.*Tableaux et langage de la chimie.* Paris: Le Seuil, 1969.

Daire, Eugène and G. de Molinari. *Mélanges d'économie politique.* Paris: Guillaumin, 1847.

Darnton, Robert. *Mesmerism and the End of the Enlightenment in France.* Cambridge, Mass.: Harvard University Press, 1968.

Darnton, Robert and Daniel Roche. *Revolution in Print: The Press in France, 1775–1800.* Berkeley: University of California Press, 1989.

Dauban, C. A. *Paris en 1794 et en 1795, histoire de la rue, du club et de la famine.* Paris: Plon, 1869.

———. *Les prisons de Paris sous la Révolution.* Paris: Plon, 1870.

Daumas, Maurice. *Les cabinets de physique au XVIIIe siècle.* Alençon: Imprimerie de Poulet-Malassis, 1951.

———. *Les instruments scientifiques aux XVIIe et XVIIIe siècles.* Paris: Presses Universitaires de France, 1953.

———. *Histoire de la Science.* Paris: Gallimard, Encyclopédie la Pléiade, 1957.

Daumas, Maurice et al. *Histoire générale des techniques.* 5 vols. Paris: Presses Universitaires de France, 1962–1979.

Delâcre, M. *Histoire de la Chimie.* Paris: 1920.

Delahante, Adrien. *Une famille de finance au XVIIIe siècle: mémoires, correspondance et papiers de famille.* 2 vols. Paris: J. Hetzel, 1881.

De Place, Dominique. "Le Bureau de Consultation pour les Arts, Paris, 1791–1796." *History and Technology* 5 (1988): 139–78.

Désortiaux, E. *Traité sur la poudre, les corps explosifs et la pyrotechnie.* Paris: Dunod, 1878.

Despois, Eugène. *Le vandalisme révolutionnaire.* Paris: Germer Baillière, 1868.

Dhombres, Nicole and Jean Dhombres. *Naissance d'un pouvoir: sciences et savants en France, 1793–1824.* Paris: Payot, 1989.

Diderot, Denis. *Eléments de Physiologie.* Paris: Didier, 1964.

Diesbach, Ghislain de. *Necker, ou la faillite de la vertu.* Paris: Germer Baillière, 1978.

Doyle, William. *Origins of the French Revolution.* Oxford: Oxford University Press, 1980.

Duhem, Pierre. *La chimie est-elle une science française?* Paris: Hermann, 1916.

Dull, Jonathan R. *The French Navy and American Independence: A Study of Arms and Diplomacy, 1774–1787.* Princeton N. J.: Princeton University Press, 1975.

———. "France and the American Revolution Seen as a Tragedy." In Ronald T. Hoffman and Peter J. Albert, eds., *Diplomacy and Revolution: The Franco-American Alliance of 1778.* Charlottesville: University Press of Virginia, 1981, pp. 73–106.

———. *Franklin the Diplomat: The French Mission.* Transactions of the American Philosophical Society 72 pt. 1, Philadelphia: American Philosophical Society, 1982.

Dumas, Jean-Baptiste. *Leçons sur la philosophie chimique.* Paris: Gauthier-Villars, 1837

Dupin, Antoine. *Rapport fait au nom des comités de Sûreté générale, des Finances et de l'examen des Comptes, réunis à la commission, sur l'administration des ci-devant Fermiers-généraux*. Paris: Imprimerie Nationale, 16 Floréal An II (1794).

———. *Motion d'ordre et exposé fidèle de tout ce qui s'est passé dans l'affaire des Fermiers-généraux, assassinés par la faction Robespierre et ses complices le 16 floréal An II, par le Tribunal révolutionnaire*. Paris: Imprimerie Nationale, Floréal An III (1795).

———. *Réponse à la dénonciation présentée par les veuves et enfants des ci-devant Fermiers-généraux*. Paris: Imprimerie Nationale, undated (1795).

Dupin, Motet, Chateauneuf, Jaquart, Godot, Vernon. *Rapport des commissaires réviseurs des trois compagnies des finances aux représentants du peuple*. Paris: 16 floréal An II (1794).

Du Pont de Nemours, Bessie Gardner. *Life of Pierre Samuel Du Pont de Nemours, 1739–1817*. 2 vols. Newark, Del.: Press of Kells, 1933.

———. *Life of Éleuthère Irénée Du Pont from Contemporary Correspondence, 1778–1834*, 11 vols. Newark, University of Delaware Press,1923–1936.

Du Pont de Nemours, Pierre Samuel. *Mémoires sur la vie et les ouvrages de M. Turgot, Ministre d'Etat*. Philadelphia, 1782.

———. *Mémoires de Pierre Samuel Du Pont adressés à ses enfants*, septembre 1792. Ms. W 2 4796, group 2, series B, box 28, Hagley Museum and Library, Wilmington, Delaware.

———. *Principes et recherches sur la philosophie de l'univers*, 22 décembre 1792. Ms. 34, group 8, series A, box 8, Hagley Museum and Library, Wilmington, Delaware. 3rd ed., Paris: Du Pont, 1799.

———. *Lettres de Du Pont de Nemours: écrites de la prison de la Force*, ed. Gilbert Chinard. Paris: Librairie Historique A. Margraff,1929.

———. *Correspondance of Mme. de Staël and Pierre Samuel Du Pont de Nemours and Other Members of the Necker and du Pont families*, ed. James F. Marshall. Madison: University of Wisconsin Press, 1968.

———. *Oeuvres politiques et économiques,1763–1817*. Intro. Elizabeth Fox Genovese. 10 vols. Nendeln: KTO Press, 1979.

———. *The autobiography of Du Pont de Nemours*, trans. Elizabeth Fox Genovese, Wilmington, Del.: Scholarly Resources Inc., 1984.

Durand de Maillane. *Histoire de la Convention nationale*. Paris: Baudouin, 1825.

Durand, Yves. *Les Fermiers généraux au XVIIIe siècle*. Paris: Faculté des Sciences Humaines de Paris Sorbonne, Recherches, vol. 70, 1971.

———. *Finance et mécénat: les Fermiers généraux au XVIIIe siècle*. Paris: Hachette, 1976.

———. *La société française au XIIIe siècle*. Paris: SEDES, 1992.

Duveyrier. *Histoire des premiers électeurs de Paris en 1789*, Bruxelles, 1858.

Echanges d'influences scientifiques et techniques entre pays européens de 1780 à 1830. Actes du 114e congrès des sociétés savantes, Paris, 3–9 avril 1989. Paris: Editions du CTHS, 1990.

Egret, Jean. *La révolution des notables: Mounier et les monarchiens, 1789*. Paris: Armand Colin, 1950.

———. *La pré-Révolution française, 1787–1788*. Paris: Presses Universitaires de France, 1962.

———. *Necker, ministre de Louis XVI*. Paris: Champion, 1975.

Ehrmann, Friedrich Ludwig. *Essai d'un art de fusion à l'aide de l'air du feu ou air vital, suivi des mémoires de M. Lavoisier sur le même sujet*. Strasbourg: Treuttel; Paris: Cuchet, 1787.

Etat, finances et économie pendant la Révolution française. Actes du colloque de Bercy organisé par le Comité pour l'histoire économique et financière de la France les 12 et 13 Octobre 1989. Paris: Imprimerie Nationale, 1991.

Etner, François. *Histoire du calcul économique en France*. Paris: Economica, 1987.

Etrennes financières ou recueil des matières les plus importantes en finance, banque et commerce. Paris: 1789.

Faccarello, Gilbert and Philippe Steiner, eds., *La pensée économique pendant la Révolution française*. Actes du colloque International de Vizille. Grenoble: Presses Universitaires de Grenoble, 1990.

Faure, Edgar. *La disgrâce de Turgot*. Paris: Gallimard, 1961.

Fay, Bernard. *Louis XVI ou la fin d'un monde*. Paris: Amiot-Dumont, 1955.

Fayet, Joseph. *La Révolution française et la science, 1789–1795*. Paris: Rivière, 1960.

Ferrières, C. E. de. *Mémoires pour servir à l'histoire de l'Assemblée Constituante et de la Révolution de 1789*. 3 vols. Paris: Marchands de Nouveautés, An VII (1799).

Fichman, M. "French Stahlism and Chemical Studies of Air, 1751–1779." *Ambix* 18 (1971): 94–122.

Fiechter, Jean-Jacques. *Un diplomate américain sous la Terreur: les années européennes de Gouverneur Morris, 1789–1798*. Paris: Fayard, 1983.

Finocchiaro, Maurice A. *History of Science as Explanation*. Detroit: Wayne State University Press, 1973.

Flori, Sabien. *Le Comité de Trésorerie 1791*. Thèse pour le doctorat. Paris: Daumat-Chrétien, 1939.

Forbonnais, François Véron de. *Recherches et considérations sur les finances de la France*, 2 vols. Bâle: Cramer Frères, 1758.

Fourastié, Jean. *Prix de vente et prix de revient*. Paris: Domat-Monchrestien, 1949.

Fourcroy, Antoine François de. *Philosophie chimique ou vérités fondamentales de la chimie moderne*. Paris: Cl. Simon, 1792.

———. *Système des connaissances chimiques et de leurs Applications, aux phénomènes de la nature et de l'art*. 6 vols. Paris: Baudouin, An IX (1801).

Fourquet, F. *Les comptes de la puissance, histoire de la comptabilité nationale et du plan*. Paris: 1980.

Fox, Robert. *The Caloric Theory of Gases, from Lavoisier to Regnault*, Oxford: Oxford University Press, 1971.

Franklin, Benjamin. *Correspondance inédite et secrète [. . .] depuis 1753 jusqu'en 1790*. Paris: Janet Père, 1817.

Frénilly, François-Auguste Fauveau, baron de. *Souvenirs*, ed. Arthur Chuquet. Paris: Plon-Nourrit, 1909.

Furet, François and Denis Richet. *La Révolution française*. 2 vols. Paris: Hachette, 1965–1966.

Gabbay, John. "Clinical Medicine in Revolution." *British Medical Journal* 299 (1989): 106–9, 166–69.

Galiani, Ferdinando, Abbé. *Lettres*. 2 vols. Paris: Charpentier, 1881–1882.

Garat, Dominique Joseph, comte. *Mémoires historiques sur le XVIIIe siècle et sur M. Suard*. Paris: Belin, 1821.

Gascar, Pierre. *Album des écrivains de la Révolution*. Paris: Gallimard, 1988.

Gatteaux. *Aperçu sur la fabrication des assignats*. Paris: Imprimerie de la Rue Mélé, 1793.

Gaudin, Michel, duc de Gaëte. *Mémoires, souvenirs, opinions et écrits*. 3 vols. Paris: Baudouin, 1826.

————. *Considérations sur la dette publique de France, sur l'emprunt en général et sur l'amortissement*. Paris: J. Tastu, 1828.

Gayot, Gérard and Jean-Pierre Hirsch, eds. *La Révolution française et le développement du capitalisme*. Actes du colloque de Lille, 19–21 novembre 1987. *Revue du Nord*, special issue 5, 1989.

Getman, F. H. "Sir Charles Blagden." *Osiris* 3 (1937): 69–87.

Gide, Charles and Charles Rist. *Histoire des doctrines économiques depuis les physiocrates jusqu'à nos jours*. Paris: Librairie du Recueil Sirey, 1926.

Gignoux, Claude Joseph. *La planche à assignats*. Paris: 1933.

Gignoux, C. J. *Turgot*. Paris: A. Fayard, 1945.

Gille, B. *Histoire des Techniques: techniques et civilisations*. Paris: Encyclopédie Pléiade, Gallimard, 1978.

Gille, Bertrand. *Les sources statistiques de l'histoire de france: les enquêtes du XVIIIe siècle à 1870*. Geneva, 1964. 2d ed. Paris: Droz, 1988.

Gillispie, Charles Coulston. The *Encyclopédie* and the Jacobin Philosophy of Science: A Study in Ideas and Consequences." In Marshall Clagett, ed., *Critical Problems in the History of Science*. Madison: University of Wisconsin Press, 1959, pp. 255–89.

————. *The Edge of Objectivity: An Essay in the History of Scientific Ideas*. Princeton, N. J.: Princeton University Press, 1960.

————. *Science and Polity in France at the End of the Old Regime*. Princeton, N. J.: Princeton University Press, 1980.

————. *The Montgolfier Brothers and the Invention of Aviation, 1783-1784*. Princeton N. J.: Princeton University Press, 1983

————, ed. *Dictionary of Scientific Biography*. 16 vols. New York: Scribner, 1970–80.

Glaser, Christophle. *Traité de la chymie*, Lyon: Chez Bailly, 1670.

Godechot, Jacques. *La prise de la Bastille, 14 juillet 1789*. Paris: Gallimard, 1965.

————. *Les institutions de la France sous la Révolution et l'Empire*. Paris: Presses Universitaires de France, 1968.

Gomel, Charles. *Les causes financières de la Révolution française*. 2 vols. Paris: Guillaumin, 1892.

————. *Histoire financière de l'Assemblée Constituante*. 2 vols. Paris: Guilaumin, 1896.

————. *Histoire financière de la Legislative et de la Convention*. 2 vols. Paris: Guillaumin, 1902.

Gondolff, Édouard. *Le tabac sous l'ancienne monarchie: la Ferme Royale, 1639-1791*. Vesoul, 1914.

Goupil, Michelle. *Le chimiste Claude Louis Berthollet, 1748-1822: sa vie, son oeuvre*. Paris: Vrin, 1977.

Grange, Henri. *Les idées de Necker*. Paris: Klincksieck, 1974.

Grégoire, Henri, Abbé. *Mémoires ecclésiastiques, politiques et littéraires*. Paris: A. Dupont, 1837.

Grison, Emmanuel, Michelle Goupil and Patrice Bret, eds. *A Scientific Correspondence During the Chemical Revolution: Louis Bernard Guyton de Morveau and Richard Kirwan, 1782-1802*. Berkeley: University of California Office for History of Science and Technology, 1994.

Grouchy, Vicomte E. de and P. Cottin. *Journal inédit du duc de Croÿ (1718–1784)*. 4 vols. Paris: Flammarion, 1907.

Grouchy, Vicomte E. de and A. Guillois. *La Révolution française racontée par un diplomate étranger: Correspondance du Bailly de Virieu, Ministre plénipotentiaire de Parme (1788–1798)*. Paris: E. Flammarion, undated. Bibliothèque Nationale: Microfiche 8° La32 771.

Gruber, Howard, E. "On the Relation Between the Experiences and the Construction of Ideas." *History of Science* 19 (1981): 41–59.

Guedj, Denis. *La méridienne (1792–1799)*. Paris: Seghers, 1987.

Guedj, D. *La révolution des savants*. Paris: Gallimard, 1988.

Guerlac, Henry. "Joseph Priestley's First Papers on Gases and Their Reception in France." *Journal for the History of Medicine and Allied Sciences* 12 (1957): 1–12.

———. "Some French Antecedents of the Chemical Revolution." *Chymia* 5 (1959): 73–112.

———. "Quantification in Chemistry." *Isis* 52 (1961): 194–214.

Guichard, Marcel. *Essais historiques sur les mesures en chimie*. Paris: 1937.

Guichen, vicomte de. *Crépuscule d'Ancien Régime*. Paris: Perrin, 1909.

Guillaume, James. *Procès verbaux du comité d'Instruction publique de la Convention nationale*. Vol. II. Paris: Imprimerie Nationale, 1894.

———. "Un mot légendaire: la République n'a pas besoin de savants." *Révolution Française* (May 1900). Also *Etudes Révolutionnaires* (1908): 136–55.

Guillois, Antoine. *Le salon de Madame Helvétius, Cabanis et les idéologues*. Paris: Calmann Lévy, 1894, pp. 240–43. (BN: microfiche 16° Li2 119 B.

Hahn, Roger. *The Anatomy of a Scientific Institution: The Paris Academy of Sciences 1666–1803*. Berkeley-Los Angeles-London: University of California Press,1971.

———. "Scientific Research as an Occupation in Eighteenth Century Paris." *Minerva* 13 (1975): 501–13.

Hales, Stephen. *Vegetable Staticks: or An Account of some Statical Experiments on theSap in Vegetables: Being an Essay Towards a Natural History of Vegetation*. London: W. and J. Innys, 1727. French. *La statique des végétaux et celle des animaux*, trans. Buffon. Paris: Imprimerie de Monsieur, 1779.

Hall, A. Rupert. *The Scientific Revolution, 1500–1800: The Formation of the Modern Scientific Attitude*, Boston: Beacon Press, 1956.

———. "L'Académie Royale des Sciences et la réforme de ses statuts en 1789." *Revue d'Histoire des Sciences* 18 (1965): 15–28.

Harris, Robert D. "Necker's Compte Rendu of 1781: A Reconsideration." *Journal of Modern History* 42 (June 1970): 170–76.

———. "French Finances and the American War, 1777–1783." *Journal of Modern History* 48 (June 1976): 233–58.

———. *Necker, Reform Statesman of the Ancien Régime*. Berkeley: University of California Press, 1977.

———. *Necker and the Revolution of 1789*. Lanham-New York-London: University Press of America, 1986.

Harris, S. E. *The Assignats*. Cambridge, Mass.: Harvard University Press, 1930.

Hays, Isaac M. *Calendar of the Papers of Benjamin Franklin in the Library of the American Philosophical Society*. Philadelphia: American Philosophical Society, 1908.

Heffert J., J. Maraisse and J. M. Chanut. "La culture du blé au milieu du 19e siècle. Le rendement, prix salaires et autres coûts." *Annales Économies, Sociétés, Civilisation* (Nov–Dec 1986): 1273–1301.

Henry, Charles. *Correspondance inédite de Condorcet et de Turgot, 1770–1779*. Geneva: Slatkine, 1970.

Hersin, Paul. *Crédit public et banque d'état en France du XVIe au XVIIIe siècle*, Geneva: Droz, 1833.

Hincker, François. *Expériences bancaires sous l'Ancien Régime*. Paris: Flammarion, 1974.

Hindie Lemay, Edna. *Dictionnaire des Constituants, 1789–1791*. Paris: Universitas, 1991.

Hoefer, Ferdinand. *Histoire de la chimie*. 2 vols. Paris: F. Didot, 1866–1869.

Jolly, Pierre. *Turgot*. Paris: Les Oeuvres Françaises, 1944.

———. *Dupont de Nemours, soldat de la liberté*. Paris: Presses Universitaires de France, 1956.

Kaplan, Steven Lawrence. *The Famine Plot Persuasion in Eighteenth Century France*. Transactions of the American Philosophical Society 72. Philadelphia: American Philosophical Society, 1982.

Kersaint, Georges. *Antoine François de Fourcroy: sa vie, son oeuvre*. Paris: Editions du Muséum, 1966.

Kirwan, Richard. *An Essay on Phlogiston and the Constitution of Acids*. London: Printed by J. Davis for P. Elmsley in the Strand, 1787.

Klotz, Gérard. "Réforme fiscale, physiocratie et statistique, le cas Lavoisier." In J. M. Servet, ed., *Idées économiques sous la Révolution, 1789–1794*. Lyon: Presses Universitaires de Lyon, 1989, pp. 125–44.

Laborde de Méréville. *Discours sur l'établissement d'une banque publique prononcé à l'Assemblée nationale le 5 décembre 1789*. Paris: Imprimerie Nationale, 1789.

Labrousse, Christian. *Les grand problèmes de l'économie contemporaine*. Paris: Les Cours de Droit, 1991.

Labrousse, Ernest. *La crise de l'économie française à la fin de l'ancien régime et au début de la Révolution*. Thèse de Droit. Paris: Presses Universitaires de France, 1946.

Lacretelle, Charles. *Histoire de France pendant le XVIIIe siècle*. 6 vols. Paris: Marescy, 1884.

Lacroix, Sigismond. *Actes de la Commune de Paris pendant la Révolution*. Paris: Cerf-Noblet-Maison Quantin,1894.

La Fayette, Marie Joseph Paul Yves Roch Gilbert Motier, marquis de. *Mémoires, correspondance publiée par sa famille*. 6 vols. Paris: Fournier, 1837–1838.

Laffon de Ladebat. *Tableau de la situation et des opérations de la Caisse d'Escompte établi en 1807*. Paris: Archives de la Banque de France.

Lakanal, Joseph. *Exposé sommaire des travaux de J. Lakanal pour sauver durant la Révolution les sciences, les lettres*. Paris: Didot, 1838.

Lamarck, Jean-Baptiste. *Réfutation de la théorie pneumatique ou de la nouvelle doctrine des chimistes modernes*. Paris: Agasse, An IV (1796).

Lamerville, J. L. T. Heurtault de. *De l'impôt territorial, combiné avec les principes de l'administration de Sully et de Colbert, adaptés à la situation actuelle de la France*. Strasbourg: Imprimerie de Rolland et Jacob, 1788.

Langins, Janis. *La République avait besoin de savants*. Paris: Belin, 1987.

Larrère, Christine. *L'invention de l'économie au XVIIIe siècle: du droit naturel à la physiocratie*. Paris: Presses Universitaires de France, 1992.

Laugier, Lucien. *Turgot, ou le mythe des réformes*. Paris: Albatros, 1979.

Lavaquery, Eugène. *Necker, fourrier de la Révolution,1732–1804*. Paris: Plon, 1933.

Lavergne, Léonce de. "La Société d'Agriculture de Paris." Paris: Revue des Deux Mondes, 1859.

———. *Les assemblées provinciales sous Louis XVI*. Paris: Michel Lévy, 1864.

———. *Les économistes français du dix-huitième siècle*. Paris, 1870. Geneva: Slatkine, 1970.

Lebeau, Auguste. *Condillac économiste*. Paris: Guillaumin, 1903.

Le Bihan, Alain. *Francs-maçons et ateliers parisiens de la grande loge de France au XVIIIe siècle, 1760–1795*. Paris: Bibliothèque Nationale, 1973.

Lebouchet, Odet Julien. *Histoire de la dernière guerre entre la Grande Bretagne et les Etats-Unis de l'Amérique, la France, l'Espagne et la Hollande, depuis son commencement en 1775 jusqu'à sa fin en 1783*. Paris: Brocas, 1787.

Le Couteulx de Canteleu. *Rapport fait au nom de la Commission de surveillance de la Trésorerie Nationale composée des citoyens Lebrun, Vernier, Cretet, Dedelay d'Agier et Le Couteulx, séance du 9 fructidor An VI*. Paris: Imprimerie Nationale, vendémiaire AN VII. Bibliothèque de la Banque de France, 12380.

Legrand, Jean-Pierre and Maxime Le Goff. *L'activité des savants pendant la Révolution française*. Paris: J. P. Legrand and M. Le Goff, 1989.

Le Mercier de La Rivière, Paul Pierre. *L'ordre naturel et essentiel des sociétés politiques*. Londres: Jean Nourse; Paris: Desaint, 1767.

Lémery, Nicolas. *Pharmacopée universelle*. Paris: d'Houry, 1697.

———. *Traité universel des drogues simples*. Paris: d'Houry, 1698.

———. *Cours de Chymie*. Lyon: Claude Rey, 1703.

Lesch, J. E. *Science and Medicine in France: the Emergence of Experimental Physiology, 1790–1855*, Cambridge, Mass. and London: Harvard University Press, 1984.

Lescure, M. de. *Correspondance secrète inédite sur Louis XVI, Marie-Antoinette, la cour et la ville de 1777 à 1792*. 2 vols. Paris: Plon, 1866.

Levere, Trevor H. and William R. Shea, eds. *Nature, Experiment and the Sciences: Essays on Galileo and the History of Science*. Kluwer, 1990.

Lévis, Pierre Marc Gaston, duc de. *Souvenirs et portraits, 1780–1789*. Paris: Beaupré, 1815.

Lüthy, Herbert. *La banque protestante en France*. 2 vols. Paris: SEVPEN, 1959–1961.

———. "Necker et la Compagnie des Indes." *Annales Economies, Sociétés, Civilisation* 15 (1960): 851–81.

MacBride, David. *Experimental Essays on Medical and Philosophical Subjects*. London: A. Millar and T. Cadell, 1767. French *Essais d'expériences (sur la fermentation des aliments, la nature de l'air fixe, les vertus des antiseptiques, le scorbut et son traitement, la vertu dissolvante de la chaux vive*, trans. Abbadie. Paris: Cavelier, 1766.

Macquer, Pierre Joseph. *Éléments de chymie pratique*. 2 vols. Paris: Jean Thomas Hérissant, 1751.

———. *Éléments de chymie théorique*. Paris: Jean Thomas Hérissant, 1756.

———. *Dictionnaire de Chymie*. 4 vols. Paris: P. F. Didot,1778.

Maddison, R. E. W. "A Summary of Former Accounts of the Life and Work of Robert Boyle." *Annals of Science* 13 (1957): 90–108.

Mallet, Georges. *La politique financière des Jacobins*. Thèse pour le Doctorat de l'Université de Paris, Faculté de Droit. Paris: Arthur Rousseau, 1913.

Malouet, Pierre Victor. *Mémoires*. 2 vols. Paris: Viguier, 1868.

Marat, Jean Paul. *Les charlatans modernes, ou Lettres sur le charlatanisme académique*. Paris: Imprimerie de Marat, 1791.

Margerison, Kenneth. *P.-L. Roederer: Political Thought and Practice During the French Revolution*. Transactions of the American Philosophical Society 73, pt. 1. Philadelphia: American Philosophical Society, 1983.

Marion, Marcel. *Histoire financière de la France depuis 1715*. 6 vols. Paris: Rousseau et cie, 1927–1931.

Marmontel, Jean François. *Les mémoires d'un père*. Paris: Stock, 1943.

Massain, Robert. *Chimie et chimistes*. Paris: Magnard, 1952.

Massin, Jean. *Almanach de la Révolution française*. Paris: Club Français du Livre, 1963.

Mathiez, Albert. "La mobilisation des savants en l'An II." *Revue de Paris* 24 (1917): 524–65

———. "L'institut et la liberté scientifique." *Annales de l'Histoire de la Révolution Française* (1917): pp. 577–82.

———. "La constitution de 1793." *Annales de l'Histoire de la Révolution Française* 5 (1928): 497–521.

———. *La Révolution française*. 2 vols. Paris: Collection 10/18, 1972.

Matthews, George T. *The Royal General Farms in Eighteenth Century France*. New York: Columbia University Press, 1958.

Mauskopf, Seymour H. "Gunpowder and the Chemical Revolution." *Osiris* 4 (1988): 93–118.

Mazé, Jules. *Louis XVI et Marie-Antoinette, la famille royale et la Révolution*. Paris: Hachette, 1943.

McCann, H. Gilman. *Chemistry Transformed: The Paradigmatic Shift from Phlogiston to Oxygen*. Norwood, N. J.: Ablex, 1978.

McKie, Douglas. "The Observations of the Abbé François Rozier (1734–93)." *Annals of Science* 13 (1957): 73–89.

———. "La chimie du XVIIIᵉ siècle avant Lavoisier." Conférence faite le 2 nov. 1957 au palais de la Découverte. Imprimerie Alençonienne, 1958.

McKie, Douglas and Heathcote, N.H. de. *Discovery of Specific and Latent Heats*, London: Edward Arnold, 1935.

Meilhan, Gabriel Sénac de. *Portraits et caractères des personnages distingués de la fin du dix-huitième siècle suivis de pièces sur l'histoire et la politique*. Paris: J. G. Dentu, 1813.

Meldrum, Andrew Norman. *The Eighteenth Century Revolution in Science: The First Phase*. Calcutta, London, and New York: Longmans, Green, 1930.

Melhado, Evan M. "Oxygen, Phlogiston, and Caloric, The Case of Guyton." *Historical Studies in Physical Science* 13 (1983): 311–34.

Mendelsohn, E. "The Controversy over Heat Production in the Body." *Proceedings of the American Philosophical Society* 105 (1961): 412–20.

Mercier, Louis Sébastien. *Le tableau de Paris*. 12 vols. Amsterdam: 1782–88.

———. *Le nouveau Paris*. 6 vols. Paris: Fuchs-Pougens-Cramer, 10 Frimaire An VII (1797).

Mériot, Claude. *La comptabilité publique au XVIIIᵉ siècle*. Thèse de Droit, Université de Paris 2, 1973.

Métra, François. *Portefeuille d'un talon rouge*. Paris: Rouveyre, 1881.

Messance. *Nouvelles recherches sur la population de la France*. Lyon: Les Frères Périsse, 1788.

Metzger, Hélène. *Newton, Stahl, Boerhaave et la doctrine chimique*. Paris: Alcan, 1930.

———. *Les doctrines chimiques en France du début du XVIIᵉ siècle à la fin du XVIIIᵉ siècle*. Paris: A. Blanchard, 1969.

————. *La méthode philosophique en histoire des sciences*. Paris: Fayard, 1987.

Meyerson, Émile. *De l'explication dans l'histoire des sciences*. Paris: Payot, 1927.

————. *Identité et réalité*. Paris: Vrin, 1951.

Michelet, Jules. *Histoire de la Révolution française*. Paris: La Pléiade Gallimard, 1976.

Mignet, François Auguste Marie Alexis. *Histoire de la Révolution française*. 2 vols. Paris: Didot,1869.

Mill, John Stuart. *Principes d'économie politique avec quelques unes de leurs applications à l'économie sociale*. 2 vols. Paris: Guillaumin,1854.

Mirabeau, Honoré Gabriel de Riquetti, comte de. *De la banque d'Espagne dite de Saint-Charles*. Paris, 1785.

————. *De la Caisse d'Escompte*. Paris, 1785.

————. *Lettre à M. Le Couteulx de La Noraye, sur la banque de Saint-Charles et sur la Caisse d'Escompte*. Bruxelles, 1785.

————. *Réponse à l'écrivain des administrateurs de la compagnie des eaux de Paris*. 2d ed. Bruxelles, 1786.

————. *Sur les actions de la compagnie des eaux de Paris*. London, 1786.

————. *Dénonciation de l'agiotage au Roi et à l'assemblée des Notables*. Paris, 1787.

————. *Lettre sur l'administration de M. Necker*. Paris, 1787.

————. *Suite de la dénonciation de l'agiotage*. 1788.

————. *Discours prononcé dans la séance du vendredi 20 novembre sur le projet de banque Nationale présenté par le premier ministre des Finances*. Paris: Baudouin, 1789.

Mirabeau, Victor de Riquetti, marquis de. *L'ami des hommes ou traité de la population*. 3 vols. 1759.

Mitchell, Samuel Latham. *Explanation of the Synopsis of Chemical Nomenclature and Arrangement, Containing Several Important Alterations of the Plan Originally Reported by the French Academicians*. New York: T. and J. Swords, 1801.

Moheau, Jean-Baptiste. *Recherches et considérations sur la population de la France (1778)*, ed. Éric Vilquin. Paris: Institut National d'Etudes Démographiques, 1987.

Molinier, J. "Les calculs d'agrégats en France, antérieurement à 1850." *Revue d'Économie Politique* (Nov–Dec 1957): 875–97.

Mollien, comte. *Mémoires d'un ministre du Trésor public, 1780–1815*. 4 vols. Paris: Fournier, 1845.

Monchanin, M. de. *Notice sur la vie de Dupont (de Nemours)*. Paris: Delaunay, Pélicier et Petit, 1818.

Monnet, Antoine Grimoald. *Traité des eaux minérales avec plusieurs mémoires de chimie relatifs à cet objet*. Paris: Didot, 1768.

Montcloux, Hippolyte de. *De la comptabilité publique en France*. Paris: H. Bossange, 1840.

Montesquiou Fezensac, Anne Pierre, marquis de. *Opinion sur le rapport du comité chargé d'examiner les plans de banque et de finance*. Paris, 18 décembre 1789.

————. *Opinion sur l'organisation du Trésor public*. Paris, 10 mars 1791.

Montyon, J. B. Auget, baron de. *Particularités et observations sur les ministres des finances de France les plus célèbres, depuis 1660 jusqu'en 1791*. Paris: Le Normant, 1822.

Moore, Ruth. *Les précurseurs de la biologie*. Paris: Hachette, 1962.

Morris, Gouverneur. *A Diary of the French Revolution*, ed. Beatrix Carry Davenport, 2 vols. Boston: Houghton Mifflin, 1939.

Mortimer Ternaux, Louis. *Histoire de la Terreur (1792-1794) d'après des documents authentiques et inédits*. 8 vols. Paris: C. Lévy, 1862.

Morveau, Louis Bernard Guyton de. *Traité des moyens de désinfecter l'air*. Paris: Bernard, 1801.

Motin, C. M. *De la Trésorerie Nationale considérée sous ses rapports constitutionnels*. Paris: L'ami des Lois, undated. Bibliothèque Nationale: Lf157 13.

Multhauf, Robert P. "On the Use of the Balance in Chemistry." *Proceedings of the American Philosophical Society* 106 (1962): 210–18.

———. *The Origin of Chemistry*, New York: Franklin Watts, 1966.

———. "The French Crash Program for Saltpeter Production, 1776–1794." *Technology and Culture* 12 (1971): 163–81.

Neave, E. W. J. "Chemistry in Rozier's Journal." *Annals of Science* 7 (1951): 101–6, 144–48, 284–99, 393–400.

Necker, Jacques. *Réponse au mémoire de M. l'abbé Morellet sur la Compagnie des Indes*. Paris: Imprimerie Royale, 1769.

———. *Éloge de Jean-Baptiste Colbert. Discours qui a remporté le prix de l'Académie française en 1773, suivi de 17 notes sur le contrôle général des Finances*. Paris: J. B. Brunet; 1773.

———. *Sur la législation et le commerce des grains*. 2 vols. Paris: Pissot, 1775.

———. *Mémoire donné au Roi par M. Necker en 1778*. 1781.

———. *Compte-rendu au Roi par M. Necker, Directeur général des Finances, au mois de Janvier 1781*. Paris: Imprimerie Royale, 1781.

———. *De l'administration des finances de la France*, 3 vols. Lausanne: J. P. Heubach, 1784.

———. *Mémoire en réponse au discours prononcé par M. de Calonne devant l'Assemblée des Notables*. Londres: J. Debrett, 1787.

———. *Sur le compte-rendu au Roi en 1781, nouveaux éclaircissements*. Lyon: Bernuset, 1788.

———. *Sur l'administration de M. Necker par lui-même*. Lausanne: Mourer cadet, 1791.

———. *Du pouvoir exécutif dans les grands Etats*. 1792.

———. *De la Révolution Française, suivi de réflexions philosophiqes sur l'égalité*. 4 vols. Paris: Drisonnier, 1797.

———. *Dernières vues de politique et de finances*. 1802.

Orieux, Jean. *Talleyrand ou le sphynx incompris*. Paris: Flammarion, 1986.

Palmer, R. R. *The Improvement of Humanity. Education and the French Revolution*. Princeton, N. J.: Princeton University Press, 1985.

Parascandola, John and Aaron Ihde. "History of the Pneumatic Trough." *Isis* 60 (1969): 350–61.

Parker, Harold T. "French Administrators and French Scientists during the Old Regime and the Early Years of the Revolution." In Richard Herr and Harold T. Parker eds., *Ideas in History: Essays Presented to Louis Gottschalk by His Former Students*. Durham, N. C.: Duke University Press, 1965, pp. 85–109.

Partington, James R. *A History of Greek Fire and Gunpowder*. Cambridge: Cambridge University Press, 1960.

———. *A History of Chemistry*. 4 vols. London: Macmillan, 1962.

Partington, James R. and Douglas McKie. "Historical Studies on the Phlogiston Theories." *Annals of Science* part I, 2 (1937): 361–404; part II, 3 (1938): 1–58; part III, 3 (1938): 337–71; part IV, 4 (1939): 113–49.

Passy, Louis Paulin. *Histoire de la société nationale d'agriculture de France*, vol. 1 (1761–1763). Paris: Typo. P. Renouard, 1912. No further volumes appeared.

Payen, Jacques. *Capital et machine à vapeur au XVIIIe siècle: les frères Périer et l'introduction en France de la machine à vapeur de Watt*. Paris and The Hague: Mouton, 1969.

Perrot, Jean-Claude. "Les économistes, les philosophes et la population." In Jacques Dupâquier, ed., *Histoire de la population française*. 4 vols. Paris: Presses Universitaires de France, 1988, 2, pp. 499–551.

———. *Une histoire intellectuelle de l'économie politique (XVIe–XVIIIe siècle)*. Paris: Editions de l'Ecole des Hautes Etudes en Sciences Sociales, 1992.

Peuchet, Jacques. *Dictionnaire universel de géographie commerçante*. 5 vols. Paris, 1799–1800.

———. *Statistique élémentaire de la France*. Paris: Gilbert, 1805.

Pigeonneau, Henri and A. de Foville. *De l'administration de l'Agriculture au contrôle général des Finances (1785-1787). Procès verbaux et Rapports*. Paris: Guillaumin, 1882.

Piquet Marchal, Marie Odile. "Gregory King, précurseur de la comptabilité nationale." *Revue Economique* (1968): 212–45.

Plessis, Alain. "La Révolution française et les banques: de la Caisse d'Escompte à la Banque de France." *Revue d'Economie* 40 (1989): 1001–14.

Porter, Theodore M. "The Promotion of Mining and the Advancement of Science: The Chemical Revolution of Mineralogy." *Annals of Science* 38 (1981): 543–70.

Pouchet, Georges. *Les sciences pendant la Terreur d'après les documents du temps et les pièces des Archives Nationales*. Paris: Société d'Histoire de la Révolution Française. 1896.

Price, Jacob. *France and the Chesapeake: A History of the French Tobacco Monopoly, 1674–1791, and of Its Relationship to the British and American Tobacco Trades*. 2 vols. Ann Arbor: University of Michigan Press, 1973.

Priestley, Joseph. *Experiments and Observations on Different Kinds of Air*. 3 vols. London: J. Johnson, 1774–1777.

———. *Experiments and Observations Relating to Various Branches of Natural Philosophy*. 3 vols. London-Birmingham: J. Johnson,1779–1786.

———. *Considerations on the Doctrine of Phlogiston and the Decomposition of Water*, Philadelphia: Thomas Dobson, 1796.

———. *A Scientific Autobiography*, ed. Robert E. Schofield. Cambridge, Mass.: MIT Press, 1966.

Ramon, Gabriel. *Histoire de la Banque de France*. Paris: Bernard Grasset, 1929.

Rappaport, Rhoda. "G. F. Rouelle, an Eighteenth Century Chemist and Teacher." *Chymia* 6 (1960): 68–101.

———. "Rouelle and Stahl, Phlogistic Revolution in France." *Chymia* 7 (1961): 73–102.

Read, John. *De l'alchimie à la chimie*. Paris: Fayard, 1959.

Révolution de 1789, guerres et croissance économique. Actes de la table ronde de l'Association française des historiens économistes (16 décembre 1789). Special issue, *Revue d'Economie* 40 (1989): 927–1203.

Rey, Jean. *Essays sur la recherche de la cause pour laquelle l'étain et le plomb augmentent de poids quand on les calcine*, Bazas, 1630. Bibliothèque Nationale: 8° Rés. pS 158.

Robiquet, Jean. *La vie quotidienne au temps de la Révolution*. Paris: Hachette, 1938.

Roederer, Pïerre Louis. *Opuscules mêlés de littérature et de philosophie*. Paris: Imprimerie du Journal de Paris, vendémiaire An VIII (1796).

Roux, Pierre. *Les fermes d'Impôt sous l'ancien régime*. Paris: Rousseau, 1916.

Roy, Antoine. *Réclamations des créanciers des ci-devant Fermiers-généraux, et des intéressés à la liquidation des créances de la Républiques sur leurs biens*. Paris: Ballard, undated.

Ruault, Nicolas. *Gazette d'un Parisien sous la Révolution, lettres à son frère, 1783–1796*. Paris: Librairie Académique Perrin, 1976.

Russo, François. *Eléments de bibliographie d'histoire des sciences et des techniques*. Paris: Hermann, 1969.

Sagnac, Philippe. *La Révolution du 10 août 1792: la chute de la royauté*. Paris, 1909.

Sahut, Marie-Catherine and Régis Michel. *David, l'art et la politique*. Paris: Découvertes Gallimard,1989.

Saigey, Émile. *Les sciences au XVIIIᵉ siècle*. Paris: Librairie Germer Baillière, 1873.

Sauvy, Alfred. "Historique de la comptabilité nationale." *Économie et Statistique* 14 (1970): 19–32

Say, Jean-Baptiste. *Traité d'économie politique*. 3 vols. Paris: Rapilly, 1826.

Scheele, Charles Guillaume. *Traité chimique de l'air et du feu*, trans. Baron de Dietrich. Paris: Rue Serpente, 1781.

Schneider, Hans-Georg. "The 'Fatherland of Chemistry': Early Nationalistic Currents in Late Eighteenth Century German Chemistry." *Ambix* 36 (1989): 14–21.

Sénac de Meilhan, Gabriel. *Considérations sur les richesses et le luxe*. Amsterdam-Paris: Valade, 1787.

———. *Particularités et observations sur les ministres des Finances de France les plus célèbres depuis 1660 jusqu'en 1791*. Paris: Le Normand, 1812.

———. *Du gouvernement, des moeurs et des conditions*. Paris: 1814.

Servet, Jean-Michel. *Idées économiques sous la Révolution 1789-1794*, Lyon: Presses Universitaires de Lyon,1989.

Sieyès, Emmanuel Joseph. *Qu'est-ce que le Tiers-Etat?* Paris: Flammarion, 1988.

Silvestre, A. F. *Essai sur les moyens de perfectionner les arts économiques en France*. Paris: Imprimerie de Madame Huzard, An IX (1801).

Smeaton, William A. "Contributions of P. J. Macquer, T. O. Bergman, and L. B. Guyton de Morveau to the Reform of Chemical Nomenclature." *Annals of Science* 10 (1954): 87–106.

———. *Fourcroy, Chemist and Revolutionary, 1755-1809*. Cambridge, Mass: W. Heffer, 1962.

———. "Some Large Burning Lenses and Their Use by Eighteenth Century French and British Chemists." *Annals of Science* 44 (1987): 265–76.

Soboul, Albert. *Histoire de la Révolution française*. 2 vols. Paris: Gallimard, 1987.

Solé, Jacques. *La Révolution en question*. Paris: Seuil,1988.

Staël, Germaine, baronne de. *Considérations sur les principaux évènements de la Révolution française*, 3 vols. Paris: Delaumay-Bossange-Masson, 1818.

Stahl, George Ernst. *Traité du soufre*. trans. Baron d'Holbach. Paris: Didot le Jeune, 1766.

Stapleton, Darwin H. *Accounts of European Science, Technology, and Medicine Written by American Travelers Abroad, 1735-1860*. In the Collections of the American Philosophical Society. Philadelphia: American Philosophical Society, 1985.

———. *The Transfer of Early Industrial Technologies to America*, Philadelphia: American Philosophical Society, 1987

Stephenson, O. W. "The Supply of Gunpowder in 1776." *American Historical Review* 30 (1925): 271–81.

Stourm, René. *Les finances de l'ancien régime et de la Révolution.* 2 vols. Paris: Guillaumin, 1885.

———. *Bibliographie historique des finances de la France au XVIIIe siècle.* Paris: Guillaumin, 1895.

Taine, Hippolyte. *Les origines de la France contemporaine.* Paris: R. Laffont, 1986.

Taton, René ed. *Histoire générale des sciences.* 4 vols. Paris: Presses Universitaires de France, 1958.

———. *Enseignement et diffusion des sciences en France au XVIIIe siècle.* Paris: Hermann, 1986.

Thackray, Arnold. *Atoms and Powers: An Essay on Newtonian Matter Theory and the Development of Chemistry.* Cambridge, Mass.: Harvard University Press, 1970.

Thibaudeaux, Antoine, Clair. *Mémoires sur la Convention et sur le Directoire.* 2 vols. Paris, 1824.

Thirion, H. *La vie des financiers au XVIIIe siècle.* Paris: Plon, Nourrit, 1895.

Thorpe, Thomas E. *Essays in Historical Chemistry.* London: Macmillan, 1902.

Tocqueville, Alexis de. *L'Ancien Régime et la Révolution.* Paris: Michel Lévy, 1856. Reprint Paris: Gallimard, 1967.

Tolosan, Jean François. *Mémoire sur le commerce de la France et de ses colonies.* Paris: Imprimerie Moutard, 1789.

Toutain, Jean-Claude. *Le produit intérieur brut de la France de 1789 à 1982,* Grenoble: Presses Universitaires de Grenoble, Economie et Sociétés, ser. AF15, 1987.

Trésorerie Nationale. *Bureaux qui formeront la consistance habituelle et permanente de la Trésorerie Nationale à compter du 1er octobre 1791.* In André Rémy, Arnoult, *Collection des décrets de l'Assemblée nationale Constituante rédigée suivant l'ordre des matières,* Dijon: Causse, 1792, vol. 5, pp. 99–127.

———. *Etat des bureaux de la Trésorerie Nationale.* Paris: Imprimerie Nationale, 1791. Bibliothèque Nationale: Lf157 11; Archives de la Banque de France, Trésorerie III, 1790–1793, box 31.

———. *Etat des recettes et des dépenses faites à la Trésorerie 1° pendant les trois derniers mois de l'Assemblée Constituante, 2° pendant les 11 mois de la Législative actuelle, 1791–1794.* Bibliothèque Nationale: Nouvelles acquisitions françaises, Ms 22375, 88 leaves.

———. *Compte rendu du 1er juillet 1791 au 1er septembre 1793, notice des divers comptes et états joints au compte rendu par les Commissaires de la Trésorerie Nationale, suivi de 25 états in folio: recettes et dépenses (2), Guerre (1), Marine et Colonies (6), Dette publique (2), Numéraire (4), Assignats (2), déficits (4) salaires (3).* Bibliothèque Nationale: Lf158 19.

———. *Deuxième compte rendu par les Commissaires de la Trésorerie Nationale de leur administration, dans lequel on trouve les principaux détails de l'organisation de cet établissement.* Bibliothèque Nationale: Lf158 20.

Tulard, Jean. *Histoire de France.* 4 vols. Paris: Fayard, 1985.

Tulard, Jean, Jean François Fayard, and Alfred Fierro. *Histoire et dictionnaire de la Révolution française, 1789–1799.* Paris: Laffont, 1988.

Turgot, Anne Robert Jacques. *Des administrations provinciales.* Lausanne, 1788.

———. *Oeuvres,* ed. Eugène Daire. 2 vols. Paris: Guillaumin, 1844.

———. *Oeuvres,* ed. Gustave Schelle. 5 vols. Paris: Félix Alcan-Guillaumin, 1913–1923.

Vacher de Lapouge. *Necker économiste.* Paris: Marcel Rivière, 1914.

Vauban, Sébastien Le Prestre de. *Projet d'une dixme royale*. Bruxelles: Georges de Backer, 1708.

Veuves et enfants des ci-devant Fermiers-généraux. *Dénonciation présentée au comité de Législation de la Convention nationale contre le représentant du peuple Dupin par les veuves et enfants des ci-devant Fermiers-généraux (22 messidor). Addition à la dénonciation, trois pièces justificatives*. Paris: Du Pont, An III (1795).

———. *Seconde addition à la dénonciation présentée contre Dupin au Comité de Législation*. Paris: Du Pont, An III (1795).

Vigié, Marc and Muriel Vigié. *L'herbe à Nicot, amateurs de tabac, fermiers généraux et contrebandiers sous l'Ancien Régime*. Paris: Fayard, 1989.

Voltaire. *L'homme aux quarante écus*. Paris: Editions de la Couronne, 1946.

Vovelle, Michel. *L'État de la France pendant la Révolution (1789-1799)*. Paris: La Découverte, 1988.

Wallerius, Johann G. *Eléments d'agriculture physique et chimique*. Yverdon, 1766.

Wallon, Henri. *Histoire du Tribunal révolutionnaire de Paris avec le Journal des actes*. 6 vols. Paris: Hachette, 1881.

———. *La Révolution française vue par ses journaux*. Reprint Paris: Tardy, 1948.

———. *Actes du Tribunal révolutionnaire*. Paris: Mercure de France-Temps retrouvé, 1968.

Weulersse, Georges. *La mouvement physiocratique en France de 1756 à 1770*. 2 vols. Paris: F. Alcan, 1910.

———. *La physiocratie sous les ministères Turgot et Necker*. Paris: Presses Universitaires de France, 1950.

———. *La physiocratie à la fin du règne de Louis XV (1770-1774)*. Paris: Presses Universitaires de France, 1959.

———. *La physiocratie à l'aube de la Révolution, 1781-1792*. Paris: Editions EHSS, 1985.

White, Eugene N. "Was There a Solution to the Financial Dilemma of the Ancien Régime?" *Journal of Economic History* 49 (1989): 545–68.

———. "The Evolution of Banking Theory During the French Revolution." In Gilbert Faccarello and Philippe Steiner, eds., *La pensée économique pendant la Révolution française*, pp. 451–63.

White, John. *The History of the Phlogiston Theory*. London: E. Arnold, 1932

Williams, L. Pearce. "Science Education and the French Revolution." *Isis* 44 (1953): 311–30.

———. "The Politics of Science in the French Revolution." In Marshall Clagett, ed., *Critical Problems in the History of Science*. Madison: University of Wisconsin Press, 1959, pp. 291–308.

Wilson, Leonard G. "The Transformation of Ancient Concepts of Respiration in the Seventeenth Century." *Isis* 51 (1960): 161–72.

Wise, Norton. "Mediations: Enlightenment Balancing Acts, or the Technologies of Rationalism." In Paul Horwich, ed., *World Changes: Thomas Kuhn and the Nature of Science*. Cambridge, Mass. and London: A Bradford Book, MIT Press, 1992, pp. 207–56.

Wohl, Robert. "Buffon and His Project of a New Science." *Isis* 51 (1960): 186–99.

Wojtkowiak, Bruno. *Histoire de la chimie*. Paris: Technique et Documentation Lavoisier, 1988.

Wurtz, A. *Histoire des doctrines chimiques depuis Lavoisier*. Paris: Hachette, 1769. Published in *Dictionnaire de chimie pure et appliquée* 5 vols. Paris: 1869–1878, vol. 1, pp. i–xciv.

Young, Arthur. *Travels During the Years 1787, 1788, 1789; Undertaken More Particularly with a View of Ascertaining the Cultivation, Wealth, Resources and National Prosperity of the Kingdom of France*. 2 vols. 2d ed. London: Richardson, 1794.

Index of Names